Index to the 1800 Massachusetts Federal Census
for the County of
Worcester

Rebecca M. Sullivan
Deborah Lee Larsson

Index to the 1800 Massachusetts Federal Census
for the County of
Worcester

September 2014

ISBN: 978-1502440020

FOREWARD:

This is the second volume of several containing the heads of household that were enumerated in the 1800 United States Federal Census in Massachusetts. Our second volume is comprised of those towns in Worcester County. In order to make it easy for the researcher, towns are alphabetized, followed by an alphabetical index of Worcester county.

We have made every attempt at correctly transcribing each town. However, many of these documents are torn, covered with ink, tape marks, rips and poor handwriting. Spelling errors have been left as they were originally written. Any names & enumerations illegible are denoted with an asterisk.

This book should be used as a guide and research aid. When possible the actual image should be obtained for proper verification and citation. Visit the National Archives website to find out more on how to obtain census images. www.archives.gov/research/census.

In order to get all of the information on one page to make for easy reading we had to reduce the size of the font.

Drop us a line, we'd love to hear what you're researching: rsulli1219@aol.com

Becky & Deb
September 2014

Check out our other books:

Index to the 1800 Massachusetts Federal Census for the Counties of Barnstable, Dukes & Nantucket, Volume 1

INDEX

Worcester County

INDEX CONTINUED

Worcester County Stats

Microfilm Reel Number: M32-16

Town:	Page Numbers:	Enumerated By:
Ashburnham	455-460	Unknown
Athol	281-290	Unknown
Barre	399-412	Unknown
Berlin	211-216	Unknown
Bolton	207-216	Unknown
Boylston	369-378	Unknown
Brookfield	245-270	Unknown
Charlton	325-340	Unknown
Douglas	475-482	Unknown
Dudley	339-344	Unknown
Fitchburg	423-432	Josiah Stearns
Gardner	447-454	Unknown
Garry	274-280	Unknown
Grafton	193-206	Unknown
Hardwick	293-306	Abijah Biggelow
Harvard	215-222	Unknown
Holden	509-516	Unknown
Hubbardston	413-420	Unknown
Lancaster	345-358	Unknown
Leicester	485-498	Unknown
Leominster	431-438	Josiah Stearns
Lunenberg	421-432	Josiah Stearns
Mendon	379-394	Unknown
Milford	359-396	Unknown
New Braintree	308-313	Unknown
Northborough	361-370	Unknown
Northbridge	473-478	Unknown

Worcester County Stats

Microfilm Reel Number: M32-16

Town:	Page Numbers:	Enumerated By:
Oakham	315-322	Unknown
Oxford	153-164	Ebenezer Waters
Paxton	499-504	Unknown
Petersham	271-287	Unknown
Princeton	513-518	Unknown
Royalston	231-242	Unknown
Rutland	505-514	Jonas How
Shrewsbury	361-370	Unknown
Southborough	200-206	Unknown
Spencer	485-502	Unknown
Sterling	348-358	Unknown
Sturbridge	327-340	Unknown
Sutton	149-168	Unknown
Templeton	231-242	Unknown
Upton	383-390	Unknown
Uxbridge	461-474	Unknown
Ward	175-180	Unknown
Westborough	189-199	Unknown
Western	249-261	Unknown
Westminster	441-456	Unknown
Winchendon	223-230	Unknown
Worcester	171-188	Benjamin Heywood

TOWN	PG#	LN#	LAST NAME	FIRST NAME	M under 10	M 10 to 16	M 16 to 26	M 26 to 45	M 45 and over	F under 10	F 10 to 16	F 16 to 26	F 26 to 45	F 45 and over	TOTAL ALL OTHER	TOTAL SLAVES	TOTALS	DISTRICT/ TOWNSHIP	NOTES
Ashburnham	455	1	Townsend	Joshua				1						1			2		
Ashburnham	455	2	Taylor	Phenihas	2			1		2			1				6		
Ashburnham	455	3	Tottingham	Moses	3			1			2		1				7		
Ashburnham	455	4	Demster	Samuel		1		1					1				3		
Ashburnham	455	5	Whitman	John	2			1	1		1	1	1	1			8		
Ashburnham	455	6	Ward	William	3	1		1					1	1			7		
Ashburnham	455	7	Whitman	Nicholas	2		1	1		1			1	1			7		
Ashburnham	455	8	Willmer	Jacob SG	2			1	1	3	1		1	1			10		
Ashburnham	455	9	Willard	Jacob				1	1			2		1			5		
Ashburnham	455	10	Wit	John	1	1		1		2			1				6		
Ashburnham	455	11	Winter	John	1			1	1	1			1	1			6		
Ashburnham	455	12	Wilder	Caleb 2d				1						1			2		
Ashburnham	455	13	Wilder	Nahum			1										1		
Ashburnham	455	14	Whitney	Sarah		2	2			2		1		1			8		
Ashburnham	455	15	Wilder	Bulah									1				1		
Ashburnham	455	16	Willard	Silas		2	1	1		4		2		1			11		
Ashburnham	455	17	Whitney	Abner				1						1			2		
Ashburnham	455	18	Winchester	Ann											1		1		
Ashburnham	456	1	Willard	Henery			1										1		
Ashburnham	456	2	Winchester	Jonathan	2	2		1		2	1			1			9		
Ashburnham	456	3	Willard	Simon	3		1			1			1				6		
Ashburnham	456	4	Whitman	Edward	1	1		1		3	1		1				8		
Ashburnham	456	5	Willard	John	2	1		1		1			1				6		
Ashburnham	456	6	Wetherbee	Thomas		1		1					1				3		
Ashburnham	456	7	Wilder	Caleb		2	1	1			1	2					7		
Ashburnham	456	8	White	Elisha	2		1	1		2	1		1				8		
Ashburnham	456	9	Ward	Caleb		1	3	1		1	1	1		1			9		
Ashburnham	456	10	Whitmore	Isaac	1	1	1	1		2			1	1			8		
Ashburnham	456	11	Wetherbee	Amos	2	1		1		3			1				8		
Ashburnham	456	12	Whitmore	Joseph				1						1			2		
Ashburnham	457	1	Cushing	John Revd		1	1	1		1		2	1				7		
Ashburnham	457	2	Cushing	David	2	1		1		2	1	1	1				9		
Ashburnham	457	3	Corey	Hezekiah			1	1		1	1	1	1	1			7		
Ashburnham	457	4	Cutting	Eunis		1		1				1	2	1			6		
Ashburnham	457	5	Corey	Hezekiah Jr	1			1		4			1				7		
Ashburnham	457	6	Cobleigh	Ephraim		1		1					1				3		
Ashburnham	457	7	Clerk	David				1						1			2		
Ashburnham	457	8	Crosby	Fitch	1			1				1					3		
Ashburnham	457	9	Crosby	Fredrick	1	3		1		3			1				9		
Ashburnham	457	10	Conn	John				1						1			2		
Ashburnham	457	11	Crehore	Timothy	1	1	2		1		1		1				7		
Ashburnham	457	12	Corey	John	3			1		1		1					6		
Ashburnham	457	13	Cumings	Abraham	4	1		1		1			1				8		
Ashburnham	457	14	Conn	John Jr	1			1			1		1				4		
Ashburnham	457	15	Clark	David Jr	2			1		4			1				8		
Ashburnham	457	16	Clerk	Daniel		1		1		3	1		1				7		
Ashburnham	457	17	Constantine	Jacob	1	1	1		1			2	1				7		
Ashburnham	457	18	Russell	David	3			1		1			1				6		
Ashburnham	457	19	Rice	Reuben	2	1		1		2	1	1	1				9		
Ashburnham	457	20	Randall	Stephen Jr	2	2		1		1	1		1				8		
Ashburnham	457	21	Rice	Phinias				1					1				2		
Ashburnham	457	22	Rice	Jonah	3			1		1	1		1				7		
Ashburnham	457	23	Randall	Phinihas		1		1				2	1	1			6		
Ashburnham	457	24	Randall	Stephen		1	1	1				1					4		
Ashburnham	457	25	Russell	Thomas	3		1	1		1			1	1			8		
Ashburnham	457	26	Randall	Ephraim		1		1		2			1				5		
Ashburnham	457	27	Stone	Joseph		1	1		1	1			1	1			6		
Ashburnham	457	28	Sampson	John			1						1				2		
Ashburnham	457	29	Stone	Nancy						1	1		1				3		
Ashburnham	457	30	Stone	Adams	2	1		1		2	1	1					8		
Ashburnham	457	31	Scolley	Grover		2	1	1			1			1			6		
Ashburnham	457	32	Stimson	Phenihm	3			1			2		1				7		
Ashburnham	457	33	Sampson	Ephraim	3			1		1			1				6		
Ashburnham	457	34	Sampson	Jonathan				1			1	1		1			4		
Ashburnham	458	1	Stone	Hosea			1										1		
Ashburnham	458	2	Stone	Oliver				1			1		1	1			4		
Ashburnham	458	3	Scolley	John			1	1					1				3		
Ashburnham	458	4	Shaw	John				1									2		
Ashburnham	458	5	Sawin	Asa			1			2			1				4		
Ashburnham	458	6	Sanderson	Moses	2	2		1		1	1		1				8		
Ashburnham	458	7	Stearns	Isaac	1	1	1		1	2	2	1		1			10		
Ashburnham	458	8	Spaulding	James	1	2	1	1		1	1	1		1			9		
Ashburnham	458	9	Starnes	James	1	1	1	1		2	1		1				8		
Ashburnham	458	10	Stearns	William	1	2			1	2	1		1				8		
Ashburnham	458	11	Stimson	Lemuel	2	1		1		2		1	1				8		
Ashburnham	458	12	Steel	Joseph				1					1				2		
Ashburnham	458	13	Smith	Joshua		1		1			1	3		2			8		
Ashburnham	458	14	Sampson	Oliver	2			1		2			1				6		
Ashburnham	458	15	Talor	Jonathan	1	1		1				1	1				5		
Ashburnham	458	16	Taylor	David			2	1					3	1			7		
Ashburnham	458	17	Townsend	Abraham	2			1		3	1	1					8		
Ashburnham	458	18	Townsend	Reuben	2	1		1		1	1	1	1				8		
Ashburnham	458	19	Anger	Timothy				1					1	1			3		
Ashburnham	458	20	Adams	John			2	1		2	1		1				7		
Ashburnham	458	21	Adams	John Jr	1			1					1				3		
Ashburnham	458	22	Adams	Ebezn Thoms	1	2		1		3			1	1			9		
Ashburnham	458	23	Adams	Levi		1		1		1			1				4		
Ashburnham	458	24	Adams	Nathaniel		1			1			1	1	1			5		
Ashburnham	458	25	Broughton	Wait	2	2	1		1	1			1				8		
Ashburnham	458	26	Brown	Josiah	2			1					1				4		

TOWN	PG#	LN#	LAST NAME	FIRST NAME	FREE WHITE MALES under 10	10 to 16	16 to 26	26 to 45	45 and over	FREE WHITE FEMALES under 10	10 to 16	16 to 26	26 to 45	45 and over	TOTAL ALL OTHER	TOTAL SLAVES	TOTALS	DISTRICT/ TOWNSHIP	NOTES
Ashburnham	458	27	Brooks	Simeon	2	2			1		1	1		1			8		
Ashburnham	458	28	Bennet	Thomas	1			1		2		1					5		
Ashburnham	458	29	Brooks	Thadus	2	1		1		1			1				6		
Ashburnham	458	30	Banding	Barnard	1		1			2		1					5		
Ashburnham	458	31	Billings	Joshua	1		1	1			1	1		1			6		
Ashburnham	458	32	Brooks	Jonathan	4			1		1			1				7		
Ashburnham	458	33	Brooks	Luther		1		1			1			1			4		
Ashburnham	458	34	Benjamin	Daniel	1	1	1	1		2	2	2	1				11		
Ashburnham	458	35	Burges	Ebenezar		1		1		2			1				5		
Ashburnham	458	36	Burges	Joseph	1		1					1					3		
Ashburnham	459	1	Gates	Henery Jr	1		1			1		1					4		
Ashburnham	459	2	Hunt	Sheribiah		1		1		2		1	1				6		
Ashburnham	459	3	Hobart	Shubiel		1		1					1				3		
Ashburnham	459	4	Hastings	Charles	2	2		1		2	1	1	1				10		
Ashburnham	459	5	Hobart	Thomas	1			1				1					3		
Ashburnham	459	6	Haynes	James				1		3	1	2	1				8		
Ashburnham	459	7	Harris	Jacob		1		1			1	1		1			5		
Ashburnham	459	8	Haven	Jonathan	1		1			1			1				4		
Ashburnham	459	9	Holden	Joshua	1			1				1					3		
Ashburnham	459	10	Harris	William	3		1			2	1		1				8		
Ashburnham	459	11	Hall	Henary				1		1	1	1					4		
Ashburnham	459	12	Holden	James	1	1		1		1			1				5		
Ashburnham	459	13	Gates	Samuel	1		1			1		1					4		
Ashburnham	459	14	Hudson	Me*ar	2			1		2			1				6		
Ashburnham	459	15	Holbrook	William	1	2	1		1	1			1				7		
Ashburnham	459	16	Haven	John				1									1		
Ashburnham	459	17	Hastings	Ezra	2			1		1		1					5		
Ashburnham	459	18	Hall	Mary										1			1		
Ashburnham	459	19	Hill	Isaac		2		1		4		1					8		
Ashburnham	459	20	Joslin	Abijah		1	1		1	1		2	1	1			8		
Ashburnham	459	21	Jewett	Joseph	2	2		1		1		1	1				8		
Ashburnham	459	22	Jones	Enos		1		1				3		1			6		
Ashburnham	459	23	Jones	Nathan	2	1	1		1	1	1			1			8		
Ashburnham	459	24	Jones	Edmund				1				1					2		
Ashburnham	459	25	Kiblinger	Jacob	1	1	1		1	2	1	2	1	1			11		
Ashburnham	459	26	Kiblinger	Henery		1		1		1		1					3		
Ashburnham	459	27	Kendall	William	1			1		1			1				4		
Ashburnham	459	28	Keyes	Thomas	2		1			2			1				6		
Ashburnham	459	29	Kelton	Lemuel		1		1		1			1				3		
Ashburnham	459	30	Lane	Benjm	1		1	1		4	2		1				10		
Ashburnham	459	31	Low	Abraham	1	1		1		2			1				6		
Ashburnham	459	32	Lawrence	Wm John			1					1					2		
Ashburnham	459	33	Lane	Frances	1	2		1		1	2						7		
Ashburnham	459	34	Lawrence	Moses	1	1						1					3		
Ashburnham	460	1	Mann	Bela	2		1			3	2		1				9		
Ashburnham	460	2	Marble	Oliver	2	1	1		1	2	1	1	1				10		
Ashburnham	460	3	Medclif	Ezekiel		2	1		2	2	1		1				9		
Ashburnham	460	4	Miles	Asahel	1			1		1			1				4		
Ashburnham	460	5	Maynard	Nehemiah		1	3		1	1	1		1				8		
Ashburnham	460	6	Merraim	William	2	1		1		2			1				7		
Ashburnham	460	7	Manning	Solomon	1			1		2			1				5		
Ashburnham	460	8	Merraim	Joseph		2	1			1	1	1	1				7		
Ashburnham	460	9	Marble	Jabez	2	2			1	3	1	1	1				11		
Ashburnham	460	10	Munroe	Ebenzr	2	1	2		1	1		1	1				9		
Ashburnham	460	11	Pollard	William		1		1				1		1			4		
Ashburnham	460	12	Peirce	Asa			1							1			2		
Ashburnham	460	13	Polley	Peter	2	2		1		2	1		1				9		
Ashburnham	460	14	Parmenter	Jacob	4	1	1	1			1		1				9		
Ashburnham	460	15	Peirce	Amos	1			1		2			1				5		
Ashburnham	460	16	Rice	Jonas	2	1			1	2	2	2	1				11		
Ashburnham	460	17	Reed	Isaac	1			1		3			1				6		
Ashburnham	460	18	Dickson	Elizabeth		1						1		1			3		
Ashburnham	460	19	Davis	Eben & Benj	3	1		1		2	1		1				9		
Ashburnham	460	20	Ellis	Jesse		1			1			2		1			5		
Ashburnham	460	21	Foster	James				1		4	1		1				7		
Ashburnham	460	22	Foster	Nathanll	1		1	1		2	2		1				8		
Ashburnham	460	23	Fletcher	Josiah	4			1		1			1				7		
Ashburnham	460	24	Foster	Abram	1			1		3			1				6		
Ashburnham	460	25	Foster	Nathll Jr	1	1		1		2			1				6		
Ashburnham	460	26	Foster	Susanna			1			1	1			1			4		
Ashburnham	460	27	Fairbanks	Ithamer	1			1		3	1		1				7		
Ashburnham	460	28	Fairbanks	Cyrus	1	1			1	1	2	1	1				8		
Ashburnham	460	29	Fenno	Joseph	2	2		1		1	1		1				8		
Ashburnham	460	30	Gates	Levi			1					1					2		
Ashburnham	460	31	Gibbs	Joseph	2	2		1		1			1				7		
Ashburnham	460	32	Gibson	Thomas	2		1		1	1	2		1				8		
Ashburnham	460	33	Garter	John	1	1	1		1	1		1	2		1		9		
Ashburnham	460	34	Gates	Henery		1	1		1					1			4		

TOWN	PG#	LN#	LAST NAME	FIRST NAME	FREE WHITE MALES under 10	10 to 16	16 to 26	26 to 45	45 and over	FREE WHITE FEMALES under 10	10 to 16	16 to 26	26 to 45	45 and over	TOTAL ALL OTHER	TOTAL SLAVES	TOTALS	DISTRICT/ TOWNSHIP	NOTES
Athol	281	1	Vining	Levet	1		1	1		2			1				6		
Athol	281	2	Wood	Elijah			1					1					2		
Athol	281	3	Ward	Alphus		2	2	1		2		1	1	2			11		
Athol	281	4	Wood	Kimball					1			1		1			3		
Athol	281	5	Willmouth	David					1				1	1			3		
Athol	281	6	Walker	Daniel	1			1					1				3		
Athol	281	7	Wait	Joseph		1		1					1	1			4		
Athol	281	8	Wheeler	Paul	1			1		1		2					5		
Athol	281	9	Wilson	Willm			1	1						1			3		
Athol	281	10	Young	Joel	1			1					1				3		
Athol	281	11	Young	David	2	3		1	1	3			1	1			12		
Athol	281	12	Young	Saml	1	1	2		1	1	1	1		1			9		
Athol	281	13	Young	Willm	1		1		1	1		2	1				7		
Athol	283	1	Stockwell	Noah	1		1		1	1		1		1			6		
Athol	283	2	Stearns	Saml	2			1			1		1				5		
Athol	283	3	Sprague	Joshua	3			1		1		1	1				7		
Athol	283	4	Stratton	Joseph	3			1		1			1				6		
Athol	283	5	Stratton	Jabez				1					1				2		
Athol	283	6	Stratton	Elias					1			1		1			3		
Athol	283	7	Stratton	Elias Jur	4	1		1					1				7		
Athol	283	8	Stratton	Eben	1	1		1		2			1	1			7		
Athol	283	9	Stockwell	Peter				1				1					2		
Athol	283	10	Stratton	Stephen			2		1		1	1		1			6		
Athol	283	11	Stratton	Levi				1		1		1					3		
Athol	283	12	Stratton	Willm		1	2		1	3	1			1			9		
Athol	283	13	Smith	Caleb			1		1					1			3		
Athol	283	14	Smith	Joshua			1	1		1			1				4		
Athol	283	15	Smith	Elihu	1			1		1	1	1					5		
Athol	283	16	Smith	Aaron	2				1	3	3	2	1				12		
Athol	283	17	Smith	Asa			1		1		2	2		1			7		
Athol	283	18	Sibley	Perley	1			1				1					3		
Athol	284	1	Stockwell	Simon	1			1				1					3		
Athol	284	2	Totman	Saml		2	1	1		2	1		1				8		
Athol	284	3	Townsend	Thomas	3		2	1				1	1				8		
Athol	284	4	Twichell	Josiah	1			1		4			1				7		
Athol	284	5	Twichell	Abner	2				1	1			2				6		
Athol	284	6	Twichell	Enos	2			1		1			1				5		
Athol	284	7	Twichell	Jereh			1	1				1	1	1			5		
Athol	284	8	Twichell	Benonah		1				1			1				3		
Athol	284	9	Twichell	Bailey	1			1		2		1					5		
Athol	284	10	Toney	Caesar											6		6		
Athol	284	11	Toney	Abram											3		3		
Athol	284	12	Twichell	Seth	3	1	2	1		1			1				9		
Athol	284	13	Tolbert	George	3			1		2			1				7		
Athol	284	14	Toney	Calvin				1									1		
Athol	284	15	Rogers	Jonah	1	2	2	1	1			2		1			10		
Athol	284	16	Rogers	Abel	1			1	1	1	2			1			7		
Athol	284	17	Rogers	Abel Jr	2			1		3			1				7		
Athol	284	18	Robinson	Jereh	1			1		3	1		1				7		
Athol	284	19	Stone	David Jr		1			1	1	1			1			5		
Athol	284	20	Spooner	Wing			1		1			2	1	1			6		
Athol	284	21	Spooner	Clap	4	1	1	1		1	1		1				10		
Athol	284	22	Stone	Saml	3	2	1		1	1	1	1	1				11		
Athol	284	23	Smith	Robert	2			1		1			1				5		
Athol	284	24	Smith	Nathan	1				1	1	1	1	1				6		
Athol	284	25	Stowell	David			1		1		1	1	1	1			6		
Athol	284	26	Shumway	Perez			1			1	1	1					4		
Athol	284	27	Stowell	John	3	2			1	1	1	1					9		
Athol	284	28	Stowell	Asahel	1	1				2		2					7		
Athol	284	29	Stowell	Abel	3		1	1		1		1	1	1			9		
Athol	284	30	Stowell	Joal	1		1		1		1		1				5		
Athol	284	31	Stowell	Lemuel		1	1	1		1			1				5		
Athol	285	1	Moore	Joshua			1			1		1		1			4		
Athol	285	2	Morton	Samuel		1	3			3	2		1				12		
Athol	285	3	Morton	Phinehas	1			1					1				3		
Athol	285	4	Morton	Reuben	1	1	1		1	2		2		1			9		
Athol	285	5	Morton	Joshua	1	1	1		1	1		1	1				7		
Athol	285	6	Moss	Willm Jur	2			1		1			1	1			6		
Athol	285	7	Moss	Samiel	1			1					1				3		
Athol	285	8	Moss	Willm					1			2	1	1			5		
Athol	285	9	Mundall	Paul		1	1	1			1	1		1			6		
Athol	285	10	Moore	Eliphalet				1						1			2		
Athol	285	11	Newhall	Jonah			1					1					2		
Athol	285	12	Newhall	Hiram Esq	1	1	1		1	1	2		1		1		9		
Athol	285	13	Newhall	Joshua	2			1		2			1				6		
Athol	285	14	Oliver	Aaron			2		2	1	1	1	1	1			9		
Athol	285	15	Oliver	John Jur	3			1		1			1				6		
Athol	285	16	Oliver	John					1			1		1			3		
Athol	285	17	Oliver	George			2										4		

TOWN	PG#	LN#	HEADS OF HOUSEHOLD		FREE WHITE MALES					FREE WHITE FEMALES					TOTAL ALL OTHER	TOTAL SLAVES	TOTALS	DISTRICT/ TOWNSHIP	NOTES
			LAST NAME	FIRST NAME	under 10	10 to 16	16 to 26	26 to 45	45 and over	under 10	10 to 16	16 to 26	26 to 45	45 and over					
Athol	286	1	Oakes	Daniel			1						1	1			3		
Athol	286	2	Pierce	Joseph	1			1		2	1	1	1				7		
Athol	286	3	Paine	Joseph			1		1					1			3		
Athol	286	4	Paine	Barnabas	2	1		1		1			1				6		
Athol	286	5	Philips	Nathl		1	1		1	1	2			1			7		
Athol	286	6	Presson	Pereicles	2			1		1			1				5		
Athol	286	7	Rice	Samuel				1		1			1				3		
Athol	286	8	Raymond	Freeborn	1	2	1		1	1	2	1		1			10		
Athol	286	9	Raymond	Freeborn Jur		1		1		2			1				5		
Athol	286	10	Richardson	Amos				1		2	1			1			5		
Athol	286	11	Rich	David	2	1			1	1	2	2	1				10		
Athol	286	12	Raymond	Edwd	1			1		3	4		1				10		
Athol	286	13	Robbins	Luke	1				1	1	1	2					6		
Athol	286	14	Reed	Israel	3	1			1		2		1				8		
Athol	286	15	Straton	Peleg	3	2	2	1	1			2		2			13		
Athol	286	16	Swatson	Samuel	2		1	2		2		1	2				10		
Athol	287	1	Holman	John	3			1		1	1		1				7		
Athol	287	2	Holman	Stephen	1	1		1				1					4		
Athol	287	3	Hill	John 2nd	1		2							1			4		
Athol	287	4	Jones	Presket	1	1		1			1		1				5		
Athol	287	5	Jacobs	John	1	2	2	1		2			1	1			10		
Athol	287	6	Jones	Amos		2		1		3			1				7		
Athol	287	7	Jones	Amos Jr			1				1						2		
Athol	287	8	Kendall	Calvin	1			1		2	1	1					6		
Athol	287	9	Ketchum	Roger	1		1				1						3		
Athol	287	10	Kendall	Seth	1			1		1		1	1				5		
Athol	287	11	Kelton	Calvin			1				1						2		
Athol	287	12	Kelton	Jonah				1						1			2		
Athol	287	13	Ketchum	Justus			1						1				2		
Athol	287	14	Kelton	James	1			1		1			1				4		
Athol	287	15	Knight	Ebenz				1						1			2		
Athol	288	1	Knight	Isaac	1	1	1		1	3	1			1			9		
Athol	288	2	Kelton	Jonah				1			1		1				3		
Athol	288	3	Kelton	George				1			1	1	1				4		
Athol	288	4	Kendall	Jona		1		1			2		1				5		
Athol	288	5	Kendall	John	1			1			1						3		
Athol	288	6	Kendall	Joel		1	1	1		4		2	1				10		
Athol	288	7	Lovering	Levi		2					1						3		
Athol	288	8	Lucus	James	1			1						1			3		
Athol	288	9	Lincoln	Ebenz	1		2		1	1	1	1	1				8		
Athol	288	10	Lord	Thomas		2	2	1		1	1			1			8		
Athol	288	11	Lilley	David	3			1			1						5		
Athol	288	12	Lewis	Thomas	4	1		1					1				7		
Athol	288	13	Lewis	Willm	1	2	1	1	2	3		1	1	1			13		
Athol	288	14	Morton	Joel				1					1				2		
Athol	288	15	Morton	Daniel			1	1		2			1	1			6		
Athol	289	1	Crosby	Jona	2	1	1	1		1	1		1				8		
Athol	289	2	Church	Paul	1			1			2			1			5		
Athol	289	3	Crosby	John		1		1				1	1				4		
Athol	289	4	Capran	Ephm	1			1		2			1				6		
Athol	289	5	Crosman	Danl	1		2	1		2	1		1				8		
Athol	289	6	Chase	Ebenz			1				1						2		
Athol	289	7	Clark	Benja	2	2			1	1	1			1			8		
Athol	289	8	Danforth	John	3			1		2			1				7		
Athol	289	9	Dike	John				1						1			2		
Athol	289	10	Dike	David	1			1		2			1				5		
Athol	289	11	Drury	John			2	1		1	1			1			6		
Athol	289	12	Drury	Saml	2		1						1				4		
Athol	289	13	Dyre	Shubnow	2			1		1	2			1			7		
Athol	289	14	Dyre	Shubnow Jr	2			1		1	2			1			7		
Athol	289	15	Drury	Joel	1			1		3			1				6		
Athol	289	16	Dexter	Benja		1	1				1						3		
Athol	289	17	Davis	Mary	2					2		1					5		
Athol	289	18	Elmwood	Daniel			2				1	1	1	1			6		
Athol	289	19	Estabrooks	Joseph Revd	2	1	2	1		2			2	1			11		
Athol	289	20	Fairbank	Benja	2	2			1	1			1				7		
Athol	289	21	Fish	Samuel	2			1		1		1					5		
Athol	289	22	Fay	Joseph	1		2		1	2	2			1			9		
Athol	289	23	Fay	Josiah			1			1			1				3		
Athol	289	24	Fairbank	John Capt	1	1	1		1	3			1				8		
Athol	289	25	Fay	Solomon		1			1	1	1			1			5		
Athol	289	26	Fairbank	Thos				1			1			1			3		
Athol	289	27	Fairbank	John			1	1		1				1			4		
Athol	289	28	Fish	Simeon		1				1		2		1			6		
Athol	289	29	Fish	Ezra	1			1					1				3		
Athol	289	30	Fuller	Joseph	1			1				2					4		
Athol	289	31	Fuller	Sarah	1									1			2		
Athol	290	1	Graves	Eliazer	1	1		1	1	3	1	1	2	2			13		
Athol	290	2	Graves	Nathl	1		1	1		2				1			8		

12

TOWN	PG#	LN#	LAST NAME	FIRST NAME	FREE WHITE MALES					FREE WHITE FEMALES					TOTAL ALL OTHER	TOTAL SLAVES	TOTALS	DISTRICT/ TOWNSHIP	NOTES
					under 10	10 to 16	16 to 26	26 to 45	45 and over	under 10	10 to 16	16 to 26	26 to 45	45 and over					
Athol	290	3	Graves	Abner		1	2	1	1			1	2	1			9		
Athol	290	4	Goddard	Josiah Esq	2	2	1		1	2		2		1			11		
Athol	290	5	Goddard	James			1	1	1			3		1			7		
Athol	290	6	Goddard	Elijah	4	1		1			1		1				8		
Athol	290	7	Goddard	Edwd	1		1		1		2	2		1			8		
Athol	290	8	Goddard	Ebenz			1		1			1		1			4		
Athol	290	9	Goddard	Joseph			1			2			1				4		
Athol	290	10	Goddard	Ephm				1		1			1				3		
Athol	290	11	Humphrey	Royal	2	1		1		1			1				6		
Athol	290	12	Humphrey	John			2	1		3	1	1	2				10		
Athol	290	13	Humphrey	James		2	1	1		1		2					7		
Athol	290	14	Hill	John	1			1		1		1					4		
Athol	290	15	Hill	Moses		2	1		1					1			5		
Athol	290	16	Haven	John	1		2		1			1		1			6		
Athol	290	17	Haven	John Jur	2	1	3	1		3	1	1	1				13		
Athol	290	18	Holman	Edwd			1	1				1		1			4		
Athol	290	19	Ballard	Joshua	3	2	1		2	1	1		1	1			12		
Athol	290	20	Briggs	Isaac	2	1		2		4	2		1				12		
Athol	290	21	Barret	John	1	1		1		2			1	1			7		
Athol	290	22	Bigelow	David	1	2	1		1	1	1	2	1				10		
Athol	290	23	Bigelow	Willm				1						1			2		
Athol	290	24	Blake	Timothy	1		1	1		2			1				6		
Athol	290	25	Baker	Marshall	1		1			2	1	1					6		
Athol	290	26	Blanchard	Benja					1	1			1	1			4		
Athol	290	27	Ball	Nathan	2			1		3			1				7		
Athol	290	28	Ball	Moses	1		2		1			1		1			6		
Athol	290	29	Ball	Adanijah	3	1		1				1	1				7		
Athol	290	30	Chase	Moses	1			1				1					3		
Athol	290	31	Crosby	Joseph	1		1	1		3	1		1				8		
Athol	290	32	Crosby	Willm	1	1		1				1		1			5		

TOWN	PG#	LN#	LAST NAME	FIRST NAME	FREE WHITE MALES					FREE WHITE FEMALES					TOTAL ALL OTHER	TOTAL SLAVES	TOTALS	DISTRICT/ TOWNSHIP	NOTES
					under 10	10 to 16	16 to 26	26 to 45	45 and over	under 10	10 to 16	16 to 26	26 to 45	45 and over					
Barre	399	1	Adams	Daniel	1	1	1		1	1			1				6		
Barre	399	2	Adams	Nathan					1	1		1		1			4		
Barre	399	3	Allen	Nehem	1		1	2					2				6		
Barre	399	4	Allen	Jonathan	1		1		1			1	1	1			6		
Barre	399	5	Ames	John			1		1				1	1			4		
Barre	399	6	Allen	Nathan	1			1		2	1		1				6		
Barre	399	7	Adams	Luther	2	2	1	1	1	1	1		1	1			11		
Barre	399	8	Allen	Saml	4	2		1					1				8		
Barre	399	9	Allen	John	2	1		1		2		1	1				8		
Barre	399	10	Allen	Zeb		1		1				1	1	1			5		
Barre	399	11	Allen	Joseph	1			1		1			1				4		
Barre	399	12	Adams	Jesse	1			1		1			1				4		
Barre	399	13	Atwood	Zack		2	2	1		1	1		1				8		
Barre	399	14	Adams	Daniel 2d	1	1	1	1		1			1				6		
Barre	399	15	Adams	John		1		1	2			1					5		
Barre	399	16	Allen	Moses	1	1		1		1		1					5		
Barre	399	17	Adams	James	3	1		1		1			1				7		
Barre	399	18	Atwood	Wait		1		1						1			3		
Barre	399	19	Ainsworth	Moss	1			1		1			1	1			5		
Barre	400	1	Allen	David		1		1					1				3		
Barre	400	2	Adams	Daniel 2d		1		1		1	1		1				5		
Barre	400	3	Bursley	Barnabas				1					1				2		
Barre	400	4	Ball	Adonijah			1					1					2		
Barre	400	5	Brimball	Sylvanus	4	2		1		1			1				9		
Barre	400	6	Bixby	Saml	1	1		1		1	1		1	1			7		
Barre	400	7	Black	James	1	1		1		1			1		1		6		
Barre	400	8	Boydon	Moses			1	1					1				3		
Barre	400	9	Bullard	Saml		1		1		1		1		2			6		
Barre	400	10	Brimstall	Peter			1	1				1	1				4		
Barre	400	11	Brimstall	Phins				1					1				2		
Barre	400	12	Brimstall	Phinas 2d	1	2	1	1		4			1				10		
Barre	400	13	Brooks	Eph Dr.	1		1	1	1	1			1	1			7		
Barre	400	14	Bangs	Want		1		1					1	1	1		5		
Barre	400	15	Bacon	Joseph				1				2		1			4		
Barre	400	16	Broad	Elisah	1		1	2						3			7		
Barre	400	17	Broad	Joseph	3		1			1		1					6		
Barre	400	18	Black	James Lt.		1	1	1		1		1	3	1	1		10		
Barre	401	1	Bacon	John 2d	2			2					1		1		6		
Barre	401	2	Barrett	Joseph	2		1	1		1	1		1				7		
Barre	401	3	Bent	Thaddeus	2			1		1				1			5		
Barre	401	4	Black	John			1	1									2		
Barre	401	5	Black	Elizabeth Wid		1								1			2		
Barre	401	6	Barrows	Thomas		1								1			2		
Barre	401	7	Bacon	Ephm	1			1		3			1				7		
Barre	401	8	Bent	Joel Capt.			1	1				1	1	2	1		7		
Barre	401	9	Brigham	Henry	1	1	1	1		1	1	1	1				8		
Barre	401	10	Bacon	John	4	2		1		1			1				9		
Barre	401	11	Biglow	David	3			1		1			1				6		
Barre	401	12	Bangs	Edmand		2	1					2		1			6		
Barre	401	13	Bacon	Josiah	2			1		2			1				6		
Barre	401	14	Babbit	Erasmus			1	1		2			1				5		
Barre	401	15	Barnaby	Joseph	1			1		4			1				7		
Barre	401	16	Barber	Nathan	3		1	1		1	1		1				8		
Barre	401	17	Brick	John				1					1	1			3		
Barre	401	18	Biglow	Saml Capt.	3		2	1		3			1				10		
Barre	401	19	Barol	Isaac	2	1	1	1		1	1		1				8		
Barre	402	1	Caldwell	David Dr.			2	1		1	1			1			6		
Barre	402	2	Chipman	Stephen	2		2	1					1				6		
Barre	402	3	Chipman	Perez			1	1					1				3		
Barre	402	4	Caldwell	Wm	3		2			1	1	1	1				10		
Barre	402	5	Caldwell	Wm 3d	3	1		1	1	1				1			8		
Barre	402	6	Clark	Wm		2	1	2					3	2			10		
Barre	402	7	Childs	Jona	3	1		1		1		3	2	2			13		
Barre	402	8	Caldwell	John & Benj				3									3		
Barre	402	9	Chace	Elias	1			1					1				3		
Barre	402	10	Caldwell	Saml	1			1					1				3		
Barre	402	11	Caldwell	Seth Maj	3	2	1	3	1	2	2	1	1	2			18		
Barre	402	12	Caldwell	James Maj				1									1		
Barre	402	13	Carruth	Saml	2	2	1		1	1		1	2	1			11		
Barre	402	14	Cunningham	Robert	1	1		1		3		1					7		
Barre	402	15	Cushing	William	1	1	1	1		1	1		1				7		
Barre	403	1	French	Leml	3	1		1		1			1				7		
Barre	403	2	Fesendon	Peter	1	2		1		3			1				8		
Barre	403	3	Fisk	Jason	2		1	1				1		1			6		
Barre	403	4	Fisk	Saml	4	1		1					1	1			8		
Barre	403	5	Farrar	Joseph Maj			3	1	1	3	2	2					12		
Barre	403	6	Fisk	David Col		2	1	1					1	1	1		7		
Barre	403	7	Fellows	John			1	1					2	1			5		
Barre	403	8	Felton	Shelton	2	3		1	1	1		3	1	1			13		
Barre	403	9	Flagg	Earle	1	3	1	1		1		4		1			12		
Barre	403	10	Freeman	Haskell Capt	1	2		1		2	1	1	1				9		
Barre	403	11	Foster	Laml Capt	1			1		2	1	1	1				7		
Barre	403	12	Forbes	Martha Wid									1	1			2		
Barre	403	13	Fay	Adam	3	1		1					1				5		
Barre	403	14	Forbes	Charles	3			1				1	1				6		
Barre	403	15	Farrar	Saml	2	1		1					1				5		
Barre	403	16	Flagg	Earle Jr				1					1				2		
Barre	403	17	Foster	Leml	1	1		1					1				4		
Barre	403	18	Fesendon	Mary Wid							1	2		1			4		
Barre	404	1	Caldwell	Moses		1	1		1	1			1	1			6		

TOWN	PG#	LN#	LAST NAME	FIRST NAME	FREE WHITE MALES under 10	10 to 16	16 to 26	26 to 45	45 and over	FREE WHITE FEMALES under 10	10 to 16	16 to 26	26 to 45	45 and over	TOTAL ALL OTHER	TOTAL SLAVES	TOTALS	DISTRICT/ TOWNSHIP	NOTES
Barre	404	2	Chattock	Ezekiel		1		1			2		1				5		
Barre	404	3	Clark	John			1			2		1					4		
Barre	404	4	Coolidge	Thoms				1		2			1				4		
Barre	404	5	Dana	Josiah				1		1	1	1	2		1		7		
Barre	404	6	Dennis	Thomas	1	1	1	1					1				5		
Barre	404	7	Denton	Gershom		1		1						1			3		
Barre	404	8	Dimmond	Israel	2	1		1		2	1		1				8		
Barre	404	9	Duncan	John	1			1		2		3		1			8		
Barre	404	10	Dennis	Isaac	1		1			1		1					4		
Barre	404	11	Eaton	Jonas Deac		1	1	1			1	1	1				6		
Barre	404	12	Eaton	James Jr	1		3	1		3			1				9		
Barre	404	13	Elit	Wm	1			1		1			1	1	5		10		
Barre	404	14	Danton	George Wasn	1		1					1					3		
Barre	405	1	Hapgood	Winsor		1		1					1				3		
Barre	405	2	Hapgood	Artemas	1	1		1			2						5		
Barre	405	3	Hanes	Dan Capt		2		1		1	1		1				6		
Barre	405	4	Henry	Wm Capt				1			1		1				3		
Barre	405	5	Hinds	Corlis Lt				1					1				2		
Barre	405	6	How	Eliphalet	1	1		1	1	3	1		1	1			10		
Barre	405	7	Harding	Abijah Capt	2	1	2	1	1			1	2	1			11		
Barre	405	8	Hastins	Timy				1			1		1				3		
Barre	405	9	Hinds	Corlis Jr				1		1			1				3		
Barre	405	10	Hinds	Eli	2			1	1	2			2				8		
Barre	405	11	Hemenway	Jonathan				1			1			1			3		
Barre	405	12	Hemenway	Daniel	1	2	2	1		1			1	1			9		
Barre	405	13	Hemenway	Solomon	1	1	1		1			1		1			6		
Barre	405	14	Holdon	Moses Lt	1		1		1	3		1	2				9		
Barre	405	15	Hamilton	Michael				1					1	1			3		
Barre	405	16	Hamilton	Micah Lt		1		1					1				3		
Barre	405	17	Hinkley	Judah	3			1		1	1		1				7		
Barre	405	18	Hamilton	James			1		1				1				3		
Barre	405	19	Willis	John	2	1			1	4			1				9		
Barre	405	20	Woodbury	Ezekiel			1		1			1		1			4		
Barre	405	21	Woodbury	Hubbard			2			1		1					4		
Barre	405	22	Wetherel	Jacob	2	2	1		1			2		1			9		
Barre	405	23	Warner	Leml	3	1		1		1			1	1			8		
Barre	405	24	Wintworth	Daniel				1		1	1	1	1				4		
Barre	405	25	Wheeler	John			1			5			1				7		
Barre	405	26	Winch	Aaron				1			1	1		1			4		
Barre	405	27	Winch	Jonathan		1		1			1	1					4		
Barre	405	28	Winslow	Rhoda Wid		1						1		1			3		
Barre	405	29	Winslow	Seth	3		1	1		3		1	1				10		
Barre	405	30	Winslow	Zens Col.			2	1	1	2			1		1		8		
Barre	405	31	Wheeler	Abial			1			4			1	1			7		
Barre	405	32	Whetherel	Sampson				1					1				2		
Barre	405	33	Wardsworth	David Capt.	3		2	2		2	1		1	1			12		
Barre	405	34	Wardsworth	John	1		1	1		1	1	1					6		
Barre	405	35	Walker	Asa Dr.		1	1	3		3			1	1			10		
Barre	406	1	Weston	Abner	1	1		1		1			1				5		
Barre	406	2	Willis	Seth		1			1			1		1			4		
Barre	406	3	White	James	1	1	1		1	2			1				7		
Barre	406	4	White	Peter		1			1	3	1		1				7		
Barre	406	5	Wetherly	George	2	1		1					1				5		
Barre	406	6	Wetherly	Ephraim	2	1			1					1			5		
Barre	406	7	Wallis	Margaret Wid			1		1				1				3		
Barre	406	8	Willson	Saml				1					1				2		
Barre	406	9	Wheeler	Abigal	1					1			1				3		
Barre	406	10	Walker	Prince											4		4		
Barre	406	11	Wilder	Wid			1			1		2		1			5		
Barre	406	12	Gates	Makw	1	1	2	1	1		1	2		1			10		
Barre	406	13	Gates	Exp Wid		1	1			1		1		1	1		6		
Barre	406	14	Gates	Aaron	1		3			1		1	1	1			8		
Barre	406	15	Green	Jedn	1	1			1			2		1			6		
Barre	406	16	Gorham	John	1	1		1	1	1	1		1	1			8		
Barre	406	17	Gorham	David	1			1		2			1				5		
Barre	406	18	Green	Keziah Wid							1	1		1			3		
Barre	406	19	Grant	Phillip	3	1		1			1	1	1				8		
Barre	406	20	Gorham	Joseph	1			1					1				3		
Barre	406	21	Gates	Jonathan	1			1		1		1					4		
Barre	406	22	Harwood	Peter			1	1		1	2	1					6		
Barre	406	23	Haywood	Stephen	1		2			1	1	1					6		
Barre	406	24	How	Wm	1			1				1					3		
Barre	406	25	Haistins	John	3							1					4		
Barre	406	26	Henry	Adam		1		1			2	1					5		
Barre	406	27	Holden	Aaron Capt		1		1				1	1				4		
Barre	407	1	Hastins	Theophs	2	1		1			2		1				7		
Barre	407	2	Herrick	Saml		1		1			1		1				4		
Barre	407	3	Jones	Ezra Capt				1					1				2		
Barre	407	4	Jones	Nathl Lt		1		1		2		1		1	1		7		
Barre	407	5	Jenison	Nathl			1	1						2			4		
Barre	407	6	Johnson	Ebenz	2	1		1		3		1	1				9		
Barre	407	7	Jenkins	Benj Esq		1		1					1				3		
Barre	407	8	Jenkins	Timith	2	1		1		2		3	1				11		
Barre	407	9	Jenkins	South		1	1		1	1	1		1				6		
Barre	407	10	Johnson	Zachr		1	1		1	1	1		1				6		
Barre	407	11	James	Eleazer Esq		1		1		2		1	1				6		
Barre	407	12	Jones	Saml											3		3		
Barre	407	13	Johnson	John				1				1		1			3		
Barre	407	14	Johnson	John	3					1	1		1				7		
Barre	407	15	Smith	Robert	1				1	2			1				5		

15

TOWN	PG#	LN#	LAST NAME	FIRST NAME	FREE WHITE MALES					FREE WHITE FEMALES					TOTAL ALL OTHER	TOTAL SLAVES	TOTALS	DISTRICT/ TOWNSHIP	NOTES
					under 10	10 to 16	16 to 26	26 to 45	45 and over	under 10	10 to 16	16 to 26	26 to 45	45 and over					
Barre	407	16	Stephens	Luther	2	1			1	1			1				6		
Barre	407	17	Stone	Benj Esq	1		1					1					3		
Barre	407	18	Thomas	Robert	3		1	1					1				6		
Barre	407	19	Totman	Nathl				1				1	1				3		
Barre	407	20	Thompson	Andrew	1		1		1			1	1	1	1		7		
Barre	407	21	Totman	Martha Wid				1					1				2		
Barre	407	22	Totman	Ebenezer	1			1				1	1	2			7		
Barre	407	23	Twitchel	Timy		3	1	1			1	1	2	1			10		
Barre	407	24	Taft	Robert	1		1	1		1	2		1				7		
Barre	407	25	Thompson	Richard			1	1	1	1		1		1	5		10		
Barre	408	1	Underwood	David	1		1		1				2	1			6		
Barre	408	2	Underwood	Jonas	1			1		2	1		1				6		
Barre	408	3	Underwood	Ithamar			1	1		2		1					5		
Barre	408	4	Unfred	Thomas	2		1	1		1		1			4		10		
Barre	408	5	Varney	John Jr		1		2	1	1	1		1				7		
Barre	408	6	Varney	Sirus	1			1		1			1				4		
Barre	408	7	Varney	Dennis	2			1		1			1				5		
Barre	408	8	Vokes	Robert	2			1		2			1				6		
Barre	408	9	Wheelock	Moses B.	3			1		1			1	1			7		
Barre	408	10	White	Noah				1						1			2		
Barre	408	11	White	Josiah			1	1		1			2	1			6		
Barre	408	12	Whiting	Jason				1		1				1			3		
Barre	408	13	Whiting	Josiah				1						1			2		
Barre	408	14	Whiting	Elijah	2			1		1			1				5		
Barre	408	15	Hanes	Jason	3			1			1	1	1				7		
Barre	408	16	Hastings	Timy Jr	1	1		1		4	1		1				9		
Barre	408	17	Hines	Forbes	2	1		1		2	2	1	1				10		
Barre	408	18	Hines	Jesse				1		2			1				4		
Barre	408	19	How	Francis Esq			1	1		2			1	1			6		
Barre	408	20	Herrick	Amos	2			1					1				4		
Barre	408	21	Howes	Edmond Capt	1	2	1	1	1	1		1	2	1			11		
Barre	408	22	Haywood	Ezekiel				1				1		1			3		
Barre	408	23	Hicks	Joshua	3			1		2			1				7		
Barre	408	24	Henry	Robert	2			1					1				4		
Barre	408	25	Holland	James Lt	3			1					1				5		
Barre	408	26	Herington	David	3	1		1					1				6		
Barre	408	27	Holland	Joab	3	1		1		1	1	1	1				9		
Barre	408	28	Holland	Nathan	1		1			1			1				4		
Barre	408	29	Holden	James	1			1		2	2		1				7		
Barre	408	30	Holden	James Jr			1	1		1		1					4		
Barre	408	31	How	Saml	2		1	2	1	1		2		1			10		
Barre	408	32	Henry	Saml			1	1					2				4		
Barre	409	1	Low	Jenison	2			1		1	1			1			6		
Barre	409	2	Loring	Abel		1			1		1	1		1			5		
Barre	409	3	Luce	Reuben	4			1		3			1				9		
Barre	409	4	Lewis	Peter											6		6		
Barre	409	5	Lee	Henry	1			1		2		1	1				6		
Barre	409	6	Lee	Seth	2		1	1		1		3		1			9		
Barre	409	7	Mayhew	Luce	4			1					1				6		
Barre	409	8	Loring	Reuben	2			1		2			1				6		
Barre	409	9	Lee	Benj Esq	2	1		1		1	1		1				7		
Barre	409	10	McFarsan	Hugh	1			1		2	1	2	1				8		
Barre	409	11	Mann	Elijah		1	1	1									3		
Barre	409	12	McFarland	Andrew		1	1										2		
Barre	409	13	Mason	Lot	4		1						1				6		
Barre	409	14	Metcalf	John Lt	4	1			1	1	3	2	1				13		
Barre	409	15	Richardson	David		1		1		4			1				7		
Barre	409	16	Randall	Josiah	2	1		1	1					1			6		
Barre	409	17	Rice	Henry	2	1		1	1	1	1	1	1				9		
Barre	409	18	Robinson	Saml Lt.				1		3	2		1				7		
Barre	409	19	Rice	Ezekiel				1		1		1					3		
Barre	409	20	Rypley	Noah	2		1		1	2	1		1				8		
Barre	409	21	Richardson	Abigal						1			1				2		
Barre	409	22	Robinson	Hannah Wid	2	1	1					1		1			6		
Barre	409	23	Rice	Phineas		1							1				2		
Barre	409	24	Sibley	Job	1	1		1		2	1		1				7		
Barre	409	25	Smith	Nathl Lt.		1	2		1	1		1	1	1			8		
Barre	409	26	Smith	Joseph Capt	1	1		1		1	1	1	1				7		
Barre	409	27	Smith	Moses Lt.			1		1			2		1			5		
Barre	409	28	Smith	John	2	1	1	1		1		1	1	1			9		
Barre	409	29	Sherman	Jason			1		2	1	4		1				9		
Barre	410	1	Smith	Wm		2		1					2	1			6		
Barre	410	2	Smith	Saml	2	2	1	1	1		1			1			9		
Barre	410	3	Smith	Saml Dea.		4		1		2	2		1				10		
Barre	410	4	Smith	Saml Jr	1			1		2			1				5		
Barre	410	5	Smith	Stephen	3	1		1		2			1				8		
Barre	410	6	Smith	David	1	2	1	1		1			2				8		
Barre	410	7	Smith	Francis					1								1		
Barre	410	8	Sibley	Saml	1	2	1	1		1		1		1			8		
Barre	410	9	Smith	Seth	2			1		1	1		1				6		
Barre	410	10	Stearns	John	2	3	2	1		3	1		1				13		
Barre	410	11	Smith	Sarah Wid									1	1			2		
Barre	410	12	Stone	Seth	4			1		1			1				7		
Barre	410	13	Stone	Elijah		1	2	1		2		1	1				8		
Barre	410	14	Sprout	Leml				1									1		
Barre	410	15	Sears	Elisha		1			1	1		1	1	1			6		
Barre	410	16	King	Saml	1		1										2		
Barre	410	17	Kendall	Saml	2			1					1				4		
Barre	410	18	King	Wm	1	1	1		1		1			1			6		
Barre	410	19	Kelley	John	1	1			1	1		2	1	1	1		9		

TOWN	PG#	LN#	HEADS OF HOUSEHOLD LAST NAME	FIRST NAME	FREE WHITE MALES under 10	10 to 16	16 to 26	26 to 45	45 and over	FREE WHITE FEMALES under 10	10 to 16	16 to 26	26 to 45	45 and over	TOTAL ALL OTHER	TOTAL SLAVES	TOTALS	DISTRICT/ TOWNSHIP	NOTES
Barre	410	20	Kelley	Joel				1									1		
Barre	410	21	Kelley	Robert		1				2		1					4		
Barre	410	22	Lee	Saml 2d	1		1			2			1				5		
Barre	410	23	Lyon	Josiah	2	1	1		1	1				1			7		
Barre	410	24	Lee	Joshua		1		1			3		2				7		
Barre	410	25	Lee	Saml	1		1	1	1			1	1	1			7		
Barre	410	26	Lee	Saml Jr	3			1		2			1				7		
Barre	410	27	Lee	Ezekiel	1		1	1	1		1	1		1			7		
Barre	411	1	Nurss	Francis													1		
Barre	411	2	Nurss	Jonathan Capt				1			1	1		1			4		
Barre	411	3	Nurss	Timothy	1	1	1		1		1	1	1				7		
Barre	411	4	Nurss	Daniel	3	2		1		1	1		1				9		
Barre	411	5	Nurss	Caleb															No enumeration listed
Barre	411	6	Nye	Simeon		1		2				2	1	2			8		
Barre	411	7	Nipton					1						1	2		4		First name blank
Barre	411	8	Oliver	Ana Wid	1		1				1			1			4		
Barre	411	9	Osgood	Asahel		1		1		1	1			1			5		
Barre	411	10	Osgood	Manas	1		1		1	1	1	1	1				7		
Barre	411	11	Oliver	Simon											9		9		
Barre	411	12	Oliver	Crumwell											3		3		
Barre	411	13	Oliver	Thoms											4		4		
Barre	411	14	Pattrick	John Lt	1		1		1	2	1		1				7		
Barre	411	15	Pike	Mary Wid									1				1		
Barre	411	16	Perry	Calvin			2	1			1			1			5		
Barre	411	17	Partridge	John 2d	1	1		1				1	1				5		
Barre	411	18	Plumer	Alphus		1		1		1		1					4		
Barre	411	19	Perry	Seth		1		1				1	1	1			5		
Barre	411	20	Parling	Daniel	3	1		1		2			1				8		
Barre	411	21	Partridge	Thaddeus	1			1	1	1		2	1	1			8		
Barre	411	22	Partridge	John			1		1	1		1		1			5		
Barre	411	23	Quamens	Daniel											3		3		
Barre	412	1	Rice	Ebenz Esq			2		1					1			4		
Barre	412	2	Rice	Thomas Lt.		2	1	1				1					5		
Barre	412	3	Rice	Jotham		2	2	1		1	1			2			9		
Barre	412	4	Rice	Daniel		1		1						1			3		
Barre	412	5	Rice	James	1		2		1		1	1		1			7		
Barre	412	6	Rice	Benj Esq		3		1		1		1		2			8		
Barre	412	7	Rice	Abel Capt.	3			1		1			1				6		
Barre	412	8	Robinson	Deneson				1			1	1		1			4		
Barre	412	9	Robinson	Deneson Jr	2		1	1		2			1				7		
Barre	412	10	Robinson	Benj			1					1					2		
Barre	412	11	Robinson	Joseph				1				1		1	1		4		
Barre	412	12	Ruggles	John		2	1					2		1	2		8		
Barre	412	13	Robinson	Leml	3	1		1		1	1		1				8		
Barre	412	14	Rice	Eliza Wid		1		1						1			3		
Barre	412	15	Robinson	Elijah	1	1		1		2	1		1				7		
Barre	412	16	Rice	Thoms Jr	1	1		1					1				4		
Barre	412	17	Rice	John		1		1		2			1				5		
Barre	412	18	Rainger	Amos Lt.	1		1	2		2			1				7		
Barre	412	19	Rice	Willis	2			1		2			1				6		
Barre	412	20	Metcalf	Simeon	2		1	1		2	1	1	1				9		
Barre	412	21	Mead	Tilly Lt			2	1						1			4		
Barre	412	22	Mills	Richard Lt.	1		1		1		1		1				5		
Barre	412	23	Mayson	Thaddeus Lt	1			1	1	5	1		1	1			11		
Barre	412	24	Mann	Asa	1			1				1					3		
Barre	412	25	McCallock	Joseph	2	1			1		1	1		1			7		
Barre	412	26	Mayhew	Sally Wd		2				1	1		1				5		
Barre	412	27	Mayo	Benj Capt.	1	1		1		2		1	1				7		
Barre	412	28	Moolet	John	2			1		2			1				6		
Barre	412	29	Moss	Timothy		1			1		1		1	1			5		
Barre	412	30	Mason	Daniel	1				1	2			1				5		
Barre	412	31	Mendall	Sylvester	3		1	1		4			1				10		
Barre	412	32	Moos	Ashbil	1			1		4			1				7		
Barre	412	33	Maldra	Moses	3	1		1		2	1		1		9		18		
Barre	412	34	Nye	Benj Maj.				1			1			1			3		
Barre	412	35	Nye	Benj Jr	1			1					1				3		
Barre	412	36	Nye	John		1							1				2		
Barre	412	37	Nichols	Robert Capt.			2		1	1	1	1		1			7		
Barre	412	38	Nurss	Jane Wid	1			1		1		1		1	1		6		

| TOWN | PG# | LN# | HEADS OF HOUSEHOLD | | FREE WHITE MALES | | | | | FREE WHITE FEMALES | | | | | TOTAL ALL OTHER | TOTAL SLAVES | TOTALS | DISTRICT/ TOWNSHIP | NOTES |
			LAST NAME	FIRST NAME	under 10	10 to 16	16 to 26	26 to 45	45 and over	under 10	10 to 16	16 to 26	26 to 45	45 and over					
Berlin	211	1	Carter	Sanderson		1		1		2		1	1				6		
Berlin	211	2	Jewett	Jesse	1		1		1	1	1		2				7		
Berlin	211	3	Baley	Stephen	2		2		1	2	1			1			9		
Berlin	211	4	Barber	Nathan		1		1						1			3		
Berlin	211	5	McBride	James	2		1	1	1		1	1	1	1			9		
Berlin	211	6	Baker	Samuel	3	2	1		1	1		1	1				10		
Berlin	211	7	Bowman	Simeon				1		2			1				4		
Berlin	211	8	Priest	Holman		1		1			1			2			5		
Berlin	211	9	Brigham	Willard			1			1		1					3		
Berlin	211	10	Bigelow	Banister			1			1	3		1				6		
Berlin	211	11	Baley	Jedediah		1						1					2		
Berlin	211	12	Barnard	Martha	1						1			1			3		
Berlin	211	13	Houghton	Silas				1		3			1				5		
Berlin	211	14	Houghton	Cyrus	1		1		1		2		1				6		
Berlin	211	15	Merriam	Levi	1	1	2	1		1	1	2	1				10		
Berlin	211	16	Knowlton	Daniel	1	1		1			1		1				5		
Berlin	211	17	Bartlett	Adam	3			1		2			1				7		
Berlin	211	18	G*	Aaron	2			1		1			1				5		Name covered by tape mark
Berlin	211	19	Maynard	*			1			2				1			4		Name covered by tape mark
Berlin	211	20	E*	J			1										1		Name covered by tape mark
Berlin	212	1	Jones	Nathan		1		1					1				3		
Berlin	212	2	Bruce	Calvin	1		1			1		1					4		
Berlin	212	3	Wheeler	Stephen	1	1	2		1	1	1		1				8		
Berlin	212	4	Crossman	Elizabeth									1				1		
Berlin	212	5	Baley	Ebenezar				1					1				2		
Berlin	212	6	Sawyer	Alvin	1			1		2			1				5		
Berlin	212	7	Brigham	Thomas	2			1		1			1				5		
Berlin	212	8	Goddard	James		1	1	1					1				4		
Berlin	212	9	Wheeler	Levi	2		1		2			1					6		
Berlin	212	10	Holder	Thomas	3	2			1		2		2				10		
Berlin	212	11	Hastings	Nathaniel		1	1		1			1		1			5		
Berlin	212	12	Baker	Benjamin				1					1				2		
Berlin	212	13	Baker	Stephen	1			1		1			1				4		
Berlin	212	14	Whitcomb	Enoch	2	2		1		2		1	1				9		
Berlin	212	15	Bruce	John	1	1	1		1	1	2	1		1			9		
Berlin	212	16	Pollard	William		1		1					1				3		
Berlin	212	17	Sawyer	Josiah				1									1		
Berlin	212	18	Sawyer	Josiah Junr	3	1		1		2	1	1		1			10		
Berlin	212	19	Faulkner	William	1		1						1				3		
Berlin	212	20	Moore	Isaac	2			1	1	1	2	1	2				10		
Berlin	213	1	Maynard	Levi	3		1		1			1					6		
Berlin	213	2	Brigham	Daniel	1	1		1		1		1	1				6		
Berlin	213	3	Merriam	Jonathan	1		1	1		1		1		1			6		
Berlin	213	4	Hoar	David			1						1				2		
Berlin	213	5	Sawyer	Amos	2			2		3			1				8		
Berlin	213	6	Maynard	Barnabas		1	1	1	1		1	1		1			7		
Berlin	213	7	Morse	William		1	1						1				3		
Berlin	213	8	Baker	Obediah	1			1		2		1					5		
Berlin	213	9	Southick	David	2	2	1		1	2	1	2	1				12		
Berlin	213	10	Southick	Enoch	1	2			1	3	1	2	1				11		
Berlin	213	11	Wheeler	Daniel	1	1	1			1	2	1	1				8		
Berlin	213	12	Wheeler	Perigrine								1					1		
Berlin	213	13	Fairbank	Jonathan		1				4			1				6		
Berlin	213	14	Barnard	Josiah				1						1			2		
Berlin	213	15	Stephens	Abel	2	1		1			1		1				6		
Berlin	213	16	Goddard	Eber	2			1		2			1				6		
Berlin	213	17	Baley	Amhurst	2		1	1		2	1	1		1			9		
Berlin	213	18	Coolidge	Stephen	3	1		1		1	1	1		1			9		
Berlin	213	19	Barns	David	2		1	1					1				5		
Berlin	213	20	Barns	Fortenatus		1		1			1			1			4		
Berlin	214	1	Barns	William	1		1		1					1			4		
Berlin	214	2	Bruce	Hugh	1		1			1		1					4		
Berlin	214	3	Johnson	Elizabeth									1				1		
Berlin	214	4	Badcock	Ephraim	2			1		1		1					5		
Berlin	214	5	Fosgate	Joel		2	3		1	4	1		1				12		
Berlin	214	6	Welsh	Jonas				1					1				2		
Berlin	214	7	Badcock	William		2	1	1		2		1					7		
Berlin	214	8	Jones	Jonathan			1	1					1				3		
Berlin	214	9	Sawyer	Silas	2			1		3	1		1				8		
Berlin	214	10	Sawyer	William		2		1			2		1				6		
Berlin	214	11	Holt	Amasa		2	1			1			1				5		
Berlin	214	12	Nurse	Sibella						1		1	1				3		
Berlin	214	13	Bruce	Benjamin		1			1			1		1			4		
Berlin	214	14	Baker	Jonathan	1			1		1			1				4		
Berlin	214	15	Jones	Timothy				1									1		
Berlin	214	16	Witt	Asa	1			1			1		1				4		
Berlin	214	17	Priest	Luthar	1			1	1	1		1					5		
Berlin	214	18	Carter	Daniel	2	3		1		3			1				10		
Berlin	214	19	Peiffer	Reubin Rev	2	1		1		1	2	1	1				9		
Berlin	214	20	Whitcomb	John			1	1		2		1					5		
Berlin	214	21	Pollard	Aaron			1	2		1							4		
Berlin	214	22	Priest	John	1			1					1				3		
Berlin	214	23	Ross	William				1		1							2		
Berlin	214	24	Russell	Thaddeus		1		1		1	1			1			5		
Berlin	214	25	Townsend	James		3		1		2		1	1				8		
Berlin	214	26	Townsend	Joshua				1						1			2		
Berlin	214	27	Townsend	Joshua Junr			1			2		1					4		
Berlin	214	28	Hastings	Benjamin	1	1		1	1	3	1		1				9		
Berlin	214	29	Ball	Nathan	1			2				1		2			6		
Berlin	214	30	Pollard	Oliver		1	1		1		1			1			5		

TOWN	PG#	LN#	LAST NAME	FIRST NAME	FREE WHITE MALES					FREE WHITE FEMALES					TOTAL ALL OTHER	TOTAL SLAVES	TOTALS	DISTRICT/ TOWNSHIP	NOTES
					under 10	10 to 16	16 to 26	26 to 45	45 and over	under 10	10 to 16	16 to 26	26 to 45	45 and over					
Berlin	214	31	Pollard	Oliver Junr		1		1		2			1				5		
Berlin	214	32	Pollard	Abijah			2		1		1	1		1			6		
Berlin	214	33	Sawyer	Josiah		1			1		2			1			5		
Berlin	214	34	Moore	Desire			1							1			2		
Berlin	214	35	Fry	William	1			1		3			1				6		
Berlin	214	36	Fife	William		3		1		3		1	1	1			10		
Berlin	214	37	Ball	Jonathan	1				1	3			1				6		
Berlin	214	38	Hastings	William	1			1		3	1		1				7		
Berlin	214	39	Moore	Tille					1								1		
Berlin	216	1	Bruce	Timothy					1	3	2		1				7		
Berlin	216	2	Pollard	Thomas			2		1			1		1			5		
Berlin	216	3	Johnson	Nathan	1	2	1		1	1	1	1		3			11		
Berlin	216	4	Spafford	Job	1		1		1	1		1	2	1			8		
Berlin	216	5	Larkin	John	1	1		1	1	2	2		1	1			10		
Berlin	216	6	Goddard	James Junr	3	2	1				1		1	1			9		
Berlin	216	7	How	Ephraim	2	1		2		2		1	1				9		
Berlin	216	8	Park	James R.		1		1		1	1		2				6		
Berlin	216	9	Bigelow	Agustus		1	1			1		1		1			5		
Berlin	216	10	Johnson	Laban	1	1		1	1	1		1		1			7		
Berlin	216	11	Fairbank	Caleb	2	1		1		2			1				7		
Berlin	216	12	McBride	Josiah	1			1		1			1				4		
Berlin	216	13	Fairbank	Manassah	2			1		2	2		1	2			10		
Berlin	216	14	Johnson	Amos		1	2		1		1		1	1			7		
Berlin	216	15	Powers	Henry	1		1		1	2	1		1				7		
Berlin	216	16	Spafford	Samuel	2			1		2	1		1				7		
Berlin	216	17	Jones	Samuel		1	3	1		2	2	2	1	1			13		
Berlin	216	18	Larkin	Ephraim	3			1		1			1				6		
Berlin	216	19	Newton	William	1		1					2					4		
Berlin	216	20	Dexter	John	2	1		1				1	1				6		

TOWN	PG#	LN#	LAST NAME	FIRST NAME	FREE WHITE MALES					FREE WHITE FEMALES					TOTAL ALL OTHER	TOTAL SLAVES	TOTALS	DISTRICT/ TOWNSHIP	NOTES
					under 10	10 to 16	16 to 26	26 to 45	45 and over	under 10	10 to 16	16 to 26	26 to 45	45 and over					
Bolton	207	1	*	*		1	1		1				1	1			5		Name is obscured by tape mark
Bolton	207	2	Adams	Oliver	1	1	1	1						1			5		
Bolton	207	3	Atherton	Benjamin			1				2			1			4		
Bolton	207	4	Bush	Jonathan			1			3		1		1			6		
Bolton	207	5	Bush	Calvin	1		2	2				1	2	1			9		
Bolton	207	6	Burnham	Lemuel			1			1		1					3		
Bolton	207	7	Fallass	William				1						1			2		
Bolton	207	8	Houghton	Susannah			2							1			3		
Bolton	207	9	Houghton	Henery	3		1						1				5		
Bolton	207	10	Houghton	Jonathan				1						1			2		
Bolton	207	11	Houghton	Rufus	2			1			1	1					5		
Bolton	207	12	Houghton	John				1						1			2		
Bolton	207	13	Houghton	James	2			1		2			1				6		
Bolton	207	14	Houghton	Simon	1	2	1	1	1	1		1	2	1			11		
Bolton	207	15	Gates	Abraham	2			1		1			1				5		
Bolton	207	16	Lewis	Timothy			1			1		2		1			5		
Bolton	207	17	Houghton	Jona P				1				1		1			3		
Bolton	207	18	Houghton	Jona P. Junr		1	1					1					3		
Bolton	207	19	Holman	Nathaniel		1		1					1				3		
Bolton	207	20	Holman	Nathaniel Junr	2		1					1					4		
Bolton	207	21	Houghton	Jonas		2		1		1	1						5		
Bolton	207	22	Houghton	Jonas Junr	2	*	*	*		2	2	1					7		Enumeration numbers obscured
Bolton	209	1	Wheeler	Thankful										1			1		
Bolton	209	2	Pollard	Thaddeus	1	1	1	1				2					7		
Bolton	209	3	Whitney	John		2	1		1	1	1	1	1				8		
Bolton	209	4	Newton	Haven			1				2						3		
Bolton	209	5	Woodbury	William	1	1	1			4		1	1	1			10		
Bolton	209	6	Nurse	Oliver	2		1			2	1		1				7		
Bolton	209	7	Bigelow	William			1	1		1	2			1			5		
Bolton	209	8	Nurse	Stephen	2	1	1			1			1				6		
Bolton	209	9	Woodbury	Samuel				1						2			3		
Bolton	209	10	Woodbury	Israel	3	1		1		1	1	1	1	1			10		
Bolton	209	11	Dammon	Ebenezer			1						1				2		
Bolton	209	12	Fairbank	Jotham		1		1					1	1			4		
Bolton	209	13	Welsh	Thomas	4			2	2				1	1			10		
Bolton	209	14	McBride	Abigail						2		1					3		
Bolton	209	15	Whitcomb	Ephraim	3		2		1	3	1	1					11		
Bolton	209	16	Wheeler	Samuel	1	2	1			1			1				6		
Bolton	209	17	Houghton	Joseph 3d	1	1	1				1		1				5		
Bolton	209	18	Sawyer	Ezekah									1	1			2		
Bolton	209	19	Whitcomb	Abel	1		1	1		1			1				5		
Bolton	209	20	Littlejohn	Sarah										1			1		
Bolton	209	21	Baley	Libella							1			1			2		
Bolton	209	22	Hudson	Wd								1		1			2		
Bolton	209	23	Baley	Elizabeth										1			1		
Bolton	210	1	Houghton	Silas	1		1						1				3		
Bolton	210	2	Howard	Job	1	1	1	1		1			1	1			7		
Bolton	210	3	Hopping	John	2		1			1	3	1	1				10		
Bolton	210	4	Haynes	Silas	3		1						1				5		
Bolton	210	5	Merriam	Simon		1			1	3		1		1			7		
Bolton	210	6	Nurse	David		1	1					2	3	1			9		
Bolton	210	7	Barrett	Oliver		1	1					1					5		
Bolton	210	8	Whitcomb	Asa	1	1	1	2	1	2	1	1	2	1			13		
Bolton	210	9	Longley	Nathaniel Junr		1	1			1			1				5		
Bolton	210	10	Holman	Abraham			4	1		2		1	1	2			11		
Bolton	210	11	Whitcomb	Silas			1			4	1	1	1				8		
Bolton	210	12	Houghton	Jonas Junr	1	1	1	1		3	1		1	1			10		
Bolton	210	13	Whitcomb	Paul		1	1					1		2			6		
Bolton	210	14	Longley	Nathaniel				1				1		1			3		
Bolton	210	15	Moore	Caleb	1		2	1				1	2		1		8		
Bolton	210	16	Moore	Henry	1		1	1					1				4		
Bolton	210	17	Moore	Josiah				1					1	1			3		
Bolton	210	18	Moore	James			1					1					2		
Bolton	210	19	Nurse	Jonathan	1	2	2	1				2		1			9		
Bolton	210	20	Knight	Carter				1									1		
Bolton	211	1	Davis	Nathan	1	2	1		1		1	2		1			9		
Bolton	211	2	Jewett	John	1	1			1	1	1	1		1			7		
Bolton	211	3	Houghton	Abel	2		1			2		1	1				7		
Bolton	211	4	Badcock	Josiah			1			1			1				3		
Bolton	211	5	Sawyer	Elijah		2	1			1	1	1					6		
Bolton	211	6	Gates	Calvin			1			1		1					3		
Bolton	211	7	Gates	Joseph				1						1			2		
Bolton	211	8	Walcutt	Mary	1									1			2		
Bolton	211	9	Whitcomb	Molley											1		1		
Bolton	211	10	Walcutt	Rebeckah		1	1	1		1	2		1				7		
Bolton	211	11	Blood	Samuel	2	1	3	3	1	1	2	2	1	2			18		
Bolton	211	12	Blood	Thomas	2	1		2					1				6		
Bolton	211	13	Pollard	Armory		1	1	1		1			1	1			6		
Bolton	211	14	Smith	David	1	1		1				1					4		
Bolton	211	15	Sawyer	Benjamin	2	2	1	1		2		1	1				10		
Bolton	211	16	Burnham	Hannah									1				1		
Bolton	211	17	Burnham	Benjamin		1			1	1		1	1	1			6		
Bolton	211	18	Welsh	John				1						1			2		
Bolton	211	19	McClary	Hannah										1			1		
Bolton	212	1	Sawyer	Joshua				1						1			2		
Bolton	212	2	Sawyer	Peter		1		1		1				1			4		
Bolton	212	3	Parmiter	Asa			1	1						1			3		
Bolton	212	4	Whitcomb	Richard			1						1				2		
Bolton	212	5	Whitcomb	Joel		1		1					1	1			4		
Bolton	212	6	Whitcomb	Jonas			1		1			1					3		

TOWN	PG#	LN#	LAST NAME	FIRST NAME	M <10	M 10-16	M 16-26	M 26-45	M 45+	F <10	F 10-16	F 16-26	F 26-45	F 45+	TOTAL ALL OTHER	TOTAL SLAVES	TOTALS	DISTRICT/ TOWNSHIP	NOTES
Bolton	212	7	Whitcomb	Azubah						2	1		1				4		
Bolton	212	8	Osborn	Thomas			2		2	1	2	2	1	1			11		
Bolton	212	9	Longley	Robert				1					1				2		
Bolton	212	10	Longley	Robert Junr		1		1		1		1					4		
Bolton	212	11	Osborn	Ephraim		1				1			1				3		
Bolton	212	12	Hastings	John				1		1	1			1			4		
Bolton	212	13	Sawyer	Joseph	1	1		1		3	1	1	1	1			10		
Bolton	212	14	Barnard	Mary						1	1		1	1			4		
Bolton	212	15	Munroe	William	1		1						1				3		
Bolton	212	16	Gardner	Stephen P.		1	1			1		1	1				5		
Bolton	212	17	Oak	Tabitha								2		1			3		
Bolton	212	18	Oak	James		1	1			1		1					4		
Bolton	212	19	Oak	Abraham	1		1			1		1					4		
Bolton	212	20	Wetherbee	Reuben		1						1					2		
Bolton	213	1	Nutlar	Isaac				1				1		1			3		
Bolton	213	2	Butlar	Joseph	2		1			4			1				8		
Bolton	213	3	Houghton	Jaazariah		1		1					1				3		
Bolton	213	4	Houghton	Martin		1						1					2		
Bolton	213	5	Holman	Asa	1		1			1		1					4		
Bolton	213	6	Greenleaf	Calvin		1	1	1									3		
Bolton	213	7	Moore	Phineas	1	1		1		1		2	2				8		
Bolton	213	8	Whitney	Elijah		1	2	1		2	1	2		1			10		
Bolton	213	9	Fay	John	1	1	1	1		2			1	1			8		
Bolton	213	10	Fay	John Junr		1		1	1	1	1	1					6		
Bolton	213	11	Moore	Levi	1	1	1					1	1				5		
Bolton	213	12	Heminway	Joshua				1		2	1		1				5		
Bolton	213	13	Cooledge	Phillip					1					1			2		
Bolton	213	14	K*mings	John	1		1			1		1					4		
Bolton	213	15	Wheeler	Asa	2	1	1			2			1				7		
Bolton	213	16	Wheeler	Abraham	1	1	1		1	3		1	1	1			10		
Bolton	213	17	Wheeler	Moses	1	1			1	1	1		1				6		
Bolton	213	18	Fairbank	Phineas			2			1		2					5		
Bolton	213	19	Prescott	Levi	1		4					1					6		
Bolton	215	1	Wheeler	Joshua	3			1		1	1		1				7		
Bolton	215	2	Rice	Jonathan	1	1			1	2	1		1				7		
Bolton	215	3	Kelley	Micajah	1	2	1	1		2			1				8		
Bolton	215	4	Maynard	John					1		2	2		1			6		
Bolton	215	5	Stratton	David			1		1	1	2	1		2			8		
Bolton	215	6	Whitcomb	Joseph	2			1		2		1					6		
Bolton	215	7	Moore	Ebenezer	2			1		1		1					5		
Bolton	215	8	Elmwood	Nathan	2			1		1			1				5		
Bolton	215	9	Chapin	Coffin	2			1		1			1				5		
Bolton	215	10	Cutting	Joseph	2		1						1				4		
Bolton	215	11	Read	John	1	2	6	1	1	2		2	2	1			16		
Bolton	215	12	Ruggles	Robert				1	2				2				5		
Bolton	215	13	Maynard	Uriah			1			2			1				4		
Bolton	215	14	Cooledge	Isaiah	1		1					1					3		
Bolton	215	15	Houghton	Joseph					1		1			1			3		
Bolton	215	16	Holman	Silas	2	1		1		1	1	1	1				8		
Bolton	215	17	Houghton	Benja				1					1				2		
Bolton	215	18	Moore	Abraham			2	1			1						4		
Bolton	215	19	Hooker	Silas	1	1		1		1			1	1			6		
Bolton	215	20	Houghton	Timothy	1		1			1	1						4		
Bolton	216	1	Clark	Peter	1		1						1				3		
Bolton	216	2	Holman	Oliver			2	1		1		1	1				6		
Bolton	216	3	Edwards	Susannah	1					1			1				3		
Bolton	216	4	Houghton	Jacob Junr	2			1		1			1				5		
Bolton	216	5	Sawyer	Keziah		1						1		2			4		
Bolton	216	6	Sawyer	Lydia	2								1				3		
Bolton	216	7	Moore	William	1	2		1		4			1				9		
Bolton	216	8	Watson	Thomas	1	1			1	1	1	1		1			7		
Bolton	216	9	Brown	John					1		1	3		1			6		
Bolton	216	10	Pierce	Calvin	2	1		1		4	1		1				10		
Bolton	216	11	Sawyer	John		1			1		2	1		1			6		
Bolton	216	12	Hagar	Lois										1			1		
Bolton	216	13	Sawyer	Jonathan				1						1			2		
Bolton	216	14	Draper	Samuel	1			1		3			1				6		
Bolton	216	15	Nurse	Barnard	1		1	1		1			1				5		
Bolton	216	16	Nurse	Abigail										1			1		
Bolton	216	17	Fletcher	Joseph	2		1		1					1			5		
Bolton	216	18	Knight	Amaziah			1	1	1				1				4		
Bolton	216	19	Cooledge	Silas		2		1		1	1	1					6		
Bolton	216	20	Fallass	William				1					1				2		

TOWN	PG#	LN#	LAST NAME	FIRST NAME	FREE WHITE MALES					FREE WHITE FEMALES					TOTAL ALL OTHER	TOTAL SLAVES	TOTALS	DISTRICT/ TOWNSHIP	NOTES
					under 10	10 to 16	16 to 26	26 to 45	45 and over	under 10	10 to 16	16 to 26	26 to 45	45 and over					
Boylston	369	1	White	Aaron	1		2	1					2				6		
Boylston	369	2	Whitney	Timothy		2	1	2	1	1		1	2		1		11		
Boylston	369	3	White	Peter	1			1					1				3		
Boylston	369	4	Winn	William		1			1	1		1					4		
Boylston	369	5	Winn	John	2			1		1	1		2				7		
Boylston	369	6	Whipple	John	1	1	1	1	1		1	1		1			8		
Boylston	369	7	Wheeler	John				1			1			1			3		
Boylston	369	8	Wheeler	John Jr		1						1					2		
Boylston	369	9	Whiting	John L.	1		1	1	1	1			1				6		
Boylston	371	1	Pratt	Abijah Jun	2			1		2	1		1				7		
Boylston	371	2	Prouty	Elijah	1	2	1		1	1			1				7		
Boylston	371	3	Peirce	Levi	2	1		1		1			1				6		
Boylston	371	4	Partridge	Asel	2		1										3		
Boylston	371	5	Rice	Luther	1			1		1	1	1	1				6		
Boylston	371	6	Sawyer	Hooker				1					1				2		
Boylston	371	7	Sawyer	Aaron	2	2	1	1				2		2			10		
Boylston	371	8	Sawyer	Oliver		2	1	1		1	1	1	2				9		
Boylston	371	9	Smith	Isaac		2		1		1	1		1	1			7		
Boylston	371	10	Sawyer	Amariah		1	1	1		3		1	1	1			9		
Boylston	371	11	Sampson	Jonathan	2	1		1		2	3	1	1				11		
Boylston	371	12	Stiles	Joshua	1	1	1		1	3	1	1	1	1			11		
Boylston	371	13	Morse	Jeremiah	2		1	1		2	1	1	1				9		
Boylston	371	14	Maynard	Artemas				1					1				2		
Boylston	371	15	Moor	Jacob				1		2			1				4		
Boylston	372	1	Smith	John	1		2	1		1			1	1			7		
Boylston	372	2	Stone	John			1						1				2		
Boylston	372	3	Sever	Persis						1			2				3		
Boylston	372	4	Sarvtell	Zechariah	1		1	1		3			1	1			8		
Boylston	372	5	Tilton	Joseph	1	2		1				2	1				8		
Boylston	372	6	Temple	Jonas		1	3	1					1				6		
Boylston	372	7	Temple	John		3	2			2	2	1	1				11		
Boylston	372	8	Temple	Timothy		1		1			1		1				4		
Boylston	372	9	Tucker	Jedediah				1					1				2		
Boylston	372	10	Tombs	Lydia		1							1				3		
Boylston	372	11	Temple	Aaron	1			1				1	1				4		
Boylston	372	12	Temple	Joshua	2	1	1	1			1		1	1			8		
Boylston	372	13	Temple	Emary	1		1			1		1					4		
Boylston	372	14	Temple	Benja			1			2		1					4		
Boylston	372	15	Tacker	Jedediah	3		1					1					5		
Boylston	373	1	Hadley	Ephraim		1				1		1					3		
Boylston	373	2	Hunter	Uriah		1				1		1	1				4		
Boylston	373	3	Hannah	John	1			1		1	1	1		1			6		
Boylston	373	4	Howard	Timothy			1					1					2		
Boylston	373	5	Keyes	Thomas		1		1				1					3		
Boylston	373	6	Keyes	Thomas Junr	1		1			3			1				6		
Boylston	373	7	Keyes	Benjamin		1							1				2		
Boylston	373	8	Keyes	Reuben	1		1						1				3		
Boylston	373	9	Kendal	Caleb	2		3		1	3	2		1				12		
Boylston	373	10	Keyes	Benja Junr	2		1			1			1				5		
Boylston	373	11	Keyes	Amasa	1		1					1					3		
Boylston	373	12	Lampson	Nathll		1	2		1		1		1				6		
Boylston	373	13	Longley	James	3	2		1		1	1		1				9		
Boylston	374	1	Larkin	Edmond	1	1	1	1				1					5		
Boylston	374	2	Lewis	Catherine								1			2		3		
Boylston	374	3	Morse	Ebenezer		2		1					1		1		5		
Boylston	374	4	Morse	Joseph	2	3		1		1		1	1	1			10		
Boylston	374	5	Morse	Mary				1				2	1				4		
Boylston	374	6	Moore	Hugh	2	2	2	1		1	2	3		2			15		
Boylston	374	7	Moore	Levi		1	1	1				1	1				5		
Boylston	374	8	Moor	Molly	1		1			2	1		1				6		
Boylston	374	9	Osgood	Abel				1			1	2	1				5		
Boylston	374	10	Osgood	Abel Jun	1		1			2			1				5		
Boylston	374	11	Peirce	Oliver		2		1		4	1		1				9		
Boylston	374	12	Partridge	James	1	1		1	1			2					6		
Boylston	374	13	Partridge	Ozias	1	1		1		1		1					5		
Boylston	374	14	Peirce	Josiah	2			1		1	1	1					6		
Boylston	374	15	Pratt	Abijah				2			1		1				4		
Boylston	375	1	Andrews	John	1		2	1	1	2		1	1	1	1		11		
Boylston	375	2	Andrews	Daniel		1	1	1		1		1	1				6		
Boylston	375	3	Andrews	Samuel				1									1		
Boylston	375	4	Andrews	Robert	1	1	2		1		1		1				7		
Boylston	375	5	Andrews	Robert Jr	1		1					1		1			4		
Boylston	375	6	Abbot	Jason		1		1		2	1	1	1				8		
Boylston	375	7	Anderson	Allen		1		1				1					3		
Boylston	375	8	Andrews	Jotham			1					1					2		
Boylston	375	9	Beaman	Ezra Esq		1	1	3	1	1	3	1		1	1		13		
Boylston	375	10	Bush	Jotham Cap		1	1	2	4	1	1	1	1				12		
Boylston	375	11	Bennet	Asa	2	1		1		2	1		1				8		
Boylston	375	12	Bennet	Ephraim	2	1		1		2	1		1				8		

TOWN	PG#	LN#	HEADS OF HOUSEHOLD LAST NAME	FIRST NAME	FREE WHITE MALES under 10	10 to 16	16 to 26	26 to 45	45 and over	FREE WHITE FEMALES under 10	10 to 16	16 to 26	26 to 45	45 and over	TOTAL ALL OTHER	TOTAL SLAVES	TOTALS	DISTRICT/ TOWNSHIP	NOTES
Boylston	375	13	Beaman	Ephraim	1		1	1	1	2	2		1	1			10		
Boylston	375	14	Bigelow	Andrew	3			1		1	2		1				8		
Boylston	375	15	Barns	Peter	1		1	1					1				4		
Boylston	375	16	Glazier	Jason	2			1		1			1				5		
Boylston	375	17	Goodale	Peter		2	3		1	1		1		3			11		
Boylston	375	18	Gale	Jonathan	1			1		1	1		1				5		
Boylston	375	19	Goodenow	Elijah	3		2	1		2			1	1			10		
Boylston	375	20	Goodale	Aaron		2			1			1	1	1			6		
Boylston	375	21	Goddard	Gardner	2			1		1	1		1				6		
Boylston	375	22	Goodenow	Jonas	2	1			1		1			1			6		
Boylston	375	23	Glazier	Oliver	3			2			1		1				7		
Boylston	375	24	Hinds	Jacob	1		2	1		1			1				6		
Boylston	375	25	Hinds	Tabatha			2	1						1			4		
Boylston	375	26	Hastings	Eliakim	3	2		1		2	1	1					10		
Boylston	375	27	Hastings	Jonathan	1		2		1	1			1				6		
Boylston	375	28	Hastings	David			1		1			1		1			4		
Boylston	375	29	Hastings	David Jn	3			1					1				5		
Boylston	376	1	Hastings	Benjamin				1					1				2		
Boylston	376	2	Hastings	Nathan	1		1						1				3		
Boylston	376	3	Hastings	John		1	1						1	1			4		
Boylston	376	4	Howe	Levi	2	1	1	2		1	1		1				9		
Boylston	376	5	Howe	Silas		2	3		2	1		2		1			11		
Boylston	376	6	Hastings	Silas	2	1	1		1	3	1	2	1				12		
Boylston	376	7	Hathern	David	2	1		1		2		1	1				8		
Boylston	376	8	Hastings	Timothy F.			1	1		2			1				5		
Boylston	376	9	Holt	Abel	1	1	1		1			1		1			6		
Boylston	376	10	Howe	John	1			1		3	1		1				7		
Boylston	376	11	Harris	Daniel	2	1		1		1	1	1	1				8		
Boylston	376	12	Hathern	Micah	1		1		1			1	2				6		
Boylston	376	13	Houghton	Benja	2			1		4			1				8		
Boylston	376	14	Hatherly	Thomas				1					1				2		
Boylston	376	15	Hildrick	Timothy	1	1	4	1		1	2		2				12		
Boylston	376	16	Holt	Abel Junr			1			1	1						3		
Boylston	377	1	Ball	William	1				2	1			1	1			6		
Boylston	377	2	Bennet	Elias	1	1		1		3		1	1				8		
Boylston	377	3	Bondman	Cato											6		6		
Boylston	377	4	Bennet	Mary										1			1		
Boylston	377	5	Barns	John			1	1		2		1					5		
Boylston	377	6	Brewer	James	2	2	1		1	2			1				9		
Boylston	377	7	Cutting	David	2			1		1			1	1			6		
Boylston	377	8	Chinnery	Thaddeus	3			1			1		1				6		
Boylston	377	9	Child	David					1					2			3		
Boylston	377	10	Child	Amos				1		4	1		1				7		
Boylston	377	11	Cutting	Silas	2			1			1		1				5		
Boylston	377	12	Cutting	Josiah	1				1	3		1	1				7		
Boylston	377	13	Cutting	Thannel		1		1			1						3		
Boylston	377	14	Cotton	Ward Revd				1				2			1		4		
Boylston	377	15	Child	Zechariah	3	1		1		2	3	1					11		
Boylston	377	16	Crosman	Abisha	1			1		1		1					4		
Boylston	377	17	Devenport	Mathew	1	2	3		1	1		2		1	1		12		
Boylston	377	18	Densmore	John			1		1		1		1				4		
Boylston	377	19	Davis	Simon		1	2	1		1							5		
Boylston	377	20	Day	Solomon		2		1	1	1		1		1			7		
Boylston	377	21	Danton	Reuben			2		1	1	1		1				6		
Boylston	377	22	Daken	Oliver				1	2			1	1				5		
Boylston	377	23	Daken	David	1	1		1				1					4		
Boylston	377	24	Densmore	Silvanus	2			1		1		1					5		
Boylston	377	25	Eames	William	1	1	1		1	1	1	1		1			8		
Boylston	377	26	Eames	Gershom	1	1			1	1	2		1				7		
Boylston	377	27	Eager	Joseph		1	1	1	1			1		1			6		
Boylston	377	28	Earls	Jacob					1				1				2		
Boylston	377	29	Fuller	Amasa		1		1					1				3		
Boylston	378	1	Fosset	Abel	3			1		1			1				6		
Boylston	378	2	Flagg	Ebenezer					1					1			2		
Boylston	378	3	Fosset	Jonathan		1	1				1	2		1			7		
Boylston	378	4	Fosset	Jonathan Jun	3		1	1		2			2	1			10		
Boylston	378	5	Flagg	Stephen				1	1				1	1			4		
Boylston	378	6	Flagg	Gershom	3		2	1		1			1				8		
Boylston	378	7	Faulkner	Paul					1					1			2		
Boylston	378	8	Flagg	Benjamin	3	1		1	1	2	1		1				10		
Boylston	378	9	Flagg	Stephen Jun	2	2		1		2	2	1	1				11		
Boylston	378	10	Fuller	Amos	1			1	1				3	1			7		
Boylston	378	11	Flagg	Rebeckah						3			1				4		
Boylston	378	12	Flagg	Rufus	1				1	1			1				4		
Boylston	378	13	Goodale	Moses			1		1					1			3		
Boylston	378	14	Gibs	Jonathan	1			1					1				3		
Boylston	378	15	Gay	William	2			1					1				4		
Boylston	378	16	Goodman	Abel	2		1	1		2			1				7		
Boylston	378	17	Barns	Oliver			1		1					3			6		

TOWN	PG#	LN#	LAST NAME	FIRST NAME	FREE WHITE MALES					FREE WHITE FEMALES					TOTAL ALL OTHER	TOTAL SLAVES	TOTALS	DISTRICT/ TOWNSHIP	NOTES
					under 10	10 to 16	16 to 26	26 to 45	45 and over	under 10	10 to 16	16 to 26	26 to 45	45 and over					
Boylston	378	18	Barns	Thd. B	1			1		1	1		1				5		
Boylston	378	19	Barns	Oliver Jun	1			1					1				3		
Boylston	378	20	Banister	Nathan	1	1	1		1		1			2			7		
Boylston	378	21	Bond	John	1	1	1	1		1		2					7		
Boylston	378	22	Bond	Jonathan	2	1		1		1	1		1	1			8		
Boylston	378	23	Brigham	Samuel	2		1	1		3	2		1				10		
Boylston	378	24	Ball	Elijah	1	2			1	1	1	1		1			8		
Boylston	378	25	Ball	Amaziah	1		1			1	1						4		
Boylston	378	26	Bigelow	Joseph					1			1		1			3		
Boylston	378	27	Bigelow	Abel	2	1	1	1	1		1	1		1			9		
Boylston	378	28	Ball	John				1	1	1		1			1		5		
Boylston	378	29	Brigham	Stephen		1	1		1	1		1		2			7		
Boylston	378	30	Brigham	Edmond				1		2	1						4		
Boylston	378	31	Ball	Elijah Jun	2		1	1		2			1				7		
Boylston	378	32	Bartlett	Phinehas	4	1		1		2	2		1				11		

			HEADS OF HOUSEHOLD		FREE WHITE MALES					FREE WHITE FEMALES					TOTAL ALL OTHER	TOTAL SLAVES	TOTALS	DISTRICT/ TOWNSHIP	NOTES
TOWN	PG#	LN#	LAST NAME	FIRST NAME	under 10	10 to 16	16 to 26	26 to 45	45 and over	under 10	10 to 16	16 to 26	26 to 45	45 and over					
Brookfield	245	1	Allen	Nathan	2	2			1	1			1	1			8	First Parish	
Brookfield	245	2	Adams	Ephraim	2		1	1	1	2	1	3	1				12	First Parish	
Brookfield	245	3	Abbott	Jonathan		1			1	1	1	1		1			6	First Parish	
Brookfield	245	4	Abbot	John		1		1		4		2	1		1		10	First Parish	
Brookfield	245	5	Abbot	Moses		1	1	1		1		1					5	First Parish	
Brookfield	245	6	Allen	Molly								2		1			3	First Parish	
Brookfield	245	7	Adams	Benjamin		1						1					2	First Parish	
Brookfield	245	8	Banister	Jesse	2	2			1			1	1	1			8	First Parish	
Brookfield	245	9	Babbit	Seth	2	1			1	1	1	1		1			8	First Parish	
Brookfield	245	10	Barns	Moses Jr			2		1	1		1		1			6	First Parish	
Brookfield	245	11	Barbro	Isaac	3			1	1	1			1	1			8	First Parish	
Brookfield	245	12	Bliss	Samuel	2	1		1		1	1		1				7	First Parish	
Brookfield	245	13	Blair	Joseph		1	1		1			2		1			6	First Parish	
Brookfield	245	14	Barnett	Benjamin	1	1	1	1		1			1	1			7	First Parish	
Brookfield	245	15	Barns	Samuel		1		1		1	1		1	1			6	First Parish	
Brookfield	245	16	Bartlet	Elijah		1		1		1	1		1	1			6	First Parish	
Brookfield	245	17	Barns	Asa		1	2		1	1				1			6	First Parish	
Brookfield	245	18	Barns	Aaron	2			1		2	2		2	1			10	First Parish	
Brookfield	245	19	Bailey	Ephraim	2		1	1		3		1	1				9	First Parish	
Brookfield	247	1	Cutler	Thomas B.	1		1					1					3	First Parish	
Brookfield	247	2	Davis	Timothy	2			1		2		1					6	First Parish	
Brookfield	247	3	Dorr	Joseph		1	1	1	1	1		2	1	1			9	First Parish	
Brookfield	247	4	Dane	Joseph		1		1		2	1	1					6	First Parish	
Brookfield	247	5	Dodge	Thaddeus	1	1	1	1		3	2	1	1	1			12	First Parish	
Brookfield	247	6	Dorr	Moses	2	1		1		1		1	1				7	First Parish	
Brookfield	247	7	Ellis	Asa				1						1			2	First Parish	
Brookfield	247	8	Ellis	Asa Junior		1		1		1	1	1	1				6	First Parish	
Brookfield	247	9	Ellis	Nathan B.	2	1	1	1		1	1		3				10	First Parish	
Brookfield	247	10	Eddy	John		1		1	1	1				2			5	First Parish	
Brookfield	247	11	Eddy	Seth	1			1		2		1					5	First Parish	
Brookfield	247	12	Fiske	Abner	1	2	1	1						1			6	First Parish	
Brookfield	247	13	Foster	Dwight	1	1		2		1	1	2	1	1			10	First Parish	
Brookfield	247	14	Field	Seth	1	1		1		3		2					8	First Parish	
Brookfield	247	15	Gleason	John		1	2	1	1		1	2		1			9	First Parish	
Brookfield	247	16	Gilbert	Solomon Jr	2		1	1			1	2					7	First Parish	
Brookfield	247	17	Gilbert	Nathan	1		2		1	1	2			1			8	First Parish	
Brookfield	247	18	Gilbert	Levi		1	1		1	1		1		1			6	First Parish	
Brookfield	247	19	Gilbert	Pelatiah	1		3		1	2	1	1	1				10	First Parish	
Brookfield	247	20	Gilbert	Pearley	2			1		3		1					7	First Parish	
Brookfield	247	21	Gilbert	John				1						1			2	First Parish	
Brookfield	247	22	Gilbert	Jonas	1		1	1		2			1				6	First Parish	
Brookfield	247	23	Gilbert	Joel	1	1		1				1	1				5	First Parish	
Brookfield	247	24	Gilbert	Lemuel	2		2		1		1	2		1			9	First Parish	
Brookfield	247	25	Gilbert	Gershom				1						1			2	First Parish	
Brookfield	247	26	Gilbert	Philip			1		1			1					4	First Parish	
Brookfield	247	27	Gilbert	Aaron		1	1	1						1			4	First Parish	
Brookfield	247	28	Gilbert	John 2		1	1	1		2	1			1			7	First Parish	
Brookfield	247	29	Gilbert	Estes	1		2	1				1		1			6	First Parish	
Brookfield	247	30	Gilbert	David		1	1	1				2		1			6	First Parish	
Brookfield	247	31	Gilbert	Benjamin				1		2		1					4	First Parish	
Brookfield	247	32	Gilbert	Henry	1		2		1				1	1			6	First Parish	
Brookfield	247	33	Gilbert	Bernard	2			1				1					4	First Parish	
Brookfield	247	34	Howland	Southwerth			4	4					1				9	First Parish	
Brookfield	248	1	Hitchcock	Moses	1	2	5			1	1	1	1	1			13	First Parish	
Brookfield	248	2	Holmes	Abraham	2	1	1	1		1				1			7	First Parish	
Brookfield	248	3	Hitchcock	Caleb		2		1		2			1				6	First Parish	
Brookfield	248	4	Hincher	Josiah	2	2		2	1	2	2		1				12	First Parish	
Brookfield	248	5	Hitchcock	David		1	1	1	1		1	2	1	1			9	First Parish	
Brookfield	248	6	Hitchcock	Peletiah	2			2		1		1	1				7	First Parish	
Brookfield	248	7	Howard	Barzela 2d	1		1					1					3	First Parish	
Brookfield	248	8	Howe	Amasa	2	1		1		2			1				7	First Parish	
Brookfield	248	9	Howard	Barzela	1				1		1	1	1				5	First Parish	
Brookfield	248	10	Hoyt	Robert	2	1			1				1	1			6	First Parish	
Brookfield	248	11	Harrison	Mary		1						1	1				3	First Parish	
Brookfield	248	12	Jennison	Josiah					1					1			2	First Parish	
Brookfield	248	13	Jordan	Dudley			3		1			1					5	First Parish	
Brookfield	248	14	Johnson	Eli	1	1		2		1	1		1				7	First Parish	
Brookfield	248	15	Jennings	John	1				1			2	1				5	First Parish	
Brookfield	248	16	Kent	Jacob	2		2	1	1	2			1	1			10	First Parish	
Brookfield	248	17	Leertourer	Maria W							1		1				2	First Parish	
Brookfield	248	18	Livermore	Elisha	2		2		1	2	2			1			10	First Parish	
Brookfield	248	19	Baldwin	Luke	3			1		1	1	1	1				8	First Parish	
Brookfield	248	20	Bradish	John	2	2			1	1		1		1			8	First Parish	
Brookfield	248	21	Beard	Daniel	1			2			1	1					5	First Parish	
Brookfield	248	22	Barnett	Rufus	2			1		2		1	1		1		8	First Parish	
Brookfield	248	23	Barns	Thomas	1	1			1	1	2	1		1			8	First Parish	
Brookfield	248	24	Blair	Mary										1			1	First Parish	
Brookfield	248	25	Crandal	Caleb	1			1		1			1				4	First Parish	
Brookfield	248	26	Coney	Daniel	3		1	1						1			6	First Parish	

TOWN	PG#	LN#	LAST NAME	FIRST NAME	FREE WHITE MALES under 10	10 to 16	16 to 26	26 to 45	45 and over	FREE WHITE FEMALES under 10	10 to 16	16 to 26	26 to 45	45 and over	TOTAL ALL OTHER	TOTAL SLAVES	TOTALS	DISTRICT/TOWNSHIP	NOTES
Brookfield	248	27	Cony	William			1		1		1			1			4	First Parish	
Brookfield	248	28	Combs	Jacob	1		2		1	2	2	1					9	First Parish	
Brookfield	248	29	Cutler	Joseph		1	1		1	1		2	1	1			8	First Parish	
Brookfield	248	30	Cutler	Asa		2		1		1		1	1				6	First Parish	
Brookfield	248	31	Clap	Elijah		2	1		1				3	2			9	First Parish	
Brookfield	248	32	Crowell	Mary	1	1	4					1	1	1			9	First Parish	
Brookfield	248	33	Crowell	Paul		1	1		1	3	2	2		1			11	First Parish	
Brookfield	249	1	Parkis	James	1	1	1	1		2			2				8	First Parish	
Brookfield	249	2	Richardson	Harmon	1	1	2		1	1		2		1			9	First Parish	
Brookfield	249	3	Richardson	Nathaniel				1	1		1	2		1			6	First Parish	
Brookfield	249	4	Richardson	Ralph	3	1	1		1	1		1	1	1			10	First Parish	
Brookfield	249	5	Richardson	Nathan	2		1	1		1			1				6	First Parish	
Brookfield	249	6	Ranger	Thomas	2			1	1	1	1	3	1				10	First Parish	
Brookfield	249	7	Ross	John		2		1	1	5		1	1				11	First Parish	
Brookfield	249	8	Rice	Thomas 2d	1		2	2		1		1	1				8	First Parish	
Brookfield	249	9	Rice	Tilly	1			3	1	2			1	1	1		10	First Parish	
Brookfield	249	10	Rich	John	1		1		1	1			1	1			6	First Parish	
Brookfield	249	11	Ross	Lemuel	1					1			1	1			4	First Parish	
Brookfield	249	12	Sampson	Perez		1		1		2	1	1					6	First Parish	
Brookfield	249	13	Stone	Silas	1	1	2		1	1		1		1			8	First Parish	
Brookfield	249	14	Snow	David	2			1		3				1			7	First Parish	
Brookfield	249	15	Snow	Jonathan Jun	2			1	1	1		1	1	1			8	First Parish	
Brookfield	249	16	Sanford	Thomas			1		1					1			3	First Parish	
Brookfield	249	17	Sanderson	David		1			1	1				1			4	First Parish	
Brookfield	249	18	Snow	Joseph			1		1			1	1	1			5	First Parish	
Brookfield	251	1	Wood	Samuel		1	2		1	1		2		1			8	First Parish	
Brookfield	251	2	Willis	Azariah		1	1					1	1				5	First Parish	
Brookfield	251	3	Waterman	Theophilus	2		1		1	2		2	1				9	First Parish	
Brookfield	251	4	Waterman	Jonathan			1		1	1	1	2	1				7	First Parish	
Brookfield	251	5	Witt	Thomas				1	1					2			4	First Parish	
Brookfield	251	6	Wood	Mathew	2	1	1	1		2	1	1		1			11	First Parish	
Brookfield	251	7	William	Samuel	2			1		1		1	1				6	First Parish	
Brookfield	252	1	Shepard	John	2	1	2		1	2	1			1			10	First Parish	
Brookfield	252	2	Shaw	William	1				1	3			1				6	First Parish	
Brookfield	252	3	Sanford	Josiah		1				2		1					4	First Parish	
Brookfield	252	4	Snow	Joseph Jun				1		2			1				4	First Parish	
Brookfield	252	5	Sampson	Charles	4	1		1				1	1				8	First Parish	
Brookfield	252	6	Smith	Levi	3			1		2	1		1				8	First Parish	
Brookfield	252	7	Tyler	Gideon				1	1	1	1			1			5	First Parish	
Brookfield	252	8	Tyler	Moses	1	2	1	1		2	1	2		1			11	First Parish	
Brookfield	252	9	Thomas	William			2	1	1				1				5	First Parish	
Brookfield	252	10	Tuffs	John	1	1	2					2		1			8	First Parish	
Brookfield	252	11	Thomas	Naaman	3	1	1			2			1				8	First Parish	
Brookfield	252	12	Thomas	Silas	2			1					1				4	First Parish	
Brookfield	252	13	Upham	Jabez	1	1	2		1	2			2				9	First Parish	
Brookfield	252	14	Ward	Ephm Revd	1	1	1	1				2		1	1		8	First Parish	
Brookfield	252	15	White	Asa		1		2				2		2			7	First Parish	
Brookfield	252	16	Wood	Saml Jur				1		1		1					3	First Parish	
Brookfield	253	1	Ayres	William 2d	1	1		1		2		1	1				7	Second Parish	
Brookfield	253	2	Ayres	Jude		1		1		1	2		1				6	Second Parish	
Brookfield	253	3	Ayres	Increase	2	1	1			1			1	1			7	Second Parish	
Brookfield	253	4	Ayres	Moses		2	1		1	1		2	1				8	Second Parish	
Brookfield	253	5	Ayres	Eli	1			1		6			1				9	Second Parish	
Brookfield	253	6	Adams	Benjamin	1	2	3		1	1				2			10	Second Parish	
Brookfield	253	7	Ayres	Onesephorus				1	1			1		1			4	Second Parish	
Brookfield	253	8	Ayres	Jabez	1		1	1		1			1				5	Second Parish	
Brookfield	253	9	Ayres	William			1	1		1		1	2	1			7	Second Parish	
Brookfield	253	10	Ayres	Cyrus			1	1					1				3	Second Parish	
Brookfield	253	11	Barns	Solomon		2	1	2		1		1	1	1			9	Second Parish	
Brookfield	253	12	Barns	Thomas 2d	2			1		1				1			6	Second Parish	
Brookfield	253	13	Barns	Dorothy								1		1			2	Second Parish	
Brookfield	253	14	Bridges	Stephen	1			1		3			1				6	Second Parish	
Brookfield	253	15	Bigelow	Jonas			1	1					1				3	Second Parish	
Brookfield	255	1	Bartlet	Eli		1	1	1	1	3	2	2		2			13	Second Parish	
Brookfield	255	2	Barns	William	3	1				1	2	1	1	1			10	Second Parish	
Brookfield	255	3	Barns	Moses				2					1	1			4	Second Parish	
Brookfield	255	4	Barns	Samuel	1		1		1	1	2	1		1			8	Second Parish	
Brookfield	255	5	Barns	Mary										1			1	Second Parish	
Brookfield	255	6	Barns	Nathan				1						1			2	Second Parish	
Brookfield	255	7	Clark	James			1	1					3	1			6	Second Parish	
Brookfield	255	8	Corruth	Nathan		1	1					1	1	1			5	Second Parish	
Brookfield	255	9	Cutler	Abijah	2	1		1		2			1				7	Second Parish	
Brookfield	255	10	Cunningham	Hugh			1	1				1		2			5	Second Parish	
Brookfield	255	11	Converse	James		1		2					2	1			6	Second Parish	
Brookfield	255	12	Converse	Samuel	1			1		2			1				5	Second Parish	
Brookfield	255	13	Cutler	Robert	3	1		2		2			1	1			10	Second Parish	
Brookfield	255	14	Casey	Josiah	3	1		1		1	2		1				9	Second Parish	
Brookfield	255	15	Cheever	Samuel	2	2		1			1	3	1				10	Second Parish	
Brookfield	255	16	Cutler	Jesse				1				1	1				3	Second Parish	

TOWN	PG#	LN#	LAST NAME	FIRST NAME	FREE WHITE MALES under 10	10 to 16	16 to 26	26 to 45	45 and over	FREE WHITE FEMALES under 10	10 to 16	16 to 26	26 to 45	45 and over	TOTAL ALL OTHER	TOTAL SLAVES	TOTALS	DISTRICT/ TOWNSHIP	NOTES
Brookfield	255	17	Carter	Jacob											4		4	Second Parish	
Brookfield	256	1	Barstow	Jeremiah	1	1	1	1		3	1		1				9	Second Parish	
Brookfield	256	2	Bush	Joseph	1	1			1	1	1		1				6	Second Parish	
Brookfield	256	3	Bradshaw	Eleazer				2				1	1				4	Second Parish	
Brookfield	256	4	Ball	Thomas			4	1		1			1	1			8	Second Parish	
Brookfield	256	5	Bruce	Roger				1						1			2	Second Parish	
Brookfield	256	6	Bush	Josiah	3			1		1			1				6	Second Parish	
Brookfield	256	7	Bush	Joseph W.			1										1	Second Parish	
Brookfield	256	8	Bell	Simpson		1		1					1				3	Second Parish	
Brookfield	256	9	Brigham	Barnabas	2			1		1			1				5	Second Parish	
Brookfield	256	10	Brewer	Jonas		1	2		2			2		1			8	Second Parish	
Brookfield	256	11	Brewer	Jonas Jun			1			2		1					4	Second Parish	
Brookfield	256	12	Ballch	Wyman	1			1		4		2		1			9	Second Parish	
Brookfield	256	13	Bigelow	Jason	2		2	1		1	1	2		2			11	Second Parish	
Brookfield	256	14	Bond	Thomas		1	2	1		1	1	1	1				8	Second Parish	
Brookfield	256	15	Bond	Amos			2				1	1					4	Second Parish	
Brookfield	256	16	Bullard	Rachel	1		1	1		1	1		1				6	Second Parish	
Brookfield	256	17	Babbit	Elkanah				1		1	1		1				4	Second Parish	
Brookfield	257	1	Fiske	Frances	1		1			1		1	1				5	Second Parish	
Brookfield	257	2	Foster	William		1	1	1				2					5	Second Parish	
Brookfield	257	3	Gilbert	Daniel		1		1					1				3	Second Parish	
Brookfield	257	4	Gilbert	Humphrey	4		1	1		1			1				8	Second Parish	
Brookfield	257	5	Glass	John	1			1		1			1				4	Second Parish	
Brookfield	257	6	Gilbert	Hannah		1							1	1			3	Second Parish	
Brookfield	257	7	Gilbert	Reuben			1		1	3	1		1	1			8	Second Parish	
Brookfield	257	8	Goodale	Josiah	3	1			2	2		1	1				10	Second Parish	
Brookfield	257	9	Horton	Andrew	1		1	1		4	1		2	1			11	Second Parish	
Brookfield	257	10	Haskall	Simeon	4		1				1		1				7	Second Parish	
Brookfield	257	11	Hunter	William	1	1	1	1				1		1			6	Second Parish	
Brookfield	257	12	Hale	Thomas			3		1		1	2	1	2			10	Second Parish	
Brookfield	257	13	Hill	Thomas		1	1		2	3	1	1		1			10	Second Parish	
Brookfield	257	14	Hamilton	Rufus	2	2	2	1		3	1	2	2				15	Second Parish	
Brookfield	257	15	Hathway	Robert	1		1	1		3	4	1		1			12	Second Parish	
Brookfield	257	16	Hinds	Oliver	1		2	1		1		1	1				7	Second Parish	
Brookfield	257	17	Hardy	Thomas		1		1		1			1				4	Second Parish	
Brookfield	258	1	Davis	Benjamin			1			1	1	1					4	Second Parish	
Brookfield	258	2	Doane	David	2	1		1				2	2	1			9	Second Parish	
Brookfield	258	3	Dodge	Nath Jun		1		1					1				3	Second Parish	
Brookfield	258	4	Dean	Abiel			2	1						1			4	Second Parish	
Brookfield	258	5	Doane	Benjamin			1	1		1		1		1			5	Second Parish	
Brookfield	258	6	Dane	William				1			1			1			3	Second Parish	
Brookfield	258	7	Dane	William Jun	2	1		1				1		1			6	Second Parish	
Brookfield	258	8	Deland	Philip		1	1	1					1	1			5	Second Parish	
Brookfield	258	9	Deland	Charles	1			1		2		1					5	Second Parish	
Brookfield	258	10	Dodge	Nathll			1	1	1			2		1			6	Second Parish	
Brookfield	258	11	Deland	Jedidiah	2	2		1		1			1				7	Second Parish	
Brookfield	258	12	Dodge	Artemas	2			1		2			1				6	Second Parish	
Brookfield	258	13	Dodge	Nathll 2d	2	2		1		1			1				7	Second Parish	
Brookfield	258	14	Deuing	Solomon	1	1	1	1		2			1	1			8	Second Parish	
Brookfield	258	15	Edmands	John	1		1	1		1		1	1				6	Second Parish	
Brookfield	258	16	Edmands	Samll				1		1		2	1	1			6	Second Parish	
Brookfield	259	1	Harwood	Katey	1					1			1				3	Second Parish	
Brookfield	259	2	Hutchins	Pearly	1		2	1				1					5	Second Parish	
Brookfield	259	3	Hathway	Levi	1			1			1	1					4	Second Parish	
Brookfield	259	4	Jenks	Lucy		1	2	1			1	1		1			7	Second Parish	
Brookfield	259	5	Jenks	Nicholas		3		1	1	1			2				8	Second Parish	
Brookfield	259	6	Jordan	Bathsheba	1	1	1			3		2	1	3			12	Second Parish	
Brookfield	259	7	Kittredge	Jacob	2	1	6		1	1			1	1			13	Second Parish	
Brookfield	259	8	Knowlton	Charles	1	1	2		1	1	2	1	1	2			12	Second Parish	
Brookfield	259	9	Kimbal	Aaron	2	1		1		2	1	3	1				11	Second Parish	
Brookfield	259	10	Kindrick	Thomas	2	2	2		1	2	1	1	1	1			13	Second Parish	
Brookfield	259	11	Kingsbury	John	1			1					1				3	Second Parish	
Brookfield	259	12	Kendal	Lucy		1				1	1	1					4	Second Parish	
Brookfield	259	13	Lampron	John		1		2	1			3					7	Second Parish	
Brookfield	259	14	Lyscom	John				1						1			2	Second Parish	
Brookfield	259	15	Mathews	Solomon	2			2		1			2	1			8	Second Parish	
Brookfield	259	16	Mellen	David	2		1						1				4	Second Parish	
Brookfield	259	17	Moore	Thomas Jun	1	1			1	1		2		1			7	Second Parish	
Brookfield	259	18	Makepiece	Gershom	1	1	1		1			2		1			7	First Parish	
Brookfield	259	19	Makepiece	Knights		1		1					1		1		4	First Parish	
Brookfield	259	20	March	Ebenezer	2			1		2			1				6	First Parish	
Brookfield	259	21	Morse	Daniel		2	1	1				1	1				6	First Parish	
Brookfield	259	22	Martin	Stephen	2			1	1	1			1				6	First Parish	
Brookfield	259	23	Moor	Elizabeth								1		1			2	First Parish	
Brookfield	259	24	Merriam	Ebenezer			5	1				1	1				8	First Parish	
Brookfield	259	25	Nicholls	Asa		1	3	2					1	1			8	First Parish	
Brookfield	259	26	Nicholls	Isaac	1		2	1		1	1	2		1			9	First Parish	
Brookfield	259	27	Newton	John	3			1		1	2		1				8	First Parish	
Brookfield	259	28	Newell	Joseph	2	1	2		1	2			1	1			10	First Parish	

TOWN	PG#	LN#	HEADS OF HOUSEHOLD		FREE WHITE MALES					FREE WHITE FEMALES					TOTAL ALL OTHER	TOTAL SLAVES	TOTALS	DISTRICT/ TOWNSHIP	NOTES
			LAST NAME	FIRST NAME	under 10	10 to 16	16 to 26	26 to 45	45 and over	under 10	10 to 16	16 to 26	26 to 45	45 and over					
Brookfield	259	29	Orcut	Sylvanus	2			1		3		1					7	First Parish	
Brookfield	259	30	Phips	Samuel		1	1	1	1		1	1		2			8	First Parish	
Brookfield	259	31	Paul	Edward		1	1		1			1	1	1			6	First Parish	
Brookfield	259	32	Peasoe	Francis		1							1				2	First Parish	
Brookfield	259	33	Peasoe	William	3			1		1	1		1				7	First Parish	
Brookfield	260	1	Harwood	Abel	1	1		1		1	1	1					6	Second Parish	
Brookfield	260	2	Hamilton	Israel	3		1	1		2		1	1				9	Second Parish	
Brookfield	260	3	Hall	Eli		1		1		3			2	1			8	Second Parish	
Brookfield	260	4	Hinds	John				1		1			1	1			4	Second Parish	
Brookfield	260	5	Hair	Mary		1								1			2	Second Parish	
Brookfield	260	6	Howe	Eli		1	2		1	1	3			1			9	Second Parish	
Brookfield	260	7	Harwood	Peter		1		1		5			1	1			9	Second Parish	
Brookfield	260	8	Hathway	Jonathan	3	1		1				1		1			7	Second Parish	
Brookfield	260	9	Hoar	Samuel			2		1	2	2	1	1				9	Second Parish	
Brookfield	260	10	Hathway	Wilson				1				1	1	1			4	Second Parish	
Brookfield	260	11	Hathway	Thomas		1			1	1				1			4	Second Parish	
Brookfield	260	12	Hubbard	William				1			1	1		1			4	Second Parish	
Brookfield	260	13	Haskall	Samuel	1	1		1	1	1			1	1			7	Second Parish	
Brookfield	260	14	Howe	Josiah	2	1		1				1	2	1			8	Second Parish	
Brookfield	260	15	Haskal	Silas	1			2			1	1					5	Second Parish	
Brookfield	260	16	Howe	Silas				1									1	Second Parish	
Brookfield	261	1	Pike	Jonas N				2		4	1		1				8	Second Parish	
Brookfield	261	2	Potter	John	3	2		1		2			1	2			11	Second Parish	
Brookfield	261	3	Parkman	Ebenz	1			1					1				3	Second Parish	
Brookfield	261	4	Rice	John	1	1		1		2			1				6	Second Parish	
Brookfield	261	5	Rice	Cheney	2	1		1		1			1				6	Second Parish	
Brookfield	261	6	Richmond	Ezra				1		2		1	3	1			8	Second Parish	
Brookfield	261	7	Raymond	Barnabas		1				1		1	1				4	Second Parish	
Brookfield	261	8	Rainger	William		1						1	1	2			5	Second Parish	
Brookfield	261	9	Rickey	Robert	2	1		1		1		1		1			7	Second Parish	
Brookfield	261	10	Rainger	Joshua	1	1	2	1					1	1			7	Second Parish	
Brookfield	261	11	Rawson	Thomson	3	2		1		2		1	1	1			11	Second Parish	
Brookfield	261	12	Raymond	John	1		2	1		1		1	2	1			9	Second Parish	
Brookfield	261	13	Richards	Ephraim	4	1		1					1				7	Second Parish	
Brookfield	261	14	Snow	Joseph	2	1		1						1			5	Second Parish	
Brookfield	261	15	Snow	Nathl				1						1			2	Second Parish	
Brookfield	261	16	Stephens	Silas				1		1	1	1		1			5	Second Parish	
Brookfield	261	17	Stevens	Jeduthan	4		2	1		2			1	1			11	Second Parish	
Brookfield	261	18	Stevens	Jude				1				1	1				3	Second Parish	
Brookfield	262	1	Moor	Thomas				1		1							2	Second Parish	
Brookfield	262	2	Moor	Holland			1										1	Second Parish	
Brookfield	262	3	Moor	Isaac	1	1		1		2		1	1				7	Second Parish	
Brookfield	262	4	Moor	Nathan	2		1	1		4	1	2	1				12	Second Parish	
Brookfield	262	5	Marcy	Lemuel	1	1		1		1		1	2				7	Second Parish	
Brookfield	262	6	Nye	Ebenezer	2		1			2			1				6	Second Parish	
Brookfield	262	7	Olds	Ezekiel	2		1			2			1				6	Second Parish	
Brookfield	262	8	Pellel	Jonathan	2	1	1		1	3	3			1			12	Second Parish	
Brookfield	262	9	Parks	Hannah	1							1	1				3	Second Parish	
Brookfield	262	10	Parker	Jonah	1					1		1	1	1			5	Second Parish	
Brookfield	262	11	Patrick	Jacob											3		3	Second Parish	
Brookfield	262	12	Potter	Silas	1	1		1		1		1	1	1			7	Second Parish	
Brookfield	262	13	Potter	Luke	1		1	1		3			1	1			8	First Parish	
Brookfield	262	14	Poland	Joseph	1	2		1		3		1	1				9	Second Parish	
Brookfield	262	15	Park	William		1					2			1			4	Second Parish	
Brookfield	262	16	Packard	Jonathan				1				1		1			3	Second Parish	
Brookfield	262	17	Packard	Samuel	1	1		1					1				4	Second Parish	
Brookfield	263	1	Wait	John			2	1		1				2			6	Second Parish	
Brookfield	263	2	Wetherbee	Jonathan		1		1		2	1	2		1			8	Second Parish	
Brookfield	263	3	Wait	Joseph	2		1	1		1	1	1					8	Second Parish	
Brookfield	263	4	Wait	Nathaniel				1						1			2	Second Parish	
Brookfield	263	5	Wait	Nathaniel 2d		1		1		2	1		1				6	Second Parish	
Brookfield	263	6	Woolcot	John				1				2	1				4	Second Parish	
Brookfield	263	7	Woolcot	John Junr	2			1		2			1				6	Second Parish	
Brookfield	263	8	Little	Joseph			1			3			1				5	Second Parish	
Brookfield	263	9	Wait	Samuel			1			1		1					3	Second Parish	
Brookfield	263	10	Walker	Walter	2		1	1				2					6	Second Parish	
Brookfield	263	11	Watson	David	2	2	1	1		2				1			9	Second Parish	
Brookfield	263	12	Forbes	Daniel	2	1	2	1		1	1		1				9	Second Parish	
Brookfield	263	13	Walker	Adoniram		1	1	1			1			2			6	Third Parish	
Brookfield	263	14	Walker	William				1		3		1					5	Third Parish	
Brookfield	263	15	Walker	Oliver			1	1						1			3	Third Parish	
Brookfield	263	16	Wood	Thomas			1	1			1	1		1			5	Third Parish	
Brookfield	263	17	Wright	Ithamar				1	1					2			4	Third Parish	
Brookfield	263	18	Walker	Jason	1	1		1		3	2		1				9	Third Parish	
Brookfield	263	19	Wetherbee	Calvin	3		1	1				1	1				7	Third Parish	
Brookfield	263	20	Westers	James		1			1			1	2	1			6	Third Parish	
Brookfield	263	21	Walker	Joseph Jun	2			1						1			4	Third Parish	
Brookfield	263	22	Wood	Buckmeister			3							1			4	Third Parish	
Brookfield	263	23	Ward	John Junr	2			1						1			4	Third Parish	
Brookfield	263	24	Walker	Moses				1		2		1					4	Third Parish	

TOWN	PG#	LN#	HEADS OF HOUSEHOLD LAST NAME	FIRST NAME	FREE WHITE MALES under 10	10 to 16	16 to 26	26 to 45	45 and over	FREE WHITE FEMALES under 10	10 to 16	16 to 26	26 to 45	45 and over	TOTAL ALL OTHER	TOTAL SLAVES	TOTALS	DISTRICT/ TOWNSHIP	NOTES
Brookfield	263	25	Walker	Oliver Jun	1		1			1		1					4	Third Parish	
Brookfield	264	1	Streeter	Eunice										3			3	Third Parish	
Brookfield	264	2	Stevens	Justus	2			1		3			1				7	Third Parish	
Brookfield	264	3	Simmonds	Job		1			1		1	1		1			5	Third Parish	
Brookfield	264	4	Loomis	Caleb		1		1	1			2		1			6	Third Parish	
Brookfield	264	5	Stephens	Roger			1	1									2	Second Parish	
Brookfield	264	6	Stone	Francis			1	1					2	2			6	Second Parish	
Brookfield	264	7	Stoddard	Bela C.	2	1		1					1				5	Second Parish	
Brookfield	264	8	Spooner	Joshua				1				1	1				4	Second Parish	
Brookfield	264	9	Sabin	John			1										1	Second Parish	
Brookfield	264	10	Tyler	John		1	3		1				1	1			7	Second Parish	
Brookfield	264	11	Tyler	Royal	3			1		1	1	1	1				8	Second Parish	
Brookfield	264	12	Thurston	Joseph	2			1					1				4	Second Parish	
Brookfield	264	13	Tucker	Ezra	1	1	2		1	1		2		1			9	Second Parish	
Brookfield	264	14	Tyler	Phinehas	2	1		1					1				5	Second Parish	
Brookfield	264	15	Townshend	George					1		1			2			4	Second Parish	
Brookfield	264	16	Winslow	Ebenezer			1		1	2		2		1			7	Second Parish	
Brookfield	264	17	Washburn	Peter		2	2		1	2		2		1			10	Second Parish	
Brookfield	264	18	Witt	Jonah	1		1	1		1			1				5	Second Parish	
Brookfield	264	19	Wright	Abijah				1						3			4	Second Parish	
Brookfield	264	20	Wetherbee	Charles			1	1						1			3	Second Parish	
Brookfield	265	1	Abbot	Jesse		1		1	1		1	2		1			7	Third Parish	
Brookfield	265	2	Abbot	Zephaniah	2	1		1		1			1				6	Third Parish	
Brookfield	265	3	Ainsworth	Daniel				1	1	1				1			3	Third Parish	
Brookfield	265	4	Ainsworth	Eunice	1		1					2	1				5	Third Parish	
Brookfield	265	5	Abbot	Joel		2	2		1			2	2	1			10	Third Parish	
Brookfield	265	6	Adams	Amos		2		1		2	1	1	2				9	Third Parish	
Brookfield	265	7	Adams	Moses			1	1		2	1	1					6	Third Parish	
Brookfield	265	8	Adams	William	1			1		2			1				5	Third Parish	
Brookfield	265	9	Adams	Jude		2	1		1	1		1		1			7	Third Parish	
Brookfield	265	10	Adams	John				1						2			3	Third Parish	
Brookfield	265	11	Adams	Jesse	2	2	1			2	1		1				10	Third Parish	
Brookfield	265	12	Ainsworth	Hannah										1			1	Third Parish	
Brookfield	265	13	Adams	Eleazer		1			1		1			2			5	Third Parish	
Brookfield	265	14	Allen	John		1	3		1		1		2	1			9	Third Parish	
Brookfield	265	15	Adams	James	1			1	1		1		1				4	Third Parish	
Brookfield	265	16	Adams	Lemuel	1			1		1	1		1				5	Third Parish	
Brookfield	265	17	Adams	Jude Junr	1		1			1		1					4	Third Parish	
Brookfield	265	18	Rice	Tilley Jun	2	1	1	1		1	1	1	1		1		10	Third Parish	
Brookfield	265	19	Rice	Moses	3	1		1		1			2				8	Third Parish	
Brookfield	265	20	Rice	Jesse	3	1		1			2	1	1				9	Third Parish	
Brookfield	265	21	Rice	John	2	2		1		1	1	1	2	1			11	Third Parish	
Brookfield	265	22	Rice	Elnathan			1	1		1			1				4	Third Parish	
Brookfield	265	23	Rice	William	2			1			1	1		2			7	Third Parish	
Brookfield	265	24	Rich	Salmon	2	2	2	1		2	2		1				12	Third Parish	
Brookfield	265	25	Richardson	Thos	1			1		1			1				4	Third Parish	
Brookfield	265	26	Russell	Asa	2		1						1	1			5	Third Parish	
Brookfield	265	27	Slayton	Isaac	1			1		1			1	1			5	Third Parish	
Brookfield	265	28	Slayton	Thomas				1						1			2	Third Parish	
Brookfield	265	29	Staples	Elias Junr	2	1		1		1			1				6	Third Parish	
Brookfield	265	30	Staples	Elias	3	1			1	2			1				8	Third Parish	
Brookfield	265	31	Stoddard	Samuel		2	1		1	1	2			1			8	Third Parish	
Brookfield	265	32	Stratton	Sarah								1	1	1			4	Third Parish	
Brookfield	265	33	Slayton	Phinehas	1		2		1			1	1	1			7	Third Parish	
Brookfield	266	1	Thurber	Lakan				1					1				2	Third Parish	
Brookfield	266	2	Tufts	John	1		1						1				3	Third Parish	
Brookfield	266	3	Taft	Martha									1	1			2	Third Parish	
Brookfield	266	4	Upham	Nathan		2	1		1			2		1			7	Third Parish	
Brookfield	266	5	Upham	Daniel	1	2		1		3			1	2			10	Third Parish	
Brookfield	266	6	Upham	Phinehas		1	2	1				2	1	1	1		9	Third Parish	
Brookfield	266	7	Walker	Nathan		1		1		2			1				5	Third Parish	
Brookfield	266	8	Woolcot	John			1	1						1			3	Third Parish	
Brookfield	266	9	Walker	Ezekiel		2	2				2		1				7	Third Parish	
Brookfield	266	10	Walker	Daniel	1	1			1		1			1			5	Third Parish	
Brookfield	266	11	Walker	Benjamin	1	1	1	1	1		1	1	1				8	Third Parish	
Brookfield	266	12	Whettemore	James	3			1					1				5	Third Parish	
Brookfield	266	13	Wood	Eli	3	1			1	1		1	2	1			10	Third Parish	
Brookfield	266	14	Willister	Gad			1	1	1			1	1	1			6	Third Parish	
Brookfield	266	15	Ward	Thomas	2		3	1		1		2	1	1			11	Third Parish	
Brookfield	266	16	Walker	Joseph			1		1				1	1			4	Third Parish	
Brookfield	267	1	Bliss	David				1									1	Third Parish	
Brookfield	267	2	Cutler	John		3			1	2		3		1			10	Third Parish	
Brookfield	267	3	Clark	Francis		2	3		1		1			2			9	Third Parish	
Brookfield	267	4	Clark	Francis O	2			1					1				4	Third Parish	
Brookfield	267	5	Cooley	Obadiah Junr	2		1	1		1	1	1	1				8	Third Parish	
Brookfield	267	6	Chadwick	Joseph	2		1	1		2		1	1				8	Third Parish	
Brookfield	267	7	Crosby	Jabez					1			1		1			3	Third Parish	
Brookfield	267	8	Crosby	Oliver		1		1	1	1		1	2	1			8	Third Parish	
Brookfield	267	9	Cooley	Ephraim	1		1		1		1		1				5	Third Parish	
Brookfield	267	10	Cooley	Obadiah			1		1			2					4	Third Parish	
Brookfield	267	11	Chillson	Levi	3	2			1			1	1				9	Third Parish	
Brookfield	267	12	Crosby	Amos	2			1		1			1				5	Third Parish	
Brookfield	267	13	Cooley	Moses			1					1					2	Third Parish	
Brookfield	267	14	Chaffee	Nathan		2		1				1	1	1			6	Third Parish	
Brookfield	267	15	Carpenter	Oliver			1			3			1				5	Third Parish	
Brookfield	267	16	Draper	Simeon	3		1	1		1		1	1	1			9	Third Parish	
Brookfield	267	17	Doane	Nathan	5	1		1				1	1				9	Third Parish	
Brookfield	267	18	Draper	Ellis	2		1			1			1				8	Third Parish	
Brookfield	267	19	Makepiece	Jason		1			1	1			1	1			5	Third Parish	

TOWN	PG#	LN#	LAST NAME	FIRST NAME	FREE WHITE MALES					FREE WHITE FEMALES					TOTAL ALL OTHER	TOTAL SLAVES	TOTALS	DISTRICT/ TOWNSHIP	NOTES
					under 10	10 to 16	16 to 26	26 to 45	45 and over	under 10	10 to 16	16 to 26	26 to 45	45 and over					
Brookfield	267	20	Nowell	John	3			1						1			5	Third Parish	
Brookfield	267	21	Olds	Jonathan		1											1	Third Parish	
Brookfield	267	22	Olds	Reuben	2		1			2	2	1					8	Third Parish	
Brookfield	267	23	Olds	Silas	2	1	1		1	1	1	1	1	1			10	Third Parish	
Brookfield	267	24	Olds	William		1		1					3	1			6	Third Parish	
Brookfield	267	25	Olds	Joseph	3	2		1		2	2	1					11	Third Parish	
Brookfield	267	26	Olds	Simion	1		2		1		1	1		1			7	Third Parish	
Brookfield	267	27	Olds	Dorothy										1			1	Third Parish	
Brookfield	267	28	Olds	Nathan			2			2			2				6	Third Parish	
Brookfield	267	29	Olds	Luke			1			1			1				3	Third Parish	
Brookfield	267	30	Porter	Nathan				1		1		1	1				4	Third Parish	
Brookfield	267	31	Parker	Jesse			1			1			1				3	Third Parish	
Brookfield	267	32	Porter	Nathan Junr	1		1			1		1					4	Third Parish	
Brookfield	267	33	Paddock	Oliver			1				1		1	1			4	Third Parish	
Brookfield	267	34	Parks	Bethiah						1			2	1			4	Third Parish	
Brookfield	267	35	Pendleton	Ephrm			1					1					2	Third Parish	
Brookfield	268	1	Rockwood	Simeon	1	1			1	1		2		1			7	Third Parish	
Brookfield	268	2	Rice	Rufus	4	1	1		1		2			1			10	Third Parish	
Brookfield	268	3	Reed	Cheney		2		2			2		1				7	Third Parish	
Brookfield	268	4	Richardson	Nathan	3	3	1		1	1		1		1			11	Third Parish	
Brookfield	268	5	Rice	Mary		1	1						1	1			4	Third Parish	
Brookfield	268	6	Rice	Semion	2			1					1				4	Third Parish	
Brookfield	268	7	Rice	James	1			1		1		1	1				5	Third Parish	
Brookfield	268	8	Rice	Ephraim				1						1			2	Third Parish	
Brookfield	268	9	Rice	Ephraim Junr	1			1					1				3	Third Parish	
Brookfield	268	10	Rice	Amos	2		1	1			2		1				7	Third Parish	
Brookfield	268	11	Rice	Oliver				1						1			2	Third Parish	
Brookfield	268	12	Rice	Phinehas	2	1		1					1	1			6	Third Parish	
Brookfield	268	13	Rice	Elisha	1			1		4			1				7	Third Parish	
Brookfield	268	14	Rice	Elijah	1	2	1	1		1	1		1				8	Third Parish	
Brookfield	268	15	Rice	Peter	2	1		1		1	2		1				8	Third Parish	
Brookfield	268	16	Richardson	Joseph	1	2	2		1	2		1	1				10	Third Parish	
Brookfield	268	17	Richardson	Ezekiel	2	1	1	1		2			2	1			10	Third Parish	
Brookfield	268	18	Reed	Joseph		1	2	1		1		1		1			8	Third Parish	
Brookfield	268	19	Brigham	Michael	2		2	1		1		2					8	Third Parish	
Brookfield	268	20	Beemis	Moses			1			1			1				3	Third Parish	
Brookfield	268	21	Brigham	Elisha		1	1			1		1					5	Third Parish	
Brookfield	268	22	Brigham	Tilley		2	1	2	1	3	1	1					12	Third Parish	
Brookfield	268	23	Brigham	Jonathan	1		1		1	3		1					7	Third Parish	
Brookfield	268	24	Bridger	Silas		1		1					1	1			4	Third Parish	
Brookfield	268	25	Blanchard	William			2		1			1		1			5	Third Parish	
Brookfield	268	26	Blanchard	Amasa		1		1		1		1					4	Third Parish	
Brookfield	268	27	Bowen	Peter			1	1		1				1			4	Third Parish	
Brookfield	268	28	Bigelow	Asa			2	1	1	1		1	1	1			8	Third Parish	
Brookfield	268	29	Banister	Seth		1	3	1				1		1			7	Third Parish	
Brookfield	268	30	Blanchard	Isaac	2		2				1	1					6	Third Parish	
Brookfield	268	31	Bigelow	Samuel	1		1			1			1				4	Third Parish	
Brookfield	268	32	Bartlet	Ezra	1		1			2		1	1				6	Third Parish	
Brookfield	268	33	Banister	Aaron	1		1			2		1	1				6	Third Parish	
Brookfield	268	34	Banister	Solomon			1			1			1				3	Third Parish	
Brookfield	268	35	Brigham	Lot		1				2			1				4	Third Parish	
Brookfield	268	36	Bowen	Moses			1			1			1				3	Third Parish	
Brookfield	269	1	Humphrey	Asa				1						2			3	Third Parish	
Brookfield	269	2	Harwood	Nathaniel	1		1			1			1		1		5	Third Parish	
Brookfield	269	3	Hastings	Nevenson	1	1	1			3	1	2	1	1			11	Third Parish	
Brookfield	269	4	Hastings	Moses		1		1		2	1	1	1				7	Third Parish	
Brookfield	269	5	Howe	Joseph				1				1		1			3	Third Parish	
Brookfield	269	6	Howe	Joseph Jun	1		1			1			1				4	Third Parish	
Brookfield	269	7	Hyde	Joseph			1			4			1				6	Third Parish	
Brookfield	269	8	Hamilton	Josiah		1	5	1				1	1				9	Third Parish	
Brookfield	269	9	Holbrook	Elihu	1		1	1		3	1	1					8	Third Parish	
Brookfield	269	10	Holbrook	George	1	2	2					1					6	Third Parish	
Brookfield	269	11	Hamilton	Amos	1								1				3	Third Parish	
Brookfield	269	12	Harrington	Amos			1			1		2		1			5	Third Parish	
Brookfield	269	13	Harrington	Rufus	1		1	1		1			1				5	Third Parish	
Brookfield	269	14	Hobbs	Silas	2	1		1		1	1		1				7	Third Parish	
Brookfield	269	15	Howe	William	4	2		1			1	1	2				11	Third Parish	
Brookfield	269	16	Howe	Ebenezer				1									1	Third Parish	
Brookfield	269	17	Hobbs	Jesse	3	2		1		2	1	1	1				11	Third Parish	
Brookfield	269	18	Hill	John				1									1	Third Parish	
Brookfield	269	19	Hamilton	William		2	2	1		2			1	1			9	Third Parish	
Brookfield	269	20	Hamilton	Rhoda	1					3			1				5	Third Parish	
Brookfield	269	21	Holbrook	Isaiah D.	1			1		1		1					4	Third Parish	
Brookfield	269	22	Hersey	Elijah	1	3			1	3		1		1			10	Third Parish	
Brookfield	269	23	Hamilton	Joseph	2	2		1		3	2		1				11	Third Parish	
Brookfield	269	24	Hincher	Thomas	1			1		1	1		1				5	Third Parish	
Brookfield	269	25	Hincher	William				1						1			2	Third Parish	
Brookfield	269	26	Hincher	Joshua	4			1			1		1				7	Third Parish	
Brookfield	269	27	Hamilton	Erastus			2	1	1			1		1			6	Third Parish	
Brookfield	269	28	Hobbs	Josiah				1						1			2	Third Parish	
Brookfield	269	29	Hobbs	Moses	1	1	1	1		4	1		1				10	Third Parish	
Brookfield	269	30	Hamilton	Seth	1	1		1		2			1	1			7	Third Parish	
Brookfield	269	31	Howard	Hannah	1	1	1		1	1	1	1	1	2			9	Third Parish	
Brookfield	269	32	Hamilton	Levi	2			1		1		1					5	Third Parish	
Brookfield	269	33	Howland	John				1		1				1			3	Third Parish	
Brookfield	269	34	Hamilton	Lydia								1	1				2	Third Parish	
Brookfield	269	35	Harrington	Amos		1											1	Third Parish	
Brookfield	270	1	Hamilton	Beemis	1			1		3			1				6	Third Parish	
Brookfield	270	2	Hamilton	Polly						2			1				3	Third Parish	
Brookfield	270	3	Jenks	Francis	2		1	1		1							6	Third Parish	

TOWN	PG#	LN#	LAST NAME	FIRST NAME	FREE WHITE MALES					FREE WHITE FEMALES					TOTAL ALL OTHER	TOTAL SLAVES	TOTALS	DISTRICT/ TOWNSHIP	NOTES
					under 10	10 to 16	16 to 26	26 to 45	45 and over	under 10	10 to 16	16 to 26	26 to 45	45 and over					
Brookfield	270	4	Jennings	Jonathan	2	1		2			2		2				9	Third Parish	
Brookfield	270	5	Jennings	Gershom		1		1		1		1	1				5	Third Parish	
Brookfield	270	6	Jennings	Moses		1			1					1			3	Third Parish	
Brookfield	270	7	Jennings	Roswell	1			1				1					3	Third Parish	
Brookfield	270	8	Jennings	Joel	1	1		1		1			1				5	Third Parish	
Brookfield	270	9	Johnson	William	1	1		1		3			1				7	Third Parish	
Brookfield	270	10	Kenney	Isaac	1			1		2	1	1					6	Third Parish	
Brookfield	270	11	Kendal	Peter	1	1			1	1	1	1		1			7	Third Parish	
Brookfield	270	12	Kingsbury	Edward			1							1			2	Third Parish	
Brookfield	270	13	Moor	Daniel		1	1		1	2				1			6	Third Parish	
Brookfield	270	14	Murry	John	2		1	1		2	1		1				8	Third Parish	
Brookfield	270	15	McClenathan	William	1			1		1	1		1				5	Third Parish	
Brookfield	270	16	Menick	Pliny	3	1	1	1		2	1	1	1				11	Third Parish	
Brookfield	270	17	McClure	Nicholas		2	3	1			1	1	1	2			11	Third Parish	
Brookfield	270	18	Daniels	Levi		2		1		1	1		1				6	Third Parish	
Brookfield	270	19	Drury	Winsor	1			1		4			1				7	Third Parish	
Brookfield	270	20	Doane	Elisha	1		1		1		1	1					5	Third Parish	
Brookfield	270	21	Dunn	Anna						1				2			3	Third Parish	
Brookfield	270	22	Doane	Eunice			1							3			4	Third Parish	
Brookfield	270	23	Force	Ebenezer	2	1		1			1		1				6	Third Parish	
Brookfield	270	24	Felton	Benjamin	1	2	2		1	1	1	1		1			10	Third Parish	
Brookfield	270	25	Foxcoft	Francis		2			1			3	2	1			9	Third Parish	
Brookfield	270	26	Forbes	Aaron		2		1		2	1	1	1				8	Third Parish	
Brookfield	270	27	Fenner	Sion			1			3		1	1				6	Third Parish	
Brookfield	270	28	Flagg	Josiah		1		1					1				3	Third Parish	
Brookfield	270	29	Furbush	Benja Junr	4	1		1					1				7	Third Parish	
Brookfield	270	30	Furbush	Benjamin			1	1		1		1	1	1			5	Third Parish	
Brookfield	270	31	Eaton	Thomas			1			1		1					3	Third Parish	
Brookfield	270	32	Guilford	John	1			1		2			1				5	Third Parish	
Brookfield	270	33	Guilford	William	1	1	2	1		3	1	1	1				11	Third Parish	

TOWN	PG#	LN#	LAST NAME	FIRST NAME	FREE WHITE MALES					FREE WHITE FEMALES					TOTAL ALL OTHER	TOTAL SLAVES	TOTALS	DISTRICT/ TOWNSHIP	NOTES
					under 10	10 to 16	16 to 26	26 to 45	45 and over	under 10	10 to 16	16 to 26	26 to 45	45 and over					
Charlton	325	1	Ammidon	Calvin	1			1		5			1	1			9		
Charlton	325	2	Alexander	Daniel		1		1				1	1	1			5		
Charlton	325	3	Aldrich	Barlow	3		1						1				5		
Charlton	325	4	Albee	Silas	1			1		1		1					4		
Charlton	325	5	Allen	Abner	2	1		1		1			1				6		
Charlton	325	6	Alton	Moses	2	1						1	1				5		
Charlton	325	7	Albee	Benja	1	2			1	1	2	2		1			10		
Charlton	325	8	Albee	Benja Jun		1				2		1					4		
Charlton	325	9	Abbot	Zebina			1			1	1		1				4		
Charlton	325	10	Addams	Emerson		1				2		1					4		
Charlton	325	11	Bacon	Asa	1		2	1			1		1				6		
Charlton	325	12	Bachelor	Perin				1					1				2		
Charlton	325	13	Bates	David		1	1	1				2					5		
Charlton	325	14	Brown	David	1	1		1		1			1				5		
Charlton	325	15	Brown	Nathan	4			1					1				6		
Charlton	325	16	Beals	Enos	2	1		1		1	1		1				7		
Charlton	325	17	Bullen	Samuel	2		1			1		1					5		
Charlton	325	18	Blood	Richard		2	2		2					2			8		
Charlton	325	19	Blood	Nathl	3	1	1		2	2		2	1	1			13		
Charlton	325	20	Blood	Joseph	1	2		1		1		2		1			8		
Charlton	325	21	Billings	William		1	1	1					1				4		
Charlton	325	22	Bullen	Stephen Jun	3		1			2			1	4			11		
Charlton	325	23	Baker	Joseph C.		3	2	1		1		1		1			9		
Charlton	325	24	Brown	Alexander		1		1					1				3		
Charlton	325	25	Bacon	Daniel		1		1				1	1				4		
Charlton	325	26	Bates	Obediah		1		1			1		1				4		
Charlton	325	27	Brown	David Jun	2			1		1			1				5		
Charlton	325	28	Bacon	Daniel Jun	3		1	1		3	3	1	1				13		
Charlton	327	1	Clemons	Benjm				1					1				2		
Charlton	327	2	Clemons	Benjm Jun			1					1					2		
Charlton	327	3	Clemons	Ebenzr	1	1	1				1			1			5		
Charlton	327	4	Coburn	John	1	1		1		1			1				5		
Charlton	327	5	Comins	Free	2	1	1	1		1		1	1				8		
Charlton	327	6	Craige	David		1		1		4	1		1				8		
Charlton	327	7	Coburn	John Junr	3		1	1		1			1				7		
Charlton	327	8	Clemons	Jacob	1			1		1		1					4		
Charlton	327	9	Coburn	Joseph	1		1			2		1					5		
Charlton	327	10	Curtis	Caleb				1		1			2				4		
Charlton	327	11	Converse	Luke			1	1		1		1	1				5		
Charlton	327	12	Commins	Cooledge			1			1		1					3		
Charlton	327	13	Comins	Wm	2	1		1		3			1				8		
Charlton	327	14	Comins	James	2	1		1		1			1				6		
Charlton	327	15	Curtis	Jonathan	2		1	1		1			1				6		
Charlton	327	16	Comins	Reuben				1					1				2		
Charlton	327	17	Comins	Reuben Junr		1		1		1		1	1				5		
Charlton	327	18	Clark	John		1	1			3		1					6		
Charlton	327	19	Comins	Barnabas		1	1			3		1					6		
Charlton	327	20	Clap	Mathew S.	2			1		2			1				7		
Charlton	327	21	Coller	John	1			1		2		1					5		
Charlton	327	22	Coller	Ezra	1			1				1					3		
Charlton	327	23	Child	John			2		1		1			1			5		
Charlton	327	24	Clemons	Reuben		1		1		2			1				5		
Charlton	327	25	Curtis	Mary Wd							1			1			2		
Charlton	327	26	Cleavland	Edward		1		1		1		1					4		
Charlton	327	27	Clough	Obediah				1					1				2		
Charlton	327	28	Chace	Waite	1					2		1	1				5		
Charlton	328	1	Bacon	David		1							1				2		
Charlton	328	2	Bacon	Ebenezer	1			1		1			1				4		
Charlton	328	3	Blanchard	Joseph		1		2		1				1			5		
Charlton	328	4	Blanchard	James Junr	2			1				1					4		
Charlton	328	5	Bates	David 2d	4		1						1				6		
Charlton	328	6	Bacon	John	3	1		1		1	1		2				9		
Charlton	328	7	Burden	Nathl		1		1		1		3	1		3		10		
Charlton	328	8	Brown	Rufus	6			1		2	1	1	1				12		
Charlton	328	9	Bachelor	Elijah			1	1			3	1		1			7		
Charlton	328	10	Bragg	William	1		1		1	3	2		1				9		
Charlton	328	11	Batten	Mehitable Wid	1	1						2		1			5		
Charlton	328	12	Blanchard	Moses	1		1					2		1			5		
Charlton	328	13	Babit	Erasmus	1	1		1		1			2				6		
Charlton	328	14	Bigelow	Phillip			1			1			1	1			4		
Charlton	328	15	Barttlet	Roger		2		1		1							4		
Charlton	328	16	Brown	Abijah	1		1	1		2		2	1				8		
Charlton	328	17	Butler	Stephen			1	1					1				3		
Charlton	328	18	Barton	Sibley	3		1			2			1	1			8		
Charlton	328	19	Belknap	Stephen	3	1		1		1				1			7		
Charlton	328	20	Blood	William	2		1				1						4		
Charlton	328	21	Bacon	Rufus	1					2	1	1	1				6		
Charlton	328	22	Conant	Harvey			1					1					2		
Charlton	328	23	Chamberlain	Timothy				1			1		1				3		

TOWN	PG#	LN#	LAST NAME	FIRST NAME	FREE WHITE MALES					FREE WHITE FEMALES					TOTAL ALL OTHER	TOTAL SLAVES	TOTALS	DISTRICT/ TOWNSHIP	NOTES
					under 10	10 to 16	16 to 26	26 to 45	45 and over	under 10	10 to 16	16 to 26	26 to 45	45 and over					
Charlton	328	24	Coburn	Jacob	1			1		1			1				4		
Charlton	328	25	Chamberlain	Eliakim	2	2	1		1	1	1	2	1				11		
Charlton	328	26	Clemons	Phillip		1			1			2	2	1			7		
Charlton	328	27	Clemons	Asa	3	1		1		2		1	1				9		
Charlton	328	28	Clemons	Jonathan Junr		1		1		4		1	1				8		
Charlton	328	29	Clemons	Jonathan		1			1					1			3		
Charlton	329	1	Dresser	Aaron	3				1		1	1		1			7		
Charlton	329	2	Dresser	Richard					1	1	1		1				4		
Charlton	329	3	Dresser	Moses	1	2	1		1	1	1	2					9		
Charlton	329	4	Denis	Jonathan		1	2		1	1	1		1				7		
Charlton	329	5	Dugor	Charles		1	2		1	1	1						6		
Charlton	329	6	Dugor	Charles Junr				1		2		1					4		
Charlton	329	7	Davis	Amasa	2	1	1	1		2	1		1				9		
Charlton	329	8	Dresser	Asa		1	1		1			2		1			6		
Charlton	329	9	Davison	Ebenzr					1	1		2		1			5		
Charlton	329	10	Danilson	Lothario				1		2		1					4		
Charlton	329	11	Davis	Levi		1	2		1	1	1	1		1			8		
Charlton	329	12	Davis	Asa		1	1	1				1	1				5		
Charlton	329	13	Denis	Isaac	2			1					1				4		
Charlton	329	14	Denis	Silas	1	1	2		1				1				6		
Charlton	329	15	Denis	Nathan					1					1			2		
Charlton	329	16	Dunbar	David	1		1		1		1		1				5		
Charlton	329	17	Dunbar	Samuel	1	1		1		4	2		1				10		
Charlton	329	18	Douty	Benjm			1		1			1		1			4		
Charlton	329	19	Douty	Benjm Junr	1		1					1					3		
Charlton	329	20	Davis	Moses	1		1			2		1					5		
Charlton	329	21	Dodge	Moses	1	1		1				1					4		
Charlton	329	22	Dugor	Gload			2			1		1		2			6		
Charlton	329	23	Dodge	David	2			1				1					4		
Charlton	329	24	Edwards	John		1			1	1	2	2	1	1			9		
Charlton	329	25	Edwards	Thomas	2	1	1	1					1				6		
Charlton	329	26	Edwards	Robert		1		1		2	2		1				7		
Charlton	329	27	Eustice	Thomas		1	1			3		1					6		
Charlton	330	1	Eddy	Edmund	2		1		1	2		1					7		
Charlton	330	2	Edwards	Joseph					1		1	1					3		
Charlton	330	3	Doskett	Thomas	1	1	1		1		2	2		1			9		
Charlton	330	4	Doskett	Samuel		2	1		1			1		2			7		
Charlton	330	5	Fitts	John	1	1	2		1	2	1	1	1				10		
Charlton	330	6	Fletcher	Nathan	1				1			1	1				4		
Charlton	330	7	Farnum	Thomas	1			1	1	1		1		1			6		
Charlton	330	8	Fitts	Caleb	1		1	1		3	1		1	4			12		
Charlton	330	9	Fuller	Jonathn					1			1	1				3		
Charlton	330	10	Fay	Stephen		1		1	1			2		1			6		
Charlton	330	11	Farnum	Joshua				1	1					1			3		
Charlton	330	12	Fitts	Robert	2	1	1	1	1	1	1		1				9		
Charlton	330	13	Goodale	Nathl	1	1	1		1			1	2	2			9		
Charlton	330	14	Goodale	Nathl Junr	2				1	1			2				6		
Charlton	330	15	Gates	Levi	1			1		4			1				7		
Charlton	330	16	Green	Thomas					1			1		1			3		
Charlton	330	17	Gould	Thomas	2	2	1		1	2	1		1	1			11		
Charlton	330	18	Gould	Jonathan				1		2			1				4		
Charlton	330	19	Gibbs	Joseph					1			1					2		
Charlton	330	20	Gibbs	Nathl	1	1	3		1					1			7		
Charlton	330	21	Gibbs	John	2			1		3	1		1				8		
Charlton	330	22	Goodale	Zacheriah			1	1				1		1			4		
Charlton	330	23	Gulley	William	1	3	2	1	1			1					9		
Charlton	330	24	Gorton	John	3	1		1		2	1		1				9		
Charlton	330	25	George	John	1		1	1		1	1						5		
Charlton	330	26	Goodale	Jonathan	3			1		1			1				6		
Charlton	331	1	Laflin	Parley	1			1		2			1				5		
Charlton	331	2	Lamb	Richard	3		1			1			1				6		
Charlton	331	3	Lamb	David	1	2			1	1	2			1			8		
Charlton	331	4	Lee	Chartman			1										1		
Charlton	331	5	Lampson	Isaac	3	1		1		2	1		1				9		
Charlton	331	6	Lampson	Ebenzr					1					1			2		
Charlton	331	7	Leavens	Elijah			1		1	1	3			1			7		
Charlton	331	8	Lamb	Abijah			2		1		1	1		1			6		
Charlton	331	9	Lamb	Abijah Junr	1		1					1					3		
Charlton	331	10	Lamb	Samuel		1	1		1		1	1		1			6		
Charlton	331	11	Lamb	Ebenzr		1	1	1	1			1		1			6		
Charlton	331	12	Lamb	Jarvis	1			1		3			1				6		
Charlton	331	13	Lamb	Reuben	2			1		1	1		1				6		
Charlton	331	14	Lamb	Nahum	2	1		1		2	1		1				8		
Charlton	331	15	Litchfield	Comins	1		1					1					3		
Charlton	331	16	Lathe	Jabez		2			1	2	2			1			8		
Charlton	331	17	Learned	David				1		2			1				4		
Charlton	331	18	Lyon	Abner Junr			1	1		4			1				7		
Charlton	331	19	Learned	Erastus	1		1	1	1	3	1	2					10		
Charlton	331	20	Merit	Walter				1				2					3		

TOWN	PG#	LN#	LAST NAME	FIRST NAME	M under 10	M 10 to 16	M 16 to 26	M 26 to 45	M 45 and over	F under 10	F 10 to 16	F 16 to 26	F 26 to 45	F 45 and over	TOTAL ALL OTHER	TOTAL SLAVES	TOTALS	DISTRICT/TOWNSHIP	NOTES
Charlton	331	21	Merit	Moses	3			1						1			5		
Charlton	331	22	McIntire	Ezra	2				1	3	1	1	1				9		
Charlton	331	23	McIntire	Elijah		1	1		1				1				4		
Charlton	331	24	McIntire	Amos	1			2		2			1	1			7		
Charlton	331	25	Marsh	Jonathan					1					1			2		
Charlton	331	26	Merit	Amos			1			4	2	1	1				9		
Charlton	331	27	Moffit	Elihu	1			1					1				3		
Charlton	332	1	Harwood	Nicholas		1			1	1	1	2		1			7		
Charlton	332	2	Heath	John	1				1	1	2	1		1			7		
Charlton	332	3	Harwood	Ezra Junr				1		1	1						3		
Charlton	332	4	Harwood	Daniel				1		2	2		1	1			7		
Charlton	332	5	Harwood	Ezra				1					1	1			3		
Charlton	332	6	Holbrook	Josiah		1		1		2	1		1				6		
Charlton	332	7	Harwood	Jonathan	1	1		1			3			1			7		
Charlton	332	8	Haven	John D.	1		1	1		2			1				6		
Charlton	332	9	Harwood	Gershom	1	2		1		1	1		1				7		
Charlton	332	10	Hammond	Moses	3	2		1		1		1	1				9		
Charlton	332	11	Hammond	Aaron	2	2		1		3	2		1				11		
Charlton	332	12	Hammond	David		1								1			3		
Charlton	332	13	Hammond	David Junr	1		1					1					3		
Charlton	332	14	Hooker	Parker		1						1					2		
Charlton	332	15	Hayward	Samuel Junr			1	1					1	1			4		
Charlton	332	16	Hill	John		1		1				1		1			4		
Charlton	332	17	Hayward	Jonathn			1			1							2		
Charlton	332	18	Hovey	Josiah		2	1		1		2	2		1			9		
Charlton	332	19	Jones	Eli	1	2		1		3			1				8		
Charlton	332	20	Jones	Seth		1		1		2		3	1				8		
Charlton	332	21	Jones	Mary Wd									1				1		
Charlton	332	22	Jenison	Peter	2	1	1		1	1	1			1			9		
Charlton	332	23	Jenison	Peter Junr	1		1			2			1				5		
Charlton	332	24	Joslin	Saml	1			1			1		1				4		
Charlton	332	25	King	Daniel	1			1		2			1				5		
Charlton	333	1	McIntire	Ebenzr		1		1		2	2		1				7		
Charlton	333	2	McIntire	Elias	3			1					1				5		
Charlton	333	3	McIntire	Stephanus	2			1		1			1				5		
Charlton	333	4	McIntire	Isaiah		1		1					1				3		
Charlton	333	5	More	Marshal	1			1		3			1				6		
Charlton	333	6	McIntire	Deborah						1			1	1			3		
Charlton	333	7	Morey	Ephraim	1	2	2		1	1		2		1			10		
Charlton	333	8	McIntire	Elnathan	1			1	1	3	2	1	1				10		
Charlton	333	9	McIntire	Alpheus			1				1						2		
Charlton	333	10	Munroe	Lemuel	3	1		1		1			1				7		
Charlton	333	11	McIntire	Nathl	2			1			1		1				5		
Charlton	333	12	Nichols	Wm	2	1					1		1	1			6		
Charlton	333	13	Newell	Joseph			1	1		1		1		1			5		
Charlton	333	14	Needham	Thomas				1			1			1			3		
Charlton	333	15	Needham	Wm	2			1		4		1					8		
Charlton	333	16	Nichols	John	1	1		1		3		1					7		
Charlton	333	17	Nichols	Alexander		1		1		3		1					6		
Charlton	333	18	Nichols	Jeremiah	3			1		1		1					6		
Charlton	333	19	Nichols	Jonathn		1		1		1		1					4		
Charlton	333	20	Newell	Asa	3			1		1		1					6		
Charlton	333	21	Oaks	Amos	2			1		2		1					6		
Charlton	333	22	Oaks	Abijah		1	1		1	1			1	1			6		
Charlton	333	23	Pratt	Nathan			1						1				2		
Charlton	333	24	Pratt	Jonathan			1			2	1	1					5		
Charlton	333	25	Putney	Jonathn			1		1	1	2	1		1			7		
Charlton	333	26	Pratt	Jesse			1			1	2	1		1			6		
Charlton	333	27	Pratt	Joseph		1	2		1		2	2		1			9		
Charlton	334	1	Morse	Timothy		1		1		3	2	2	1	1			12		
Charlton	334	2	McIntire	Zebulon		3	1		1		1		1				7		
Charlton	334	3	McIntire	Robert				1					1				2		
Charlton	334	4	McIntire	Robert Junr			1						1				2		
Charlton	334	5	McIngtry	James	1	2	1		1		1	1		1			8		
Charlton	334	6	Miner	Ezra		2	1		2	1				2			9		
Charlton	334	7	Mory	Nathl	2			1					1	1			5		
Charlton	334	8	Merit	Jesse	1			1		4	1		1				8		
Charlton	334	9	Melody	James		2		1					1				4		
Charlton	334	10	McIntire	Nehemiah		1	1		1				1				4		
Charlton	334	11	Moris	Elijah G.	2			1		3			1				7		
Charlton	334	12	Moris	Wm			1			1		1					3		
Charlton	334	13	Morse	Ruggles		1		1			1	1					4		
Charlton	334	14	McFarlen	Elijah				1		2			1				4		
Charlton	334	15	McIntire	Joseph			1	1					1	2			5		
Charlton	334	16	Marble	Daniel	2			1		1	1		1	1	1		7		
Charlton	334	17	More	Jonathan				1					1				2		
Charlton	334	18	Marble	Thadeus	2	2		1		1		1					7		
Charlton	334	19	Marble	Aaron	1	2		1		2	1	1					8		
Charlton	334	20	McIntire	Ephraim	1		1		1	3		1					8		

TOWN	PG#	LN#	HEADS OF HOUSEHOLD LAST NAME	FIRST NAME	FREE WHITE MALES under 10	10 to 16	16 to 26	26 to 45	45 and over	FREE WHITE FEMALES under 10	10 to 16	16 to 26	26 to 45	45 and over	TOTAL ALL OTHER	TOTAL SLAVES	TOTALS	DISTRICT/ TOWNSHIP	NOTES
Charlton	334	21	Madin	Edward					1					1			2		
Charlton	334	22	McIntire	Elihu		2	2	1	1		1	1	1	1			10		
Charlton	334	23	McIntire	Nathan	1	3	2		1		1	1		1			10		
Charlton	334	24	Morey	Thomas	3			1		1	1		1				7		
Charlton	334	25	Merit	Henry					1		1		1				3		
Charlton	334	26	Merit	Henry Junr	1			1		4			1				7		
Charlton	334	27	Merit	Benjm	1	1			1		1			1			5		
Charlton	334	28	Merit	Amos	2			1		2			1				6		
Charlton	335	1	Russel	John	1			1		1			1				4		
Charlton	335	2	Price	George R	1			1		1			1				4		
Charlton	335	3	Richardson	Zachriah					1				1				2		
Charlton	335	4	Stutson	Deborah						1			1				2		
Charlton	335	5	Sawyer	Bazaleel	1			1		1			1				4		
Charlton	335	6	Stone	Benjm				1		2		1	1				5		
Charlton	335	7	Streeter	Daniel					1					2			3		
Charlton	335	8	Spurr	John	2		3	1			1	2					9		
Charlton	335	9	Stephens	Moses				1									1		
Charlton	335	10	Stephens	Peter	1	1		1		4	1		1	1			10		
Charlton	335	11	Stephen	Saml	3			1				1					5		
Charlton	335	12	Stephens	John					1					1			2		
Charlton	335	13	Smith	Joshua					1					1			2		
Charlton	335	14	Streeter	Mary										1			1		
Charlton	335	15	Smith	Oliver			1	1		1			1	1			5		
Charlton	335	16	Stephens	John Junr	1	1	3		1	3	1		1				11		
Charlton	335	17	Sabin	Edmund	1	1				1	1		1				6		
Charlton	335	18	Stone	Nehemiah	1		1	1		2	4	1	1	1			12		
Charlton	335	19	Stone	Ebenzr		1		1		1	1	1	1				6		
Charlton	335	20	Smith	Jesse	1	1		1				1	1				5		
Charlton	335	21	Stone	Josiah				1									1		
Charlton	335	22	Stone	Sampson	2	1		1		2	1		1				8		
Charlton	335	23	Searles	Andrew	1			1		1		1					4		
Charlton	335	24	Smith	Reuben				1		2		1					4		
Charlton	335	25	Smith	William		2			1	3	1		1				8		
Charlton	335	26	Twist	Ebenzr		1			1					1			3		
Charlton	335	27	Sampson	Aaron	1				1					1			3		
Charlton	336	1	Pike	Saml	1	1	1		1					1			5		
Charlton	336	2	Pike	George	1		1			2	3	2	1	1			11		
Charlton	336	3	Pike	Saml Junr	1		1	1					1	1			5		
Charlton	336	4	Putney	Isaiah					1				1				2		
Charlton	336	5	Putney	Isaiah Jun		1				1		1					3		
Charlton	336	6	Putney	Ezra	1			1		2			1				5		
Charlton	336	7	Perry	Jonathan	1	1			1	2	1		1				7		
Charlton	336	8	Putman	Simeon				1		2			1				4		
Charlton	336	9	Phillips	Ebenzr H.	1			1		1	1	1	1				6		
Charlton	336	10	Parker	Saml			1			1			1				4		
Charlton	336	11	Parker	Joel			1			1			1	2			5		
Charlton	336	12	Putnam	Gideon	2			1			1		1				5		
Charlton	336	13	Phillips	Edward	1			1		2		2	1				7		
Charlton	336	14	Parker	Saml Junr	1			1		3			1				6		
Charlton	336	15	Parker	Aaron	1	2		1		4	1		1				10		
Charlton	336	16	Patridge	Benjm			1					1					2		
Charlton	336	17	Putney	Saml	1			1		3			1				6		
Charlton	336	18	Rich	David	2	1	3		1	2		2	1				12		
Charlton	336	19	Rich	Paul		1			1		1		1				4		
Charlton	336	20	Rich	Benjm		1		1	1		1			1			5		
Charlton	336	21	Rich	Jacob	2	1		1		1			1				6		
Charlton	336	22	Rider	Mary Wdw	1	1	1					1		1			5		
Charlton	336	23	Rider	Wm P.			2			1		1					4		
Charlton	336	24	Rider	Eliezer		3	1		1	1		1		1			8		
Charlton	336	25	Rich	Benj Jun				1									1		
Charlton	336	26	Robinson	Saml		2		2		1	2	1	2		1		11		
Charlton	336	27	Rich	Jonathan		3			1	1		1		1			7		
Charlton	337	1	White	Ebenzr 2d	1	1	1		1	1	1	2		1			9		
Charlton	337	2	Wakefield	Luther		1	1		1	1			1				5		
Charlton	337	3	Woodard	Joshua			1										1		
Charlton	337	4	Woodard	Sarah	2			1		1				1			6		
Charlton	337	5	Wyman	Levi	1	1		1		1			1	1			6		
Charlton	337	6	Wyman	Daniel	3			1		2		1	1				8		
Charlton	337	7	Wing	Benj	3	1			1			1	1	1			8		
Charlton	337	8	Wheelock	Aaron	2	1		1		1		1		1			7		
Charlton	337	9	Wheelock	Seth		2			1	1			1	1			6		
Charlton	337	10	Wheelock	Benj	1		2		1	2	1			1			8		
Charlton	337	11	Wheelock	John		2		1		1		1	1				6		
Charlton	337	12	Watters	Israel	1	1	2		1		1	1		1			8		
Charlton	337	13	Wheelock	Amos	3	1	1	1		1			1				8		
Charlton	337	14	Wheelock	Abner	1	1			1	1	1	1		1			7		
Charlton	337	15	Ward	Elijah	1		1		1	1	1	2		1			8		
Charlton	337	16	Ward	Benj			1	1						2			4		
Charlton	337	17	Ward	Benj Junr	3			1						1			5		
Charlton	337	18	Ward	David				1		4	1		1				7		

TOWN	PG#	LN#	LAST NAME	FIRST NAME	Males under 10	10 to 16	16 to 26	26 to 45	45 and over	Females under 10	10 to 16	16 to 26	26 to 45	45 and over	TOTAL ALL OTHER	TOTAL SLAVES	TOTALS	DISTRICT/ TOWNSHIP	NOTES
Charlton	337	19	Ward	Jonas		1	2		1				1	1			6		
Charlton	337	20	Ward	Levi			1		1				1	1			4		
Charlton	337	21	Ward	Simon	2			1		1			1				5		
Charlton	337	22	White	Ebenzr 2d		1	1		1			2		1			6		
Charlton	337	23	Ward	Artemas	1			1		2	1		1				6		
Charlton	337	24	Williams	Daniel		1			1		1	2		1			6		
Charlton	337	25	William	Alpheus	1			1	1	3			1	1			8		
Charlton	337	26	Watters	Simeon		2			1		1		1				5		
Charlton	337	27	Wills	Jabez	1			1		2			1				5		
Charlton	338	1	Town	Richard Jr	1				1	1			1	1			5		
Charlton	338	2	Twichell	Benjm	3				1				1				5		
Charlton	338	3	Town	Elisha	1			1		1			1				4		
Charlton	338	4	Town	Daniel			1			1			1				3		
Charlton	338	5	Town	Josiah				1						1			2		
Charlton	338	6	Town	Josiah Junr			1	1			2	1		1			6		
Charlton	338	7	Tucker	Wm	1	2			1		1	1		1			7		
Charlton	338	8	Tucker	Lucy	1									1			2		
Charlton	338	9	Tucker	Wm Junr	2	1		1		1				1			6		
Charlton	338	10	Tucker	Jonathan			2		1			1	1				6		
Charlton	338	11	Twiss	James	1		1	1		3			1	1			8		
Charlton	338	12	Tucker	Loas										1			1		
Charlton	338	13	Town	Salem		2	1		1		1	1	1	2			9		
Charlton	338	14	Twiss	Moses	1		1	1		3			1	1			8		
Charlton	338	15	Tucker	Tamerson	1	2						2	1	1			7		
Charlton	338	16	Thompson	Elisha		1		1			2	1		1			6		
Charlton	338	17	Thompson	Elijah 2d	2		1						1				4		
Charlton	338	18	Town	Thomas			1			1			1				3		
Charlton	338	19	Twiss	Stephen	1			1						1			3		
Charlton	338	20	Thompson	Elijah 1st	1			1		3			1				6		
Charlton	338	21	Vinton	Joshua			1			3			1				5		
Charlton	338	22	Vinton	Lyman			1			3			1				5		
Charlton	338	23	Vinton	John					1			1	1	1			4		
Charlton	338	24	Vassal	Benjm		1	1		1		1		1	1			6		
Charlton	338	25	Weld	Asa				1									1		
Charlton	338	26	Walker	Asa	2	1			1				1	1			6		
Charlton	338	27	White	John	3	1			1			1	1	1			8		
Charlton	340	1	Weld	Mary			1							1			2		
Charlton	340	2	Weld	Esquire	1	1			1	1	2		1	1	1		9		
Charlton	340	3	Wale	Abel	2			1		2			1				6		
Charlton	340	4	Watters	Phillip	2			1		2			1				6		
Charlton	340	5	Winslow	Jonathan		1	2		1	1	1	2	1				9		
Charlton	340	6	Wood	Wm	1			1		3			1				6		
Charlton	340	7	Williams	Daniel Maj	1			1				1	1				4		
Charlton	340	8	Williams	Daniel Junr	1			1		1	2		1				6		
Charlton	340	9	Walcot	James	1	1		1				2	1				6		
Charlton	340	10	Weto	Daniel				1						1			2		
Charlton	340	11	Willard	Ephraim	2		2	1		3	3	1	1				13		
Charlton	340	12	Wheelock	Addams		1	1	1				1					4		
Charlton	340	13	Woodbury	Caleb	1		1	1				1					4		
Charlton	340	14	Wheeler	Abel				1		1				1			3		
Charlton	340	15	Wyman	John				1						1			2		
Charlton	340	16	Wakefield	Amos	2	2		1		2	2		1	1			11		
Charlton	340	17	Weld	William				1		1			1	1			4		

TOWN	PG#	LN#	LAST NAME	FIRST NAME	FREE WHITE MALES					FREE WHITE FEMALES					TOTAL ALL OTHER	TOTAL SLAVES	TOTALS	DISTRICT/ TOWNSHIP	NOTES
					under 10	10 to 16	16 to 26	26 to 45	45 and over	under 10	10 to 16	16 to 26	26 to 45	45 and over					
Douglas	475	1	Ammidon	John			1			2	1		1				5		
Douglas	475	2	Aldrich	Daniel			1		1			3		1			6		
Douglas	475	3	Aldrich	Aaron		1	3		1			1		1			7		
Douglas	475	4	Aldrich	Israel	2	1		1		1	2		1				8		
Douglas	475	5	Aldrich	Noah	4	1		1					1				7		
Douglas	475	6	Aldrich	Amos	3			1			1		1				6		
Douglas	475	7	Aldrich	Jacob			1		1		1	2		1			6		
Douglas	475	8	Aldrich	Calvin		1		1		1			1				4		
Douglas	475	9	Aldrich	Amariah			1	1		1			1				4		
Douglas	475	10	Aldrich	Ananias				1		4			1				6		
Douglas	475	11	Aldrich	Jesse	1			1		2			1				5		
Douglas	475	12	Aldrich	Ebenezer	1		1			1			1				4		
Douglas	475	13	Aldrich	Seth			1						1				2		
Douglas	475	14	Balkcom	Mark	3			1					1				5		
Douglas	475	15	Balkcom	Ellis	1		1						1				3		
Douglas	475	16	Brown	John		1	1		2		1	3		1			9		
Douglas	475	17	Bigelow	Thomas	2	2	2		1				1	1			9		
Douglas	477	1	Bowen	Eaner	1	1		1		3			1				7		
Douglas	477	2	Briggs	Greenlief			1	1					1				3		
Douglas	477	3	Balkcom	Luke	1		1			1			1				4		
Douglas	477	4	Collar	Jonas				1				1		1			3		
Douglas	477	5	Chase	David		1	1		2	1				1			6		
Douglas	477	6	Claflin	Oliver	3			1			1		1	1			7		
Douglas	477	7	Carpenter	Edmund			1		1			1		1			4		
Douglas	477	8	Corrary	Benja				2						1			3		
Douglas	477	9	Craggin	Benjamin			1	1		2		1					5		
Douglas	477	10	Carpenter	Nathl			1	1		4	1		1				8		
Douglas	477	11	Cummings	Samuel				1						1			2		
Douglas	477	12	Curtis	Ebenezer	1			2		3		1	1	1			9		
Douglas	477	13	Chase	Asa	1			1		2	1		1				6		
Douglas	477	14	Craggin	Timothy		1				1			2				4		
Douglas	477	15	Cummings	Abel	2	1		1		1	1		1				7		
Douglas	477	16	Chase	Joseph		3		1		3			1				8		
Douglas	477	17	Chase	Amasa	1		2		1	2			1	1			8		
Douglas	478	1	Brown	John 2d	1	2		1		1	1	3		1			10		
Douglas	478	2	Brown	Nathl				1						2			3		
Douglas	478	3	Brown	Nathl Jun	1			1		3			1				6		
Douglas	478	4	Brown	Samuel				1		1	1	1	1				5		
Douglas	478	5	Balkcom	John	2	1			1	3	1	1	1				10		
Douglas	478	6	Balkcom	David		1	1		1	3	2	1	1				10		
Douglas	478	7	Balkcom	Aaron			1			1			1				3		
Douglas	478	8	Brown	Elijah	2			1		1			1	1			6		
Douglas	478	9	Briggs	Abraham			1			1			1				3		
Douglas	478	10	Benson	Aaron	1	1	1			1	1		1				7		
Douglas	478	11	Buffam	Benjamin		1	1		1	2	2	2		1			10		
Douglas	478	12	Billing	Erastus		1				2			1				4		
Douglas	478	13	Bucklin	Lonnon											2		2		
Douglas	478	14	Baker	John	1	1	2	1	1	3		3		1			13		
Douglas	478	15	Balkcom	Bezaleel	2	1	1	1		1	1	1	1				9		
Douglas	478	16	Bolster	Richard		1	2		1	1	2	1		1			9		
Douglas	479	1	Farnum	John	2	1		1	1	3	1		1	1			11		
Douglas	479	2	Fairbanks	Amos		1	1		1		1	1		1			6		
Douglas	479	3	Fuller	John		1			1			3		1			6		
Douglas	479	4	Fairbanks	Joshua	2	1		1		1			2				8		
Douglas	479	5	Gould	Ebenezer	1	2		1		3	1		1	1			10		
Douglas	479	6	Gould	Eleazer		1	2		1			1	1	1			7		
Douglas	479	7	Gould	Jedidiah	1			1	1	1	1		1	1			7		
Douglas	479	8	Humes	Josiah		1			1			1		1			4		
Douglas	479	9	Howell	Richard				1						1			2		
Douglas	479	10	Howell	Barnebus			1						1				2		
Douglas	479	11	Howell	Philip	1			1		2		1					5		
Douglas	479	12	Hill	Moses	3	1	2	1				2	1				10		
Douglas	479	13	Hale	Elisha		1	2		1				1	1			6		
Douglas	479	14	Hill	Aaron		2	1		1			2		1			7		
Douglas	479	15	Humes	David			1			2			1				4		
Douglas	479	16	Humes	Moses	2	1		1		1			1	1			7		
Douglas	479	17	Humes	Nahum			1			1		1					3		
Douglas	479	18	Thayer	Thadeus		2	3		1	4	2		1				13		
Douglas	479	19	Tiffany	Lemuel	3			1		1			1				6		
Douglas	479	20	Thayer	Israel	1		1	1		3	2		3	1			12		
Douglas	479	21	Thayer	Moses	1			1		4			1				7		
Douglas	479	22	Tyler	Henry			1			2			1				4		
Douglas	479	23	Upham	Samuel				1						1			2		
Douglas	479	24	Whiting	Caleb		1		1						1			3		
Douglas	479	25	Williams	Samuel	2		1	1	2				1	1			8		
Douglas	479	26	Wallis	Benja				1						1			2		
Douglas	479	27	Wallis	Aaron	2		1	1		2			1				7		
Douglas	479	28	White	Peter				1						1			2		
Douglas	479	29	White	David	1	1		1		3			1				7		

TOWN	PG#	LN#	HEADS OF HOUSEHOLD LAST NAME	FIRST NAME	FWM under 10	FWM 10 to 16	FWM 16 to 26	FWM 26 to 45	FWM 45 and over	FWF under 10	FWF 10 to 16	FWF 16 to 26	FWF 26 to 45	FWF 45 and over	TOTAL ALL OTHER	TOTAL SLAVES	TOTALS	DISTRICT/ TOWNSHIP	NOTES
Douglas	479	30	Whiting	Timothy	2		1	1		1	2		1				8		
Douglas	479	31	Wallis	Samuel	1	1	2	1		3	1		1				10		
Douglas	479	32	Whiting	Abner		1		1		1			1				4		
Douglas	479	33	Wallis	David		2	1		1	1		1	1				7		
Douglas	479	34	Wallis	James		1	2	1		1	1		1				7		
Douglas	480	1	Wallis	Benja Junr	2	1	2		1		1	1	1				9		
Douglas	480	2	Whiting	David	2			1	1	2			1	1			8		
Douglas	480	3	White	Seth	1	2		1		5	1		1				11		
Douglas	480	4	White	Chloe			1				1			1			3		
Douglas	480	5	White	Paul	1		1						1	1			4		
Douglas	480	6	Walker	Benja		2	2		1		1			1			7		
Douglas	480	7	Whiting	John	1	1			1			1		1			5		
Douglas	480	8	Yates	Abner		2			1					1			4		
Douglas	480	9	Yates	John	2			1					1				4		
Douglas	480	10	Chase	William	2			1			1		1				5		
Douglas	480	11	Caswell	Nathan	3			1		2	1		1				8		
Douglas	480	12	Crowd	William											7		7		
Douglas	480	13	Cook	Ebenezer	2			1		1		1					5		
Douglas	480	14	Corbit	Edward				1						1			2		
Douglas	480	15	Cook	Jesse			1			2		1					4		
Douglas	480	16	Dudley	Benja		2		1		3	1	1	2				10		
Douglas	480	17	Davis	William			1	1			1	1	1				5		
Douglas	480	18	Davis	Benja			1					1					2		
Douglas	480	19	Davidson	Samuel	1	1		1					3				6		
Douglas	480	20	Davidson	Douglas	1			1		4			1				7		
Douglas	480	21	Dudley	Paul	3	1	5	2				1	1				13		
Douglas	480	22	Dudley	Lemuel	1			1		1			1				4		
Douglas	480	23	Drake	Stephen	2	1	1		1			2		1			8		
Douglas	480	24	Dixon	Polladore											4		4		
Douglas	480	25	Emerson	Joseph		1		1		1	1		1				5		
Douglas	481	1	Learned	Hezekiah			1	1				1	1				4		
Douglas	481	2	Learned	Benja	3		2			1		1	1				8		
Douglas	481	3	Lee	Ephraim		1	1	1					1				4		
Douglas	481	4	Lee	Comfort		1		1		2			1		1		6		
Douglas	481	5	Lee	Richard	2	1	1	1		1		1	1				8		
Douglas	481	6	Lee	James		1	1	1					1				4		
Douglas	481	7	Lee	John	2			1					1				4		
Douglas	481	8	Lee	Simeon	1			1					1				3		
Douglas	481	9	Luther	William	1				1	2	1	1	1				7		
Douglas	481	10	Long	Elizabeth			1						1	2			4		
Douglas	481	11	Moore	Elijah	1	1	1		1		1		1				6		
Douglas	481	12	Marsh	Aaron	2	1		1	2	3	1		1	1			12		
Douglas	481	13	Morse	Abel	2		1	1		3	1		1				9		
Douglas	481	14	Morse	Jacob		1	1		1	2	1		1				7		
Douglas	481	15	Morse	Obadiah	3	1	1	1		2			1				9		
Douglas	481	16	Morse	Levi	2	1		1		1	1	1	1				8		
Douglas	481	17	Martin	Comfort	1		1		1	3	2	1		1			10		
Douglas	481	18	Mowry	David		1		1		1	1	1	1				6		
Douglas	481	19	McKnight	James	3		1	1			1		1	1			8		
Douglas	481	20	Marsh	John	1		1					1					3		
Douglas	481	21	Marsh	Ebenezer		1		1					1				3		
Douglas	481	22	Marsh	Nahum	2		1				1						4		
Douglas	481	23	Parker	Samuel		1		1		3			1				6		
Douglas	481	24	Parker	David			1	1	1	2							5		
Douglas	481	25	Pettefaw	Hosea	2			1		2		1	1				7		
Douglas	481	26	Parker	Archilaus	1	1	2		1	1	2		1				9		
Douglas	481	27	Potter	Asa		2		1		1		1					5		
Douglas	481	28	Parker	Joseph	2	1	1	1		1	1		1	1			9		
Douglas	481	29	Preston	Ezekiel		1					1		1	1			4		
Douglas	481	30	Pulsipher	Lovel				1		1	1	1					4		
Douglas	481	31	Riedel	Polly	2	2	1			2	1	2		1			11		
Douglas	481	32	Robbins	Benja	2	1			1	2			1				7		
Douglas	481	33	Robbins	Abel	1		1						1				3		
Douglas	481	34	Read	Peter			1		1			1		1			4		
Douglas	481	35	Smith	Elijah	1	1	2		1		1		1				7		
Douglas	481	36	Smith	Robert			1				1						2		
Douglas	481	37	Stockwell	Eli	2			1					1				4		
Douglas	482	1	Sprague	Mercy						1	1		1				3		
Douglas	482	2	Sprague	Jonathan	3	2		1		1	2		1				10		
Douglas	482	3	Streeter	Stephen				1					1				2		
Douglas	482	4	Streeter	Asa	3			1		2			1				7		
Douglas	482	5	Southworth	Stephen	1		1	1		1	2	1		1			8		
Douglas	482	6	Smith	Ebenezer			1	1					1	2			5		
Douglas	482	7	Stone	Moses		1	1			1		1					4		
Douglas	482	8	Stone	Isaac	1		1	1		1	2		1				7		
Douglas	482	9	Sibley	Abel	1		1			3			1				6		
Douglas	482	10	Thayer	Gideon	1			1					1				3		
Douglas	482	11	Thompson	Elisha	2	1	1		1	1	1						7		
Douglas	482	12	Taylor	Daniel				2			2		2				6		

TOWN	PG#	LN#	HEADS OF HOUSEHOLD LAST NAME	FIRST NAME	FREE WHITE MALES under 10	10 to 16	16 to 26	26 to 45	45 and over	FREE WHITE FEMALES under 10	10 to 16	16 to 26	26 to 45	45 and over	TOTAL ALL OTHER	TOTAL SLAVES	TOTALS	DISTRICT/ TOWNSHIP	NOTES
Douglas	482	13	Thayer	Elisha	2			1					1				4		
Douglas	482	14	Thayer	Abijah	1	1		1		2	1		1				7		
Douglas	482	15	Tilly	James			2		1	1	1		1				6		
Douglas	482	16	Thayer	Joseph		1			1					1			3		
Douglas	482	17	Thayer	John	1	1	1		1		1	1	1				7		
Douglas	482	18	Hunt	Ezekiel			1		1					1			3		
Douglas	482	19	Hunt	Joseph	1			1				1					3		
Douglas	482	20	Hunt	Oliver	1		1					1					3		
Douglas	482	21	Howland	Thomas	1	1	1		1		1		1	1			7		
Douglas	482	22	Howland	Joseph	2			1				2	2				8		
Douglas	482	23	Herendeen	Simeon			3		1	1	1	1		1			8		
Douglas	482	24	Holbrook	Sylvanus		1			1		1			1			4		
Douglas	482	25	Harwood	David		1			1			1		1			4		
Douglas	482	26	Hill	Noah		1		1			1	1					4		
Douglas	482	27	Hill	Job	1				1			1	1	2			6		
Douglas	482	28	Ide	Reuben	1	1		1				1					3		
Douglas	482	29	Jepherson	William				1					1	1			3		
Douglas	482	30	Jepherson	Wm Junr			1		1								2		
Douglas	482	31	Jepherson	Seth	1	1	1	1		1	1		1				7		
Douglas	482	32	Jepherson	Reuben	3	2		1		1	1	2	1				11		
Douglas	482	33	Jepherson	Aaron	3	1		1		2	2		1				10		
Douglas	482	34	Knap	Job	2		1	1		2		2	1				9		
Douglas	482	35	Kelly	Mercy		1	1				1		1				4		

TOWN	PG#	LN#	LAST NAME	FIRST NAME	FWM under 10	FWM 10 to 16	FWM 16 to 26	FWM 26 to 45	FWM 45 and over	FWF under 10	FWF 10 to 16	FWF 16 to 26	FWF 26 to 45	FWF 45 and over	TOTAL ALL OTHER	TOTAL SLAVES	TOTALS	DISTRICT/ TOWNSHIP	NOTES
Dudley	339	1	Ammidown	John	2	3	1	1		2			1				10		
Dudley	339	2	Ammidown	Ebenz		1	1		1		1		1				5		
Dudley	339	3	Alexander	Daniel	1			1		1			1				4		
Dudley	339	4	Albee	John		1	1		1	1		1	1				6		
Dudley	339	5	Allen	Eleazer	1	2		1				1	1				6		
Dudley	339	6	Arnold	Joseph			2		1	1	1	1	1				7		
Dudley	339	7	Alexander	Israel			1			1			1				3		
Dudley	339	8	Abbit	Daniel	1		1			1	1	1					5		
Dudley	339	9	Bacon	Cyrel	1		1	1		1		1	1				6		
Dudley	339	10	Bracket	Moses	1	3		1			2	2	1				10		
Dudley	339	11	Brown	Ezekiel	1		2		1		1	3		1			9		
Dudley	339	12	Burns	Josiah	2	1	1		1	1	1	1	1				9		
Dudley	339	13	Blackmore	Joseph	2		1			1			1				5		
Dudley	339	14	Blackmore	Adonijah			1			1	1		1				4		
Dudley	339	15	Bacon	Jonathan 2d			1		1	1	1	1	1				6		
Dudley	339	16	Brown	Charles 1st	2	2		1					1				6		
Dudley	339	17	Brown	Charles 2d	4	1	1	1					1				8		
Dudley	339	18	Brown	Ebenz	3	1		1	1	1	1		1				9		
Dudley	339	19	Bracket	Ebenz	1			1		4	1		1				8		
Dudley	339	20	Brown	Chad		1	1					1					3		
Dudley	339	21	Bacon	Jonathan		1		1	1	1			1	1			6		
Dudley	341	1	Carter	William	1			1	1				1				4		
Dudley	341	2	Cudworth	Lemuel	1			1		1		2		1			6		
Dudley	341	3	Curtis	Charles	2	1		1		1	1		1				7		
Dudley	341	4	Coburn	Edward			1	1		1			1				4		
Dudley	341	5	Carpenter	Harvey			1					1					2		
Dudley	341	6	Corbin	Timothy	2			1		2	1	1		1			8		
Dudley	341	7	Cody	John	1	1		1		2	2		1	1			9		
Dudley	341	8	Carter	Esborn	2		1	2		2		2	1	1			11		
Dudley	341	9	Curtis	Edward		4		1			1	1		1			8		
Dudley	341	10	Curtis	Bethiah									2				2		
Dudley	341	11	Conant	Josiah	1		1	1		1		1					5		
Dudley	341	12	Conant	Rufus	2			1		2	1		1				7		
Dudley	341	13	Corbin	Joshua	3	1		1		1	1	2	1				10		
Dudley	341	14	Corbin	Ephraim				1					1				2		
Dudley	341	15	Corbin	Rufus			1					1					2		
Dudley	341	16	Davis	Joseph Jun	1			1		2			1		1		6		
Dudley	341	17	Davis	Joshua	1		1					1					3		
Dudley	341	18	Davis	Edward		1	1	1		4	1	1	1				10		
Dudley	341	19	Day	Jonathan		1	2		1			2		1			7		
Dudley	341	20	Davis	Saml	2			1		3			1				7		
Dudley	341	21	Davis	Joseph				1				1	1				3		
Dudley	341	22	Duncan	Wm		1		1				1		1			4		
Dudley	341	23	Upham	Simeon	2			1			2		1				6		
Dudley	341	24	Upham	Eunice								1		1			2		
Dudley	341	25	Upham	Ephraim	1		1	1		2			1	1			7		
Dudley	341	26	Upham	Nathan	3	1		1			1		1				7		
Dudley	341	27	Vinton	Joseph	4	1	1	1			2		1				10		
Dudley	341	28	Vinton	Wm	3	1	1	1		1	1	2					10		
Dudley	341	29	Vinton	Ralph	2	1	1		1	1	1		1				8		
Dudley	341	30	Vorse	Olive	1					1			1				3		
Dudley	341	31	Wood	Simeon		2		1			1	1					5		
Dudley	341	32	Wood	Nathan	1		1			1		1					4		
Dudley	341	33	Wakefield	Solomon	1	1		1		3	1		1				8		
Dudley	341	34	Wakefield	Simeon	3		1	1		1	1		1				8		
Dudley	341	35	Walden	Nathan	3	2		1					1	1			8		
Dudley	341	36	Willard	Hezekiah	1			1		2			1	1			6		
Dudley	341	37	Weatheril	Joshua			1						1				2		
Dudley	341	38	Willard	Jonathan				1					1				2		
Dudley	341	39	Willard	Jonath Junr		1		1	1	2		1	1				8		
Dudley	341	40	Willard	Henry	1			1		2	1	1					6		
Dudley	341	41	Warren	Mansir	1			1		1	1		1				5		
Dudley	341	42	Warren	John			2		1	1	1		2				7		
Dudley	341	43	Warren	Jacob				1					1				2		
Dudley	341	44	Wakefield	Joel	2			1		2			1				6		
Dudley	341	45	Wood	Jesse		1				1	1						3		
Dudley	341	46	Willard	Nathan		1					1						2		
Dudley	342	1	Willard	Elijah		1					1		1				3		
Dudley	342	2	Webster	John			1			2			1				4		
Dudley	342	3	Webster	Wm	1		1			2			1	1			6		
Dudley	342	4	Weatherly	Hannah	1	1	1						1				4		
Dudley	342	5	Williams	Henry	2			1					1	1			5		
Dudley	342	6	Webster	Coburn	1			1				1	1				5		
Dudley	342	7	Weatherly	Joseph				1					1				2		
Dudley	342	8	Weaver	William			1	1					1				3		
Dudley	342	9	Warren	Jacob 2d		1					1						2		
Dudley	342	10	Windsor	William		1					1						2		
Dudley	342	11	Bates	Alanson	3		1	1			2		1				8		
Dudley	342	12	Bracket	John									2				5		

TOWN	PG#	LN#	HEADS OF HOUSEHOLD — LAST NAME	FIRST NAME	FREE WHITE MALES under 10	10 to 16	16 to 26	26 to 45	45 and over	FREE WHITE FEMALES under 10	10 to 16	16 to 26	26 to 45	45 and over	TOTAL ALL OTHER	TOTAL SLAVES	TOTALS	DISTRICT/ TOWNSHIP	NOTES
Dudley	342	13	Bowers	John	3	2		1		2	2		1				11		
Dudley	342	14	Bullard	Lynde	1		2			2		2					7		
Dudley	342	15	Bartlet	Zepheniah	1	1		1				1					4		
Dudley	342	16	Brown	Wm 2d			1		1	1		1					4		
Dudley	342	17	Brown	Zepheniah	1	1	1					2					5		
Dudley	342	18	Brown	Wm	1		2		1	2	1	1	1				9		
Dudley	342	19	Curtis	Asa			1		1			2		1			5		
Dudley	342	20	Curtis	John	2	2	1		2	1		2	1	1			12		
Dudley	342	21	Cotril	Thomas	3			1				1	1				6		
Dudley	342	22	Chamberlain	Edward		2		1				1	1				6		
Dudley	342	23	Chamberlain	John	1	1	1	1		3		1	2	1			11		
Dudley	342	24	Chamberlain	Luther	2	1		1				1		1			6		
Dudley	342	25	Cheney	Thomas		2	2		1	1	2	1		1			10		
Dudley	342	26	Chamberlain	Joshua			2										2		
Dudley	342	27	Corbin	Jedediah	3	1	2		1	2	1	1		1			12		
Dudley	342	28	Corbin	Lemuel		1		1		1	1		1				5		
Dudley	342	29	Corbin	Leml Junr	1			1		1	1	1					5		
Dudley	342	30	Corbin	Hannah						2			1	1			4		
Dudley	342	31	Chamberlain	Calvin	1			1		2		1		1			6		
Dudley	342	32	Chace	Isaac				1					1				2		
Dudley	342	33	Cotril	Benja		2	1	1				1	1				6		
Dudley	343	1	Healey	Nathl Jun	1	1		1		3		1					7		
Dudley	343	2	Healey	Wm	2			1		3	1	1					8		
Dudley	343	3	Healey	Moses	2	1		1		1		2	1				8		
Dudley	343	4	Healey	Saml	1		1	1	1	1	1		1				7		
Dudley	343	5	Healey	Joseph		1		1		1	1		1				5		
Dudley	343	6	Healey	Leml	1		1	1		3		1	1				8		
Dudley	343	7	Hancock	Allen	2		1		1	1		1	1				7		
Dudley	343	8	Haskil	John		1		1			1		2				5		
Dudley	343	9	Haskil	John Junr	1	1	1	1		1	2		1				9		
Dudley	343	10	Hillman	James	1		1		1		1	1		1			6		
Dudley	343	11	Haskil	Stephen	1	1		1		2			1				6		
Dudley	343	12	Haskil	James	1	1		1		1	1	1	1				7		
Dudley	343	13	Healey	John	2	1		1		1		1	1				7		
Dudley	343	14	Hillman	Ebenz	2			1					1				4		
Dudley	343	15	Jewett	Moses		1	1		1		1	1		1			6		
Dudley	343	16	Johnson	Smith				1			1			1			3		
Dudley	343	17	Jewett	Roger			1			2		1					4		
Dudley	343	18	Keith	Joseph		1	2		1			2		1			7		
Dudley	343	19	Kidder	Benja				1				1	1				3		
Dudley	343	20	Keith	Thos	1			1		2			1				5		
Dudley	343	21	Lawton	John	3		2		1	3	1	1	1				12		
Dudley	343	22	Learnard	Wm				1					1				2		
Dudley	343	23	Learnard	Thomas		2		1		2			2				7		
Dudley	343	24	Lee	Benja			1	1				1		1			4		
Dudley	343	25	Lee	Isaac		1	2	1				1		2			7		
Dudley	343	26	May	Samuel	1	2	1		1	2	1	1		1			10		
Dudley	343	27	McIntire	Gardner				1		2	1	3		1			8		
Dudley	343	28	Moris	John				1					1				2		
Dudley	343	29	Moris	Edward		2	2	1					1				6		
Dudley	343	30	Marcy	Theodore		1			1	2				1			5		
Dudley	343	31	Morse	David 2d	2			1				1					4		
Dudley	343	32	Morse	Jesse	1		1			2		1					5		
Dudley	343	33	Marcy	Daniel	4	1		1		1	2	1					10		
Dudley	343	34	Moris	Zebulon	1	1	1	2		1		1	1	1			9		
Dudley	343	35	Marsh	Lot			2			2	1	2		1			8		
Dudley	343	36	Mansfield	Daniel	3			1		4			1		1		10		
Dudley	343	37	Nichols	Aaron		1		1			1		1				4		
Dudley	343	38	Nichols	David		1			1			2	1				5		
Dudley	343	39	Nichols	David Jun		2		1				1	1				5		
Dudley	343	40	Nichols	Amasa		1	1					1	1				4		
Dudley	343	41	Putney	Eleazer				1					1	1			3		
Dudley	343	42	Putney	Eleazer Junr	1	2	1	1		3		1					9		
Dudley	343	43	Pratt	Elisha	1			1		1		1					4		
Dudley	343	44	Perry	Eliaphas	1	1		1	1	1	1	1	1				8		
Dudley	343	45	Palmer	Joseph	1		1			1		1					4		
Dudley	343	46	Perry	Rowland	1		1			1		1					4		
Dudley	343	47	Reynolds	Albro	1	1			1		2			1			6		
Dudley	344	1	Reynolds	Stephen	2		1			2		1					6		
Dudley	344	2	Roberson	Asa	3		1		1	2				1			8		
Dudley	344	3	Roberson	William	3		1	1	1	1	1		1		1		10		
Dudley	344	4	Roberson	Saml	2		1	1		1			1				6		
Dudley	344	5	Roberson	Eliakim		2			1			2		1			6		
Dudley	344	6	Sabin	Daniel	2	1	1		1	3	1	1		1			11		
Dudley	344	7	Sabin	Royal			1					1		2			4		
Dudley	344	8	Stone	Reuben	3	1		1		2			1				8		
Dudley	344	9	Sales	Royal	3	1		1	1				1	1			8		
Dudley	344	10	Stone	Benj				1				1		1			3		
Dudley	344	11	Stone	Parley	2			1		1			1				5		

TOWN	PG#	LN#	LAST NAME	FIRST NAME	under 10	10 to 16	16 to 26	26 to 45	45 and over	under 10	10 to 16	16 to 26	26 to 45	45 and over	TOTAL ALL OTHER	TOTAL SLAVES	TOTALS	DISTRICT/ TOWNSHIP	NOTES
					\<FREE WHITE MALES\>					\<FREE WHITE FEMALES\>									
Dudley	344	12	Smith	Wm Jun	1		1			1		1			1		5		
Dudley	344	13	Shepherd	Simeon	1	1			1	2	1	1	1				8		
Dudley	344	14	Stone	Henry			1		1								2		
Dudley	344	15	Sabin	Joseph			1		1					2			4		
Dudley	344	16	Sly	Nathan	1	1	1	1		2	1		1				8		
Dudley	344	17	Streeter	John				1					1				2		
Dudley	344	18	Town	Simon	1	1	1		1		1	2		1	1		9		
Dudley	344	19	Town	John	1		1			1		1					4		
Dudley	344	20	Town	Joel			2										2		
Dudley	344	21	Tufts	Aaron	1	1		1				1	1				5		
Dudley	344	22	Upham	Thomas	2		1		1	1	1	1					7		
Dudley	344	23	Upham	Benj		1	2		1				1				5		
Dudley	344	24	Dodge	Mark		1			1			1		1			4		
Dudley	344	25	Dyre	John			1			1			1				3		
Dudley	344	26	Dalrimple	Robert	2		1	1		1			1				6		
Dudley	344	27	Dalrimple	John	1		1					1					3		
Dudley	344	28	Dodge	Paul	2		1					1					4		
Dudley	344	29	Day	Jabez	1	1	1			1		2					6		
Dudley	344	30	Dagget	Ebenzr	1			1		1		1					4		
Dudley	344	31	Dyer	Thomas	2			1		3	3		1				10		
Dudley	344	32	Edmunds	John	4	1		1		2	2		1				11		
Dudley	344	33	Eddy	John	4	1	2		1		1	1	1				11		
Dudley	344	34	Eaton	John S.			2	1		3		2	1				9		
Dudley	344	35	Eddy	Augustus			4	1				1					6		
Dudley	344	36	Foster	Timothy			2				1	1		1			6		
Dudley	344	37	Foster	Ebenze	1		1	1						1			4		
Dudley	344	38	Freeman	David			1						1				2		
Dudley	344	39	Foster	Abel	1	1		1		2			1				6		
Dudley	344	40	Fishel	Wm		1		1		1		1		1			5		
Dudley	344	41	Fishel	Wm Jun	1		1			1		1					4		
Dudley	344	42	Foster	Mary						1		1		1			3		
Dudley	344	43	Farnam	Calvin	1		1			1	1	1					5		
Dudley	344	44	Gore	John		1			1	2	1	3		1			9		
Dudley	344	45	Healey	Hezekiah			1	1					1				3		
Dudley	344	46	Healey	Nathl			1		1				1	1			4		

TOWN	PG#	LN#	LAST NAME	FIRST NAME	FREE WHITE MALES					FREE WHITE FEMALES					TOTAL ALL OTHER	TOTAL SLAVES	TOTALS	DISTRICT/ TOWNSHIP	NOTES
					under 10	10 to 16	16 to 26	26 to 45	45 and over	under 10	10 to 16	16 to 26	26 to 45	45 and over					
Fitchburg	423	1	Turner	Consider		2		2	2		1			2			9		
Fitchburg	423	2	Thurlo	Rhoda	1					3			1				5		
Fitchburg	423	3	Taylor	Samuel	2	1		1		1			1	1			7		
Fitchburg	423	4	Thurston	John					1		1			1			3		
Fitchburg	423	5	Thurston	John Jun	1	2				2	1	1	1				9		
Fitchburg	423	6	Thurston	Thomas	1	1	1	1		2		1	1				8		
Fitchburg	423	7	Thurston	Ebenz		1		1			1			1			4		
Fitchburg	423	8	Thurston	Stephen	2	1		1	1	1			1	1			8		
Fitchburg	423	9	Underwood	Mary								1	1	1			3		
Fitchburg	423	10	Upton	John	1	1	1	1		2		1					8		
Fitchburg	423	11	Upton	Jacob		2	1	1				1		1	2		8		
Fitchburg	423	12	Willard	Abraham		1	2		1					1			5		
Fitchburg	423	13	Whittemore	Jona	2			1		1			1				5		
Fitchburg	423	14	Wood	Jonathan		1	1	1	1		1		1	1			7		
Fitchburg	423	15	Worcester	Samuel			1	1		3	1	1					7		
Fitchburg	423	16	Wilson	Benja				1		3			1	1			6		
Fitchburg	423	17	Willard	Charles		2		1			2	1	2				8		
Fitchburg	423	18	Willard	Daniel		1			1	3	2		1				8		
Fitchburg	424	1	Woods	John			1				1		1				3		
Fitchburg	424	2	Whitmore	David	2			1		2			1				6		
Fitchburg	424	3	Whitmore	Daniel	1			1		1	1	1					5		
Fitchburg	424	4	Wood	George	4	2		1		3	1		1				12		
Fitchburg	424	5	Wheeler	Aaron	2			1	1	3			1	1			9		
Fitchburg	424	6	Ware	Jonathan	1		2	1	1				2	1			8		
Fitchburg	424	7	Wheeler	Amos	1			1				1	1				4		
Fitchburg	424	8	Wheeler	Joseph	3	1			1	1		1	1				8		
Fitchburg	424	9	Weatherbee	Paul		1	2		1	2	1			1			8		
Fitchburg	424	10	Weatherbee	Daniel	3	3		1		2	1		1				11		
Fitchburg	425	1	Phelps	Samuel	1	1		1		2			2	1			8		
Fitchburg	425	2	Perly	Eliph	1		2		1	1	2	2		1			10		
Fitchburg	425	3	Pratt	John	2			1		3	1		1	1			9		
Fitchburg	425	4	Pool	James				2					1	2			5		
Fitchburg	425	5	Perry	Joseph	1	2		1		1	1	1	1				8		
Fitchburg	425	6	Pirkins	Petmadus		1		1						1			3		
Fitchburg	425	7	Phelps	Joseph			1	4		2			1				8		
Fitchburg	425	8	Richardson	Joseph				1		3			1				5		
Fitchburg	425	9	Rider	William	1	1			1	1		2		1			7		
Fitchburg	425	10	Ritter	Ezra	1			1		3			1				6		
Fitchburg	425	11	Reed	James	1			1			1			1			4		
Fitchburg	425	12	Storer	Solomon	3	1			1	3		1		2			11		
Fitchburg	425	13	Sawyer	Joseph	3	2			1	1	1	3		1			12		
Fitchburg	425	14	Sheldon	Zachh	2	1			1		2		1				7		
Fitchburg	425	15	Sheldon	Benja	3			1			1		1				6		
Fitchburg	425	16	Scott	Edward			1		1		1			1			4		
Fitchburg	425	17	Shattuck	Simon		2		1	1	1	1	1	1				7		
Fitchburg	426	1	Smith	Benja	2	2	1	1	1	1		1	1	1			11		
Fitchburg	426	2	Simonds	Joseph	1			1		2			1				5		
Fitchburg	426	3	Stearns	Daniel M.	1	1	2			1	1	1					8		
Fitchburg	426	4	Small	William			1		1		1			1			4		
Fitchburg	426	5	Sampson	Robert	1	2			1	2			1				7		
Fitchburg	426	6	Sawyer	Jabez	4			1			1		1				7		
Fitchburg	426	7	Smith	Reuben	3			2	1			2	1				9		
Fitchburg	426	8	Sawyer	Luke	2			1		2			1				6		
Fitchburg	426	9	Sheldon	Amos	1			1		3	1		1				7		
Fitchburg	426	10	Stickney	Oliver			1	1						1			3		
Fitchburg	426	11	Sawin	Stephen			1	1					1				3		
Fitchburg	426	12	Snow	Peter	3		1	1				1	1				7		
Fitchburg	426	13	Scott	John	2			1					1				4		
Fitchburg	426	14	Stickney	Joshua			1					1					2		
Fitchburg	426	15	Steward	Daniel				1				1		1			3		
Fitchburg	426	16	Turner	Israel			2		1	1	2	1		1			8		
Fitchburg	427	1	Kendall	William				1			1		2				4		
Fitchburg	427	2	Lawrence	Amos		1	1		1		2	2		1			8		
Fitchburg	427	3	Low	Joseph Jun	4		1	1	1	1			2	1			11		
Fitchburg	427	4	Low	Jonathan Jun	2	2	2		2	2	1	2		3			16		
Fitchburg	427	5	Mace	Abraham	2	1		1		3			1				8		
Fitchburg	427	6	Marshall	Jonas	1		3		1	1		1	1	1			9		
Fitchburg	427	7	Messinger	John	1			1		3	2		1				8		
Fitchburg	427	8	McIntire	Daniel	2	2	1		1	1		1	1				9		
Fitchburg	427	9	McIntire	Gartrude					1			1	1		1		4		
Fitchburg	427	10	McIntire	Elijah	1	1	1	1	1	1	1	1	1	1			10		
Fitchburg	427	11	McIntire	Elias	2	1		1		2	1		1				8		
Fitchburg	427	12	Marshall	Jonas Jun	1		1	1		1	1	1	1				7		
Fitchburg	427	13	Marshall	Benja			1					1					2		
Fitchburg	427	14	McIntire	Jacob	1		1	1				1					4		
Fitchburg	427	15	Mace	James			1							1			2		
Fitchburg	427	16	Messinger	Thomas	3		3		1	1	1	1		1			11		
Fitchburg	427	17	Messinger	Elias	1			1				1					3		
Fitchburg	427	18	Miles	Thomas	1			1			2						6		

TOWN	PG#	LN#	HEADS OF HOUSEHOLD		FREE WHITE MALES					FREE WHITE FEMALES					TOTAL ALL OTHER	TOTAL SLAVES	TOTALS	DISTRICT/ TOWNSHIP	NOTES
			LAST NAME	FIRST NAME	under 10	10 to 16	16 to 26	26 to 45	45 and over	under 10	10 to 16	16 to 26	26 to 45	45 and over					
Fitchburg	427	19	Martin	Barzilla									1				1		
Fitchburg	427	20	Miles	Richard			1						1	1			3		
Fitchburg	428	1	Ordway	Amos	1	1	1	1	1			2	1	1			9		
Fitchburg	428	2	Osborn	Ephm	4	2			1			1	1	1			10		
Fitchburg	428	3	Osborn	John	2			1		1	1		1				6		
Fitchburg	428	4	Osborn	Jacob				1		2	2		1				6		
Fitchburg	428	5	Osgood	Joseph		3			1					1			5		
Fitchburg	428	6	Pierce	Joshua			1	1				1		2			5		
Fitchburg	428	7	Putman	John				1				1		1			3		
Fitchburg	428	8	Parkhurst	James	3	1		1					1				6		
Fitchburg	428	9	Putman	Amos			1		1	1	1	1		1			6		
Fitchburg	428	10	Perry	Asa	1	1	3	1	1			2	2	1			12		
Fitchburg	428	11	Phillips	Seth	2	2	1		1	1	1			1			9		
Fitchburg	428	12	Phillips	Blany			1		1			1	3	1			7		
Fitchburg	428	13	Pratt	David	2	1	2		1				3		2		11		
Fitchburg	428	14	Pierce	Amos	4	2		1	1				1				9		
Fitchburg	428	15	Payson	John			2		1	1	1		1				6		
Fitchburg	428	16	Polley	Joseph	3	2	2	1		2		1	1	1			13		
Fitchburg	428	17	Putnam	Daniel		1	2	1				1		1			6		
Fitchburg	428	18	Putnam	Daniel Jun			1	1		2		4					8		
Fitchburg	428	19	Page	Jonathan		1	1		1			1		1			5		
Fitchburg	429	1	Farnsworth	Joseph	1		1	1		3	3		1				10		
Fitchburg	429	2	Fuller	Nehemiah Jun	5			1		1			1				8		
Fitchburg	429	3	Gibson	Thomas	2		1	1		3			1				8		
Fitchburg	429	4	Gray	Joseph	1		1	1	1	2	2		2				10		
Fitchburg	429	5	Goodridge	Asaph		2		1		1		1		1			6		
Fitchburg	429	6	Goodridge	John			1	1		1	2	1		2			8		
Fitchburg	429	7	Goodridge	Abijah	2	1			1	2	1	2		2			11		
Fitchburg	429	8	Gibson	Samuel			1	1				1		1			4		
Fitchburg	429	9	Garfield	Timothy	2	1	1	1				1	1				7		
Fitchburg	429	10	Gibson	Jacob	1	1	1		1		1	2		1			8		
Fitchburg	429	11	Gibson	Ephraim	1			1		2			1				5		
Fitchburg	429	12	Giddings	William	2			1		1			1				5		
Fitchburg	429	13	Gibson	Reuben		1	1		1	2	3	2		1			11		
Fitchburg	429	14	Gibson	Solomon	2			1		2	2		1				8		
Fitchburg	429	15	Godfrey	Daniel		1		1		1			1	1			5		
Fitchburg	429	16	Gibson	Samiel Jun	1	1	1		1				1				5		
Fitchburg	429	17	Gleason	William	1			1		1	1						4		
Fitchburg	429	18	Gibson	Armington		2			1			1		1			5		
Fitchburg	429	19	Garfield	Jane								1	1	1			3		
Fitchburg	429	20	Herrick	Benjamin	2				1								3		
Fitchburg	429	21	Holt	Joseph			1		1	1	2	1		1			7		
Fitchburg	430	1	Bartell	Kendall Jun		1	2	1		3	1	2					10		
Fitchburg	430	2	Baldwin	Abel				1						1			2		
Fitchburg	430	3	Baldwin	David	3		1	1		1			1				7		
Fitchburg	430	4	Bolton	William	1	1		1					1				4		
Fitchburg	430	5	Battle	Joseph				1				2		1			4		
Fitchburg	430	6	Battle	Joseph Jun	1		1			2			1				5		
Fitchburg	430	7	Battle	John	4	1		1		1	1		1				9		
Fitchburg	430	8	Brown	Phinehas		2	2		1			1	1	1			8		
Fitchburg	430	9	Bartlett	Nathaniel			1			3			1				5		
Fitchburg	430	10	Bartell	David	2		1	1		2	1	2	1				10		
Fitchburg	430	11	Battle	Nathan		1				1		1					3		
Fitchburg	430	12	Brown	William		1			1	1		2					5		
Fitchburg	430	13	Badcock	Nathan		1		1		2	2		1				7		
Fitchburg	430	14	Blodget	Thomas	1			1	1	1	1		1				5		
Fitchburg	430	15	Badcock	Nathan Jun		1				1		1					3		
Fitchburg	430	16	Burnap	Jacob	3			1		2	1		1				8		
Fitchburg	430	17	Bennet	Abraham		1	1	1						1			4		
Fitchburg	430	18	Berry	Samuel	1	2		1		1	1		1				7		
Fitchburg	430	19	Batchelder	Timothy	1				1	2	3	1		1			9		
Fitchburg	430	20	Burnap	Edward	2			1		2	2		1				8		
Fitchburg	430	21	Brooks	Isaac	1			1		1			1				4		
Fitchburg	431	1	Berns	Edmund				1					1				2		
Fitchburg	431	2	Carlton	Solomon		1		1				2		1			5		
Fitchburg	431	3	Caswell	Samuel		1	1		1			2		1			6		
Fitchburg	431	4	Chase	Warren			1		4			1	1				7		
Fitchburg	431	5	Condin	Hannah		1			1	2	1	1	1				7		
Fitchburg	431	6	Condin	Thomas	1	1	2		1	1	1	2		1			10		
Fitchburg	431	7	Crague	William	1		1			1			1	1			5		
Fitchburg	431	8	Cummings	Jonathan		1		1					1				3		
Fitchburg	431	9	Carter	Elijah	1	1	2		1		1	1		1			8		
Fitchburg	431	10	Carter	John		1	1	1	1	1	2			1			8		
Fitchburg	431	11	Chamberlain	Elisha	2			1		2		2	1				8		
Fitchburg	431	12	Carlisle	Silas			1	1				1		1			4		
Fitchburg	431	13	Condin	James	1	1		1		1	1	1					6		
Fitchburg	431	14	Davis	Levi			1		2			1					4		
Fitchburg	431	15	Downe	Joseph		1	3		1			2		2			9		
Fitchburg	431	16	Downe	Joseph Jun	1		1	1				1					4		

TOWN	PG#	LN#	LAST NAME	FIRST NAME	FREE WHITE MALES under 10	10 to 16	16 to 26	26 to 45	45 and over	FREE WHITE FEMALES under 10	10 to 16	16 to 26	26 to 45	45 and over	TOTAL ALL OTHER	TOTAL SLAVES	TOTALS	DISTRICT/ TOWNSHIP	NOTES
Fitchburg	431	17	Darby	Aaron	3	1		1		2			1				8		
Fitchburg	431	18	Durant	Edward	2	2	3	2		2		1	1				13		
Fitchburg	432	1	Darby	Jonathan	1		1		1	3	2	1		1			10		
Fitchburg	432	2	Durant	Jackson	2			1		2			1				6		
Fitchburg	432	3	Eaton	Thomas			1		1			1		1			4		
Fitchburg	432	4	Eaton	Thomas 3d			1					1					2		
Fitchburg	432	5	Eaton	Aaron	1	1	3		1		1	1	1	1			10		
Fitchburg	432	6	Flint	Benjamin	1	1		1		1	1	3	1				9		
Fitchburg	432	7	Fox	Joseph	1		2	1	1	1	1	4					11		
Fitchburg	432	8	Flagg	Levi	3			5		2			1				11		
Fitchburg	432	9	Flint	Jonathan	1		2		1					1			5		
Fitchburg	432	10	Farwell	Abraham		2			1	1	1		1				6		
Fitchburg	432	11	Farwell	Zacheus	3	1	1		1	2	1	1	1	1			12		
Fitchburg	432	12	Fuller	Nehemiah			1	1		1	1	1		1			7		
Fitchburg	432	13	Fitzgerald	Elizabeth		1								1			2		
Fitchburg	432	14	Fullam	Oliver	1			1		4	1		1				8		
Fitchburg	432	15	Farwell	Daniel	1			1	1	1		1	1	1			7		
Fitchburg	432	16	Fullam	Jacob	4	1		1	1		2		1	1			11		
Fitchburg	432	17	Farwell	Simeon	3			1	1	1			1				6		
Fitchburg	432	18	Fuller	Joseph	2	2		1		2	1	1	1				10		
Fitchburg	432	19	Farwell	Asa	1			1		1			1				4		
Fitchburg	432	20	French	Thomas	4			1		1			1				7		
Fitchburg	432	21	Farwell	John		1			1					1			3		

TOWN	PG#	LN#	LAST NAME	FIRST NAME	FREE WHITE MALES under 10	10 to 16	16 to 26	26 to 45	45 and over	FREE WHITE FEMALES under 10	10 to 16	16 to 26	26 to 45	45 and over	TOTAL ALL OTHER	TOTAL SLAVES	TOTALS	DISTRICT/ TOWNSHIP	NOTES
Gardner	447	1	Pratt	Ephraim					1					1			2		
Gardner	447	2	Pratt	Aaron	1			1		1							3		
Gardner	447	3	Partridge	Jabez	1		1		1	2	2		1				8		
Gardner	447	4	Pennamon	Ezra	1			1		3	1	1	1	1			9		
Gardner	447	5	Parley	Allen	1	1	1		1	1			1	1			7		
Gardner	447	6	Pratt	Joseph	1	1	1		1		1		1				6		
Gardner	447	7	Payson	Joseph			1		1			2					4		
Gardner	447	8	Putnam	John	2			1		1			1				5		
Gardner	447	9	Partridge	Reuben		1			1					1			3		
Gardner	447	10	Peirce	John	2	1		1		2			1				7		
Gardner	447	11	Richardson	Jonas		1	1		1				1	1			5		
Gardner	447	12	Reed	David	2	1			1				1				5		
Gardner	447	13	Simonds	Elijah	1	1	3		1	2				1			9		
Gardner	447	14	Sawyer	Jude	1				1					1			3		
Gardner	447	15	Simonds	Joseph			1			1				1			3		
Gardner	447	16	Stone	Simon	1			1		1							3		
Gardner	447	17	Stone	Samuel	1	1	2		1	3	1	1	1				11		
Gardner	447	18	Sandson	Samuel	1			1						1			3		
Gardner	448	1	Sanderson	Moses			1			2		1					4		
Gardner	448	2	Sever	Eathan	2			1		1			1				5		
Gardner	448	3	Temple	Ahio	1			1		3			1				6		
Gardner	448	4	Temple	Ephraim			1			1	1		1				4		
Gardner	448	5	Whitney	Joshua	4		1		1	1	1		1				9		
Gardner	448	6	Wood	Jonathan	1		2	1	1			1	1				7		
Gardner	448	7	Wood	Nahum		1						1					2		
Gardner	448	8	Wilson	Joseph	2			1		2			1				6		
Gardner	448	9	Wood	Aaron	1		1	1		2			1				6		
Gardner	448	10	Wright	Joseph	3			1		2			1				7		
Gardner	448	11	Whitney	William	3			1		2			1				7		
Gardner	448	12	Wheeler	Joel	1		1		1	2	1		1				7		
Gardner	448	13	Wilder	Josiah	1	2			1	1	1	2		1			9		
Gardner	448	14	Wheeler	Josiah		1	2		1			1		1			6		
Gardner	448	15	Wheeler	John B.	3			1		1			1				6		
Gardner	448	16	Wood	Isabel		1							1	1			3		
Gardner	449	1	Larnard	Samuel	2	1	1			1			1				6		
Gardner	449	2	Glazor	Smarna	1			1			1	1					4		
Gardner	449	3	Green	Nathan		1			1					2			4		
Gardner	449	4	Gates	Nathan	5			1		1			1				8		
Gardner	449	5	Gates	Jonathan	4			1				1	1				7		
Gardner	449	6	Gates	Simon	1	2	2		1				1	1			8		
Gardner	449	7	Hill	Jesse	2		1	1		1	1		1				7		
Gardner	449	8	Hill	Moses	2	1	2		1	3	1	1	1				12		
Gardner	449	9	Haynes	Reuben		1		1		3	1	2	1				9		
Gardner	449	10	Hill	Silvanus	1		1						1				3		
Gardner	449	11	Hill	Barzelial	2			1		3	1		1				8		
Gardner	449	12	Hill	Abigail						1				1			2		
Gardner	449	13	Hill	Nathll			1	1		4	1		1				8		
Gardner	449	14	How	Elezer		1	1	1	1	1		1		1			7		
Gardner	449	15	How	Parley			1			1		1					3		
Gardner	449	16	Haywood	Seth			1		1			1		1			4		
Gardner	449	17	Haywood	Benje			1						1				2		
Gardner	449	18	Hall	Edward		1							1				2		
Gardner	450	1	Johnson	Elisha		1	4		1		1	1		1			9		
Gardner	450	2	Keyes	Ebenzar	3	1	1		1				1				7		
Gardner	450	3	Kneeland	Timothy			1		1			1	1	2			6		
Gardner	450	4	Kilton	Samuel		1	2		1	1			1	1			7		
Gardner	450	5	Kendall	Abel	2			1		3			1				7		
Gardner	450	6	Linds	William	2			1					1				4		
Gardner	450	7	Miles	Oliver	1		1	1		1			1				5		
Gardner	450	8	Martain	Jonathn			1		1	1	2		1	1			7		
Gardner	450	9	Moor	Ezra	1		1	1		1	1		1				6		
Gardner	450	10	Merraim	Jonathan	2			1					1				4		
Gardner	450	11	Mathews	John		1		1				1		1			4		
Gardner	450	12	Nichols	Rebeckah										1			1		
Gardner	450	13	Nichols	Isaac	1		1						1				3		
Gardner	450	14	Nichols	Kendal	2			1					1				4		
Gardner	450	15	Nichols	David	3			1		2	1		1				8		
Gardner	450	16	Nichols	Zachariah	3			1					1				5		
Gardner	450	17	Osgood	Jonath Revd			2	1		2			2				7		
Gardner	450	18	Pruett	Jonathan	2			1					1				4		
Gardner	451	1	Bacon	Joseph	1	1			1	1	2			1			7		
Gardner	451	2	Banister	Daniel		1							1				2		
Gardner	451	3	Barker	Artimas		1							1				2		
Gardner	451	4	Currier	Nathll	1		1						1				3		
Gardner	451	5	Clerk	Joseph		1	1							1			3		
Gardner	451	6	Clerk	Benjamin	1		1			4	1		1				8		
Gardner	451	7	Cole	John	2		1	1					1				5		
Gardner	451	8	Clap	Stephen		1			1		1						3		
Gardner	451	9	Currier	Jonathan			1			1		1		1			4		

TOWN	PG#	LN#	LAST NAME	FIRST NAME	under 10	10 to 16	16 to 26	26 to 45	45 and over	under 10	10 to 16	16 to 26	26 to 45	45 and over	TOTAL ALL OTHER	TOTAL SLAVES	TOTALS	DISTRICT/ TOWNSHIP	NOTES
					FREE WHITE MALES					FREE WHITE FEMALES									
Gardner	451	10	Cooledge	James			2		1			1		1			5		
Gardner	451	11	Childs	Daniel	1	2	1		1	4	1		1				11		
Gardner	451	12	Comee	David		1			1	3	1	1	1				8		
Gardner	451	13	Comee	David Jr			3						1				4		
Gardner	451	14	Cower	James	2	1		1		4		1	1				10		
Gardner	451	15	Cower	David	1	1		1					1				4		
Gardner	451	16	Conant	Josiah	2	1		1		3	2		1				10		
Gardner	451	17	Chappell	William			1				2			1			4		
Gardner	451	18	Dunn	Lewis				1					1	1			3		
Gardner	452	1	Dunster	Hubard	1		1			1		1					4		
Gardner	452	2	Eaton	Joanna		1							1				2		
Gardner	452	3	Eaton	Sally								1					1		
Gardner	452	4	Eager	Jonathan	1	1		1		3	1		1				8		
Gardner	452	5	Eaton	Jonathan	1			1		1			1				4		
Gardner	452	6	Edgell	Benjamin	1	1		1		3			1				7		
Gardner	452	7	Eaton	John	2	1		1		1	1	1	1				8		
Gardner	452	8	Edgell	Samuel	3		1			2	2		1				9		
Gardner	452	9	Edgell	Joseph	1		1			2			1				5		
Gardner	452	10	Foster	David		1		1		1		1	1				5		
Gardner	452	11	Fenno	William	3		1				1		1				6		
Gardner	452	12	Fairbanks	Levi	1	2	2		1	2			1				9		
Gardner	452	13	Flint	Ezekiel		1		1		1			1				4		
Gardner	452	14	Glazor	John				1				1		1			3		
Gardner	452	15	Glazor	Levi	1			1				1					3		
Gardner	452	16	Greenwood	Aaron		1		1		1		1					4		
Gardner	452	17	Greenwood	Jonathan		2	1	1		1	1		1				7		
Gardner	452	18	Lealand	Simeon	3	1		1				1	1				7		
Gardner	454	1	Brick	Jonas	2			1		1	2		1				7		
Gardner	454	2	Bond	Andrew		2		1		3	1			1			8		
Gardner	454	3	Bancroft	Jonathan		1		1		2	3			1			8		
Gardner	454	4	Brigham	Seth	1	2		1		1			1				6		
Gardner	454	5	Bancroft	Jonathan Jr		1				1	1						3		
Gardner	454	6	Brooks	Joel	2	1		1		3			1				8		
Gardner	454	7	Brown	Jonathan	4			1					1				6		
Gardner	454	8	Bigford	William Jr			1						1				2		
Gardner	454	9	Bigford	William		1	1	1				1		1			5		
Gardner	454	10	Bond	Andrew Jr	1			1					1				3		
Gardner	454	11	Corey	Stephen	1			1		2	1						5		
Gardner	454	12	Barker	Thomas	2	1		1		1			1				6		
Gardner	454	13	Bolton	Ebezr			1	1			1			1			4		
Gardner	454	14	Barker	George	1	1		1		1		1	1				6		
Gardner	454	15	Barker	John		1		1				1		1			4		
Gardner	454	16	Bennet	Thomas	1			1					1	1			4		

TOWN	PG#	LN#	LAST NAME	FIRST NAME	FREE WHITE MALES					FREE WHITE FEMALES					TOTAL ALL OTHER	TOTAL SLAVES	TOTALS	DISTRICT/ TOWNSHIP	NOTES
					under 10	10 to 16	16 to 26	26 to 45	45 and over	under 10	10 to 16	16 to 26	26 to 45	45 and over					
Garry	274	1	Upham	Benj		2	2						1				5		
Garry	274	2	Ward	Jabez	1	1		1		3			1	1			8		
Garry	274	3	Ward	Thomas	2		2		1	2		2	1				10		
Garry	274	4	Whitemore	Joseph	2				1	2		1	1				7		
Garry	274	5	Write	Nehemiah	1	2			1	1		2		1			8		
Garry	274	6	Wheeler	Thomas			1		1		1		1				4		
Garry	274	7	Whitehead	Gad	1			1		1	1		1				5		
Garry	274	8	White	Abel	1		1						1				3		
Garry	274	9	White	Thomas	1		1	1	1				1				5		
Garry	274	10	White	Simion			1			1		1					3		
Garry	274	11	White	Samuel			1			1	1	1					4		
Garry	274	12	Whitehead	George	4	1		1					1				7		
Garry	274	13	White	Lucy			1							1			2		
Garry	274	14	Cuming	Samuel	1		1							1			3		
Garry	274	15	Homans	Jonas	1			1					1				3		
Garry	275	1	McClallen	Willm			1			2		1	1				5		
Garry	275	2	Moore	Saml	2			2		1			1				6		
Garry	275	3	Moore	Peter					1			1	1				3		
Garry	275	4	Moore	Luther	3			1					1				5		
Garry	275	5	Mills	Brigham	1		1	1		1		1		1			6		
Garry	275	6	Maynard	Abner		1		1						1			3		
Garry	275	7	Maynard	Francis		1		1		3			1				6		
Garry	275	8	Maynard	Gardner		1	2		1	1	2		1				8		
Garry	275	9	Maynard	Abraham	1		1						1				3		
Garry	275	10	Newton	Isaaac	1	1			1			1		1			5		
Garry	275	11	Newton	Edmond	4	1	1		1		1		1				9		
Garry	275	12	Newo	Iva			1		1		1		1				4		
Garry	275	13	Nickerson	Nathan	2		1	1		3			1				8		
Garry	275	14	Osborn	Mary			1							1			2		
Garry	275	15	Philips	Saml				1						1			2		
Garry	275	16	Philips	Seth	2	1		1			1		1				6		
Garry	275	17	Peckham	Mordica	2	1		1		1		1	1				7		
Garry	275	18	Powers	Edwd	1		1		1	2	1	1					7		
Garry	275	19	Parker	Moses				1						2			3		
Garry	276	1	Pike	David	3	1		1		1	1		1				8		
Garry	276	2	Piper	Abel		1	2		1		3	1	2				10		
Garry	276	3	Piper	Amos	1		1			1		1					4		
Garry	276	4	Piper	Asa	3			1					1				5		
Garry	276	5	Pike	Michal	2			1		2			1				6		
Garry	276	6	Powers	Jonas	1			1		1			2				5		
Garry	276	7	Parker	Elisha	2	2			1	1		1	3	1			11		
Garry	276	8	Perry	Ezra				1			1		1				3		
Garry	276	9	Rich	Zacheus Jr			1			1	1	1			1		5		
Garry	276	10	Rich	Zacheus				1			2	1	1				5		
Garry	276	11	Rich	Joseph		1	1			3			1				6		
Garry	276	12	Rich	Joshua	1		1			3			1				6		
Garry	276	13	Rich	Benja			1			1		1					3		
Garry	276	14	Richardson	Person	2	1	1	1				1		2			8		
Garry	276	15	Rich	Thacher		1	2		1	2	1	1	1				10		
Garry	276	16	Ross	Simon		1		1					1				3		
Garry	276	17	Richardson	Amos	4	1				2			1				8		
Garry	276	18	Rice	Reuben	1			1					1				3		
Garry	277	1	Eaton	Maltiah		1		1	1	1	1		1				6		
Garry	277	2	Eaton	Jonas			1										1		
Garry	277	3	Earl	Stephen	1		3		1	2	2		1				10		
Garry	277	4	Fuller	Elisha	1			2		1		1	1				6		
Garry	277	5	Farnsworth	Phinehas				1		2			1				4		
Garry	277	6	Foster	Abner	1		1	1	1	1			1	1			7		
Garry	277	7	Fletcher	Peter	2		2	1		3		1	1				10		
Garry	277	8	Goddard	Simeon	2	1	2		1			2		1			9		
Garry	277	9	Gould	Elijah	4	1		2				1	1				9		
Garry	277	10	Goulding	Abel	1	1	1		1				1				5		
Garry	277	11	Goss	Stephen	1		2			2		1	1				7		
Garry	277	12	Hale	Silas		1	1		1		1			1			5		
Garry	277	13	Hager	John	2	1	1	1	1	2	1		1	1			11		
Garry	278	1	Johnson	Elizabeth		1				2	1		1				5		
Garry	278	2	Jones	Jona	2	1	1		1	2			1				8		
Garry	278	3	Jones	Nathan			1						1				2		
Garry	278	4	Knight	Ebenz	3	2		1		1			1				8		
Garry	278	5	Knolton	Joseph		1		1		3		1	1				7		
Garry	278	6	Kendall	Willm		1		1	2	1		1		1			7		
Garry	278	7	Knight	Daniel		1		1		1			1				4		
Garry	278	8	Knight	Thadeus		1		1		1		1					4		
Garry	278	9	Kendall	Jesse	2	1		1		2	3		1				10		
Garry	278	10	Lamb	Joshua				1		1	1			1			4		
Garry	278	11	Lamb	Isaac		2	3		1					1			7		
Garry	278	12	Lamb	Bezaleel			1	1				1	1				4		
Garry	278	13	Lovering	Rufus				1		4	1		1				7		
Garry	278	14	Lamb	John	2		1	1		2	2	1	1				10		

TOWN	PG#	LN#	LAST NAME	FIRST NAME	FREE WHITE MALES					FREE WHITE FEMALES					TOTAL ALL OTHER	TOTAL SLAVES	TOTALS	DISTRICT/ TOWNSHIP	NOTES
					under 10	10 to 16	16 to 26	26 to 45	45 and over	under 10	10 to 16	16 to 26	26 to 45	45 and over					
Garry	278	15	Lamb	Saml	2		2		1		2			1			8		
Garry	278	16	Lamb	Jonas	3			1		1			1				6		
Garry	278	17	Lamb	Willm		1				1		1		1			4		
Garry	279	1	Atwood	Martha			1		1	1		2	1	1			7		
Garry	279	2	Ayres	Jason	2			1		2			1				6		
Garry	279	3	Allard	Isaac	2			1					1				4		
Garry	279	4	Baker	Charles Esq				1					1	1			3		
Garry	279	5	Baker	Levi		1	1	1		1			1	1			6		
Garry	279	6	Bigelow	Jotham					1		2	2		1			6		
Garry	279	7	Baits	Asa				1					1				2		
Garry	279	8	Brumdell	Willm	1	1	1		1	1	1		2				8		
Garry	279	9	Baldwin	Thadeus	1	3	1		1	3			1	1			11		
Garry	279	10	Baits	Noah	2	2			1	1			1	1			8		
Garry	279	11	Bruce	Simeon	1		1		1		1	2		1			7		
Garry	279	12	Brigham	John		1	1			1				1			5		
Garry	279	13	Bancroft	Nathll	1			1						1			3		
Garry	279	14	Baker	Charles Jr		3	1		1	2		1	1				9		
Garry	279	15	Baker	Joseph	2			1		1	1		1				6		
Garry	279	16	Bowker	Jona	2			1		2			1				6		
Garry	279	17	Brown	Thadeus	1		1	1	1		2	1		1			8		
Garry	280	1	Bowker	Susannah	2		2			2	3		1				10		
Garry	280	2	Baker	Silas		2		1		2	1			1			7		
Garry	280	3	Brown	Nathan	1	1		1		2		1	1				7		
Garry	280	4	Cluney	James		1	1		1			2	1	1			7		
Garry	280	5	Cutting	Earl	1	1		1		1		1	1	1			8		
Garry	280	6	Cumings	Joseph				1						1			2		
Garry	280	7	Cumings	Stephen	1		1	1		4			1				8		
Garry	280	8	Cole	Elkanah	1	1			1	2	1	1	1	1			9		
Garry	280	9	Carreth	James		2	2		1		1	1		1			8		
Garry	280	10	Carliss	Thomas	1			1					1				3		
Garry	280	11	Cook	Elisha	1		1	1		2		1	1				7		
Garry	280	12	Cutting	Saml		1	1		1	1				1			5		
Garry	280	13	Cobb	Jacob	2			1		2	1		1				7		
Garry	280	14	Dunton	Eben	1		2		1	1	1		1				7		
Garry	280	15	Drury	Huldah				1					1	1			3		

TOWN	PG#	LN#	LAST NAME	FIRST NAME	FREE WHITE MALES under 10	10 to 16	16 to 26	26 to 45	45 and over	FREE WHITE FEMALES under 10	10 to 16	16 to 26	26 to 45	45 and over	TOTAL ALL OTHER	TOTAL SLAVES	TOTALS	DISTRICT/ TOWNSHIP	NOTES
Grafton	193	1	Goddard	Benj		1		1						1			3		
Grafton	193	2	Goddard	Levi	1			1				1					3		
Grafton	193	3	Golding	Ephraim	2		2	1		2		1	1				9		
Grafton	193	4	Fay	Jedithen	2				2	3			1	3			11		
Grafton	193	5	Holdbrook	Moses Jun	2			1		3	1		1				8		
Grafton	193	6	Wesson	Abel	1	1	2		1		2	1	1	1			10		
Grafton	193	7	Wesson	Joel		2	1	1	1	1		2		1			9		
Grafton	193	8	Thurston	John		1		1					1	1			4		
Grafton	193	9	Harrington	Mary								1		1			2		
Grafton	195	1	Wheeler	Jonathan	1	1	3	1				1		2			11		
Grafton	195	2	Turner	Asa	3			1		1			1				6		
Grafton	195	3	Temple	Abner		1		1					1				3		
Grafton	195	4	Wait	Simon			1	1			2	1	1				6		
Grafton	195	5	Wadsworth	Ebenz	1	1	2		1	1	1	1	1	1			10		
Grafton	195	6	Brooks	Joel				1					1				2		
Grafton	195	7	Brooks	Elijah		1	1	1		2	1		1				7		
Grafton	195	8	Cutler	Ebenz				1					1				2		
Grafton	195	9	Cutler	Ebenz Jun	2	1	1	1					1				6		
Grafton	195	10	Cutler	Moses Jun	1			1					1				3		
Grafton	195	11	Cutler	Moses			1						1	1			4		
Grafton	195	12	Brooks	Noah				1					1				2		
Grafton	195	13	Kimball	Aaron		1		1					1				3		
Grafton	195	14	Kimball	Aaron Jun	2		1	1		1	2	2	1				10		
Grafton	195	15	Willard	Benj		1		2		2	1	1	1				8		
Grafton	196	1	Willard	Josephus	1			1		2			1				5		
Grafton	196	2	Fairbank	Isaiah	1		1	1	1	2		1	1				8		
Grafton	196	3	Willard	Hannah								1		1			2		
Grafton	196	4	Aaron	Joseph											2		2		
Grafton	196	5	Axtell	Thomas			1			1	2		1				6		
Grafton	196	6	Axtel	Mary								1		3			4		
Grafton	196	7	Adams	Samuel				1		1		1					3		
Grafton	196	8	Kimball	Isaac			1			1			1				3		
Grafton	196	9	Harrington	Moses		1	2			2			1				6		
Grafton	196	10	Reding	Zebede Jun	1			1		2		1					5		
Grafton	196	11	Reding	Zebede				1						1			2		
Grafton	196	12	Abbot	Abner	3		1	1		1		1	1				8		
Grafton	196	13	Adams	Nathll	4	1	3	1		1	2	1	1				14		
Grafton	196	14	How	Anna	2		1			1			1	1			6		
Grafton	196	15	Rider	Samuel	3		1			1		1	1	1			8		
Grafton	196	16	Adams	Andrew	2	1	2	1		2	2		1				11		
Grafton	197	1	Lealand	Ebenz	1	1	2		1	1	2	1	1				10		
Grafton	197	2	Brigham	John		1	1	1									3		
Grafton	197	3	Brigham	Millitent								1		1			2		
Grafton	197	4	Brigham	Ezekiel	2	1		1		1	2		1				8		
Grafton	197	5	Gimbe	Lucy											4		4		
Grafton	197	6	Stow	Ithimer	2		1	1		2			1	1			8		
Grafton	197	7	Stow	Lucy						1		1		1			3		
Grafton	197	8	Harmon	Timothy				1		2	2			1			6		
Grafton	197	9	Goddard	Joseph			1			1		1					3		
Grafton	197	10	Harrington	Joshua	1	1	1					1					5		
Grafton	197	11	Harrington	Anna									1				1		
Grafton	197	12	Brigham	William	1	1	2		1		1	2		1			9		
Grafton	197	13	Brigham	Charles	1	1		1				1					4		
Grafton	197	14	Brigham	Solomon			1					1					2		
Grafton	197	15	Greenwood	Enoch	2			1		2			1				6		
Grafton	197	16	Cannon	James			1			1			1				3		
Grafton	197	17	Packard	Ephm	3		1			1			1				6		
Grafton	198	1	Rice	Stephen Jun	1		1			1		1					4		
Grafton	198	2	Rice	Stephen		1		1			1	1		1			5		
Grafton	198	3	Kimball	Noah		1	2	1		2	2	1					9		
Grafton	198	4	Drewry	Luke		2	1	1				1		1			6		
Grafton	198	5	Harrington	Samuel	2		1		1		1						5		
Grafton	198	6	Putnam	Zadock		3		1		1		1					6		
Grafton	198	7	Putnam	John	1		1			1		1					4		
Grafton	198	8	Stone	Nahum		1	2	1		1	1	1					7		
Grafton	198	9	Johnson	Timothy		1	1			1			1				4		
Grafton	198	10	Johnson	Widow								1		1			2		
Grafton	198	11	Whiple	Pearle	1		2	1		1		1					6		
Grafton	198	12	Adams	Moses		1	1						1				3		
Grafton	198	13	Drewry	Sarah										1			1		
Grafton	198	14	Flagg	Robartus	3	1			1	4			1				10		
Grafton	198	15	Nayson	Oliver	2		1			3	1		1				8		
Grafton	198	16	Disau	Joseph	1		1			1		1					4		
Grafton	199	1	Sadler	Ebenz			1	1	1					1			4		
Grafton	199	2	Parker	James	2	1	1	1		1				1			7		
Grafton	199	3	Browning	John	3	1		1		1	2	1	1				10		
Grafton	199	4	Holdbrook	Moses		1		1					1				3		
Grafton	199	5	Lealand	Phine	1	2	1	1		1	1	2		1			10		
Grafton	199	6	Smith	Eliphalet			1					1		1			3		

TOWN	PG#	LN#	HEADS OF HOUSEHOLD LAST NAME	FIRST NAME	FREE WHITE MALES under 10	10 to 16	16 to 26	26 to 45	45 and over	FREE WHITE FEMALES under 10	10 to 16	16 to 26	26 to 45	45 and over	TOTAL ALL OTHER	TOTAL SLAVES	TOTALS	DISTRICT/ TOWNSHIP	NOTES
Grafton	199	7	Peirce	Abijah	1			1		1			1				4		
Grafton	199	8	Lealand	David W.	3	1		1		1	2	1	1				10		
Grafton	199	9	Brown	Clark	1	1	1	1		1		1					6		
Grafton	199	10	Brown	Jonas			1	1		3	2		1				8		
Grafton	199	11	White	John	3	1		1		2	2		1				10		
Grafton	199	12	Howard	Levi			2					1					3		
Grafton	199	13	Lathe	Zephaniah	2				1	3			1				7		
Grafton	199	14	Lathe	Benjn		2	3	1	1		2	4		2			15		
Grafton	199	15	New	James	1				1	3	1		1				7		
Grafton	199	16	Perry	Timothy	1	1		1		2	1		1				7		
Grafton	200	1	Lealand	Samuel	1	1			1	1	1	1					6		
Grafton	200	2	Phillips	Ebenz				1		4	1		1				7		
Grafton	200	3	Temple	Timothy			1	1				1					3		
Grafton	200	4	Minor	Samuel				1					1				2		
Grafton	200	5	Roberts	John			1	1		1	1		1				5		
Grafton	200	6	Ames	Jack											6		6		
Grafton	200	7	Brooks	Ephr		1		1					1				3		
Grafton	200	8	Harrington	Solomon	1			1		2			1				5		
Grafton	200	9	Godward	Pearly			1			1		1		1			4		
Grafton	200	10	Printice	Daniel	3	1	2	1		1	1		1				10		
Grafton	200	11	White	Benjn	4	1	1	1					1				8		
Grafton	200	12	Daniels	Zebulon	2	1	1	1		1	1	1	1				9		
Grafton	200	13	Brigham	Elisha				1				1	1				3		
Grafton	200	14	Holdbrook	Stephen		1		1		1		2					5		
Grafton	200	15	Holdbrook	Sarah									1				1		
Grafton	201	1	Warren	Joseph				1		1			1				3		
Grafton	201	2	Warren	Samuel	1			1		2			1				5		
Grafton	201	3	Lesure	Edward	2			1				1	1				5		
Grafton	201	4	Darling	Nathan	1			1		1			1	1			5		
Grafton	201	5	Bruce	Ellis									1				1		
Grafton	201	6	Bruce	Sarah		1				2			1				4		
Grafton	201	7	Miles	John	1			1		1			1				4		
Grafton	201	8	Bennet	John	1			1		1		1					4		
Grafton	201	9	Harrington	Ephraim		3	3			4	1	2	1				14		
Grafton	201	10	Harrington	Jacob	1		1			1		1					4		
Grafton	201	11	Bruce	Eunice									2				2		
Grafton	201	12	Lamb	William	2			1		2	1		1				7		
Grafton	201	13	Wood	Samuel	1		1	1				1	1				5		
Grafton	201	14	Whiple	Thads	2		1	1			1	1					6		
Grafton	201	15	Stow	Eliza									1				1		
Grafton	201	16	Wood	Joseph	1	1	1		1	1		2	1				8		
Grafton	201	17	Warren	John			2			1	1		1				5		
Grafton	202	1	Knox	John	1			1		2			1				5		
Grafton	202	2	Wheeler	Jonathan Jun			1				1		1				3		
Grafton	202	3	Barns	Francis	1	1			1	1		2		1			7		
Grafton	202	4	Whiple	Joseph				1			1	1	1				4		
Grafton	202	5	Heywood	Amasiah	1	1		1		3			1				7		
Grafton	202	6	Whiple	James	1		2		1			2		1			7		
Grafton	202	7	Whiple	John				1					1				2		
Grafton	202	8	Whiple	John Jun	2		1	1					1				5		
Grafton	202	9	Sharman	Ephm				1				1		1			3		
Grafton	202	10	Sharman	Moses	3	2	1	1				2	1				10		
Grafton	202	11	Sharman	Ephm Jun	1		1	1		5	1		1				10		
Grafton	202	12	Sharman	David				1					1				2		
Grafton	202	13	Wadsworth	Jonath			1	1		3		1	1				7		
Grafton	202	14	Hayden	Solomon			1				1						2		
Grafton	202	15	Wadsworth	David				1					1				2		
Grafton	202	16	Wadsworth	Samuel		2							1				3		
Grafton	204	1	Sibley	William	2	2			1	1		1	1				8		
Grafton	204	2	Mores	Prince											4		4		
Grafton	204	3	Boney	Sarah											1		1		
Grafton	204	4	Flagg	Samuel		1	3		1				1	1			7		
Grafton	204	5	Rocket	Benjn				1					1	1			3		
Grafton	204	6	Rocket	Moses	1		1	1		1			1				5		
Grafton	204	7	Reed	Thaddeus	1				1	2	1		3		1		9		
Grafton	204	8	Lealand	Benjn			1		1			1	1				4		
Grafton	204	9	Lealand	Daniel			1			1		1					3		
Grafton	204	10	Kieth	Royal		1	3	1		2		2		1			10		
Grafton	204	11	Batcheller	Nathll	3	1	1		1	2	2	1					11		
Grafton	204	12	Pratt	John	3			1		1	1		1				7		
Grafton	204	13	Clap	Jeremiah	1		1			1	1						4		
Grafton	204	14	Grover	Benjn			1		1				1				3		
Grafton	204	15	Drak	Francis	2			1		1			1				5		
Grafton	204	16	Batcheller	Pearly		2		1				1		1			5		
Grafton	206	1	Wood	Joseph Jun	2		3		1	2	1	1					10		
Grafton	206	2	Williams	Moses	1			1				1					3		
Grafton	206	3	Davis	Amos	1		1		1	1	1			1			6		
Grafton	206	4	Miller	James	2	1		1			1		1				6		
Grafton	206	5	Hayden	Moses		1	1		1		1			1			5		

51

TOWN	PG#	LN#	HEADS OF HOUSEHOLD		FREE WHITE MALES					FREE WHITE FEMALES					TOTAL ALL OTHER	TOTAL SLAVES	TOTALS	DISTRICT/ TOWNSHIP	NOTES
			LAST NAME	FIRST NAME	under 10	10 to 16	16 to 26	26 to 45	45 and over	under 10	10 to 16	16 to 26	26 to 45	45 and over					
Grafton	206	6	Warren	Jonathan	3		2	2		2	1		2				12		
Grafton	206	7	Perham	Lemuel		1			1		1			1			4		
Grafton	206	8	Child	Elizabeth					1					1			2		

TOWN	PG#	LN#	LAST NAME	FIRST NAME	FREE WHITE MALES					FREE WHITE FEMALES					TOTAL ALL OTHER	TOTAL SLAVES	TOTALS	DISTRICT/ TOWNSHIP	NOTES
					under 10	10 to 16	16 to 26	26 to 45	45 and over	under 10	10 to 16	16 to 26	26 to 45	45 and over					
Hardwick	293	1	Atkins	John		1	1	1		3	2		1				9		
Hardwick	293	2	Aikin	David		1		1				2		1			5		
Hardwick	293	3	Allen	David	1		1					2		1			5		
Hardwick	293	4	Allen	Keziah	1			1		3		1	1	1			8		
Hardwick	293	5	Allen	Moses			1	1			1	1					4		
Hardwick	293	6	Allen	Joseph		1		1	1			1					4		
Hardwick	293	7	Amesden	Joel			1	1		1		1					4		
Hardwick	293	8	Amesdenn	Rhoda						3	1		1				5		
Hardwick	293	9	Amesdenn	John		1	1		1			1	1	1			6		
Hardwick	293	10	Allen	Jonas	2	2	1		1	2			1				9		
Hardwick	293	11	Atwood	Zechh		1		1				1					3		
Hardwick	293	12	Beal	Saml			2		1			1		1			5		
Hardwick	293	13	Billings	Asael		1	2		1		1	2		1			8		
Hardwick	293	14	Billings	Elisha	1		1		1		1			2			6		
Hardwick	293	15	Billings	Elijah	2	1		1		1			1				6		
Hardwick	293	16	Billings	Asael Jr				1			1		1				3		
Hardwick	293	17	Barns	Jesse				1			1	2		1			5		
Hardwick	293	18	Barns	Jonas		1		1		2			1				5		
Hardwick	293	19	Barns	Eli	4			1		2	1		1				9		
Hardwick	293	20	Billings	Timothy	1		2				1	1		1			6		
Hardwick	293	21	Barlow	Wyat		2	1		1	1	1	3		1			10		
Hardwick	293	22	Bruce	Josph	1		1			1							3		
Hardwick	295	1	Basset	Wm		2		1									3		
Hardwick	295	2	Basset	Wm Jr			1					1					2		
Hardwick	295	3	Bowen	Samll		1	1			4		1	1				8		
Hardwick	295	4	Barns	Adonijah	2		1			3		1					7		
Hardwick	295	5	Bonney	Job		2	1		1	1		1		1			7		
Hardwick	295	6	Billings	Daniel		1	2	1				1	1				6		
Hardwick	295	7	Bangs	Elijah	2	2	1	1		2		1	1				10		
Hardwick	295	8	Bruce	John	1		2	1	1		1			1			7		
Hardwick	295	9	Brown	Luke			1			2			1				4		
Hardwick	295	10	Burges	Luther	2		1						1				4		
Hardwick	295	11	Barnard	Joseph				1		2	1			1			5		
Hardwick	295	12	Bridges	Isaac		2		1						1			4		
Hardwick	295	13	Bridges	Isaac Jr	3		1			1			1				6		
Hardwick	295	14	Bryant	Wm		1	1		1	1	1	1	1	1			8		
Hardwick	295	15	Bryant	Calvin	2		1			2	1		1				7		
Hardwick	295	16	Butterfield	Aaron	2		1						1				4		
Hardwick	295	17	Bartlett	Bethuel	2	1	1			2			1				7		
Hardwick	295	18	Beluo	Hosea	1		1			1	1	1					5		
Hardwick	295	19	Burt	Ebenz	1		1			4			1				7		
Hardwick	295	20	Borden	Luba				2			1		1				4		
Hardwick	295	21	Butler	Isaac	1	1	2		1		1			1			7		
Hardwick	295	22	Cobb	Sherabiah			2		1			1	1	1			6		
Hardwick	296	1	Collings	Rachel		1	1					1					4		
Hardwick	296	2	Cutler	Convers	2		1			1	1	1					6		
Hardwick	296	3	Crowell	Joshua			1	1					1				3		
Hardwick	296	4	Cleveland	Ebenz	3		1			1		1					6		
Hardwick	296	5	Cobb	Gershom	3	1		1			1			1			7		
Hardwick	296	6	Cobb	Ebenz	1	1		1				1					4		
Hardwick	296	7	Collings	Jonah			1			1		1					3		
Hardwick	296	8	Cleveland	Ephraim	2			1	1	3	1		1	1			10		
Hardwick	296	9	Chamberlain	Moses		1		1	1	1					1		5		
Hardwick	296	10	Cobb	Lemll			1		1	1	1			1			5		
Hardwick	296	11	Cummings	Isaac	2	1	3		1	3	1			1			12		
Hardwick	296	12	Campbell	Jeremiah	1			1		1	2		1				6		
Hardwick	296	13	Cleveland	Elijah	3			1		3		1	1				9		
Hardwick	296	14	Carpenter	Gideon	1			1	1				1	1			5		
Hardwick	296	15	Clark	Isaac	1	1		1				1	1				6		
Hardwick	296	16	Carpenter	Elijah	1		1			3	1		1				7		
Hardwick	296	17	Cutler	Wm	2		2	1	1	2		1	1		1		11		
Hardwick	296	18	Cox	Elizabeth			1					1		1			3		
Hardwick	296	19	Child	Ebenz	3	1	2		1			2		2			11		
Hardwick	296	20	Clark	Edward		1	1		1	1	1						5		
Hardwick	297	1	Cobb	Sylvanus			3		1		2	2	1	1			10		
Hardwick	297	2	Cleveland	Joseph			3		1		2	1					8		
Hardwick	297	3	Clark	Isaac Jr	1	1	1		1			1	1	1			7		
Hardwick	297	4	Covel	Philip	4			1				1		1			7		
Hardwick	297	5	Crowell	Joshua Jr	2			2	1	2			1	1			9		
Hardwick	297	6	Chess	Luther				1		3		1					5		
Hardwick	297	7	Chandler	Josiah	1		1	1	1			1					5		
Hardwick	297	8	Clark	Simeon	3			1		1		1					6		
Hardwick	297	9	Doane	Uriah	3	1		1		1	1		1				8		
Hardwick	297	10	Dexter	Job		1	2	1	1		1			1			7		
Hardwick	297	11	Dennis	Adonijah		1	2	1		1		1	1	1			8		
Hardwick	297	12	Dexter	Samll	3	2	2		1	1		2		1			12		
Hardwick	297	13	Dean	Paul	3	1	2		1			1	1	1			10		
Hardwick	297	14	Doty	John		1	1	1		2	2	1	1				9		
Hardwick	297	15	Danforth	Jno	2	1	4		1	2	1	1		1	1		17		

TOWN	PG#	LN#	HEADS OF HOUSEHOLD LAST NAME	FIRST NAME	FREE WHITE MALES under 10	10 to 16	16 to 26	26 to 45	45 and over	FREE WHITE FEMALES under 10	10 to 16	16 to 26	26 to 45	45 and over	TOTAL ALL OTHER	TOTAL SLAVES	TOTALS	DISTRICT/ TOWNSHIP	NOTES
Hardwick	297	16	Dexter	Ebenz	2				1	5			1		1		10		
Hardwick	297	17	Edson	Oliver		1	1	1					1				4		
Hardwick	297	18	Easterbrook	Benn					1		2	1		1			5		
Hardwick	297	19	Ellwell	David	3			1		1			1	1			7		
Hardwick	297	20	Egery	Daniel			1	1				2		1			5		
Hardwick	297	21	Earl	Jacob				1		1			1				3		
Hardwick	297	22	Eager	Paul				1		1				1			3		
Hardwick	298	1	Egery	Thos	1			1				1	1	1			5		
Hardwick	298	2	Earl	John	1	1		1		1	1	1					6		
Hardwick	298	3	Field	George		1	2		1			1	1				7		
Hardwick	298	4	Furbush	Moses		1		1	1	1			1	1			6		
Hardwick	298	5	Fish	Henry	1			1		1	2		1				6		
Hardwick	298	6	Freeman	Nathan	4		1	1		1	1		1				9		
Hardwick	298	7	Fay	Timothy	3	2	1		1	1		1	1	1			11		
Hardwick	298	8	Freeman	Eli				1	2	1		1		1			6		
Hardwick	298	9	Fay	Reuben			1	1		1	2	1					6		
Hardwick	298	10	Gilbert	Samll	1			1		1			1				4		
Hardwick	298	11	Gilbert	Timothy	1	1	1	1	1			2		1			8		
Hardwick	298	12	Giffen	John	3	2	3	1	1	3	2		2				17		
Hardwick	298	13	Gleason	Nathaniel		2	2					1	1	1			8		
Hardwick	298	14	Gorham	Stephen	1			1	1			1		1			5		
Hardwick	298	15	Gates	Jonah	2	1		1		3			1				8		
Hardwick	298	16	Green	Larkin			1	1	1					1			4		
Hardwick	298	17	Hale	Joseph	3			2		2	1		1				9		
Hardwick	298	18	Hathaway	Jereh	1	1	1	1		2	1		1				8		
Hardwick	298	19	Haskel	Sheveriah	4	1		1		1			1				8		
Hardwick	298	20	Hinkley	Barnabas	1		1	1					1	2			6		
Hardwick	298	21	Hastings	John	1	2	2		1	1	1	1		1			10		
Hardwick	298	22	Haskell	Ephraim		1		1		2			1				5		
Hardwick	299	1	Haskell	Nathl				1					1				2		
Hardwick	299	2	Hatheway	Timothy	2	2		1		2	1		1				9		
Hardwick	299	3	Hinkley	Samll	1		1	1		1	2		1	1			8		
Hardwick	299	4	Hinkley	Seth	1			1		1	3		1				7		
Hardwick	299	5	Haskins	Samll	2			1	1	3			2	1			10		
Hardwick	299	6	Haskell	Micah	1			1					1				3		
Hardwick	299	7	Harmon	Elijah	2	1		1		1			1				6		
Hardwick	299	8	Holt	Thos	1	1		1		2		1	1				7		
Hardwick	299	9	Haskins	Samll Jr	3	3	1	1		1		1	1				11		
Hardwick	299	10	Hammond	Gideon				1						1			2		
Hardwick	299	11	Jackson	Nathll	2	1		1		4	2		1	1			12		
Hardwick	299	12	Jennings	John	4	1		2			1		2	1	1		12		
Hardwick	299	13	Johnson	Seth			1	1	1		1			1			5		
Hardwick	299	14	Johnson	Daniel	2			1				1					4		
Hardwick	299	15	Johnson	Zebediah	1		1	1		1	1						5		
Hardwick	299	16	Johnson	Joel				1			1		1				3		
Hardwick	299	17	Johnson	Silas	1	1		1	1			1		1			6		
Hardwick	299	18	Johnson	Seth Jr			1										1		
Hardwick	299	19	Jones	John	1			1						1			3		
Hardwick	299	20	Johnson	Joshua	2			1			1						4		
Hardwick	299	21	Knowles	Simeon	3			1	1	1			1	1			8		
Hardwick	299	22	Knoulton	Abm	2			1	1			1		2			7		
Hardwick	299	23	Lathe	Asa			1						1				2		
Hardwick	300	1	Lawton	James	1	2	1		1			3		1			9		
Hardwick	300	2	Luce	Experience		1		1		1	1	3		1			8		
Hardwick	300	3	Lawrence	Moses	3	3	1	1	1	2		1	1				13		
Hardwick	300	4	Lathrop	Nathan	2			1		3	1			1			8		
Hardwick	300	5	Lawrence	Ebenz			3		1			3		1			8		
Hardwick	300	6	Larned	James	2	1		1		5		1	1				11		
Hardwick	300	7	Lane	Elijah	2			2				1					5		
Hardwick	300	8	Marsh	Joel	1	1	1			2		1					6		
Hardwick	300	9	Mendal	Moses	2	4		1		2	2		1				12		
Hardwick	300	10	Marble	Daniel	3			1	1				1	1			7		
Hardwick	300	11	Merrick	Nathl			1										1		
Hardwick	300	12	Mendall	Paul				1						1			2		
Hardwick	300	13	Manly	Josiah	3		1	1				1		1			7		
Hardwick	300	14	Newton	Lemll		1		1		3	3	1		2			11		
Hardwick	300	15	Newton	Timothy	1		1	1		1			2	1			7		
Hardwick	300	16	Newton	Silas	2	1		1		3			1				8		
Hardwick	300	17	Nye	Prince	2	2	2		1	2	1	1		1			12		
Hardwick	300	18	Nye	Joseph	1	2	2		1	2			1	1			10		
Hardwick	300	19	Newcomb	Annis		1		1		3	1		1				7		
Hardwick	300	20	Nye	John R	1		1						1				3		
Hardwick	300	21	Nye	Caleb				1						1	1		3		
Hardwick	301	1	Parkust	Jonathan				1						1			2		
Hardwick	301	2	Phinney	Zenas	2	1		1		2	2		1				9		
Hardwick	301	3	Paige	Moses	2			1		2		1					6		
Hardwick	301	4	Paige	Jesse	1	1	1		1	1	1			1			8		
Hardwick	301	5	Paige	Paul	1	1		1		4		1	1	1			10		
Hardwick	301	6	Paige	Nathl	3	1		1			2			2			9		

TOWN	PG#	LN#	LAST NAME	FIRST NAME	FREE WHITE MALES					FREE WHITE FEMALES					TOTAL ALL OTHER	TOTAL SLAVES	TOTALS	DISTRICT/ TOWNSHIP	NOTES
					under 10	10 to 16	16 to 26	26 to 45	45 and over	under 10	10 to 16	16 to 26	26 to 45	45 and over					
Hardwick	301	7	Paige	Charles	1	1		1		1		1	2				7		
Hardwick	301	8	Paige	Benm		1	1					1	1	1			5		
Hardwick	301	9	Paige	James		2	1		1			1		2	1		8		
Hardwick	301	10	Paige	Timt	1	3			3	1		3	1	1			13		
Hardwick	301	11	Paige	John	1			1					1		2		5		
Hardwick	301	12	Perkins	James	1		2					1	1				5		
Hardwick	301	13	Paige	Luther			2	1	1			2		1			7		
Hardwick	301	14	Paige	David	2	1		1		2	1		1				8		
Hardwick	301	15	Perry	Nathan			3	1					1				5		
Hardwick	301	16	Peirce	Seth		1			1		1			1			4		
Hardwick	301	17	Pike	Samll			1							1			2		
Hardwick	301	18	Penniman	Chiron			2			2		1					5		
Hardwick	301	19	Rice	Stephan	1		1	1	1			2	1	1			8		
Hardwick	301	20	Robinson	Samll	1			1		3		1					6		
Hardwick	301	21	Raimond	John		1	1		1			1		2			6		
Hardwick	301	22	Rice	Antipah		2	1		2			3	1	1			10		
Hardwick	302	1	Ruggles	Benm			1		1	2		1	1				6		
Hardwick	302	2	Ramsdel	Sylvanus	1	1		1		1		1	1				6		
Hardwick	302	3	Ruggles	Ephm			1	1		6	2		1				11		
Hardwick	302	4	Robinson	Joseph		1						1	1				3		
Hardwick	302	5	Richardson	Silas	2		1			2			1				6		
Hardwick	302	6	Richards	David	2	2	1	1	1	1		1					9		
Hardwick	302	7	Roggers	Elkenah	4	3		1				1	1	1			11		
Hardwick	302	8	Robinson	Phebe		2						1		1			4		
Hardwick	302	9	Roggers	James	1	1		1	1			1	1				6		
Hardwick	302	10	Ruggles	Benm Jr	1		1			1	1	1		1			7		
Hardwick	302	11	Ruggles	Constant	2	1	1	1	1	2	1	1	1	1			12		
Hardwick	302	12	Ruggles	Edward	2	1	1		1	2	1	1		1			10		
Hardwick	302	13	Ruggles	Welthy			1							1			2		
Hardwick	302	14	Ruggles	Lemll		1	1				1			1			4		
Hardwick	302	15	Ruggles	Seth	3			1		1		1	1				7		
Hardwick	302	16	Ruggles	Daniel	1	1	2		1	3	1		1				10		
Hardwick	302	17	Rice	Ashbel	1	2		1		1			1				6		
Hardwick	302	18	Robinson	Sally		1	1	1		1	1						5		
Hardwick	302	19	Robinson	Danl		1		1		2		1					5		
Hardwick	302	20	Studson	Robert			2		2			1	1				6		
Hardwick	303	1	Studson	Ezra				1				1	1				3		
Hardwick	303	2	Sprout	James	1	1			3	1	1			2			9		
Hardwick	303	3	Snow	Jesse	1		1	1					1	1			5		
Hardwick	303	4	Sprout	Nathan	1				1	2			1				5		
Hardwick	303	5	Snow	Apollos	1		1			1			1				4		
Hardwick	303	6	Smith	Wm	1		1	1	1	1	1	3	2	1			12		
Hardwick	303	7	Smith	Thos R	3			1					1				5		
Hardwick	303	8	Sellen	John	2	2			2	1		1		2			10		
Hardwick	303	9	Spooner	Zepheniah	3				1				1				5		
Hardwick	303	10	Stephans	Thos		1	2		1			2	1	1			8		
Hardwick	303	11	Spooner	Samll				1		1		1					3		
Hardwick	303	12	Sibley	Jeremiah					1					1			2		
Hardwick	303	13	Smith	Nathl				1		2	1		1				5		
Hardwick	303	14	Sibley	Samll		1			1			1		1			4		
Hardwick	303	15	Sibley	Abijah	1			1		1	2		1				6		
Hardwick	303	16	Stimpson	Thos	2			1		1		1					5		
Hardwick	303	17	Sprout	Robert	1				1	1	1		1				5		
Hardwick	303	18	Spooner	Seth				1		2		1	2	1			7		
Hardwick	303	19	Spooner	Jeduthan	3	1	1		1	1	2	1		1			11		
Hardwick	303	20	Stanford	Polly								1		1			2		
Hardwick	304	1	Sloane	Ezekial	4			1		2				1			8		
Hardwick	304	2	Stephens	Jacob				1		2				1			4		
Hardwick	304	3	Shirtlif	Jedediah	2	1		1				1					5		
Hardwick	304	4	Stearns	Elizabeth	2	1					1	2	1				7		
Hardwick	304	5	Stearns	Jno		1			1		1	1		1			5		
Hardwick	304	6	Trow	Israel	3		1	1	1	1		1		1			9		
Hardwick	304	7	Tucker	Seth		1		1	1	1	1		1				6		
Hardwick	304	8	Terry	John	3	1	2	1					1	1			9		
Hardwick	304	9	Thayer	James	3			1		1			1				6		
Hardwick	304	10	Thayer	John					1			1		1			3		
Hardwick	304	11	Thayer	Ephraim	1	2	1		1	1		2		1			9		
Hardwick	304	12	Tailor	Seth			2		1		1			1			5		
Hardwick	304	13	Taylor	Sylvanus		1											1		
Hardwick	304	14	Taylor	Samll	2			1		3	2		1				9		
Hardwick	304	15	Taylor	Uel		1		1					1				3		
Hardwick	304	16	Taylor	Jonathan		1		1		1	1		1				5		
Hardwick	304	17	Thomas	Daniel	1			1			1		1				4		
Hardwick	304	18	Tailor	Wm	2			1				1					4		
Hardwick	304	19	Taylor	Benn	1			1		2			1				5		
Hardwick	304	20	Utley	James	2	2		1	2			1		1			10		
Hardwick	304	21	Warner	Daniel		1			1		2		1				5		
Hardwick	305	1	Warren	Isaac	1			1	1			1		1			5		
Hardwick	305	2	Wheeler	Thos					1					1			2		

TOWN	PG#	LN#	LAST NAME	FIRST NAME	under 10	10 to 16	16 to 26	26 to 45	45 and over	under 10	10 to 16	16 to 26	26 to 45	45 and over	TOTAL ALL OTHER	TOTAL SLAVES	TOTALS	DISTRICT/ TOWNSHIP	NOTES
Hardwick	305	3	Weeks	Joseph	1	2	2		1			1		1			8		
Hardwick	305	4	Wheeler	Thos Jr	1	1		1		1			1				5		
Hardwick	305	5	Warner	Daniel		1			1			2		1			5		
Hardwick	305	6	Warner	Jno	1		2	2	2	1	2	3		1			14		
Hardwick	305	7	Washburn	Eliphalet		1		1	1	1		2	1	1			8		
Hardwick	305	8	Warner	Elijah	1		3		2	1	1	3		2			13		
Hardwick	305	9	Whipple	James	2	1		1		3	1		1				9		
Hardwick	305	10	Willis	Ebenz	2	1		1	1	1		1		1			8		
Hardwick	305	11	Winchester	Moses		1			1					2			4		
Hardwick	305	12	Wicker	Wm		3	2	1	1	2				1			10		
Hardwick	305	13	Walker	Abel		1	2	1	1			2		1			8		
Hardwick	305	14	Webb	John	1	2	2		1		1	2	1				10		
Hardwick	305	15	Wheelock	David					1					1			2		
Hardwick	305	16	Whipple	Samll		2	2			1	1	1		1			8		
Hardwick	305	17	Willis	Lemll		1		1	1	1	1			1			6		
Hardwick	305	18	Wing	Rebeckah										1			1		
Hardwick	305	19	Wheeler	Daniel	1	1	1	1	1			1		1			7		
Hardwick	305	20	White	Elias	2			1		1	1		1				6		
Hardwick	305	21	Whipple	David	4			1		1	1		1				8		
Hardwick	306	1	Whiting	Ebenz	1			1					1				3		
Hardwick	306	2	Whipple	Jacob	1		1	1				1	1				5		
Hardwick	306	3	Whipple	Simon			1		1			1		1			4		
Hardwick	306	4	Wheeler	Lemll				1				1	1				3		
Hardwick	306	5	Winchester	Thos	3			1			1		1				6		
Hardwick	306	6	White	Joseph	1			1				2					4		
Hardwick	306	7	Weeks	David	3			1					1				5		
Hardwick	306	8	Whitney	Ebenz				1		1		2					4		
Hardwick	306	9	Woods	Wm	1			1				1					3		
Hardwick	306	10	Woods	Nathl	1	1		1					1				4		
Hardwick	306	11	Waner	Jno Jr	4			1			1		1				8		
Hardwick	306	12	Washburn	Siris				1				1					2		
Hardwick	306	13	Wing	James	1			1				1					3		
Hardwick	306	14	Thayer	John Jr				1					1				2		
Hardwick	306	15	Winslow	Rozamond		1	1			1				1			4		
Hardwick	306	16	Wheeler	Nathan					1					1			2		
Hardwick	306	17	Winchester	Benn				1									1		

TOWN	PG#	LN#	LAST NAME	FIRST NAME	FREE WHITE MALES					FREE WHITE FEMALES					TOTAL ALL OTHER	TOTAL SLAVES	TOTALS	DISTRICT/ TOWNSHIP	NOTES
					under 10	10 to 16	16 to 26	26 to 45	45 and over	under 10	10 to 16	16 to 26	26 to 45	45 and over					
Harvard	215	1	Nurse	David	2		1	1					1	1			6		
Harvard	215	2	Turner	Luthar		1	2			1			1	1			6		
Harvard	215	3	Turner	Rebeckah	1					2	2	1					6		
Harvard	215	4	Farr	Francis	2	1			1	3		1	1	1			10		
Harvard	215	5	Barnard	Jesse	1			1		3			1				6		
Harvard	215	6	Stacy	John	2		1	1		1			1				6		
Harvard	215	7	Steadman	Thomas	2	1		1	1	2	2	2	1				12		
Harvard	215	8	Stow	Benjamin	2		1	1			1	1	1	1			8		
Harvard	215	9	Priest	Phillimon	3	2	1		1				2	2			12		
Harvard	215	10	Sampson	Willis	1		1			1			1				4		
Harvard	215	11	Sprague	Nathan			1	1					1				3		
Harvard	215	12	Barnard	Abigail										1			1		
Harvard	217	1	Whitney	Aaron		1	1		1				1	1			5		
Harvard	217	2	Whitney	Moses		1	1			1			1				4		
Harvard	217	3	Robbins	Daniel			1				1		1				3		
Harvard	217	4	Whitney	Solmon	2	1		1		1			1	1			7		
Harvard	217	5	Fairbank	Jabez	1			1		2			1				5		
Harvard	217	6	Fairbank	Ephraim	2			1		3	2		1				9		
Harvard	217	7	Woods	Jabez	1		1						1				3		
Harvard	217	8	Woods	Eliphalet				1		1			1				3		
Harvard	217	9	Fairbank	Jonathan		2	1			1			1				5		
Harvard	217	10	Fairbank	Joseph				1			1						2		
Harvard	217	11	Dickinson	Francis		1	1		1	1	1	1	1				7		
Harvard	217	12	Fairbank	Phineas				1						1			2		
Harvard	217	13	Meads	Samuel Junr	2			1	2				1				6		
Harvard	217	14	Burges	Marritt	3			1		2	1		1				8		
Harvard	217	15	Burges	Loammi	2			1		2			1				6		
Harvard	217	16	Burges	Ebenz				1						1			2		
Harvard	217	17	Daby	Asa	2		1	1		1	1						6		
Harvard	217	18	Fairbank	Amos		1		1					1	1			4		
Harvard	217	19	Fairbank	Noah		1		1		1			1				4		
Harvard	217	20	Priest	John				1					1	1			3		
Harvard	217	21	Grugg	Samuel	4			1		1	1	1		1			9		
Harvard	217	22	Sprague	Samuel			1	1		1			1	1			5		
Harvard	217	23	Clark	Matthew	1			1		1	1		1				5		
Harvard	217	24	Dickinson	Samuel		1		1				1	1				4		
Harvard	217	25	Darby	John				1						1			2		
Harvard	217	26	Willard	William	3	2		1		1			1				8		
Harvard	217	27	Hill	John		1		1		1				1			4		
Harvard	217	28	Hill	Sarah						1	1		1				3		
Harvard	217	29	Gary	John	1			1					1				3		
Harvard	217	30	Pollard	Thaddeus Junr	4	1		1		1	2	1	1				11		
Harvard	217	31	Woodbury	Samuel	1	1			1	2	1		1	1			8		
Harvard	217	32	Pollard	Jonathan				1			1			1			3		
Harvard	217	33	Barnard	Samuel	2	2		1					1	1			7		
Harvard	217	34	Albertson	Jacob				1		1	2			1			5		
Harvard	217	35	Sawyer	Manasah Junr	2	1		1		1		1	1				7		
Harvard	217	36	Forbush	Sarah										1			1		
Harvard	217	37	Kelley	Morris				1				1	1				3		
Harvard	217	38	Patterson	Lemue	1	2	1	1		1			1	1			8		
Harvard	217	39	Hayden	Polly	3					1			1				5		
Harvard	218	1	Willard	Caleb		1	1						1				3		
Harvard	218	2	Willard	Daniel	4		2	1	1	1	1		1				11		
Harvard	218	3	Knight	Daniel				1					1				2		
Harvard	218	4	Willard	Joel	2		1	1		3			1				8		
Harvard	218	5	Willard	Phineas			1	1						1			2		
Harvard	218	6	Hill	Levi	2			1				2					5		
Harvard	218	7	Fullam	Elisha		1	1							1			3		
Harvard	218	8	Knight	Joseph			2	1	2				1	1			7		
Harvard	218	9	Turner	Simeon		2		1				1	1				5		
Harvard	218	10	Emmerson	Peter	1	1	1	1	1				1	1			7		
Harvard	218	11	Barnard	David				1					1				2		
Harvard	218	12	Barnard	Benjamin			1	1				1	1	1			5		
Harvard	218	13	Sawyer	Caleb				1						1			2		
Harvard	218	14	Sawyer	Jonathan	2	1		1					2				6		
Harvard	218	15	Whitney	Israel		2			1	1		2	1				7		
Harvard	218	16	Whitney	Isaiah	3	2			1		2	1	1	1			11		
Harvard	218	17	Whitney	Abraham		1	3	1		3			1				9		
Harvard	218	18	Barnard	Jotham	2	1	1		1			1	2	2			10		
Harvard	218	19	Fairbank	Thomas	2	1		1		2			1	1			8		
Harvard	218	20	Polley	Elnathan	1	1		1		3			1				7		
Harvard	218	21	Warner	Calvin	2	1		1	1	3			1				9		
Harvard	218	22	Priest	Jacob	1	1		1				1	1				5		
Harvard	218	23	Warner	John				1						1			2		
Harvard	218	24	Warner	Elias	1	1	1	2		1			1				7		
Harvard	218	25	Warner	Phineas				1						1			2		
Harvard	218	26	Warner	Ephraim	1		2			1		1					5		
Harvard	218	27	Sawyer	Phineas	2		2	1	1		1		1	1			9		
Harvard	218	28	Whitney	Ebenezar	3	1		1		2			1				8		

TOWN	PG#	LN#	HEADS OF HOUSEHOLD		FREE WHITE MALES					FREE WHITE FEMALES					TOTAL ALL OTHER	TOTAL SLAVES	TOTALS	DISTRICT/ TOWNSHIP	NOTES
			LAST NAME	FIRST NAME	under 10	10 to 16	16 to 26	26 to 45	45 and over	under 10	10 to 16	16 to 26	26 to 45	45 and over					
Harvard	218	29	Whitcomb	Phineas	2			1				1		1			5		
Harvard	218	30	Priest	Jeremiah	2				1	2	1		1				7		
Harvard	218	31	Gates	Submit								1	1	1			3		
Harvard	218	32	Houghton	Cyrus	1	1	1						1				4		
Harvard	218	33	Sawyer	Manassah				1					1	1			3		
Harvard	218	34	Sawyer	Luthar	1	1		1		1	1		1				6		
Harvard	218	35	Sawyer	Elizabeth									1	1	1		3		
Harvard	218	36	Robins	Jacob	2			1		2			1				6		
Harvard	218	37	Robbins	Anna										1			1		
Harvard	219	1	Atherton	David	3	1		1		1	1		1				8		
Harvard	219	2	Haskell	Josiah		1		1						1			3		
Harvard	219	3	Haskell	Jacob	2		1	1		2		1	1				8		
Harvard	219	4	Willard	Abel			2						1				3		
Harvard	219	5	Haskell	Samuel	1	1		1	1	1	1	5		1			12		
Harvard	219	6	Robertson	George			2	1		1			3		1		8		
Harvard	219	7	Whiting	Lucy									1	1			2		
Harvard	219	8	Stone	Ephraim			1					1	1				3		
Harvard	219	9	Dawes	Robert	2		1	1		3			1				8		
Harvard	219	10	Hyde	John	2			1		1			1				5		
Harvard	219	11	Davis	Flint		1		1		1			1				4		
Harvard	219	12	Haskell	Josiah Jun		1		1		1							3		
Harvard	219	13	Atherton	Oliver		1	1	1	1			2		1			7		
Harvard	219	14	Mical	John			3		1	1	1	1		1			8		
Harvard	219	15	Willard	Josiah		1	3		2	1	1	2		1			11		
Harvard	219	16	Willard	Barzilla	1		1		1	1	2	1		2			9		
Harvard	219	17	Tousant	Joseph		1		1		1			1				4		
Harvard	219	18	Farwell	John				1					1	1			3		
Harvard	219	19	Chaffin	Gladwin	1		1	1		3	2		1				9		
Harvard	219	20	Cushing	James			1							1			2		
Harvard	219	21	Meads	Jason	1			1		2	1		1				6		
Harvard	219	22	Patterson	Abigail						1	1		1				3		
Harvard	219	23	Dudley	Zacheus		1		1					1				3		
Harvard	219	24	Merriam	Jonas		1						1					2		
Harvard	219	25	Stone	Joseph			2	1				1		1			5		
Harvard	219	26	Hammon	Thomas			1			1			1				3		
Harvard	219	27	Dickinson	David		2							1				3		
Harvard	219	28	Read	Israel	3		1	1			1	1					7		
Harvard	219	29	Conant	Levi	1	1		1		2			1				6		
Harvard	219	30	Conant	William			1						1				2		
Harvard	219	31	Sampson	David			1					1		1			3		
Harvard	219	32	Hapgood	John	1			1				1					3		
Harvard	219	33	Hapgood	Shadrack	1	1	1		1			2		1			7		
Harvard	219	34	Taylor	Charles				1						1			2		
Harvard	219	35	Meeds	Francis	1	1		1		2			1	1			7		
Harvard	219	36	Harlow	William	1		1			1			1	1	1		6		
Harvard	219	37	Gould	Joseph		1		1						1			3		
Harvard	219	38	Wares	Moses	1		1						1				3		
Harvard	220	1	Garfield	Reubin		1		1				1	1				4		
Harvard	220	2	Sanderson	Oliver	1			1		2			1				5		
Harvard	220	3	Wetherbee	Joseph		1		1		1		1	1				5		
Harvard	220	4	Sisson	George	1			1		2	1		1				6		
Harvard	220	5	Robbins	Ephraim		3	1	1					1				6		
Harvard	220	6	Pollard	David		1		1				1	1				4		
Harvard	220	7	Read	Abijah	1		1					1	1				4		
Harvard	220	8	Gibson	John	2		1			1			1				5		
Harvard	220	9	Farnsworth	Abel		1		1				2		1			5		
Harvard	220	10	Wetherbee	Abel	1			1		1		1					4		
Harvard	220	11	Huse	Enoch				1						1			2		
Harvard	220	12	Cond	George		1		1				1		1			4		
Harvard	220	13	Safford	Ward		1								2			4		
Harvard	220	14	Davis	Aaron Junr			1			1		1	1				4		
Harvard	220	15	Read	Jonathan	1		1			3	1		1				7		
Harvard	220	16	Whitcomb	Reubin	1		1						1				3		
Harvard	220	17	Priest	Abel	2	2	1						1				6		
Harvard	220	18	Houghton	John				1						1			2		
Harvard	220	19	Houghton	Peter	3			1		2		1	1				8		
Harvard	220	20	Fairbank	Jacob			1	1		2			1				5		
Harvard	220	21	Stone	Micah		2		1						1			4		
Harvard	220	22	Houghton	Asa				1						1			2		
Harvard	220	23	Houghton	Asa Junr	2	2	2	1		2		1	1				11		
Harvard	220	24	Pollard	Thaddeus Junr	1	1	2	1			2		1				8		
Harvard	220	25	Whitney	Oliver		1		1		1				1			4		
Harvard	220	26	Houghton	Elijah				1		3				1			5		
Harvard	220	27	Houghton	Thomas	4	3		1						1			9		
Harvard	220	28	Houghton	Elijah Junr	2			2		2			1				7		
Harvard	220	29	Scott	Mary			1						1	1			3		
Harvard	220	30	Pierce	John		1		1		1			1	1			5		
Harvard	220	31	Dudley	Samuel	1		2	1		1			1				6		
Harvard	220	32	Atherton	Sarah										1			1		

| | | | HEADS OF HOUSEHOLD | | FREE WHITE MALES | | | | | FREE WHITE FEMALES | | | | | | | | | |
TOWN	PG#	LN#	LAST NAME	FIRST NAME	under 10	10 to 16	16 to 26	26 to 45	45 and over	under 10	10 to 16	16 to 26	26 to 45	45 and over	TOTAL ALL OTHER	TOTAL SLAVES	TOTALS	DISTRICT/TOWNSHIP	NOTES
Harvard	220	33	Willard	Lemuel		3	1		1	1	1		1				8		
Harvard	220	34	Hartwell	Hannah							1		1				2		
Harvard	221	1	Bromfield	Hennery				1			1			1	1		4		
Harvard	221	2	Forbush	Samuel		2	1		1	1	1		1	1			8		
Harvard	221	3	Forbush	John				1					3				4		
Harvard	221	4	Whitney	Richard	1	1			1		1			1			5		
Harvard	221	5	Barnard	Phineas			1				1						2		
Harvard	221	6	Goldsmith	Richard	1	1		1	1	1		1		1			7		
Harvard	221	7	Lawrance	Stephen		1		1					1				3		
Harvard	221	8	Clark	Jonathan				1	1					2			4		
Harvard	221	9	Fairbanks	Amos Junr	2			1				1	1				5		
Harvard	221	10	Dwinnel	Elijah	1		2	1		1			1	1			7		
Harvard	221	11	Willard	Joseph				1					1				2		
Harvard	221	12	Willard	Joseph Junr	4	1	1	1					1				8		
Harvard	221	13	Mead	Samuel				1					1	1			3		
Harvard	221	14	Whitney	Isaac	1	1		1		1	1			1			6		
Harvard	221	15	Goldsmith	Theodore		2					1						3		
Harvard	221	16	Rand	Silas		1		1				1		1			4		
Harvard	221	17	Rand	Silas Junr		1				1		1					3		
Harvard	221	18	Cotton	Edward			1							1			2		
Harvard	221	19	Whitney	Isaiah		1		1		1				1			4		
Harvard	221	20	Cotton	John	1	1	1	1		1		1					6		
Harvard	221	21	Forbush	Daniel	1		1	1				1	1	1			6		
Harvard	221	22	Haskell	James Junr	2					1		1					4		
Harvard	221	23	Haskell	James			1	1		1	1		1				5		
Harvard	221	24	Brooks	Samuel				1		4		2	1				8		
Harvard	221	25	Davis	Isaiah	1		1	1		1		1					5		
Harvard	221	26	Fairwell	Edmund	1	1	3		1	1	1			1			9		
Harvard	221	27	Wood	Timothy				1				1	1				3		
Harvard	221	28	Wood	John			1						1				2		
Harvard	221	29	Haskell	Jonathan			1	1		2	2		1				7		
Harvard	221	30	Jewett	Aaron		6	12	3			10	21	2				54		
Harvard	221	31	Bridges	Jonathan			2	3			3	2	10				20		
Harvard	221	32	Willard	Jeremiah		1		1	12		3	6	20				43		
Harvard	221	33	Farnsworth	Mathias				1					1				2		
Harvard	221	34	Ramsdell	Nehemiah	1			1		1			1				4		
Harvard	221	35	Cotton	Josiah	1	1		1		2			1				6		
Harvard	221	36	Holmes	William		1	1	1					1	1			5		
Harvard	221	37	Park	Thomas		1	3	1			1	1	1				8		
Harvard	222	1	Farrer	Stephen			1	1					1				3		
Harvard	222	2	Park	William	1		1	1		2			1				6		
Harvard	222	3	Blanchard	Lycias				1		1			1				3		
Harvard	222	4	Perminan	Joseph				1		1	2		1				5		
Harvard	222	5	Nurse	Samuel		1		1		1		1					4		
Harvard	222	6	Burdeen	Thomas			1	1		1		1	1				5		
Harvard	222	7	Burt	William		1		1				1	1				4		
Harvard	222	8	Blanchard	Abel		1		1			1	1					4		
Harvard	222	9	Harlow	Ellis	2	2		1		1	1		1				8		
Harvard	222	10	Farnsworth	Nathl	1		1	1			1			1			5		
Harvard	222	11	Blanchard	Simon	2	1		1		1		2	1				8		
Harvard	222	12	Whitney	James	1	1	1	1			1		1				6		
Harvard	222	13	Whitney	Enoch		1		1			1	1	1				5		
Harvard	222	14	Whitney	David				1					1				2		
Harvard	222	15	Davis	Josiah		1		1					1				3		
Harvard	222	16	Davis	Mary						2			1				3		
Harvard	222	17	Whitney	Reuben	1		1	1				2	1				6		
Harvard	222	18	Bateman	Jonas	2			1		3	1		1				8		
Harvard	222	19	Pierce	Nathaniel				1					1				2		
Harvard	222	20	Whitney	Hezikiah		1		1				1	1				4		
Harvard	222	21	Taylor	Solomon	1			1		1	2	2	1				10		
Harvard	222	22	Harris	Lydia		1								1			2		
Harvard	222	23	Whitney	Cyrus				1		1		1					3		
Harvard	222	24	Hill	Oliver	2		2	1				2					7		
Harvard	222	25	Mead	John				1					1				2		
Harvard	222	26	Chaffin	Elias				1			1						2		
Harvard	222	27	Bigelow	Roger	2	1		1					1				5		
Harvard	222	28	Stone	Lemuel				1					1				2		
Harvard	222	29	Godfrey	Lucy	1								1				2		
Harvard	222	30	Whitney	Jonas	1		1	1		2	3	1	1		1		11		
Harvard	222	31	Parkhurst	Silas		1						2	1				5		
Harvard	222	32	Kimball	Benjamin		1		1	1	1	1	2	1				9		
Harvard	222	33	Meads	Samuel		1	1	1					1	1			5		
Harvard	222	34	Wetherbee	Ezra			2					2					4		
Harvard	222	35	Pollard	Luke		1		1		1	1	1					5		
Harvard	222	36	Stone	Phineas	2		1	1		1		1	1				7		
Harvard	222	37	Simons	Jonathan	1		1	1			1		1				5		
Harvard	222	38	Henney	Joseph				1				1	1	1			4		
Harvard	222	39	Fairfield	John				1					2	1			4		

TOWN	PG#	LN#	LAST NAME	FIRST NAME	FWM under 10	FWM 10 to 16	FWM 16 to 26	FWM 26 to 45	FWM 45 and over	FWF under 10	FWF 10 to 16	FWF 16 to 26	FWF 26 to 45	FWF 45 and over	TOTAL ALL OTHER	TOTAL SLAVES	TOTALS	DISTRICT/TOWNSHIP	NOTES
Holden	509	1	Parmenter	John	1			1		2			1				5		
Holden	509	2	Read	John	1			1		1			1				4		
Holden	509	3	Rice	Jonathan				1					2	1			4		
Holden	509	4	Rice	Jasen			1			3			1				5		
Holden	509	5	Rice	David	1			1		3			1				6		
Holden	509	6	Rice	John	2			1		2	2		1				8		
Holden	509	7	Rice	Ezra	2	1		1		2	1		1				8		
Holden	509	8	Richardson	Thomas		1			1	1		1		1			5		
Holden	509	9	Richardson	Heman	1			2		3			1				7		
Holden	509	10	Rogers	Nathan		2	1			1		1		1			6		
Holden	509	11	Rogers	Aaron	2	1	1	1		1	1		1				8		
Holden	509	12	Rogers	Jonathan	5	1			1			1	1				9		
Holden	509	13	Rowe	Samuel	2				1	3	1		1				8		
Holden	509	14	Spring	John	1			1				1	1				4		
Holden	509	15	Smith	Moses			2	1				2	1	1			7		
Holden	509	16	Smith	Moses 2d				1		2	3		1				7		
Holden	509	17	Smith	Amos		2		1		3	1		1				8		
Holden	509	18	Smith	David	2	1	1	1		2	1		1				9		
Holden	509	19	Stratton	Josiah		1		1				1	1				4		
Holden	509	20	Stratton	Israel	2			1					1				4		
Holden	509	21	Stratton	Thomas	1			1		2		1					5		
Holden	509	22	Symonds	John		1		1						1			3		
Holden	510	1	Sargeant	Daniel	1	1	*	*	*	1				1			4		
Holden	510	2	Stearns	Joseph			2	1						1			4		
Holden	510	3	Smith	Nathan	2			1						1			4		
Holden	510	4	Shepherd	Paul		1							1				2		
Holden	510	5	Turner	Bezaleel		1		1						1			3		
Holden	510	6	Turner	Bezaleel Junr		1				2		1					4		
Holden	510	7	Temple	Aaron			1			4			1				6		
Holden	510	8	Townsend	Jacob				1						1			2		
Holden	510	9	Tuttle	Joseph		1	1	1		3	1	1	1	1			10		
Holden	510	10	Viner	John	1	1		1		3			1				7		
Holden	510	11	Walker	Hezekiah	1	1	1	1		3	2	1		1			11		
Holden	510	12	Winch	John	1	1		1						1			4		
Holden	510	13	Winch	Francis	2	1		1		1			1	1			7		
Holden	510	14	Wilson	Francis			1	1				1		1			4		
Holden	510	15	Wheeler	Moses		2		1					1	2			6		
Holden	510	16	Wheeler	Thomas	2			1		1			2				6		
Holden	510	17	Webb	George				1				3		1			5		
Holden	510	18	Webb	Barnabas		1						1					2		
Holden	510	19	Willard	Thomas				1						1			2		
Holden	510	20	Willard	Jacob			1			1			1				3		
Holden	510	21	Willard	Joseph	1			1		1			1				4		
Holden	510	22	Willard	Ashbel	1			1					1	1			4		
Holden	511	1	Hubbard	Samuel	1		1	1		1				1			5		
Holden	511	2	Heywood	Samuel	1	1		1		2	1		1				7		
Holden	511	3	Heywood	Thaddeus			1						1				2		
Holden	511	4	Heywood	Alpheus			1			1			1				3		
Holden	511	5	Harrington	Nathan				1					2	1			4		
Holden	511	6	Harrington	Samuel			2	1		2			1				6		
Holden	511	7	Harrington	Micah			1	1		1			1				4		
Holden	511	8	Harrington	Ephraim			1						2				3		
Holden	511	9	Hubbard	W. Moore			1			1		1					3		
Holden	511	10	Harvy	James	3		1						1				5		
Holden	511	11	Haskell	Ebenezer				1		2	2	3	1				9		
Holden	511	12	Kimbel	David	1	1		1		1			2				6		
Holden	511	13	Knowlton	Jesse	1			1		3			1				6		
Holden	511	14	Jenkins	Lucy	1					1		1					3		
Holden	511	15	Lovell	Asa		1			1	2	1		2	2			9		
Holden	511	16	Lovell	Amos	1	1	1		2	2	2	1	1				12		
Holden	511	17	Lovering	Jesse			3	1		1							5		
Holden	511	18	Lovering	Jesse Junr	1	1		1		1			1				5		
Holden	511	19	Mirick	Elisha				1					1	1			3		
Holden	511	20	Mirick	Tilly	1			1					1	1			4		
Holden	511	21	Morse	Joseph	4	2	1	1		2	1		1				12		
Holden	511	22	Moore	Jonathan		1	1	1		1	1		1				6		
Holden	511	23	Mann	Nathan		1		2						1			4		
Holden	512	1	Mead	William	1		1	1					1				4		
Holden	512	2	Marshall	Timothy		1						1	1				4		
Holden	512	3	Marshall	Abel	1	1	1	1	1	2		2	2	1			12		
Holden	512	4	Marshall	Mary						2			1	1			4		
Holden	512	5	Metcalf	Jabez		1		1		1	2			1			6		
Holden	512	6	Merrifield	Asaph		1	1	1		3	2	1	1				10		
Holden	512	7	Newel	Aaron			1			1		1	3	1			8		
Holden	512	8	Nichols	Jonathan	1	2		1		3		1	1				9		
Holden	512	9	Nichols	Thaddeus	2	1		1		1			2	1			8		
Holden	512	10	Nash	Samuel	3	1		1		2			2	1			10		
Holden	512	11	Newel	Rufus	1			1					1				3		
Holden	512	12	Obens	John				1									1		

TOWN	PG#	LN#	HEADS OF HOUSEHOLD		FREE WHITE MALES					FREE WHITE FEMALES					TOTAL ALL OTHER	TOTAL SLAVES	TOTALS	DISTRICT/ TOWNSHIP	NOTES
			LAST NAME	FIRST NAME	under 10	10 to 16	16 to 26	26 to 45	45 and over	under 10	10 to 16	16 to 26	26 to 45	45 and over					
Holden	512	13	Peirce	David Junr	2		1	1	1	1	2		1	1			9		
Holden	512	14	Partridge	Jesse		1	1		1	1			1	1			6		
Holden	512	15	Paddock	Reuben					1		1	1		1			4		
Holden	512	16	Paddock	Reuben Jr	1			1		1			1				4		
Holden	512	17	Parker	Timothy		1	2	1	1			1	2				8		
Holden	512	18	Parker	Aaron	3			1					1				5		
Holden	512	19	Perry	John				1						1			2		
Holden	512	20	Perry	Abner	1	1		1		1			1				5		
Holden	512	21	Perry	Simeon	2			1		2			1				6		
Holden	512	22	Potter	James	3	1		1		2		1	1				9		
Holden	512	23	Parmenter	Soloman		2		1		1		1		1			6		
Holden	513	1	Damon	Samuel		1	4	1	1			2		1			10		
Holden	513	2	Damon	Stephen	2	1			2	2		1	1				9		
Holden	513	3	Dryden	Artimas	2	2			1	1				2			8		
Holden	513	4	Dreary	William	4	1	1	1		1	2		1				11		
Holden	513	5	Dunton	Beulah		1				1	1		1				4		
Holden	513	6	Dunsmore	Reuben	1	1		1					1				4		
Holden	513	7	Estabrook	Ebenezer	1		2		1			1	1				6		
Holden	513	8	Estabrook	Jonathan	2		2	1		2			2				9		
Holden	513	9	Estabrook	James	2	1	1	1		1		1					7		
Holden	513	10	Estabrook	Samuel		1			1			1		1			4		
Holden	513	11	Eaton	Uriah					1								1		
Holden	513	12	Farr	Simeon					1					1			2		
Holden	513	13	Felton	John	1			1		1			1				4		
Holden	513	14	Flagg	Benjamin		1	1		1	1		2		2			8		
Holden	513	15	Fisk	Nahum	3	1		1		1	2		1				9		
Holden	513	16	Fisk	Jonathan		1	1		1	1	1	1					6		
Holden	513	17	Fisk	Lemuel		1		1		1		1	1				5		
Holden	513	18	Fales	Lemuel	2	1	1			1			1	1			7		
Holden	513	19	Flagg	Jonathan	3	2	1	1		1			1				9		
Holden	513	20	Flagg	Silas	2			1		1	1		1				6		
Holden	513	21	Glezen	Jason				1				1					2		
Holden	513	22	Glezen	Jason Junr		1		1				1	1				4		
Holden	513	23	Glezen	Joel	1		2			1		1	1				6		
Holden	513	24	Goulding	Ignatius			1	1	1			1	1	1			6		
Holden	514	1	Goodale	Paul		2	2		1	1		1		1			8		
Holden	514	2	Goulding	Winsor			2	1	1				1				5		
Holden	514	3	Goulding	John M.	2	2		1			1		1				7		
Holden	514	4	Gale	Mary		1				1	1			1			4		
Holden	514	5	Gale	Isaac	1	1		1		2			1				6		
Holden	514	6	Gale	Oliver		1	2					1					4		
Holden	514	7	Grant	Samuel				1			1		1				3		
Holden	514	8	Greenwood	Asa				1					1				2		
Holden	514	9	Hemmenway	Daniel	4	1		1					1				7		
Holden	514	10	Hayden	Jonathan				1					1				2		
Holden	514	11	Holt	Ephraim				1				1		2			4		
Holden	514	12	Holt	Aaron			1					1					2		
Holden	514	13	Holt	Amos			1			3		1					5		
Holden	514	14	Hubbard	Joseph	2	3	1	1	1	2			1	1			12		
Holden	514	15	Hubbard	Elisha		1	2		1		1		2	1			8		
Holden	514	16	Hubbard	John	1			1		2			1				5		
Holden	514	17	Hubbard	Peter	1	1	2		1			1		1			7		
Holden	514	18	How	Abraham		1			1					1			3		
Holden	514	19	How	Jotham	2	1	1		1			1		1			7		
Holden	514	20	How	Jonathan		1			1	2		3		1			8		
Holden	514	21	Hastings	Ezra	1	2	1	1		1	1		1				8		
Holden	514	22	Holbrook	David	1	1	1	1		1	1		1				7		
Holden	514	23	Howard	Joseph		1	1	1	1			3		2			9		
Holden	514	24	Hubbard	Isaac			1		2				2	1			6		
Holden	515	1	Avery	Joseph		1	1	1				1	2	1			7		
Holden	515	2	Abbott	Samuel	4		3	2		1		1	1	1			13		
Holden	515	3	Abbott	John	2	2		1		2	1		1				9		
Holden	515	4	Allen	Ephraim			1	1	1	2		3	1	1			10		
Holden	515	5	Allen	Peletiah			1				1		1	1			4		
Holden	515	6	Brannan	Daniel	2	1	2		1	1	1	1		1			10		
Holden	515	7	Bartlett	John	1			1		2			1				5		
Holden	515	8	Bartlett	Artimas	1	1	1			1	1	1		2			8		
Holden	515	9	Black	Daniel				1						1			2		
Holden	515	10	Broad	Josiah	1	1	2	1	1	2	1	4		1			14		
Holden	515	11	Blake	Jeremiah	1	2		1		1		2	1	1			9		
Holden	515	12	Boynton	Ebenezer	2	2	2	1				2		2			11		
Holden	515	13	Ball	Phinehas	1			1		3	2		1	1			9		
Holden	515	14	Boyden	Daniel	1		3		1			2	2	1			10		
Holden	515	15	Ball	Jotham	1	1		1		3	1		1				8		
Holden	515	16	Ball	Jonah	2			1					1				4		
Holden	515	17	Bigelow	Stephen	1			1		4			1				7		
Holden	515	18	Cheeney	Josiah				1						1			2		
Holden	515	19	Cheeney	Josephus			1						1				2		
Holden	515	20	Crosby	Sparrow	3	2		1		3		2	1				12		

TOWN	PG#	LN#	LAST NAME	FIRST NAME	FREE WHITE MALES					FREE WHITE FEMALES					TOTAL ALL OTHER	TOTAL SLAVES	TOTALS	DISTRICT/ TOWNSHIP	NOTES
					under 10	10 to 16	16 to 26	26 to 45	45 and over	under 10	10 to 16	16 to 26	26 to 45	45 and over					
Holden	515	21	Chaffin	Samuel		1	2	1	1			1	1	1			8		
Holden	515	22	Chaffin	Tilly	3		1	1			2		1				8		
Holden	515	23	Chaffin	Nathan	3	1		1		3			1				9		
Holden	516	1	Cheeney	S Clark		2		1		2			1				6		
Holden	516	2	Chickering	Samuel	2	1	1		1			1	1				7		
Holden	516	3	Church	Alexander		1		1		2				1			5		
Holden	516	4	Clap	Seth	2		1		1	2	1			1			8		
Holden	516	5	Colburn	Alpheus			1							1			2		
Holden	516	6	Colburn	Thaddeus	1			1	1	3			1				7		
Holden	516	7	Cheeney	Isaac	2	1	1		1		1	1	1	1			9		
Holden	516	8	Cordwell	Martha	2					1			1				4		
Holden	516	9	Daniels	Joseph		2	1	1				1	1				6		
Holden	516	10	Davis	Lemuel	1	1	1	1		3	1		1	1			10		
Holden	516	11	Dodds	John	2		1		1			1	1				6		
Holden	516	12	Davis	Paul			2		1			1	1	1			6		
Holden	516	13	Dodds	James		2			1		1	2		1			7		
Holden	516	14	Davis	Thomas	2	2	1		1		1		1				8		
Holden	516	15	Dwelly	Joseph				1						1			2		
Holden	516	16	Dwelly	Joseph Junr	1			1					1				3		
Holden	516	17	Davis	James			1	1					1				3		
Holden	516	18	Davis	Edmund	1	1		1		3		1	1				8		
Holden	516	19	Davis	Elnathan		1		1		3		2					7		
Holden	516	20	Davis	Ethan	2		1	1		2			1				7		
Holden	516	21	Davis	James 2d			1	1		1				1			4		
Holden	516	22	Davis	Israel		1	1		1	1	1			1			6		
Holden	516	23	Davis	John			2		1	1			1				5		

TOWN	PG#	LN#	HEADS OF HOUSEHOLD		FREE WHITE MALES					FREE WHITE FEMALES					TOTAL ALL OTHER	TOTAL SLAVES	TOTALS	DISTRICT/ TOWNSHIP	NOTES
			LAST NAME	FIRST NAME	under 10	10 to 16	16 to 26	26 to 45	45 and over	under 10	10 to 16	16 to 26	26 to 45	45 and over					
Hubbardston	413	1	Bullard	Isekiah		1			1					1			3		
Hubbardston	413	2	Bartlett	Saml	2			1		1	1		1	1			7		
Hubbardston	413	3	Boynton	Edward			1		1		2			1			5		
Hubbardston	413	4	Boardman	Ebenezer			1				1		1		3		6		
Hubbardston	413	5	Brown	John			1						1				2		
Hubbardston	415	1	Allen	Simon		1		1	1	2		3		1			9		
Hubbardston	415	2	Allen	Ephraim	2	1		1		1	1	1					7		
Hubbardston	415	3	Adams	Elijah		1			1	1	1	1		1			6		
Hubbardston	415	4	Adams	Isachar	2		1		1	2	2	2		1			11		
Hubbardston	415	5	Adams	Eben				1					1				2		
Hubbardston	415	6	Ames	Jonathan	1			1					1				3		
Hubbardston	415	7	Adams	Titus	1	1		1		2	1		1				7		
Hubbardston	415	8	Barnes	Daniel	1			1				1	1				4		
Hubbardston	415	9	Bellows	Asaph	3			1		1			1				6		
Hubbardston	415	10	Burditt	Jesse		1	4		1	1	2			1			10		
Hubbardston	415	11	Brigham	Hosea		1	2		1	1		1		1			7		
Hubbardston	415	12	Browning	John Lt.	3	2		1		2	1		2				11		
Hubbardston	415	13	Brown	Asa			2		1			1		1			5		
Hubbardston	415	14	Benson	Abner					1		1		1	1			4		
Hubbardston	415	15	Bennet	David	1		1		1	2	1		1				8		
Hubbardston	415	16	Bellows	Isaac	1				1			1		1			4		
Hubbardston	415	17	Brown	Eben	4	2			1	1			1	1			10		
Hubbardston	415	18	Brown	Oliver	1		1						1				3		
Hubbardston	415	19	Clark	John Jr		2	1		1	1	3			1			9		
Hubbardston	415	20	Clark	Ezra	3	1		1		1		1	1				8		
Hubbardston	415	21	Clark	Wm.	1	3			1	1	1	1		1			9		
Hubbardston	415	22	Clark	Moses	2	1	2	1	1		2	1	2				12		
Hubbardston	415	23	Clark	Isaac	4	1		1			2						8		
Hubbardston	415	24	Clark	Joseph	2	2	1	1		1	2		1				10		
Hubbardston	415	25	Clark	Saml	1		2		1	2	1		1				8		
Hubbardston	415	26	Clark	Peter	3			1			2		1		1		8		
Hubbardston	415	27	Clark	Jenny Wid								1	1		2		4		
Hubbardston	415	28	Clark	Eli Lt.		2	1	1	1	2		1		1			9		
Hubbardston	415	29	Clark	Thos	2			1	1	1	1		1				6		
Hubbardston	415	30	McClanathan	John	2		1		1	1	2		1				8		
Hubbardston	415	31	McClanathan	Thoms	1	1	1	1		4	2		1				11		
Hubbardston	415	32	Clifford	Jonath	2		1		1	2	1	2	1				10		
Hubbardston	415	33	Church	Asa Capt.	3	2	1		1			2		1			10		
Hubbardston	415	34	Cutting	Abraham	1	1		1		2			1				6		
Hubbardston	415	35	Clark	John Capt.				2			1						3		
Hubbardston	415	36	Clark	Aaron R.	1	1		1			1		1				5		
Hubbardston	415	37	Clark	Luther	2	1		1		1			1				6		
Hubbardston	415	38	Cutting	Jonathan			1						1				2		
Hubbardston	415	39	Davis	Israel		1		1					1				3		
Hubbardston	415	40	Davis	Benjm	1			1		1			1				4		
Hubbardston	415	41	Clark	Amos	1			1		1	1		1		5		10		
Hubbardston	415	42	Dunster	David				1					1				2		
Hubbardston	416	1	Woodward	Philemon		1	1	1	1	1		1		1			7		
Hubbardston	416	2	Woodward	Daniel	3	1		1		2	2		1				10		
Hubbardston	416	3	Witt	Oliver Capt.	4	2	1	1	1	1		1	3	1			15		
Hubbardston	416	4	Williams	John	3	1	1	1				1					8		
Hubbardston	416	5	Williams	Jona	1	1		1		2		1	1				7		
Hubbardston	416	6	Warren	Luke	2	1		1		1	1		1				7		
Hubbardston	416	7	Woodward	Ebenz				1									2		
Hubbardston	416	8	Woodward	Edward	3			2					1				6		
Hubbardston	416	9	Wait	Nathl Jr.				2					1				3		
Hubbardston	416	10	Whitemore	Isaac	1			1		1		1					4		
Hubbardston	416	11	Witt	Eunas Wid	1	1	2					1		1			6		
Hubbardston	416	12	Willard	Joshua		3			1				1				5		
Hubbardston	416	13	Wheeler	Oliver					1			1	1				3		
Hubbardston	417	1	Marcan	Wm. Maj.		1	1		1	1	1	1		1			7		
Hubbardston	417	2	Marcan	Timy P.	1	1		1		1	1	1					6		
Hubbardston	417	3	Murdock	Robert Lt.		1	1		1			1					4		
Hubbardston	417	4	Murdock	Joshua				1			1		1				3		
Hubbardston	417	5	Murdock	Abial	1	1	1		1			1		1			6		
Hubbardston	417	6	Muzzy	Wm. Lt					1			1	1				3		
Hubbardston	417	7	Morss	Katharine Wid.		1	1					1	1				4		
Hubbardston	417	8	Morss	Samuel	5	2	1	2		1			1	1			13		
Hubbardston	417	9	Morss	Wm.	2		1	1		2			1				7		
Hubbardston	417	10	Meriam	David		1	1		1		1	2	1	1			8		
Hubbardston	417	11	Merrick	Paul	1			1				1	1				4		
Hubbardston	417	12	Mann	Ebenezer Capt.	2	1	1		1	2	1		1				9		
Hubbardston	417	13	Mandell	Daniel	1	1		1		1		1		1			6		
Hubbardston	417	14	Marsh	Joseph	3			1			1		1				6		
Hubbardston	417	15	Nightingale	Wm Capt.	3			1		3			1				9		
Hubbardston	417	16	Newton	Joel	1			1		2			1				5		
Hubbardston	417	17	Newton	Emial			1			1		2	1				5		
Hubbardston	417	18	Follit	Saml		2	1		4		1	1	1	1			11		
Hubbardston	417	19	Falis	John H.	1		2	1			1		1	1			7		
Hubbardston	417	20	Frost	Stephen		2	1	1		3			1				8		
Hubbardston	417	21	Goodspeed	Ann Wid	1								1	1			3		
Hubbardston	417	22	Gage	Abraham			1			1			1				3		
Hubbardston	417	23	Goodspeed	Isaac	1		1	1		2	1		1				7		
Hubbardston	417	24	Green	Joseph	1		2		1	3		2		1			10		
Hubbardston	417	25	Gage	Daniel	1		2		1	1	1	1	1				8		
Hubbardston	417	26	Grimes	Bill		2		1	1	1	1	1					7		
Hubbardston	417	27	Grimes	Joseph			1		1	1	2						5		
Hubbardston	417	28	Grimes	Ephraim	3			1	1				1				6		
Hubbardston	417	29	Gates	Jonathan		1	1					2		1			6		
Hubbardston	417	30	Gates	Henry	2		1		1	4		1		1			10		

TOWN	PG#	LN#	LAST NAME	FIRST NAME	FREE WHITE MALES					FREE WHITE FEMALES					TOTAL ALL OTHER	TOTAL SLAVES	TOTALS	DISTRICT/ TOWNSHIP	NOTES
					under 10	10 to 16	16 to 26	26 to 45	45 and over	under 10	10 to 16	16 to 26	26 to 45	45 and over					
Hubbardston	417	31	Gates	Benj	2			1		2			1				6		
Hubbardston	417	32	Greenwood	Abijah		1	2		1	1	2		1	1			9		
Hubbardston	417	33	Greenwood	Moses Mj	1	1	3		2	1			1	1			12		
Hubbardston	417	34	Greenwood	Levi				1		2	1	1		1			4		
Hubbardston	417	35	Goodspeed	Luther				1		2			1				4		
Hubbardston	417	36	Goodspeed	Elijah	3			1					1				5		
Hubbardston	417	37	Goodspeed	Heman	1			1	1	1			1				5		
Hubbardston	417	38	Gay	Abner	1			1				1					3		
Hubbardston	417	39	Gleazon	Barzeleel					1					1			2		
Hubbardston	417	40	Gleazon	Clark	1		1	1		1		1					5		
Hubbardston	417	41	Green	Robert			1	1		1		1					4		
Hubbardston	418	1	Heald	Ebenezer		1			1	1		1	1				5		
Hubbardston	418	2	Heald	Stephen Lt	2		1		1				1	1			6		
Hubbardston	418	3	Heald	Timy Capt	2	2		1	1	2	1		1	1			11		
Hubbardston	418	4	Heald	Luther	3	1		1		2	1		1				9		
Hubbardston	418	5	Holden	Nathan	3	1	1		1	1			1	1			9		
Hubbardston	418	6	How	Daniel Capt		1		1					1	1			4		
Hubbardston	418	7	Hunting	Stephen Jr				1		2			1				4		
Hubbardston	418	8	Hunting	Wm.		1	2		1		1			1			6		
Hubbardston	418	9	Hunting	Convas	2	3		1	1				1	1			10		
Hubbardston	418	10	Hunting	Alexander	1			1		2			1				5		
Hubbardston	418	11	Hapgood	Thomas Esq		1		1	1				1	1			5		
Hubbardston	418	12	Hinds	Howard	3	1	1		1	1	1	1	1				10		
Hubbardston	418	13	Hagar	David	2	2	2		2	1	1			2			12		
Hubbardston	418	14	Hinds	Abner				1	1				1	1			4		
Hubbardston	418	15	Hasey	Zanus					1					1			2		
Hubbardston	418	16	Hunting	Moses	3				1				1				5		
Hubbardston	418	17	Josling	Ebenezer		1	2		2			1	1	1			8		
Hubbardston	418	18	Josling	Silas	1			1					1				3		
Hubbardston	418	19	Josling	Wm.			1	1		1			1				3		
Hubbardston	418	20	Kendall	Jonathan	3			1	1			1	1	1			8		
Hubbardston	418	21	Kinsman	Daniel	1		4		1	1	1	2		1			11		
Hubbardston	418	22	Lyon	Asa	1			1			1	1					4		
Hubbardston	418	23	Lamb	James			2		1	1	1		1				7		
Hubbardston	418	24	Lyon	Mary Wid.						1			1				2		
Hubbardston	419	1	Upham	Nathl		2		1	1	1		1		1			7		
Hubbardston	419	2	Underwood	Timothy	2	1			1		1	1	1				7		
Hubbardston	419	3	Underwood	Israel		1		1		4			1				7		
Hubbardston	419	4	Upham	Calven	1			1		1			2				5		
Hubbardston	419	5	Wheeler	Adam Capt		1		1						1			3		
Hubbardston	419	6	Wheeler	Silas	1	3		1		1	1		1				8		
Hubbardston	419	7	Wheeler	Asa Lt.	4			1					1				6		
Hubbardston	419	8	Woods	John Capt.		1		1				2		1			5		
Hubbardston	419	9	Wright	Joseph		2	3		1	3			2				12		
Hubbardston	419	10	Wait	Joseph	1	1	1		1	3	2	2	1				12		
Hubbardston	419	11	Wait	Nathl			1		1	1		1	1	1			6		
Hubbardston	419	12	Wait	Jacob	1		1						1				3		
Hubbardston	419	13	Warren	Ebenz	4	2	1		1	1	1	1	1				12		
Hubbardston	419	14	Woodward	Elisha Esq		1			1	1		1		1			5		
Hubbardston	419	15	Newton	Ebenr		1	2			1		2	1	1			8		
Hubbardston	419	16	Newton	Timothy			3	1	1				1	1			7		
Hubbardston	419	17	Nichols	Jonathan	1	1			1				4	1			8		
Hubbardston	419	18	Partridge	Liberty			1			1							2		
Hubbardston	419	19	Persons	Kendall					1		1	1					3		
Hubbardston	419	20	Pierce	Moses H.	3			1		1			1				6		
Hubbardston	419	21	Pond	Levi	3	1		1		1	2		1				9		
Hubbardston	419	22	Parker	Nahl Rev		1		1		1				1			4		
Hubbardston	419	23	Pond	Ezra Ens				1						1			2		
Hubbardston	419	24	Pond	Joseph	2	1		1		1	1		1				7		
Hubbardston	419	25	Pollard	Joel	2		2		1	3	1	3	1				13		
Hubbardston	419	26	Phelps	Moses Dr.	1	3	1		1				1	1			8		
Hubbardston	419	27	Parker	Amos			3		1		1	1	1				7		
Hubbardston	419	28	Pierce	Thoms					1				1	1			3		
Hubbardston	419	29	Parkis	Daniel Maj		1	2	1				1	2	1			8		
Hubbardston	419	30	Peck	Ezra	1	1	1			1			2				6		
Hubbardston	420	1	Richardson	Job		1			1	1			1				4		
Hubbardston	420	2	Rice	Abigal Wid		1				1			1	2			5		
Hubbardston	420	3	Slocomb	Saml Capt		1	1	2	1				1	1			7		
Hubbardston	420	4	Slocomb	James	2	1	1	1		2	1		1				9		
Hubbardston	420	5	Smith	Warren	1	1	1		1		1			1			6		
Hubbardston	420	6	Selfredge	Edward		1		1				3		1	1		7		
Hubbardston	420	7	Shattock	Abraham		2				1		1					4		
Hubbardston	420	8	Springe	Saml	3	1		1		1	1		1				8		
Hubbardston	420	9	Seargeant	John	1	1	1	1		3	2	1	1	1			12		
Hubbardston	420	10	Seargeant	John Jr	1		1	1		1		1					5		
Hubbardston	420	11	Seargeant	Ebenezer	2	1		1		2			1				7		
Hubbardston	420	12	Stone	Nathan Lt		2	1		1		1			1			6		
Hubbardston	420	13	Stone	Eliphalet	1			1				2					4		
Hubbardston	420	14	Stone	Ebenezer	1		1		1			2		1			6		
Hubbardston	420	15	Sawyer	Luther	1			1		1			1				4		
Hubbardston	420	16	Slocumb	Peleg	1		1						1				3		
Hubbardston	420	17	Smith	Abel		1		1					1				3		
Hubbardston	420	18	Stone	Sary										1			1		
Hubbardston	420	19	Thompson	James	2	1	1		1			2	2	1			10		
Hubbardston	420	20	Thompson	Saml	2			1		2			1				6		
Hubbardston	420	21	Tenney	Abel	4	3	1		1		1	2					12		
Hubbardston	420	22	Tabour	Joseph	1			1				1					3		
Hubbardston	420	23	Tucker		1			1		1			1				4		First name blank

TOWN	PG#	LN#	LAST NAME	FIRST NAME	FREE WHITE MALES under 10	10 to 16	16 to 26	26 to 45	45 and over	FREE WHITE FEMALES under 10	10 to 16	16 to 26	26 to 45	45 and over	TOTAL ALL OTHER	TOTAL SLAVES	TOTALS	DISTRICT/ TOWNSHIP	NOTES
Lancaster	345	1	Arnold	Nathaniel			2	1		3			1				7		
Lancaster	345	2	Arnold	William		1			1	3	1	1		2			9		
Lancaster	345	3	Atherton	Israel			1	1	1		1	4	1	2	1		12		
Lancaster	345	4	Allen	Samuel	2	1		1	1	1	1		1	2			10		
Lancaster	345	5	Allen	Daniel	1	1			1	1	1	1	1				7		
Lancaster	345	6	Atherton	Peter					1	1	1	1	1				5		
Lancaster	345	7	Allen	Phillemon	1	1			1	1	1		1				6		
Lancaster	345	8	Butler	Simon	2		1	1	1	1	1	1	1				8		
Lancaster	345	9	Ballard	Thomas	1			1			1	2	2				7		
Lancaster	345	10	Bridge	William	2			1		3			1	1			8		
Lancaster	345	11	Ballard	Samuel	1			1		1	1		1				5		
Lancaster	345	12	Ballard	Jeremiah		2			1	1		2	1				7		
Lancaster	345	13	Bowers	Jonah				1			1		1				3		
Lancaster	345	14	Ballard	John	1	2		1		2		2	1				9		
Lancaster	345	15	Burbank	Nathaniel	4	1				1	2	1			2		11		
Lancaster	345	16	Bennett	Jonathan	1	1		1		1		2	1				7		
Lancaster	345	17	Beaman	Joseph				1			1	1	2				5		
Lancaster	345	18	Butler	Ebenezer	1	1		1		1					1		5		
Lancaster	345	19	Bennett	Elisha Junr			1					1					2		
Lancaster	347	1	Cleverly	John				1					1				2		
Lancaster	347	2	Cook	Finnis			1										1		
Lancaster	347	3	Colburn	Eijah	2			1		1		1					5		
Lancaster	347	4	Chambers	David	2			1		1			1				5		
Lancaster	347	5	Curtis	Timothy				1					2				3		
Lancaster	347	6	Chaplin	Joseph	1	1		1					1				4		
Lancaster	347	7	Dunlap	Samuel	2			1		1			1				5		
Lancaster	347	8	Deputson	William Jun			1			1		1	1				4		
Lancaster	347	9	Divol	Ephraim				1			2	1					5		
Lancaster	347	10	Dollison	John	2	1	1	1		3	1	1	1	1			12		
Lancaster	347	11	Danson	Samuel		1		1			2			1			5		
Lancaster	347	12	Divol	Menasseh		1	1	1			1		2	2			8		
Lancaster	347	13	Davis	Francis											4		4		
Lancaster	347	14	Deputson	William				1			1		1				3		
Lancaster	347	15	Dickerson	Moses			1	1					1				3		
Lancaster	347	16	Divol	Thomas	1			1		2	1		1				6		
Lancaster	347	17	Elder	James	1			1					1				3		
Lancaster	347	18	Eaton	Nathaniel		1		1		2			1				5		
Lancaster	347	19	Eager	Aaron				1					1				2		
Lancaster	347	20	Everton	Benjamin	3	1		1					1				6		
Lancaster	347	21	Fletcher	Rufus	2			1		1			1				7		
Lancaster	348	1	Barnard	Jonathan	1	1		1	1	2			1				7		
Lancaster	348	2	Bruce	Joel	2		1		1	1		2					7		
Lancaster	348	3	Baldwin	Oliver			1			1		1					3		
Lancaster	348	4	Bennitt	Thomas Jun	1		1	1		2		1	1	1			8		
Lancaster	348	5	Bennitt	Elisha Junr			1				1			1			3		
Lancaster	348	6	Bennitt	Nathan			1			1			1				3		
Lancaster	348	7	Butler	Israel		1		1						1			3		
Lancaster	348	8	Brooks	Thomas				1						1			2		
Lancaster	348	9	Chase	Charles	2	1		1		1			1				6		
Lancaster	348	10	Carter	Oliver	3	1		1				1	1	1			8		
Lancaster	348	11	Carter	James	1	1	7		1	1	1	2	2				16		
Lancaster	348	12	Carter	Joseph	1	1	3		1		3	2		1			12		
Lancaster	348	13	Carter	John		1	1		1	1				2			6		
Lancaster	348	14	Carter	Thomas	5	2			1	2			2				12		
Lancaster	348	15	Carter	Ephraim	1		3	1		1	1	2		2			11		
Lancaster	348	16	Cook	Aaron	1			1		2			2				6		
Lancaster	348	17	Clarke	James		1		1						1			3		
Lancaster	349	1	Goodwin	Edward	1	1		1		1		2		1			7		
Lancaster	349	2	Goodwin	James Junr	1		1	1		1			1				5		
Lancaster	349	3	Goss	Daniel		1		1		1	1		1				5		
Lancaster	349	4	Goss	John	2			1				1					4		
Lancaster	349	5	Goodwin	James				1				3	1				5		
Lancaster	349	6	Godfrey	Salmon	1		1	1		1		1	1				6		
Lancaster	349	7	Goss	Daniel Jun	1			1		1			1				4		
Lancaster	349	8	Goodwin	John	1		1	1				1					4		
Lancaster	349	9	Heard	Edmund	2			1		1			1				5		
Lancaster	349	10	Hudson	Robert	1				1	2		1		1			6		
Lancaster	349	11	Houghton	Abijah					1					2			3		
Lancaster	349	12	Harskell	Elias	1				1	1	2	1	1				7		
Lancaster	349	13	Hosley	David		1	2	1					1				6		
Lancaster	349	14	Haven	Ebenezer		1		1			1		1	2			6		
Lancaster	349	15	Hawks	John	1			1				3		1			6		
Lancaster	349	16	Hawks	John Jun	2			1		2		1					6		
Lancaster	349	17	Houghton	Benjmn	3	1		1		1		1	1	1			10		
Lancaster	349	18	Haven	Richard	3		1	1		1		2					8		
Lancaster	349	19	Harskell	Henry		1		1						1			3		
Lancaster	349	20	Hunt	John	1	2	2		1	4		1		1			12		
Lancaster	349	21	Houghton	Elijah Jun	2			1	1	1			1	1			7		
Lancaster	350	1	Fairbank	Cyrus Jun			1					1					2		

TOWN	PG#	LN#	LAST NAME	FIRST NAME	FWM under 10	FWM 10 to 16	FWM 16 to 26	FWM 26 to 45	FWM 45 and over	FWF under 10	FWF 10 to 16	FWF 16 to 26	FWF 26 to 45	FWF 45 and over	TOTAL ALL OTHER	TOTAL SLAVES	TOTALS	DISTRICT/ TOWNSHIP	NOTES
Lancaster	350	2	Farnsworth	Benjamin	1			1		1			1				4		
Lancaster	350	3	Fisher	Jacob	2	1	1	1		3		3					11		
Lancaster	350	4	Farwell	Joseph	1		1	1		1	1		1				6		
Lancaster	350	5	Flagg	Josiah	1	1	1	1		3	1		1				9		
Lancaster	350	6	Fletcher	Joshua			1	1		1				1			4		
Lancaster	350	7	Fales	Jeremiah		1	1		1	3	2		1				9		
Lancaster	350	8	Fairbank	Cyrus	2	1			1	2	1		1		1		9		
Lancaster	350	9	Fairbank	Jonas		1	2		1	1	1	1	1				8		
Lancaster	350	10	Flagg	Rebeca	5					1			3	1			10		
Lancaster	350	11	Fletcher	Timothy	2		1		1	1			1				6		
Lancaster	350	12	Farwell	Leonard	2	1	3	1	1	1	1		1				11		
Lancaster	350	13	Fuller	James				1			2		1				4		
Lancaster	350	14	Faulkner	Paul	2			1					1				4		
Lancaster	350	15	Flood	William	3				1	2			1				7		
Lancaster	350	16	Fuller	Edward			2	1					1				4		
Lancaster	350	17	Frye	Obediah	1			1		3			1				6		
Lancaster	350	18	Farwell	Amsa						1		1					2		
Lancaster	350	19	Goold	Benjamin	1	1			1	1	1	1		1			7		
Lancaster	350	20	Goold	William			2		1	1	2			1			7		
Lancaster	350	21	Gates	Thomas		1					1	1		1			5		
Lancaster	351	1	Low	Nathaniel Jun			1	1		2	1		1				6		
Lancaster	351	2	Leach	Joseph	1	1		1		2			1	1			7		
Lancaster	351	3	Laughton	Daniel	2	1	1		1	2	1			1			9		
Lancaster	351	4	Langley	Ezekiel	2	1		1		1	1		1				7		
Lancaster	351	5	Langley	William	2			1		1			1				5		
Lancaster	351	6	Lewis	Timothy Jun	1			1				1					3		
Lancaster	351	7	Maynard	John	1	1	1		1	3	2	1	1				11		
Lancaster	351	8	McIntosh	Archabald	1			1					1				3		
Lancaster	351	9	Moore	John				1					1				2		
Lancaster	351	10	Mitchel	Abner											5		5		
Lancaster	351	11	Newman	Gawen B.	2		1	1		1			2				7		
Lancaster	351	12	Newman	Joseph			1	1		1			1				3		
Lancaster	351	13	Nichols	Joseph	1			1				1		1			4		
Lancaster	351	14	Osgood	Ephraim	1			1		1	2		2	1			8		
Lancaster	351	15	Osgood	Joel	4		1		1	1	2	3		4			16		
Lancaster	351	16	Osgood	Joel Jun	3		1						1				5		
Lancaster	351	17	Phelps	Calvin	1			1		1			1				4		
Lancaster	351	18	Puffer	Nathan	1			1		2		1					5		
Lancaster	351	19	Phelps	Ruth									2				2		
Lancaster	351	20	Poor	Eunice									1				1		
Lancaster	352	1	Haskell	William	1		1	1	1	2	1	1	1				9		
Lancaster	352	2	Haskell	Louis						2	2		1	1			6		
Lancaster	352	3	Hammond	Casar											5		5		
Lancaster	352	4	Jones	Moses	2			1		3			1				7		
Lancaster	352	5	Jones	Aaron		1		1		1			1				4		
Lancaster	352	6	Joslyn	Jonas	3		1	1		1		1		1			9		
Lancaster	352	7	Jones	Samuel	2	1	2	1		2	1	1	1	1			12		
Lancaster	352	8	Johnson	Aaron	2		1	1	1			3		1			9		
Lancaster	352	9	Johnson	Daniel				1		1	1		1				4		
Lancaster	352	10	Joslyn	Samuel			2		1			1		2			6		
Lancaster	352	11	Johnson	Ruth									1				1		
Lancaster	352	12	Kies	Daniel	2			1	1	1	1		2	1			9		
Lancaster	352	13	Knights	Menasseh		1		1				2	1	1			6		
Lancaster	352	14	Larkin	William				1					1				2		
Lancaster	352	15	Lincoln	Jacob	2			1		2			1				6		
Lancaster	352	16	Littayce	Noel	1	1		1		1	1	1	1				7		
Lancaster	352	17	Lawson	James				1			2		1				4		
Lancaster	352	18	Lyon	Aaron			4		10	3	4	5	22				48		
Lancaster	352	19	Liswell	James		1		1				2	1				5		
Lancaster	352	20	Lincoln	Caleb			1	1					1				3		
Lancaster	352	21	Lee	Benjamin	1	1		1				1	3		1		8		
Lancaster	352	22	Lane	Jonas	2	2		1					1	1			7		
Lancaster	353	1	Rugg	Isaac	1	1			1	1		1	1	1			7		
Lancaster	353	2	Rugg	Abijah	3			1		1				1			6		
Lancaster	353	3	Rice	Joseph	1			1		1			1				4		
Lancaster	353	4	Rogers	Joseph				1			1		1	1			4		
Lancaster	353	5	Russell	Eleazer	1			1		1			1				4		
Lancaster	353	6	Rice	William	1		1						1				3		
Lancaster	353	7	Russell	Caleb	2			1		2			1				6		
Lancaster	353	8	Stone	Jemima	1					1			1				3		
Lancaster	353	9	Studley	Consider		2		1		2			1	1			7		
Lancaster	353	10	Sergeant	Seth		1			1	1			1				4		
Lancaster	353	11	Stearns	Eli	1	2	3	1		4			1	1			13		
Lancaster	353	12	Sergeant	Richard Junr	4			1					1				6		
Lancaster	353	13	Safford	Thomas	4	1	1	1		1		1	1	1			11		
Lancaster	353	14	Stone	Jacob	2			1	1				1	1			6		
Lancaster	353	15	Solenstine	Isaac				1						1			2		
Lancaster	353	16	Stedman	William	2	1		1		1		1	1				7		
Lancaster	353	17	Sweetser	Jacob						1	2	2		1			7		

TOWN	PG#	LN#	LAST NAME	FIRST NAME	FREE WHITE MALES					FREE WHITE FEMALES					TOTAL ALL OTHER	TOTAL SLAVES	TOTALS	DISTRICT/ TOWNSHIP	NOTES
					under 10	10 to 16	16 to 26	26 to 45	45 and over	under 10	10 to 16	16 to 26	26 to 45	45 and over					
Lancaster	353	18	Sawyer	Luther	1	1		2		2	1	1	1				9		
Lancaster	353	19	Smith	Moses		1	2	1					1	2			7		
Lancaster	353	20	Sergeant	Anson			1	1		1		1	1				5		
Lancaster	353	21	Sawyer	Amos	1			1					1				3		
Lancaster	354	1	Prentiss	John	3	1		1		2		2	1				10		
Lancaster	354	2	Phelps	Sylvester	2	1	1	1	1	1		2		1			10		
Lancaster	354	3	Phelps	Elisha	1	1		1	1	1			1	1			7		
Lancaster	354	4	Pollard	John			1	1				1		1			4		
Lancaster	354	5	Pollard	Abner	1			1		4		1	1				8		
Lancaster	354	6	Prescott	John					1			1	1				3		
Lancaster	354	7	Phelps	Abijah		1		1		1	1			2			6		
Lancaster	354	8	Phillips	Micah	2		1	1		2	1	1		1			9		
Lancaster	354	9	Pratt	James	1			1		3			1				6		
Lancaster	354	10	Phelps	Jacob			1			3	1		1				6		
Lancaster	354	11	Phelps	Anson				1				1	1				3		
Lancaster	354	12	Phelps	Gardner	1			1		2	1		1				6		
Lancaster	354	13	Phelps	Robert				1		1		1					3		
Lancaster	354	14	Rugg	Jonph	2			1		2			1				6		
Lancaster	354	15	Rugg	Daniel		2	1	1				2		1			7		
Lancaster	354	16	Robbins	Eleazer			1	1		2			1				5		
Lancaster	354	17	Robbins	John		1		1				1	1	1			5		
Lancaster	354	18	Rice	Merrick				1				1		1	1		4		
Lancaster	354	19	Rugg	Samuel				1		2			1				4		
Lancaster	354	20	Rugg	Abel	1		1	1		1			1	2			7		
Lancaster	354	21	Rugg	Elisha	2			2		1		1	1	1			8		
Lancaster	355	1	Thurston	Peter				1						2			3		
Lancaster	355	2	Turner	Joshua			1	1				1					3		
Lancaster	355	3	Thomas	Thompson			1			1			1				3		
Lancaster	355	4	Thurston	John	2	1	1	1		2	2		1				10		
Lancaster	355	5	Tower	Asahel	2	1		1		1	2		1				8		
Lancaster	355	6	Tinney	Jonathan		1		1		1			1	1			5		
Lancaster	355	7	Tinney	Oliver	1			1		2	1		1				6		
Lancaster	355	8	Wyman	Benjamin	1			1		3	2		1	1			9		
Lancaster	355	9	Whitney	Jonathan		1	1	1	1		1	3		1			9		
Lancaster	355	10	Whiting	Timothy	1	2	1	1		1	1	2		1			10		
Lancaster	355	11	Wilder	Stephen			2		1					1			4		
Lancaster	355	12	Wiles	Joseph				1			1	2	2	1			7		
Lancaster	355	13	Whiting	John	2	2		1		2	2	1	1	1			12		
Lancaster	355	14	Wilder	Jonathan	5	2		1			1	1	1				11		
Lancaster	355	15	Whitemore	Nathaniel		2		1	1			2		1			7		
Lancaster	355	16	Whitney	Paul	1	1		1		3			1				7		
Lancaster	355	17	White	John				1					1				2		
Lancaster	355	18	Wilder	Samuel 2d	2	1	1	1		2		1	1				9		
Lancaster	355	19	Willard	Paul	3			1		1		1					6		
Lancaster	355	20	Willard	James	1		2	1		1		1	1	1			8		
Lancaster	355	21	Willard	Benjamin W.		1	1	1		1				2			6		
Lancaster	356	1	Sawyer	Israel	1		1	1		1			2	2			8		
Lancaster	356	2	Stearns	Daniel				1		2			1				4		
Lancaster	356	3	Sawyer	Moses		1	2	1		2	1		1				8		
Lancaster	356	4	Sawyer	Moses Jun	2			1		1			1				5		
Lancaster	356	5	Sergeant	Richard			1	1		2	1	1	1				7		
Lancaster	356	6	Sanderson	Samuel				1		2			1				4		
Lancaster	356	7	Sawyer	Polly (or Calvin)	2					1	1		1				5		
Lancaster	356	8	Sawyer	Elias				1		1	1	1		1			5		
Lancaster	356	9	Sprague	John		1	3	1		1	3		1				10		
Lancaster	356	10	Solendice	John		1		1						3			5		
Lancaster	356	11	Sawyer	Amos 2d	1			1		1			1				4		
Lancaster	356	12	Stevens	Samuel	1			1		1	1		1				5		
Lancaster	356	13	Sanderson	Elisha	2	2		1		1	1		1				8		
Lancaster	356	14	Sergeant	Ebenezer	1		1			1			1				4		
Lancaster	356	15	Townsand	Robert	1		1	1		2		1	1		1		8		
Lancaster	356	16	Torrey	Ebenezer		1	1		1	1			2	1			7		
Lancaster	356	17	Thurston	Peter Junr			1	1		2	1	1					6		
Lancaster	356	18	Thurston	Gates	4			1		1	1		1				8		
Lancaster	356	19	Thurston	Samuel					1		1	1	1	1			5		
Lancaster	356	20	Thurston	Silas	2	1		1		3		1	1				9		
Lancaster	356	21	Thayer	Nathaniel			2	1		3	1	1	1				9		
Lancaster	356	22	Thomas	Joshua				1			1	1		1			4		
Lancaster	357	1	Willard	William	3			1			1		1				6		
Lancaster	357	2	Willard	John	1	2		1	1	1	1	1		1			9		
Lancaster	357	3	Willard	Kenneth (or Silas)	2								1				3		
Lancaster	357	4	White	Nathaniel	2			1		1			1	1			6		
Lancaster	357	5	Whitcomb	Leonard	1			1					1	1			4		
Lancaster	357	6	Warner	Ebenezer	3	1		1				2	1				8		
Lancaster	357	7	Zware	Jacob				1					1	1			3		
Lancaster	357	8	Zware	Reuben	1		1						1				3		
Lancaster	358	9	Willard	Simon		1		1	1			1		1			5		
Lancaster	358	10	White	Joseph	3	1			1		2		1	1			9		
Lancaster	358	11	Whitcomb	Chapman	1			1		1			1				4		

TOWN	PG#	LN#	LAST NAME	FIRST NAME	FREE WHITE MALES					FREE WHITE FEMALES					TOTAL ALL OTHER	TOTAL SLAVES	TOTALS	DISTRICT/ TOWNSHIP	NOTES
					under 10	10 to 16	16 to 26	26 to 45	45 and over	under 10	10 to 16	16 to 26	26 to 45	45 and over					
Lancaster	358	12	Warner	Asa	1	1	1		1		1	1	1				7		
Lancaster	358	13	Wilder	Gardner					1	1				1			3		
Lancaster	358	14	Ward	Samuel	1	1	2	1	1		1	2	2	1			12		
Lancaster	358	15	Wilder	Samuel	1				1					1			3		
Lancaster	358	16	Wilder	Calvin				1					1				2		
Lancaster	358	17	Wilder	William			1		1		1		1				4		
Lancaster	358	18	Wilder	John	2				1	1	1	1		1			7		
Lancaster	358	19	Wilder	Moses		1	1		1	1		2					6		
Lancaster	358	20	Wilder	Menasseh		1			1		1	1		1			5		
Lancaster	358	21	Wilder	Titus	1	1	1		1	1		2		1			8		
Lancaster	358	22	Worcester	Samuel	1				1	2			1				5		
Lancaster	358	23	White	Abijah	1		1	1					1				4		
Lancaster	358	24	Wheelock	Benjamin	2	1		3		2	1	1	1				11		
Lancaster	358	25	Willard	Solomon	3			1					1				5		
Lancaster	358	26	Wilder	John 3d	2			1				1					4		
Lancaster	358	27	White	John Jun	1			1		2			1				5		
Lancaster	358	28	Willard	Ezra		1		1		1	1		1				5		

68

TOWN	PG#	LN#	LAST NAME	FIRST NAME	FREE WHITE MALES					FREE WHITE FEMALES					TOTAL ALL OTHER	TOTAL SLAVES	TOTALS	DISTRICT/ TOWNSHIP	NOTES
					under 10	10 to 16	16 to 26	26 to 45	45 and over	under 10	10 to 16	16 to 26	26 to 45	45 and over					
Leicester	485	1	Arnold	*has			1	1		2		1	1				6		First name obscured by tape mark
Leicester	485	2	Arnold	Oliver			1					1					2		
Leicester	485	3	Arnold	Ahab		3		1		1			1				6		
Leicester	485	4	Adams	Ebenezer	1	4	4	1		2	2	3	1				18		
Leicester	485	5	Adams	John				1					1	1			3		
Leicester	485	6	Brooks	Thomas				1					1				2		
Leicester	485	7	Bond	Benja			1		1			2		1			5		
Leicester	485	8	Bryant	Jona	2		1		1		1			1			6		
Leicester	485	9	Bryant	David			1		1			1		1	1		5		
Leicester	485	10	Bond	Richard		1	1		1			1	2	1			7		
Leicester	485	11	Brooks	Thomas				1					1				2		
Leicester	485	12	Bond	Benja			1		1			2		1			5		
Leicester	485	13	Bryant	Jona	2	1		1		1			1				6		
Leicester	485	14	Bryant	David			1		1		1		1	1			5		
Leicester	485	15	Bond	Richard		1	1		1			1	2	1			7		
Leicester	485	16	Bond	Richard Jun			2			1		1	1	1			6		
Leicester	485	17	Bond	Jona		2	1			1	1	1		1			7		
Leicester	485	18	Bond	Thomas	2	1		1		2			1				7		
Leicester	485	19	Baldwin	James				1		1			1				3		
Leicester	485	20	Baldwin	Ebenz				1					1				2		
Leicester	487	1	Convers	Reuben	2			1		2			1				6		
Leicester	487	2	Craige	Amos		1		1		1			1				4		
Leicester	487	3	Craige	Robert	1			1					1				3		
Leicester	487	4	Denny	Joseph	1			1				1					3		
Leicester	487	5	Denny	Thomas 2d			1			1			1				3		
Leicester	487	6	Denny	Samuel		1		1						2			4		
Leicester	487	7	Denny	Thomas	1		3	1	1	3		3	1	1			14		
Leicester	487	8	Dunbar	Abnor	1		1	1	1	1			1	1			7		
Leicester	487	9	Dunbar	Lucretia	1						1	1	1				4		
Leicester	487	10	Earle	Antipas			2	1	1	1		1		2			8		
Leicester	487	11	Earle	John			1			1		1					3		
Leicester	487	12	Earle	Jonah	3		1	1		1		2		1	1		10		
Leicester	487	13	Earle	Robert			2		1			1		1			5		
Leicester	487	14	Earle	Pliny	2	1	1	1		2		1	1				9		
Leicester	487	15	Earle	James	4	1	1		1		1		1				9		
Leicester	488	1	Baldwin	Benja			1	1				2	1	1			6		
Leicester	488	2	Baldwin	David		1		1				1		1			4		
Leicester	488	3	Baldwin	Stephen			2	1				2	2	1			8		
Leicester	488	4	Baldwin	Steph Jun				1									1		
Leicester	488	5	Barton	Caleb	2			1		2	1		1				7		
Leicester	488	6	Barton	Joshua	1	1		1		1			1	1			6		
Leicester	488	7	Beers	Nathan		1	1			1	1		1				5		
Leicester	488	8	Barton	Phinehas	2			1		2		2		1			8		
Leicester	488	9	Burr	Luther	2	2		1			1		1				7		
Leicester	488	10	Bates	Robert	1			1				1					3		
Leicester	488	11	Baldwin	Benja Jun				1					1				2		
Leicester	488	12	Comstock	George			1		1			1		1			4		
Leicester	488	13	Convers	Joshua		1		1					1	2			5		
Leicester	488	14	Cutting	Darius	2	2	5			2	2		1				15		
Leicester	488	15	Copeland	Ephraim	2			1		1			1				5		
Leicester	489	1	Green	Isaac	2	1	1		1	1		1	1	1			9		
Leicester	489	2	Greaton	John Jun	1		2		1		1	3		1			9		
Leicester	489	3	Green	Jabez Jun	4		1		1		2			1			9		
Leicester	489	4	Green	Samuel	1		1		1			1	1	1			6		
Leicester	489	5	Green	Samuel Jun		2	1	1		1		1	1	1			8		
Leicester	489	6	Greaton	John				1						1			2		
Leicester	489	7	Hemsey	Calvin	2	1		1	1	2	1	1					9		
Leicester	489	8	Henshaw	William		1	3		1	1	1	1		1			9		
Leicester	489	9	Holden	John	2			1		3			1				7		
Leicester	489	10	Howard	John	2	1	1	1				1	1	1			8		
Leicester	489	11	Hubbard	Daniel				1		1				1			3		
Leicester	489	12	Hubbard	Daniel Jun	1		1		1	3	2	2	1				11		
Leicester	489	13	Hobart	John	2	1		2		1	1	1	1				9		
Leicester	489	14	Harwood	James			2						2	1			6		
Leicester	489	15	Haven	Elkanah	2	1		1		1	1		1				7		
Leicester	489	16	Haven	Hannah								1	1				2		
Leicester	490	1	Earle	Asahel	1			1		2		1	1				6		
Leicester	490	2	Earle	Silas	1		2	1		2		3					9		
Leicester	490	3	Earle	Henry			1					1	1				3		
Leicester	490	4	Earle	William				1				1		1			3		
Leicester	490	5	Earle	Winthrop		2	2			1		1	1				7		
Leicester	490	6	Earle	Thomas				1				1	1				3		
Leicester	490	7	Elliot	Joseph		1	2		1			1	2		1		8		
Leicester	490	8	Eddy	Azariah	1				1				1	1			4		
Leicester	490	9	Eddy	John	3			1						1			5		
Leicester	490	10	Flint	Austin	2	5	3	2		2	1		1				16		
Leicester	490	11	Green	Jabez Jun				1						1			2		
Leicester	490	12	Green	Abel		1		1		2	1		1				6		
Leicester	490	13	Gage	Jonathan	2	1			1				1				6		
Leicester	490	14	Gilmore	Adam			1		1					1			3		

TOWN	PG#	LN#	LAST NAME	FIRST NAME	FREE WHITE MALES under 10	10 to 16	16 to 26	26 to 45	45 and over	FREE WHITE FEMALES under 10	10 to 16	16 to 26	26 to 45	45 and over	TOTAL ALL OTHER	TOTAL SLAVES	TOTALS	DISTRICT/ TOWNSHIP	NOTES
Leicester	491	1	Livermore	Isaac		1			1					1			3		
Leicester	491	2	Livermore	Jonas				1					1	1			3		
Leicester	491	3	Livermore	Salem			1	1		2			1				5		
Leicester	491	4	Mathews	Asahel		1	1						1	1			4		
Leicester	491	5	Morse	Joseph	2	1		1		1	1	1	1				8		
Leicester	491	6	Morse	Hannah		1						1		1			3		
Leicester	491	7	Moover	Samuel	1	1		1						1			4		
Leicester	491	8	Moore	Zephl L.		2	4	1				2	1		1		11		
Leicester	491	9	Newhall	Phinehas		1	1		1		2			1			6		
Leicester	491	10	Newhall	Thomas				1					1				2		
Leicester	491	11	Newhall	Thomas 2d			2			1		1					4		
Leicester	491	12	Newhall	Mary	1					2			1				4		
Leicester	491	13	Phipps	Moses	3	1		1		1	1		1				8		
Leicester	491	14	Paine	Jabez				1				1	1				3		
Leicester	492	1	Henshaw	David	2	1	2		1	1		1	2	1			11		
Leicester	492	2	Hearkness	James	1		3	1				2		1			8		
Leicester	492	3	Hood	Daniel			1	1					1				3		
Leicester	492	4	Hill	John			1						1				2		
Leicester	492	5	Huntington	Asahel			1			1		1					3		
Leicester	492	6	Jackson	Marthew		1	3	1		2		1					8		
Leicester	492	7	Kent	Ebenezer		1		1		1	1		1				5		
Leicester	492	8	Knight	Jonathan			1	1		1			1				3		
Leicester	492	9	Knight	Jona Jun	1			1				1					3		
Leicester	492	10	Knapp	Joseph			2		1	2	1		1				7		
Leicester	492	11	King	Henry		1	1	1		1			1				5		
Leicester	492	12	Lynde	Thomas	2		2	1		1	2		1				9		
Leicester	492	13	Livermore	Micah		1		1				1	1				4		
Leicester	492	14	Lyscum	John	2		1			1	1	1	1				7		
Leicester	493	1	Sprague	William	2		1	1		1	3		1	1			10		
Leicester	493	2	Snow	Abner	3		1	1		1	1		1				8		
Leicester	493	3	Snow	Thomas				1						1			2		
Leicester	493	4	Snow	Nathan				1						1			2		
Leicester	493	5	Snow	James	2			1		1	1	1					6		
Leicester	493	6	Stickney	John			2	2					1	1			6		
Leicester	493	7	Stetson	Laban		1		1				3					5		
Leicester	493	8	Sprague	Knight			2	1		1			1	1			6		
Leicester	493	9	Southgate	Susannah						1		1					2		
Leicester	493	10	Searle	Ambrose				1				1	1				3		
Leicester	493	11	Sargeant	John	2		1	1		2	2		1	1			10		
Leicester	493	12	Sargeant	Joseph				1					2				3		
Leicester	493	13	Sargeant	Stephen	1	1		1					1				4		
Leicester	493	14	Studly	Benj		1	1	1		1	1	1	1				7		
Leicester	493	15	Studly	Zenas			1						1				2		
Leicester	493	16	Southgate	John	1		1		1	1		1	1				6		
Leicester	493	17	Southgate	Isaac				1				1		1			3		
Leicester	494	1	Paine	William		1		1		1	1	1					5		
Leicester	494	2	Parker	William	1		1	1		3			1				7		
Leicester	494	3	Parker	Thomas					2			1		1			4		
Leicester	494	4	Parker	John			1			1			1				3		
Leicester	494	5	Parker	David				1		2			1				4		
Leicester	494	6	Parsons	Solomon	2		1	1			3		1				8		
Leicester	494	7	Rawson	Edward			1		1				1	1			4		
Leicester	494	8	Robinson	Luther		1		1		1				1			4		
Leicester	494	9	Richardson	Samuel	1		1	1		1		3	1				8		
Leicester	494	10	Reed	Simon	1		1			1			1				4		
Leicester	494	11	Richardson	William			1			1			1				3		
Leicester	494	12	Steel	Mary						1			1	1			3		
Leicester	494	13	Sylvester	Joshua	1			1		1	1		1				5		
Leicester	494	14	Sylvester	John			2						1				3		
Leicester	494	15	Sylvester	Peter Jun	1	1		1		1	1	1					8		
Leicester	494	16	Sprague	Timothy		1	1		1		2	1	1		1		8		
Leicester	495	1	Upham	Ebenz Jun	2		1	1		1			1	1			7		
Leicester	495	2	Upham	Samuel	3		1	1					1	1			7		
Leicester	495	3	Very	Isaac	3			1		1	1	1	1				8		
Leicester	495	4	Wickery	Benja				1				1		1			3		
Leicester	495	5	Waite	Samuel	4		1		1			1	1				8		
Leicester	495	6	Ward	Luther	2			1		2	2		1				8		
Leicester	495	7	Washburn	Joseph	4	3		1		2			1	2			13		
Leicester	495	8	Whittemore	James		1	1		1			2	1	1			7		
Leicester	495	9	Watson	Samuel	1		2		1	1		2	4		1		12		
Leicester	495	10	Waters	Thomas	2			1		1	1		1				6		
Leicester	495	11	Washburn	Jacob				1						1			2		
Leicester	495	12	Washburn	Francis	1	1		1					1				4		
Leicester	495	13	Wheaton	Abigail	1		1	1		1			2	1			7		
Leicester	495	14	White	Stephen		2		1					1				4		
Leicester	495	15	Warren	Jonathan	1		2	1		1	1		1				7		
Leicester	495	16	Warren	Elijah		2	1	1		1	3						8		
Leicester	496	1	Swan	Reuben B			1					1	1				3		
Leicester	496	2	Sargeant	Mary	1							1	1				3		

TOWN	PG#	LN#	LAST NAME	FIRST NAME	FREE WHITE MALES					FREE WHITE FEMALES					TOTAL ALL OTHER	TOTAL SLAVES	TOTALS	DISTRICT/ TOWNSHIP	NOTES
					under 10	10 to 16	16 to 26	26 to 45	45 and over	under 10	10 to 16	16 to 26	26 to 45	45 and over					
Leicester	496	3	Sargeant	Samuel	4	1		1	1	3	1		1				12		
Leicester	496	4	Scott	Andrew		2	1	1				1	1	1			7		
Leicester	496	5	Swan	Reuben				1	1		1	1		1	1		6		
Leicester	496	6	Stone	Jonas	2	3	11	1		1	4	6	1				29		
Leicester	496	7	Trask	David			1	1		1	1	2					6		
Leicester	496	8	Tucker	Joseph		2	4	1		1	1	1	1				11		
Leicester	496	9	Trask	Samuel	1	2	2		1	1	1		1				9		
Leicester	496	10	Town	Elisha		1		1		3			1				6		
Leicester	496	11	Taintor	Nahum		1		1		2	2	1	1				8		
Leicester	496	12	Trask	Saml Junr	1			1					1				3		
Leicester	496	13	Trumbull	Peter	1	1	1	1		3			1				8		
Leicester	496	14	Thompson	Abner	3	2		1		2			1				9		
Leicester	496	15	Thompson	Edward				1		2				1			4		
Leicester	496	16	Upham	Thaddeus	2		5	1		1				1			10		
Leicester	496	17	Upham	Ebenz				1						1			2		
Leicester	497	1	Woodward	Benja				1						1			2		
Leicester	497	2	Willson	John				1						1			2		
Leicester	498	1	Wilder	Joseph			2					1					3		
Leicester	498	2	Waite	Asa			1			1		1					3		
Leicester	498	3	Waite	Phinehas				1			1	1					3		
Leicester	498	4	Waite	Nathan			3	1	1			2		1	1		9		
Leicester	498	5	Watson	William	1		1		1		1	2	1		2		9		
Leicester	498	6	Whittemore	Asa Jun			1					1					2		
Leicester	498	7	Worcester	John			1		1	1		1					4		
Leicester	498	8	Woodward	Caleb			1		1				1				3		
Leicester	498	9	Woodward	John				1					1				2		
Leicester	498	10	Washburn	Asahel		1		1		2			1				5		
Leicester	498	11	Watson	Matthew			2	1				3	1	1			8		
Leicester	498	12	Watson	Benjamin		1	1		1	2	1	1		1			8		
Leicester	498	13	Whittemore	Asa	2	2			1	2	1	2		1			11		
Leicester	498	14	Woodbury	Aaron	3	1		1					1				6		
Leicester	498	15	Willington	Josiah				1					1				2		

TOWN	PG#	LN#	LAST NAME	FIRST NAME	FREE WHITE MALES					FREE WHITE FEMALES					TOTAL ALL OTHER	TOTAL SLAVES	TOTALS	DISTRICT/ TOWNSHIP	NOTES
					under 10	10 to 16	16 to 26	26 to 45	45 and over	under 10	10 to 16	16 to 26	26 to 45	45 and over					
Leominster	431	1	Allen	Silas	1			1		2			1				5		
Leominster	431	2	Belcher	Elizabeth	1	1				1	1			1			5		
Leominster	431	3	Bagwell	James	1		1						1				3		
Leominster	431	4	Bowers	Mary							1	2	2	1			6		
Leominster	431	5	Bowers	Samuel	2	1	2		1	1	1	1	1				10		
Leominster	431	6	Bontell	James			1		1	2	2		1				7		
Leominster	431	7	Bontell	Timothy			4		1			1		2			8		
Leominster	431	8	Bontell	John	2		1	1		1	1		2	1			9		
Leominster	431	9	Burdit	John	2	1	1		1			2		1			8		
Leominster	431	10	Brigham	Joel	2	2			1	3	2	1					11		
Leominster	431	11	Bass	John	1		1	1		3	2		1				9		
Leominster	431	12	Bennet	Jacob	1		1		2	2		2	1	1			10		
Leominster	431	13	Burridge	Wm				1		1	1	2	1	1			7		
Leominster	431	14	Burridge	Josiah			1					1					2		
Leominster	431	15	Butter	Abijah	1		2		1	2		2	1	2			11		
Leominster	431	16	Beaman	John	1			1						1			3		
Leominster	431	17	Burridge	Wm Jun	1		2	1		2			1				7		
Leominster	431	18	Butter	Phino				1						1			2		
Leominster	431	19	Badcock	Malicai	1			1		1		1	1				5		
Leominster	431	20	Burt	Daniel	2	1		1				1	1				6		
Leominster	431	21	Battle	David				1		2			1	1			5		
Leominster	431	22	Bennet	John				1									1		
Leominster	433	1	Chase	Stephen		1		1						1			3		
Leominster	433	2	Carter	Jacob	2			1				1	1				5		
Leominster	433	3	Chase	Metaphor	2	1	2	1		2	1	2	1				12		
Leominster	433	4	Carter	Warren	1		1			1		1					4		
Leominster	433	5	Colburn	Nathaniel	1			1		1		1		1			5		
Leominster	433	6	Crooker	Samuel		1						1					2		
Leominster	433	7	Carter	Ephm Jun	2			1		1			1	1			6		
Leominster	433	8	Carter	Nathl Jun		1		1			1			1			4		
Leominster	433	9	Carter	Nathl Jun			1			2			1				4		
Leominster	433	10	Darby	Simon		1		1				1	1				4		
Leominster	433	11	Darby	Joseph				1				2		1			4		
Leominster	433	12	Darby	Nathan	4			1					1				6		
Leominster	433	13	Darby	Deliverance				1				1		1			3		
Leominster	433	14	Davis	Elisha				1			1			1			3		
Leominster	433	15	Divoll	John Jun		1		1		1		1					4		
Leominster	433	16	Daniel	Elias	1		1					1					3		
Leominster	433	17	Divoll	John				1				1		1			3		
Leominster	433	18	Divoll	Oliver	1	1		1		3	1		1				8		
Leominster	433	19	Divoll	Luke	3			1		2		1					7		
Leominster	433	20	Darby	Joshua	1		1					1					3		
Leominster	433	21	Wood	Joshua				1				1		1			3		
Leominster	433	22	Wood	Caleb		1		1					1				3		
Leominster	433	23	Walker	Samuel	1			1		1				1			4		
Leominster	433	24	Warren	William				1						1			2		
Leominster	433	25	Wood	Michal				1				1		1			3		
Leominster	433	26	Wilder	Jemima		1						1		1			3		
Leominster	433	27	Woods	James			1				1						2		
Leominster	433	28	Walker	John	1			1		1	1		1				5		
Leominster	433	29	Wilder	James	4	1	1	1		1	2		1	1			12		
Leominster	433	30	Warren	Oliver	2		2	2		3		2					11		
Leominster	433	31	Whitcomb	Nathan				1		1		1					3		
Leominster	433	32	Woods	John Jun	2			1				1					4		
Leominster	433	33	Allen	Phinehas	3	1		1		2		1	1				9		
Leominster	433	34	Andrews	Daniel	4	2	1		1		1		1				10		
Leominster	433	35	Brown	Oliver	2	2	1		1	1	1	1	1				10		
Leominster	433	36	Brown	Pearson	3	2		1	1	1			1	1			10		
Leominster	433	37	Bontell	Kendall		1		1				2	1	1			7		
Leominster	433	38	Bontell	Asaph	1			1		2			1				5		
Leominster	433	39	Burbank	Samuel	4	1		1				1	1	1			9		
Leominster	433	40	Boynton	Jonathan	1	1	1		1	1	1	1					7		
Leominster	434	1	Bigelow	Nathal	3	2		1	1	1							9		
Leominster	434	2	Colburn	Pliny	3			1					1				5		
Leominster	434	3	Colburn	Ebenz	3		1			1	1		1				7		
Leominster	434	4	Carter	Asa		1		1						1			3		
Leominster	434	5	Carter	John		1	1		1	2		2		1			8		
Leominster	434	6	Carter	Josiah	1		1	1	1	2			2	1			9		
Leominster	434	7	Carter	Ephm	1		4		1			3		2			11		
Leominster	434	8	Carter	Josiah Jun	5		1		1	1	1		1				10		
Leominster	434	9	Chase	John	3		2	2		1	3	1	1				13		
Leominster	434	10	Carter	Silas		1		1						1			3		
Leominster	434	11	Carter	Jonathan		1		1	1	1	1	1	1				7		
Leominster	434	12	Colburn	Jona			1		1			2		1			5		
Leominster	434	13	Colburn	Nathan	2		1	1		1		2	3	1			11		
Leominster	434	14	Capen	James	2	1		1		1	1		1				7		
Leominster	434	15	Colburn	Elisha	2			1					1				4		
Leominster	434	16	Colburn	John	1	1	1		1	1		2		1			8		
Leominster	434	17	Carter	Phinehas			1					2	1	1			6		

72

TOWN	PG#	LN#	HEADS OF HOUSEHOLD		FREE WHITE MALES					FREE WHITE FEMALES					TOTAL ALL OTHER	TOTAL SLAVES	TOTALS	DISTRICT/ TOWNSHIP	NOTES
			LAST NAME	FIRST NAME	under 10	10 to 16	16 to 26	26 to 45	45 and over	under 10	10 to 16	16 to 26	26 to 45	45 and over					
Leominster	434	18	Carter	Silas Jun			1					1					2		
Leominster	435	1	Henderson	John				1						2			3		
Leominster	435	2	Hyde	Joseph				1					1				2		
Leominster	435	3	Houghton	Ebenezer	1			1		3	1		2	2			10		
Leominster	435	4	Hale	Samuel Jun	2	2		2		2	1		1				10		
Leominster	435	5	Hawks	Benjm			4	1		4	1		2		2		14		
Leominster	435	6	Haws	Benjm	2		1	1				1	1				6		
Leominster	435	7	Hall	Jacob	2		1	1			1		1				6		
Leominster	435	8	Hills	John	2		3	1		1			1				8		
Leominster	435	9	Hayns	Samuel	3	2		1					1				7		
Leominster	435	10	Hale	Calvin	1	1	3	1		3	1	1	1	1			13		
Leominster	435	11	Hale	Thomas	2		2	1		2	2	1	1	1			12		
Leominster	435	12	Haven	John	1		1					1					3		
Leominster	435	13	Hale	Ezra	2		1		1					2			6		
Leominster	435	14	Houghton	Abiathar			1				1		1				4		
Leominster	435	15	Hills	Sarah									1				1		
Leominster	435	16	Hills	Smith	1		2	1		1			1	1			7		
Leominster	435	17	Holbrook	Elijah		1		1		3			1				6		
Leominster	435	18	Jones	Samuel	1	1		1			2	1	1				7		
Leominster	435	19	Johnson	Stephen					1				1				2		
Leominster	435	20	Johnson	Stephen Jun	2	1		1					1				5		
Leominster	435	21	Stewart	Richard	1	2	1	1	1	1		2	2	1			12		
Leominster	435	22	Stewart	John		4			2			1	1				8		
Leominster	435	23	Stewart	Alpheus	3			1		1		1					6		
Leominster	435	24	Smith	Samuel	1		1	1		1	2		1				7		
Leominster	435	25	Smith	Lydia									1				1		
Leominster	435	26	Smith	Mary			1				1		1				3		
Leominster	435	27	Stearns	Samuel Jun	2			1		2			1				6		
Leominster	435	28	Stearns	Thomas	1	1	1		1	2			1				8		
Leominster	435	29	Stearns	Josiah	1		1	1		2			1				6		
Leominster	435	30	Stearns	Samuel				1		1		1		1			4		
Leominster	435	31	Snow	Moses	2		1			3				1			7		
Leominster	435	32	Simonds	Mehitable	1					1			1				3		
Leominster	435	33	Turner	Nathl		1		1			1			1			4		
Leominster	435	34	Tylor	Phinehas	1				1		1	2		1			6		
Leominster	435	35	Tylor	Phinehas Jun	3	1		1		1			1				7		
Leominster	435	36	Tylor	Joshua		1			1	3	2	1	1				9		
Leominster	435	37	Tylor	Simeon	2			1		1			1				5		
Leominster	435	38	Tainter	Ayers	1			1	1			1					4		
Leominster	435	39	Tylor	Parker	2	1	1		1	3	2		1				11		
Leominster	436	1	Tenny	Joseph	1	2	1		1	1	1	1		1			9		
Leominster	436	2	Tulip	Peter											6		6		
Leominster	436	3	Taylor	John	1			1		1			1				4		
Leominster	436	4	Tainter	Catherine			5	3		1	1		1				11		
Leominster	436	5	Thurston	Mehitable										1			1		
Leominster	436	6	Thompson	Benja	1			1		3			1				6		
Leominster	436	7	Warner	Levi	1		2		1		2			1			7		
Leominster	436	8	Waters	Samel	2	1	2	1		2	1		1				10		
Leominster	436	9	Warner	Phinehas				1					1				2		
Leominster	436	10	Wilder	Sarah									3				3		
Leominster	436	11	Woods	Asa	2	2		1		3			1				9		
Leominster	436	12	Wilder	Edward	3	2		1		1			2				9		
Leominster	436	13	Woods	John			1	1				2		1			5		
Leominster	436	14	Woods	Samuel	3			1		2	2		1				9		
Leominster	436	15	Wood	John	1	2	2		1			1		1			8		
Leominster	436	16	Wilder	David Jun	1		2					1					4		
Leominster	436	17	Wilder	Elisha	1		1	1		1				2			6		
Leominster	436	18	Wilder	Joseph		1	2	1	1	1	1	1		1			9		
Leominster	436	19	Wilder	Thomas	1	1	1	1	1	2		1	1	1			10		
Leominster	436	20	Wilder	David	1		1				1	2		1			7		
Leominster	436	21	Darby	Joseph Jun	1			1		3			1				5		
Leominster	436	22	Davis	Oliver	1	1	1		1		1			1			6		
Leominster	436	23	Darby	Benjamin		1	3		1	2	1	1		1			10		
Leominster	436	24	Evans	Samuel		1		1	1		1		2	1			7		
Leominster	436	25	Folliensbee	Francis	1	1	1		1	1	1	1	1				8		
Leominster	436	26	Fuller	Edward	3	2		1		1	1		1				9		
Leominster	436	27	Folinsbee	Edward	3			1		2			1	1			8		
Leominster	436	28	Fairbank	Elijah		1			1	1	1	1	1	1			7		
Leominster	436	29	Fairbank	Elizabeth	1					2			1				4		
Leominster	436	30	Fisk	Jonas			1			1		1	1	1			5		
Leominster	436	31	Fullam	Jacob	1	1	1		1			2	3	1			10		
Leominster	436	32	Fletcher	Rebeckah									2				2		
Leominster	436	33	Farnsworth	Elias	2	1	2		1	2	2		1				11		
Leominster	436	34	Gary	Thomas	2		1		1	2		2	1	1			10		
Leominster	436	35	Glover	John	1	3			1			2	1				8		
Leominster	436	36	Gary	David	1			1		1	1		2				6		
Leominster	436	37	Gardner	John	1			1		4			1		1		8		
Leominster	436	38	Gardner	Francis	1	1			1	1		1	6	2	1		14		
Leominster	436	39	Gates	Reuben	2		2		1	2		2		1			10		

73

TOWN	PG#	LN#	LAST NAME	FIRST NAME	M under 10	M 10 to 16	M 16 to 26	M 26 to 45	M 45 and over	F under 10	F 10 to 16	F 16 to 26	F 26 to 45	F 45 and over	TOTAL ALL OTHER	TOTAL SLAVES	TOTALS	DISTRICT/ TOWNSHIP	NOTES
Leominster	436	40	Gates	Jonas	3	1		2					3				9		
Leominster	436	41	Hills	Silas	3	1	1	2		2	2		1				12		
Leominster	437	1	Lincoln	Jesse	2			1		2	1		1				7		
Leominster	437	2	Lealand	Caleb		1			1		1	1		1			5		
Leominster	437	3	Lawrence	Bazalel		1	2	1		3		3	1	1			12		
Leominster	437	4	Lincoln	Ephraim			2	1		3	1		1				8		
Leominster	437	5	Lincoln	William					1			3		1			5		
Leominster	437	6	Legate	Thomas		1	4		1			1	1	1			9		
Leominster	437	7	Legate	Thomas Jun	2	2	2	1	1		1	3	1	1			14		
Leominster	437	8	Lowe	Edward		2			1		1	2		1			7		
Leominster	437	9	Lincoln	Wm Jun		1		1			1		1				4		
Leominster	437	10	Low	Nathl					1		1	1	1				4		
Leominster	437	11	Lincoln	Thomas			1	1		3	1		1				7		
Leominster	437	12	Meriam	Amos	1			1	1	3	1	1	1	1			10		
Leominster	437	13	May	Jacob			1			3			1				5		
Leominster	437	14	May	James Jun	2		1				1	1					5		
Leominster	437	15	Maynard	John	1		1					1					3		
Leominster	437	16	May	James				1				2	1				4		
Leominster	437	17	May	Moses	1			1		4			1				7		
Leominster	437	18	May	Aaron	3		1				1		1				6		
Leominster	437	19	Mosman	Mark		1				2		1					4		
Leominster	437	20	Meriam	Jonathan	1			1		3		1	1				7		
Leominster	437	21	Mead	Abijah	3	1			2	4	1						11		
Leominster	437	22	Mills	Collins		1					1						2		
Leominster	437	23	Nichols	Israel Jun		1	1				1		1				4		
Leominster	437	24	Nichols	Israel				1		1			1				3		
Leominster	437	25	Nichols	William		1	3	1			1	1					7		
Leominster	437	26	Newhall	Michael				1						3			4		
Leominster	437	27	Nichols	Levi	1	1		1		3			2	1			9		
Leominster	437	28	Newhall	Daniel	2		1	1					1				5		
Leominster	437	29	Pike	Ephraim	2	2		1		2		2	2				11		
Leominster	437	30	Pierce	Jonathan	1			1		2			1				5		
Leominster	437	31	Platts	Isaac	2	1			1		1	1		1			7		
Leominster	437	32	Priest	Joseph				1				1					2		
Leominster	437	33	Pierce	Joshua	1	1	1	2				1	1				9		
Leominster	437	34	Phelps	John		1				1		2					4		
Leominster	437	35	Parmeter	Silas		1	1	1				2		1			6		
Leominster	437	36	Powers	Levi	2			1		3	2		1				9		
Leominster	437	37	Priest	Lydia						3	1	1	1	1			7		
Leominster	437	38	Payson	Sarah						3			1				4		
Leominster	437	39	Potter	Jacob	2			1		2	2		1				8		
Leominster	437	40	Pierce	Reuben		1	1		1			1		1			5		
Leominster	438	1	Perkins	Benja	2	2		1		1		3		1			10		
Leominster	438	2	Perry	Ichabod	2	1		1		1	1	3	1				10		
Leominster	438	3	Phelps	Abel	2	1		1					1				5		
Leominster	438	4	Pierce	Thomas	2			1		2			1				6		
Leominster	438	5	Parmeter	David		1	1			1		1	1	1			6		
Leominster	438	6	Parker	Willard			1					1					2		
Leominster	438	7	Rice	John	2			1				1					4		
Leominster	438	8	Rogers	Benja				1				1					2		
Leominster	438	9	Robbins	Thomas	1	1		1		1	2		1	1			8		
Leominster	438	10	Rugg	Jacob	1			1		3			1				6		
Leominster	438	11	Richardson	John	2	1	1	1	1			4	1	1			12		
Leominster	438	12	Richardson	Silas	1		1		1	1		1	1				6		
Leominster	438	13	Richardson	Luke	2		2	1	1	1		2	1	1			11		
Leominster	438	14	Rugg	aaron			1			1	1		1	1			5		
Leominster	438	15	Richardson	Luke Jun	1	1		1		2	1		1				7		
Leominster	438	16	Smith	Mary										2			2		
Leominster	438	17	Snow	Samuel	2		1			1	2		1				8		
Leominster	438	18	Simonds	John	1	1	1		1	2	2	1					10		
Leominster	438	19	Stewart	Huldah									1				1		
Leominster	438	20	Joslin	Elias	2	1	1	1		1	1	1	1				9		
Leominster	438	21	Johnson	Ephraim		1		1		3			1				6		
Leominster	438	22	Johnson	Joseph	2	1		1		2			1				7		
Leominster	438	23	Johnson	Asa			2				1		1				4		
Leominster	438	24	Jones	Amasa		1		1				1	1				4		
Leominster	438	25	Johnson	Jotham	1		1	2	1	2	1		1				9		
Leominster	438	26	Joslin	John			2	1						1			4		
Leominster	438	27	Joslin	Luke		1	1	1				1					4		
Leominster	438	28	Joslin	James			2	1			1		1				5		
Leominster	438	29	Joslin	Samuel	2		1	1				1					5		
Leominster	438	30	Joslin	Joseph		1		1				1		1			4		
Leominster	438	31	Johnson	Luke	1			1		2			1	1			6		
Leominster	438	32	Joslin	Peter	1	1		1		1			1				5		
Leominster	438	33	Jones	Aaron	1			1				1					3		
Leominster	438	34	Johnson	Benja	1			1			2		1				5		
Leominster	438	35	Kendall	David	1	1	1		1	1	1	1		1			8		
Leominster	438	36	Knight	William			1			3	2		1				7		
Leominster	438	37	Kendall	John		2	1	2			1		1	1			8		

TOWN	PG#	LN#	HEADS OF HOUSEHOLD		FREE WHITE MALES					FREE WHITE FEMALES					TOTAL ALL OTHER	TOTAL SLAVES	TOTALS	DISTRICT/ TOWNSHIP	NOTES
			LAST NAME	FIRST NAME	under 10	10 to 16	16 to 26	26 to 45	45 and over	under 10	10 to 16	16 to 26	26 to 45	45 and over					
Leominster	438	38	Kilburn	Jacob	2				1	1			1				5		
Leominster	438	39	Kendall	Jonas	1	1	3	1		1	2	3	1				13		
Leominster	438	40	Kendall	Abel	1	1	2	1		1	1	1	2	1			11		
Leominster	438	41	Kendall	Asa	2	1	1		1	1	1	1	1	1			10		

TOWN	PG#	LN#	HEADS OF HOUSEHOLD		FREE WHITE MALES					FREE WHITE FEMALES					TOTAL ALL OTHER	TOTAL SLAVES	TOTALS	DISTRICT/ TOWNSHIP	NOTES
			LAST NAME	FIRST NAME	under 10	10 to 16	16 to 26	26 to 45	45 and over	under 10	10 to 16	16 to 26	26 to 45	45 and over					
Lunenberg	421	1	Adams	*iel		1	1		1			4	1	1			9		
Lunenberg	421	2	Adams	Jonathan		1			1		1			1			4		
Lunenberg	421	3	Adams	Jona Jun	1	1	2	1		2	1		1				9		
Lunenberg	421	4	Adams	Edward	3			1		1	1	1					7		
Lunenberg	421	5	Allexander	John		1			1				1				3		
Lunenberg	421	6	Austin	Timothy	3	1	1	1		1			1		1		9		
Lunenberg	421	7	Austin	John			3				1		1				5		
Lunenberg	421	8	Allen	Benjamin			1						1				2		
Lunenberg	421	9	Bathrick	Reuben			2		1				1				4		
Lunenberg	421	10	Bathrick	Samuel	1			1		2		1					5		
Lunenberg	421	11	Billings	Samuel		1	2		1	2	1	1		2			10		
Lunenberg	421	12	Billings	John	1	2	1		1	4	1	1	1				12		
Lunenberg	421	13	Brown	Philemon		1		1				2		1			5		
Lunenberg	421	14	Bennett	James			2		1	3	3		1				10		
Lunenberg	421	15	Boynton	Wm	4			2		1			2				9		
Lunenberg	421	16	Bailey	Benja		1			1			2		1			5		
Lunenberg	421	17	Bryant	Amos	1	1		1		2	1		1				7		
Lunenberg	421	18	Bicknell	Daniel	2	1	1	1		1	2	1	1				10		
Lunenberg	421	19	Bicknell	Joseph	1	2			2	1		2	1				10		
Lunenberg	421	20	Brown	Peter	2	2	1		1	2	1	1	1				11		
Lunenberg	421	21	Bicknell	James	1		1					1					3		
Lunenberg	421	22	Bailey	Jedidiah	1			1	1	1			1	1			6		
Lunenberg	421	23	Boynton	Jona				1				2	1				4		
Lunenberg	421	24	Boynton	David		1		1			1		1				4		
Lunenberg	421	25	Ba*	Josiah				1					1				2		
Lunenberg	423	1	Cushing	Charles			1		1		1	1		1			5		
Lunenberg	423	2	Cowdry	Ezra	3			1		1	1		1				7		
Lunenberg	423	3	Cushing	Edmund			3					1	1				5		
Lunenberg	423	4	Conant	Simeon	4			1		2	1		1				9		
Lunenberg	423	5	Cuningham	Nath	1			1		1		1	1				5		
Lunenberg	423	6	Clap	Ezra				1					1				2		
Lunenberg	423	7	Chute	Paul G.	2			1		1			1	1			6		
Lunenberg	423	8	Chute	George W.		1						1					2		
Lunenberg	423	9	Divol	Asahel	4		1						1				6		
Lunenberg	423	10	Divol	Sarah		1						1		1			3		
Lunenberg	423	11	Divol	Phinehas	1				2			2	1	1			7		
Lunenberg	423	12	Dressor	Ama		1	1		1			2		1			6		
Lunenberg	423	13	Damon	Thomas	2	1	1				1	1	1				7		
Lunenberg	423	14	Dunsmoor	Phinehas	1	2			1	3			1				8		
Lunenberg	423	15	Dunsmoor	Ebenezer	2	3	2	1			1		2				11		
Lunenberg	423	16	Dole	John		1		1			1		1				4		
Lunenberg	423	17	Dodge	Elijah	1			1		1			1				4		
Lunenberg	423	18	Dodge	James	2			1		1		1					5		
Lunenberg	423	19	Eaton	Pearson			1										1		
Lunenberg	423	20	Foster	Isaac Jun		1	1	1				1		1			5		
Lunenberg	423	21	Fuller	John	1			1	1	1			1	1			6		
Lunenberg	423	22	France	Hannah	1			1					1				3		
Lunenberg	423	23	Foster	Samuel			1						1				2		
Lunenberg	424	1	Bailey	Josiah Jun	2	1		1				2					6		
Lunenberg	424	2	Bancroft	Edmand	1		1	1		1	1		1				6		
Lunenberg	424	3	Bennett	David	2	1	1	1		4	1	3	1				14		
Lunenberg	424	4	Barnard	Jacob	1			1		1		1					4		
Lunenberg	424	5	Bancroft	Joseph	3			1		1			1				6		
Lunenberg	424	6	Brooks	Aaron	1	1		1					1				4		
Lunenberg	424	7	Burridge	Jonathan				1		1	1	1	1				5		
Lunenberg	424	8	Boston	Phillip											5		5		
Lunenberg	424	9	Curtis	Joseph				1				1					2		
Lunenberg	424	10	Crocker	Paul				1					1		1		3		
Lunenberg	424	11	Chaplin	Joseph				1			1		1				3		
Lunenberg	424	12	Caldwell	Jacob		1	1		1		1	1		1			6		
Lunenberg	424	13	Carlton	Asahel	1	1	1	1			1	1	1				8		
Lunenberg	424	14	Cook	Enoch	1	2			1	2		1		1			8		
Lunenberg	424	15	Clark	Wm				1					3				4		
Lunenberg	424	16	Cummings	Thaddeus	1			1				1	1	1			5		
Lunenberg	424	17	Carleton	Calvin	1	1		1				1					4		
Lunenberg	424	18	Carter	Thomas	1	2	3	1					1				8		
Lunenberg	424	19	Carter	Phinehas	1	2	3			3			1				11		
Lunenberg	424	20	Choate	Robert	2	1		1			2		1				7		
Lunenberg	424	21	Cunningham	Wm	1		1	1			1		1				5		
Lunenberg	424	22	Cogswell	Wm	2	1		1		1	2		2				10		
Lunenberg	425	1	Houghton	Stephen	2		1						1				4		
Lunenberg	425	2	Hovey	Solomon	1	2	1		1		1		2				9		
Lunenberg	425	3	Harrington	Wm	1	1	1		1	1	1	3		2			11		
Lunenberg	425	4	Heywood	John T.	2	2	1		1		1	1	1				9		
Lunenberg	425	5	Hilton	Samuel			1	1					1				3		
Lunenberg	425	6	Harrad	Noah	2	1		1		2	2		1				9		
Lunenberg	425	7	Houghton	Asahel	1		1						1	1			4		
Lunenberg	425	8	Hartwell	Josiah		1		2				1		1			5		
Lunenberg	425	9	Hartwell	Jonathan		1			1		1	2	1				6		
Lunenberg	425	10	Harris	Wm			2		1		1			1			5		
Lunenberg	425	11	Henry	John	2	1		1		3	1		1				9		
Lunenberg	425	12	Henry	George Jun	1			1		1	1		1				5		
Lunenberg	425	13	Hastings	David				1									1		
Lunenberg	425	14	Hastings	Caleb				1		1			1				3		
Lunenberg	425	15	Holt	Jonathan				1					1				2		
Lunenberg	425	16	Houghton	Levi Jun		1	1	1				1					4		
Lunenberg	425	17	Hastings	Jonathan	2			1		3			1				7		
Lunenberg	425	18	Hartwell	Joseph				1				1					3		
Lunenberg	425	19	Henry	George				1									1		
Lunenberg	425	20	Hartwell	John	1		2	1			2		1				7		

TOWN	PG#	LN#	HEADS OF HOUSEHOLD LAST NAME	FIRST NAME	FREE WHITE MALES under 10	10 to 16	16 to 26	26 to 45	45 and over	FREE WHITE FEMALES under 10	10 to 16	16 to 26	26 to 45	45 and over	TOTAL ALL OTHER	TOTAL SLAVES	TOTALS	DISTRICT/ TOWNSHIP	NOTES
Lunenberg	426	1	Farmer	John				1						1			2		
Lunenberg	426	2	Fairchild	Elijah	2	1		1				1					5		
Lunenberg	426	3	Goodridge	Benja	1		2	1				1		1			6		
Lunenberg	426	4	Goodridge	Oliver		1	2	1		2		1					7		
Lunenberg	426	5	Gould	Sampson				1		2			1				4		
Lunenberg	426	6	Goodridge	Phinehas	2	1		1		1			2	1			8		
Lunenberg	426	7	Gould	Thomas		1		1					1	1			4		
Lunenberg	426	8	Going	Jonathan	1	1	2	1		1			1	1			8		
Lunenberg	426	9	Goodridge	Simon	1			1		1			1	1			5		
Lunenberg	426	10	Gilchrist	James	2	1		1		3	1		2	1			11		
Lunenberg	426	11	Goodridge	Ezekiel		1		1		3	1	1	1				9		
Lunenberg	426	12	Gardner	Daniel	3			1		1			1	1			7		
Lunenberg	426	13	Giddings	Mehitable								1	1	1			3		
Lunenberg	426	14	Gibson	Timothy	1		1		1	1				1			5		
Lunenberg	426	15	Green	Jabez	2		1	1					1				5		
Lunenberg	426	16	Holt	Abiel	2			1		1			1				5		
Lunenberg	426	17	Holden	Sylvanus	4			1		1			1				7		
Lunenberg	426	18	Haskell	Abraham		2	3	1		2	1	1					10		
Lunenberg	426	19	Harkness	Thomas	1		1	1		2	4	1	2				12		
Lunenberg	426	20	Hartwell	Jacob	1			1		2		1					5		
Lunenberg	426	21	Howard	Timothy	3	1		1		2			1				8		
Lunenberg	426	22	Houghton	Levi Jun		1		1					1	1			4		
Lunenberg	426	23	Houghton	Eleazer				1				2	1	1			5		
Lunenberg	427	1	Lowe	Wm		2	2	2		1	1			1			9		
Lunenberg	427	2	Lincoln	Jeremiah		1	1	1					1	1			5		
Lunenberg	427	3	Mitchell	Andrew			2	1		1				1			5		
Lunenberg	427	4	Moffett	Joseph			1			1				1			4		
Lunenberg	427	5	Mead	Thomas	2			1		1		1	1	1			7		
Lunenberg	427	6	Marshall	Samuel		1	1	1		1				1			5		
Lunenberg	427	7	Marshall	Samuel Jun		1	1			3		1					6		
Lunenberg	427	8	Mills	James				1			1			1			3		
Lunenberg	427	9	Marshall	David			2	1		4		1					8		
Lunenberg	427	10	Masson	Jona	4			1		1		1					7		
Lunenberg	427	11	Marshall	Jacob	1	1	3	1		2	1		1				10		
Lunenberg	427	12	Moffett	Hannah							1		1				2		
Lunenberg	427	13	Martin	Eunice									1				1		
Lunenberg	427	14	Mallikin	Benja	3	1		1		2	2	1					10		
Lunenberg	427	15	Newell	Thomas				1			1			2			4		
Lunenberg	427	16	Oldham	Thomas				1						1			2		
Lunenberg	427	17	Pierce	Oliver		1		1		1				1			4		
Lunenberg	427	18	Parker	Elisha			1	1		1				2			5		
Lunenberg	427	19	Parker	Elisha Jun	3			1					1				5		
Lunenberg	427	20	Perkins	Frances				1						1			2		
Lunenberg	428	1	Johnson	Samuel	1			1		1	3		1				7		
Lunenberg	428	2	Japson	Wm	2		1			1			1				5		
Lunenberg	428	3	Johnson	Benja	2	1		1		2		1	1	1			9		
Lunenberg	428	4	Jones	Wm				1					1				2		
Lunenberg	428	5	Jones	Wm Jun	1	1		1		2			1				6		
Lunenberg	428	6	Jones	John	1			1		2			1				5		
Lunenberg	428	7	Jackman	Joseph			1			2			1				4		
Lunenberg	428	8	Jones	Joseph			1	1						1			3		
Lunenberg	428	9	Kimball	Thomas	1		2	1		1	1	1	1				8		
Lunenberg	428	10	Kilburn	Jona			1	1					1	1			4		
Lunenberg	428	11	Kilburn	David	2			1		1			1				5		
Lunenberg	428	12	Kilburn	Wm				1						1			2		
Lunenberg	428	13	Keys	Simon	3			1		1			1				6		
Lunenberg	428	14	Kilburn	Wm Jun	1		1	1		1		1					5		
Lunenberg	428	15	Kelly	John				1									1		
Lunenberg	428	16	Kimball	Saml				1		3	3			1			8		
Lunenberg	428	17	Little	John		1		1		1			1	1			5		
Lunenberg	428	18	Lain	Eleazer	1	1		1		3			1	1			8		
Lunenberg	428	19	Lowe	Samuel				2				1		1			4		
Lunenberg	428	20	Litch	John		1	1	1	1		2	1		1			8		
Lunenberg	429	1	Ritter	David		1	1	1	1				1	2			7		
Lunenberg	429	2	Rea	Gideon	1	1		1	1	1		1	2				10		
Lunenberg	429	3	Stewart	Benja				1									1		
Lunenberg	429	4	Shed	John		1		1					1				3		
Lunenberg	429	5	Stickney	Stephen			2			1			1	1			5		
Lunenberg	429	6	Stiles	Jonathan	4	1		1		1			1	1			9		
Lunenberg	429	7	Smith	Ebenezer	4	2	1	1		1			1	1			11		
Lunenberg	429	8	Searls	Mary									2	1			3		
Lunenberg	429	9	Sanderson	Isaac		1		1			1	3		1			7		
Lunenberg	429	10	Snow	Silas	1		1	1		1				1			5		
Lunenberg	429	11	Stearns	Josiah		1	1	1		2		3		1			9		
Lunenberg	429	12	Snow	Silas Jun	4			1		1			1				7		
Lunenberg	429	13	Simonds	daniel	1	2		1		3	1	1	1				10		
Lunenberg	429	14	Sanderson	Jacob				1				2		1			4		
Lunenberg	429	15	Sanderson	Jonan	3			1		2		1					7		
Lunenberg	429	16	Stearns	Levi	5			1		1		1	1	1			10		
Lunenberg	429	17	Stiles	Caleb	1			1		1			1	1			6		
Lunenberg	429	18	Sylvester	Lot				1		1				1			4		
Lunenberg	429	19	Stiles	Nahum	1			1		1				1			4		
Lunenberg	429	20	Stiles	Levi	1			1	1			1	1	1			6		
Lunenberg	429	21	Turner	Joseph	2	2		1		3	1		1				10		
Lunenberg	430	1	Pierce	Abraham	2			1		1			1	1			7		
Lunenberg	430	2	Pirkins	Jonathan	3	1		1					1				6		
Lunenberg	430	3	Pierce	Ephraim			1		1				1	1			4		
Lunenberg	430	4	Patterson	John	2		1	1		2	3	2					11		
Lunenberg	430	5	Pierce	Jonathan		1	2		1					2			6		
Lunenberg	430	6	Perrin	Charles				1				1					2		

TOWN	PG#	LN#	LAST NAME	FIRST NAME	under 10	10 to 16	16 to 26	26 to 45	45 and over	under 10	10 to 16	16 to 26	26 to 45	45 and over	TOTAL ALL OTHER	TOTAL SLAVES	TOTALS	DISTRICT/ TOWNSHIP	NOTES
			HEADS OF HOUSEHOLD		FREE WHITE MALES					FREE WHITE FEMALES									
Lunenberg	430	7	Page	Amos					1		1			1			3		
Lunenberg	430	8	Pierce	Benja		1	1			3		1					6		
Lunenberg	430	9	Prentice	Thaddeus		1			1	1	2			1			6		
Lunenberg	430	10	Peabody	Phinehas	2		1						1				4		
Lunenberg	430	11	Proctor	Mary			1	1					1				3		
Lunenberg	430	12	Peabody	John	3	1		1		2			1				8		
Lunenberg	430	13	Pratt	Eleazer					1		1			2			4		
Lunenberg	430	14	Page	Abel	1	1		1		1	1		1				6		
Lunenberg	430	15	Russell	Ephraim	2	1		1		1	2		1				8		
Lunenberg	430	16	Rand	Jonathan				1		4			1				6		
Lunenberg	430	17	Richards	Mitchell				1						1			2		
Lunenberg	430	18	Ramsdell	Seth	1			1		1			1				4		
Lunenberg	430	19	Richards	John	2			1		2		1					6		
Lunenberg	430	20	Richards	Mitchell Jun	2			1		2			1				6		
Lunenberg	432	1	Taylor	Caleb		1			1	1			2	1			6		
Lunenberg	432	2	Tylor	Moses	1	1			1				2	1			6		
Lunenberg	432	3	Tylor	Nathan				1		2			1				4		
Lunenberg	432	4	Taylor	Nathan				1		3			1				5		
Lunenberg	432	5	Taylor	Isreal	2			1		2			1				6		
Lunenberg	432	6	Wheeler	Josiah G.	1		3	1		1			1				7		
Lunenberg	432	7	Weatherbee	Ephrm		2	1	1				1	1				6		
Lunenberg	432	8	Whitney	Zachariah		1	1	1			1	2	1				7		
Lunenberg	432	9	Wood	David	3	1		1				2	1	1			9		
Lunenberg	432	10	Weatherbee	David	1			1		3	1	3	1				10		
Lunenberg	432	11	Wood	Zephaniah		1		1					1				3		
Lunenberg	432	12	Whiting	Esek	2		2	1		1			1				7		
Lunenberg	432	13	Whiting	Nathaniel	1			1		3			1				6		
Lunenberg	432	14	willard	Jepzibah								1		1			2		
Lunenberg	432	15	Wood	Joseph				1							1		2		
Lunenberg	432	16	Whiting	Luther		1		1					1				3		
Lunenberg	432	17	Wood	David Jun	2			1		2		1	1				7		
Lunenberg	432	18	Watson	Elizabeth		2						2	1				5		
Lunenberg	432	19	Whitney	John	1		2		1	1			1				6		
Lunenberg	432	20	Whitney	Abigail									1				1		
Lunenberg	432	21	Whitney	Stephen		1	1	1	1	1	2	1	2				10		
Lunenberg	432	22	Wallis	Ebenezer	2	1		1		1			1				6		
Lunenberg	432	23	Whitney	Lemuel		1	1		1			1	1	1			6		

TOWN	PG#	LN#	LAST NAME	FIRST NAME	under 10	10 to 16	16 to 26	26 to 45	45 and over	under 10	10 to 16	16 to 26	26 to 45	45 and over	TOTAL ALL OTHER	TOTAL SLAVES	TOTALS	DISTRICT/ TOWNSHIP	NOTES
					FREE WHITE MALES					FREE WHITE FEMALES									
Mendon	379	1	Alexander	Caleb	1	1	1	1		3	2	2	1				12	1st Parish	
Mendon	379	2	Ammidon	Philip Esq		1	1	1	1			1	1	2			8	1st Parish	
Mendon	379	3	Adams	Polly Wd.		1						1	1				3	1st Parish	
Mendon	379	4	Adams	Josiah Deac.				1						1			2	1st Parish	
Mendon	379	5	Adams	Joseph Dr.	2	1		1		1	1	2	1				9	1st Parish	
Mendon	379	6	Allen	Samuel Capt.	2	1		1			1		1				6	1st Parish	
Mendon	379	7	Aldrich	Benoni	1			1		1		1					4	1st Parish	
Mendon	379	8	Aldrich	Jasan	1			1		2		1					5	1st Parish	
Mendon	379	9	Aldrich	Charles				1		2		1	1				5	1st Parish	
Mendon	379	10	Aldrich	George	3			1		1	2		1				8	1st Parish	
Mendon	379	11	Aldrich	Jacob				1									1	1st Parish	
Mendon	379	12	Aldrich	Silas		1		1				1		1			4	1st Parish	
Mendon	379	13	Allen	Ezra	1			1						1			3	1st Parish	
Mendon	379	14	Allen	Ezra Junr		1						1					2	1st Parish	
Mendon	379	15	Aldrich	Luke		1	1	1		1				2			6	1st Parish	
Mendon	379	16	Albee	Simeon	2	1		1		4			1				9	1st Parish	
Mendon	379	17	Aldrich	Pardon	2		1						1				4	1st Parish	
Mendon	379	18	Allen	Ahaz	1	1		1		1			2				6	1st Parish	
Mendon	379	19	Allen	Alvan	1	1		1		1		1					5	1st Parish	
Mendon	379	20	Allen	Joseph				1						1			2	1st Parish	
Mendon	381	1	Daniels	Darius			1	1	1			1		1			5	1st Parish	
Mendon	381	2	Daniels	Joseph			1			2		2					5	1st Parish	
Mendon	381	3	Daniels	Nathan	1		1			2		2					6	1st Parish	
Mendon	381	4	Dexter	Andrew	1	1	2	1				1	1				7	1st Parish	
Mendon	381	5	Daniels	Adams	1		1				1	1					4	1st Parish	
Mendon	381	6	Darling	John Jr	3		1						1				5	1st Parish	
Mendon	381	7	Eames	John				1				2	1				4	1st Parish	
Mendon	381	8	Fox	Joseph	1		1			1			1				4	1st Parish	
Mendon	381	9	Fuller	Charlotte Mrs.	1								1				2	1st Parish	
Mendon	381	10	Freeman	Ralph		1				2			1				4	1st Parish	
Mendon	381	11	Fairbanks	Nancy Wd.	2			1		2	1		1				7	1st Parish	
Mendon	381	12	Fletcher	Asa		1		1					1	2			5	1st Parish	
Mendon	381	13	French	William	1			1					1	1			4	1st Parish	
Mendon	381	14	French	Royal	1		1			3	2	1	1				9	1st Parish	
Mendon	381	15	Freeman	William	3		1	1		1		1	1				8	1st Parish	
Mendon	381	16	Goodale	Ephm	1	3	2	1		3	1	1	1				13	1st Parish	
Mendon	381	17	Goss	Zebulon		1		1			1	1		2			6	1st Parish	
Mendon	381	18	Hill	John				1				1		1			3	1st Parish	
Mendon	381	19	Holden	John Capt.		1		1				1					3	1st Parish	
Mendon	382	1	Aldrich	Luke 2d	3	1	1	1		1	1	1	1				10	1st Parish	
Mendon	382	2	Aldrich	Ebenezer		1	1			1	1		1				5	1st Parish	
Mendon	382	3	Albee	Levi				1		2	2		1				6	1st Parish	
Mendon	382	4	Albee	Samuel	1		1	1		2	1		1				7	1st Parish	
Mendon	382	5	Brown	Aaron		1	1	1			1			1			5	1st Parish	
Mendon	382	6	Ballou	Hepzibah Wd	1							1	1	1			4	1st Parish	
Mendon	382	7	Bosworth	Joseph	3		1					1	1				6	1st Parish	
Mendon	382	8	Bates	Nahum	2		1	1			1	1					6	1st Parish	
Mendon	382	9	Bates	Martha Wd		1					1			1			3	1st Parish	
Mendon	382	10	Chapin	Seth Deac		1	1		1		1	1		1			8	1st Parish	
Mendon	382	11	Chapin	Ebenezer				1						1			2	1st Parish	
Mendon	382	12	Chapin	Ebenezer Jr	1	1	1	1		2	1	2	1				10	1st Parish	
Mendon	382	13	Craggin	John		1		1	1		1	2		1			7	1st Parish	
Mendon	382	14	Carpenter	Oliver			2		1	2	2		1				8	1st Parish	
Mendon	382	15	Davenport	Seth Jr	2		1					2			1		6	1st Parish	
Mendon	382	16	Davenport	Seth		2	1		2			2		1			8	1st Parish	
Mendon	382	17	Davenport	David	2		3	1					2				8	1st Parish	
Mendon	383	1	Lasall	Joshua	2		2	1			1		1				7	1st Parish	
Mendon	383	2	Legg	Joel	2	2		1		2			1				8	1st Parish	
Mendon	383	3	Fuller	Miller	2	1		2		1		1	2				9	1st Parish	
Mendon	383	4	Miller	Lewis			1										1	1st Parish	
Mendon	383	5	Maynard	Windsor	3			1				1	1				6	1st Parish	
Mendon	383	6	McClintock	Joseph	2	1		1		2	1		1		1		9	1st Parish	
Mendon	383	7	Mowry	Isreal		1	1	1	1		1	2					7	1st Parish	
Mendon	383	8	Mowry	Henry	2			1		2			2				7	1st Parish	
Mendon	383	9	Mason	Chad	3		1			1			1				6	1st Parish	
Mendon	383	10	Mellen	James Col.	1		2	1				1		2	4		11	1st Parish	
Mendon	383	11	Marsh	Douglas	1	1		1					1	1			5	1st Parish	
Mendon	383	12	Nicholas	Mary Wd		1				1	1			2			5	1st Parish	
Mendon	383	13	Penniman	Peter Esq				1					1				2	1st Parish	
Mendon	383	14	Penniman	Andrew		1	1					2					4	1st Parish	
Mendon	383	15	Peters	Elinor Mrs.							1		1				2	1st Parish	
Mendon	383	16	Penniman	Baruch	2		1	2		2			1				8	1st Parish	
Mendon	383	17	Penniman	John				1						1			2	1st Parish	
Mendon	383	18	Penniman	Josiah Jr	2		1	1		3			1				8	1st Parish	
Mendon	383	19	Penniman	Josiah		1			1					1			3	1st Parish	
Mendon	384	1	Hastings	Seth Esq	1		2	2		1			1	1			8	1st Parish	
Mendon	384	2	Holbrook	Peter Lt.	2		1	1					1				5	1st Parish	
Mendon	384	3	Hill	Elizabeth Wd	1							1	1	1			4	1st Parish	
Mendon	384	4	Hayward	Elisha	2		1	1		1		1					7	1st Parish	

| | | | HEADS OF HOUSEHOLD | | FREE WHITE MALES | | | | | FREE WHITE FEMALES | | | | | | | | | |
TOWN	PG#	LN#	LAST NAME	FIRST NAME	under 10	10 to 16	16 to 26	26 to 45	45 and over	under 10	10 to 16	16 to 26	26 to 45	45 and over	TOTAL ALL OTHER	TOTAL SLAVES	TOTALS	DISTRICT/ TOWNSHIP	NOTES
Mendon	384	5	Hayward	Elijah		1	2		1					1			5	1st Parish	
Mendon	384	6	Hayward	Ichabod				1						1			2	1st Parish	
Mendon	384	7	Hayward	John		1	2		2			1	1	1			8	1st Parish	
Mendon	384	8	Hill	Joel				1		3			1				5	1st Parish	
Mendon	384	9	Johnson	Solomon	2			1		3		1	1				8	1st Parish	
Mendon	384	10	Jennison	Willm	1		1						1				3	1st Parish	
Mendon	384	11	Johnson	Stephen	1	1			1	1	2	2		1			9	1st Parish	
Mendon	384	12	Johnson	Baxter	4	1		1		2		1	1				10	1st Parish	
Mendon	384	13	Keith	Nathan Lt.		1	1	1	1			1	1	1			7	1st Parish	
Mendon	384	14	Lovett	James				1					4	1			6	1st Parish	
Mendon	384	15	Lovett	Phinehas		1						1					2	1st Parish	
Mendon	384	16	Lovett	James Jr			1					1					2	1st Parish	
Mendon	384	17	Lord	Thomas		1				1		1					3	1st Parish	
Mendon	384	18	Legg	Benjamin		1			1	2	1	1	1				7	1st Parish	
Mendon	384	19	Legg	John				1						1			2	1st Parish	
Mendon	384	20	Legg	Susannah Wd						1		1		1			3	1st Parish	
Mendon	385	1	Torrey	Willm Capt.	2	1		1	1	1			1				7	1st Parish	
Mendon	385	2	Torrey	Joseph Capt.	4		1					1					6	1st Parish	
Mendon	385	3	Torrey	Stephen	1			2		1			1				5	1st Parish	
Mendon	385	4	Tyler	Urana Wd		1	2			1	1	1	1				7	1st Parish	
Mendon	385	5	Thayer	Smith	1	1	1	1		2	1	1	1				9	1st Parish	
Mendon	385	6	Taft	Enos	1	1	1	1		1	1			1			7	1st Parish	
Mendon	385	7	Taft	Zacheus	2	1		1		2			1				7	1st Parish	
Mendon	385	8	Taft	Seth	3	1	1		1	2	1		1				10	1st Parish	
Mendon	385	9	Taft	Nathaniel	3	3		1	1	1		1	1	1			12	1st Parish	
Mendon	385	10	Taft	Thomas	3	1	1		1	2	1	3	1		2		15	1st Parish	
Mendon	385	11	Taft	Amasa	1		1					1					3	1st Parish	
Mendon	385	12	Taft	Jotham		1	1		1			1		1			5	1st Parish	
Mendon	385	13	Thurston	Daniel	1		1						1				3	1st Parish	
Mendon	385	14	Taft	Elijah	1		1		1	2			1				6	1st Parish	
Mendon	385	15	Taft	George	2		1						1				4	1st Parish	
Mendon	385	16	Thayer	Increase Lt.		1	1		1	1	1			1			6	1st Parish	
Mendon	385	17	Thayer	Alexander	1			1	1			2					5	1st Parish	
Mendon	385	18	Thayer	Amos	1			2				1					4	1st Parish	
Mendon	385	19	Thayer	Benjamin	2		2		1	2	1	1	2				11	1st Parish	
Mendon	385	20	Thayer	Aaron Capt.	3	1	3	1		2	1	2	1		1		15	1st Parish	
Mendon	385	21	Thurber	Daniel Dr.		1		1					1				3	1st Parish	
Mendon	386	1	Rawson	Levi	1	2	2		1			2		2			10	1st Parish	
Mendon	386	2	Ramsdale	Saul	1	1	1		1	1				1			6	1st Parish	
Mendon	386	3	Rawson	Secretary	1			1				1	1				6	1st Parish	
Mendon	386	4	Russell	Abigail Wd	2	1				2		2	1	1			9	1st Parish	
Mendon	386	5	Rawson	Parn	1	1	2		1			1	1				7	1st Parish	
Mendon	386	6	Rhodes	Zebulon	1		1	1		1			1				5	1st Parish	
Mendon	386	7	Reed	Benjm Esq		1	1		1		1			1			5	1st Parish	
Mendon	386	8	Staples	Simeon	3	2	1	1		1	1	2		1			12	1st Parish	
Mendon	386	9	Sweeting	Job	1		1		1			1					4	1st Parish	
Mendon	386	10	Stone	Thomas	1	1		1		3			1				7	1st Parish	
Mendon	386	11	Searles	James			1			3		1					5	1st Parish	
Mendon	386	12	Staples	Thomas				1						1			2	1st Parish	
Mendon	386	13	Stimson	Charles	2		1	1		1			1				6	1st Parish	
Mendon	386	14	Smith	Calvin Col.				1					1				2	1st Parish	
Mendon	386	15	Southland	Willm	1			1		2		1					5	1st Parish	
Mendon	386	16	Staples	Nahor	2	1	1	1		2	1	1	1				10	1st Parish	
Mendon	386	17	Staples	George	1	2		1		2	1		1				8	1st Parish	
Mendon	386	18	Southland	Joel			1					1					2	1st Parish	
Mendon	387	1	Aldrich	Luther	1	1		1				1	1	1			6	2d Parish	
Mendon	387	2	Aldrich	Calvin	1	1	1	1		1			1				6	2d Parish	
Mendon	387	3	Aldrich	Phinehas Capt		1	1	2			1		2				7	2d Parish	
Mendon	387	4	Aldrich	Dan				1						1			2	2d Parish	
Mendon	387	5	Aldrich	Willm		1	2				1			1			5	2d Parish	
Mendon	387	6	Aldrich	Rufas Majr	1		1		1			1		1			5	2d Parish	
Mendon	387	7	Alexander	Timothy	1		1		1	1	2	1	1				8	2d Parish	
Mendon	387	8	Brayley	Solomon	1	1			1	2		1		1			7	2d Parish	
Mendon	387	9	Bowen	Willm			1	1		1			1				4	2d Parish	
Mendon	387	10	Benson	John Lt.	2		2		1	2	2		2				12	2d Parish	
Mendon	387	11	Benson	Benoni		1			1					1			3	2d Parish	
Mendon	387	12	Benson	Amasa	1			1				1					3	2d Parish	
Mendon	387	13	Benson	Henry	1			1		2			1				5	2d Parish	
Mendon	387	14	Blake	Asa	1			1	1	1	1						5	2d Parish	
Mendon	387	15	Blake	Benjamin				1						1			2	2d Parish	
Mendon	387	16	Blake	Reuben	1		1			1	2	1					6	2d Parish	
Mendon	387	17	Blake	Zacheus	2			1		2	1		1				7	2d Parish	
Mendon	387	18	Bennett	Hosea		1			1				1	1			4	2d Parish	
Mendon	387	19	Boyden	Amos	1			1		3			1				6	2d Parish	
Mendon	388	1	Wood	Grindal			1	1	1		1	2					7	1st Parish	
Mendon	388	2	Wood	Stephen		2	1		1	4	2	2	1				13	1st Parish	
Mendon	388	3	Wood	Obadiah			1			1			1				3	1st Parish	
Mendon	388	4	Wood	Solomon Lt.			2		1	2	1	1	1				8	1st Parish	
Mendon	388	5	Wheelock	Calvin	1							2	1				6	1st Parish	

TOWN	PG#	LN#	LAST NAME	FIRST NAME	FREE WHITE MALES					FREE WHITE FEMALES					TOTAL ALL OTHER	TOTAL SLAVES	TOTALS	DISTRICT/ TOWNSHIP	NOTES
					under 10	10 to 16	16 to 26	26 to 45	45 and over	under 10	10 to 16	16 to 26	26 to 45	45 and over					
Mendon	388	6	White	Ebenezer				1				1		1			3	1st Parish	
Mendon	388	7	Willard	Levi Dr.	1		3	1				1	1	1			8	1st Parish	
Mendon	388	8	Westcott	Reuben			1			1		1					3	1st Parish	
Mendon	388	9	Warfield	John	1		1	1				1	1				5	1st Parish	
Mendon	388	10	Wheelock	Nahum	3	2		1		2	2		1				11	1st Parish	
Mendon	388	11	Wheelock	Peter				1						1			2	1st Parish	
Mendon	388	12	Wheelock	Seth Lt.		1	1	1				1		2			6	1st Parish	
Mendon	389	1	Darling	Jesse			1	1									2	2d Parish	
Mendon	389	2	Darling	Matthew			1			1	1	1	1				8	2d Parish	
Mendon	389	3	Darling	Benson			1			2			1	1			5	2d Parish	
Mendon	389	4	Darling	John		1	1	1		1	1	1		1			7	2d Parish	
Mendon	389	5	Darling	Phinehas				1						3			4	2d Parish	
Mendon	389	6	Darling	Abigail	1	1							1	1			4	2d Parish	
Mendon	389	7	Darling	Job		1		1		4	2		1				9	2d Parish	
Mendon	389	8	Engly	Timothy	2			1		3			1				7	2d Parish	
Mendon	389	9	Easty	Abijah	1		1		1	1		2		1			7	2d Parish	
Mendon	389	10	Fisher	Nathan	1		1						1				3	2d Parish	
Mendon	389	11	Gaskill	George			1	1					2	1			5	2d Parish	
Mendon	389	12	Gaskill	Peter	2		1	1		3			1				8	2d Parish	
Mendon	389	13	Green	Job	2		1			3		1	1				8	2d Parish	
Mendon	389	14	Harkness	Samuel	3		1			2	1		1				8	2d Parish	
Mendon	389	15	Handy	David	3		1						1				5	2d Parish	
Mendon	389	16	Hunt	John				1			1	1	1				4	2d Parish	
Mendon	389	17	Hill	John 2d	2		1			1			1				5	2d Parish	
Mendon	389	18	Hill	Daniel	2		1			2	1	2	1				9	2d Parish	
Mendon	389	19	Handy	Mary Wd			1			1		1		1			4	2d Parish	
Mendon	389	20	Himpton	John				1		1			3	1			6	2d Parish	
Mendon	390	1	Cook	Ezekiel	1			1		1			1				4	2d Parish	
Mendon	390	2	Cook	Thaddeus	2	1		1		1	2						8	2d Parish	
Mendon	390	3	Cook	Arthur	1			2		2			2				7	2d Parish	
Mendon	390	4	Cook	Ichabod	1	1	2		1			2		1			8	2d Parish	
Mendon	390	5	Cook	Stephen	1			1		1	2			1			6	2d Parish	
Mendon	390	6	Chace	Coggsall		1	2	1				1		1			6	2d Parish	
Mendon	390	7	Chace	Timothy	1			1		1			1				4	2d Parish	
Mendon	390	8	Chace	Anthony				1						2			3	2d Parish	
Mendon	390	9	Cook	Adanis	3		1			1			1				6	2d Parish	
Mendon	390	10	Cook	Joseph	2		1			2	1						6	2d Parish	
Mendon	390	11	Cass	John	3	1		1		2			1				8	2d Parish	
Mendon	390	12	Callum	Ebenezer				1						1			2	2d Parish	
Mendon	390	13	Cook	Pasco	2			1		1			1				5	2d Parish	
Mendon	390	14	Cook	John	1		1						1				3	2d Parish	
Mendon	390	15	Capron	Nathl	2			1		2			1				6	2d Parish	
Mendon	390	16	Cook	Daniel				1						1			2	2d Parish	
Mendon	390	17	Cook	Margaret									2	1			3	2d Parish	
Mendon	390	18	Callum	Caleb	2			1		2			1				6	2d Parish	
Mendon	390	19	Daniels	David	1	1	3		1	2		1		1			10	2d Parish	
Mendon	390	20	Daniels	Moses	2	1	1	1	1	1	2	1	2				12	2d Parish	
Mendon	390	21	Day	Daniel	3		1	1		1	1		2				9	2d Parish	
Mendon	391	1	Scott	Nathl	2			1		1	1			1			6	2d Parish	
Mendon	391	2	Swift	Joseph		1		1						1			3	2d Parish	
Mendon	391	3	Swift	Abraham			1					1					2	2d Parish	
Mendon	391	4	Smith	Saml Jr	2			1		2			1				6	2d Parish	
Mendon	391	5	Southwick	Seth	1		1	1		2			1				6	2d Parish	
Mendon	391	6	Southwick	Edward			1	1			1	1		1			5	2d Parish	
Mendon	391	7	Southwick	John 3d	3			1		1			1				6	2d Parish	
Mendon	391	8	Southwick	Joseph			1	1				2		1			5	2d Parish	
Mendon	391	9	Southwick	John 2d		1		1		3	2		1				8	2d Parish	
Mendon	391	10	Sibley	David			1			3			1				5	2d Parish	
Mendon	391	11	Southwick	Jacob	1		1			1			1				4	2d Parish	
Mendon	391	12	Shove	Josiah	1	2		1				2		1			7	2d Parish	
Mendon	391	13	Smith	Asa			1		1	1	1		1				5	2d Parish	
Mendon	391	14	Southwick	Theophilus	1	1	2		1	1	1		1	1			9	2d Parish	
Mendon	391	15	Southwick	John	1		3	1	1		1	2		1			10	2d Parish	
Mendon	391	16	Thompson	John				2				1	1	2			6	2d Parish	
Mendon	391	17	Thayer	Thomas	2			1				1	1				5	2d Parish	
Mendon	391	18	Thayer	Joseph		2	2	1				1		2			8	2d Parish	
Mendon	391	19	Thayer	Benjamin 2d			1	1		1		1	1				5	2d Parish	
Mendon	391	20	Thayer	Nicholas		2		1		3		1	1				8	2d Parish	
Mendon	391	21	Thayer	Nahum	2			1		3		1	1				8	2d Parish	
Mendon	392	1	Joslin	Abraham				1					1	1			3	2d Parish	
Mendon	392	2	Kelley	Seth	4		1	1		1		1	1				9	2d Parish	
Mendon	392	3	Kelley	Wyllis	2		1	1		1			1				6	2d Parish	
Mendon	392	4	Kelley	John		1	2					2		2			7	2d Parish	
Mendon	392	5	Legg	Samuel		1		1					1				3	2d Parish	
Mendon	392	6	Lesure	Levi		1	1		1	1	1	2		3			10	2d Parish	
Mendon	392	7	Mann	Benedic	3	1		1		1	2	1	1	1			11	2d Parish	
Mendon	392	8	Philips	Israel	2			1					1				4	2d Parish	
Mendon	392	9	Pickering	David	1			1		2			1				5	2d Parish	
Mendon	392	10	Pickering	Jona				1						1			2	2d Parish	

TOWN	PG#	LN#	LAST NAME	FIRST NAME	FREE WHITE MALES					FREE WHITE FEMALES					TOTAL ALL OTHER	TOTAL SLAVES	TOTALS	DISTRICT/ TOWNSHIP	NOTES
					under 10	10 to 16	16 to 26	26 to 45	45 and over	under 10	10 to 16	16 to 26	26 to 45	45 and over					
Mendon	392	11	Pickering	Willm	4	1			1	1			3	1			11	2d Parish	
Mendon	392	12	Pickering	Benjm Jr		1	1	1		1		1	1				6	2d Parish	
Mendon	392	13	Pickering	Asa	2	1	1	1		1			1				7	2d Parish	
Mendon	392	14	Pickering	Benjm	1	1			1		2			2			7	2d Parish	
Mendon	392	15	Prentice	Saml	2		1	1		2	1		1				8	2d Parish	
Mendon	392	16	Remmington	Benedic	2	1	1	1	1	1		1		1			9	2d Parish	
Mendon	392	17	Smith	George	1	1	1	1		4	1			1			10	2d Parish	
Mendon	392	18	Smith	Saml	2			1	1	2	2		1	1			10	2d Parish	
Mendon	394	1	Taft	Enos 2d			1					1					2	2d Parish	
Mendon	394	2	Taft	Ebenezer	2		1	1		2	3		1	1			11	2d Parish	
Mendon	394	3	Thayer	Robert			1				1						2	2d Parish	
Mendon	394	4	Thayer	Artemas	2	1		1		1			2				7	2d Parish	
Mendon	394	5	Thayer	Caleb	1	1		1		3			1				7	2d Parish	
Mendon	394	6	Taft	Nahum			1	1						2			4	2d Parish	
Mendon	394	7	Tourtellotte	Jesse	1		3	1		2				1			8	2d Parish	
Mendon	394	8	Tourtellotte	Stephen			1			1		1					3	2d Parish	
Mendon	394	9	Thayer	Ichabod	3			2		1			1	1			8	2d Parish	
Mendon	394	10	Tourtellotte	Asahel	1		2			1		1					5	2d Parish	
Mendon	394	11	Taft	Japheth	4	1		1		1	1		1	1			10	2d Parish	
Mendon	394	12	Trask	Jonathan	1	2	1		1	1		2		1			9	2d Parish	
Mendon	394	13	Verry	Nathan Jr			2	1		3	1	1	1				9	2d Parish	
Mendon	394	14	Verry	Nathan		1	1		1	1		1	1				6	2d Parish	
Mendon	394	15	Walkup	Henderson				2		3	1			1			7	2d Parish	
Mendon	394	16	White	Smith	2		1		1	1	3		1				9	2d Parish	
Mendon	394	17	Wilson	Alexander	3	1	1	1		2	1		1				10	2d Parish	
Mendon	394	18	Wilson	Caleb	1			1		2		1	1				6	2d Parish	
Mendon	394	19	Warfield	Samuel Lt.		2	1	1		3	1	1	1				10	2d Parish	
Mendon	394	20	Wilson	Jeddediah		1	1		1		1	1					5	2d Parish	
Mendon	394	21	Wilson	John				1									1	2d Parish	
Mendon	394	22	Wood	Peleg	3			1		2	1		1				8	2d Parish	

TOWN	PG#	LN#	HEADS OF HOUSEHOLD		FREE WHITE MALES					FREE WHITE FEMALES					TOTAL ALL OTHER	TOTAL SLAVES	TOTALS	DISTRICT/ TOWNSHIP	NOTES
			LAST NAME	FIRST NAME	under 10	10 to 16	16 to 26	26 to 45	45 and over	under 10	10 to 16	16 to 26	26 to 45	45 and over					
Milford	389	1	Wheelock	Luther	1		1	1			1	1	1				6		
Milford	389	2	Wood	Obadiah		2		1		1				1			5		
Milford	389	3	Wood	Nathan			1						1				2		
Milford	389	4	Wheelock	Obadiah	1	2		1		1		1	2	2			10		
Milford	389	5	Wedge	Daniel	1			1					1				3		
Milford	389	6	Wedge	Jepthah				1			1		1				3		
Milford	389	7	Wedge	Eli			1						1				2		
Milford	389	8	Whitney	Elias Jr			1	1	1	1	3		1	1			9		
Milford	389	9	Whitney	Elias				1					1				2		
Milford	389	10	Wiswall	Timothy	1	1	1		1		2	1		2			9		
Milford	389	11	Wiswall	Noah		1		1		1			1				4		
Milford	389	12	Whitney	Hachaliah	1	1		1					1				4		
Milford	389	13	Whitney	Jesse				1					1				2		
Milford	389	14	Wales	John	2	1		1		3			1				8		
Milford	389	15	White	Daniel		1	1	1					1				4		
Milford	389	16	Wood	Robert				1					1				2		
Milford	389	17	White	John	2			1		1			1				5		
Milford	389	18	Wood	Ebenezer		1	1	1				1		1			5		
Milford	389	19	Williamson	John				1					1				2		
Milford	389	20	Warfield	Abijah	2	1		1		3	2		1				10		
Milford	391	1	Pond	Abner	1		1	1		1	1		1				6		
Milford	391	2	Parkhurst	Amasa	1			1		1	1	1					5		
Milford	391	3	Pool	William	1		1						1				3		
Milford	391	4	Parkhurst	Nathan	1		1	1		1		1	1				6		
Milford	391	5	Parkhurst	Athiel	1		1			3			1				6		
Milford	391	6	Parkhurst	Nathl Capt.		1	3		1	4	2	1		1			13		
Milford	391	7	Parkhurst	Elisha			1	1		1	1			1			5		
Milford	391	8	Parkhurst	Jonas		1	2	1	1	2	1			1			9		
Milford	391	9	Perry	Elihu	1			1		2	1		1				6		
Milford	391	10	Rockwood	Saml	1	1		1		2	1		1	1			8		
Milford	391	11	Rawson	Nathl Deac			2		1		2	2		1			8		
Milford	391	12	Rawson	Thomas				1					1	1			3		
Milford	391	13	Stodard	Jeremiah				1						1			2		
Milford	391	14	Stodard	Sarah Wd	2						1		1				4		
Milford	391	15	Sumner	Joseph	1			1		1	2		2				7		
Milford	391	16	Sumner	Darius	1	1	2		1	1	2		1				9		
Milford	391	17	Stearns	David			3		1	3		1	2				10		
Milford	391	18	Sumner	Ebenz				1			1						2		
Milford	391	19	Sumner	Ebenz Junr	2	2	1	1		1	1		1				9		
Milford	391	20	Scammel	Alexander	1	1				1		2					5		
Milford	391	21	Saunders	Robert Jr	2	1	2	1	1	1			2				10		
Milford	391	22	Saunders	John	2	1		1		2	1		1				8		
Milford	391	23	Saunders	Nathl	1	2		1				1	1				6		
Milford	391	24	Thayer	Seth				1					1				2		
Milford	391	25	Thayer	Seth Junr	2			1		3			1				7		
Milford	391	26	Twitchell	Garshom	1		2		1	1	1		1				7		
Milford	391	27	Twitchell	Ephm				1			2						3		
Milford	391	28	Thayer	Elijah	2	1	2	1	1		1	1	1	1			11		
Milford	391	29	Thayer	Ichabod Col.		1	3		1		1	2		1			9		
Milford	391	30	Wight	Abner	4			1		1			1				7		
Milford	391	31	Wheelock	Ebenz			1		2					2			5		
Milford	391	32	Wheelock	Cyrus	1	1		1		2			1				6		
Milford	393	1	Albee	Elijah	2			3		1		1	1	1			9		
Milford	393	2	Albee	Seth			2			1			4	2			9		
Milford	393	3	Albee	Abel	2			1		2		1	1				8		
Milford	393	4	Allen	Seth		1	1	1	1			1		1			6		
Milford	393	5	Atwood	Eldad				1			1			1			3		
Milford	393	6	Albee	Caleb	1			1		3		1					6		
Milford	393	7	Albee	Mary Wd									1	1			2		
Milford	393	8	Albee	Thomas	2	1		1		1			1				6		
Milford	393	9	Andrews	William			2						1				3		
Milford	393	10	Aldrich	Caleb	2	1		1		2	1		1				8		
Milford	393	11	Adams	Enoch Deac				1					1	1			3		
Milford	393	12	Adams	Oliver			2			1	1						4		
Milford	393	13	Bullard	Aaron	1			1		1			1				4		
Milford	393	14	Barber	Hamlet	2	1	2		1	3	2	1	1				13		
Milford	393	15	Ball	Lazarus	1			1				1	1				4		
Milford	393	16	Battle	James				1			1			1			3		
Milford	393	17	Ball	Josiah			2		1	1		1	2	1			8		
Milford	393	18	Hall	Sarah Wd										1			1		
Milford	393	19	Johnson	Joseph	1	1		1					1				5		
Milford	393	20	Jones	Saml Esq				1						2			3		
Milford	393	21	Jones	Ezekiel Lt.	1			1			2	1	1				6		
Milford	393	22	Jones	David	2		1	1		1			1				6		
Milford	393	23	Jones	Ruth Wd.	1	1							4	1	1		8		
Milford	393	24	Kelley	Luke	1		1	1		2	1	1	1				8		
Milford	393	25	Kelley	George	1	1		1	1	3	1		1				9		
Milford	393	26	Kilburne	Josiah				1						1			2		
Milford	393	27	Kilburne	Stephen	1		1	1		1	1	1	1				7		

TOWN	PG#	LN#	LAST NAME	FIRST NAME	M <10	M 10–16	M 16–26	M 26–45	M 45+	F <10	F 10–16	F 16–26	F 26–45	F 45+	TOTAL ALL OTHER	TOTAL SLAVES	TOTALS	DISTRICT/ TOWNSHIP	NOTES
Milford	393	28	Littlefield	Isaac		2			1	1			1	1			6		
Milford	393	29	Legg	Nathl		1			1			2		2			6		
Milford	393	30	Lefure	John	1				2				1				4		
Milford	393	31	Lefure	Simeon	1	1		1		2	2	1	1				9		
Milford	393	32	Madden	Levi	2			2			1	1					6		
Milford	394	1	Madden	Michael			1		1				1				3		
Milford	394	2	McFarland	Ebenz		1		1		1	1			1			5		
Milford	394	3	Madden	David	2	1		1			1	1					6		
Milford	394	4	Nelson	Simeon Lt.	1	1		1			1		1				5		
Milford	394	5	Nelson	Seth Deac			2		1				1	1			5		
Milford	394	6	Nelson	Garshom Capt				1			1			1			3		
Milford	394	7	Nelson	Saml Majr	2	1	1	1			1		2				8		
Milford	394	8	Nelson	Anna Wd										1			1		
Milford	394	9	Nelson	Josiah		1	1		1		1	1	1				6		
Milford	394	10	Nelson	Ezra		1						1					2		
Milford	394	11	Pickering	Ichabod		3		1		1	1			1			7		
Milford	394	12	Parkman	Elias Lt.		3		1		1	1			1			7		
Milford	394	13	Penniman	Saml Jr	1	1	1	1		1			1	1			7		
Milford	394	14	Penniman	Saml				1					1				2		
Milford	394	15	Perry	James		1	1	1			1	1					5		
Milford	394	16	Plumb	Samuel	1			1		1			1				4		
Milford	395	1	Cobb	Lewis	3			1				1					5		
Milford	395	2	Corbett	John	1	2		1		3			1				8		
Milford	395	3	Chapin	Mary Wd										1			1		
Milford	395	4	Carter	Daniel		1		1					2				4		
Milford	395	5	Chapin	Marvel	1		1			2			1				5		
Milford	395	6	Claflin	John		3						2					5		
Milford	395	7	Chapin	John Deac		1		1	1	1			1	1			6		
Milford	395	8	Cornell	Philip		1	1	1	1			1	1				6		
Milford	395	9	Chapin	Joel	1		2			1		1	1				6		
Milford	395	10	Chapin	Stephen		1	1		1				1				4		
Milford	395	11	Chapin	Moses		2		1				1		1			5		
Milford	395	12	Chapin	Nathan Lt	2			1		1	1		1				6		
Milford	395	13	Cheney	Calvin			1			1		1					3		
Milford	395	14	Clark	Lovell	2			1		1		2					6		
Milford	395	15	Daniels	Oliver		2		1				1		1			5		
Milford	395	16	Disper	Edward				1	1	1			1				4		
Milford	395	17	Day	Mordecai				1			1		1				3		
Milford	395	18	Day	Joel		1				1		1					3		
Milford	395	19	Duno	Andrew											6		6		
Milford	395	20	Davis	Phinehas		1		1	1	1		1	1	1			6		
Milford	395	21	Davis	Moses	1			1		2			1				5		
Milford	395	22	Dixen	Marvel											5		5		
Milford	395	23	Eames	Phinehas		1		1		5			1				8		
Milford	395	24	Earl	Elizabeth Wd										1			1		
Milford	395	25	Godfrey	Benjm Capt	1	2	2	1	1	3		3	1	1			15		
Milford	395	26	Green	Moses	4		1	1		1			1				8		
Milford	395	27	Gibbs	Joseph Lt				1					1				2		
Milford	395	28	Gage	David	1			2		3		1					7		
Milford	395	29	Gage	Moses				1			1		1				3		
Milford	395	30	Hayward	David				1					1				2		
Milford	395	31	Hayward	Ephm				1		2			1				4		
Milford	395	32	Highland	Ruth						2			1				3		
Milford	396	1	Hardy	Nathan				1		1	1		1				4		
Milford	396	2	Hayward	Adam	5	1		1		2		2	1	1			13		
Milford	396	3	Hayward	Jonathan	1	1		1		2		1	1				7		
Milford	396	4	Hayward	Hannah Wd	1	1					1	1		1			5		
Milford	396	5	Hayward	Warfield				1			1	1	1				4		
Milford	396	6	Hayward	Joel	1	1	1	1		2			1				7		
Milford	396	7	Hayward	Samuel				1		1			1				3		
Milford	396	8	Holbrook	Calvin	2		1	1	1	2		2		1			10		
Milford	396	9	Holbrook	Ziba	1			1		2	1	1					6		
Milford	396	10	Hayward	Amos			1			1		1					3		
Milford	396	11	Hayward	Margaret Wd										2			2		
Milford	396	12	Hayward	Jacob			1		1	1	2			1			6		
Milford	396	13	Hunt	Pearley		1	1					1					3		
Milford	396	14	Hancock	Joseph	1			1		1	1	1		1			6		
Milford	396	15	Hunting	Joseph Jr	1			1					1				3		
Milford	396	16	Hunting	Joseph				1					1				2		
Milford	396	17	Hunt	Daniel		3	1		1		1		1				7		
Milford	396	18	Hunt	Joseph		1				1		1					3		
Milford	396	19	Bowker	Edmond	1		1	1		1	1	1		1			7		
Milford	396	20	Brown	Peter		1			1			1		1			4		
Milford	396	21	Brigham	Isaac Dr	1	1		2				1	1				6		
Milford	396	22	Bruce	Abijah	1	1	1			2			1				6		
Milford	396	23	Babcock	Stephen			2			1		1					4		
Milford	396	24	Brown	Peter Junr	1			1		1			1				4		
Milford	396	25	Beall	Daniel		1				1		1					3		
Milford	396	26	Beall	Asa	1			1		5			1				8		

TOWN	PG#	LN#	LAST NAME	FIRST NAME	FREE WHITE MALES					FREE WHITE FEMALES					TOTAL ALL OTHER	TOTAL SLAVES	TOTALS	DISTRICT/ TOWNSHIP	NOTES
					under 10	10 to 16	16 to 26	26 to 45	45 and over	under 10	10 to 16	16 to 26	26 to 45	45 and over					
Milford	396	27	Corbett	Ichabod	1	2		1		2	1	1	1				9		
Milford	396	28	Chapin	Ephm Lt.			2		1			1		1			5		
Milford	396	29	Chapin	Levi	1	1		1		2		1	1				7		
Milford	396	30	Cheney	Caleb	2			1					1				4		
Milford	396	31	Cheney	Mary Wd			1					1	1	1			4		
Milford	396	32	Cheney	Charles			1			2		1					4		
Milford	396	33	Cutler	Moses				1						1			2		
Milford	396	34	Chapin	Adam	1	2	2	1		1		1	1				9		
Milford	396	35	Cheney	Wales			1		1			1		1			4		

TOWN	PG#	LN#	LAST NAME	FIRST NAME	FREE WHITE MALES					FREE WHITE FEMALES					TOTAL ALL OTHER	TOTAL SLAVES	TOTALS	DISTRICT/ TOWNSHIP	NOTES
					under 10	10 to 16	16 to 26	26 to 45	45 and over	under 10	10 to 16	16 to 26	26 to 45	45 and over					
New Braintree	308	1	Ayres	Joseph		1			1	1				1			4		
New Braintree	308	2	Adams	John	1	1			1		1	2	1	1			8		
New Braintree	308	3	Ayres	Moses	1	1		1		2	1	1	1				8		
New Braintree	308	4	Anderson	John	5			1				1	2				9		
New Braintree	308	5	Ayrez	Jabez	3			1	1	2			1				8		
New Braintree	308	6	Adams	Jno	2		1	1		2	1		1				8		
New Braintree	308	7	Adams	James	2		2		1	2	2		1				10		
New Braintree	308	8	Bigelow	Abijah	3	1	4	1	1	2	1	2	1				16		
New Braintree	308	9	Bowker	Jerusha	1				1	1				1			4		
New Braintree	308	10	Barr	James		2			1					1			4		
New Braintree	308	11	Bowman	Joseph	2	1			1			1	1	1			7		
New Braintree	308	12	Barr	Joseph	1	1		1	1	1	1	1	1	1			9		
New Braintree	308	13	Barr	Davidson	2			1		2			1				6		
New Braintree	308	14	Barnes	Joseph		1	2					2		1			7		
New Braintree	308	15	Barr	John			1	1				2	1				5		
New Braintree	308	16	Burk	James			1			3			1	1	4		10		
New Braintree	308	17	Barr	George		1	1	1	1	1	2	2	1				11		
New Braintree	308	18	Bowman	Joseph Jr	1	1		1		1	1	1					6		
New Braintree	308	19	Cobb	Perez	2			1		1			1				6		
New Braintree	308	20	Denny	Isaac			1	1		3		1	1				7		
New Braintree	308	21	Dow	Joseph	2	2	1		1			1		1			8		
New Braintree	308	22	Delano	Abisha				1						1			2		
New Braintree	309	1	Delano	Gideon	1	1		2		1	1	1					7		
New Braintree	309	2	Delano	Philip	4			1					1				6		
New Braintree	309	3	Eager	Paul				1		1			1				3		
New Braintree	309	4	Edson	Elijah		2		1	1	1	2		1				8		
New Braintree	309	5	Evens	Robert	1			1				1					3		
New Braintree	309	6	Fay	Stephan		1	1		1	1	1	1					6		
New Braintree	309	7	Frost	Seth	1	1		1		2			1				6		
New Braintree	309	8	Force	Jno Jr	1		2	1		2	1						8		
New Braintree	309	9	Foster	Betsey						1		1	1				3		
New Braintree	309	10	Foster	Nathl	3		1		2	3	3		1	1			14		
New Braintree	309	11	Force	Jno	1			1						1			3		
New Braintree	309	12	Fisk	John	1	2					1	1	1		2		9		
New Braintree	309	13	Gilbert	Josiah			1			1		1					3		
New Braintree	309	14	Gould	Jno			1	1	2		1		1				6		
New Braintree	309	15	Gould	George	2		1	1		3			2				9		
New Braintree	309	16	Glazier	Jotham	1	1			1	2	2	1	1				11		
New Braintree	309	17	Granger	Noah	2	1	1	1		2	1		2	1			11		
New Braintree	309	18	Hunter	John	1		3	1	1	1	1		1				9		
New Braintree	309	19	Hunter	Wm	2	1		2		1	1		1				9		
New Braintree	309	20	Hunter	Isaac		2	2	1		1	2		1				9		
New Braintree	309	21	Hawes	Paul		1	2			1	1		1				6		
New Braintree	310	1	Harrington	Samll	1			2	1	1			2				7		
New Braintree	310	2	Hoyt	Wyman	1	1		1	1		1		1				6		
New Braintree	310	3	Hudson	Edward		1		1	1		2						5		
New Braintree	310	4	Holms	James	1	1	2		1	1	3	1	1	1			12		
New Braintree	310	5	Hall	Elias	1		2	1		2	3	1	3				13		
New Braintree	310	6	Hamilton	Moses			1	2			1		1				5		
New Braintree	310	7	Holms	Wm	1			1		3	1		1				7		
New Braintree	310	8	Hall	Nathan	2			1		2			1				6		
New Braintree	310	9	Hunter	Isaac Jr		1	1	1		1		1	1				6		
New Braintree	310	10	Joslyn	Henry	1			1		2			1				5		
New Braintree	310	11	Joslyn	Benm	1	1		1	1	2		1	1				9		
New Braintree	310	12	Joslyn	Samll			1	1				2	1				5		
New Braintree	310	13	Joslyn	Matthew	1	1		1		2			1				6		
New Braintree	310	14	Kennada	Lemll	2			1		2	1	2	1				9		
New Braintree	310	15	Larned	James	2	1		1		5		1	1				11		
New Braintree	310	16	Little	Benm		2		1				1	2				6		
New Braintree	310	17	Matthews	Elisha	4	1	2	1				2	1	2			13		
New Braintree	310	18	Mixter	Samll		1	1		1		2	1	1				7		
New Braintree	310	19	Newel	Jonas		1	1		1	1		1	1				6		
New Braintree	310	20	Norton	Elijah	3		1		1		1	1					7		
New Braintree	310	21	Norton	Burrows	4			1		2			1				8		
New Braintree	311	1	Nye	Jno	1	1	1		1	3	2	3		1			13		
New Braintree	311	2	Nye	Philip	1	2	1	1	1		3	1	1				11		
New Braintree	311	3	Nichols	Davidson		1	1	1			2	1					6		
New Braintree	311	4	Pope	Asa		1		1		1	1		1				5		
New Braintree	311	5	Pollard	Jno	2			1		3	1		1				8		
New Braintree	311	6	Pepper	Ezra	1	1	2		1	1	1		1				7		
New Braintree	311	7	Pepper	Jacob	4	1		1	1	1	1	1	1				11		
New Braintree	311	8	Penniman	Henry		1	4		2	1	2	1	1				12		
New Braintree	311	9	Robertson	Joseph	2		2		1	1	1	1					8		
New Braintree	311	10	Reed	Micah		1	1	1	1	1	1	2		1			9		
New Braintree	311	11	Richmond	Silvester	2	2	1	2	2	3		2	1				15		
New Braintree	311	12	Reed	Jeremiah	2		2	1	1	1		1	1	1			10		
New Braintree	311	13	Ruggles	Lucy										1			1		
New Braintree	311	14	Richmond	Desire							1		1				2		
New Braintree	311	15	Rixford	Henry	1			1		3			1				6		

TOWN	PG#	LN#	LAST NAME	FIRST NAME	FREE WHITE MALES					FREE WHITE FEMALES					TOTAL ALL OTHER	TOTAL SLAVES	TOTALS	DISTRICT/ TOWNSHIP	NOTES
					under 10	10 to 16	16 to 26	26 to 45	45 and over	under 10	10 to 16	16 to 26	26 to 45	45 and over					
New Braintree	311	16	Severance	Benm			1	1		2	1	1		1			7		
New Braintree	311	17	Stone	Silas	3			1		1			1	1			7		
New Braintree	311	18	Shaw	Joseph		1			1				1				3		
New Braintree	311	19	Swetzer	John	2			1		4			1				8		
New Braintree	311	20	Sargant	Nathan		2	1		1	1		2		1			8		
New Braintree	312	1	Field	Ebenz	1	1	2	1	1	2		2	1	1			12		
New Braintree	312	2	Field	Benm		1	1		1			2		1			6		
New Braintree	312	3	Thompson	John					1			1	1	1			4		
New Braintree	312	4	Thrasher	Stephan	2			2	1		1	3		1			10		
New Braintree	312	5	Thompson	Nathan	1	1	1		1	1	1	2	1				9		
New Braintree	312	6	Tufts	John			1	1									2		
New Braintree	312	7	Thrasher	Wm			1		1			2		1			5		
New Braintree	312	8	Thrasher	Samll	1	2			1	3		1					8		
New Braintree	312	9	Thompson	John	2	1			1	2	1		1				8		
New Braintree	312	10	Trow	Israel				1	1				1	1			4		
New Braintree	312	11	Tidd	Wm	1				1	3	1	1	1				8		
New Braintree	312	12	Tufts	Wm	1				1			2		1			5		
New Braintree	312	13	Thompson	Hugh	2				1	3			1				7		
New Braintree	312	14	Wetherill	Jno	1		2	2					1				6		
New Braintree	312	15	Whipple	Francis		1	1		1			1		1			5		
New Braintree	312	16	Whipple	Thos					1					1			2		
New Braintree	312	17	Wilson	James	1				1	1	1		1	1			6		
New Braintree	312	18	Wilson	Robert			1		1					1			3		
New Braintree	312	19	Woods	James	3	1	1		1	1		2	1	1			11		
New Braintree	312	20	Woods	Jno	3			1	1	1	2	1	1	1			11		
New Braintree	312	21	White	Jonah	1		1	1				1					4		
New Braintree	313	1	Ware	Pelatiah			1	1						1			3		
New Braintree	313	2	Wilder	Ephraim	1				1	1		1					4		
New Braintree	313	3	Woods	George	2		1	1	1			1		1			7		
New Braintree	313	4	Warren	Warham	1		2	1				1		1			6		
New Braintree	313	5	Weston	Joshua	3			1		1		1	1				7		
New Braintree	313	6	Woods	Daniel	1	1		1	1	2	1	1	1	2			11		
New Braintree	313	7	Wait	David		1	1	1	1		2	2		1			9		
New Braintree	313	8	Wetherill	Mehitable		1		1						1			3		
New Braintree	313	9	Weston	Paul	2	2			1		1		1				7		
New Braintree	313	10	Warner	Meriba	2	1						1		1			2		
New Braintree	313	11	Woods	Asa	1	1		1	1	2	1	1	1	2			11		
New Braintree	313	12	Wilcox	David	1		1	1	1			1	1	1			7		
New Braintree	313	13	Warren	Elisha	4		4	1			1	3	2				15		
New Braintree	313	14	Thompson	Wm	1	1	1				1	1					5		
New Braintree	313	15	Hooper	Isaac				1				1					2		
New Braintree	313	16	Warner	Phinehas		2	1	1		2		1	1				8		
New Braintree	313	17	Wait	Wm		1		1	1	1			1				5		
New Braintree	313	18	Wilcox	Stephan				1		1			1				3		

TOWN	PG#	LN#	HEADS OF HOUSEHOLD		FREE WHITE MALES					FREE WHITE FEMALES					TOTAL ALL OTHER	TOTAL SLAVES	TOTALS	DISTRICT/ TOWNSHIP	NOTES
			LAST NAME	FIRST NAME	under 10	10 to 16	16 to 26	26 to 45	45 and over	under 10	10 to 16	16 to 26	26 to 45	45 and over					
Northborough	361	1	Newton	Martin	1			1		3			1	1			7		
Northborough	361	2	Newton	Moses		1			1	2	1		1				6		
Northborough	361	3	Parker	Abigail							1		1				2		
Northborough	361	4	Parker	Jabez M.			1			1			1				3		
Northborough	361	5	Parminter	Joel		1		1		3	1		1				7		
Northborough	361	6	Parminter	Asa	2			1		1	1		1				6		
Northborough	361	7	Patterson	James				1		1		1					3		
Northborough	361	8	Pond	Adam	2	1		1	1	1			1	1			9		
Northborough	361	9	Rice	Seth		1			1			1	1	1			5		
Northborough	361	10	Rice	William	1	1	2					1	1				6		
Northborough	361	11	Rice	Ezekiel		1		1		2			1				5		
Northborough	361	12	Rice	Amos	1		2		1		1	1	1	1			8		
Northborough	361	13	Rice	Baxter		1		1		2			1				5		
Northborough	361	14	Rice	Joseph	2	3		1		2	1	1	1				11		
Northborough	361	15	Rice	Asaph	2	2	1	1					1				7		
Northborough	362	1	Rice	Nathan	3				1	1	1		1				7		
Northborough	362	2	Rice	Samuel	2	2		1		1	1		1				8		
Northborough	362	3	Southick	Nathl					1	2	1	1		1			6		
Northborough	362	4	Segar	Caleb					1		2			2			5		
Northborough	362	5	Sever	Joseph	2			1						1			4		
Northborough	362	6	Stephens	Jacob				1			1		1				3		
Northborough	362	7	Sawyer	William			1			1	1	1			1		5		
Northborough	362	8	Sibley	Stephen	1	1	2	1		2	1	1					10		
Northborough	362	9	Stratten	Windsor	1			1		1			1				4		
Northborough	362	10	Tenny	Gideon	2	1		1		2	1		1				8		
Northborough	362	11	Temple	Henry	2			1		2			1				6		
Northborough	362	12	Underwood	Timothy			1	1		5			2				9		
Northborough	362	13	Wood	Abraham	2	1		1	1	3	1	2		1			12		
Northborough	362	14	Wood	Samuel					1					1			2		
Northborough	363	1	White	John			1	1				1					3		
Northborough	363	2	Warren	Elipatet		1	2		1		1	1		1			7		
Northborough	363	3	Wyman	John		1	1		1	1	1	1		1			7		
Northborough	363	4	Williams	Stephen		2	2	2		1	1	1	2				11		
Northborough	363	5	Whitney	Peter Revd		1					1		3	1			6		
Northborough	363	6	Wheelock	Eliab	1	1		1		1		1	1				6		
Northborough	363	7	Wheeler	Obadiah	2	2	1		1	1	1	2		1			11		
Northborough	363	8	Whitney	Tho. L.			1	1		1			1				5		
Northborough	363	9	Wright	James			1	1	1		1		1				5		
Northborough	365	1	Fay	Abigail						2	1	1					4		
Northborough	365	2	Green	Nathan		2	3		1			2		1			9		
Northborough	365	3	Goodenow	Asa				1						2			3		
Northborough	365	4	Gasset	Henry	1		1		1			2		1			6		
Northborough	365	5	Goddard	Solomon				1						1			2		
Northborough	365	6	Garfield	Mary								1		1			2		
Northborough	365	7	Gasset	Winslow	1			1					1				3		
Northborough	365	8	Harrington	Caleb	2	2	1		1				1	1			8		
Northborough	365	9	Hunt	John	1			1					1				3		
Northborough	365	10	Hunt	Jeremiah		1		1		1	2		1				6		
Northborough	365	11	Henderson	Nathan	1			1		1			1				4		
Northborough	365	12	Henderson	William			1	1					1				3		
Northborough	365	13	Holbrook	Daniel	4	1		1		1			1				8		
Northborough	365	14	How	Isaac	1	1	2		1	4	1	1	1				12		
Northborough	366	1	How	Benjamin	1			1					1				3		
Northborough	366	2	Keyes	James	1	2	1		1	2		1	1	1			10		
Northborough	366	3	Keyes	Silas	2	1		1		3		1	1				9		
Northborough	366	4	Keyes	Tho.	3	1			2		1	1	1	1			10		
Northborough	366	5	Munroe	Abraham	1	1	1	3	1		1	4		1			13		
Northborough	366	6	Maynard	David					1		1			1			3		
Northborough	366	7	Maynard	Nathan		2	1			1		1	2	1			8		
Northborough	366	8	Morse	Samuel			2		1			1		1			5		
Northborough	366	9	Miller	Caleb	1			1		1		1	1				5		
Northborough	366	10	Mahan	David	4			1				1		1			7		
Northborough	366	11	Munroe	Oliver	1	1						1	1				5		
Northborough	366	12	Maynard	Reuben				1		4				1			6		
Northborough	366	13	Maynard	Taylor			1			2		1		1			5		
Northborough	366	14	Norcross	Moses			2						1				3		
Northborough	366	15	Newton	Nahum	2			1		1			1	1			6		
Northborough	367	1	Bailey	Silas	2	2	2	1		1	1	1	1				11		
Northborough	367	2	Badcock	Jonas			1		1	1			1	1			5		
Northborough	367	3	Bartlett	Antiphas		1	2		1	1		1	1	2			9		
Northborough	367	4	Ball	Stephen			1	2				1	1				5		
Northborough	367	5	Bartlett	Jonas	1	1		1		2			1				6		
Northborough	367	6	Badcock	Reuben	1	2	1		1	4	1		1				11		
Northborough	367	7	Badcock	William				1					1				2		
Northborough	367	8	Ball	Jonas	1		2		1		1	1	1				7		
Northborough	367	9	Brigham	Henry	1			1			1		1				4		
Northborough	367	10	Bartlett	Gill	1			1					1	1			4		
Northborough	367	11	Barnard	Ephraim		1			1		1	2		1			6		
Northborough	367	12	Con	Polly									1				1		

88

TOWN	PG#	LN#	LAST NAME	FIRST NAME	under 10	10 to 16	16 to 26	26 to 45	45 and over	under 10	10 to 16	16 to 26	26 to 45	45 and over	TOTAL ALL OTHER	TOTAL SLAVES	TOTALS	DISTRICT/ TOWNSHIP	NOTES
					FREE WHITE MALES					FREE WHITE FEMALES									
Northborough	367	13	Corruth	Joseph				2			1		1				4		
Northborough	367	14	Corruth	John					1					1			2		
Northborough	367	15	Crawford	John	1		1	2		2	1	1	1				9		
Northborough	368	1	Davis	Isaac		1	2		1	1	1	3		1			10		
Northborough	368	2	Davis	Joseph	1		2	1				1					5		
Northborough	368	3	Davis	Phinehas	2		2	1		1	1		1				8		
Northborough	368	4	Delane	Partrick				1		2			1				4		
Northborough	368	5	Dalrymple	Samuel	1	1		1		3			1				7		
Northborough	368	6	Eager	Francis			1		1		1	1		2			6		
Northborough	368	7	Eager	Oliver	1	1	1	1		1	1		1				7		
Northborough	368	8	Eager	William	1		1	1		1			1				5		
Northborough	368	9	Eager	Ephron	3		1					1					5		
Northborough	368	10	Fay	Adam			3		1					2			6		
Northborough	368	11	Fay	Timothy	2		1	1	1			1		1			7		
Northborough	368	12	Fay	Thaddeus	1		2	1	1		1		2	1			9		
Northborough	368	13	Fay	Asa	2			1			1		1	1			6		
Northborough	368	14	Fay	David				1						1			2		
Northborough	368	15	Fay	Nahum Esq		1	1	1		1		1	1				6		
Northborough	370	1	Allen	Samuel	2	1	2	1		1		2	1	2			12		
Northborough	370	2	Brigham	Antiphas	1		1	1		2	2	1	1				9		
Northborough	370	3	Brigham	Artemas		1	1		1			2		1			6		
Northborough	370	4	Bruce	Jonathan					1			1	1	1			4		
Northborough	370	5	Bruce	Silas		1		2		2			1				6		
Northborough	370	6	Brigham	Winslow	2	2	1	1		3	2		1	1			13		
Northborough	370	7	Bartlett	Jotham	3		1	1		2		1	1				9		
Northborough	370	8	Bartlett	Jonathan		1		1		3		1	1	1			8		
Northborough	370	9	Brigham	Gardner		1	1	1				1	1				5		
Northborough	370	10	Brigham	Moses	1			1		1	1		2				6		
Northborough	370	11	Ball	John	1	1	2		1			2		1			8		
Northborough	370	12	Ball	Nathan	3		1	1		2		1	1	1			10		
Northborough	370	13	Booker	Josiah				1	1			1		2			5		
Northborough	370	14	Brooks	Jacob	1		1			3		1					6		
Northborough	370	15	Brigham	Jonah		1			1			1		1			4		

TOWN	PG#	LN#	LAST NAME	FIRST NAME	FREE WHITE MALES under 10	10 to 16	16 to 26	26 to 45	45 and over	FREE WHITE FEMALES under 10	10 to 16	16 to 26	26 to 45	45 and over	TOTAL ALL OTHER	TOTAL SLAVES	TOTALS	DISTRICT/ TOWNSHIP	NOTES
Northbridge	473	1	Hill	Jacob			2	1	1			1	2	1			8		
Northbridge	473	2	Hill	Joseph				1					1	1			3		
Northbridge	473	3	Hayward	Amasa	1			1		1			1				4		
Northbridge	473	4	Morse	James				1			1	1	1				4		
Northbridge	473	5	Morse	Henry	2	1		1		1	1		1				7		
Northbridge	473	6	Mcnamara	Hugh	2	2		1		3	1		1	1			11		
Northbridge	473	7	Moffit	Jeremiah			2	1		2			1				6		
Northbridge	473	8	Persons	George			1	1		5			1				8		
Northbridge	473	9	Preston	Amariah		1	1		1			1	2		1		7		
Northbridge	473	10	Parks	Nathan					1				2				3		
Northbridge	473	11	Parks	Nathan Jun	2			1		1			1				5		
Northbridge	473	12	Read	Mary			3						2	1	1		7		
Northbridge	473	13	Slocum	Joshua	3	2		1		1	1		1				9		
Northbridge	473	14	Smith	Jacob	1			1		1			1				4		
Northbridge	473	15	Spring	Adolphus	2		3	2		2	1	1	1	2	1		15		
Northbridge	474	1	Southwick	Jacob		3	1		1	4	1	2		1			13		
Northbridge	474	2	Taft	Israel	1	1		1		3	1	1	2				10		
Northbridge	474	3	Taft	Keith			1	1		1			1	1			5		
Northbridge	474	4	Taft	Marvel	3		3	1		1		1	1	1			11		
Northbridge	474	5	Vilas	Samuel		1		1		1			1				4		
Northbridge	474	6	Williams	Chester		2		2		1			1				6		
Northbridge	474	7	Whiten	Paul	1		2	1					1				5		
Northbridge	474	8	Winter	John	3	1			1	1			1				7		
Northbridge	474	9	Winter	David		1		1		2	2	1	1				8		
Northbridge	474	10	Winter	William			2	1		1			1				5		
Northbridge	474	11	Wing	Jabez	1			1		2			1				5		
Northbridge	474	12	White	Joel		1		1		2	1			1			6		
Northbridge	474	13	White	Jesse	2		3	1		1				1			10		
Northbridge	474	14	White	Abisha			1										2		
Northbridge	474	15	Young	Levi	1	1	2		1	4	1	1		1			12		
Northbridge	475	1	Bullard	Artemus		1		1		1			1				4		
Northbridge	475	2	Batchellor	David		1		1						1			3		
Northbridge	475	3	Batchellor	Joel	1			1		2			1				5		
Northbridge	475	4	Bowen	Thomas		1	1	1		1	1		1				6		
Northbridge	475	5	Bennet	Robert			1	1					1	1			4		
Northbridge	475	6	Benson	Benjamin	1	1	1	1		1	1	3		1			10		
Northbridge	475	7	Batchellor	Simeon	1			1		2			1				5		
Northbridge	475	8	Bassett	Simeon	2		2			3			1				8		
Northbridge	475	9	Bassett	Benjamin				1				2		1			4		
Northbridge	475	10	Bardeen	Samuel				1				3		1			5		
Northbridge	475	11	Briant	Asa	5	1		1					1				8		
Northbridge	475	12	Croney	John		1		1		1		1		1			5		
Northbridge	475	13	Cooper	Nathll		2	2	1	1				1	1			8		
Northbridge	475	14	Congdon	Joshua	4			1					1				6		
Northbridge	475	15	Combs	Reuben	2			1					1				4		
Northbridge	475	16	Chapin	Henry	3		4	1					1				9		
Northbridge	475	17	Crane	John	2	2	4	1				2	1				12		
Northbridge	476	1	Cooper	John		2		1	1	1			1				8		
Northbridge	476	2	Dunn	Henry		2		1	1	1			1				8		
Northbridge	476	3	Ellison	Thomas	1				1	2	1	1	1				7		
Northbridge	476	4	Eddy	Jesse	1		1	1	1	2			1	1			8		
Northbridge	476	5	Ellison	Eliab	1		1						1				3		
Northbridge	476	6	Fletcher	James	2		3	1		1	2	1	1				11		
Northbridge	476	7	Fowler	Jonathan			1			1			1				3		
Northbridge	476	8	Fowler	John		1		1		3		1					6		
Northbridge	476	9	Fowler	Barnard	2			1		2			1				6		
Northbridge	476	10	Fowler	Samuel		1		1		1			3	1			7		
Northbridge	476	11	Flagg	Eleazer	2			1		2			1				6		
Northbridge	476	12	Farrow	Benjamin	2		1	1		1			1				6		
Northbridge	476	13	Goldthwait	Stephen			2	1		1				1			5		
Northbridge	476	14	Goldthwait	Jacob	1		1		1	2			1				6		
Northbridge	476	15	Goldthwait	Thomas	2	1		1		1			1	1			7		
Northbridge	476	16	Glasco	Jacob											4		4		
Northbridge	476	17	Hayward	Elisha		1		1		1				1			4		
Northbridge	478	1	Adams	Francis	1			1		1		2	1				6		
Northbridge	478	2	Adams	John	1	1	1	1		1	1		1				7		
Northbridge	478	3	Adams	Nehemiah	1	1	1	1		3	1	1	1				10		
Northbridge	478	4	Adams	Oliver	1			1		1			1				4		
Northbridge	478	5	Adams	Nathll			1	1		3		2	1				8		
Northbridge	478	6	Adams	Aaron	3	1	1	1		1		1	1				9		
Northbridge	478	7	Aldrich	John	1	1		1		2			1				6		
Northbridge	478	8	Aldrich	Samuel Jun	1	1		1		2	1		1				7		
Northbridge	478	9	Aldrich	Lyman	1		1	1	1	4			3	1			12		
Northbridge	478	10	Aldrich	David	2	1	1	1		1	1		1				8		
Northbridge	478	11	Aldrich	Jesse			2				1	1	1				6		
Northbridge	478	12	Aldrich	Paul	2	1		1		2	2	1	1				10		
Northbridge	478	13	Adams	Andrew	3		1	1		1		1	1				8		
Northbridge	478	14	Aldrich	Alexander	2			1	1	1			1	1			7		
Northbridge	478	15	Aldrich	Barnebus	2						1						4		

| TOWN | PG# | LN# | HEADS OF HOUSEHOLD | | FREE WHITE MALES | | | | | FREE WHITE FEMALES | | | | | TOTAL ALL OTHER | TOTAL SLAVES | TOTALS | DISTRICT/ TOWNSHIP | NOTES |
			LAST NAME	FIRST NAME	under 10	10 to 16	16 to 26	26 to 45	45 and over	under 10	10 to 16	16 to 26	26 to 45	45 and over					
Northbridge	478	16	Adams	Clark	2		1					1					4		
Northbridge	478	17	Aldrich	Ahaz	1		2			2		1	1				7		

TOWN	PG#	LN#	LAST NAME	FIRST NAME	FREE WHITE MALES					FREE WHITE FEMALES					TOTAL ALL OTHER	TOTAL SLAVES	TOTALS	DISTRICT/ TOWNSHIP	NOTES
					under 10	10 to 16	16 to 26	26 to 45	45 and over	under 10	10 to 16	16 to 26	26 to 45	45 and over					
Oakham	315	1	Adams	Jacob					1			1		1			3		
Oakham	315	2	Allen	Abia		1	2					1		1			5		
Oakham	315	3	Allen	Jesse	1		1	1	1	2	2	1		1			10		
Oakham	315	4	Adams	Hannah						2	1		1				4		
Oakham	315	5	Bullard	Silas	2	1	2		1	1	1	1		1			10		
Oakham	315	6	Bullard	Jno	4	1	1	1		2		1					10		
Oakham	315	7	Burbank	John	1		1	1	1	1				1			6		
Oakham	315	8	Boid	John	2	1		1	1	2	1		1	1			10		
Oakham	315	9	Boid	James	1	1	1	1		2	1	1					9		
Oakham	315	10	Blake	George		1		1		1				1			4		
Oakham	315	11	Botherill	John	1	1		1				1	1	1			6		
Oakham	315	12	Blair	James	1	2	1	1				1		1			7		
Oakham	315	13	Blake	Sarah		1		2			1		2	1			7		
Oakham	315	14	Bullard	Phinehas	3			1				2	1				7		
Oakham	315	15	Bell	James				1	4					1			6		
Oakham	315	16	Butler	John	2		1		1	1	2			1			8		
Oakham	315	17	Brimhall	Saml	3	1	1	1		1	1	1	3				12		
Oakham	315	18	Brown	James				1	1				2	1			5		
Oakham	317	1	Dunbar	Benson	1			1		2	1	1	1	1			9		
Oakham	317	2	Dean	Isaiah	1			1		1		1					4		
Oakham	317	3	Edson	Calvin		1				1			1				3		
Oakham	317	4	Esterbrook	Joel	3			1					1				5		
Oakham	317	5	Fitts	Peter	3		1		1	1	1	1		3			11		
Oakham	317	6	Field	Spencer			6	1		1	1	3	1				13		
Oakham	317	7	Foster	Ebenzr	1			1	1	1	1		1				6		
Oakham	317	8	Fobes	Jno		1		1		1			1				4		
Oakham	317	9	French	John	1		1	1				3	1	1			8		
Oakham	317	10	Flint	John	1	1	1	1		1	1			1			7		
Oakham	317	11	Freeman	Elijah			1					1					2		
Oakham	317	12	French	Asa		1	1	1				1	1	1			7		
Oakham	317	13	Stone	Daniel	3	1			1			1	1				7		
Oakham	317	14	Foster	Samll	1		1			1		1					4		
Oakham	317	15	Fobes	Joseph	1		1	1		2			1	1			7		
Oakham	317	16	Forbs	Elenor	2		1			2			1				6		
Oakham	317	17	Gault	Matthew	3		1		1			1		1			7		
Oakham	317	18	Howe	Artemas		2	3		1	1	2	1	1				11		
Oakham	318	1	Boulton	Nathl		1			1			1		1			4		
Oakham	318	2	Bullard	Vonentine	2			1		3	1		1				8		
Oakham	318	3	Bullard	Moses		1	1	1		1			2	1			7		
Oakham	318	4	Barnard	David	2	1	2	1				1					7		
Oakham	318	5	Chadwick	Bowman	2		1	1		1	1		1				7		
Oakham	318	6	Conant	Oliver	1		1			1		1					4		
Oakham	318	7	Crafford	Calvin	3			1					1				5		
Oakham	318	8	Crafford	John		1			1	4	2		1				9		
Oakham	318	9	Crafford	Alexander			1			3	1		1				6		
Oakham	318	10	Conant	Thos	5			1					1				7		
Oakham	318	11	Conant	Luther		2		1		3	1		1				8		
Oakham	318	12	Crafford	Wm	1	1	2		1	1	1	2		1			10		
Oakham	318	13	Chadwick	Joseph		1		1		1				1			4		
Oakham	318	14	Caldwell	Wm				1		2	1		1				5		
Oakham	318	15	Conant	James	2	1	1	1		3	1	1	1				11		
Oakham	318	16	Dean	James	1	2			1	1				1			6		
Oakham	318	17	Dean	Samll	1	1		1		1			1				5		
Oakham	318	18	Dean	Zebulon				1	1				1				3		
Oakham	318	19	Davis	Samll			1		1	2	2		1				7		
Oakham	319	1	Hall	Percivil	1			2		2			1	1			7		
Oakham	319	2	Haskell	George			1			2		1					4		
Oakham	319	3	Hammond	Elijah		1			1	2	1		1	1			7		
Oakham	319	4	Haskell	Roger		1	1							1			4		
Oakham	319	5	Hale	Dolly									1	2			3		
Oakham	319	6	Kelly	Richard		2		1			2		1		1		7		
Oakham	319	7	Lincoln	Stephan	3		2	1		2	1	2		1			12		
Oakham	319	8	Leonard	Ezra	1			1				4		1			8		
Oakham	319	9	Lee	Philip			1			2			1				4		
Oakham	319	10	Long	John		1		1				1		1			4		
Oakham	319	11	Leonard	Andrew			1							1			2		
Oakham	319	12	McFarland	Reuben	4	2		1		1	1	1					10		
Oakham	319	13	Macumber	John	1	1		1		3		1					7		
Oakham	319	14	Marsh	Elias	2	2	1	1				2	1				9		
Oakham	319	15	Maynard	Amasa	2			1		2		1	2	1			9		
Oakham	319	16	Mullet	Abm	2			1		2			1				6		
Oakham	319	17	Nye	Crocker		1		2			1	1		1			6		
Oakham	319	18	Nye	Timothy				1		4		1					6		
Oakham	320	1	Parmenter	Wm			1		1	3	1		1				7		
Oakham	320	2	Packard	Nehemh	1	1		1		1	1	2	1				8		
Oakham	320	3	Presho	Isaac	2			1					1				4		
Oakham	320	4	Packard	Ichabod				1					1	1			3		
Oakham	320	5	Packard	Caleb	1			1			1	1					4		
Oakham	320	6	Patridge	Edward	1	1	1		1			1		1			6		

TOWN	PG#	LN#	HEADS OF HOUSEHOLD		FREE WHITE MALES					FREE WHITE FEMALES					TOTAL ALL OTHER	TOTAL SLAVES	TOTALS	DISTRICT/ TOWNSHIP	NOTES
			LAST NAME	FIRST NAME	under 10	10 to 16	16 to 26	26 to 45	45 and over	under 10	10 to 16	16 to 26	26 to 45	45 and over					
Oakham	320	7	Presho	James	1	1		1			1	1	1				6		
Oakham	320	8	Parmenter	Rufus	1		1		1		2			1			6		
Oakham	320	9	Patridge	Silas			1		1		1			1			4		
Oakham	320	10	Piper	James	1	1		1		1	1		1				6		
Oakham	320	11	Parmenter	Daniel	1	1	1	1	1		1	1	1	1			9		
Oakham	320	12	Packard	James		1	2			1	1	1					6		
Oakham	320	13	Powers	John	2	1			1	1	1	1	1				8		
Oakham	320	14	Reed	Silas	3	3		1		2			1				10		
Oakham	320	15	Richardson	George		1		1		3	2		1				8		
Oakham	320	16	Robinson	John	1	1	2		1	4	1	1	1				12		
Oakham	320	17	Ripley	Zenas	1	1		1		1			1				5		
Oakham	320	18	Ripley	Jepthah	2	1	1	1		1		3	2	1			12		
Oakham	321	1	Ruggles	Thos	2		1		1	1	3	2	1				11		
Oakham	321	2	Redding	Zachh	3	1			1	1			1				7		
Oakham	321	3	Rich	Reed	1			1				1					3		
Oakham	321	4	Stone	Alpheus	1	1	1	2	1		2	3	2	1			14		
Oakham	321	5	Spooner	Eleazer	3	1	2	1	1	2		1	1	1			13		
Oakham	321	6	Spooner	Benn			1	1			1	1		1			5		
Oakham	321	7	Stone	Frederick	3	2		1			1			1			8		
Oakham	321	8	Stone	Isaac	1	1			1	1	1	1					6		
Oakham	321	9	Spooner	Moses		1		1					1				3		
Oakham	321	10	Starbuck	Uriah	1	2		1		2			2				8		
Oakham	321	11	Tomlinson	Daniel	1	1		2		1		1	1				7		
Oakham	321	12	Wilson	Robert	4		1	1		2	1	2	1				12		
Oakham	321	13	Wilcot	Oliver		2		1	1		1	1	1				7		
Oakham	321	14	Ware	Archabald	4			1		1	1		1				8		
Oakham	321	15	Whitaker	Wm	1		1		1	2	1	1					7		
Oakham	321	16	Wilson	Samll		1		1				2	1				5		
Oakham	321	17	Willis	Azariah	2			1		1	1	1	1				7		
Oakham	321	18	Weaks	Nathl	1		1		1				1				4		
Oakham	322	1	Whitmore	Ebenzr	1			1		2	1		1				6		
Oakham	322	2	Witt	Stephan	3				1	1			1				6		
Oakham	322	3	Woodis	Dorothy		1	1						1				3		
Oakham	322	4	Wilton	Simon		1		1			1		1				4		
Oakham	322	5	Woodis	Edward	1	1		1	1		1		1	1			7		
Oakham	322	6	Woodis	Ebenzr	2			1		1			1				5		
Oakham	322	7	Waterman	Perez			1		1		1		3	1			7		
Oakham	322	8	Witt	Benm	2				1	2		1					6		
Oakham	322	9	Waterman	Calvin				1		3		1	1				6		
Oakham	322	10	Woodis	Reuben	1			1			1		1				4		

TOWN	PG#	LN#	LAST NAME	FIRST NAME	FREE WHITE MALES under 10	10 to 16	16 to 26	26 to 45	45 and over	FREE WHITE FEMALES under 10	10 to 16	16 to 26	26 to 45	45 and over	TOTAL ALL OTHER	TOTAL SLAVES	TOTALS	DISTRICT/ TOWNSHIP	NOTES
Oxford	153	1	Seary	Joseph				1		3			1				5		
Oxford	153	2	Sibley	Jonathan		1		1		1		1	1				5		
Oxford	153	3	Stone	Luther	1		3	2		1	1	1		1			10		
Oxford	153	4	Shumway	Ebenz	1	1			1		1			1			5		
Oxford	153	5	Stone	Ambrose			1		2			2		1			6		
Oxford	153	6	Sparhawk	Timo	1	1			1	1	1	1	1				7		
Oxford	153	7	Sparhawk	Joseph		1			1			1	1	1			5		
Oxford	153	8	Shumway	David	2			1		1			1				5		
Oxford	153	9	Stone	David	1		2		1	1		1	1				7		
Oxford	153	10	Shumway	John				1					1				2		
Oxford	153	11	Shumway	Jonah	4			1		2			1				8		
Oxford	153	12	Sparhawk	Ezra				1		1		1					3		
Oxford	153	13	Sibley	Aaron			1		1	2			1				5		
Oxford	153	14	Stone	Samuel	2	1			1	1	1			1			7		
Oxford	153	15	Turner	Joshua			1		1			3		1			6		
Oxford	153	16	Trumbull	James	2			1		2	1		1				7		
Oxford	153	17	Town	Silvanus	1	1			1		1		1				5		
Oxford	153	18	Town	Moses					2					3			5		
Oxford	153	19	Trumbull	Ebenz	3			1		3				1			8		
Oxford	153	20	Wakefield	Aaron	2		1		1		2	1		1			8		
Oxford	154	1	Wakefield	Beza			1			1		1					3		
Oxford	154	2	Wakefield	Timo	5			1						1			7		
Oxford	154	3	Wolcott	Naomi Wd				1						2			3		
Oxford	154	4	Walker	Solomon		1	1	1					1				4		
Oxford	154	5	Whitmore	Nathl	1		2	1		1	1	1	1				8		
Oxford	154	6	Williams	James		1	1	1					1	1			5		
Oxford	154	7	Work	Jacob	1	1		1		1				1			5		
Oxford	154	8	Wolcott	Joshua			1	1					1				3		
Oxford	154	9	Woodward	Amos	1			1		1			1				4		
Oxford	154	10	Woodward	Caleb			1	1						1			3		
Oxford	154	11	Moshier	Samuel	1			1		1		1	1				5		
Oxford	154	12	Radford	John	3					1	1		1				6		
Oxford	154	13	Taylor	Eliphalet				1					1				2		
Oxford	154	14	Knight	Elisha				1					1				2		
Oxford	154	15	Lincoln	Collin	1			1					1				3		
Oxford	155	1	Meriam	John	2		1	1		2		1					7		
Oxford	155	2	Meriam	Ebenz	5	1	1	1					1				9		
Oxford	155	3	Meriam	Joel			2										2		
Oxford	155	4	Marsh	Joshua	3			1		2	2		1				9		
Oxford	155	5	Nichols	John		1		1						1			3		
Oxford	155	6	Nichols	John Junr	1			1	1	1			1	1			5		
Oxford	155	7	Nichols	David			1	2		3			1				7		
Oxford	155	8	Nichols	Daniel	1			1		1			1	1			5		
Oxford	155	9	Putnam	Calvin				1				1					2		
Oxford	155	10	Prince	Stephen					1			1	1				3		
Oxford	155	11	Prince	Stephen Junr	1		2						1				4		
Oxford	155	12	Pratt	Joseph		1	1	1	1				1	1			6		
Oxford	155	13	Pray	Jonathan	2			1		2			1	1			7		
Oxford	155	14	Prince	Jonathan	3			1		2			1				7		
Oxford	155	15	Prince	David	1		1	1				1					4		
Oxford	155	16	Pratt	Elias		1		1	1		1			1			5		
Oxford	155	17	Pratt	Elijah	1	1	1	1				1	1				6		
Oxford	155	18	Pratt	Nahum			1			2			1				4		
Oxford	155	19	Pratt	Jonathan				1			1	2	1				5		
Oxford	156	1	Pratt	John	1		2	1	1	1	2			2			10		
Oxford	156	2	Parker	Aaron				1			1		1				3		
Oxford	156	3	Parker	Thomas	2	1			1	1			1				6		
Oxford	156	4	Pratt	Benja		1		1		2			1				5		
Oxford	156	5	Pray	Ebenz	2			1		1	1			1			6		
Oxford	156	6	Phipps	Abigail Wd										1			1		
Oxford	156	7	Rawson	Joseph			1		1			2		1			5		
Oxford	156	8	Rawson	Daniel		2		1		4	1	1	1				10		
Oxford	156	9	Russell	Ephraim	1		1		1	1		1		1			6		
Oxford	156	10	Rockwood	Joseph	2			1		2	2		1				8		
Oxford	156	11	Rich	Elijah	1	1		1		2			1				6		
Oxford	156	12	Reading	Ebenz	2			1		1							4		
Oxford	156	13	Russell	Thomas	1	1			1	2	1		1				7		
Oxford	156	14	Riaford	Elijah	2		1	1		1		1					6		
Oxford	156	15	Sigourney	Andrew	2	1		2		4		1	1	1			12		
Oxford	156	16	Shumway	Peter	1		1	1		1	2			1			7		
Oxford	156	17	Stockwell	Joshua	1			1					1				3		
Oxford	156	18	Sibley	Gideon			3	1				1		1			6		
Oxford	156	19	Shumway	Jacon Junr	2	2		1		1	1	1					8		
Oxford	156	20	Shumway	Amos				1									1		
Oxford	156	21	Shumway	Amos Junr	2		1			3	1		1				9		
Oxford	156	22	Shumway	Noah			1						1				2		
Oxford	156	23	Spaulding	Peter			1			2		1	1				5		
Oxford	157	1	Kingsbury	Jer				1					1				2		
Oxford	157	2	Kingsbury	Jer Junr	2	1		1		1			1				6		

TOWN	PG#	LN#	LAST NAME	FIRST NAME	under 10	10 to 16	16 to 26	26 to 45	45 and over	under 10	10 to 16	16 to 26	26 to 45	45 and over	TOTAL ALL OTHER	TOTAL SLAVES	TOTALS	DISTRICT/ TOWNSHIP	NOTES
Oxford	157	3	Kingsbury	Josiah	1			1		1			1				4		
Oxford	157	4	Kingsbury	Amasa					1	1			1				3		
Oxford	157	5	Kingsbury	Danl		1	2	1		4	1		1				10		
Oxford	157	6	Kingsbury	Simeon			1						1				2		
Oxford	157	7	Kingsbury	Jacob	1		1		1	1		1	1	2			8		
Oxford	157	8	Kingsbury	Ephm			1			1		1					3		
Oxford	157	9	Kingsbury	Saml	1		1			2			1				5		
Oxford	157	10	Kingsbury	Joseph			1							1			2		
Oxford	157	11	Kidder	Jonathan		1	1		1				2	3			8		
Oxford	157	12	Kidder	Jesse				1					1				2		
Oxford	157	13	Learned	Asa		1	1		1					1			4		
Oxford	157	14	Learned	Elijah			1	1	1	1				1			5		
Oxford	157	15	Learned	John			1	1	1				2	1			6		
Oxford	157	16	Learned	John Junr	1		1	1		4	3		1				11		
Oxford	157	17	Learned	Jacob	1	1				2	1		1	1			8		
Oxford	157	18	Lamb	Levi		1	1		2	1		1		2			8		
Oxford	157	19	Lilley	Ebenezer			1	1					1	1			4		
Oxford	157	20	Learned	Ebenz		1			1				1	1			4		
Oxford	158	1	Learned	Silvanus		2	1	1		3	2		1	1			11		
Oxford	158	2	Learned	Rufus		1		1		1				1			4		
Oxford	158	3	Learned	Jeremiah	3	1		1	1				1	1			8		
Oxford	158	4	Learned	Benja	3	1		1		2			1	1			9		
Oxford	158	5	Learned	Jona	3	1	1	1		1			1				8		
Oxford	158	6	Learned	Simpson		1		1					1	1			4		
Oxford	158	7	Samson	William	2		1	1					1				5		
Oxford	158	8	Lamb	Reuben		2	1		1				1	1			6		
Oxford	158	9	Lamb	Abijah	1	1		1					2				5		
Oxford	158	10	Mayo	John	1		1		1	2	2	2		1			10		
Oxford	158	11	Morse	Joshua	1		1	1		2	2		1				8		
Oxford	158	12	Mayo	John Junr			1					1					2		
Oxford	158	13	Moore	Marvin	1	1	2		1	1			1	1			8		
Oxford	158	14	Moore	Collins	2		2		1	3			1				9		
Oxford	158	15	Millen	Abner			1		1			1		1			4		
Oxford	158	16	Moffit	Isaac				1		1				1			3		
Oxford	158	17	Moffit	Elihu	2			1		1			1				5		
Oxford	158	18	Moffit	Lemuel	1		1			1			1				4		
Oxford	158	19	McFarling	Josiah	3		1			1			1				6		
Oxford	158	20	Meriam	Sarah Wd	1	1	1				1	2		1			7		
Oxford	158	21	Moore	Margaret Wd										1			1		
Oxford	158	22	Meriam	Joshua					1								1		
Oxford	158	23	Meriam	James		2			1	1		1	2	1			8		
Oxford	159	1	Fith	Benja Junr	2			1					1				4		
Oxford	159	2	Fuller	Lemuel				1		1	1		1	1			5		
Oxford	159	3	Gould	Lyman	1		1			1		1					4		
Oxford	159	4	Gould	Ebenz				1		1				1			3		
Oxford	159	5	Gleason	Jona & Jesse	1		1	1	1			1		1	1		7		
Oxford	159	6	Gleason	James Junr		2	1	1	1	1		1	1	1			9		
Oxford	159	7	Gleason	James	1			1		1	1	1	1				6		
Oxford	159	8	Gleason	Josiah	1			1		1			1	1			5		
Oxford	159	9	Gale	Abijah					1				1	1			3		
Oxford	159	10	Holley	Joseph		2			1	1				1			5		
Oxford	159	11	Hall	Nathan	2	2			1			1	1				7		
Oxford	159	12	Harwood	David				1						1			2		
Oxford	159	13	Harwood	David Junr	1			1					1				3		
Oxford	159	14	Harwood	Solomon	1		1	1		1			1				5		
Oxford	159	15	Harwood	Elihu	2			1					1				4		
Oxford	159	16	Harwood	Stephen		1	1	1	1		1	2		1			8		
Oxford	159	17	Howard	John			1		1		1	1		1			5		
Oxford	160	1	Howard	John Junr				1		2			1				4		
Oxford	160	2	Howard	Stephen	3			1		1				1			6		
Oxford	160	3	Howard	Simeon	1		1						1				3		
Oxford	160	4	Humphrey	Ebenz	1	1	1		1	1	1	1	1	1			9		
Oxford	160	5	Harris	Jonathan	2	1	1	1		2	1	1	1	1			11		
Oxford	160	6	Harris	Abijah				1						1			2		
Oxford	160	7	Harris	Asa			2	1		1		1					5		
Oxford	160	8	Healy	Ruth Wd	1		2			1		1	1	1			7		
Oxford	160	9	Hurd	Joseph			1		1			1	1	2			6		
Oxford	160	10	Hager	Benja	1		1	1		2		1	1				7		
Oxford	160	11	Howard	Asahel	3	3		1		1			1				9		
Oxford	160	12	Hartwell	Saml	3	1	1	1		1		1	1				9		
Oxford	160	13	Hill	Aaron	3				1	1	1		1				7		
Oxford	160	14	Hovey	Gideon	2		2	1				1	1				7		
Oxford	160	15	Hudson	William			1		2	1	1	1	1				7		
Oxford	160	16	Hudson	John	1			1		2			1	1			6		
Oxford	160	17	Hardin	Amos	2			1		1	2		1				7		
Oxford	160	18	Ide	Timothy	1	1			1	1	1			1			6		
Oxford	160	19	Ide	Nathan			1					1					2		
Oxford	160	20	Ide	Liberty			1			1		1					3		
Oxford	161	1	Coburn	Richard		1			2			1		1			5		

95

TOWN	PG#	LN#	LAST NAME	FIRST NAME	FREE WHITE MALES					FREE WHITE FEMALES					TOTAL ALL OTHER	TOTAL SLAVES	TOTALS	DISTRICT/ TOWNSHIP	NOTES
					under 10	10 to 16	16 to 26	26 to 45	45 and over	under 10	10 to 16	16 to 26	26 to 45	45 and over					
Oxford	161	2	Carey	William	2	1			1	1	1	1		1			8		
Oxford	161	3	Campbell	Archibald			2					1		1			4		
Oxford	161	4	Coburn	Samuel	1		1						1				3		
Oxford	161	5	Conant	Asa				1		1				1			3		
Oxford	161	6	Crane	Lemuel	1	1	1		1			2		1			7		
Oxford	161	7	Clark	Thomas				1						1			2		
Oxford	161	8	Crane	Gilbert			2			1			2				5		
Oxford	161	9	Cudworth	Warren	1		1			2			1				5		
Oxford	161	10	Davis	Benjamin	3			1		1	2	1	1				9		
Oxford	161	11	Davis	Mary Wd		2	2			2			1				7		
Oxford	161	12	Davis	Ezekiel	1	1			1	3	1	1	1				9		
Oxford	161	13	Davenport	Richard		1			1		1		1	1			5		
Oxford	161	14	Davis	Jeremiah			3		1			2	1	1			8		
Oxford	161	15	Davis	Abijah			1	1				1					3		
Oxford	161	16	Davis	Thomas	1		1	1		1			1				5		
Oxford	161	17	Davis	Nehemiah			2	1					1				4		
Oxford	161	18	Davis	Samuel		1			1			2		1			5		
Oxford	162	1	Davis	Elijah			1		1	1		2		1			6		
Oxford	162	2	Davis	Learned	1	1	1		1	1	1		1				7		
Oxford	162	3	Davis	Jonathan	2	2		1				1	2	1			9		
Oxford	162	4	Davis	Joseph	1	2	1		2				1	4			11		
Oxford	162	5	Davis	Craft	2	1			1	1		1	1				7		
Oxford	162	6	Davis	James	1		1						1				3		
Oxford	162	7	Davis	John	1	1	1	1	1			1	1	1			8		
Oxford	162	8	Davis	John		1	1	1	1	1			2	1			8		
Oxford	162	9	Day	David		1	1					1					3		
Oxford	162	10	Eddy	Silas	2		2		1		1			1			7		
Oxford	162	11	Eddy	William				1						2			3		
Oxford	162	12	Eddy	Reuben	1	2			1	2		1	1				8		
Oxford	162	13	Eddy	Jonas			2		1		1		1	1			6		
Oxford	162	14	Eddy	Parley	1	1		1			1		1				5		
Oxford	162	15	Edson	Rhodolphus		1		1			1	1					4		
Oxford	162	16	Fuller	Daniel	3	1		1		2			1				8		
Oxford	162	17	Fitts	Bena & Andrew			2		1			1		1			5		
Oxford	162	18	Fitts	David	1		1			1			1				4		
Oxford	162	19	Fisk	Daniel	1		3		1	2	1	2	1		1		12		
Oxford	162	20	Forbes	William			3	1				1	1				6		
Oxford	162	21	Fitts	Daniel	2	1			1	2	1		1				8		
Oxford	164	1	Amedown	Jeremiah				1				1		1			3		
Oxford	164	2	Atwood	Abial				1		2				1			4		
Oxford	164	3	Alverson	George		1		1		1			1	1			5		
Oxford	164	4	Bound	John				1			1			1			3		
Oxford	164	5	Bixby	Jonathan				1		1				1			3		
Oxford	164	6	Brown	Philip	1	2	2	1		1	1			1			9		
Oxford	164	7	Barret	Jacob				1						2			3		
Oxford	164	8	Brown	Josiah		1		1		3			1				6		
Oxford	164	9	Brown	Joseph	1			1		1			1				4		
Oxford	164	10	Briggs	Abraham	1	1	1		1	2				1			7		
Oxford	164	11	Brown	James	1		1	1		2				1			5		
Oxford	164	12	Blanchard	Saml	1	1			1	1	1			1			7		
Oxford	164	13	Ballard	John				1						1			2		
Oxford	164	14	Ballard	John Junr	1			1				1					3		
Oxford	164	15	Butter	James	1		2		1	1		2		1			8		
Oxford	164	16	Burr	Daniel	1	1		1					1				6		
Oxford	164	17	Bonzey	Peter A	2		1		1	2	2		1				9		
Oxford	164	18	Blandin	Francis	3				1	2	1		1				8		
Oxford	164	19	Cudworth	James				1		1	1		1				4		
Oxford	164	20	Campbell	Saml	1	2	3		1	2	1	1	1	1	3		16		
Oxford	164	21	Collar	James	3	2	1	1	1	1	2	1	1	1			14		

TOWN	PG#	LN#	HEADS OF HOUSEHOLD		FREE WHITE MALES					FREE WHITE FEMALES					TOTAL ALL OTHER	TOTAL SLAVES	TOTALS	DISTRICT/ TOWNSHIP	NOTES
			LAST NAME	FIRST NAME	under 10	10 to 16	16 to 26	26 to 45	45 and over	under 10	10 to 16	16 to 26	26 to 45	45 and over					
Paxton	499	1	Allen	Ichabod			1					1					2		
Paxton	499	2	Abbot	Abijah			1		1	2	1	2	1				8		
Paxton	499	3	Bigelow	Timothy				1		1			1				3		
Paxton	499	4	Bigelow	Ithamar		1	2		1			1		1			6		
Paxton	499	5	Bellows	Ezekiel	1	1			1			2		1			6		
Paxton	499	6	Bellows	John	1		1	1		2			1				6		
Paxton	499	7	Brewer	Eliab	1	1		1	1	2	1	2	1				10		
Paxton	499	8	Brigham	John	1			1		4			1		1		8		
Paxton	499	9	Brown	Samuel				1	2				1				4		
Paxton	499	10	Brown	Abel		1		1				1	1	1			5		
Paxton	499	11	Barnes	Abijah	2	1	1		1	3			1				9		
Paxton	499	12	Carruth	Ephraim			1			3			1				5		
Paxton	499	13	Clarke	Simeon	1	2		1	1			3	1	1			10		
Paxton	499	14	Clarke	Amos	1	1		1		3	1	1					9		
Paxton	499	15	Chase	Jonathan	1	1	1		1	1	1	2		1			9		
Paxton	499	16	Crocker	Nathl	2	3		1	1	1			1	1			10		
Paxton	499	17	Cogswell	Ebenn				1						2			3		
Paxton	501	1	Grosvenor	Daniel	2		4		1	2	1	1					11		
Paxton	501	2	Goodenough	David	1			1	1	1	2	1	1	1			9		
Paxton	501	3	Howe	Jonah		1			1	2	1			2			7		
Paxton	501	4	Howe	Jonah Jun			1			1		1					3		
Paxton	501	5	Howard	William	1		1		1	1	1	1		1			7		
Paxton	501	6	Hubbard	Jona			1	2						3			6		
Paxton	501	7	Howe	John	3	1		2		2	2	1	2				13		
Paxton	501	8	Hunt	Aaron			2	1		1	1		1				6		
Paxton	501	9	Jennison	Saml	3	1		1					1				6		
Paxton	501	10	King	Samuel	2		1					1					4		
Paxton	501	11	Lynde	Johnson	2	1			1			4	1				9		
Paxton	501	12	Livermore	Bradl	2	2		1		1		2	1				10		
Paxton	501	13	Lamb	Thomas	1	1	1		1		1	1		1			7		
Paxton	501	14	Mann	Phinehas		2	1		1					1			5		
Paxton	502	1	Cass	Jonathan				1						1			2		
Paxton	502	2	Cogswell	Aaron			1			2		1					4		
Paxton	502	3	Davis	David			2		1	2		1					6		
Paxton	502	4	Davis	David Junr		1	1			2		1					5		
Paxton	502	5	Day	Joseph		2		1						2			5		
Paxton	502	6	Estabrook	Jonah	1	1		1		2		1					6		
Paxton	502	7	Estabrook	Thads	2	1			1		1	2	1				8		
Paxton	502	8	Earle	Clark		1	1	2		1	1						6		
Paxton	502	9	Earle	Oliver		1	3	1		1		2	1				9		
Paxton	502	10	Earle	Marmaduke	2	1			1	3	1		1				9		
Paxton	502	11	Fuller	Azariah	2	1		1		2			1				7		
Paxton	502	12	Fuller	Josiah		1			1			1		1			4		
Paxton	502	13	Frost	Jonathan		1		1		4			2	1			9		
Paxton	502	14	Estabrook	Ebenz	2	1		1		2	1		1				8		
Paxton	503	1	Pierce	David	1			1	1			1					4		
Paxton	503	2	Penniman	Joseph			1		1	1		1	1				5		
Paxton	503	3	Penniman	Simeon			1					1					2		
Paxton	503	4	Penniman	Sarrell	1		1			1			1				4		
Paxton	503	5	Pike	Francis		1	1					1					3		
Paxton	503	6	Partridge	Samuel	2		1			2	1	1	1				8		
Paxton	503	7	Pike	John	2	2		1		1	1		1				8		
Paxton	503	8	Pond	Darius	2			1				1	1				5		
Paxton	503	9	Peirce	Aaron			1			3	1	1					6		
Paxton	503	10	Robbins	Nathl	2	1		1		2		1	1				8		
Paxton	503	11	Sweetzer	Jacob F.			1							1			2		
Paxton	503	12	Swan	Nathan		1		1				1		1			4		
Paxton	503	13	Snow	Nathan				1									1		
Paxton	503	14	Sweetzer	Benja			1	1	1	1		2		1			7		
Paxton	503	15	Smith	Reuben	2		1	1	1	3		1	1	1			11		
Paxton	503	16	Smith	Joel	2			1		1		1					5		
Paxton	503	17	Sweetzer	Jacob			1	1	1					1			4		
Paxton	503	18	Shattuck	Caleb	1		2			1	1	1					6		
Paxton	503	19	Smith	David	2			1		1	1	1	1				7		
Paxton	503	20	Snow	John		1		1		1				1			4		
Paxton	503	21	Snow	Willard	2		1			1	1	1					6		
Paxton	503	22	Snow	Seth		1	1		1	1		1	1	1			7		
Paxton	503	23	Slade	Henry	1	1	2		1	1		1		1			8		
Paxton	503	24	Stebbins	Peter	1	1			1	1	1	2	1				8		
Paxton	503	25	Sweetzer	Benja Jun				1			1		1				3		
Paxton	503	26	Thompson	James		1			1				2				4		
Paxton	503	27	Thompson	William	2	1		1		3		1			2		10		
Paxton	503	28	Ward	Hezekiah				1						1			2		
Paxton	503	29	Ward	Calvin	1	1							2	1			6		
Paxton	504	1	Warren	John				1		1	1	1	1				5		
Paxton	504	2	Warren	William	1			1		1			1				4		
Paxton	504	3	Waite	Ebenezer		2	1		1			4		1			9		
Paxton	504	4	Waite	Samuel	1			1		1	1	1					5		
Paxton	504	5	Ware	Amos	2	2							1				7		

TOWN	PG#	LN#	LAST NAME	FIRST NAME	FREE WHITE MALES					FREE WHITE FEMALES					TOTAL ALL OTHER	TOTAL SLAVES	TOTALS	DISTRICT/ TOWNSHIP	NOTES
					under 10	10 to 16	16 to 26	26 to 45	45 and over	under 10	10 to 16	16 to 26	26 to 45	45 and over					
Paxton	504	6	Wicker	Samuel					1								1		
Paxton	504	7	Wicker	David		1	1		1			1	2	1			7		
Paxton	504	8	Willson	Benjamin	2	1			1	2	1		1				8		
Paxton	504	9	McDonald	Archd			1		1					1			3		
Paxton	504	10	Morse	Elijah	2	1		1		2	1		1				8		
Paxton	504	11	Morse	Abner		1			1					1			3		
Paxton	504	12	Morse	Aaron		1		1			2	1	1				6		
Paxton	504	13	Moore	Phins			1	1					1	1	1		5		
Paxton	504	14	Moore	Pliny			1	1				1	1				4		
Paxton	504	15	Metcalf	Seth	1			1		1		1		1			5		
Paxton	504	16	Newton	Silas	1		3	1	1	1		3					10		
Paxton	504	17	Newton	Merriam		1								1			2		
Paxton	504	18	Newton	Jonah	1				1				1	1			4		
Paxton	504	19	Newhall	Joseph		1		1					1				3		
Paxton	504	20	Needham	Daniel		1			1	2		1	1				6		
Paxton	504	21	Newton	Nahum	2	1			1	2		1		1			8		
Paxton	504	22	Osland	Jona	1	1			1	1	1	3	1				9		

			HEADS OF HOUSEHOLD		FREE WHITE MALES					FREE WHITE FEMALES									
TOWN	PG#	LN#	LAST NAME	FIRST NAME	under 10	10 to 16	16 to 26	26 to 45	45 and over	under 10	10 to 16	16 to 26	26 to 45	45 and over	TOTAL ALL OTHER	TOTAL SLAVES	TOTALS	DISTRICT/ TOWNSHIP	NOTES
Petersham	271	1	Aldrich	Simeon		1		1				1	1				4		
Petersham	271	2	Amsden	Thomas	1				1	1	1			1			5		
Petersham	271	3	Amsden	Jacob	3	1	1	1			2		1				9		
Petersham	271	4	Allen	David	2	1			1	3			1				8		
Petersham	271	5	Ainsworth	Samuel	1		1						1				3		
Petersham	271	6	Abbot	Lewis	1			1		2			1				5		
Petersham	271	7	Amsbury	Jesse	2			1		1		4	1				9		
Petersham	271	8	Allen	Elijah	1	1		1		1		1	1				6		
Petersham	271	9	Alexander	Jesse	1			1		2		1	1				6		
Petersham	271	10	Ainsworth	Jacob	1		2		1		1	1		1			7		
Petersham	271	11	Amsden	Ephm	3			1		1	2		2	1			10		
Petersham	271	12	Amsden	Bozaleel	1		1	1		1	1		1				6		
Petersham	271	13	Burroughs	Wellsworth	1			1					1				3		
Petersham	271	14	Bridge	Nancy	1	1				1		2	1		1		7		
Petersham	271	15	Brown	Joseph		1	2	1		1	1		1	1			8		
Petersham	271	16	Babcock	James	1			1		2			1				5		
Petersham	271	17	Briggs	Job Jur	1			1		2			1				5		
Petersham	271	18	Briggs	Job	1				1				1				3		
Petersham	271	19	Babbit	Abner				1	1	1	1		1				5		
Petersham	271	20	Blanchard	Seth	2	1			1			2	1				7		
Petersham	273	1	Bancroft	Willm		1	2		1	1	1		1				7		
Petersham	273	2	Bosworth	Benja	1	2	1		1	1			1				7		
Petersham	273	3	Bosworth	George	3			1	1	2		1	1	1			10		
Petersham	273	4	Blackmore	Solo	2	2		1		1	1		1				8		
Petersham	273	5	Bliss	Moses				1		2			1				4		
Petersham	273	6	Cross	Silas	1			1		1	1		1				5		
Petersham	273	7	Cutler	Samuel	1		3	1		4	1		1		1		12		
Petersham	273	8	Chamberlin	Saml Jr	3			1		2			1				7		
Petersham	273	9	Crowl	Artimus	2		1						1				4		
Petersham	273	10	Chandler	Benja	2	1	1	1		1			1				7		
Petersham	273	11	Carter	John	6			1					1				8		
Petersham	273	12	Clark	Edwd			1	1			1						3		
Petersham	273	13	Clark	Nathl	2	1	1	1		2	2						9		
Petersham	273	14	Chandler	Willm	3			1		1	1		1				7		
Petersham	273	15	Chamberlin	Saml		2			1	1	1		2		1		8		
Petersham	273	16	Chamberlin	Joshua	1	1		1		2			1				6		
Petersham	273	17	Carruth	Jonas				1	1			1		1			4		
Petersham	273	18	Curtis	David				1						1			2		
Petersham	273	19	Curtis	Thomas	3	2			1	3	1	1	1				12		
Petersham	273	20	Chase	Peter	1	1		1		1		2	1				7		
Petersham	273	21	Clark	David		1		1				1	1				4		
Petersham	274	1	Buckwith	Eliot		1	1			1		1	1				5		
Petersham	274	2	Bruce	Rueben	1			2				1		2			6		
Petersham	274	3	Babcock	Enoch		1		1				2	1				5		
Petersham	274	4	Babbit	Silas	2			1		1	1		1				6		
Petersham	274	5	Briggs	Amos	1		1	1		2	1		1				7		
Petersham	274	6	Brown	Frederick F	4	1		1		1	2		1		1		11		
Petersham	274	7	Bryant	Joel	2	1	1	1		2		1		1			10		
Petersham	274	8	Bowker	Ezekel	1				1		1			1			4		
Petersham	274	9	Bowker	Jotham	3		2		1	2			1				9		
Petersham	274	10	Brown	Thomas	1		1			1			1				4		
Petersham	274	11	Brigham	Edwd	1	1		1		3		1	1				8		
Petersham	274	12	Baker	Edwd					1		1			2			4		
Petersham	274	13	Baker	Cyprian		2		1					1				4		
Petersham	274	14	Bigelow	Daniel Esq		2	2		1	1	1	1	1	1	1		11		
Petersham	274	15	Bond	Willm	1			1		1			1				4		
Petersham	274	16	Brooks	Joel	4	1		1			1		1				8		
Petersham	274	17	Brooks	Aaron	2	1		1		2	1		1				8		
Petersham	274	18	Bancroft	Benja				1		2	2	1					7		
Petersham	274	19	Bagg	Solomon	1			1		2		1	1				7		
Petersham	274	20	Burt	Alven	2	1		1		1	1		1				7		
Petersham	275	1	Duncan	John				1									1		
Petersham	275	2	Doan	Noah				1					1				2		
Petersham	275	3	Doan	Edwd	1			1				1					3		
Petersham	275	4	Demula	Jesse		1		1					1				3		
Petersham	275	5	Dickerson	David		1	1						1	1			4		
Petersham	275	6	Dudley	Francis		2	1	1		1			1	1			7		
Petersham	275	7	Duncan	Willm				1		5			1				7		
Petersham	275	8	Doolittle	Joel		2	3	1				2	1	1			10		
Petersham	275	9	Dean	Jereh	1			1	1			2					5		
Petersham	275	10	Eames	Peter	2			1		2			1				6		
Petersham	275	11	Eager	Winslow	2			1				1	1				5		
Petersham	275	12	Fisk	Ebenz				1					1				2		
Petersham	275	13	Flagg	Elisha	1		1			1			1				5		
Petersham	275	14	Fisk	John	1	1		1		4		1	1				9		
Petersham	275	15	Fiske	Abigail								1		1			2		
Petersham	275	16	Farnsworth	Ephm		1	1	1	1				1	1			6		
Petersham	276	1	Clark	Hardin	3			1		1			1				6		
Petersham	276	2	Clark	Jonah				1	1	1			1				5		

TOWN	PG#	LN#	LAST NAME	FIRST NAME	FREE WHITE MALES under 10	10 to 16	16 to 26	26 to 45	45 and over	FREE WHITE FEMALES under 10	10 to 16	16 to 26	26 to 45	45 and over	TOTAL ALL OTHER	TOTAL SLAVES	TOTALS	DISTRICT/ TOWNSHIP	NOTES
Petersham	276	3	Chandler	John Esq			3	2				2	2	1			10		
Petersham	276	4	Clements	Saml		1		1		1			1				4		
Petersham	276	5	Canning	Reuben					1			1		1			3		
Petersham	276	6	Conner	Joseph											2		2		
Petersham	276	7	Clements	Mary				1		1				1			3		
Petersham	276	8	Clements	Thomas				1				1					2		
Petersham	276	9	Clements	John Jr			1					1					2		
Petersham	276	10	Crosset	Susannah		1								1			2		
Petersham	276	11	Clap	Samuel	1			1		1		1					4		
Petersham	276	12	Curtis	Ebenz	2			1		2		1	1	1			8		
Petersham	276	13	Chamberlin	Caleb	2			1				1					4		
Petersham	276	14	Clements	John	1	2	1		1	1	1		1				8		
Petersham	276	15	Crowl	Alpheus				1		1			1				3		
Petersham	276	16	Crowl	John					1				3	1			5		
Petersham	276	17	Crowl	Cyrus	1			1		3			1				6		
Petersham	276	18	Calhoon	James	3			1		2			1				7		
Petersham	276	19	Cuming	Nathan	1	1		1		2		1					6		
Petersham	276	20	Calhoon	John				1									1		
Petersham	277	1	Gale	Daniel	1	1	3		1	1		1	1				9		
Petersham	277	2	Goddard	David	2		1	1					1				5		
Petersham	277	3	Gleson	Joseph		1	1		1	1	3			1	1		10		
Petersham	277	4	Gould	Daniel		1		1		2			1				5		
Petersham	277	5	Gates	John		1	1	1		1		1	2	1			8		
Petersham	277	6	Holland	John	2	3		1		2		2	1				11		
Petersham	277	7	Hunter	Jona	1	1	1	1	1	2	1	1		1			11		
Petersham	277	8	Haskins	Elkanah		1		1		2		1	1				6		
Petersham	277	9	Hathaway	Joel	2	2	1	1		2	1		1				10		
Petersham	277	10	Hammond	Elisha		3	1		1		1	4	1	1			12		
Petersham	277	11	Howard	Nehemiah	1	1	1		1	2	2	2		1			11		
Petersham	277	12	Howard	John					1					1			2		
Petersham	277	13	Hapgood	Hutchins	2		2	1		2			2				9		
Petersham	277	14	Holden	Nathan	1		1	1		3	3		1				10		
Petersham	277	15	Hopkins	Saml			2		1	3	1		1				8		
Petersham	277	16	Handy	Ebenz	2		1	1		1		1					6		
Petersham	277	17	Houghton	Zarah	1	2			1		1		1	1			7		
Petersham	277	18	Houghton	Jemima			1			2	2		1				6		
Petersham	278	1	Fulton	George	3	1		1		1	2		1				9		
Petersham	278	2	Farrar	Joseph	1	1	1		1	2	1		1				8		
Petersham	278	3	Furness	Benja	1			1		2			1				5		
Petersham	278	4	Goddard	Nathl	3	1		1		2			1				9		
Petersham	278	5	Goddard	Joel	4	1		1			1	1	1				9		
Petersham	278	6	Goddard	Robert	1		1	1	1		1	2	1				8		
Petersham	278	7	Goodale	Enoch	1	1		1		3			1				7		
Petersham	278	8	Gates	Silas	2	2		1		1		1	1				8		
Petersham	278	9	Gardenor	Jesse	1	2	2		1	1			1				8		
Petersham	278	10	Goodale	Joseph	2	1	1		2	1	1	1		1			10		
Petersham	278	11	Gollund	Jereh			2		1			2	1	1			7		
Petersham	278	12	Gollund	Joseph	1		1	1		1			1				5		
Petersham	278	13	Gore	Peter											3		3		
Petersham	278	14	Gates	Saml	3			1	1	2			1				8		
Petersham	278	15	Geningson	John	1		1	1				1	1				5		
Petersham	278	16	Gross	Thomas				1									1		
Petersham	278	17	Grout	Jona Esq	1	1	4		1		2	1	2				12		
Petersham	279	1	Jackson	James	1			1				1		1			4		
Petersham	279	2	Jackson	James Jur	2			1		1			1				5		
Petersham	279	3	Jackson	Nathan			2	1				1	1				5		
Petersham	279	4	Johnson	Jona	1	2	1		1				1				6		
Petersham	279	5	Johnson	Levi			2			2	1		1				6		
Petersham	279	6	King	Stephen	1	1			1	1			1				5		
Petersham	279	7	King	Henry	3			1		1			1				6		
Petersham	279	8	King	Jona					1					1			2		
Petersham	279	9	Knapp	John		1			1			1	3	1			7		
Petersham	279	10	Knapp	Jezneah				1		1			1				3		
Petersham	279	11	Kendall	Samuel	1		1	1		3	1		1				8		
Petersham	279	12	Lamson	Samuel	2			1		1	1		1				6		
Petersham	279	13	Lincoln	Caleb	3	1		1					1	1			7		
Petersham	279	14	Loring	Abel	2		1	1		2			1				7		
Petersham	279	15	Lincoln	Enos		2	1		1	3	1	1		1			10		
Petersham	279	16	Maundry	Nathll		1	3	1				1	1	1			8		
Petersham	279	17	McClallen	Reuben	1		1	2		1		1					6		
Petersham	280	1	Hapgood	Seth		1		1	1				1	1			5		
Petersham	280	2	Hammond	Enoch Junr	2		1	1		2			1				7		
Petersham	280	3	Hammond	Enoch					1	1	1			1			4		
Petersham	280	4	Hastings	Henry	1			1	1	2		1	1				7		
Petersham	280	5	How	Benja		1	1	1		3	1		1				9		
Petersham	280	6	How	John		1	1		1			1		1			5		
Petersham	280	7	How	Silvanus	1		2	1	1			1	1	1			8		
Petersham	280	8	Holland	Wilder			1			1		1					3		
Petersham	280	9	Holman	Jona		1	1	1	1		1	2	1	1			9		

TOWN	PG#	LN#	HEADS OF HOUSEHOLD LAST NAME	HEADS OF HOUSEHOLD FIRST NAME	FREE WHITE MALES under 10	10 to 16	16 to 26	26 to 45	45 and over	FREE WHITE FEMALES under 10	10 to 16	16 to 26	26 to 45	45 and over	TOTAL ALL OTHER	TOTAL SLAVES	TOTALS	DISTRICT/ TOWNSHIP	NOTES
Petersham	280	10	Holland	Luther	1		3		1	2	1		1				9		
Petersham	280	11	Hodges	Abiel			1	1					2	1			5		
Petersham	280	12	Hatstall	George	2	3			1	3			1				10		
Petersham	280	13	Hildruth	John	1		2		1	1	2	2		1			10		
Petersham	280	14	Hildruth	Elijah	1	1		1		1			1				5		
Petersham	280	15	Hildruth	John	1			1					1				3		
Petersham	280	16	Houghton	Levi				1			1						2		
Petersham	281	1	Partridge	John				1				1		1			3		
Petersham	281	2	Prentiss	Nathan	1			1		3		1					6		
Petersham	281	3	Peekham	John		1	1		1	1		1		1			6		
Petersham	281	4	Parmenter	John	1	1		1				3		1			7		
Petersham	281	5	Parmenter	Abiel	2	1		1		3	1		1				9		
Petersham	281	6	Pike	Saml			1				1	1					3		
Petersham	281	7	Powers	Jacob	3		1	1		3	1	1	1				12		
Petersham	281	8	Pebody	Phinihas	3	1		1					1				6		
Petersham	281	9	Pratt	Abigail						1		1					2		
Petersham	281	10	Patterson	Andrew		1		1	1			1		1			5		
Petersham	281	11	Pierce	Willm				1		2		1					4		
Petersham	281	12	Peekham	Elis	1			1		2			1				5		
Petersham	281	13	Pierce	Jona	1	1		1		3			1				7		
Petersham	281	14	Rice	Martin	4		1	1		2	1	1	1				11		
Petersham	281	15	Rand	Solomon Revd	4		1		1	1	3	1	1				12		
Petersham	281	16	Rice	Willm			2			1		1					4		
Petersham	281	17	Ross	Seth	3	1		1		2	1		1		1		10		
Petersham	281	18	Rice	Abel	2		1			3			1				7		
Petersham	281	19	Randall	Benja		1				1	1						3		
Petersham	282	1	Mead	John	2		1			1		1					5		
Petersham	282	2	Moss	Samuel				1						1			2		
Petersham	282	3	Miles	Joab	2			1		2	1		1				7		
Petersham	282	4	Marsh	Moses	1	2	1	1		2	1	1	1				10		
Petersham	282	5	Mahan	Thomas				1				1	1				3		
Petersham	282	6	Mahan	John	3	1	2	1			1	1		1			10		
Petersham	282	7	Miles	Daniel		2		1		1	1	1	1				7		
Petersham	282	8	McClallen	Moses				1				1	2				4		
Petersham	282	9	McClallen	David		1	1		1	1	1		1				6		
Petersham	282	10	Mann	Ensign		2	2		1	1	1	3		1			11		
Petersham	282	11	Mason	Newhall	1	1	1	1		1	1		1				7		
Petersham	282	12	Negus	Joel	2			1		3	1	2	1				10		
Petersham	282	13	Negus	Paul	1		1	1					1				4		
Petersham	282	14	Negus	John			1			4			1				6		
Petersham	282	15	Pond	Asa		3		1		2	1		2				9		
Petersham	282	16	Peekham	Robert		1		1					1				3		
Petersham	282	17	Peekham	Willm	1		1		1	1		1		1			6		
Petersham	283	1	Stone	Jesse		1			1	3	1	1		1			8		
Petersham	283	2	Smith	Joseph		1		1		2	2		1				7		
Petersham	283	3	Stears	Ephm		3		1		1	1		1				7		
Petersham	283	4	Spooner	Ruggles		1			1	1	1	1					5		
Petersham	283	5	Stevens	Gardner	4	2		1	1	1	1		1	1			12		
Petersham	283	6	Stow	Lydia	1								1				2		
Petersham	283	7	Schaal	Abraham				1		1			1				3		
Petersham	283	8	Stone	Jona	1		2			1	1	1		1			7		
Petersham	283	9	Sanderson	Nathl			1			1	1		1				4		
Petersham	283	10	Sanderson	David				1					1				2		
Petersham	283	11	Sanderson	Jona		1		2				2		1			7		
Petersham	283	12	Sprague	Joseph		1	1	1				2		1			6		
Petersham	283	13	Stone	David				1				2	2				5		
Petersham	283	14	Spooner	Philip	1			1	1			3		1			7		
Petersham	283	15	Simmons	Benja		1	1	1				2	1	1			8		
Petersham	283	16	Sibley	Elisha	4	1	1	1		1		1					10		
Petersham	283	17	Stone	John	1			1				1					3		
Petersham	283	18	Sanderson	Moses	2	1		1		2	1		1				8		
Petersham	283	19	Stearns	Martha							1	1	1				3		
Petersham	283	20	Stone	Amos	2		1		1	1	1		1				7		
Petersham	284	1	Rogers	Josiah	1	2	2	1				2		1			10		
Petersham	284	2	Rogers	Abel	1			1	1	1	2			1			7		
Petersham	284	3	Rogers	Abel Jr	2			1		3			1				7		
Petersham	284	4	Robinson	Jereh	1			1		3	1		1				7		
Petersham	284	5	Stone	David Jr		1			1	1	1			1			5		
Petersham	284	6	Spooner	Wing			1		1			2	1	1			6		
Petersham	284	7	Spooner	Clap	4	1	1	1		1		1		1			10		
Petersham	284	8	Stone	Saml	3	2	1		1	1	1	1	1				11		
Petersham	284	9	Smith	Robert	2		1			1			1				5		
Petersham	284	10	Smith	Nathan	1			1		1	1		1	1			6		
Petersham	284	11	Stowell	David			1			1	1	1	1	1			6		
Petersham	284	12	Shumway	Perez			1			1	1	1					4		
Petersham	284	13	Stowell	John	3	2			1		1	1	1				9		
Petersham	284	14	Stowell	Asahel	1	1		1		2		2					7		
Petersham	284	15	Stowell	Abel	3		1	1		1		1	1	1			9		
Petersham	284	16	Stowell	Joab	1			1		1							5		

TOWN	PG#	LN#	LAST NAME	FIRST NAME	FREE WHITE MALES					FREE WHITE FEMALES					TOTAL ALL OTHER	TOTAL SLAVES	TOTALS	DISTRICT/ TOWNSHIP	NOTES
					under 10	10 to 16	16 to 26	26 to 45	45 and over	under 10	10 to 16	16 to 26	26 to 45	45 and over					
Petersham	284	17	Stowell	Lemuel		1	1	1		1			1				5		
Petersham	285	1	Whitney	Simon	3	1	1	1		2	1		1				10		
Petersham	285	2	Wheeler	Jonus	1	1		1		3	1	1	1	1			10		
Petersham	285	3	Wilder	Manasah			1	1						1			3		
Petersham	285	4	Wilder	Abel	2	2	2	1		3	2		1	1			14		
Petersham	285	5	Wilder	Cornelius		1	1		1	1		1					5		
Petersham	285	6	Walker	Willm		1			1		2	2	1	1			8		
Petersham	285	7	Walker	Jotham		1	1	1			1		1	1			6		
Petersham	285	8	Wilder	John	1	1	1		1	1	1						6		
Petersham	285	9	Wheeler	Nathan	3	1		1		1			1				7		
Petersham	285	10	Ward	Daniel	1	1	1		1	2	1	1		1			9		
Petersham	285	11	Wheeler	Margaret									1	1			2		
Petersham	285	12	Willard	Wilm		1	2	1	1			1	1	1			8		
Petersham	285	13	Willson	John	1			1		3		1	1				7		
Petersham	285	14	Ward	Nahum		1		1		1		1	1				5		
Petersham	285	15	Ward	Elisha				1					1	1			3		
Petersham	285	16	Whiple	John		1	1		1			2		1			6		
Petersham	285	17	Whiple	William	2			1			1		1				5		
Petersham	285	18	Whiple	Richard	2			1		2		1	1		1		8		
Petersham	285	19	Willard	Josiah				1					1				2		
Petersham	285	20	Willard	Willm Jr	1			1		3		1	1				7		
Petersham	285	21	Wheeler	Joel				1				1		1			3		
Petersham	286	1	Tolman	Willm	1		2		1	1	2		1				8		
Petersham	286	2	Tower	Jonas	2		1	1		1		1	1	1			8		
Petersham	286	3	Tame	Joseph		2		1		2			1				6		
Petersham	286	4	Trumball	Joseph	1			1				1	1	1			5		
Petersham	286	5	Town	Jedadiah	5	1		1		1			1				9		
Petersham	286	6	Town	Amos		1		1					1				3		
Petersham	286	7	Thayne	Ephm	3	1			1	2	1	2	1				11		
Petersham	286	8	Underwood	Timothy	2			1		1			1				5		
Petersham	286	9	Williams	Jarus	1			1		3			1				6		
Petersham	286	10	Whitney	Benja	1		2		1	1	2	1		1			9		
Petersham	286	11	Woodward	Joseph		2			1	3	1			1			8		
Petersham	286	12	Woodward	Nathl			1			1			1				3		
Petersham	286	13	Woodward	Willm	1				1		1	1	1				5		
Petersham	286	14	White	Stephen	3			1		2			1	1			8		
Petersham	286	15	Woodward	Elisha	1	2			1			1	1				6		
Petersham	287	1	Wheeler	David	1			1		1			1				4		
Petersham	287	2	Willis	Caleb		1			1	2	1	1		2			8		
Petersham	287	3	Wood	Carver	1			1		1			1				4		
Petersham	287	4	West	Charles			1			1		1					3		
Petersham	287	5	Walker	Josiah	1	1		1		3	1		1				8		
Petersham	287	6	Williams	Seth	2	1	1		1	1	2		1				9		
Petersham	287	7	Wardin	Thomas		1		1		4	1		1				8		
Petersham	287	8	Weeks	Roland	3	1	1		1		1			1			8		
Petersham	287	9	Weeks	John	1			1		1			1				4		
Petersham	287	10	Walker	Reuben	1			1		1	1		1				5		

| TOWN | PG# | LN# | HEADS OF HOUSEHOLD | | FREE WHITE MALES | | | | | FREE WHITE FEMALES | | | | | TOTAL ALL OTHER | TOTAL SLAVES | TOTALS | DISTRICT/ TOWNSHIP | NOTES |
			LAST NAME	FIRST NAME	under 10	10 to 16	16 to 26	26 to 45	45 and over	under 10	10 to 16	16 to 26	26 to 45	45 and over					
Princeton	513	1	Bennet	Abner			1			3			1				5		
Princeton	513	2	Babcock	Amos	2	2		1		1			1				7		
Princeton	513	3	Ball	Aaron	1		1	1		1	2	1	1				8		
Princeton	513	4	Brooks	Mary		1	1				1			1			4		
Princeton	513	5	Brooks	Jonas	2		1	1				1					5		
Princeton	513	6	Brooks	David	3	2	1		1	2	1	3		1			14		
Princeton	513	7	Brigham	Stephen	1	1	1	1	1	4			2				11		
Princeton	513	8	Baxter	Joseph				1					2	1			4		
Princeton	513	9	Baxter	Richard				1				1		1			3		
Princeton	513	10	Baker	Joseph		1	1	1					1				4		
Princeton	513	11	Brown	James	2	2		1					1				6		
Princeton	513	12	Beaman	Phinehas			2		1		1	1	1	1			7		
Princeton	513	13	Beaman	Jonas	1	1	1	1	2	1	1	2		1			11		
Princeton	513	14	Brooks	Enoch		1	2		1			1		1			6		
Princeton	513	15	Brown	Jesse	1			1		1			1				4		
Princeton	515	1	Everett	Joshua Junr	2			1					1				4		
Princeton	515	2	Everett	William	1	1		1					1				4		
Princeton	515	3	Ellis	James	1	1			1	1	1		1				6		
Princeton	515	4	Fisher	Ichabod			2		1		2			1			6		
Princeton	515	5	Fay	Silas		2	3		1	1	2	1		1			10		
Princeton	515	6	Gill	Moses	1		3	3	2	2	2	3	2				18		
Princeton	515	7	Gill	Michael	2	1	2		1	1	1	1	1				10		
Princeton	515	8	Gill	John		1		1	1	1	2	2	1	1			10		
Princeton	515	9	Graves	Richard				1					1				2		
Princeton	515	10	Gregory	Phinehas			2		2	2	1	1					9		
Princeton	515	11	Glezon	John	1		1	1					1	1			5		
Princeton	515	12	Goodenow	Lois	1	3	1						1				6		
Princeton	515	13	Glezon	Thomas	2	3		1	1				1	1			9		
Princeton	515	14	Garfield	Moses	2		1			1			1				5		
Princeton	515	15	Gould	Benjamin			1			1			1				3		
Princeton	515	16	How	Israel		2			1		1	1		1			6		
Princeton	515	17	How	Abner			1	2	1			1	1	1			7		
Princeton	515	18	How	Adonijah			1	2	1			2		1			7		
Princeton	515	19	How	Peabody			1	2						2			4		
Princeton	515	20	How	Artimas				1		2	1	1					5		
Princeton	515	21	Houghton	Thankful	1	1	1			1		1		1			6		
Princeton	515	22	Harrington	Abijah			1	1		1	1			1			5		
Princeton	515	23	Hobbs	Elisha			3		1			1		1			6		
Princeton	515	24	Hobbs	Elisha Junr	4			1			1		1				7		
Princeton	516	1	Bartlett	John	4	2	1	1		1			1				10		
Princeton	516	2	Baker	Luke			1					1					2		
Princeton	516	3	Chillenden	Isaac	1	1			1	1	2	1		2			9		
Princeton	516	4	Ballard	Martha	2		1			1	2		1				7		
Princeton	516	5	Clark	Norman	1	1		1	1	3			1				8		
Princeton	516	6	Chandler	John			2		1	1				1			5		
Princeton	516	7	Cheever	Daniel	3			1		2	2		1				9		
Princeton	516	8	Clark	Benjamin	3	2		1		1		1	1				9		
Princeton	516	9	Cutting	Josiah	1	2		1		3			1				8		
Princeton	516	10	Copeland	Eliphalet	3			1		1	1		1				7		
Princeton	516	11	Dodds	William			2		1	1		2		1			7		
Princeton	516	12	Dadnum	Samuel	2			1		1	1		1				6		
Princeton	516	13	Davis	Josiah Junr			1		1		2			1			5		
Princeton	516	14	Davis	Samuel			1		1	1	2	1		1			7		
Princeton	516	15	Dana	John	2	1		1		3			1				8		
Princeton	516	16	Davis	Solomon	1	1		1		2	2	1	1				9		
Princeton	516	17	Davis	John P.	1		1	1		4	1		1				9		
Princeton	516	18	Davis	Oliver			1		1		1			1			4		
Princeton	516	19	Davis	Simon	2	1		1		1			1				6		
Princeton	516	20	Dale	David	2			1		1			1				5		
Princeton	516	21	Eldridge	Hezekiah	1			1			1	1					4		
Princeton	516	22	Eveleth	Abishai				1		2		1	1	1			6		
Princeton	516	23	Eveleth	Joshua Junr	1			1		4			2				8		
Princeton	516	24	Everett	Joshua			1		1				1	2			5		
Princeton	517	1	Mason	Sadey				1					1	1			3		
Princeton	517	2	Mason	Thomas			1		1	1			2	1			6		
Princeton	517	3	Mason	Silas	2	3		1		1			1				8		
Princeton	517	4	Moore	Molley			2						2	1			5		
Princeton	517	5	Moore	Uriah	1	2			1	2	2	1	1				10		
Princeton	517	6	Moore	Boaz		1			1				1	1			4		
Princeton	517	7	Newton	Uriah		1		1	1	1			1	1			6		
Princeton	517	8	Newton	Charles			1	1				2		1			5		
Princeton	517	9	Norcross	Jacob				1		1	2	2	1				7		
Princeton	517	10	Osgood	Ephraim				1		1	1		1	1			5		
Princeton	517	11	Osgood	Houghton				1		2				1			4		
Princeton	517	12	Parker	Nehemiah	2	2		1		2		1		1			9		
Princeton	517	13	Parker	Philemon	3	2	1		1	2	1	1	1				12		
Princeton	517	14	Parker	Ebenezer		1	1	1	1		1	2		3			10		
Princeton	517	15	Parker	John	1	1	1		1	2	2	1					10		
Princeton	517	16	Parker	Solomon P.			1										3		

TOWN	PG#	LN#	LAST NAME	FIRST NAME	FREE WHITE MALES					FREE WHITE FEMALES					TOTAL ALL OTHER	TOTAL SLAVES	TOTALS	DISTRICT/ TOWNSHIP	NOTES
					under 10	10 to 16	16 to 26	26 to 45	45 and over	under 10	10 to 16	16 to 26	26 to 45	45 and over					
Princeton	517	17	Powers	John	1			1		3			1				6		
Princeton	517	18	Perry	Aaron				1	1			1		1			4		
Princeton	517	19	Parmenter	Luther		1		1		1		2					5		
Princeton	517	20	Parmenter	Reuben					1					1			2		
Princeton	517	21	Prentiss	Henry				1					1				2		
Princeton	517	22	Proctor	John	1			1	1	2		1		1			7		
Princeton	517	23	Priest	Nathan	1	1			1	1	1	1	1				7		
Princeton	517	24	Raymore	Thomas					1					1			2		
Princeton	517	25	Raymore	Thomas Jr				1		1			1				3		
Princeton	517	26	Raymore	Edward	1			1					1				3		
Princeton	517	27	Roper	Benjamin	2			1		2				1			6		
Princeton	517	28	Roper	John	1			1		3			1	1			7		
Princeton	517	29	Russel	Joseph				1				1	1				3		
Princeton	517	30	Russel	Eunice	1	1				1	1		1				5		
Princeton	517	31	Richardson	William				1				2		1			4		
Princeton	517	32	Richardson	Samuel	2	1		1		2	1	1					9		
Princeton	517	33	Rice	Asa	1		2	1			1		1				6		
Princeton	517	34	Rolph	Solomon		1	3		1	3	1	1		2			12		
Princeton	517	35	Rice	David	3	1	1	1			1		1				8		
Princeton	517	36	Reed	Benjamin	3			1	1	1	1			1			7		
Princeton	517	37	Raymore	Timson	1			1		2		1					5		
Princeton	517	38	Spence	Frederick	2		1		1	1	1		1				7		
Princeton	517	39	Smith	Nathan					1	3		1	1	1			7		
Princeton	517	40	Stratton	Samuel	2		1	1		3	3		1				11		
Princeton	517	41	Savage	Seth	2			1	1	2			2	1			9		
Princeton	517	42	Stearns	Jonas			2	1		2			1				6		
Princeton	517	43	Sargeant	Amos				1		5			1	1			8		
Princeton	517	44	Sargeant	Joseph	1			1		1		1					4		
Princeton	517	45	Smith	Jonas	2	2	2		1	1		1		1			10		
Princeton	517	46	Sawin	Ezekiel	3	2	1		1	2		1	1				11		
Princeton	517	47	Sawin	Jesse	1	1		1		4			1				8		
Princeton	517	48	Symonds	Isaac	1			1		2			1				5		
Princeton	517	49	Thacher	Obediah	1	3		1		2		1	1				9		
Princeton	518	1	Thacher	John A.	4			1					2				7		
Princeton	518	2	Thomson	William	2			1		2			1	2			8		
Princeton	518	3	Thomson	Isaac		1		1			1			1			4		
Princeton	518	4	Thomson	John	1	1		1		1			1				5		
Princeton	518	5	Woods	Samuel				1				2		1			4		
Princeton	518	6	Woods	Asa	1		2						1				4		
Princeton	518	7	Wilson	Ephraim	3	1	2	1		1	1	2	1				12		
Princeton	518	8	Wilson	Solomon				1				2					3		
Princeton	518	9	Whitcomb	Asa				1						1			2		
Princeton	518	10	Watson	John	1	1	1		1	2		1					7		
Princeton	518	11	Wheeler	Joseph			1	1		3	1		1				7		
Princeton	518	12	Whiteker	William	3	1	3		1	1	1	1	1				12		
Princeton	518	13	Whitney	Andrew	2	2	1		1	1			1				8		
Princeton	518	14	Wyman	Thomas	4		1	1	1	1		1	1				10		
Princeton	518	15	Worster	Samson	2			1					1				4		
Princeton	518	16	West	Amos				1		1		1		1			4		
Princeton	518	17	Whitcomb	John			1	1		3		1	1				7		

| TOWN | PG# | LN# | LAST NAME | FIRST NAME | FREE WHITE MALES | | | | | FREE WHITE FEMALES | | | | | TOTAL ALL OTHER | TOTAL SLAVES | TOTALS | DISTRICT/ TOWNSHIP | NOTES |
					under 10	10 to 16	16 to 26	26 to 45	45 and over	under 10	10 to 16	16 to 26	26 to 45	45 and over					
Royalston	231	1	Williams	Joseph H			1	1		4	1		2				9		
Royalston	231	2	Bliss	Sylvanus			1			3	1						5		
Royalston	231	3	Wheelor	Russell	3		1			1			1				6		
Royalston	231	4	Dean	Joshua	1	1	1		1		2		1				7		
Royalston	231	5	Bosworth	Ichabod	1				2		1		1				5		
Royalston	231	6	Walker	Reuben			1				1			1			3		
Royalston	231	7	Turner	Samll	1	2	1		1	3			1	1			10		
Royalston	231	8	Stockwell	John	2	2		1		2			1	1			9		
Royalston	231	9	Hill	Ephraim	1			1		3	1		1				7		
Royalston	231	10	Walker	Elijah	2	2	1		1	1		1	1				9		
Royalston	231	11	White	Elisha															No Enumeration Listed
Royalston	231	12	Davis	Joseph	1			1		1							3		
Royalston	231	13	Dexter	James	2	1			1	1	1		1				7		
Royalston	231	14	Walker	Moses	2			1		4			1				8		
Royalston	232	1	Biglow	Gershom				1				1		1			3		
Royalston	232	2	Metcalf	Enos	1	1	1			3	1		1				8		
Royalston	232	3	Shephardson	Isaac	1	1	1	1					1				5		
Royalston	232	4	Shephardson	Jonathan	1	1		1	1				2	1			7		
Royalston	232	5	Metcalf	Michael		2		1		2		1	1				7		
Royalston	232	6	Whitney	Levi	1	1		1		2	1		1				7		
Royalston	232	7	Thurstin	Lewis	1	2	1		1		1	1	1				8		
Royalston	232	8	Kenny	Elizbath Widow		2					2	1	1				6		
Royalston	232	9	Gregory	Isaac	2	2						1	1	1			7		
Royalston	232	10	Lyon	David	4		1		1	3	1	1	1				12		
Royalston	232	11	Bartlet	Nathan	1	1			1	1	1			1			6		
Royalston	232	12	Nurse	Joel	2		3				1	1					7		
Royalston	232	13	Cutler	Ebenz	1		1			2	2		2	1			9		
Royalston	232	14	Taft	David	1		1			3			1				6		
Royalston	233	1	Kinsley	Elisha	1	1		1		4	2		1				10		
Royalston	233	2	Bullock	Ebenz	1		1			1	2		1				6		
Royalston	233	3	Bullock	Nathan	1			1		2				1			5		
Royalston	233	4	Fisher	David	2		1			3			1				7		
Royalston	233	5	Foster	John		1		1		1	1						4		
Royalston	233	6	Hinsley	Peleg	2	2	1			2			1	1			9		
Royalston	233	7	Deck	John				1				1		1			3		
Royalston	233	8	Deck	Squire	1			1		1		1					4		
Royalston	233	9	Bliss	Timothy				1				1		1			3		
Royalston	233	10	Bliss	Timothy Junr	2		2	1		2	2		1				10		
Royalston	233	11	Bliss	Israel	2	2		1		2			1				8		
Royalston	233	12	Bliss	Nathan		1		1		1	1		1				5		
Royalston	233	13	Peck	Daniel		2		1		2	3			1			9		
Royalston	233	14	Wood	Abiel	1			1		1		1					4		
Royalston	234	1	Briggs	Jacob				1						1			2		
Royalston	234	2	Deck	Danll Junr	2			1		2		1					6		
Royalston	234	3	Gale	Jonathan		1		1		2	1		1				6		
Royalston	234	4	Baker	Amos				1						1			2		
Royalston	234	5	Bliss	Aaron	2	1	1		1				4	1			10		
Royalston	234	6	Goddard	Samll	2	1	2	1		1	1		1				9		
Royalston	234	7	Brewer	Jonas	1		1	1		2		3		3			11		
Royalston	234	8	Garfield	Joshua		1	1	1		2	1	2	1				9		
Royalston	234	9	Matthews	Jona		1	1	1		1	1	2					7		
Royalston	234	10	Peck	Solomon	2		2	1		2	3			1			11		
Royalston	234	11	Davis	Joanna		1						1	1	1			4		
Royalston	234	12	Davis	Asahel	1		1						1				3		
Royalston	234	13	Bullock	Hugh	1	1	2		1	1	1		1				8		
Royalston	234	14	Bullock	Molten	1		1		1	1	1		1	1			7		
Royalston	234	15	Rogers	Eliphalet	3	1	1				2		1				9		
Royalston	234	16	Blending	Shubael	1		1	1		2	1	2		1			9		
Royalston	235	1	Norton	John	1			1		3			1				6		
Royalston	235	2	Batchelor	Thomas				1		2		1					4		
Royalston	235	3	Batchelor	John	1			1						1			3		
Royalston	235	4	Nichols	Jonathan	2			1		2	1		1				7		
Royalston	235	5	Leath	Benja	2	1		1		2				1			7		
Royalston	235	6	Eddy	Benja	1	1	1	1				2		2			8		
Royalston	235	7	Felch	Caleb	3	1		1		3			1				9		
Royalston	235	8	Cheney	Elisha	3	1		1		1	2	1	2				11		
Royalston	235	9	Derry	Thaddeus	1	1		1		2	1		1				7		
Royalston	235	10	Michard	Eliphaley Jun	2	1		1		1	1		1				7		
Royalston	235	11	Whitney	Ephm	1			1		3				1			6		Name crossed off on census
Royalston	235	12	Jacobs	Whitman			1		1	1				1			4		
Royalston	235	13	Jacobs	Joseph			1			3			1				5		
Royalston	235	14	Jacobs	Simeon	1	1	1	1		2	2		1				9		
Royalston	235	15	Chamberlain	John	2		1	1			1	1	1				7		
Royalston	235	16	Pratt	Jabez	1			1						1			3		
Royalston	236	1	Metcalf	Pelatiah	1	1			1					1			5		
Royalston	236	2	Walker	Obadiah		2		1		1		1	1	1			7		
Royalston	236	3	Grant	Aaron		1	1	1					1	1			5		
Royalston	236	4	Kelton	Lovell		1				1		1					3		
Royalston	236	5	Raymond	Stephen	1			1		1		1					4		
Royalston	236	6	Davis	Squire	2	2		1		1	1		1				8		
Royalston	236	7	Forbes	James	1	1	1	1		3	1	1	1				10		
Royalston	236	8	Hix	Josiah		1			1	1		1	1	1			6		
Royalston	236	9	Hix	Ephrm	1			1		2			1				5		
Royalston	236	10	Blanding	Ebenz	2		1		1	3			1				8		
Royalston	236	11	Pine	William	2			2						1			5		
Royalston	236	12	Blanding	Ebenz Jr			1			1			1				3		
Royalston	236	13	Ingolls	Ebenz	2	1	1		1	1			1				7		
Royalston	236	14	Fuller	George			1			1			1				3		
Royalston	236	15	Bullock	Christopher		1			1			1	1	1			5		
Royalston	236	16	Bullock	Christopher Jr	1	2		1		1		2		1			8		

TOWN	PG#	LN#	LAST NAME	FIRST NAME	FREE WHITE MALES					FREE WHITE FEMALES					TOTAL ALL OTHER	TOTAL SLAVES	TOTALS	DISTRICT/ TOWNSHIP	NOTES
					under 10	10 to 16	16 to 26	26 to 45	45 and over	under 10	10 to 16	16 to 26	26 to 45	45 and over					
Royalston	237	1	Chamberain	Josiah	1			1		2	1			1			6		
Royalston	237	2	Piper	Isaac			1			2		1					4		
Royalston	237	3	Peirce	William	2		1	1		4			1				9		
Royalston	237	4	Whitmore	Isaac	1			1		2			1	1			6		
Royalston	237	5	Sanders	William	1		1						1				3		
Royalston	237	6	Burbank	John	1			1					1	1			4		
Royalston	237	7	Stockwell	Simeon	2	1		1		1				1			6		
Royalston	237	8	Whitmore	John	2		1	1		1				1			6		
Royalston	237	9	Holman	Smith	1			1		3				1			6		
Royalston	237	10	Chubb	Silas	1	1	1		1	1	2	1	1				9		
Royalston	237	11	Woodcock	Jeremiah			1					1		1			3		
Royalston	237	12	Bosworth	Jona	2	2	2		1	2	1			1			11		
Royalston	237	13	Green	Samuel	1		1			2			1				5		
Royalston	237	14	Fry	James	1		1			2			1				5		
Royalston	237	15	Davis	Alexander P.		1		1		1	2			1			6		
Royalston	237	16	Bowker	Samll W.	2		1					1					4		
Royalston	237	17	Gregory	Samll			2		1		1		1				5		
Royalston	238	1	Chase	David	2	2		1		2	1			1			9		
Royalston	238	2	Chase	William	1		1	1		2			1	1			7		
Royalston	238	3	Fith	Isaac	1			1		3			1				6		
Royalston	238	4	Clements	Widow									1	1			2		
Royalston	238	5	Thomson	Margaret		1								2			3		
Royalston	238	6	Carrol	Anna		1	2			2		1	2	2			10		
Royalston	238	7	Thomson	Jonas	1	2	2		1	1	2	1		2			12		
Royalston	238	8	Newton	Nathan B.	2	2	2		1	3	1			1			12		
Royalston	238	9	Nichols	Solomon	5			1						1			7		
Royalston	238	10	Fry	David		1		1						1			3		
Royalston	238	11	Gregory	Amasa	1		1						1				3		
Royalston	238	12	Nichols	William				1					1	1			3		
Royalston	238	13	Nichols	William Junr	1			1		2			1				5		
Royalston	238	14	Nichols	Robert	1			1		1		1					4		
Royalston	238	15	Fith	Robert	2			1					1				4		
Royalston	238	16	Bartlet	Jonas	1			1		1	1						4		
Royalston	238	17	Gary	Aaron			1			2	1						4		
Royalston	239	1	Nichols	Elijah			1						1				2		
Royalston	239	2	Brown	William 2d	1	1		1		2	1		1				7		
Royalston	239	3	Felch	Samll				1					1	1			3		
Royalston	239	4	Felch	Samll Junr		2	1					1	1				5		
Royalston	239	5	Emerson	Joseph	1			1				1	3	1			7		
Royalston	239	6	Hewes	Joshua				1					1				2		
Royalston	239	7	Eager	Solomon	1	1		1					1	1			5		
Royalston	239	8	Upham	Willard			2			1			1				4		
Royalston	239	9	Heywood	Silas	1	1	1	1				1		1			6		
Royalston	239	10	Perry	Thomas				1						1			2		
Royalston	239	11	Lee	Joseph		1		1	1	1	1	2		1			8		
Royalston	239	12	Furbush	David	1	1	1	1		1	1			1			7		
Royalston	239	13	Soverein	Joseph	1			1						1			3		
Royalston	239	14	Manning	Joseph	1	1		1		1		1	1				6		
Royalston	239	15	Bullock	Molton	1		1	1		1		1	1	1			7		
Royalston	240	1	Peirce	Gad Junr	2	1		1		2			1				7		
Royalston	240	2	Ellis	Adams			1	1		1		1	1	1			6		
Royalston	240	3	Stockwell	Judah	3			1		3			1				8		
Royalston	240	4	Ellis	Ezekiel	2	1	1	1		1	1		1				8		
Royalston	240	5	Lawrence	Samuel	1		1						1				3		
Royalston	240	6	Stockwell	Joseph		1		1					1	1			4		
Royalston	240	7	Nichols	David	1			1		2	1		1				6		
Royalston	240	8	Cutler	Jonathan			1	1		2	2			1			7		
Royalston	240	9	Peirce	John	2	1		1		2	1		1				8		
Royalston	240	10	White	Thomas	2			1			2		1				6		
Royalston	240	11	Gale	Isaac	2			1		1		1	1				6		
Royalston	240	12	Beal	John	1			1					1				3		
Royalston	240	13	Nichols	Moses		1		1		2		2					6		
Royalston	240	14	Whitmore	Enoch	1			1		3				1			6		
Royalston	240	15	Kenney	William	3	2	1	1		1	1		1				10		
Royalston	240	16	Piper	Josiah				1			1			1			3		
Royalston	240	17	Norcross	Isaac			1							1			2		
Royalston	241	1	Andrews	Ebenz				1			1		1				3		
Royalston	241	2	Bemis	Jonas	1	1		1		2	1		1				7		
Royalston	241	3	Hale	Jacob	2			1			1		1				5		
Royalston	241	4	Bud	Nathan	1	1	1	1		3	1		1				9		
Royalston	241	5	Taft	Joel	3	1				1			1				6		
Royalston	241	6	Woods	John	1	1		1		1			1				5		
Royalston	241	7	Foster	Tammy	4	1	1			2	1		1				10		
Royalston	241	8	Hubbard	James	2			1		1		1	1				6		
Royalston	241	9	Bartlet	Josiah	3			1		1			1				6		
Royalston	241	10	Stockwell	Asahel	1		1						1				3		
Royalston	241	11	Batchelor	Stephen	2		1	1		2				2			8		
Royalston	241	12	Nichols	John				1		1	1	1	1	1			6		
Royalston	241	13	Batchelor	John Jr	1			1		1			1				4		
Royalston	241	14	Goddard	Samll	2		1	1						1			5		
Royalston	241	15	Goddard	Henry				1					1				2		
Royalston	241	16	Bartlet	Ira	1	1	2	1					1				6		
Royalston	241	17	Pratt	William	1		2						1	1			5		
Royalston	241	18	Raymond	Wm	3	1	2	1		1	1		1	1			11		
Royalston	241	19	Chase	Archebald	1	1	1	1		3		1	1	1			10		
Royalston	241	20	Hill	Jonah				1						1			2		
Royalston	241	21	Hill	Oliver	2	1		1					2				6		
Royalston	241	22	Hutchinson	Benja	1		1	1		1		1		1			6		
Royalston	241	23	Whitney	Ephm	1					1		1	1	1			5		
Royalston	241	24	Fry	Ebenz	2	1	1	1				1	1				7		

TOWN	PG#	LN#	HEADS OF HOUSEHOLD LAST NAME	FIRST NAME	FREE WHITE MALES under 10	10 to 16	16 to 26	26 to 45	45 and over	FREE WHITE FEMALES under 10	10 to 16	16 to 26	26 to 45	45 and over	TOTAL ALL OTHER	TOTAL SLAVES	TOTALS	DISTRICT/ TOWNSHIP	NOTES
Royalston	241	25	Fry	John					1			1		1			3		
Royalston	241	26	Bemis	Jason	1	1	1	1		2			1				7		
Royalston	241	27	Clap	Nehemiah	1	1	2						3	1			9		
Royalston	241	28	Richardson	Thos	2			1		3	1		1				8		
Royalston	241	29	Barret	Benja	2		1	1				2					6		
Royalston	241	30	Peirce	Gad		1	1		1					1			4		
Royalston	241	31	Peirce	Jona	1		1	1					1				4		
Royalston	241	32	Chase	Roger		1			1				2	1			5		
Royalston	241	33	Davis	Peter	1			1		4			1	1			8		
Royalston	241	34	Town	William			1		1			2	1	1			6		
Royalston	241	35	Faulkner	Ammi R*	2		1	1			1		1				6		
Royalston	242	1	Woodbury	Peter			1	1	1					1			4		
Royalston	242	2	Wood	Daniel	2	1		1		1		1	1				7		
Royalston	242	3	Beal	Thomas			1		1			1		2			5		
Royalston	242	4	Sweet			1	1		1	2	1		1				7		First name left blank
Royalston	242	5	Clements	Wm		1	1	1		2	1	2	1				9		
Royalston	242	6	Allen	Jonas		1	1	1	1		1	1	1	1			8		
Royalston	242	7	French	Widow	1	1				1			1				4		
Royalston	242	8	Bowker	Stephen	1			1				1					3		
Royalston	242	9	Bowker	Silas					1			1		1			3		
Royalston	242	10	Cutting	Nathan					1		2	1		1			5		
Royalston	242	11	Piper	Josiah Junr	1			1					1				3		
Royalston	242	12	Cutting	Nathan Jr				1		1			1				3		
Royalston	242	13	Nichols	Henry		1			1	1			1				4		
Royalston	242	14	Nichols	Henry Junr				1				1					2		
Royalston	242	15	Chase	Silas	1	1		1		1	1		1				6		
Royalston	242	16	Richardson	Timo	1	1	2		1		1	1		1			8		
Royalston	242	17	Bragg	Nathl	1	1	1		1			2		1			7		

TOWN	PG#	LN#	LAST NAME	FIRST NAME	M under 10	M 10 to 16	M 16 to 26	M 26 to 45	M 45 and over	F under 10	F 10 to 16	F 16 to 26	F 26 to 45	F 45 and over	TOTAL ALL OTHER	TOTAL SLAVES	TOTALS	DISTRICT/ TOWNSHIP	NOTES
Rutland	505	1	Adams	Daniel	2	2			1				1				6		
Rutland	505	2	Adams	Asa	2	1	1	1		1	1		1				8		
Rutland	505	3	Adams	Reuben	1	1		1		3	1	1	1				9		
Rutland	505	4	Blair	James Junr	2	4			2		1			2			11		
Rutland	505	5	Bridge	William		1	1		1			1	2	1			7		
Rutland	505	6	Briant	Isaac	2			1		1	1		1				6		
Rutland	505	7	Bartlet	Daniel				1			1	1	1				4		
Rutland	505	8	Bartlet	Daniel Junr	2			1		2	1		1				7		
Rutland	505	9	Bartlet	Levi	1			1					1				3		
Rutland	505	10	Baxter	Moses		1		1			1		1				4		
Rutland	505	11	Brown	Solomon	2			1	1	2	1		1	1			9		
Rutland	505	12	Ball	Eleazer	1	3		1		3			2				10		
Rutland	505	13	Borman	John	1			1			1		1				4		
Rutland	505	14	Bigelow	Thaddeus		1		1				1	1				4		
Rutland	505	15	Bigelow	Joseph	2			1		1	1		1				6		
Rutland	505	16	Bent	Martha		1	1				1		1				4		
Rutland	505	17	Bent	Darius			2	1		2	1		1				7		
Rutland	505	18	Bent	Phinehas	1		2			1		1		1			6		
Rutland	505	19	Bartlet	Adonijah	1	1		1		1	2		2				8		
Rutland	505	20	Blake	Francis	2	1	1	2		1	1	1					9		
Rutland	505	21	Browning	William				1					1				2		
Rutland	505	22	Browning	Ephraim		1	1			1			1	1			5		
Rutland	505	23	*	*	2			1				1		1			5		Name illegible due to fading
Rutland	505	24	*	*		1				1		1					3		Name illegible due to fading
Rutland	505	25	Browning	James	3	1		1		3	3		1	1			13		
Rutland	505	26	Browning	James 2d	1	1	1	1		1			1				6		
Rutland	505	27	Boice	John		1		1			1		1				4		
Rutland	505	28	Boice	Thomas	3			2		1	1		1				8		
Rutland	505	29	Boice	John Junr	2			2		1			1				6		
Rutland	505	30	Boynes	Philip				1		1	1	1		1			5		
Rutland	505	31	Brown	Josiah			1	1		2			1				5		
Rutland	505	32	Bowker	Oliver	1	1		1		3	1	1	1				9		
Rutland	505	33	Brigham	John	3	1	1	1		1	1		1				9		
Rutland	505	34	Cowden	James	1	1		1	1	2		1	1				8		
Rutland	505	35	Child	Thomas	1			1				1	2				5		
Rutland	505	36	Child	Abiathar	1		2		1	2	1		1				8		
Rutland	505	37	Child	Amherst	5			1		1			3				10		
Rutland	505	38	Cutting	Keziah								1	1				2		
Rutland	505	39	Cunningham	Mary		1	1	1					1				4		
Rutland	505	40	Chickering	Oliver		1		1					1				3		
Rutland	505	41	Carrell	Benjamin	1	1		1				1					4		
Rutland	505	42	Clap	Asahel		1	1				1	1	1				5		
Rutland	505	43	Coggswell	Stephen	1	1		1		2	2		1				8		
Rutland	505	44	Craige	David	1			1		2			1				5		
Rutland	505	45	Capen	Lemuel			1	1		2		1					5		
Rutland	505	46	Davis	Thaddeus	1			1	1				1	1			5		
Rutland	505	47	Davis	Alpheus	1	1	1	1		2			1	1			8		
Rutland	506	1	Davis	Jesse		1		1				1		1			4		
Rutland	506	2	Davis	Eliakim	2			1	1	3	2	1	1	1			12		
Rutland	506	3	Davis	Mary		1								2			3		
Rutland	506	4	Davis	Asa				1		2		1					4		
Rutland	506	5	Davis	William	2			1		1		1					5		
Rutland	506	6	Dean	William	2			1		1		1					5		
Rutland	506	7	Davis	Rebeckah		1	1					1	1	1			5		
Rutland	506	8	Desmond	Daniel	3		1	1					1				6		
Rutland	506	9	Dean	Lavery	1			1		3			2				7		
Rutland	506	10	Daws	Cato											5		5		
Rutland	506	11	Eustis	Chamberlain		1	1	1		1			2				6		
Rutland	506	12	Eustis	Joseph	1	1	1			2		1					6		
Rutland	506	13	Estabrook	Daniel		1		1		1		1					4		
Rutland	506	14	Estabrook	Daniel Jr		1	1				1						3		
Rutland	506	15	Estabrook	Jedediah	5			1			1	1					8		
Rutland	506	16	Everett	Phinehas		1	1		1	2	1		1				7		
Rutland	506	17	Freelove	Samuel			1			2	1	1					5		
Rutland	506	18	Frost	Ruth									1				1		
Rutland	506	19	Fisk	William	1			1		2			1				5		
Rutland	506	20	Forbes	John		1	1	1		2	1		1				7		
Rutland	506	21	Fisk	Asa	2			1	1	1	1		1	1			8		
Rutland	506	22	Frink	John	1	1	1	2	1	2		1	1	1			11		
Rutland	507	1	Willington	John			2	1		2			1				6		
Rutland	507	2	Willington	Ebenezer	2			1		2			1				6		
Rutland	507	3	Wheeler	Asa	2			1		4	1		1				9		
Rutland	507	4	Wood	Nathaniel	3			1					1				5		
Rutland	507	5	Wright	Tabitha			1				1		1				3		
Rutland	509	1	Homer	Thomas	3	1	1	1		1		1	1	1			10		
Rutland	509	2	Homer	Thomas Junr				1			1						2		
Rutland	509	3	Hale	David	1			1		2			1				5		
Rutland	509	4	Heard	Mark	2		1		1	1		3		1			9		
Rutland	509	5	Hubbard	Jonathan		1		1		1	1	1	1				6		
Rutland	509	6	Hubbard	Joel	4			1					2				7		
Rutland	509	7	Henry	David			1	1				2		1			5		
Rutland	509	8	Henry	Samuel	1		1			1			1				4		
Rutland	509	9	Henry	Silas	1			1					1				3		
Rutland	509	10	Henry	William		1	1	1	1		1	1	1				7		
Rutland	509	11	Haynes	Jonathan		1	1	1			1		1				5		
Rutland	509	12	Johnson	Dillington		2	1		1	3			1				8		
Rutland	509	13	Kennan	Andrew	2	1		1		2	1		1				8		
Rutland	509	14	King	Samuel	1	1		1			1		1				5		
Rutland	509	15	King	Joseph	2	2	3		1	1			1				10		
Rutland	509	16	Linkfield	John	2		1					1					4		

Town	PG#	LN#	LAST NAME	FIRST NAME	under 10	10 to 16	16 to 26	26 to 45	45 and over	under 10	10 to 16	16 to 26	26 to 45	45 and over	TOTAL ALL OTHER	TOTAL SLAVES	TOTALS	DISTRICT/ TOWNSHIP	NOTES
			HEADS OF HOUSEHOLD		FREE WHITE MALES					FREE WHITE FEMALES									
Rutland	509	17	Lincoln	Samuel	1	1		1		2	1		1	1			8		
Rutland	509	18	Messenger	Pelitiah	1			1					1				3		
Rutland	509	19	Metcalf	Timothy	1		1		1	1		1	1	1			7		
Rutland	509	20	Morse	Elisha	2			1		1	1		1				6		
Rutland	509	21	Maynard	Moses	2	2		1		1	1		1	1			9		
Rutland	509	22	Morse	Isaac	2			1		2			1				6		
Rutland	509	23	Morse	Timothy	2	1	1		1		1	1		1			8		
Rutland	509	24	Miles	Barzillas	1		1	1		3	1		1				8		
Rutland	510	1	Fessenden	Elizabeth		1	1				1		1	1			5		
Rutland	510	2	Fessenden	Inman				1					1				2		
Rutland	510	3	Flint	Tilly	1	1		1	1	1			1				7		
Rutland	510	4	Gates	Joseph	2		1	1	1	2			1	1			9		
Rutland	510	5	Goodenow	Daniel		1		1		3			1				6		
Rutland	510	6	Graham	William			1					1	1	1			4		
Rutland	510	7	Gates	Zadock			3	1		1		1		1			7		
Rutland	510	8	Goodell	John	1	1		2				1	1				6		
Rutland	510	9	Goodenow	Asa	1			1		1			1				4		
Rutland	510	10	Gray	John			1			3	1		1				6		
Rutland	510	11	Goodrich	Hezekiah	1	1		1		1	1						5		
Rutland	510	12	Gates	Sarah	1								2	1			4		
Rutland	510	13	Hodges	Job			1	1	1			2		1			7		
Rutland	510	14	How	Jonas		1		1	1			2	1				6		
Rutland	510	15	How	David	1	2	1		1	1	1	1	1				9		
Rutland	510	16	How	Lucy		1	1					1	1	1			5		
Rutland	510	17	How	Matthias		1			1	1			1	1			5		
Rutland	510	18	Harrington	Noah				1		1			1				3		
Rutland	510	19	Holden	Phidelia	2	1	1			1	1		1				7		
Rutland	510	20	Holden	Benjamin	2	1		1		1			1				6		
Rutland	510	21	Hildreth	Ralph	1			1				2	1				5		
Rutland	510	22	Hunt	Thomas				1		1		2	1				5		
Rutland	510	23	Hooker	Samuel		1		1		1		1					4		
Rutland	510	24	Hammond	Stephen	2	1	1	1		2			1				8		
Rutland	511	1	Read	Daniel		1	1	1		2		1	1	1			8		
Rutland	511	2	Reed	Jonas	2	1	2	2	1		1		1				10		
Rutland	511	3	Rice	David			1	1	1				1	1			5		
Rutland	511	4	Rice	John	1		1		1	2	1	5	1	1			13		
Rutland	511	5	Rice	Josiah	3			1		2			1				7		
Rutland	511	6	Ruggles	Timoth		1	2		1			1	1	1			7		
Rutland	511	7	Roper	Daniel	1			1	1	1			1	1			6		
Rutland	511	8	Roper	Daniel Junr			1			2			1				4		
Rutland	511	9	Randall	Joshua				1		1				1			3		
Rutland	511	10	Reed	Edmund		2	2		1	1	1	1		1			9		
Rutland	511	11	Robinson	Samuel				1		2	2	1		1			7		
Rutland	511	12	Randall	Hannah	4					1			1				6		
Rutland	511	13	Smith	Lockert	2	2		1		2	1		1	1			10		
Rutland	511	14	Smith	William		1	1		1		1	1	1				6		
Rutland	511	15	Smith	David	4		2	1				1	1				9		
Rutland	511	16	Smith	Enoch	1	1		1		3	1		1				8		
Rutland	511	17	Smith	Andrew	1		1	1		1		1	2	1			8		
Rutland	511	18	Smith	Benoni	2	1	2		1	1				1			8		
Rutland	511	19	Smith	Jonas	1			1		1				1			4		
Rutland	511	20	Stone	John			1	1	1	1		1	1	2			8		
Rutland	511	21	Stone	Stevens			1	1			1	2		1			6		
Rutland	511	22	Stone	Elijah	1	1		1		1		1	1	1			6		
Rutland	511	23	Stone	Jedithon		2		1			1	3					8		
Rutland	511	24	Sanders	Daniel	1		1		2				2	1			7		
Rutland	512	1	Miles	Ebenezer	2	1		1		2	1		1				8		
Rutland	512	2	Mead	Benjamin	1	1		1	1	3			1	1			9		
Rutland	512	3	Merick	Silas	2			1					1				4		
Rutland	512	4	Murray	Alexander			1		1	2		2	1				7		
Rutland	512	5	Murray	Samuel	2		1						1				4		
Rutland	512	6	Messenger	Wigglesworth		1	1		1	1	1		1				7		
Rutland	512	7	Marble	Jesse	1	1		1		4			1				8		
Rutland	512	8	McGregory	Isaac											5		5		
Rutland	512	9	McCuller	Matthew	1		1						1				4		
Rutland	512	10	Newton	Peter				1						2			3		
Rutland	512	11	Newton	Asa			1					1					2		
Rutland	512	12	Newton	Hezekiah	1	3			1	1				1			7		
Rutland	512	13	Newton	Samuel			1						1				2		
Rutland	512	14	Oliver	David		1		1				1		1			4		
Rutland	512	15	Putnam	Archilaus		1			1			2		1			5		
Rutland	512	16	Putnam	Benjamin	1	1	1	1		2		1	1				8		
Rutland	512	17	Peirce	Joel	3			1		1			1				6		
Rutland	512	18	Parmenter	Jonas	1		1		1	3			1				7		
Rutland	512	19	Parmenter	Abel		1		1		1	2		1	1			7		
Rutland	512	20	Phillips	Joshua	1		1		1	1	2	2	1				9		
Rutland	512	21	Phillips	Daniel	1		1			1			1				4		
Rutland	512	22	Putnam	Andrew	1			1					1				3		
Rutland	512	23	Read	Thomas	1		1	1		2			3				8		
Rutland	512	24	Read	Jason	1		1	1	1				1	1			6		
Rutland	513	1	Woodcock	John	1		1			1			1				4		
Rutland	513	2	Wheeler	Jacob	1		1			1							3		
Rutland	513	3	Woodcock	Daniel	1		1			1			1				4		
Rutland	514	1	Stearns	Jonathan				1	1				1	1			4		
Rutland	514	2	Stearns	Elijah	1		1	1	1	1		1	1				7		
Rutland	514	3	Sawyer	Nathaniel	2	1				1	1		1				7		
Rutland	514	4	Skinner	Israel	2			1						1			4		
Rutland	514	5	Savage	Thankful				1				1		1			3		
Rutland	514	6	Savage	Charlotte	2							1	1				4		
Rutland	514	7	Smith	James	2	1	1		1	3	1	2	1				12		

TOWN	PG#	LN#	LAST NAME	FIRST NAME	FREE WHITE MALES					FREE WHITE FEMALES					TOTAL ALL OTHER	TOTAL SLAVES	TOTALS	DISTRICT/ TOWNSHIP	NOTES
					under 10	10 to 16	16 to 26	26 to 45	45 and over	under 10	10 to 16	16 to 26	26 to 45	45 and over					
Rutland	514	8	Stone	Jonas	1	1		1		3			1	1			8		
Rutland	514	9	Stratton	Alpheus	2	1		1	1	3			1	1			10		
Rutland	514	10	Stone	Jerusha	1					1	1		1				4		
Rutland	514	11	Tower	Jonathan	1			1					1				3		
Rutland	514	12	Tower	John	2			1		1			1				5		
Rutland	514	13	Wood	Rebekah		1						1		2			4		
Rutland	514	14	Walton	John					1			1		1			3		
Rutland	514	15	Walton	Samuel		1	4	1		1			1	1			9		
Rutland	514	16	Wheeler	Isaac			1	1	1			1		1			5		
Rutland	514	17	Wheeler	Abraham		1	2	1					1				5		
Rutland	514	18	Woodcock	Bela	2		1	1		2	1		1				8		
Rutland	514	19	Walker	Daniel	3		1	1		2	2	1	1	1			12		
Rutland	514	20	Warner	Thomas W			1	2				2					5		
Rutland	514	21	Williams	Samuel	2	1		1		1			1				6		
Rutland	514	22	Wheeler	James				1					1				2		
Rutland	514	23	White	Moses	5	1		3	1	1	1	2	2				16		
Rutland	514	24	Whitmore	Eber	1	1		1	1				1						

TOWN	PG#	LN#	LAST NAME	FIRST NAME	FREE WHITE MALES					FREE WHITE FEMALES					TOTAL ALL OTHER	TOTAL SLAVES	TOTALS	DISTRICT/ TOWNSHIP	NOTES
					under 10	10 to 16	16 to 26	26 to 45	45 and over	under 10	10 to 16	16 to 26	26 to 45	45 and over					
Shrewsbury	361	1	Adams	Jonathan				1	1				1	1			4		
Shrewsbury	361	2	Allen	Elnathan		1	1		1				1	1			5		
Shrewsbury	361	3	Allen	Silas		1		1					1				3		
Shrewsbury	361	4	Alexander	James	1			1	1	1	1		1				5		
Shrewsbury	361	5	Allen	Ashel			1					1					2		
Shrewsbury	361	6	Bragg	John	1	1	1		1		1		1				6		
Shrewsbury	361	7	Baker	Reuben	1		1	1		2	1		1				7		
Shrewsbury	361	8	Baker	John				1		2			1				4		
Shrewsbury	361	9	Baker	Daniel	1	2	1	1					2	1			8		
Shrewsbury	361	10	Baldwin	Azubah	1	1					1		1				4		
Shrewsbury	361	11	Brigham	Samuel		1	1		2					2			6		
Shrewsbury	361	12	Bellows	John		1	2		1			1		1			6		
Shrewsbury	361	13	Brigham	David		2	1		1			2		2			8		
Shrewsbury	361	14	Brigham	Nathl			1					1					2		
Shrewsbury	361	15	Brown	George				1					1				2		
Shrewsbury	365	1	Deane	Nathaniel	1			1		1		1					4		
Shrewsbury	365	2	Eddy	Benjamin				1	1	1	1	1		1	4		9		
Shrewsbury	365	3	Eager	Lewis	2	1	1		1	2		2	1				10		
Shrewsbury	365	4	Fay	Charles	2	1		1		1		1	1				7		
Shrewsbury	365	5	Flint	Edward Doct.	1		3		1		1		1				7		
Shrewsbury	365	6	Fitch	Charles M.		1	1			2		2					6		
Shrewsbury	365	7	Goddard	Benja	1	1	1	1	1	1	1	1		3			11		
Shrewsbury	365	8	Goddard	Daniel		1		1				1		1			4		
Shrewsbury	365	9	Goddard	Luther	1	2	1	1		4	1		2				12		
Shrewsbury	365	10	Green	Nathaniel	3			1		1			1				6		
Shrewsbury	365	11	Garfield	Abijah	2	1	1		1	3			1		1		10		
Shrewsbury	365	12	Green	John	2		1	1				1					5		
Shrewsbury	365	13	Green	Zacheus	1			1					1				3		
Shrewsbury	365	14	Henshaw	Joshua Esq		1			1			2		2			6		
Shrewsbury	365	15	Holden	Daniel	1	1			2				1	1			6		
Shrewsbury	366	1	Biglow	Humphrey	1	1	1	1		3			1				8		
Shrewsbury	366	2	Billings	Silvanus	2	2	2		1		1	1		2			11		
Shrewsbury	366	3	Bruce	Jonathan			1		1		1			1			4		
Shrewsbury	366	4	Cloyes	Eunice	1					1	1						3		
Shrewsbury	366	5	Cushing	Col Job				1						2			3		
Shrewsbury	366	6	Cutler	Jonathan			1	2	1				2	1			7		
Shrewsbury	366	7	Crosby	Philip	3		1	1					1				6		
Shrewsbury	366	8	Cary	Peter	2		1	1		1			1				6		
Shrewsbury	366	9	Chickering	Oliver				1		1		1					3		
Shrewsbury	366	10	Drane	Jonathan			1		1	1		2		1			6		
Shrewsbury	366	11	Drury	Caleb				1				1		1			3		
Shrewsbury	366	12	Drury	Joel	1	1		1		2	1		1				7		
Shrewsbury	366	13	Drury	Abijah	1		1	1		2			1				6		
Shrewsbury	366	14	Drury	Ebenezer	3		1	1	1	2		1	1				10		
Shrewsbury	366	15	Deane	Ebenezer				1		2			1				4		
Shrewsbury	367	1	Harrington	Jonathan	3		1	1			1		1				7		
Shrewsbury	367	2	Hastings	Joseph		1			1					1			3		
Shrewsbury	367	3	Hastings	Jonas	1	2	1	1		1				1			7		
Shrewsbury	367	4	Heywood	Nathaniel	1	2	3		1	1	1		1				10		
Shrewsbury	367	5	Henshaw	Sarah			1	1			1	1		1	1		6		
Shrewsbury	367	6	Harlow	Arunah		1		1				1					3		
Shrewsbury	367	7	Harlow	Thomas	1		1	1					1				4		
Shrewsbury	367	8	Howe	Daniel	3		1			1			1				6		
Shrewsbury	367	9	Haven	Samuel	2		3	1		2	2		1		3		14		
Shrewsbury	367	10	Haven	Samuel Jr	2		1						1				4		
Shrewsbury	367	11	Johnson	Daniel	2		1		1	1	2	1	1				9		
Shrewsbury	367	12	Johnson	Stephen	1		1	2		3			1				8		
Shrewsbury	367	13	Johnson	Philip		1		1	1					2			5		
Shrewsbury	367	14	Jenison	Joseph B.	4			1	2	1			1	1			10		
Shrewsbury	367	15	Jenison	William	2	2		1			1						7		
Shrewsbury	368	1	Howe	Nathan	2	1		1	1	2	1	1	1	2			12		
Shrewsbury	368	2	Howe	Gideon				1			2		1				4		
Shrewsbury	368	3	Howe	John H.	1			1		1	2		1				6		
Shrewsbury	368	4	Howe	Jonah Maj.		1			1			1		1			4		
Shrewsbury	368	5	Howe	Dennis	2	1		1	1	2	1		1	1			10		
Shrewsbury	368	6	Hapgood	Joab			1	1					1	1			4		
Shrewsbury	368	7	Hapgood	Ephraim			1			1			1				3		
Shrewsbury	368	8	Hemanway	Silas			2		1			1		1			5		
Shrewsbury	368	9	Hemanway	Jonas		1		1				1	1	1			5		
Shrewsbury	368	10	Hemanway	Vashni	2		3	1					1				7		
Shrewsbury	368	11	Howard	Timothy			1		1					1			3		
Shrewsbury	368	12	Holding	Amasa		1	1			2		1					5		
Shrewsbury	368	13	Harrington	Isaac		1	1	1	1					1			5		
Shrewsbury	368	14	Harrington	Fortunatas	1			1		1		1	1				5		
Shrewsbury	368	15	Harrington	Thomas		1					2		1				5		
Shrewsbury	368	16	Harrington	Daniel	1	1		1		2			1	1			7		
Shrewsbury	368	17	Harrington	Elijah		1	1		1	1	1	1		1			7		
Shrewsbury	370	1	Knowlton	Joseph	2			1		1	2		1				7		
Shrewsbury	370	2	Knowlton	Lucy	1		2			3			1				7		

TOWN	PG#	LN#	HEADS OF HOUSEHOLD LAST NAME	FIRST NAME	FREE WHITE MALES under 10	10 to 16	16 to 26	26 to 45	45 and over	FREE WHITE FEMALES under 10	10 to 16	16 to 26	26 to 45	45 and over	TOTAL ALL OTHER	TOTAL SLAVES	TOTALS	DISTRICT/ TOWNSHIP	NOTES
Shrewsbury	370	3	Knowlton	Thomas	1	2	1		1	1	1	1		1			9		
Shrewsbury	370	4	Knowlton	Abraham		1	1		1		1	3		1			8		
Shrewsbury	370	5	Knowlton	William		2	1		1		1			1			6		
Shrewsbury	370	6	Knowlton	Artemas	1			1					1				3		
Shrewsbury	370	7	Lyon	Ephraim		1			1					1			3		
Shrewsbury	370	8	Lyon	Ephraim Jr			1			1		1					3		
Shrewsbury	370	9	Miles	Thomas				1	1			2		1			5		
Shrewsbury	370	10	Munroe	Nathaniel		3	3		1	1				1			9		
Shrewsbury	370	11	Munroe	Aaron	1		1	1		1			1				5		
Shrewsbury	370	12	Munroe	Abraham				1		2			1				4		
Shrewsbury	370	13	Mixer	Asa		1	1		1	2				1			6		
Shrewsbury	370	14	Maynard	Daniel	3	2	1		1	1	1	1	1	1			12		

TOWN	PG#	LN#	LAST NAME	FIRST NAME	FREE WHITE MALES					FREE WHITE FEMALES					TOTAL ALL OTHER	TOTAL SLAVES	TOTALS	DISTRICT/ TOWNSHIP	NOTES
					under 10	10 to 16	16 to 26	26 to 45	45 and over	under 10	10 to 16	16 to 26	26 to 45	45 and over					
Southborough	200	1	Brigham	Elijah	1		2		1		2	1		1			8		
Southborough	200	2	Brigham	Silvester	2			1			1		1				5		
Southborough	200	3	Ward	Erasmus	3	2			1		1		1				8		
Southborough	200	4	Brigham	Silas	1			2			1	1					5		
Southborough	200	5	Walker	Barzellel				1						1			2		
Southborough	200	6	Walker	Daniel	2			1					1				4		
Southborough	200	7	Fay	Hezekiah	4	1	1	1		1	1	2	1				12		
Southborough	200	8	Morse	Isaac			1		1	1		1		1			5		
Southborough	200	9	Fay	Brigham	1	1		1		1		1		1			6		
Southborough	200	10	Newton	Barzellel	2		1	1		1		1					6		
Southborough	200	11	Newton	Aaron	1	1		1		2			1				6		
Southborough	200	12	Newton	Solomon				1			1			1			3		
Southborough	200	13	Newton	Willard	1		1	1		2			1				6		
Southborough	200	14	Newton	Rhoda									1	1			2		
Southborough	201	1	Newton	Mary	1	1		1		1	1		1	1			7		
Southborough	201	2	Taylor	Trowbridge		1		1		2		2	1				7		
Southborough	201	3	Taylor	William	2			1		2		1	1	1			8		
Southborough	201	4	Peirce	Jonathan	1	2		1		3		2	1				10		
Southborough	201	5	Brigham	Nathan		1		1	1			2		2			7		
Southborough	201	6	Bridges	Nathan	1			1				1		1			4		
Southborough	201	7	Ball	Jonas Junr		1		1		1			1				4		
Southborough	201	8	Bellows	Ebenz	2	1		1		2	1	1	1	1			10		
Southborough	201	9	Horn	Martha		1	1						1				3		
Southborough	201	10	Parker	Benjm	1		2			1		1					5		
Southborough	201	11	Parker	Jereboim			1			1		1					3		
Southborough	201	12	Parker	Abigail							1		1				2		
Southborough	201	13	Fessendon	Benjm				1						1			2		
Southborough	201	14	Newton	Caleb	4			1				1	1				7		
Southborough	201	15	Newton	Ezra				1				1	1				3		
Southborough	201	16	Newton	Elijah				1			1		1				3		
Southborough	202	1	Amsden	Ephraim				1		2			1				4		
Southborough	202	2	Fay	Nathan	1	2	1	1		1		2		1			9		
Southborough	202	3	Harrington	William	1		1				1		1				4		
Southborough	202	4	Chamberlain	Edward Junr		1				1		1					3		
Southborough	202	5	Wood	Lucrecia		1	2				1	1					6		
Southborough	202	6	Graves	Thomas			1			3			1				5		
Southborough	202	7	Amsden	John	1	2		1		2			1				7		
Southborough	202	8	Hudson	Samuel	4			1		2	1		1	1			10		
Southborough	202	9	Fay	Heman	1	1	1		1	3	1	1	1				10		
Southborough	202	10	Moor	Abigail										1			1		
Southborough	202	11	Johnson	Mary										1			1		
Southborough	202	12	Angeir	Charles	2	1			1	3	1		1				9		
Southborough	202	13	Ball	Jonas		1	1	1	1				1	1			6		
Southborough	202	14	Winchester	Willim				1			1		1				3		
Southborough	202	15	Stow	William	2			1		1		1	1				6		
Southborough	202	16	Fay	Nathl	1		2		1	3		2					9		
Southborough	203	1	Brewer	Joel	3	1	2		1		1	1	1				10		
Southborough	203	2	Onthank	William		1						1		1			4		
Southborough	203	3	Onthank	James	1		1		1	2	1			1			7		
Southborough	203	4	Wetherbee	Joseph				1						1			2		
Southborough	203	5	Gardner	David	2			1		2	2	1	1				9		
Southborough	203	6	Fay	Robert Jun	3	2		1	1	2	1	1	1				12		
Southborough	203	7	Newton	Amos				1				1	1				3		
Southborough	203	8	Newton	Stephen			1			1		1					3		
Southborough	203	9	Newton	John				1					1				2		
Southborough	203	10	Johnson	David		1						1					2		
Southborough	203	11	Newton	Abel			1			1		1					3		
Southborough	203	12	Ball	Isaac		1		1		1			1				4		
Southborough	203	13	Angier	Calvin	1		1			2		1					5		
Southborough	203	14	Angier	Mary										1			1		
Southborough	203	15	Tozer	Josiah		1		1		4	1		1				8		
Southborough	203	16	Ward	Abner		1		1				1					3		
Southborough	203	17	Newton	David				1					1				2		
Southborough	203	18	Onthank	William Jun	3	2		1		2	2	1	1				12		
Southborough	203	19	Merriam	Joseph		2	1	1		1	1		1				7		
Southborough	203	20	Whiple	James Jun	1			1				1					3		
Southborough	203	21	Merriam	Timothy	1	1	2		1	2	1		1	1			10		
Southborough	203	22	Printice	Joseph	2			1	1			1					5		
Southborough	203	23	Stow	Jonathan		1		1	1				1	1			5		
Southborough	203	24	Daniels	Abigail									1				1		
Southborough	203	25	Hayden	Jonathan		1		1	1				1				4		
Southborough	203	26	Forbush	Silas	2			1		3	1		2				9		
Southborough	203	27	Forbush	Elizabeth						3	1		2				6		
Southborough	203	28	Thurston	Timothy	3	1		1		2	1	1					9		
Southborough	203	29	Thurston	Daniel		1						1					2		
Southborough	203	30	Haden	Daniel		2		1				1		1			5		
Southborough	203	31	Fisher	Timothy				1			1		1				3		
Southborough	203	32	Ellis	Amos	2		1	1		1	1		1				7		
Southborough	203	33	Forbush	Enoch			1			1							3		

TOWN	PG#	LN#	HEADS OF HOUSEHOLD		FREE WHITE MALES					FREE WHITE FEMALES					TOTAL ALL OTHER	TOTAL SLAVES	TOTALS	DISTRICT/ TOWNSHIP	NOTES
			LAST NAME	FIRST NAME	under 10	10 to 16	16 to 26	26 to 45	45 and over	under 10	10 to 16	16 to 26	26 to 45	45 and over					
Southborough	203	34	Wheeler	James	3	1	1	1		2	1	1	1				11		
Southborough	203	35	Wheeler	Ebenezer					1		1			1			3		
Southborough	204	1	Newton	Reuben	2	2			1		1		1				7		
Southborough	204	2	Denton	James	2			1					1				4		
Southborough	204	3	Fisher	Joshua	2			2		1	1		1				7		
Southborough	204	4	Holaway	David	1			1		3	1		1				7		
Southborough	204	5	Stearns	John				1									1		
Southborough	204	6	Fay	Reuben	1	1			1	1		1	1	1			7		
Southborough	204	7	Fay	Solomon	1		2						1				4		
Southborough	204	8	Taylor	Ezra			2		1	1		1	3	1			9		
Southborough	204	9	Stone	Luther		1			1	2	2		1				7		
Southborough	204	10	Johnson	Elijah	4				1		2		1				8		
Southborough	204	11	Jenison	Samuel	3	2		1					1				7		
Southborough	204	12	Newton	Alven			1							1			2		
Southborough	204	13	Nixon	Thomas				1						2			3		
Southborough	204	14	Nichols	John	2			1		3			1				7		
Southborough	204	15	Dunton	Levi	2			1		2	1		1				7		
Southborough	204	16	Bemas	Elisa Jun	1	3	2		1	2				1			10		
Southborough	204	17	Eaton	Benjm		1		1				2		1			5		
Southborough	204	18	Onthank	Joseph		1		1		1		1	1				5		
Southborough	205	1	Chamberlain	Edmind Jun		1		2	1	1	1			1			7		
Southborough	205	2	Bellows	James		1		1						2			4		
Southborough	205	3	Rice	Lot	3		1				1		1				6		
Southborough	205	4	Collins	Mark				1						1			2		
Southborough	205	5	Collins	Aaron	3			1					1				5		
Southborough	205	6	Dunton	Samuel				1						1			2		
Southborough	205	7	Ward	Josiah	1	1		1		2			1				6		
Southborough	205	8	Collins	John	2		1					1					4		
Southborough	205	9	Prentice	John	1			1						4			6		
Southborough	205	10	Bond	John			1					1					2		
Southborough	205	11	Newton	Seth		1	2	1				1		1			6		
Southborough	205	12	Phillips	Sarah	1								1	1			3		
Southborough	205	13	Matthews	Asahel				1					1				2		
Southborough	205	14	Burnet	Charles R.	2	1		1		2	2		1	1			10		
Southborough	205	15	Newton	Isaac	1	1	1	1		2	1		1				8		
Southborough	205	16	Holden	Isaac			2	1		1	1			2			7		
Southborough	205	17	Fay	David	2	1	2	1		2	1	1	1				11		
Southborough	205	18	Bemos	Elisha				1					1				2		
Southborough	205	19	Bemos	Josiah	3		1										4		
Southborough	205	20	Bemos	Phinehas	1		3		1	2	1		1				9		
Southborough	205	21	Wetherbee	Sarah	1	1	2					2	1				7		
Southborough	205	22	Richards	John				1		5	1	1	1				9		
Southborough	205	23	Richard	Ebenezer			2	1		1		2	1				7		
Southborough	205	24	Chamberlain	Abel		1		1		1	2		1				6		
Southborough	205	25	Bridges	Hacklisah		1	1			2			1				5		
Southborough	205	26	Chamberlain	Edward				1					1				2		
Southborough	205	27	Chamberlain	Lemuel	2	1	2	1		3	1		1				11		
Southborough	205	28	Bridges	James				1				1		1			3		
Southborough	205	29	Bridges	Nathan Jr		1	1						1				3		
Southborough	205	30	Bridges	Josiah	1		1	1				1		1			5		
Southborough	205	31	Smith	Ephraim	1			1		2			1				5		
Southborough	205	32	Amsden	David	1			1		2			1				5		
Southborough	205	33	Newton	Josiah	2	1		2			2		1				8		
Southborough	205	34	Fay	Jeremiah	1			1		1			1	1			5		
Southborough	205	35	Fay	Francis	2		1	1					1				5		
Southborough	205	36	Fay	Peter	1			1		3	3		1				9		
Southborough	206	1	Fay	Mary				1						1			2		
Southborough	206	2	Johnson	Isaac				1									1		
Southborough	206	3	Johnson	Elisha			4	1			2			1			8		
Southborough	206	4	Johnson	John	1	1		1		2		2	1				10		
Southborough	206	5	Brown	Josiah				1					1				2		
Southborough	206	6	Brigham	William	1			1			1		1				4		
Southborough	206	7	Williams	William		1				1		1					3		
Southborough	206	8	Newton	Obediah	3			1		2			1				7		
Southborough	206	9	Bellows	Stephen	1			1		2	3		1				8		
Southborough	206	10	Bellows	Jotham		1		1					1	1			4		
Southborough	206	11	Bellows	Timothy	2		2	1			1		1	1			8		
Southborough	206	12	Champney	Jonathan		1		1		1			1	1			5		
Southborough	206	13	Champney	Benjm		1	2	2					1				6		
Southborough	206	14	Brigham	George			1	1		1			1	1			5		
Southborough	206	15	Brigham	Phinehas	1	2		1		2	1	1	1				9		
Southborough	206	16	Robartson	Zacheus	3			1	1	1			1				7		
Southborough	206	17	Estee	Solomon	2			1			1		1	1			6		
Southborough	206	18	Holman	John	2		2	1		1		1	1				8		
Southborough	206	19	Mixer	Bayman	1		1	1		3			1				7		
Southborough	206	20	Moor	Joel				1		1	1		1	1			5		
Southborough	206	21	Moor	Elisha				1		1			1				3		
Southborough	206	22	Newton	Ebenz Jun	1			1			1	1					4		
Southborough	206	23	Collins	William					1					1			2		

114

TOWN	PG#	LN#	HEADS OF HOUSEHOLD		FREE WHITE MALES					FREE WHITE FEMALES					TOTAL ALL OTHER	TOTAL SLAVES	TOTALS	DISTRICT/ TOWNSHIP	NOTES
			LAST NAME	FIRST NAME	under 10	10 to 16	16 to 26	26 to 45	45 and over	under 10	10 to 16	16 to 26	26 to 45	45 and over					
Southborough	206	24	Collins	Mark	1	1	1		1	1				1			6		
Southborough	206	25	Collins	William Jun			1					1					2		
Southborough	206	25	Parker	Lois	1					1			1				3		

TOWN	PG#	LN#	HEADS OF HOUSEHOLD LAST NAME	FIRST NAME	FREE WHITE MALES under 10	10 to 16	16 to 26	26 to 45	45 and over	FREE WHITE FEMALES under 10	10 to 16	16 to 26	26 to 45	45 and over	TOTAL ALL OTHER	TOTAL SLAVES	TOTALS	DISTRICT/ TOWNSHIP	NOTES
Spencer	485	1	Willson	Nathl	1		1		1	2	1		1				7		
Spencer	485	2	Willson	Lydia		1	1			2		1		1			6		
Spencer	485	3	William	Nathl			2	1	1		2	3		1			10		
Spencer	485	4	Whittemore	Reuben	2	1	1		1	2	1	1	1				10		
Spencer	485	5	Wheelock	Paul	1	2	1	1		1			1				7		
Spencer	485	6	Weld	Josiah	3			1		1			1				6		
Spencer	487	7	Sibley	Paul Junr	3			1		1			2				7		
Spencer	487	8	Sibley	Caleb	1			1		2			1				5		
Spencer	487	9	Seager	Oliver					1					2			3		
Spencer	487	10	Tucker	Ezekiel		1	1	1		2		1	1				7		
Spencer	487	11	Underwood	Reuben	1		1		1	2			1				6		
Spencer	487	12	Upham	Jesse	2	1	1	1					1	1			7		
Spencer	487	13	Upham	John			1			2		1	1				5		
Spencer	487	14	Woodward	Noah	1	2			1	5	1		1				11		
Spencer	487	15	White	Rand			2		1	1	1			1			6		
Spencer	487	16	Watson	Oliver					1				1				2		
Spencer	487	17	Watson	Robert	1	2	2		1	3	1	1		1			12		
Spencer	487	18	Watson	William	1	2	1	1	1		1	2		1			10		
Spencer	487	19	Whittemore	Jere Jun	1			1		2			1				5		
Spencer	488	1	White	Thomas			1										1		Most of enumeration covered by tape
Spencer	488	2	Whittemore	Jeremiah		1		1				1	1	1			5		
Spencer	488	3	Whittemore	Aaron	3			1	2	1			1				8		
Spencer	488	4	Willson	Isaac			1						1				2		
Spencer	488	5	Willson	Samuel		1	1		2		1	1		2			8		
Spencer	488	6	Wood	Sarah	2		1					3	1				7		
Spencer	488	7	Watson	Jacob	1		1	1		1	1	2	1	1			9		
Spencer	488	8	Watson	Oliver Junr	1		2		1	2	3	1	1				11		
Spencer	488	9	Watson	James	2		1		1	2	2	1					9		
Spencer	488	10	White	William		1			1	1	2			1	1		7		
Spencer	488	11	White	Josiah				1					1				2		
Spencer	488	12	White	John	1		1			1			1				4		
Spencer	488	13	White	Nathan	1			1					1				3		
Spencer	488	14	White	Jonathan	3			1		1	2		1				8		
Spencer	488	15	Willson	Nathan			1			1		1					3		
Spencer	488	16	Wheat	Joseph		2	1		1	3	1		1				9		
Spencer	488	17	Woodward	Wright				1		1			1				3		
Spencer	489	1	Pratt	Isaac		1			1		3				1		6		
Spencer	489	2	Prouty	James		1				1		1	1		1		5		
Spencer	489	3	Prouty	Isaac				1				2	1	1			5		
Spencer	489	4	Prouty	David Jun				1				1					2		
Spencer	489	5	Prouty	Isaac Junr		2		1		2	1			2			8		
Spencer	489	6	Prouty	David		1		1			1		1				4		
Spencer	489	7	Prouty	Johnson	3	1	1	1		2			1	1			11		
Spencer	489	8	Prouty	Asa		1	3		1		1	1		1			8		
Spencer	489	9	Prouty	Eli	1	1		1		1	1		1				6		
Spencer	489	10	Prouty	Joshua	2	1		1		2	1		1				8		
Spencer	489	11	Prouty	Elisha	1	1		1		2			1				6		
Spencer	489	12	Prouty	Joseph	3	1		1		2			1				8		
Spencer	489	13	Prouty	Jesse			1						1				2		
Spencer	489	14	Prouty	Anna		2							1				3		
Spencer	489	15	Prouty	Dolly						1		3	1				5		
Spencer	489	16	Prouty	William			1			1		1					3		
Spencer	489	17	Phillips	John	1			1		1			1				4		
Spencer	490	1	Rice	Ashur	1				1	2	1		1				6		
Spencer	490	2	Reed	John			2		1					1			4		
Spencer	490	3	Rogers	Stephen				1				1	1				3		
Spencer	490	4	Ryan	Samuel	4	2		1		2	2		1	2			14		
Spencer	490	5	Sylvester	Ichabod	2		1	1				1					5		
Spencer	490	6	Sibley	Jona		1	1				1						3		
Spencer	490	7	Snow	James	1	3		1		2			1				8		
Spencer	490	8	Snow	Seth	2	1		1			1		1				6		
Spencer	490	9	Spear	Daniel	2			1		2		1	1				7		
Spencer	490	10	Stebbins	John		1		1					1				3		
Spencer	490	11	Sumner	John	2	1	1		1	1	2			1			9		
Spencer	490	12	Sumner	William		1				1	1						3		
Spencer	490	13	Seager	Ephraim	1	1		1		3			1				7		
Spencer	490	14	Sprague	Caleb	4	3		1		1			1				10		
Spencer	490	15	Sprague	James	2	2		1		1	1		1				8		
Spencer	490	16	Sprague	Thomas			2	1						2			5		
Spencer	490	17	Sibley	Paul	1	1	1	1				3		1			8		
Spencer	491	1	Muzzey	John	1	1	2		1				3	1			9		
Spencer	491	2	Muzzey	Edmund		1		1		1			1				4		
Spencer	491	3	Mason	Enoch	3			1		1			1				6		
Spencer	491	4	Morgan	Andrew	3	1		1	1	2	1	1	1				11		
Spencer	491	5	Morgan	Robt			1	1		1			1				4		
Spencer	491	6	Muzzey	Jonas	3	1	2		1	3		1	2				13		
Spencer	491	7	Morse	Caleb	1	1	1		1	1	1	1		1			8		
Spencer	491	8	Manning	Jacob	3			1		1			1	1			7		
Spencer	491	9	Marsh	Tyler			1	1		4			1				7		
Spencer	491	10	Muzzey	Isaac			1			2		1					4		
Spencer	491	11	Mason	Ebenz	1	1		1		3	1		1				8		
Spencer	491	12	Morgan	Nicholas	1			1					1				3		
Spencer	491	13	Newton	Edmund		2		1	1		1	1	1	2			9		
Spencer	492	1	Newton	Ezekiel Jun	2	2		1		3	1	1	2				12		
Spencer	492	2	Newton	David	2		1			1	1	1					6		
Spencer	492	3	Newhall	Reuben	2	1	1	1		2	2	2	1				12		
Spencer	492	4	Ormes	James Jun			1			1			1				3		
Spencer	492	5	Ormes	James		1			1	1	2	2		2			9		
Spencer	492	6	Peirce	Shadrach				1					1				2		
Spencer	492	7	Prouty	Nathan	3	2		1		2	2		1				11		

TOWN	PG#	LN#	HEADS OF HOUSEHOLD		FREE WHITE MALES					FREE WHITE FEMALES					TOTAL ALL OTHER	TOTAL SLAVES	TOTALS	DISTRICT/ TOWNSHIP	NOTES
			LAST NAME	FIRST NAME	under 10	10 to 16	16 to 26	26 to 45	45 and over	under 10	10 to 16	16 to 26	26 to 45	45 and over					
Spencer	492	8	Prouty	Thomas	3	1		1				1					6		
Spencer	492	9	Peirce	Shadrach Jun		1		1				1		1			4		
Spencer	492	10	Peirce	John	1		1			2		1					5		
Spencer	492	11	Phelps	Simeon	1		1			1			1				4		
Spencer	492	12	Pixley	Lot	1		1					1					3		
Spencer	492	13	Parks	Jonathan	2		1		1	1	1	1					7		
Spencer	492	14	Perham	Jacob				2	1			1		1			5		
Spencer	492	15	Pope	Joseph		1	2		1		1	1		1			7		
Spencer	492	16	Pratt	Othniel	2	1			1			2	1	1			8		
Spencer	493	1	Kingsbury	Ebenz	1	1	1	1					1				5		
Spencer	493	2	Ketridge	Elijah	1		1			1		1					4		
Spencer	493	3	Kerny	Jeremiah		1	1					1					3		
Spencer	493	4	Knight	William	4			1		3	2	1		1			12		
Spencer	493	5	Knight	William Jun		1				1		1					3		
Spencer	493	6	Knapp	John		1		1		1		1		1			5		
Spencer	493	7	Knapp	Enoch	2	2	1		1	3	1		1				11		
Spencer	493	8	Knight	Joshua		1						1		1			3		
Spencer	493	9	Lamb	Isaac			1	1		3			1				6		
Spencer	493	10	Livermore	Phins			1		1	1			1				3		
Spencer	493	11	Livermore	James	1	1			1				2				5		
Spencer	493	12	Loring	Nathl	2	1	2		1	1	3	1	1				12		
Spencer	494	1	Ludden	Enoch		1		1		2	2			1			7		
Spencer	494	2	Livermore	Moses	2	3	1	1		2			2	1			12		
Spencer	494	3	Livermore	Abijah				1					1	1			3		
Spencer	494	4	Livermore	Amos	2		1			4			1				8		
Spencer	494	5	Lamb	Jonas	2	1	1		1	1	1	2		2			11		
Spencer	494	6	Luther	Robt			1	1		2				1			5		
Spencer	494	7	Livermore	David		1	2		1	2	1		1				8		
Spencer	494	8	Lamb	David		2	1		1	1				1			6		
Spencer	494	9	Luther	Thomas	1		1			1			1				4		
Spencer	494	10	Mason	Elliot		1	1	1			1	1		1			6		
Spencer	494	11	Mason	Joseph			1										1		
Spencer	494	12	May	William	5			1					1				7		
Spencer	494	13	Moulton	Daniel	1			1		2			1				5		
Spencer	494	14	Munroe	Amos	2	1	1	1						1			6		
Spencer	494	15	Munroe	Jona			1		1	1	2			1			6		
Spencer	495	1	Gleason	Benja		1	2		1			3		1			8		
Spencer	495	2	Green	Lemuel	2	1			1		1	1		1			7		
Spencer	495	3	Green	Benja	3	1		1		2	1		1				9		
Spencer	495	4	Hall	Samuel	1	1	3		1		1	2		1			10		
Spencer	495	5	Hatch	Elias	2			1		1		1					5		
Spencer	495	6	Hatch	Thomas	2	1		1		2			1				7		
Spencer	495	7	Hall	Saml Jun	1			1				1					3		
Spencer	495	8	Hatch	Joshua			1						1				2		
Spencer	495	9	Hatch	Stevens				1						1			2		
Spencer	495	10	Hathaway	James		1		1	2	1		1	1	2			9		
Spencer	495	11	Hathaway	Enos	3	1		1		2			1				8		
Spencer	495	12	How	Elijah Jun	4			2					1				7		
Spencer	495	13	How	Elijah		1	1		1	2	1		1				7		
Spencer	496	1	How	Fredk	3			1		1	1		1				7		
Spencer	496	2	How	Kerly	2	1		1		2	1		1				8		
Spencer	496	3	Harrington	Eliha	3	1	2	1		3			2				12		
Spencer	496	4	Howland	Abner	1		2	1		1	1	2	1				9		
Spencer	496	5	Hobbs	Daniel	4		1	1					1	1			8		
Spencer	496	6	Hide	William	1			1		1			1				4		
Spencer	496	7	Hill	Daniel			2		1					1			4		
Spencer	496	8	Hill	Joshua	3			1				1					5		
Spencer	496	9	Henderson	William					1	1		1	1				4		
Spencer	496	10	Hallowell	Joseph				1						1			2		
Spencer	496	11	Hallowell	David			1	1				1		1			4		
Spencer	496	12	Jenks	Isaac		1	3	1	1	2	1			1			10		
Spencer	496	13	Jones	Phinehas	2	2		1		1			1				7		
Spencer	496	14	Jones	Francis				1						1			2		
Spencer	496	15	Jones	Josiah	1			1		2			1				5		
Spencer	497	1	Cutter	Isaac				1					1	1			3		
Spencer	497	2	Cutter	Jedediah			1	1		2	1		1				6		
Spencer	497	3	Craige	Nathan	1			1		1	1	1	1				6		
Spencer	497	4	Convers	Daniel		2	2		1		1	2		1			9		
Spencer	497	5	Capon	James Jun	1	1		1	1	1			2	1			9		
Spencer	497	6	Davison	John	2			1		2	1			1			7		
Spencer	497	7	Denny	William	3			1		2	1		1				8		
Spencer	497	8	Draper	John	1	1		1		1	1	2		1			8		
Spencer	497	9	Draper	James	1		2	1			3	1		1			9		
Spencer	497	10	Draper	Zenas	1			1						1			3		
Spencer	497	11	Drury	Benja	2	1	1	1		1	2		1				9		
Spencer	497	12	Drury	Ebenz			2	1						1			4		
Spencer	497	13	Drury	Ebenz Jun	1	1		1		2			1	1			7		
Spencer	498	1	Davison	Benja					1			1					2		
Spencer	498	2	Davison	Benja Jun	2		1	1		1	2		1				8		
Spencer	498	3	Drake	Elisha		1	1		2			1		1			6		
Spencer	498	4	Darling	Zenas	1			1		3			1				6		
Spencer	498	5	Draper	David			1					1					2		
Spencer	498	6	Flagg	Saml				1						1			2		
Spencer	498	7	Fales	James		1	1		1	1	1	1		1			7		
Spencer	498	8	Garfield	Joseph	2		1						1				4		
Spencer	498	9	Gates	Silvanus	2		1		1	2	2	1	1	1			11		
Spencer	498	10	Green	Lydia			2				1	1		1			5		
Spencer	498	11	Gilford	John		3		1	1					1			6		
Spencer	498	12	Gilford	Jonas	2	3		1		3			1	1			11		
Spencer	498	13	Grout	Jona	4	1		1		2	1		1				10		

117

TOWN	PG#	LN#	LAST NAME	FIRST NAME	FREE WHITE MALES under 10	10 to 16	16 to 26	26 to 45	45 and over	FREE WHITE FEMALES under 10	10 to 16	16 to 26	26 to 45	45 and over	TOTAL ALL OTHER	TOTAL SLAVES	TOTALS	DISTRICT/TOWNSHIP	NOTES
Spencer	498	14	Grout	Thomas					1					1			2		
Spencer	499	1	Brown	Alpheus	1	1	1		1	2		2		1			9		
Spencer	499	2	Ball	Daniel		1	1		1				2	1			6		
Spencer	499	3	Barnes	David			1		1		1	2					5		
Spencer	499	4	Bacon	Noah	1				1	2	2		1				7		
Spencer	499	5	Baxter	Ezekiel	2	2	6	1		1			1	1			14		
Spencer	499	6	Bennett	Joseph	1		1		2	2	1	3		1			11		
Spencer	499	7	Bemiss	David	3	2		1		1	1		1				9		
Spencer	499	8	Bemiss	Amasa	3	1	2	1				1	3				11		
Spencer	499	9	Bemiss	William		1	1		1			1	1	1			6		
Spencer	499	10	Bisco	John				1				1		1			3		
Spencer	499	11	Bisco	Jacob	1			2	1	1		1		1			7		
Spencer	499	12	Brewer	John	2	1		1				2	1				7		
Spencer	499	13	Bemiss	John	1			1		2			1	1			6		
Spencer	499	14	Brewer	Samuel				1						1			2		
Spencer	499	15	Bemiss	Nathan	3			1		2	1	1	1	1			10		
Spencer	500	1	Bemiss	Nathl	3		1			1			1				6		
Spencer	500	2	Bemiss	Joshua	2	1		1		2			1	1			8		
Spencer	500	3	Bemiss	Joseph	2	1	1		1	2	2	1	1				11		
Spencer	500	4	Bemiss	Jonas	2	1	2	1				1	1	1			9		
Spencer	500	5	Beers	Richard Jun		1	1	1		2			1	3			9		
Spencer	500	6	Baldwin	Levi	1		1	1		1				1			5		
Spencer	500	7	Banister	Liberty			1			1		1					3		
Spencer	500	8	Bennett	Ezra	5	1	1	1					1	1			10		
Spencer	500	9	Capen	Timothy Jun		1	1	2		2		1	1	2			10		
Spencer	500	10	Clarke	John			1			3			1				5		
Spencer	500	11	Cummings	Gershom	1		1			3	2	1	1				9		
Spencer	500	12	Cunningham	Robt		1	1	1				2		1			6		
Spencer	500	13	Cunningham	Nathl	4			1		1	2		1				9		
Spencer	500	14	Cunningham	Jona		1	1					1	1				4		
Spencer	502	1	Atwood	Daniel	1	1		1					1	1			5		
Spencer	502	2	Adams	Elias	2	1	1						1				5		
Spencer	502	3	Allen	Israil		1	1	1				2		1			6		
Spencer	502	4	Allen	Silas			1	1		2			1				5		
Spencer	502	5	Adams	David			2	1		1	2			1			7		
Spencer	502	6	Adams	Abigail										1			1		
Spencer	502	7	Bowen	Asa	2		1			1			1				5		
Spencer	502	8	Bell	John	3			1		2			1				7		
Spencer	502	9	Bridges	Caleb		1		1						1			3		
Spencer	502	10	Baldwin	Samuel		1		1					1				3		
Spencer	502	11	Baldwin	Zerubl			1	1					1				3		
Spencer	502	12	Bemiss	Jesse			1	1		1			1				4		
Spencer	502	13	Bemiss	Silas	1			1		1	1	1					5		
Spencer	502	14	Barton	Abia	3		1	1		1			1				7		
Spencer	502	15	Barton	Nathl	3			1						2			6		
Spencer	502	16	Baldwin	Asa				1						1			2		

TOWN	PG#	LN#	LAST NAME	FIRST NAME	FREE WHITE MALES					FREE WHITE FEMALES					TOTAL ALL OTHER	TOTAL SLAVES	TOTALS	DISTRICT/ TOWNSHIP	NOTES
					under 10	10 to 16	16 to 26	26 to 45	45 and over	under 10	10 to 16	16 to 26	26 to 45	45 and over					
Sterling	348	1	Wilder	Elihu	2		3	1		4		1	1				12		
Sterling	348	2	Whitney	Caleb				1	1	2			1	1			6		
Sterling	348	3	Wilder	Silas	1	1	1		1			1		2			7		
Sterling	348	4	White	Josiah	1		1			1			1				4		
Sterling	348	5	Willard	Joshua	2	1		1		2		1	1				8		
Sterling	348	6	Willard	Ephraim	3			1	1			1	1				7		
Sterling	348	7	Willard	David		1		1	1	1	1		1	1			6		
Sterling	348	8	Willard	David Junr		2	1	1				1	1				6		
Sterling	348	9	Wright	Thomas	1	2	1	1		4	1		2				12		
Sterling	348	10	Wilder	Phinehas		1		1				1		1			4		
Sterling	348	11	Wilder	Ephraim		1		1	1	1	1	1	1				7		
Sterling	348	12	Wilder	Timothy	1	1		1		2		1	1				7		
Sterling	348	13	Willard	Ephraim Junr	1	2		2		1	2	1	1		1		11		
Sterling	348	14	Whitney	Mellon			1			3		1					5		
Sterling	348	15	Wilder	Phinehas Junr	2			1		1			1				5		
Sterling	348	16	Willson	Edward	2	1			1		1			1			6		
Sterling	348	17	Winn	Rheuben	2		1					1					4		
Sterling	348	18	Woodard	Pomp											2		2		
Sterling	348	19	Waldren	Edward				1				2	1				4		
Sterling	348	20	Wait	Richard	1	1		1		1		1	1				6		
Sterling	349	1	Pope	Ebenezer	1		3			1	1	2	2	1			11		
Sterling	349	2	Ruth	Solomon	1	1		1		3	1		1				8		
Sterling	349	3	Ruth	Samuel	1			1					1				3		
Sterling	349	4	Reed	William	1		1			2		1					5		
Sterling	349	5	Robbins	Jude			1					1					2		
Sterling	349	6	Raymond	Edmund	1	1	1		2	1	1		1	2			10		
Sterling	349	7	Robbins	John		1	1				1	1	1				5		
Sterling	349	8	Ross	Thomas				1		1			1				3		
Sterling	349	9	Ross	Moses	2		1			2			1				6		
Sterling	349	10	Roper	Asa	1	2		1				1	1				6		
Sterling	349	11	Roper	Silas		1	1	1		3			1				7		
Sterling	349	12	Roper	Monasseh	1	1	1	1		4			1	1			10		
Sterling	349	13	Roper	Enoch				1									1		
Sterling	349	14	Richardson	Benjamin		2	1	1	1		2	2		1			10		
Sterling	349	15	Richardson	James				1				1	1				3		
Sterling	349	16	Richardson	Abel	2	3		1		2		1	1				10		
Sterling	349	17	Roper	Sylvester	1	1		2					1				5		
Sterling	349	18	Reed	Nathan	3	1		1			1		1				7		
Sterling	349	19	Ross	William		1	1		1					1			4		
Sterling	349	20	Rugg	Luther			1					1					2		
Sterling	350	1	Richardson	Thomas		1			1	1				1			4		
Sterling	350	2	Raymond	William	3		3					1	1				8		
Sterling	350	3	Ross	Roger		2	2		1	1	1	1		1			9		
Sterling	350	4	Robbins	Daniel				1			1			1			3		
Sterling	350	5	Reed	Joshua	3	1	1	1			1		1				8		
Sterling	350	6	Ross	Ebenezer			1	1		1				1			4		
Sterling	350	7	Reed	Levi	2		1					1					4		
Sterling	350	8	Rugg	Asa	2				2	1	1			1			7		
Sterling	350	9	Richardson	Menapah	3		2	1		1	1		1				9		
Sterling	350	10	Robbins	Levi	1			1		3			1				6		
Sterling	350	11	Raymond	David				1		3			1				5		
Sterling	350	12	Rice	Ezra	2	1		1		2	1		1				8		
Sterling	350	13	Reed	Danford		1	1			2			1				5		
Sterling	350	14	Shattock	Walter		2		1						1			4		
Sterling	350	15	Sawyer	Ezra		1		1			1	1	1				5		
Sterling	350	16	Stewart	Samuel			1			2	1						4		
Sterling	350	17	Spofford	John	1	1	2	1		1	1		1				8		
Sterling	350	18	Smith	Moses	1	1		1		3			1				7		
Sterling	350	19	Smith	Richard	2			1		3	1		1				8		
Sterling	350	20	Stone	Daniel	2			1					1				4		
Sterling	350	21	Sever	Joseph		1	1	1		1	2	2		1			9		
Sterling	351	1	Kies	Asa	1	1		1					1				4		
Sterling	351	2	Kendall	Etham Junr	1			2					1				4		
Sterling	351	3	Larkin	Seth	1			1					1				3		
Sterling	351	4	Kilborn	Levi	1			1		2			1				5		
Sterling	351	5	Kowlton	Joseph	1			1		2			1				5		
Sterling	351	6	Kilborn	John	2	1	1		1	1	1		1				8		
Sterling	351	7	Loring	John	1	1	1		1		1	1		1			7		
Sterling	351	8	Loring	Joseph	1		1	1					1				4		
Sterling	351	9	Lewis	Joseph	1	1	2		1		1	1		1			8		
Sterling	351	10	Leonard	Linus											5		5		
Sterling	351	11	Morris	William	1	2		1		3		1	1				9		
Sterling	351	12	May	Levi	3	1		1			1		1				7		
Sterling	351	13	May	Daniel	1			1		1			1				4		
Sterling	351	14	Mayson	Jonas			1		1			1		1			4		
Sterling	351	15	Moore	Alvin	1			1		1	1	1	1				6		
Sterling	351	16	Moore	Israel		1	2		1			1		1			6		
Sterling	351	17	Moore	Calvin		1			1			1	1				4		
Sterling	351	18	Moore	Jonathan	1	2		2				1	1	2			10		

TOWN	PG#	LN#	LAST NAME	FIRST NAME	FREE WHITE MALES					FREE WHITE FEMALES					TOTAL ALL OTHER	TOTAL SLAVES	TOTALS	DISTRICT/ TOWNSHIP	NOTES
					under 10	10 to 16	16 to 26	26 to 45	45 and over	under 10	10 to 16	16 to 26	26 to 45	45 and over					
Sterling	351	19	Munson	Samuel			2		1			1	1				5		
Sterling	351	20	May	Ezra				1		1			1				3		
Sterling	351	21	Moore	David	1			1		2			2				6		
Sterling	351	22	Manning	Israel		1		1		2	1	3		1			9		
Sterling	352	1	May	Thomas				1									1		
Sterling	352	2	Newton	Silas	2	1	1	1		1			1				7		
Sterling	352	3	Newhall	David	2	1	1	1		2	1	1	1				10		
Sterling	352	4	Newhall	Moses	1	1	2		1	2	1		1				9		
Sterling	352	5	Nelson	Michael	4	2	1		1		1		1				10		
Sterling	352	6	Osgood	Samuel		1	1		1		1	1		2			7		
Sterling	352	7	Osborn	Daniel	1			1					1				3		
Sterling	352	8	Porter	John	1	1		1		2	1		1				7		
Sterling	352	9	Prescott	Jonathan Jun	1	1	1		2		1		2	2			10		
Sterling	352	10	Putnam	Andrew	4	1	2	1	1		1		1				11		
Sterling	352	11	Pike	David				1					1				2		
Sterling	352	12	Person	Joseph	1	2		1	1	1	1		1	2			10		
Sterling	352	13	Palmer	John		1		1				2	2	1			7		
Sterling	352	14	Palmer	William				1		3			1				5		
Sterling	352	15	Pratt	Joel	1		1	1		1	1		1				7		
Sterling	352	16	Phelps	Abisha		1	2		1	1		2		1			8		
Sterling	352	17	Putnam	William		1	1	1				1	1	1			6		
Sterling	352	18	Palmer	Joseph	1	1		1		3		1	1				8		
Sterling	352	19	Pope	Joseph				1		1				1			3		
Sterling	352	20	Perris	Joseph	1			1		1				1			4		
Sterling	353	1	Holcomb	Rheuben		1	1		1	1		1	1		1		7		
Sterling	353	2	Headley	Josiah	3	2			1		1			1			8		
Sterling	353	3	Houghton	Joshua				1		1	1	1					4		
Sterling	353	4	Hastings	Stephen	2		1	1					2				6		
Sterling	353	5	How	Silas	2	1	1	1		1	1	1					9		
Sterling	353	6	Holmes	William		1		1						1			3		
Sterling	353	7	Hart	Aaron	1		1	1		2		1					6		
Sterling	353	8	Houghton	Joel		1		1		1	1		1				5		
Sterling	353	9	Headley	John	1			1		4		1	1				8		
Sterling	353	10	Holman	Stephen	2	1	2		1	1	2	1					11		
Sterling	353	11	Houghton	Nathanl			2		1				1	1			5		
Sterling	353	12	Harris	Amasiah	1			1					1				3		
Sterling	353	13	How	Alven	1	1			1	3		1	1				8		
Sterling	353	14	Houghton	Saml			1	1						2			4		
Sterling	353	15	Houghton	Stephen	2			1		1			1				5		
Sterling	353	16	Holman	John	3			1		2	1		1				8		
Sterling	353	17	Houhgton	Menasseh			1			1			1				3		
Sterling	353	18	Haydon	Benjamin	1			1			1		1				4		
Sterling	353	19	Houghton	Benjamin	2		2			1			2				7		
Sterling	353	20	Holt	James			1					1					2		
Sterling	353	21	Houghton	Josiah R.	2	1		1		1			1				6		
Sterling	353	22	Houhgton	Ephraim	1			1		2			1				5		
Sterling	354	1	Hunt	Caleb	1		1	1		2	2		1				8		
Sterling	354	2	Headley	Josiah Jun			1						1				2		
Sterling	354	3	Holman	Rufus	1								2				4		
Sterling	354	4	Holt	Abial		1	1	1		4	1		1				9		
Sterling	354	5	How	Asa Jun	1			1					1				3		
Sterling	354	6	Jewitt	Solomon				1						1			2		
Sterling	354	7	Jewitt	David		1	2	1			1			1			6		
Sterling	354	8	Jewitt	Samuel	1		1	1				1		3			7		
Sterling	354	9	Johnson	Jonas		1	2	1			1	1		1			7		
Sterling	354	10	Johnson	Edward	1		1	1		1	2	1	1				9		
Sterling	354	11	Jewitt	Ebenezer			1			1			1				3		
Sterling	354	12	Johnson	Asa				1					1				2		
Sterling	354	13	Kendall	Josiah			1						1		1		5		
Sterling	354	14	Kendall	Ezra		1	1				1	1					4		
Sterling	354	15	Kilborn	Timothy	1	1	1	1		2		2	1	1			10		
Sterling	354	16	Kendall	Josiah Jun	3		1	1		2	1		2				10		
Sterling	354	17	Kendall	Ezekiel Jun	3	2		1	1	1				1			9		
Sterling	354	18	Kendall	Mary		1	2	1			1	2		1			9		
Sterling	354	19	Kendall	Joseph	1	1	2		1	1		2	2	1			11		
Sterling	354	20	Kendall	James	1			1		1	1		2				6		
Sterling	354	21	Kendall	Ethan		2	2	1		2	2	2		1			12		
Sterling	354	22	Kimball	Aaron		1	1			2	1		1				6		
Sterling	355	1	Brooks	Ami	4			1			1		1				7		
Sterling	355	2	Bailey	Nathaniel		1		1		1			1				4		
Sterling	355	3	Brown	William	1			1		2			1				5		
Sterling	355	4	Bigelow	Elias	1	1	1		1	1	1	1		1			8		
Sterling	355	5	Burphee	Nathan	2			1					1				4		
Sterling	355	6	Brown	John 2d	1			1		1			1	1			5		
Sterling	355	7	Boynton	Abial	1	2	1		1	4	1		1				11		
Sterling	355	8	Bellows	Jonas	2			1		1			1				5		
Sterling	355	9	Carey	Ezra	2	2			1			2		1			8		
Sterling	355	10	Conant	Samuel			2		1	2	2		2				9		
Sterling	355	11	Clarke	Samuel			2		1			2		1			6		

120

TOWN	PG#	LN#	LAST NAME	FIRST NAME	FREE WHITE MALES					FREE WHITE FEMALES					TOTAL ALL OTHER	TOTAL SLAVES	TOTALS	DISTRICT/ TOWNSHIP	NOTES
					under 10	10 to 16	16 to 26	26 to 45	45 and over	under 10	10 to 16	16 to 26	26 to 45	45 and over					
Sterling	355	12	Churchill	Samuel		1	1		1	1	1			1			6		
Sterling	355	13	Coulton	William	1				1					1			3		
Sterling	355	14	Colburn	Paul	2			1		2			1				6		
Sterling	355	15	Dale	Samuel	1	1	1	2		2	1		1				9		
Sterling	355	16	Dresser	Elijah	1			1		1			1				4		
Sterling	355	17	Dorchester	Ishmael											8		8		
Sterling	355	18	Dana	Jesse	1	1	3	1		1	1	1	1				10		
Sterling	355	19	Eager	Fortunatus		1	1	1	1			1	1	1			7		
Sterling	355	20	Eaton	Joseph	2			1					1				4		
Sterling	355	21	Emes	Patty						2			1				3		
Sterling	356	1	Eddy	Joshua	1	2			1	4			1				9		
Sterling	356	2	Fairbank	Alpheus	1			1		2	1		1				6		
Sterling	356	3	Francis	Caleb		1		1		3	1		1	1			8		
Sterling	356	4	Fairbank	Lemuel			1	1				2	1				5		
Sterling	356	5	Fairbank	Jabez	1		1	1		1			1	1			6		
Sterling	356	6	Fairbank	Seth	3		1	1		1	2	2	1				11		
Sterling	356	7	Fairbank	William			1			3	1	1	1				7		
Sterling	356	8	Fairbank	Oliver	1	2	2	1			1	1		1			9		
Sterling	356	9	Fairbank	Joseph	1		1	1				2	1				6		
Sterling	356	10	Fairbank	Abijah		1		1		1		1					4		
Sterling	356	11	Fitch	Ebenezer	3	2	1	1		1	3		1				12		
Sterling	356	12	Goss	Joseph			1	1		1	1	1	1				6		
Sterling	356	13	Goney	Rheuben	1		2	1	1	2	1	2	1	2			13		
Sterling	356	14	Gibbs	William	2	1		2		1		1	1				8		
Sterling	356	15	Goney	Thomas	2	2		1		1			1		1		8		
Sterling	356	16	Garish	Paul	2			1		2			1				6		
Sterling	356	17	Gorey	Ichabod		1		1					1				3		
Sterling	356	18	Goney	Nathan			1	1					1				4		
Sterling	356	19	Goney	Jonathan	4			1				1	1				7		
Sterling	356	20	Gates	Amos	2	1		1		2	1		1	1			9		
Sterling	356	21	House	Prudence									1				1		
Sterling	356	22	Hosmore	Timothy	1			1	1			1					4		
Sterling	356	23	Houghton	Jonas	3	2		1		2	1		1	1			11		
Sterling	356	24	How	Asa	1	1			1					2			5		
Sterling	357	1	Allen	Israel		1	1	2					1				5		
Sterling	357	2	Bigelow	Abraham	1			1		2		1					5		
Sterling	357	3	Baker	Samuel	1			1		4	1		1				8		
Sterling	357	4	Bailey	William		1	1	1		3	1		1				8		
Sterling	357	5	Bailey	Jonathan 3d	1		1						1				3		
Sterling	357	6	Brooks	Helan	1	1	1			2			1				6		
Sterling	357	7	Burrs	Ebenezer				1				3		1			5		
Sterling	357	8	Brooks	John 2d			1	1					1				3		
Sterling	357	9	Brown	Benjamin	1	1		1		3	1		1	1			9		
Sterling	357	10	Beaman	Josiah		2	1	1		1		1		1			7		
Sterling	357	11	Bailey	Shuball			1	1			2			1			5		
Sterling	357	12	Brooks	Joshua		1		1			1	1	1	1			6		
Sterling	357	13	Burrs	Silas	1	1		1		1			1				5		
Sterling	357	14	Brooks	Ebenezer			1	1				2					4		
Sterling	357	15	Belknap	Cyrus	1	1		1		2			1				6		
Sterling	357	16	Beaman	Gideon		1	1	1		4	1	1	1				10		
Sterling	357	17	Bailey	Joseph	1			1			1			1			4		
Sterling	358	1	Brown	Samuel		1		1		1		1		1			5		
Sterling	358	2	Beaman	Phinehas				1				1		1			3		
Sterling	358	3	Brown	Samuel 2d	3		2	1		2	1		1				10		
Sterling	358	4	Burphee	Moses	1		2	1		1	1	1	1				8		
Sterling	358	5	Burphee	Jeremiah	2	2		1	1	2			1	1			10		
Sterling	358	6	Blood	Reuben	1		1	1		2			1				6		
Sterling	358	7	Burrs	John	2	1		1		1			1				6		
Sterling	358	8	Burphee	Ebenezer			3	1	1	1		1	1				8		
Sterling	358	9	Burrs	Benjam	3	1		1		1			1				7		
Sterling	358	10	Burrs	Ebenezer Jun	1	1		1		2	2		1				8		
Sterling	358	11	Boynton	Ephraim			1		1		1		1				4		
Sterling	358	12	Burphee	Samuel	1			1					1	1			4		
Sterling	358	13	Bailey	Jonas	1	1								2	1		6		
Sterling	358	14	Bailey	Jonathan Jr	2	1		1	1	3		1	2				11		
Sterling	358	15	Burphee	Thomas			1						2	2			5		
Sterling	358	16	Barnard	John	1		1	1	1	1	2	2	1	1			11		
Sterling	358	17	Buterick	Jonathan		1	3		1			2		1			8		
Sterling	358	18	Bailey	Jonathan				1				1	1	1			4		
Sterling	358	19	Beaman	Elisha	3	1		1		1		1	1				8		
Sterling	358	20	Burphee	Elijah	3	2		1		1			1				8		
Sterling	358	21	Bailey	Paul	2			1	1	3			1	2			10		
Sterling	358	22	Brooks	John				1		1			1				3		

121

TOWN	PG#	LN#	LAST NAME	FIRST NAME	under 10	10 to 16	16 to 26	26 to 45	45 and over	under 10	10 to 16	16 to 26	26 to 45	45 and over	TOTAL ALL OTHER	TOTAL SLAVES	TOTALS	DISTRICT/TOWNSHIP	NOTES
			HEADS OF HOUSEHOLD		FREE WHITE MALES					FREE WHITE FEMALES									
Sturbridge	327	1	Waite	John			2			1		1					4		
Sturbridge	327	2	Wheelock	James			1										1		
Sturbridge	327	3	Winter	Asa	2	1		1		2	3	1	1				11		
Sturbridge	327	4	Weld	Caleb	3	1		1		2			1				8		
Sturbridge	327	5	Walker	Ezra		1	1		1	1	1		1				6		
Sturbridge	327	6	White	Sarah Wd										2			2		
Sturbridge	327	7	Welch	Thomas	2								1	1	8		12		
Sturbridge	327	8	Wight	David Jr	1	2	4			3	2	1	1	1			15		
Sturbridge	329	1	Upham	Lenard	3		1	1		2			1				8		
Sturbridge	329	2	Upham	Pease			2	1				1		1			5		
Sturbridge	329	3	Upham	Nathl		1	1		1		1	2		1			7		
Sturbridge	329	4	Upham	Thomas	1		1	1		1	1	1	1		1		8		
Sturbridge	329	5	Upham	Isaac Jr	1			1				1					3		
Sturbridge	329	6	Upham	Jonathan				1				1		1			3		
Sturbridge	329	7	Weld	Timothy	1	1	1	1	1		1		1	1			8		
Sturbridge	329	8	Weld	Warham	2		1	1		1			1				6		
Sturbridge	329	9	Weld	Aaron			1			1			1				3		
Sturbridge	329	10	Weld	Pennal		1	1	1				1	1				6		
Sturbridge	329	11	Wheelock	Eleazer	1					1			1				5		
Sturbridge	329	12	Wheelock	Ralph			2	1	1			1	1	2	1		9		
Sturbridge	329	13	Wheelock	Denison		1	1		1	1	1			1			6		
Sturbridge	329	14	Wheelock	Ephraim	1			1				1					3		
Sturbridge	329	15	Walker	Nathl	1		1		1	1		1		1			6		
Sturbridge	329	16	Walker	Obed			1			1		1	1				4		
Sturbridge	329	17	Watkins	Deliverance									1				1		
Sturbridge	329	18	Watkins	Hannah									1				1		
Sturbridge	329	19	Walker	Josiah	1				1	2	1		3				8		
Sturbridge	329	20	White	David			1		1	1			1				4		
Sturbridge	329	21	Wight	Oliver	1	1	2	1		4	3		1				13		
Sturbridge	329	22	Wight	Alpheus	2	1		1		3		1	1				9		
Sturbridge	329	23	Whitmore	Wm	1	2		1			1	1	1				7		
Sturbridge	329	24	Walker	Perez		1	1	1		1		1	1				6		
Sturbridge	329	25	Warner	*		1	2			1		1		1			6		
Sturbridge	329	26	Whitcomb	*	1		3						1				5		
Sturbridge	331	1	Newel	Stephen	4	1		1		1	1	1	1	1			11		
Sturbridge	331	2	Nichols	Edmund Jr	2			1					1				4		
Sturbridge	331	3	Nichols	Caleb	2	1		1		1	2	1					8		
Sturbridge	331	4	Newton	Jotham		2		1	1	1				1			6		
Sturbridge	331	5	Nichols	Edmund		1	1		1	2		2		1			8		
Sturbridge	331	6	Nichols	Jabez			1					1					2		
Sturbridge	331	7	Pitman	Benj			1										1		
Sturbridge	331	8	Phillips	John	4		2	1					1	1			9		
Sturbridge	331	9	Plimton	Gershom				1		2		1	1	1			6		
Sturbridge	331	10	Plimton	Fredric	3		1		1		2	2		1			10		
Sturbridge	331	11	Plimton	Oliver	1	1	1	2		3	3	2	1				14		
Sturbridge	331	12	Plimton	Elijah		1		1				1		1			4		
Sturbridge	331	13	Plimton	Elisha	1			1		1	1		1				5		
Sturbridge	331	14	Plimton	Raynolds	2	1		1		1			1				6		
Sturbridge	331	15	Plimton	Elias	1		1		1	3		1	1				8		
Sturbridge	331	16	Plimton	John	4		2		1				1	1			9		
Sturbridge	331	17	Plimton	James		1	2	1	1			2		1			8		
Sturbridge	331	18	Plimton	Joel	1			1		1			1				4		
Sturbridge	331	19	Pratt	Henry	2	1	1		1	1	2	1	1				10		
Sturbridge	331	20	Perry	Jonathan	1	1		1				1	1				6		
Sturbridge	331	21	Pike	Ephram	2			1		1			2	1			7		
Sturbridge	331	22	Partridge	Malicha				1					1				2		
Sturbridge	331	23	Patten	Thomas	1		2	1		1	1		1				7		
Sturbridge	331	24	Paine	Mary		1							1	1			3		
Sturbridge	332	1	Plimton	Gershom Jr	5		1	1		1			1	1			10		
Sturbridge	332	2	Pratt	Freeman			1			1			1				3		
Sturbridge	332	3	Perry	Calvin		1		1		2							4		
Sturbridge	332	4	Pike	James	1				1		1	1		1			5		
Sturbridge	332	5	Robins	Ezekiel	1	1	1		1	2		1	1	1			9		
Sturbridge	332	6	Robins	John	2			1		3	1		1				8		
Sturbridge	332	7	Robins	Saml	2			1	1	1			1	1			8		
Sturbridge	332	8	Rice	Caleb	2	1	3		1	2	1	1		1			12		
Sturbridge	332	9	Rice	Simeon	4	2		1		2			1				10		
Sturbridge	332	10	Rice	Asariah	2			1		2			1				6		
Sturbridge	332	11	Richardson	Saml	2			1		2			1				6		
Sturbridge	332	12	Richardson	Wm	2			1					1				4		
Sturbridge	332	13	Robins	Ichabod	1			1					1				3		
Sturbridge	332	14	Rofee	Solomon				1		2	1			1			5		
Sturbridge	332	15	Robin	Asa	3			1					1				5		
Sturbridge	332	16	Russel	Wm	1	1		1		1	1		1				7		
Sturbridge	332	17	Simpson	Wm	1			1			2			1			5		
Sturbridge	332	18	Shumway	Abijah		1	3		1	2	1		1	1			10		
Sturbridge	332	19	Shumway	Saml	3	1			1	1			1	1			8		
Sturbridge	332	20	Shumway	Jeremiah	2		1	1		2	1	1			1		9		
Sturbridge	332	21	Sanders	Thankful									1	1			4		

122

TOWN	PG#	LN#	HEADS OF HOUSEHOLD LAST NAME	FIRST NAME	FREE WHITE MALES under 10	10 to 16	16 to 26	26 to 45	45 and over	FREE WHITE FEMALES under 10	10 to 16	16 to 26	26 to 45	45 and over	TOTAL ALL OTHER	TOTAL SLAVES	TOTALS	DISTRICT/ TOWNSHIP	NOTES
Sturbridge	332	22	Sith	Mary										1			1		
Sturbridge	332	23	Smith	Nathan	2	1		1		1	1	1	1				8		
Sturbridge	332	24	Stephens	Cyprean		1	1		1		1	2		1			7		
Sturbridge	332	25	Shepard	*			1		1				1				3		
Sturbridge	333	1	Johnson	Comfort		2	1		1	1		2		1			8		
Sturbridge	333	2	Johnson	Timothy		1	2	1		1			1				6		
Sturbridge	333	3	Jewitt	Jesse	3	2		1		2	1	1	1				11		
Sturbridge	333	4	Lombard	Wm	2		1					1					4		
Sturbridge	333	5	Lion	Abner	1	1	1	1	1			3		1			9		
Sturbridge	333	6	Lancaster	David	1		1	1		1		1					5		
Sturbridge	333	7	Leach	Asa	2		1	1		1	1		1				7		
Sturbridge	333	8	Leonard	Ezenas		1		1			1	1					4		
Sturbridge	333	9	Lyon	Wm			3	1		1		2					7		
Sturbridge	333	10	Lane	Otis				1									1		
Sturbridge	333	11	Lane	Robert				1	1	1	1			1			4		
Sturbridge	333	12	Morse	Alphans			1						1				2		
Sturbridge	333	13	Marey	Jedediah	1	2	2	1		3		2	1				12		
Sturbridge	333	14	Morse	David		2		1		2	1		1				7		
Sturbridge	333	15	Morse	Saml	1	2	1			1	2		1				9		
Sturbridge	333	16	Morse	Daniel	1			1	1			2	1				7		
Sturbridge	333	17	Morse	Jeremiah		1	1		1			2		1			6		
Sturbridge	333	18	Morse	Oliver	2	1	1	1		2	1	1	1				10		
Sturbridge	333	19	Morse	Oliver 2d	2		1	1		1		1					6		
Sturbridge	333	20	Morse	Jason	2	1		1	1	2		1	1	1			10		
Sturbridge	333	21	Mason	Abel		2		1		2		2		1			8		
Sturbridge	333	22	Mason	Lemuel	2	1		1	1	1		1	1				8		
Sturbridge	333	23	Mason	Moses			1			1		1					3		
Sturbridge	333	24	Mallens	Henry	2		1	1				1	1				6		
Sturbridge	333	25	Mason	Simeon				1				1	1				3		
Sturbridge	333	26	Mason	Joshua	1			1	1	1	1		1	1	1		8		
Sturbridge	334	1	Marsh	Silas		1			1	4	2	3	1				12		
Sturbridge	334	2	Marsh	Duty	3	1			1	1			1	1			8		
Sturbridge	334	3	Marsh	Eli			1		1	1	1		2				6		
Sturbridge	334	4	McInstry	Wm	2	1		1		1	2		1				8		
Sturbridge	334	5	Moris	Jonathan				1				3		1			5		
Sturbridge	334	6	Morse	Asa	3	1			1	3	2						10		
Sturbridge	334	7	Morse	Asa Junr	1			1		2		1	1				6		
Sturbridge	334	8	Marsh	Israel		1		1	1	2			1	1			7		
Sturbridge	334	9	Maryfield	Ithamer				1					1				2		
Sturbridge	334	10	Morse	Monasser	1	1	1					1	1				5		
Sturbridge	334	11	Morse	Calvin	1		1						1				3		
Sturbridge	334	12	May	Eleazer	1	1		1		2		1	1				7		
Sturbridge	334	13	Moris	Jonathan Jr	2	2	1	1		2	1	1	1				11		
Sturbridge	334	14	Moris	Walter			1			1		1					3		
Sturbridge	334	15	Mason	Simeon				1		1			1				3		
Sturbridge	334	16	Macy	Daniel		2		1		1			1				5		
Sturbridge	334	17	Mayon	Jacob		1	1						1				3		
Sturbridge	334	18	Marsh	John	2	2	3		1	3				2			13		
Sturbridge	334	19	Macy	Theodore		1	2	1		1	1	2	1				9		
Sturbridge	334	20	Macy	Elijah	1		1		1	2			1				6		
Sturbridge	334	21	McInstry	Joseph			1					1					2		
Sturbridge	334	22	Marsh	Elisha	1			1				1	1				4		
Sturbridge	334	23	Newel	Timothy		1	1	1	1	2	3		1				10		
Sturbridge	335	1	Furbush	Noah	1			1		1		1					4		
Sturbridge	335	2	Freeman	Saml	1	1	1					1					4		
Sturbridge	335	3	Fisk	David	2	2	1	1		2		2	1	1	1		13		
Sturbridge	335	4	Freeman	Chester	1		1	1		2	1		1				7		
Sturbridge	335	5	Goodale	Benj	1	2	1	1				3	1				9		
Sturbridge	335	6	Gerrold	Stephen	2		1			2	1	1		1			9		
Sturbridge	335	7	Gibbs	Zephr	2		1		1	1	1		1	1			8		
Sturbridge	335	8	Goodale	John		1	1		1			1		1			5		
Sturbridge	335	9	Gibbs	Jonathan		1	2		1	3		1		1			9		
Sturbridge	335	10	Griggs	Ichabod	2				1	3	1		1				8		
Sturbridge	335	11	Gould	Amos	2	1	2	1				1	1	1			9		
Sturbridge	335	12	Grve	Peter	1			1				1					3		
Sturbridge	335	13	Holbrook	John				1	1	1			1				3		
Sturbridge	335	14	Holbrook	John 2d	2	1	2		1	1	2		1				10		
Sturbridge	335	15	Howard	Jacob	1			1		1			1				4		
Sturbridge	335	16	Howard	Nathan			1										1		
Sturbridge	335	17	Holbrook	James		1	2		1	1	1	1					7		
Sturbridge	335	18	Hill	Ziba		1		1					1				3		
Sturbridge	335	19	Howard	Benajah	1			1		1			1				4		
Sturbridge	335	20	Holbrook	John 3d	2	1	2		1	1		2	1				10		
Sturbridge	335	21	Hobbs	Nathan	1			4	1	1				2			9		
Sturbridge	335	22	Hibbard	Eleaser		1	1	1			1	1	1				6		
Sturbridge	335	23	Hammond	Seth	1			1				1					3		
Sturbridge	336	1	Hammond	Job Junr	2			1		1			1				5		
Sturbridge	336	2	Howard	Josiah		1			1			1	1	1			5		
Sturbridge	336	3	Howard	Abner			1					1					3		

TOWN	PG#	LN#	LAST NAME	FIRST NAME	FREE WHITE MALES under 10	10 to 16	16 to 26	26 to 45	45 and over	FREE WHITE FEMALES under 10	10 to 16	16 to 26	26 to 45	45 and over	TOTAL ALL OTHER	TOTAL SLAVES	TOTALS	DISTRICT/TOWNSHIP	NOTES
Sturbridge	336	4	Harding	Joshua	4	1	1		1	1	1		1				10		
Sturbridge	336	5	Harding	Ralph	2	1		1		1			1	1			7		
Sturbridge	336	6	Harding	Jabez		1		1			1		1				4		
Sturbridge	336	7	Harding	Stephen	1	1	1		1	2	1	1	1	2			11		
Sturbridge	336	8	Hobbs	Benj				1			1		1				3		
Sturbridge	336	9	Hooker	Saml	2		1		1		1	1	1	1			8		
Sturbridge	336	10	Hammond	Job	2				1		1	1	1				6		
Sturbridge	336	11	Hammond	Saml		1	2		1			2		1			7		
Sturbridge	336	12	Hobbs	Saml		3	3	1	1	1		2		1			12		
Sturbridge	336	13	Howard	Eleazer			2		1			1	1	1			6		
Sturbridge	336	14	Hyde	Joshua	1			1		2			1				5		
Sturbridge	336	15	Hooker	Oliver	2		1	1				1					5		
Sturbridge	336	16	Holbrook	Hannah	1							2		1			4		
Sturbridge	336	17	Humphrey	Benja				1			1		1				3		
Sturbridge	336	18	Haris	Wm	1			1		1				1			4		
Sturbridge	336	19	Hooker	Parker	1			1	1			2		2			7		
Sturbridge	336	20	Howard	Charles	1	1	3	2	1	1		1	2	1			13		
Sturbridge	336	21	Harding	Meriam									2				2		
Sturbridge	336	22	Hooker	Henry	1					1		2		1			6		
Sturbridge	336	23	Howard	Abijha			1						1				2		
Sturbridge	336	24	Johnson	James		1	2		1			1		1			6		
Sturbridge	337	1	Cory	David	1			1		3	2	1	1	1			10		
Sturbridge	337	2	Carpenter	Elijah	1			1	1	1		2		1			7		
Sturbridge	337	3	Child	Abijah	4	1		1	1		1	1		1			10		
Sturbridge	337	4	Child	Isaac	2			1					1				4		
Sturbridge	337	5	Child	Joseph			1	1				2		1			5		
Sturbridge	337	6	Curtis	Silvanus	1		2				2	1					6		
Sturbridge	337	7	Child	Rufus		1		1		2		1	1				6		
Sturbridge	337	8	Clark	Rufus					1				2				3		
Sturbridge	337	9	Cutting	Ebenze	1	1	1	1		2			1	1			8		
Sturbridge	337	10	Coburn	Edward	1			1			1			1			4		
Sturbridge	337	11	Crosby	Jeremiah	2		1	1		1			1	1			7		
Sturbridge	337	12	Clemons	Richard	3		1		1		1	1		1			8		
Sturbridge	337	13	Child	Ephraim			1			3		1					5		
Sturbridge	337	14	Clemons	Aaron	1		2			1	1	1					6		
Sturbridge	337	15	Coburn	Zacheus	1			1			1			1			4		
Sturbridge	337	16	Chamberlain	Ezra		1	1			3		1					6		
Sturbridge	337	17	Conant	Jonathan				1			1		1				3		
Sturbridge	337	18	Copeland	Daniel	1		1	1		2		1					6		
Sturbridge	337	19	Carter	William		1	1	1					1				4		
Sturbridge	337	20	Dix	David		1		1				1					3		
Sturbridge	337	21	Dresser	Anna							1		1				2		
Sturbridge	337	22	Dunton	Silas	1		1		1	2	2		1	1			9		
Sturbridge	337	23	Draper	Stephen				1					1				2		
Sturbridge	337	24	Dyer	James	2	1	2	1		2	2	1	1		2		14		
Sturbridge	338	1	Dresser	Caleb	2			1		1		1					5		
Sturbridge	338	2	Dodge	Ebenzr	2			1					1				4		
Sturbridge	338	3	Dyer	Thos	2			1		3	2		1				9		
Sturbridge	338	4	Dagget	Ebenzr	3		1						1				5		
Sturbridge	338	5	Draper	Jacob				1		3			1		1		6		
Sturbridge	338	6	Dunton	Ebenzr				1					1				2		
Sturbridge	338	7	Dunton	Jesse				1					1				2		
Sturbridge	338	8	Dresser	Meriam				1		1			1				3		
Sturbridge	338	9	Ellis	Saml				1					1				2		
Sturbridge	338	10	Eddy	Josiah	2			1				2	1				7		
Sturbridge	338	11	Edmunds	Ebenzr	3	1	1		1				1				7		
Sturbridge	338	12	Ellis	Jedediah	1	2	1		1	3		2	1				11		
Sturbridge	338	13	Fisk	Henry	1		3		1		2	3		2			12		
Sturbridge	338	14	Fisk	Daniel	2	2	1	1		2	2		1				12		
Sturbridge	338	15	Fisk	Simeon		1		1				1		1			4		
Sturbridge	338	16	Fisk	Saml			1										1		
Sturbridge	338	17	Fisk	Nathan	2		1	1		2		1	1				8		
Sturbridge	338	18	Faulkner	Peter				1			1		1				3		
Sturbridge	338	19	Faulkner	Daniel	1			1			1	1	1				5		
Sturbridge	338	20	Fay	Cyrus	1	2		1		2		1	1				8		
Sturbridge	338	21	Foster	Fletcher	2	2	2		1		1	1		2			11		
Sturbridge	338	22	Freeman	benj				1			1		2				4		
Sturbridge	338	23	Freeman	Comfort		1	1		1	2	1			1			7		
Sturbridge	339	1	Allen	Daniel				1									1		
Sturbridge	339	2	Allen	Aaron			2		1	1		1	1	2			8		
Sturbridge	339	3	Allen	Simeon			1	1						1			3		
Sturbridge	339	4	Allen	Elijah	1	2		1		1		2		1			8		
Sturbridge	339	5	Allen	Timothy	1	1	1	1	1					2			7		
Sturbridge	339	6	Allen	John		1	1	1			1	2		1			7		
Sturbridge	339	7	Allen	Jacob Jun		3	1	1		3	2		1	1			12		
Sturbridge	339	8	Allen	Abner	2	1	2		1		2	1		1			10		
Sturbridge	339	9	Allen	Abel	1	1		1		1			1				5		
Sturbridge	339	10	Allen	Abner 2d	1	1	1		1	1			1				6		
Sturbridge	339	11	Allen	Sabin	1					2			1				6		

TOWN	PG#	LN#	LAST NAME	FIRST NAME	FREE WHITE MALES under 10	10 to 16	16 to 26	26 to 45	45 and over	FREE WHITE FEMALES under 10	10 to 16	16 to 26	26 to 45	45 and over	TOTAL ALL OTHER	TOTAL SLAVES	TOTALS	DISTRICT/ TOWNSHIP	NOTES
Sturbridge	339	12	Ammidown	Joseph	1				1	1		2		1			6		
Sturbridge	339	13	Amidown	Cyrus	2			1	2	3			1				9		
Sturbridge	339	14	Allen	Nehemiah			1	1					1				3		
Sturbridge	339	15	Allen	Willard	2			1					1				4		
Sturbridge	339	16	Blanchard	Benj	2			1		2	1	1					7		
Sturbridge	339	17	Barret	Joseph Jr		1		1					1		1		4		
Sturbridge	339	18	Babit	Thomas	3	1	2	1			1	1	1		1		11		
Sturbridge	339	19	Boyden	Justice				1	1				1				3		
Sturbridge	339	20	Boyden	John			1	1		2		2					6		
Sturbridge	339	21	Boyden	Joseph				1	1					2			4		
Sturbridge	339	22	Borden	Isaac		1		1		1			1				4		
Sturbridge	339	23	Belknap	Peter			1	1	1			1		1			5		
Sturbridge	339	24	Barret	Joseph					1				1	1			3		
Sturbridge	340	1	Bacon	Ephraim					1					1			2		
Sturbridge	340	2	Brown	Nathan	3	1		1		2			1				8		
Sturbridge	340	3	Blodget	Edward	2		1	1		1		1	1				7		
Sturbridge	340	4	Barnum	George	1			1		1			1				4		
Sturbridge	340	5	Bullard	Elijah	1		2					1					4		
Sturbridge	340	6	Boyden	Paul				1		3		1					5		
Sturbridge	340	7	Benson	Joseph		1	1		1		1	1	1				6		
Sturbridge	340	8	Belknap	Chester			1			1		1	1				4		
Sturbridge	340	9	Bracket	Aaron				1				1	1				3		
Sturbridge	340	10	Benson	David	4	2		1		2	1	2	1				13		
Sturbridge	340	11	Blanchard	John				1					1				2		
Sturbridge	340	12	Bacon	Enoch	2			1		1	1	1					6		
Sturbridge	340	13	Clark	Isaac	1			1		2			1				5		
Sturbridge	340	14	Clark	Moses	1			1				1	1				4		
Sturbridge	340	15	Clark	Jepthed		2		1		4		1	1				9		
Sturbridge	340	16	Clark	Henry		1	1	1	1	4		1	1				10		
Sturbridge	340	17	Clark	Ebenzr	2	1	2	1		1		1	1				9		
Sturbridge	340	18	Clark	Solomon	2		2					1					5		
Sturbridge	340	19	Cheny	Joseph			2	1				2		1			6		
Sturbridge	340	20	Cheny	Nathan	1		2	1		1	1	1	1				8		
Sturbridge	340	21	Coburn	John	1	1			1	3	1		1				8		
Sturbridge	340	22	Cory	Jacob		2			1	2		2	1				8		

TOWN	PG#	LN#	LAST NAME	FIRST NAME	FREE WHITE MALES					FREE WHITE FEMALES					TOTAL ALL OTHER	TOTAL SLAVES	TOTALS	DISTRICT/ TOWNSHIP	NOTES
					under 10	10 to 16	16 to 26	26 to 45	45 and over	under 10	10 to 16	16 to 26	26 to 45	45 and over					
Sutton	149	1	Axtell	William	1			1	2					1			5		
Sutton	149	2	Axtell	William Junr			1			2		1					4		
Sutton	149	3	Adams	James				1				1					2		
Sutton	149	4	Armsby	Enos				1				1	1				3		
Sutton	149	5	Armsby	Silas			1			3	1		1	1			7		
Sutton	149	6	Axtell	Thomas	1	2	1		1	2	1	1	1				10		
Sutton	149	7	Adams	Israel	2			1		2	1		1				7		
Sutton	149	8	Atwood	Elkanah	1		1						1				3		
Sutton	149	9	Armsby	Joshua	1			1		2	1		1	1			7		
Sutton	149	10	Ambler	Christopher				1					1				2		
Sutton	149	11	Allen	Timothy				1									1		
Sutton	149	12	Adams	Abner	3			1		2	1	1					8		
Sutton	149	13	Buxton	Enos				1						2			3		
Sutton	149	14	Buxton	Enos Junr	1	1	1		1	2	2		1				9		
Sutton	149	15	Brown	Abram	1			1					3				5		
Sutton	149	16	Burden	Jonathan	2	2		1		2	1	1	1	1			11		
Sutton	149	17	Blanden	Elisha			1				1	1					3		
Sutton	149	18	Batcheller	William		2		1	1			1	1				6		
Sutton	149	19	Batcheller	William Jr		2		1				2	1				6		
Sutton	149	20	Batcheller	Abram & Amos	2			1	1	1			1				6		
Sutton	149	21	Batcheller	Abner			1				1		1				3		
Sutton	149	22	Batcheller	Benja	1		1	1				1	1				5		
Sutton	149	23	Batcheller	Ezra	3	1		1					1				6		
Sutton	149	24	Batcheller	Mark		2		1				2	1	1			7		
Sutton	151	1	Bond	Jonas				1					1				2		
Sutton	151	2	Bond	Jonas Junr	1			1		1		1	1				5		
Sutton	151	3	Bond	Josiah			1						1				2		
Sutton	151	4	Bond	Oliver	2	2	3	1				1	1				10		
Sutton	151	5	Bond	William	2			1		1			1				5		
Sutton	151	6	Bartlet	Stephen	2	1	1	1		1	1		1	1			9		
Sutton	151	7	Braman	Amasa	1			1		2		1	1				6		
Sutton	151	8	Brigham	Amariah		1		1		1				2			5		
Sutton	151	9	Buckman	Russell		2						1					3		
Sutton	151	10	Bigelow	John	1		1	1		1			1				5		
Sutton	151	11	Burnap	Abijah	1	1		1			1	1	2				7		
Sutton	151	12	Basset	Benja	1		1			1			1				4		
Sutton	151	13	Batcheller	Jonas	1		1						1				3		
Sutton	151	14	Carriel	Nathaniel	1		1	1		1	1		1				6		
Sutton	151	15	Carriel	Aaron	1		1	1	1	2	2		1				9		
Sutton	151	16	Carriel	Timothy			1	1		2			1				4		
Sutton	151	17	Carriel	John	1	1	1		1				1				5		
Sutton	151	18	Carriel	Henry	1		1				1	1					4		
Sutton	151	19	Chase	Thomas F.	2		1	1		3	1	1	1	1			11		
Sutton	152	1	Billings	Robert	1			1					1				3		
Sutton	152	2	Batcheller	Daniel			1										1		
Sutton	152	3	Briggs	Elijah				1			1	1		1			4		
Sutton	152	4	Basset	Alwan	1		1	1		2			1				6		
Sutton	152	5	Burnap	Timothy	4	2			2		1	1	1				11		
Sutton	152	6	Burden	John			2		1		1	1	1				6		
Sutton	152	7	Bartlett	John				1									1		
Sutton	152	8	Basset	Joshua				1					1				2		
Sutton	152	9	Basset	Jacob	1	1	1			1			1				5		
Sutton	152	10	Bixby	Samuel			1	1	1	1	1	1		1			7		
Sutton	152	11	Bixby	Samuel Junr			1	1		1	1	1	1				6		
Sutton	152	12	Barton	Reuben	1	1			1		2	1		1			7		
Sutton	152	13	Barton	Reuben Junr			1	1					1				3		
Sutton	152	14	Barton	Jedidiah	2	2	1		1			2	1				9		
Sutton	152	15	Buck	Samuel				1					1	1	1		3		
Sutton	152	16	Bancroft	Joseph	3	1		1				1	1	2			9		
Sutton	152	17	Burbank	Caleb		2	2	1		1		4	1				11		
Sutton	152	18	Bancroft	Benja				1			1		1				3		
Sutton	152	19	Brown	Josiah				1				2		1			7		
Sutton	152	20	Brown	Joseph	2			1		1			1	1			6		
Sutton	152	21	Brown	William			1	1				1		1			4		
Sutton	153	1	Chase	Ambrose		1	1			1		1					4		
Sutton	153	2	Chase	Samuel			1					1					2		
Sutton	153	3	Chase	March				1		1			1				3		
Sutton	153	4	Chase	Joshua	1	1		1		2	1		1				7		
Sutton	153	5	Chase	Nathan	1	1		1		2	1		1				7		
Sutton	153	6	Chase	Abel	1	1			1					1			5		
Sutton	153	7	Chase	Abel 3rd	3			1		1			1				6		
Sutton	153	8	Comings	Jacob				1			1	1					3		
Sutton	153	9	Comings	Jesse		1	2	1		1			1				6		
Sutton	153	10	Comings	Asa		1		1		1	1		1				5		
Sutton	153	11	Comings	Allen			1			3	1						5		
Sutton	153	12	Cheney	Nathaniel		1	1		1	2	2			1			8		
Sutton	153	13	Carleton	Benja		1	1		1	2			1				6		
Sutton	153	14	Carpenter	Widos S			2						1	1			4		
Sutton	153	15	Crossman	Samuel	2					2	1		1				8		

TOWN	PG#	LN#	LAST NAME	FIRST NAME	under 10	10 to 16	16 to 26	26 to 45	45 and over	under 10	10 to 16	16 to 26	26 to 45	45 and over	TOTAL ALL OTHER	TOTAL SLAVES	TOTALS	DISTRICT/ TOWNSHIP	NOTES
			HEADS OF HOUSEHOLD		FREE WHITE MALES					FREE WHITE FEMALES									
Sutton	153	16	Chaplin	Revd Ebenza		1	1		1					1			4		
Sutton	153	17	Chamberlin	Jacob	1	2			1	1	1		1				7		
Sutton	153	18	Chase	David P.		1	1		1				1				4		
Sutton	153	19	Chase	Thaddeus	1			1		1			1				4		
Sutton	153	20	Chase	Abel Junr			1		1	2	1	1	1				7		
Sutton	153	21	Carter	Joshua	2	1		1		1	1		1				7		
Sutton	153	22	Cane	John			1			3			1	1			6		
Sutton	154	1	Comings	Jacon Junr	2	1	2		1	1	1	1		2			11		
Sutton	154	2	Comings	Jonathan			1						1				2		
Sutton	154	3	Cole	Stephen	2	2		1		2			1				8		
Sutton	154	4	Comings	P. Widow						2			1				3		
Sutton	154	5	Carpenter	Simeon	3	1		1		1	1		1	2			10		
Sutton	154	6	Crossman	Noah	3		1		1	2	1		1				9		
Sutton	154	7	Carriel	Jednathan			1			2			1				4		
Sutton	154	8	Cole	John			2				1		1				4		
Sutton	154	9	Cole	David	1			1		1		2					5		
Sutton	154	10	Collins	Benjamin		1	1	1					1				4		
Sutton	154	11	Cole	Abel		1		1					1				3		
Sutton	154	12	Clark	Erasmus		1							1				2		
Sutton	154	13	Carriel	Joseph				1						1			2		
Sutton	154	14	Carleton	Joshua	2		1						1				4		
Sutton	154	15	Carpenter	John	1	1		1		1			1				5		
Sutton	154	16	Crossman	Ezra	1	1							1				3		
Sutton	154	17	Chase	Caleb				1						1			2		
Sutton	154	18	Chase	Nehemiah	1	2	1		1	1		1	1				8		
Sutton	154	19	Chase	Moses	2		1						1				4		
Sutton	155	1	Dudley	Jonathan	1	1		1		2			1				6		
Sutton	155	2	Dudley	Nabby Wd	2					1		1		1			5		
Sutton	155	3	Dodge	Richard H.			1	1	1				1	1			5		
Sutton	155	4	Dodge	Josiah	1	1		1		1	1						5		
Sutton	155	5	Day	Moses	2		1			2				2			7		
Sutton	155	6	Day	Aaron	1		1	1					1				4		
Sutton	155	7	Deane	William		1	1		1				1	1			5		
Sutton	155	8	Dudley	David	1	1	2		1	1	1	1	1				9		
Sutton	155	9	Dwinnel	Henry			1		1			1		1			4		
Sutton	155	10	Dwinnel	Solomon	2	1		1					1	1			6		
Sutton	155	11	Dwinnel	Moses	1			1					1				3		
Sutton	155	12	Dwinnel	Henry Junr	1			1		3			1				6		
Sutton	155	13	Dwinnel	Abram	1			1				1					3		
Sutton	155	14	Dudley	Samuel	3		1	1					1				6		
Sutton	155	15	Danforth	Elijah	1			1		2			1				5		
Sutton	155	16	Elliot	Aaron		1	1		1	1	1		1				6		
Sutton	155	17	Elliot	Aaron Junr	1			1		3			1				6		
Sutton	155	18	Ellis	Abel		1	1	1		1	1		1				6		
Sutton	155	19	Elliot	Jonathan		2		1	1	1				1			6		
Sutton	155	20	Elliot	Andrew			4	1	1			1		2			9		
Sutton	156	1	Curtis	Oliver	1	1	1		1	1	2	1	1				9		
Sutton	156	2	Childs	Daniel				1						2			3		
Sutton	156	3	Caldwell	Eliza Wd							1	1	1				3		
Sutton	156	4	Dodge	Isaac		1	2	1				2	1	1			8		
Sutton	156	5	Dike	Anthony		2	2		1					1			6		
Sutton	156	6	Darling	William				1						1			2		
Sutton	156	7	Darling	Zeleck	4	2		1					1				8		
Sutton	156	8	Davis	Timothy		1		1		2		2					6		
Sutton	156	9	Dwinnel	Saml	2			1		1			1				5		
Sutton	156	10	Davenport	Aaron				1				1					2		
Sutton	156	11	Davenport	William		1	1	1				3		1			7		
Sutton	156	12	Dudley	Abel		1	1	1				1		1			5		
Sutton	156	13	Daggett	Lydia Wd								2	1	1			4		
Sutton	156	14	Dudley	Peter		1	1	1				1	1	1			6		
Sutton	156	15	Dudley	John	1		1	1		3			1				7		
Sutton	156	16	Dudley	Jemima Wd						2	2			1			5		
Sutton	157	1	Greenwood	James				1						1			2		
Sutton	157	2	Greenwood	Jas Junr	1			1		2			1				5		
Sutton	157	3	Greenwood	Daniel				1						1			2		
Sutton	157	4	Goffe	Joseph Revd	1		1					1	1				4		
Sutton	157	5	Gale	Jonas				1						1			2		
Sutton	157	6	Gale	Nehemiah				1				1	1	1			4		
Sutton	157	7	Gale	Jonas Junr	1		1	1		2	1		1				7		
Sutton	157	8	Goodell	Asa	3	1	1		1			3		1			10		
Sutton	157	9	Goodell	Relief Wd	2							2		2			6		
Sutton	157	10	Gould	Jonathan	1	1		1				2		1			6		
Sutton	157	11	Gibbs	Jacob	2		1			1			1				5		
Sutton	157	12	Greenwood	Danl Junr				1		3			1				5		
Sutton	157	13	Harwood	Daniel			2	2	1			1	1	2			9		
Sutton	157	14	Hutchinson	Barthl		1	1		1			1	2	3			9		
Sutton	157	15	Haven	John				1						3			4		
Sutton	157	16	Holbrook	Stephen	2	1		1		1			1				6		
Sutton	157	17	Hayward	James	1				1	1	2	1		1			7		

TOWN	PG#	LN#	LAST NAME	FIRST NAME	FREE WHITE MALES under 10	10 to 16	16 to 26	26 to 45	45 and over	FREE WHITE FEMALES under 10	10 to 16	16 to 26	26 to 45	45 and over	TOTAL ALL OTHER	TOTAL SLAVES	TOTALS	DISTRICT/ TOWNSHIP	NOTES
Sutton	157	18	Harwood	Jos & Jerusha					1		1			2			4		
Sutton	157	19	Hurst	Timothy	1		1		1	1	1	1		1			7		
Sutton	158	1	Eager	Stephen			1	1	1					1			4		
Sutton	158	2	Eaton	Reuben	2				1			1	2	1			7		
Sutton	158	3	Eaton	Samuel					1				1				2		
Sutton	158	4	Farrar	Seth	1				1	1	1			1			5		
Sutton	158	5	Fuller	Levi	1	1	1		1	2		1		1			8		
Sutton	158	6	Fuller	Jeduthun	1	2			1		2			1			7		
Sutton	158	7	Fuller	Amos	2		1	1					1				5		
Sutton	158	8	Fisher	Aaron	2		1	1		1	1		1				7		
Sutton	158	9	Freeland	James				1					1				2		
Sutton	158	10	Fletcher	Ebenz	1	1			1	2	1			1			7		
Sutton	158	11	Farnsworth	Joseph			3						1				4		
Sutton	158	12	Goldthwait	Stephen	1				1	3	1			1			7		
Sutton	158	13	Gorton	William	2	1			1	2	1			1			8		
Sutton	158	14	Griggs	Mary Wd	1	2							1	1			5		
Sutton	158	15	Giles	James				1						1			2		
Sutton	158	16	Goodell	John				1						1			2		
Sutton	158	17	Goddard	Robert	1	1	1		1	1	1	1	1				8		
Sutton	159	1	Hayden	Asa	1			1					1				3		
Sutton	159	2	Hewit	William	3	2	1		2	1		2		1			12		
Sutton	159	3	Houghton	Jona				1		1		1					3		
Sutton	159	4	Hewit	Daniel	1			1		1		1					4		
Sutton	159	5	Holman	Jonathan		1	2		1	1		2	1				8		
Sutton	159	6	Holman	David		1	1		1			1		1			5		
Sutton	159	7	Holman	Peter	1			1		1			1				4		
Sutton	159	8	Holman	Francis	3			1		1	1	1					7		
Sutton	159	9	Hayward	Simeon		1		1		1	2			1			6		
Sutton	159	10	Hayden	Hezekiah		1		1						1			3		
Sutton	159	11	Hayward	Joseph			1							1			2		
Sutton	159	12	Hayward	Hartwell		1		1			1		1				4		
Sutton	159	13	Holland	Joseph	1	1		1		1		1	1	1			7		
Sutton	159	14	Harwood	John	2			1		2			1				6		
Sutton	159	15	Jones	Elnathan	1		1			1		1					4		
Sutton	159	16	Jones	Jesse		2	1		1	1		1		1			7		
Sutton	159	17	Jacobs	John		1	1	1		2		1	1				7		
Sutton	159	18	Jennison	Saml				1						1			2		
Sutton	159	19	Kendall	Thos Revd		1		1						1			3		
Sutton	159	20	King	Jonathan	3			1		2	1			1			8		
Sutton	160	1	Kingsbury	John	1			1						1			3		
Sutton	160	2	Hunt	Daniel	1		2		1	4	1	2	1				12		
Sutton	160	3	Hunt	Timothy Junr	2		1						1				4		
Sutton	160	4	Hall	Stephen		1	1			1	1		1				6		
Sutton	160	5	Hall	John	1	1	1		1	2			1				8		
Sutton	160	6	Hall	Josiah		1		1		3	1		1				7		
Sutton	160	7	Hall	Joseph	2	2			1	1			1	1			8		
Sutton	160	8	Hall	Joseph Junr	1	1		1		2			1				6		
Sutton	160	9	Harbach	John			1	1				1	1	1			5		
Sutton	160	10	Harbach	Thomas			2		1	1	2	2		1			9		
Sutton	160	11	Harbach	Daniel	3	1		1		2	1		1				9		
Sutton	160	12	Hicks	Benjamin		1			1		1	1		1			5		
Sutton	160	13	Hicks	Eliza Wd	1		1					1		1			4		
Sutton	160	14	Hicks	Joseph		1	2	1				1	1	1			7		
Sutton	160	15	Hicks	Caleb	1			1				1	1				4		
Sutton	160	16	Hicks	Ebenz	1	2		1		1	1		1				7		
Sutton	160	17	Hathaway	Simeon	1	2	4		2	4	1	1	1				16		
Sutton	160	18	Hart	Peter R.	1		1		1	4				1			8		
Sutton	160	19	Hall	Stephen Junr	1			1		1		1					4		
Sutton	160	20	Harris	Thomas			1	1				1		1			4		
Sutton	160	21	Hayden	Elias				1						1			2		
Sutton	161	1	Landman	Thomas	2				1	1		1	1				6		
Sutton	161	2	Lovell	Ezra		1	1		3	1		1		2			9		
Sutton	161	3	Lincoln	Isaac	3	1		1			1		1				7		
Sutton	161	4	Lathe	Zephaniah			1					1					2		
Sutton	161	5	Mills	Edmund Revd	2				1	2	1		1				7		
Sutton	161	6	Munroe	Stephen				1		4	1		1				7		
Sutton	161	7	Marble	Stephen	1	2	1	1	1	1	1	1	1				10		
Sutton	161	8	Marble	Daniel	3	1	1		1				1				7		
Sutton	161	9	Marsh	Stephen				1					1				2		
Sutton	161	10	Marsh	Stephen Junr		1		1		2	2		1				7		
Sutton	161	11	Marsh	Caleb				1			1	1	2				5		
Sutton	161	12	Marsh	Tyler	1			1		3			1				6		
Sutton	161	13	Marsh	Joshua		1		1		1			2				5		
Sutton	161	14	Marble	Nathan			1					1					2		
Sutton	161	15	Marsh	Peter				1			2		1				4		
Sutton	161	16	Morse	Ezekiel	2			1		1	1		2				7		
Sutton	161	17	Morse	Simeon	3	1		1	1	1	2		1				10		
Sutton	161	18	Martin	Abel	1	2	1		1		1			1			7		
Sutton	161	19	Morse	Moody & Fry	1	1		1	2	2	1	2					11		

128

TOWN	PG#	LN#	LAST NAME	FIRST NAME	FREE WHITE MALES					FREE WHITE FEMALES					TOTAL ALL OTHER	TOTAL SLAVES	TOTALS	DISTRICT/ TOWNSHIP	NOTES
					under 10	10 to 16	16 to 26	26 to 45	45 and over	under 10	10 to 16	16 to 26	26 to 45	45 and over					
Sutton	161	20	Morse	Benja				1		1	1		1	1			5		
Sutton	162	1	Kinney	Stephen		1	2		1			1		1			6		
Sutton	162	2	Kinney	Stephen Junr	1			1		1		1					4		
Sutton	162	3	Kinney	John	2	1		1		1			1				6		
Sutton	162	4	King	Solomon				1			1		1				3		
Sutton	162	5	Keith	Stephen	1			1		1			1				4		
Sutton	162	6	King	William			2	1									3		
Sutton	162	7	King	Samuel	1			1		2		1	1	1			7		
Sutton	162	8	King	Isaac	3			1		1	1	1	1				8		
Sutton	162	9	Kimball	Leonard	1		1	1		1			1				5		
Sutton	162	10	Kinney	Asa		1		1						1			3		
Sutton	162	11	Kittredge	Jacob			1				1						2		
Sutton	162	12	Kinney	Reuben				1						1			2		
Sutton	162	13	Lilley	David				1			1	1	1				4		
Sutton	162	14	Lilley	John	2		1			2	1		1				7		
Sutton	162	15	Lamson	Timothy		1		1		1		1		2			6		
Sutton	162	16	Leland	Solomon			1			1			1				3		
Sutton	162	17	Leland	Jonathan			1			1		1					3		
Sutton	162	18	LeBarron	Lazarus		1	1	1				1	1				5		
Sutton	162	19	Leland	Timothy	1		1	1		2	1		1				7		
Sutton	162	20	Lackey	Matthew	1	2	2	1		1			1				8		
Sutton	163	1	Putnum	Nathan	1	1	1	1	1	1		2		1			9		
Sutton	163	2	Putnum	John	1		1	1				1		1			5		
Sutton	163	3	Putnum	Charles			1			3			1				5		
Sutton	163	4	Putnum	Nathll				2						1			3		
Sutton	163	5	Putnum	Moses	1	2	2	1		2		2	1				11		
Sutton	163	6	Putnum	Eliza Wd	1									1			2		
Sutton	163	7	Putnam	Aaron	3			1		1			1				6		
Sutton	163	8	Putnam	Peter		1		1		1			1				5		
Sutton	163	9	Putnam	Batho	1		1		1		1	1	1				6		
Sutton	163	10	Putnam	Tamar Wd	1						1		1	1			4		
Sutton	163	11	Putnam	Asa	2	1	1	1		1	1		1				8		
Sutton	163	12	Putnam	Benajah	1	1		1			1			1			5		
Sutton	163	13	Prentiss	Samuel				1						1			2		
Sutton	163	14	Prentiss	William	1	1		1		1	2		1				7		
Sutton	163	15	Parker	Thomas				1			1	1	1				4		
Sutton	163	16	Phelps	Henry	3		1		1	1	1	1					8		
Sutton	163	17	Phelps	Ebenz	1			1		2			1				5		
Sutton	163	18	Putnam	John Junr	3	1	1	1		1	3	2	2	2			16		
Sutton	163	19	Putnam	Francis	1	1		1		3	1		1				8		
Sutton	163	20	Putnam	Abner		1				1		1					3		
Sutton	163	21	Peirce	John Junr		1	1			1				1			4		
Sutton	164	1	Marble	Enoch				1						1			2		
Sutton	164	2	Marble	Malachi	1	1	1	1		1	2		2				9		
Sutton	164	3	Marble	Andrew	3	1		1		2	1		1				9		
Sutton	164	4	Marble	Alpheus		2	1		1		2		1				7		
Sutton	164	5	Marble	Samuel		2				1		1					4		
Sutton	164	6	Marble	Rufus	1			1				1					3		
Sutton	164	7	McClellan	Sarah Wd			1							1			2		
Sutton	164	8	McClellan	James		1		2		4	2		1				10		
Sutton	164	9	Marsh	Andrew	2			1					1				4		
Sutton	164	10	Mann	Andrew	1			1		2	1		1				6		
Sutton	164	11	Mann	Levi	2		1	1		3		1	1				9		
Sutton	164	12	Marsh	Ebenz		1		1			1	2		1			6		
Sutton	164	13	Marble	Solomon	4	1	2	1		1	2		1	1			13		
Sutton	164	14	March	Stephen	2	1			1	1	1		1				7		
Sutton	164	15	March	Jacob	1	4			1	3			1				10		
Sutton	164	16	March	Tappan	2	1			1	2	1		1				8		
Sutton	164	17	Nelson	Joseph	2			1				1					4		
Sutton	164	18	Newton	John	1			1		2			1				5		
Sutton	164	19	Newton	Levi	1		1			1		1					4		
Sutton	165	1	Sibley	Jonas	2			1				1	1				5		
Sutton	165	2	Stockwell	Nathll		1		2		1	2			1			7		
Sutton	165	3	Stockwell	Nathll Junr	3			1		2			1				7		
Sutton	165	4	Sibley	Nathan	1	1	1	1	1	1	1	1	1	2			11		
Sutton	165	5	Smith	Timothy	2	3			1		1	1	1	1			10		
Sutton	165	6	Sibley	Simeon	1	1		1					1				4		
Sutton	165	7	Singletarry	Amos				1									1		
Sutton	165	8	Stiles	Josiah	2		1			1	1		2				8		
Sutton	165	9	Small	Samuel	1	1				1	1	1		2			8		
Sutton	165	10	Severy	John				1						2			3		
Sutton	165	11	Severy	John Junr		1	1	2		1		1					7		
Sutton	165	12	Stone	Levi				1						1			2		
Sutton	165	13	Stone	Elijah	2	1		1		2	1	1	1				9		
Sutton	165	14	Sibley	Ebenz	1	1	1		1		1			1			6		
Sutton	165	15	Sibley	Archelaus	1			1		2			1				5		
Sutton	165	16	Stockwell	Enoch	1		1	1		1			1				5		
Sutton	165	17	Snow	Warren	1		1					1					3		
Sutton	165	18	Searles	Curtis	2			1					1				4		
Sutton	165	19	Sibley	Oliver				1			2		1				4		

TOWN	PG#	LN#	LAST NAME	FIRST NAME	FREE WHITE MALES					FREE WHITE FEMALES					TOTAL ALL OTHER	TOTAL SLAVES	TOTALS	DISTRICT/ TOWNSHIP	NOTES
					under 10	10 to 16	16 to 26	26 to 45	45 and over	under 10	10 to 16	16 to 26	26 to 45	45 and over					
Sutton	165	20	Sibley	Peter Junr	1			1				1	1	1			5		
Sutton	165	21	Still	Freeman											3		3		
Sutton	165	22	Town	Asa		1		1						1			3		
Sutton	165	23	Terel	Gilbert			1	1				1		1			4		
Sutton	165	24	Tisdale	Rachel	1					2		1	1				5		
Sutton	165	25	Tinney	Daniel				1						1			2		
Sutton	165	26	Torrey	Caleb			1	2		2		1	1				7		
Sutton	165	27	Torrey	Keziah Wd	1								2	1			4		
Sutton	165	28	Torrey	Samuel		1		1		2		1	1				6		
Sutton	165	29	Titus	Jonah	4			1	1	1			1				8		
Sutton	165	30	Titus	John	2	1		1		1	1		1				7		
Sutton	165	31	Thompson	Jeremiah			1					1					2		
Sutton	165	32	Taylor	Mary Wd	1	1	2					1		1			6		
Sutton	165	33	Taylor	James	2	1		2					1				6		
Sutton	165	34	Tinney	Simon		1		1				1		1			4		
Sutton	165	35	Tinney	Danl Junr	1		1	1		1	1	1					6		
Sutton	165	36	Tainter	Abijah		1		1				1		1			4		
Sutton	165	37	Tainter	Joel	1		1	1		2			1				6		
Sutton	165	38	Trask	Jonathan	1	1		1		1			1	2			7		
Sutton	165	39	Trask	Peter			5	1		1	2						9		
Sutton	165	40	Tainter	Stephen		1							1				2		
Sutton	165	41	Tainter	Abijah Junr	1		1						1				3		
Sutton	165	42	Thurstin	Nathan	1		1	1		4	1	1	1	1			11		
Sutton	166	1	Waters	Stephen	1			1				1	1	1			5		
Sutton	166	2	Waters	John Junr	2	1		1		4		1	1				10		
Sutton	166	3	Waters	Samuel	1		2		1	1	2	2		1			10		
Sutton	166	4	Waters	Amos	1			1		1			1	1			5		
Sutton	166	5	Waters	Reuben	2		1	1		1			1				6		
Sutton	166	6	Waters	Simeon			1						1				2		
Sutton	166	7	Whitmore	Nathll			1		2	1	1			1			6		
Sutton	166	8	Woodbury	Jona				1				1	1	1			4		
Sutton	166	9	Woodbury	John Junr		2		1		1		1	1				6		
Sutton	166	10	Woodbury	Nathan	3		1						1				5		
Sutton	166	11	Woodbury	Simeon			3			1		1					5		
Sutton	166	12	Woodbury	Barthl				1				1		1			3		
Sutton	166	13	Woodbury	Lot	2	2		1		1			1				7		
Sutton	166	14	Woodbury	Benja	3			1		2	2		1				9		
Sutton	166	15	Whipple	John	1			1		2			2	1			7		
Sutton	166	16	Wheelock	Jonah			1	1					1				3		
Sutton	166	17	Wakefield	Amasa	1			1				1		1			4		
Sutton	166	18	Wakefield	Isaiah				1			1			1			3		
Sutton	166	19	Walker	Timothy	3			1				1					5		
Sutton	166	20	Woodbury	John	1	1	1		1			1	1				6		
Sutton	166	21	Woodbury	Joseph		1		1		2	1		1				6		
Sutton	166	22	Woodbury	Benja Junr	1	1		1		2			1				6		
Sutton	166	23	Walker	Asa	1	1	1		1	3	1	1	1				10		
Sutton	166	24	Sibley	Abel	1			1				2	1	2			7		
Sutton	166	25	Stone	John				1						1			2		
Sutton	166	26	Simpson	Lot	1			1		1			1				4		
Sutton	166	27	Sibley	John			1	1						1			3		
Sutton	166	28	Sibley	Arthur	1			1				1					3		
Sutton	166	29	Sibley	Abner	1			1		1			1				4		
Sutton	166	30	Sibley	Gibbs	3			1		2			1				7		
Sutton	166	31	Sibley	Elisha			1		1		1			1			4		
Sutton	166	32	Stockwell	Stephen				1				2	1				4		
Sutton	166	33	Stockwell	Stephen Junr		1	1	1					1				4		
Sutton	166	34	Severy	Jacob				1			1		1	1			4		
Sutton	166	35	Severy	Moody	3	1		1		1		1	1				8		
Sutton	166	36	Stockwell	Amos		1		1				1		1			4		
Sutton	166	37	Stockwell	Solomon		1	1	1		1	2	1	1				8		
Sutton	166	38	Smith	Thomas	1		1	1		1		1					5		
Sutton	166	39	Stone	Daniel	1			1		1				1			4		
Sutton	166	40	Simpson	William			1	1					1	1			4		
Sutton	166	41	Stockwell	Simeon	2			1		1			1				5		
Sutton	166	42	Sibley	Peter	2	1			1		1	1	1				7		
Sutton	166	43	Slocumb	William	3			1			2	1	1				9		
Sutton	166	44	Sibley	Nathll				1						1			2		
Sutton	166	45	Sibley	Reuben		1	1	1				1		1			5		
Sutton	166	46	Sibley	Reuben Junr	1	1		1		1	1		1				6		
Sutton	167	1	Rich	Samuel		1	2	1			1			1			6		
Sutton	167	2	Rich	Amos	1	1		1		2	1	1	1	1			9		
Sutton	167	3	Rich	Ebenz	1	3			1			2		1			8		
Sutton	167	4	Rich	Caleb				1			1	1					3		
Sutton	167	5	Rice	Asel			1		1	1		1	1	1			6		
Sutton	167	6	Russell	Darius			1	1					1				3		
Sutton	167	7	Rice	Ruth & Mary Harwood										2			2		
Sutton	167	8	Rawson	Ebenz	1			1	1		1	2		1			8		
Sutton	167	9	Roberts	Amasa	1			1					1				3		
Sutton	167	10	Rice	Noah			1					2		1			4		
Sutton	167	11	Rice	Daniel	2	1		1		1	1	1					8		
Sutton	167	12	Richardson	Benja	3	1		1		2	1		1				9		
Sutton	167	13	Richardson	Jona	2			1			1		1				5		
Sutton	167	14	Randall	Joshua	2			1				1	1				5		
Sutton	167	15	Sibley	Timothy				1				1		1			3		
Sutton	167	16	Sibley	Tarrant	4	2	1	1		1		1	1	1			12		
Sutton	167	17	Sibley	Molley Wd		3				1		2	1	2			9		
Sutton	167	18	Sibley	Stephen	1							1		1			3		
Sutton	167	19	Sibley	James			1			1	1			1			4		
Sutton	167	20	Sibley	Elijah				1				1	1	1			4		

130

TOWN	PG#	LN#	LAST NAME	FIRST NAME	FREE WHITE MALES					FREE WHITE FEMALES					TOTAL ALL OTHER	TOTAL SLAVES	TOTALS	DISTRICT/ TOWNSHIP	NOTES
					under 10	10 to 16	16 to 26	26 to 45	45 and over	under 10	10 to 16	16 to 26	26 to 45	45 and over					
Sutton	167	21	Sibley	Daniel		1		1		2		1	1				6		
Sutton	167	22	Sibley	Joseph			1		1					1			3		
Sutton	167	23	Wilmarth	Benoni					1					1			2		
Sutton	167	24	Whipple	Solomon		1	1		1	1		2		2			8		
Sutton	167	25	Woodbury	Jonah		1			1					1			3		
Sutton	167	26	Wakefield	Bariah Junr	1		1						1				3		
Sutton	167	27	Warren	William	2				1	1	1		1				6		
Sutton	167	28	Wakefield	Joseph					1					1			2		
Sutton	167	29	Waters	Ebenz					1								1		
Sutton	167	30	Waters	Asa		1			1				1	1			4		
Sutton	167	31	Waters	Saml Junr	1		1	1					1				4		
Sutton	167	32	Waters	John		1	1		1	1	1	1	1				7		
Sutton	167	33	Waters	Joseph	1	2	3		1					2			9		
Sutton	167	34	Waters	Elijah	1		5	1		3	1		2				13		
Sutton	167	35	Waters	Jonathan		1	1	1	1				1	1			6		
Sutton	167	36	Waters	Salmon	1	1	3						2				7		
Sutton	167	37	Woodward	Jonas					1					1			2		
Sutton	167	38	Woodward	Jonah		1	1	1		2		1	1				7		
Sutton	167	39	White	William					1					1			2		
Sutton	167	40	White	Joshua		3	1		1	2		2		1			10		
Sutton	167	41	Waite	William Junr	4	1			1		2		1				9		
Sutton	167	42	Willard	Abigail Wd								1		1			2		
Sutton	167	43	Wheelock	Paul					1					1			2		
Sutton	168	1	Wheelock	Paul	2	2	1		1	3			1				10		
Sutton	168	2	Wesson	Joel	1			1		1		1					4		
Sutton	168	3	Wheelock	John	1	1	1	1		1		1	1				7		
Sutton	168	4	Waters	Asa Junr			2	2				1					5		
Sutton	168	5	Waters	Simeon Junr			1					1		1			3		
Sutton	168	6	Woodward	Solomon				1					1				2		
Sutton	168	7	Pek	John				1	1			1		1			4		
Sutton	168	8	Peirce	Amos Junr			1	1				1					3		
Sutton	168	9	Putnam	David		1	1		1		1	1		1			6		
Sutton	168	10	Putnam	Archelaus	1			1		2			1				5		
Sutton	168	11	Putnam	Israel	1			1		1		2		1			6		
Sutton	168	12	Prentiss	James			2		1	1	1	1		1			7		
Sutton	168	13	Prentiss	Calvin	2			1					1				4		
Sutton	168	14	Putnam	Jona F	1	1		1			1		1				5		
Sutton	168	15	Putnam	Daniel	1			1		1			1				4		
Sutton	168	16	Peirce	Ebenz				1						1			2		
Sutton	168	17	Peirce	John	1	1			1	1	1	1	1				7		
Sutton	168	18	Peirce	Aaron	1			1		3			1				6		
Sutton	168	19	Phelps	Azor	2		1	1		3		1	1				9		
Sutton	168	20	Park	Moses		2	1		1				1		1		6		
Sutton	168	21	Park	Caleb		2		1		3	1	1					9		
Sutton	168	22	Park	Samuel	3			1					1	1			6		
Sutton	168	23	Park	Joseph	2				1		1		1				5		
Sutton	168	24	Peirce	Amos	1			1		1	3		1				7		
Sutton	168	25	Peirce	Jesse	4			1		1	1		1				8		
Sutton	168	26	Putnam	Luke	1			1					1	1			4		
Sutton	168	27	Pratt	Benja	2			1		2			1	2			8		

TOWN	PG#	LN#	LAST NAME	FIRST NAME	FREE WHITE MALES under 10	10 to 16	16 to 26	26 to 45	45 and over	FREE WHITE FEMALES under 10	10 to 16	16 to 26	26 to 45	45 and over	TOTAL ALL OTHER	TOTAL SLAVES	TOTALS	DISTRICT/ TOWNSHIP	NOTES
Templeton	231	1	Anderson	James			2		1	1	2	2		1			9		
Templeton	231	2	Andrews	Elisha	3			1		1		1	1				7		
Templeton	231	3	Day	John	3			1					1				5		
Templeton	231	4	Lawater	Sarah										1			1		
Templeton	231	5	Burrage	Thomas		1	1	1		4			1				8		
Templeton	231	6	Stone	Leonard		1	2		2	1		1		2			9		
Templeton	231	7	Kindall	Noah		1			1		1		1				4		
Templeton	231	8	Burpee	Samll			1						1				2		
Templeton	231	9	Baldwin	Jona		1		1	1	1			1				5		
Templeton	231	10	Sparhawk	Ebenz		2	2		1			3		2			10		
Templeton	231	11	Kindall	Pearson	1			1		1			2				5		
Templeton	231	12	Wright	Joshua	1		1		1	1			1	2			7		
Templeton	231	13	Whitcomb	Jona Jr	1			1		3			1				6		
Templeton	231	14	Wright	Rufus	1	1		1					2				5		
Templeton	231	15	Goodah	William	3			1	1	2			1				8		
Templeton	231	16	Sawyer	John	3			1		1		1	1				7		
Templeton	231	17	Sawyer	Jotham		1	1		1				1	1			5		
Templeton	231	18	Norcrop	Daniel		1	2		1	1	1		1				7		
Templeton	233	1	Cutler	Ephraim	1			1					1				3		
Templeton	233	2	Thomson	Abel			2						1				3		
Templeton	233	3	Hyde	Aaron	3			1		1			1	1			7		
Templeton	233	4	Cutler	William	1	1		1		3	1		1				8		
Templeton	233	5	Symonds	James			2	1	1		1	2	1				8		
Templeton	233	6	Symonds	Samuel	1			1					1				3		
Templeton	233	7	Byam	Samuel				1				1	1				3		
Templeton	233	8	Byam	Samll Junr	1		1					1					3		
Templeton	233	9	Fletcher	Joel			1	1				1		1			4		
Templeton	233	10	Fletcher	William	2		1			3	1		1				8		
Templeton	233	11	Brown	Cyrus			1						1				2		
Templeton	233	12	Cambridge	Edwd				1			1		1				3		
Templeton	233	13	Rice	William	1	1		1		2	1		1				7		
Templeton	233	14	Reed	Benja		2	1			1	2	1					7		
Templeton	233	15	Goodridge	Ebenz		1	2		1	3	1	1		1			10		
Templeton	233	16	Kindall	Paul			1	2	1		2	2		1			9		
Templeton	233	17	Wilder	Josiah		2		1			1	1	1				6		
Templeton	233	18	Wilder	Josiah Junr			1					1					2		
Templeton	233	19	Cobley	John	1	1	1	1			1	1	1				7		
Templeton	234	1	Patch	Jonathan	1	1	1	1			1	1	1	1			8		
Templeton	234	2	Greenleaf	Danll	1	1		1		2			1				6		
Templeton	234	3	Greenleaf	John	1			1		4	2	1	1				10		
Templeton	234	4	Church	Silas		2	3		1		1	1		2			10		
Templeton	234	5	Haynes	Jonas	2			1					1				4		
Templeton	234	6	Patch	Benja	1			1		3			1				6		
Templeton	234	7	Dolbear	Benja			1	1			1	1	1				5		
Templeton	234	8	Prescott	Ruthey	1					1		1	2				5		
Templeton	234	9	Withington	Benja	3			1		1			1				6		
Templeton	234	10	Jackson	Daniel			1					1					2		
Templeton	234	11	Jackson	Jona			1			2			1				4		
Templeton	234	12	Heyward	Samll			1										1		
Templeton	234	13	Cutting	Jonathan		2	2		1		2			1			8		
Templeton	234	14	Cutting	Jona Jr		2	1				1		1				5		
Templeton	234	15	Church	Nathan		1		1		1	1	1		1			6		
Templeton	234	16	Sawyer	Elias	2		4	1		2			1				10		
Templeton	234	17	Cutler	Silas				1				1	1				3		
Templeton	235	1	French	Ebenz Jr	2			1		1			1				5		
Templeton	235	2	French	Ebenz		1	1		1	1	1	1	1				7		
Templeton	235	3	Marret	Noah	1	1	1		1	1	1	2	1	1			10		
Templeton	235	4	Marret	Simeon	1			1					1				3		
Templeton	235	5	Parker	Timothy		1		1		1			1				4		
Templeton	235	6	Bush	Ephraim			1			3			1				5		
Templeton	235	7	Wright	Ebenz		1		1	2				1	1			6		
Templeton	235	8	Davis	Eleazer	2		1	1	1	2	2		1	1			11		
Templeton	235	9	Farnsworth	Oliver	1	1	1		1	3	1	1	1				10		
Templeton	235	10	Wyley	Moses	4		1		1		2		2	1			11		
Templeton	235	11	Spear	Richard	2	2	1	1	1	1	1			2			11		
Templeton	235	12	Davis	Solomon	3			1		1			1				6		
Templeton	235	13	Conlin	Benja	1			1		1			1				4		
Templeton	235	14	Fith	Robert		1		1			1	1		1			5		
Templeton	235	15	Learned	Thomas	2		1	1		2	1		1	1			9		
Templeton	235	16	Newton	Peter	5			1			1		1				8		
Templeton	235	17	Lewis	Jacob	2			1		1			1				5		
Templeton	235	18	Fisher	Samll		1		1		1		1	1				5		
Templeton	236	1	Cobley	David			1		1		1						3		
Templeton	236	2	Brooks	Stephen	4	2	2		1		2	1	1				13		
Templeton	236	3	Holman	Jona	5	2		1			2	1	1				12		
Templeton	236	4	Sawyer	Cooper		2	1					1					4		
Templeton	236	5	Barret	Zaccheus				1				1	1				3		
Templeton	236	6	Dolbear	James	4	1		1		1	1	1	1				10		
Templeton	236	7	Dolbear	Benja			1	1			1	1	1				5		

TOWN	PG#	LN#	LAST NAME	FIRST NAME	FREE WHITE MALES					FREE WHITE FEMALES					TOTAL ALL OTHER	TOTAL SLAVES	TOTALS	DISTRICT/ TOWNSHIP	NOTES
					under 10	10 to 16	16 to 26	26 to 45	45 and over	under 10	10 to 16	16 to 26	26 to 45	45 and over					
Templeton	236	8	Brigham	Edmund	1	1	1	1		2	1	1	1	1			10		
Templeton	236	9	Wesson	James	1	1		1		3	-		1				7		
Templeton	236	10	Pike	William			1										1		
Templeton	236	11	Fisher	Nathan				1						2			3		
Templeton	236	12	Fisher	Thomas	2	1	1	1		3	1		1				10		
Templeton	236	13	Whelor	Thos			2		1	1			1	1			6		
Templeton	236	14	Whelor	Abel	1		1					1					3		
Templeton	236	15	Hancock	Hezekiah	2	1		1		2	1			1			8		
Templeton	236	16	Jones	Benja	2	2		2		1	1	1		2			13		
Templeton	236	17	Orcott	Jona	1		1	1		1	2	1	1	1			10		
Templeton	236	18	Moor	Uriah	1		1			2			1				5		
Templeton	237	1	Knowton	Ezekiel		1		1				2		1			5		
Templeton	237	2	Knowlton	Stephen	3			1					1				5		
Templeton	237	3	Johnson	Shubael		1		1					1				3		
Templeton	237	4	Johnson	Enoch	3			1		2			1				7		
Templeton	237	5	Wallace	Abel			1			1			1				3		
Templeton	237	6	Whitcomb	Job		1		1			1	2	1				6		
Templeton	237	7	Osgood	Joseph	1			1		1		1					4		
Templeton	237	8	Osgood	Joseph Jr	1	2		1		2		1		1			8		
Templeton	237	9	Hale	Oliver			1			1			3	1			6		
Templeton	237	10	Gay	Amos	2		1						1				4		
Templeton	237	11	Mason	Asa	2		1			1			1				5		
Templeton	237	12	Symonds	Zebedia	3	1		1		2	2						9		
Templeton	237	13	Tucker	Joshua	1	1		1				1					4		
Templeton	237	14	Simson	Joshua		1		1		1		1		1			5		
Templeton	237	15	How	Artemas	1	1	1		1	1	2	2		1			10		
Templeton	237	16	Symonds	James		1	1	1			1	1	1				6		
Templeton	237	17	Symonds	Samll	1		1					1					3		
Templeton	237	18	Whelor	Beulah	1		1				2		1				5		
Templeton	237	19	Bush	Jessee		1		1		1		2					5		
Templeton	238	1	Sprague	Wm	4		1	1		1	1		1				9		
Templeton	238	2	Wilkinson	Ebenz		1	1	1			1	2	1				7		
Templeton	238	3	Horton	Jona		2		1		1	1		1				6		
Templeton	238	4	Trask	William	1			1			1			1			4		
Templeton	238	5	Trask	William Jr	2		1			1			1				5		
Templeton	238	6	Brown	Samll	2	1		1			1	1	1				7		
Templeton	238	7	Haskell	Stephen			1				1			1			3		
Templeton	238	8	Haskell	Joseph	1	1		1		1	1		1				6		
Templeton	238	9	Haskell	Oliver	1	2		1			1	1					6		
Templeton	238	10	Clap	Jonas	3	1		1		2			1				8		
Templeton	238	11	Richardson	John Junr	2	3		1		1			1				8		
Templeton	238	12	Cook	Samll		1	1		1			2		1			6		
Templeton	238	13	Byam	Phinehas	1			1		1				1			4		
Templeton	238	14	Sawyer	Moses	1		1					1	1				4		
Templeton	238	15	How	Josiah	3			1	1			1	3	1			10		
Templeton	238	16	Jones	Aaron Jun	3	1		1	1	1	1		2				10		
Templeton	239	1	Hunt	Abel			1				1						2		
Templeton	239	2	Stockwell	Abel	2		1				2		1				6		
Templeton	239	3	Bruce	Josiah	2		1	1		1			1				6		
Templeton	239	4	Dean	Seth			1					2		1			4		
Templeton	239	5	Skinner	Luther	1		1			2			1				5		
Templeton	239	6	Lamb	Israel		1		1		2	1		1				6		
Templeton	239	7	Lamb	Joseph		1		1		1	1	1	1				6		
Templeton	239	8	Patch	Benja	1			1		3			1				6		
Templeton	239	9	Patch	Jonathan	1		1	1	1			1	1	1			7		
Templeton	239	10	Balcom	Joseph	3			1		2	1	1					8		
Templeton	239	11	Whitney	Samuel				1						1			2		
Templeton	239	12	Whitney	Moses 2d	2		1					1					4		
Templeton	239	13	Richardson	John Junr	1	1		1		1	1	4		1			10		
Templeton	239	14	Richardson	Amos				1						1			2		
Templeton	239	15	Whitney	Moses	1		1		1		1	1	1	3			9		
Templeton	239	16	Gates	Laban	2		1						1				4		
Templeton	239	17	Child	William	1	1		1		2	1		1				7		
Templeton	240	1	Bush	Stephen	2	1		1		2			1				8		
Templeton	240	2	Bush	Jabez	1	3		1					1	1			7		
Templeton	240	3	Stone	Simeon		1	1		1	1	2	3		1			10		
Templeton	240	4	Turner	Asa	2	1		1		2		1	1	1			9		
Templeton	240	5	Bruce	Eli	3		1	1					1				6		
Templeton	240	6	Hancock	John	1		1						1				3		
Templeton	240	7	Knowlton	Lyman			1	1		2			1				5		
Templeton	240	8	Baldwin	Eden	2	1	2	1		1			1	1			9		
Templeton	240	9	Lawater	Elias			1						1				2		
Templeton	240	10	Holden	Robert	1	1		1		1		1	1				6		
Templeton	240	11	Holden	Jonathan			1			4		1					6		
Templeton	240	12	Atwood	James				1				1	1	1			4		
Templeton	240	13	Briant	Nathan	3	1		1	1	1	2	2	1	1			13		
Templeton	240	14	Danforth	Jesse	1	1		1	1		2		1				7		
Templeton	240	15	Hosmer	Josiah	2	2		1		1		1	1				8		
Templeton	240	16	Hosmer	Asa	3			1				1	1				6		

TOWN	PG#	LN#	LAST NAME	FIRST NAME	FREE WHITE MALES					FREE WHITE FEMALES					TOTAL ALL OTHER	TOTAL SLAVES	TOTALS	DISTRICT/ TOWNSHIP	NOTES
					under 10	10 to 16	16 to 26	26 to 45	45 and over	under 10	10 to 16	16 to 26	26 to 45	45 and over					
Templeton	240	17	Hunt	Rebecca				1			1			1			3		
Templeton	240	18	Hunt	Oliver	1	1		1			2		1				6		
Templeton	240	19	Johnson	James	2		1	1		4			1				9		
Templeton	242	1	Beal	Samuel	2	2		1		2	1		1				9		
Templeton	242	2	Cook	Cyrus		1		1				1	1				4		
Templeton	242	3	Moor	Ebenz		1	1		1				1	1			5		
Templeton	242	4	French	Lypha	1	1		1	1	2		1					7		
Templeton	242	5	How	Fisk	1	1			1	1	1	1	1				7		
Templeton	242	6	Kindall	Abijah		1	4		1	1		2	1				10		
Templeton	242	7	Knight	Daniel	4			1		1	1		1				8		
Templeton	242	8	Langer	William	3			1			2		1				7		
Templeton	242	9	Upham	Daniel		2	2		1	1		1		1			8		
Templeton	242	10	Fletcher	Caleb		1	3		1			1		1			7		
Templeton	242	11	Wesson	John	1	1		1		3	1		1				8		
Templeton	242	12	Cutting	Asa	1		1			2		1					5		
Templeton	242	13	Whitney	Hezekiah	3	1	1	1		1			1				8		

TOWN	PG#	LN#	LAST NAME	FIRST NAME	FREE WHITE MALES					FREE WHITE FEMALES					TOTAL ALL OTHER	TOTAL SLAVES	TOTALS	DISTRICT/ TOWNSHIP	NOTES
					under 10	10 to 16	16 to 26	26 to 45	45 and over	under 10	10 to 16	16 to 26	26 to 45	45 and over					
Upton	383	1	Tenney	Joshua					1					1			2		
Upton	383	2	Taft	John	1		1		1			1		1			5		
Upton	383	3	Taft	Matthew					1					1			2		
Upton	383	4	Taft	Eli	1			1		3		1	1				7		
Upton	383	5	Thurston	Pardius		1				1		1					3		
Upton	383	6	Taft	Solomon		1		1		3	1	1		1			8		
Upton	383	7	Taft	Robert Capt.	1			1					1	1			4		
Upton	383	8	Taft	Elisha Lt.	3			1		1		1	1	1			8		
Upton	383	9	Vial	James	1	1		1		2	2		1				8		
Upton	383	10	Vial	Caleb				1						1			2		
Upton	383	11	Vaile	Edward		1	1		1	1				1			5		
Upton	383	12	Wood	Seth		1		1		1	1	1		1			6		
Upton	383	13	Wood	Ezra Col.				1						1			2		
Upton	383	14	Wilson	Saml			1			2			1				4		
Upton	383	15	White	Zuba Wd								1		1			2		
Upton	383	16	Webster	Thomas			1								8		9		
Upton	383	17	Wheelock	Lucretia Mrs.	1					1			1				3		
Upton	383	18	Warren	Hepzibah Wid	1					2			1	1			5		
Upton	383	19	Warren	Jonathan			1		1	2	2	1					8		
Upton	383	20	Wood	Maynard			1					1					2		
Upton	383	21	Warren	Elisha	1	1		1		1	2	1					7		
Upton	383	22	Warren	Silas	1	1	1		1	2	1			1			8		
Upton	383	23	White	Daniel			2		1	2			1				6		
Upton	384	1	Whitney	Ezra				1			3			1			5		
Upton	384	2	Wood	Benjm Revd	1		2	1		1		1	1	1			8		
Upton	384	3	Wood	Benjamin				1						1			2		
Upton	384	4	Wood	Reuben	1	1		1		3	1		1				8		
Upton	384	5	Warren	Daniel Ens	1	1		1		2	2	1					9		
Upton	384	6	Warren	Jonas				1						1			2		
Upton	384	7	Whitney	Jacob			1	1		2			1				5		
Upton	384	8	Whitney	Oliver			1	1					1	1			4		
Upton	384	9	Whitney	Amos	2		1	1		1	1	1	1				8		
Upton	384	10	Whitney	Ephm		1	1	1		2	1	1					8		
Upton	384	11	Wood	Samuel		1						2	1	2			7		
Upton	384	12	Walker	Ebenezer	1			1	1				1	1			5		
Upton	384	13	Walker	Ebenezer Jr	4	1		1					1				7		
Upton	384	14	Ward	Nahum Capt.			1		1	1	1			1			5		
Upton	384	15	Wood	Asa	2	1	2		1	3		1		1			11		
Upton	384	16	Ward	Jonathan		1		1		2			1				5		
Upton	384	17	Wood	Hezekiah		1	1	2	1		2	1		1			9		
Upton	384	18	Wood	Ezra Esq	1	1	1	1		3	1	2	1				11		
Upton	385	1	Lackey	Samuel	1	2	1		1		1		1				7		
Upton	385	2	Lackey	Nathan			1		1		1			1			4		
Upton	385	3	Lealand	Eli		1	1		1					1			5		
Upton	385	4	Lucas	Matthew			1			1		1					3		
Upton	385	5	Merrifield	John	1	1	1		1	3		1	1				9		
Upton	385	6	Maynard	Winslow	2			1		1	2		1				7		
Upton	385	7	Miller	Elizabeth Wd						1				1			2		
Upton	385	8	Morss	John			1		1					1			3		
Upton	385	9	Nelson	Joseph	2		1	1		2		1	1	1			9		
Upton	385	10	Nelson	Thomas			1		2				1	1			5		
Upton	385	11	Nelson	Thomas Jr	1		2		1	1	3			1			9		
Upton	385	12	Nelson	Isaac		1	1	1		1	1	1	1	1			8		
Upton	385	13	Nelson	Paul Capt.	1		2	1		1	2	1	1				9		
Upton	385	14	Nobles	Eunice Wd	1	1							1				3		
Upton	385	15	Newton	Tyrus					1		1	3		1			6		
Upton	385	16	Palmer	Abner		1		1	1			2		1			6		
Upton	385	17	Pearce	Joshua	1			1	1	1			1				5		
Upton	385	18	Perham	Benjamin		1								1			3		
Upton	385	19	Perham	Aaron	1		1			2		1					5		
Upton	385	20	Perham	Benjm Jr		1	1			1	2		1				6		
Upton	385	21	Pease	Josiah			1			1					1		3		
Upton	385	22	Pease	Aaron	1		1			1	1		1				6		
Upton	385	23	Putnam	John Dr.	1			1		1			1				4		
Upton	386	1	Perham	Sarah Wd	3					2			1				6		
Upton	386	2	Rawson	Wilson		1	1		1		1	1		2			7		
Upton	386	3	Rooth	Joseph	1			1		2			1				5		
Upton	386	4	Robbins	Joseph	2			1		2	1		1				7		
Upton	386	5	Rockwood	Hezekiah	2	1		1		3	1	1	1				10		
Upton	386	6	Rutter	Jesse				1				1		1			3		
Upton	386	7	Ruggles	Jeremiah	3	1	1	1		1		1	1				9		
Upton	386	8	Rawson	Dorcas Mrs.	2	1	1			2		1	1				8		
Upton	386	9	Rawson	Joshua	3	2			1		1	2	1				10		
Upton	386	10	Southland	David	1			1		1		1					4		
Upton	386	11	Sadler	Joseph				1						1			2		
Upton	386	12	Sadler	John	1			1		4		1	1				8		
Upton	386	13	Sheffield	Isaac				1						1			2		
Upton	386	14	Stearns	Increase	5	2		1			1		1				10		
Upton	386	15	Stearns	Ebenezer		1		1						1			4		

TOWN	PG#	LN#	LAST NAME	FIRST NAME	under 10	10 to 16	16 to 26	26 to 45	45 and over	under 10	10 to 16	16 to 26	26 to 45	45 and over	TOTAL ALL OTHER	TOTAL SLAVES	TOTALS	DISTRICT/ TOWNSHIP	NOTES
					FREE WHITE MALES					FREE WHITE FEMALES									
Upton	386	16	Stanford	Jemime Mrs.								1		1			2		
Upton	386	17	Sadler	Bial				1				1		1			3		
Upton	386	18	Sadler	Stephen Capt.				1						1			2		
Upton	386	19	Stodder	Ezekiel	1	1		1		3	1		1				8		
Upton	386	20	Taft	Isreal			2			1		1					4		
Upton	386	21	Taft	Stephen	1			1				1					3		
Upton	386	22	Taft	Joseph	1		1	1		3			1	1			8		
Upton	387	1	Chapin	David	2		2	1		1	2		1				9		
Upton	387	2	Carpenter	Reuben	2	2			1	1		1	1				8		
Upton	387	3	Deane	Josiah Esq.				1					1				2		
Upton	387	4	Deane	Saml		1	1			2		1					5		
Upton	387	5	Eames	Moses		2		1		3			1				7		
Upton	387	6	Fisk	Benjamin Jr	4	3	1		1	1	1	2	1	1			15		
Upton	387	7	Farrer	Ezra	2		1	1					1				5		
Upton	387	8	Freeman	Prince											7		7		
Upton	387	9	Forbes	Susannah Wd	1	1	1			2		1	1	1			8		
Upton	387	10	Furbush	Saml		1		1		1		1		1			5		
Upton	387	11	Furbush	Saml Jr	1			1				1					3		
Upton	387	12	Farrer	Benjm Maj					1				2	1			4		
Upton	387	13	Fisher	Elias	2	2	1		1			1	1				8		
Upton	387	14	Furbush	Peter		1		1				1		1			4		
Upton	387	15	Furbush	Elijah	1		1					1					3		
Upton	387	16	Fisk	Daniel		1		1		4		1	1				8		
Upton	387	17	Fisk	Benjamin					1						1		2		
Upton	387	18	Fisk	Josiah	1	1		2	1	1		2		1			9		
Upton	387	19	Fisk	Robert			2		1				1	1			5		
Upton	387	20	Fisk	William	1		2	1	1	1		2		1			9		
Upton	388	1	Flagg	Nathaniel	2	1			1	4	1	1	1				11		
Upton	388	2	Gore	Ebenezer	1			1				1					3		
Upton	388	3	Green	John				1			1			2			4		
Upton	388	4	Green	Zalmon	2		1	1		1		1	1				7		
Upton	388	5	Green	Benjamin	2			1					1	1			5		
Upton	388	6	Hayward	Jont	1		2			3		2					8		
Upton	388	7	Hall	Abijah Capt.		1	1			4			1				8		
Upton	388	8	Hill	Edmond	2	1		1					1	1			6		
Upton	388	9	Hix	Joshua				1						1			2		
Upton	388	10	Holbrook	Simeon		1		1						1			3		
Upton	388	11	Holbrook	Daniel	1		1					1					3		
Upton	388	12	Hayward	Jont Lt.	2	1				1		1	1				7		
Upton	388	13	Holbrook	Nathan				1		2			1				4		
Upton	388	14	Hardy	Silas	1	1		1					1	1			5		
Upton	388	15	How	Ebenezer	1	1	1	1		2			1				7		
Upton	388	16	Hardy	Constant	1	1		1		4			2				9		
Upton	388	17	Jones	Sylvanus				1					1				2		
Upton	388	18	Jackson	Nathan			1					1					2		
Upton	388	19	Jackson	Joseph	3			1		1			1				6		
Upton	388	20	Kelley	David Lt.			2	1	1	2	1		1				8		
Upton	388	21	Lesure	David		2		1				2		1			6		
Upton	390	1	Aldrich	Stephen			1			1			1				3		
Upton	390	2	Aldrich	Timothy	2			1				1					4		
Upton	390	3	Alexander	Willm		1		1						1			3		
Upton	390	4	Butler	Peter				1						1			2		
Upton	390	5	Butler	Ebenezer		1	1	1				1		1			5		
Upton	390	6	Beal	Nehemiah		1		1				1	1	1			5		
Upton	390	7	Baker	Thos Capt.				1		1	1	1	1				5		
Upton	390	8	Baker	Ward		1		1		2		1	1				6		
Upton	390	9	Bachellor	Enoch	2	2		2		1		2	1				10		
Upton	390	10	Bathrick	Jasan			1	1				1		1			4		
Upton	390	11	Brooks	Peter	1		2					2					5		
Upton	390	12	Bradish	James				1						1			2		
Upton	390	13	Bradish	Amos	3		1	1		2		1	1				9		
Upton	390	14	Bradish	Elisha	1	1	1	1				3		1			8		
Upton	390	15	Brooks	Joseph	2		1			2		1					6		
Upton	390	16	Buck	Ebenezer	1	2		1		1	3		1				9		
Upton	390	17	Bachellor	Jont		1	1	1				2		1			6		
Upton	390	18	Brown	John			1			4	2		2				9		
Upton	390	19	Croxford	Willm	2			1		1	1		1				6		
Upton	390	20	Childs	Asa Lt.	2	1		1	1	2		2		1			10		
Upton	390	21	Childs	John	1	2	1	1	1	1			1				8		

TOWN	PG#	LN#	HEADS OF HOUSEHOLD		FREE WHITE MALES					FREE WHITE FEMALES					TOTAL ALL OTHER	TOTAL SLAVES	TOTALS	DISTRICT/ TOWNSHIP	NOTES
			LAST NAME	FIRST NAME	under 10	10 to 16	16 to 26	26 to 45	45 and over	under 10	10 to 16	16 to 26	26 to 45	45 and over					
Uxbridge	461	1	Adams	Joseph				1						2			3		
Uxbridge	461	2	Adams	Samuel	1		1	2		3		1	1				9		
Uxbridge	461	3	Adams	Joseph Jun		1		1		1			1				4		
Uxbridge	461	4	Aldrich	Abel	4	2	2		1	1			1	2			13		
Uxbridge	461	5	Aldrich	Nathl			2		1	1	1	1		1			7		
Uxbridge	461	6	Aldrich	William	2	1		1		1			1				6		
Uxbridge	461	7	Albee	James	1		2		1	2	2		1				9		
Uxbridge	461	8	Aldrich	Benjamin		1		1			1			2			5		
Uxbridge	461	9	Aldrich	Obadiah	2			1		1		1	1				6		
Uxbridge	461	10	Aldrich	Enoch	2	2	1		1	2			2	1			11		
Uxbridge	461	11	Aldrich	Seth	1		1	1	1		1	1		1			7		
Uxbridge	461	12	Aldrich	Ephraim		1		1		1			1				4		
Uxbridge	461	13	Aldrich	Nehemiah	1	2	2		1	1	1	2		1			11		
Uxbridge	461	14	Aldrich	Seth Junr		1	2		1		1						6		
Uxbridge	461	15	Adams	Benjamin	3	1		1	1				1	1	1		9		
Uxbridge	461	16	Aldrich	Israel			3	1		2	3		1				10		
Uxbridge	461	17	Aldrich	George	1			1		2			1				5		
Uxbridge	463	1	Carpenter	Daniel	2			2		1		1	1				7		
Uxbridge	463	2	Capron	John	3		3	1		4	2		1	1			15		
Uxbridge	463	3	Chapin	Amariah	2	1		1		2			1				7		
Uxbridge	463	4	Chilson	Jeremiah				1				1		1			3		
Uxbridge	463	5	Cumstock	Laban	1		1	1					1				4		
Uxbridge	463	6	Chapin	Gershom			2	1			1	2	1				7		
Uxbridge	463	7	Chapin	Phinehas				1		3	2						6		
Uxbridge	463	8	Capron	Charles	2	1	2		1	1	1	1	1				10		
Uxbridge	463	9	Chapin	Joseph			1	1					1				3		
Uxbridge	463	10	Chapin	Moses	2		1	1				1					5		
Uxbridge	463	11	Clap	Eleazer	1	2		1				1		1			6		
Uxbridge	463	12	Carpenter	Joseph	1	2		1				2		1			8		
Uxbridge	463	13	Carpenter	William				1		1			1				3		
Uxbridge	463	14	Crowney	Daniel	2			1		1			1				5		
Uxbridge	463	15	Chilson	Israel	4			1					1				6		
Uxbridge	463	16	Draper	David	2			1			2		1				6		
Uxbridge	463	17	Darling	Joshua	3	1		1		1	2		1				9		
Uxbridge	463	18	Darling	Pelitiah	2			1		2				1	1		7		
Uxbridge	464	1	Aldrich	Enoch 2d	1			1					1				3		
Uxbridge	464	2	Aldrich	Daniel				1		2	1		1				5		
Uxbridge	464	3	Aldrich	Jesse	2			1		1			1		1		6		
Uxbridge	464	4	Bacon	George				1		2			1				4		
Uxbridge	464	5	Barstow	Job			1		1			1		1			4		
Uxbridge	464	6	Burk	Joseph				1						1			2		
Uxbridge	464	7	Bullard	Baruch	2	2		1				1	1				7		
Uxbridge	464	8	Basset	Joseph		1		1		4	1		1				8		
Uxbridge	464	9	Baylis	Nicholas		1	1		1		2	1					6		
Uxbridge	464	10	Baylis	Alpheus	2	1		1		1	1						6		
Uxbridge	464	11	Blake	Joseph				1			1						2		
Uxbridge	464	12	Buxton	Samuel	1		1	1				1	1	1			7		
Uxbridge	464	13	Battey	Nicholas	3	2		1	1	1	1		1	1			11		
Uxbridge	464	14	Baker	Menasseh	1	1		1		2			1				6		
Uxbridge	464	15	Brown	Elihu	1			1		3			1				6		
Uxbridge	464	16	Brister	Abigail								2	1				3		
Uxbridge	465	1	Gifford	Seth	2	1	2		2	1	1		2				11		
Uxbridge	465	2	Gaskill	Benja			2		1		1	1	1	1			7		
Uxbridge	465	3	Green	David	2			1	1	1	1	2	1	1			10		
Uxbridge	465	4	Grout	Rhoda		2						1		1			4		
Uxbridge	465	5	Holbrook	Stephen	3			1			1		2				7		
Uxbridge	465	6	Holbrook	Henry				1					1	1			3		
Uxbridge	465	7	Holbrook	Amariah			1		1				1	1			4		
Uxbridge	465	8	Handy	Benja		1	1			1	1			1			6		
Uxbridge	465	9	Handy	Caleb	3	1							1				5		
Uxbridge	465	10	Hix	David	1			1		3			1				6		
Uxbridge	465	11	Humes	Amos			1						1				2		
Uxbridge	465	12	Hall	Deborah	1		1			1	3		1				7		
Uxbridge	465	13	Hall	Nehemiah	3	1		1		1	1			1			8		
Uxbridge	465	14	Hall	Jonathan	1	1	1	1		2			2	1			9		
Uxbridge	465	15	Hall	James W				1				1		2			4		
Uxbridge	465	16	Hall	William	3	1		1		1			1				7		
Uxbridge	465	17	Elliot	Mehitable	1	1				3			1				6		
Uxbridge	465	18	Emerson	Jonathan			1		1				2	1			5		
Uxbridge	465	19	Emerson	Nathl			2	1		2			2	1			8		
Uxbridge	465	20	Emerson	Nathl Jur	1		1	1		1			1				5		
Uxbridge	465	21	Ellison	Joseph		1				1	1	1					4		
Uxbridge	465	22	Farnum	David Junr	2	1		1					2				6		
Uxbridge	465	23	Fisk	Nathl	2	1		1		2	2	1	1				10		
Uxbridge	465	24	Farnum	Royal	2	2		1		2			1				8		
Uxbridge	465	25	Farnum	Moses	2			1		1			2				6		
Uxbridge	465	26	Farnum	Peter	3	1		1		1			1				7		
Uxbridge	465	27	Farnum	Caleb	2		3	1		1		1	1				9		
Uxbridge	465	28	Frost	Gideon				1		1			1		1		4		

TOWN	PG#	LN#	LAST NAME	FIRST NAME	FWM under 10	FWM 10-16	FWM 16-26	FWM 26-45	FWM 45+	FWF under 10	FWF 10-16	FWF 16-26	FWF 26-45	FWF 45+	TOTAL ALL OTHER	TOTAL SLAVES	TOTALS	DISTRICT/TOWNSHIP	NOTES
Uxbridge	465	29	Farnum	David	2	2			1	1			1	1			8		
Uxbridge	465	30	Farnum	George			2	1		1			1				5		
Uxbridge	465	31	Feechum	Samuel	2			1		1			1				5		
Uxbridge	465	32	Gaskill	Ezekiel	2	1		1				1					5		
Uxbridge	465	33	Green	Benjamin		2	1		1		1	3	3	1			12		
Uxbridge	467	1	Kempton	George	2		3		1			2		1			9		
Uxbridge	467	2	Lewis	Robert	3			1					1				5		
Uxbridge	467	3	Lesure	Gideon	2				1	2	1	1					7		
Uxbridge	467	4	Legg	David	2		1			1	1	1	1				8		
Uxbridge	467	5	Lawton	William	2				1				2				5		
Uxbridge	467	6	Miller	Philip W			1						1				2		
Uxbridge	467	7	Mitchel	John			1						1	1			3		
Uxbridge	467	8	Mowry	Wanton	1			1		4			1				7		
Uxbridge	467	9	Mowry	Richard		1	1		1	2	3		1				9		
Uxbridge	467	10	Mitchel	Hannah		1				2		1		1			5		
Uxbridge	467	11	Morse	Jesse	2			1	1				1	1			6		
Uxbridge	467	12	Morse	Jesse Jun		2	1			1	1	1	1				7		
Uxbridge	467	13	Morse	Solomon	1		1					1					3		
Uxbridge	467	14	Morse	Gideon		1		1					1				3		
Uxbridge	467	15	Morse	Joseph	1	1		1		4	2		1				10		
Uxbridge	467	16	Murdock	Elisha	2	1		1	1	1			1	1	1		9		
Uxbridge	467	17	Pottle	Simon	2			1		2			1				6		
Uxbridge	468	1	Herendun	Asa		1			1	2		1	1				6		
Uxbridge	468	2	Holbrook	Moses	1		1	1		1			1				5		
Uxbridge	468	3	Hill	Elizabeth	2			1				1	1				5		
Uxbridge	468	4	Huse	Alpheus	2			1		1			1				5		
Uxbridge	468	5	Harris	Israel				1						1			2		
Uxbridge	468	6	Jackson	David	1	1		1		3	2		1				9		
Uxbridge	468	7	Jacobs	William	1	1	1		1	1			1				6		
Uxbridge	468	8	Judson	Samuel	1			1			1		1				4		
Uxbridge	468	9	Jepherson	John	3			1					1				5		
Uxbridge	468	10	Keith	Job		1			1					1			3		
Uxbridge	468	11	Keys	Oren			1			3	2		1				7		
Uxbridge	468	12	Keith	Abijah	4			1					1				6		
Uxbridge	468	13	Keith	Comfort	1	3	1		1			2		1			9		
Uxbridge	468	14	Keith	Chapin	4		2	1					1				8		
Uxbridge	468	15	Keith	James			2	1				2		1			6		
Uxbridge	468	16	Keith	Gershom		1		1		1				1			4		
Uxbridge	469	1	Segraves	Bezaleel	1	1		1		3			1				7		
Uxbridge	469	2	Segraves	John	1	1	2	1		2		1	1				9		
Uxbridge	469	3	Severy	Reuben	2			1			1		1				5		
Uxbridge	469	4	Spring	Ephraim	2	2	1		1	3	1	1	1				12		
Uxbridge	469	5	Sibley	Stephen		1		1				1		1			4		
Uxbridge	469	6	Sibley	Joel	2			1		2			2				7		
Uxbridge	469	7	Salsbury	David	1			1						1			3		
Uxbridge	469	8	Segraves	Josiah		1	1			1		1		1			5		
Uxbridge	469	9	Shove	Thomas B	4			1		1			1				7		
Uxbridge	469	10	Southwick	Joseph	3	1	2		2	2	1	1			1		13		
Uxbridge	469	11	Southwick	Royal	2	1	1	1		2			1				8		
Uxbridge	469	12	Southwick	George	1	1	2		2	1	1	1	1	1			11		
Uxbridge	469	13	Smith	Luis			1			1	1		1				4		
Uxbridge	469	14	Taft	Sweeting	2	2			1	2	1		1				9		
Uxbridge	469	15	Taft	Amasa	1		1						1				3		
Uxbridge	469	16	Trask	Frederic			1			4	1		1				7		
Uxbridge	469	17	Tyler	Solomon	4	1	1	1			1	1	1				10		
Uxbridge	470	1	Persons	William				1					1	1			3		
Uxbridge	470	2	Persons	James	1			1					1				3		
Uxbridge	470	3	Persons	John	4	2	1	1			1		1				10		
Uxbridge	470	4	Pitts	Job	2			1	1		1	2	1				8		
Uxbridge	470	5	Paine	Licester		1			1		2		1				5		
Uxbridge	470	6	Pierce	Cuff											9		9		
Uxbridge	470	7	Pierce	Timothy	1		1						1				3		
Uxbridge	470	8	Rist	Joseph		1	1		2			1		1			6		
Uxbridge	470	9	Rawson	John	2	1		1		1			1				6		
Uxbridge	470	10	Richardson	Joseph	1	2	1		1	2			1				9		
Uxbridge	470	11	Rawson	Grindal		1	2	1				1	1	1			7		
Uxbridge	470	12	Read	Samuel	1		2	1		3	1		1	1			10		
Uxbridge	470	13	Rawson	Silas		1		1			1	1	1				5		
Uxbridge	470	14	Rawson	Charles	1			1		1			1				4		
Uxbridge	470	15	Read	Ebenezer				2					1				3		
Uxbridge	470	16	Rawson	Nathan	2			1	1				1				5		
Uxbridge	470	17	Rawson	Seth	3	1		1			2		1				8		
Uxbridge	471	1	Taft	Mijaman			2		1			1		1			5		
Uxbridge	471	2	Thompson	Benjamin	5			1		1			1				8		
Uxbridge	471	3	Tucker	Benja	4	1		1			1		1				8		
Uxbridge	471	4	Thompson	Joel	1		1		2			1	1				6		
Uxbridge	471	5	Taft	Leonard	3			1					1				5		
Uxbridge	471	6	Taft	Cummings	3	1		1	1				1				7		
Uxbridge	471	7	Taft	Paul				1						1			2		

TOWN	PG#	LN#	HEADS OF HOUSEHOLD LAST NAME	FIRST NAME	FREE WHITE MALES under 10	10 to 16	16 to 26	26 to 45	45 and over	FREE WHITE FEMALES under 10	10 to 16	16 to 26	26 to 45	45 and over	TOTAL ALL OTHER	TOTAL SLAVES	TOTALS	DISTRICT/ TOWNSHIP	NOTES
Uxbridge	471	8	Thwing	Benja	1		1		1			2		1			6		
Uxbridge	471	9	Taft	Jacob					1			1	1				3		
Uxbridge	471	10	Taft	James		1	1		1	1	1		1				6		
Uxbridge	471	11	Taft	Jacob Junr	2	1			1	1	2	1		1			9		
Uxbridge	471	12	Taft	Easmon	1		1	1		1		1					5		
Uxbridge	471	13	Taft	Aaron				1	1			1	1		1		5		
Uxbridge	471	14	Taft	Willis	3	1		1		1	1	1					8		
Uxbridge	471	15	Taft	Noah	1			2	1	2			1	1			8		
Uxbridge	471	16	Tillinghart	Sylvanus			3	1		1			2		2		9		
Uxbridge	471	17	Taft	Frederic	1	1	1	1		3	2		2				11		
Uxbridge	471	18	Thayer	Amos	1			1		1			1	1			5		
Uxbridge	472	1	Taft	Samuel		2	1		1	2				1			7		
Uxbridge	472	2	Tillinghart	Daniel		1		1	1		1		1		2		7		
Uxbridge	472	3	Thayer	Asa	3	2	1	1		1	1	1	1				11		
Uxbridge	472	4	Taft	Thadeus	2	2		1		1		2	1				9		
Uxbridge	472	5	Taft	Micajah		1		1		2		1					5		
Uxbridge	472	6	Taft	Moses	1			1		1	1	1					5		
Uxbridge	472	7	Taft	Abner					1		1		1				3		
Uxbridge	472	8	Taft	Webb	1			1		1		1					4		
Uxbridge	472	9	Taft	Darias				1		2		1					4		
Uxbridge	472	10	Taft	Joseph Junr			1		1	1	1		1				5		
Uxbridge	472	11	Taft	Gershom					1				1				2		
Uxbridge	472	12	Taft	Calvin	2	1		1		1			1				6		
Uxbridge	472	13	Taft	Ephraim			1		1	1	2	1	1	1			8		
Uxbridge	472	14	Taft	Bezeleel		2	2		1	1	1	2	2		1		12		
Uxbridge	472	15	Taft	Nathan					1		2		1				4		
Uxbridge	472	16	Taft	Nathan Jun	1			1			1						3		
Uxbridge	472	17	Thayer	Grindale			1	1		2	1		1				6		
Uxbridge	473	1	Wood	Mark	2			2				1					5		
Uxbridge	473	2	Whitney	Moses		2		1		3		2	1				9		
Uxbridge	473	3	Williams	Stephen		1	1		1		1			1			5		
Uxbridge	473	4	White	Peter	1				1			2	1				5		
Uxbridge	473	5	Whipple	Jona	1	1	3	1	1	3		3	1				14		
Uxbridge	473	6	Wood	Dexter		1	1	1				3		1			7		
Uxbridge	473	7	Willard	Samuel	2	1	5	6	1		2	1	3	1	2		24		
Uxbridge	473	8	Wood	Timothy	2	1		1	1			2	1				8		
Uxbridge	473	9	Winslow	Ebenezer	1			1		1		1					4		
Uxbridge	473	10	Wall	Phebe		1				1		1		1			4		
Uxbridge	473	11	Wood	Amery	1			1		4		1					7		
Uxbridge	473	12	White	Alpheus			1				1						2		
Uxbridge	473	13	White	Nathan			1	1				1					3		
Uxbridge	473	14	White	Thomas		3	1		1	1		2	1	1			10		
Uxbridge	473	15	Webb	Daniel	2		1			2		1					6		
Uxbridge	473	16	Were	Robert					1								1		
Uxbridge	474	1	Taft	Stephen	1	1			1		1	1		1			6		
Uxbridge	474	2	Thayer	Denis	2			1					1				4		
Uxbridge	474	3	Taft	Gerera	1			1		2		1					5		
Uxbridge	474	4	Taft	Nathan	1			1		2		1					5		
Uxbridge	474	5	Taft	Josiah	3		1	1		1	1	1					8		
Uxbridge	474	6	Wood	Samuel	1	1		1		2		1					6		
Uxbridge	474	7	Wood	David			1		1	2	2	2		2			10		
Uxbridge	474	8	Wood	Ezekiel	2	1	1		1	1		3		1			10		
Uxbridge	474	9	White	Ezra	2			1	1	1			3	1			9		
Uxbridge	474	10	Wheelock	Deborah		1						1		1			3		
Uxbridge	474	11	White	Jonathan	2				1	2	1	1					7		
Uxbridge	474	12	White	Amariah		1		1		1		1					4		
Uxbridge	474	13	Wheelock	Paul	2			1	1	1	1		1	1			8		
Uxbridge	474	14	Wilson	Samuel		1			1	1		2					5		
Uxbridge	474	15	White	William				1		1		1					3		
Uxbridge	474	16	White	John	1	1	2		1		1	2		1			9		
Uxbridge	474	17	Wood	Henry	1		1		1		1	1	1				6		

TOWN	PG#	LN#	HEADS OF HOUSEHOLD		FREE WHITE MALES					FREE WHITE FEMALES					TOTAL ALL OTHER	TOTAL SLAVES	TOTALS	DISTRICT/ TOWNSHIP	NOTES
			LAST NAME	FIRST NAME	under 10	10 to 16	16 to 26	26 to 45	45 and over	under 10	10 to 16	16 to 26	26 to 45	45 and over					
Ward	175	1	Rice	Edward		1	1			3			1				6		
Ward	175	2	Rice	Jonathan	2	2		1		1		1	1				8		
Ward	175	3	Rice	Peter		1		1		2			1				5		
Ward	175	4	Richards	David					1					1			2		
Ward	175	5	Richardson	Charles		1	1		1		2		1	1			7		
Ward	175	6	Richardson	Peter	1	1			1	1	1	2		1			8		
Ward	175	7	Rice	Gershom					1			1					2		
Ward	175	8	Rawson	Joseph	2			1		2			1				5		
Ward	175	9	Stone	Jonathan		2	1		1			1		1			6		
Ward	175	10	Stone	Jona Jr	2			1		1		1	1				6		
Ward	175	11	Stone	Joseph		1		1					1				3		
Ward	175	12	Stone	Nathl	2	1		1		3	1	2	1				11		
Ward	175	13	Stone	John	1	2		1		1	1		1				7		
Ward	175	14	Sibley	Solomon	1			1		1			1				4		
Ward	175	15	Stone	Israel	1	1			1	1				2			6		
Ward	175	16	Stockwell	John	1	1		1		4	1		1				9		
Ward	176	17	Scott	Thomas	1			1				3		1			6		
Ward	176	18	Stone	Jesse				1					1				2		
Ward	176	19	Southworth	Nethl	2		1	1		1		1	1				7		
Ward	176	20	Severy	Joseph	1			1		1			1				4		
Ward	176	21	Stevens	Phins		1	1		1	1	1	1		1			7		
Ward	176	22	Sibley	Aaron		2						1					3		
Ward	176	23	Stone	Isaac	3		1	1		1			1				7		
Ward	176	24	Scott	Thomas Junr				1				1					2		
Ward	176	25	Singletary	Amos Jur	2	2	2	1		1	1			1			10		
Ward	176	26	Town	Phinehas		1	1			3			1				6		
Ward	176	27	Waters	Judah	3	1	2	1		2	1		1				11		
Ward	176	28	Young	William		2	1		1	1	1			1			7		
Ward	177	29	Holman	Hannah	1	1							1				3		
Ward	177	30	Holman	Eliphalet		1		1		1	1		1				5		
Ward	177	31	Hart	John	1		3		1			1	1	1			8		
Ward	177	32	Holman	John	1	1	1				1	1					5		
Ward	177	33	Howard	Daniel				1					1				2		
Ward	177	34	Hart	James Jur			1			2		1					4		
Ward	177	35	Henshaw	Joseph			1			1			1				3		
Ward	177	36	Hart	Thomas	3	1		1					1				6		
Ward	177	37	Jacobs	John		1		1					1				3		
Ward	177	38	Jenison	Daniel	1		2	1			2		1				7		
Ward	177	39	Jacoby	Samuel		1	1			1		1	1				6		
Ward	177	40	Jacoby	Israel	2			1				1	1				5		
Ward	177	41	Jenison	Joseph				1					1				2		
Ward	177	42	Jenison	Nethl	1		1					1					3		
Ward	177	43	King	John		1		1			1	1					4		
Ward	178	44	Knowls	Thomas		1	1	1				3		1			7		
Ward	178	45	Knowls	Thomas Junr		1				1		1					3		
Ward	178	46	Knowlton	Joseph				1					1				2		
Ward	178	47	Livermore	Elisha	1	1	2	1		3		1	1				10		
Ward	178	48	Muzzy	Nathan	4			1	1	1		1	1	2			11		
Ward	178	49	Muzzy	Jonathan	4		2	1			1		1				9		
Ward	178	50	Mann	Elijah		1		1		1			1				4		
Ward	178	51	Meriam	James			2										2		
Ward	178	52	Pitts	Ebenz				1			1	1	1				4		
Ward	178	53	Phillips	Simon	1	1		1		1	1		2	1			8		
Ward	178	54	Prentice	John		1	2		1			1		1			6		
Ward	178	55	Rich	Reuben		1	2			1		1					5		
Ward	178	56	Rice	Comfort	1			1					1				3		
Ward	179	57	Clark	Joseph				1					1		1		3		
Ward	179	58	Craige	Abijah	1	1		1			1		1				5		
Ward	179	59	Clark	John	1	1		1				1	1				5		
Ward	179	60	Clark	Samuel			1			1		1					3		
Ward	179	61	Cary	Recompence	1	1	1	1		1	1		1				7		
Ward	179	62	Cheeney	Ephm		1		1		1	2	1	1				7		
Ward	179	63	Cudworth	Abigail		1					1	2		1			5		
Ward	179	64	Comins	Daniel	2	2		1		2			1				8		
Ward	179	65	Cheeney	Joseph			1		1			1		1			4		
Ward	179	66	Cheeney	Aquilla			1				1		1				3		
Ward	179	67	Carter	Benjamin				1						2			3		
Ward	179	68	Cutler	Amos	3			1		1			1				6		
Ward	179	69	Cariel	Daniel				1		1			1				3		
Ward	179	70	Comins	Rachel								1		1			2		
Ward	180	71	Eaton	Jonas	3		1		1	1		1	1	1			9		
Ward	180	72	Eddy	Levi	2	2	2		1	1			1				9		
Ward	180	73	Eddy	Samuel	2			1	1		1		1	1			7		
Ward	180	74	Dodge	Daniel		1		1		2			1				5		
Ward	180	75	Drury	Thomas		1			1					2			4		
Ward	180	76	Drury	Thomas Junr	2		1	1					1				5		
Ward	180	77	Fitts	Walter	2			1		2	1		1				7		
Ward	180	78	Goulding	Jonah		1	1		1		1	3		1			8		
Ward	180	79	Gleason	David	1			2					2	1			7		

TOWN	PG#	LN#	HEADS OF HOUSEHOLD		FREE WHITE MALES					FREE WHITE FEMALES					TOTAL ALL OTHER	TOTAL SLAVES	TOTALS	DISTRICT/ TOWNSHIP	NOTES
			LAST NAME	FIRST NAME	under 10	10 to 16	16 to 26	26 to 45	45 and over	under 10	10 to 16	16 to 26	26 to 45	45 and over					
Ward	180	80	Gleason	David Junr	2			1		3			1				7		
Ward	180	81	Green	Thomas		1	1	1		2		1	1				7		
Ward	180	82	Hart	Martha									1				1		
Ward	180	83	Hart	James		1		1					1				3		
Ward	180	84	Holman	Abel				1					2				3		

TOWN	PG#	LN#	LAST NAME	FIRST NAME	FREE WHITE MALES					FREE WHITE FEMALES					TOTAL ALL OTHER	TOTAL SLAVES	TOTALS	DISTRICT/TOWNSHIP	NOTES
					under 10	10 to 16	16 to 26	26 to 45	45 and over	under 10	10 to 16	16 to 26	26 to 45	45 and over					
Westborough	189	1	Brigham	Elijah	1	1	1	1	1	3	1	1	2				12		
Westborough	189	2	Parkman	Brick		1	3		2	3	1	2		2			14		
Westborough	189	3	Forbush	Isaac		1	2	2		2		1		1			9		
Westborough	189	4	Cobb	Edward	3	2	1		1	1			1				9		
Westborough	189	5	Wares	Bariah	1				1		1			1			4		
Westborough	189	6	Fisk	John	2	2		1		1		1	1				8		
Westborough	189	7	Warren	Benjm	2	3	3		1	1	1	1	1	2			15		
Westborough	189	8	Fesendon	John					1		1	1	1				4		
Westborough	189	9	Nichols	Joseph	1	1	1	1		1	1	2	1				9		
Westborough	189	10	Nichols	Fortunalus	1		1	1		2		1	1				7		
Westborough	189	11	Beaton	John	1	1	3		1	1				1			8		
Westborough	189	12	Beaton	Martha										3			3		
Westborough	189	13	Maynard	Ebenz				1						1			2		
Westborough	189	14	Maynard	Luther		1		1				1					3		
Westborough	189	15	Fisher	Samuel	2	1		1		1			1				6		
Westborough	189	16	Whitney	Thomas				1				1		1			3		
Westborough	189	17	Robbins	Daniel			2	1		1			1	1			6		
Westborough	189	18	Maynard	Nathan		2	2	2			1			1			8		
Westborough	191	19	Pratt	Martin				1						1			2		
Westborough	191	20	Miller	Moses			1			2			1				4		
Westborough	191	21	Ball	John	1		1		1	1	1		1				6		
Westborough	191	22	Lackey	Judith						1	1		1				3		
Westborough	191	23	Adams	Isaac		1		1		1			1				4		
Westborough	191	24	Ball	Lucy		1				1	1		1				4		
Westborough	191	25	Bowman	James			2	1		1			1				5		
Westborough	191	26	Hardy	Phinehas	1	1			1	1		1					5		
Westborough	191	27	Forbush	Rufus	2	2	1	1		1		1	1				9		
Westborough	191	28	Miller	James				1				1	1				3		
Westborough	191	29	Harrington	Joseph		1	3			1				3			9		
Westborough	191	30	Harrington	John			2		1	2			1	1			7		
Westborough	191	31	Thurston	Samuel		1	1	1			2		2				7		
Westborough	191	32	Forbs	Elisha	1		3		1	1	2		1				9		
Westborough	191	33	Blake	Braman	2		1	1		1	1	1					7		
Westborough	191	34	Whitney	Eli	1		1	1	1			1	1				6		
Westborough	191	35	Hide	Rachel		1				1			1				3		
Westborough	192	36	Parker	Otis	2	1		1					1				5		
Westborough	192	37	Parker	Margen							1		1				2		
Westborough	192	38	Morse	Seth		1	1		1	1			1				5		
Westborough	192	39	Whitney	Jonah		1				2		1					4		
Westborough	192	40	Miller	Willard		1				1			1				3		
Westborough	192	41	Morse	Thomas	2	1	1	2	1		1	2	1				11		
Westborough	192	42	Bigelow	Arnisa	2	1		1	1	1			1	1			8		
Westborough	192	43	Pike	Sarah		1				1			1				3		
Westborough	192	44	Fay	Catharine									1				1		
Westborough	192	45	Smith	Levi		1		1		1	1		1				5		
Westborough	192	46	Miller	Joshua	1	2	1	1		2		2					9		
Westborough	192	47	Corbet	Elisha	3	1	1	1		1		1	1				9		
Westborough	192	48	Bowman	Levi			1			1	1						3		
Westborough	192	49	Forbs	Phinehas		1		1		1	2	1	2	1			9		
Westborough	192	50	Warren	David				1		1			1				3		
Westborough	192	51	Warren	Aaron					1					1			2		
Westborough	192	52	Brigham	Joseph	1	1		1		1			1				5		
Westborough	194	53	Fisher	Nathan	2				1	1	2	1		1			8		
Westborough	194	54	Peirce	Benjm			1			1		1					3		
Westborough	194	55	Bowman	Benjm	3	1		1		3			1				9		
Westborough	194	56	Feywether	John		1	1	1	1								4		
Westborough	194	57	Wheelock	Moses				1				1		1			3		
Westborough	194	58	Fairbank	Jonathan	1		1					1	1				4		
Westborough	194	59	Blake	Elisha	4		2	1		1			1	1			10		
Westborough	194	60	Parker	Gardner	1		1	1					1				4		
Westborough	194	61	Newton	Barnabas			2	1	1		2	2	1	1			10		
Westborough	194	62	Robartson	John			1			1		1	1				4		
Westborough	194	63	Clarke	Benjm		1		1				2					4		
Westborough	194	64	Rugles	Isaac		2	1	2			1	1	1				8		
Westborough	194	65	Sandburn	John		1		1					2				4		
Westborough	194	66	Gould	James			1		1					1			3		
Westborough	194	67	Belknap	Stephen	3	1		1		1	1	1	1				9		
Westborough	194	68	Miller	Nehemiah	1			1	1	2			1				6		
Westborough	194	69	Parker	Joel				1		2		1					4		
Westborough	194	70	Forbush	Colledge	1		1	1		4			1				8		
Westborough	195	71	Batherick	Solomon	1		1	1	1					2			6		
Westborough	195	72	Batherick	Levi	1		1			1			1				4		
Westborough	195	73	Maynard	Solomon		1		1						1			3		
Westborough	195	74	Bond	Abraham	4			1		1			1	1			8		
Westborough	195	75	Barns	Richard	1		3		1		1		1				7		
Westborough	195	76	Brigham	David	2	1	1	1		2			1				8		
Westborough	195	77	Peters	Andrew				1			1	1		1			4		
Westborough	195	78	Peters	Lovet	1	1	1	1		1	1		1				7		
Westborough	195	79	Morse	Abner W.	1								1				4		

142

TOWN	PG#	LN#	LAST NAME	FIRST NAME	FREE WHITE MALES					FREE WHITE FEMALES					TOTAL ALL OTHER	TOTAL SLAVES	TOTALS	DISTRICT/ TOWNSHIP	NOTES
					under 10	10 to 16	16 to 26	26 to 45	45 and over	under 10	10 to 16	16 to 26	26 to 45	45 and over					
Westborough	195	80	Cook	Jonathan				1						1			2		
Westborough	195	81	Maynard	Stephen	1	1		2		1	1		1				7		
Westborough	195	82	Beman	John				1		3			1				5		
Westborough	195	83	Chamberlain	Ebenz		1	1		1			1		1			5		
Westborough	195	84	Wood	Seth		1			1		1	1		1			5		
Westborough	195	85	Belknap	Joseph		1	3		2	1		4		2			13		
Westborough	195	86	Bellows	Reuben	1				1	1	1		1				5		
Westborough	195	87	Johnson	William			1		1			1		1			4		
Westborough	196	88	Fay	Benjm	1	3		2	1	1		3		1			12		
Westborough	196	89	Fay	Silas	1		3	1		2			2				9		
Westborough	196	90	Nurse	Lydia										2			2		
Westborough	196	91	Forbs	Moses			1			1		2					4		
Westborough	196	92	Grout	Jonathan		1		1	1			3	1	1			8		
Westborough	196	93	Fay	David	4	1	2	1		1	1	1	1	1			13		
Westborough	196	94	Grout	Samuel	1	1		1		4		1		1			9		
Westborough	196	95	Hardy	Elijah			3		1			2	1				7		
Westborough	196	96	Miller	Isaac		1			1				2	1			5		
Westborough	196	97	Brigham	Benajah	1	1	2		1					1			6		
Westborough	196	98	Haws	James		1			1					1			3		
Westborough	196	99	Haws	James Jun			1			3			1				5		
Westborough	196	100	Forbush	Ebenz				1					1				2		
Westborough	196	101	Andrew	Thomas		1	1		1	1	1		1				6		
Westborough	196	102	Forbush	Samuel				1				1	1				3		
Westborough	196	103	Forbush	Samuel Jun	2			1					1				4		
Westborough	196	104	Batherick	Jonathan	1	2	2		1	1	1	1		1			10		
Westborough	197	105	Warren	Abner	1			1		3	1	1	1				8		
Westborough	197	106	Garfield	Susannah		1				1			1	1			4		
Westborough	197	107	Lathrop	Thomas	1			1					1				3		
Westborough	197	108	Bruce	Mary										1			1		
Westborough	197	109	Harrington	Wentworth	1		1					1					3		
Westborough	197	110	Andrew	Nathll		1	1	1		3	1		1	1			9		
Westborough	197	111	Johnson	Samuel	1		1	1				1					4		
Westborough	197	112	Bruce	Eli	2			1		1				1			5		
Westborough	197	113	Twichel	Thomas				1					1	1			3		
Westborough	197	114	Twichel	Thomas Jun		1				1	1	1	1				6		
Westborough	197	115	Brigham	Trowbridge			1					1					2		
Westborough	197	116	Forbs	Jonath		2	2		1	1	2	1		1			10		
Westborough	197	117	Brigham	Ebenz		1		1		1			1				4		
Westborough	197	118	Fay	Daniel			3					1					4		
Westborough	197	119	Chamberlain	Daniel		2	2		1	2	1	1		1			10		
Westborough	197	120	Downs	Farris											2		2		
Westborough	197	121	Bowman	Nathaniel		1		1			1		1				4		
Westborough	198	122	Snow	Susannah									1				1		
Westborough	198	123	Estee	John	3			1					2				6		
Westborough	198	124	Beman	Abraham					1				1				2		
Westborough	198	125	Beman	Levi				1					1				2		
Westborough	198	126	Forbush	Asa	1	2		1		2	2		1				9		
Westborough	198	127	Wood	John	1	1		1		3			1				7		
Westborough	198	128	Lenard	Solomon				1						1			2		
Westborough	198	129	Bellows	Samuel	1	1		1		1	1	1		1			7		
Westborough	198	130	Brigham	Edmund		2	1	1		1		2		1			8		
Westborough	198	131	Gale	Abijah		1		1	1	2		1		1			7		
Westborough	198	132	Gale	Nahum	3	1	1	1		1			1				8		
Westborough	198	133	Andrew	George Jun	1			1		3	1		2				8		
Westborough	198	134	Haskell	Phinh		1	1			1				1			4		
Westborough	198	135	Haskell	Asa	1			1		2		1	1				6		
Westborough	198	136	Bellows	Simeon		1	2		1			1	1	2			8		
Westborough	198	137	Warren	Timothy				1									1		
Westborough	198	138	Warren	John		2		1		1	1	2	1				8		
Westborough	198	139	White	Dix				1		1			1				3		
Westborough	199	140	Brigham	William	1			1			1		1				4		
Westborough	199	141	Newton	Silas	3			1		2	2		1				9		
Westborough	199	142	Newton	Ebenezer	1			1		1	1		1				5		
Westborough	199	143	Johnson	Daniel				1						1			2		
Westborough	199	144	Johnson	Joseph		1		1		5	2		1				10		
Westborough	199	145	Newton	Jeremiah	2	1		1		1			2				7		
Westborough	199	146	Fay	Elisha		1	2		1		1	2		1			8		
Westborough	199	147	Bullard	Joseph	2			1				1					4		
Westborough	199	148	Cutting	Merrick	1			1		1			1				4		
Westborough	199	149	Parker	Jidediah			3		1					1			5		
Westborough	199	150	Parker	Abner		1			1			1	1				4		
Westborough	199	151	Sumner	Samuel			1						1				2		
Westborough	199	152	Williams	Cutting			2			1		1					4		
Westborough	199	153	Estee	Nathaniel	1			1		2			1				5		
Westborough	199	154	Ward	Solomon				1					1				2		

TOWN	PG#	LN#	LAST NAME	FIRST NAME	FREE WHITE MALES					FREE WHITE FEMALES					TOTAL ALL OTHER	TOTAL SLAVES	TOTALS	DISTRICT/ TOWNSHIP	NOTES
					under 10	10 to 16	16 to 26	26 to 45	45 and over	under 10	10 to 16	16 to 26	26 to 45	45 and over					
Western	249	1	Brooks	John	3	1	3			3	2	2	1				15		
Western	249	2	Brown	John	2				1	1				1			5		
Western	249	3	Dennison	David		1	1	1		2		2	1				8		
Western	249	4	Dow	Jonathan			2	1				1					4		
Western	249	5	Stephens	James		1				1		1					3		
Western	249	6	Chadwick	Lucy				1					2	2			5		
Western	251	1	Tyler	Isaac		1	1		1		1		1				5		
Western	251	2	Tyler	Isaac 2d	2		1	1		1	1	1	1				8		
Western	251	3	Tyler	Abner	2	2	2		1	1	1	2		1			12		
Western	251	4	Tyler	Moses	1	1	1		1	1	1	1	1				8		
Western	251	5	Town	Elisha			1			1			1				3		
Western	251	6	White	William Jr	4	1		1	1		1	1	1				10		
Western	251	7	Wheeler	Rice		1			2	1	1	3		2			10		
Western	251	8	White	Robert	1	1		1		1			1				5		
Western	251	9	Winslow	Jona	1			1		1			1				4		
Western	251	10	Woodworth	Arad	2		2	2		1			1				8		
Western	251	11	Williams		2			1		1			1				5		First name left blank
Western	251	12	Alexander	Joseph	1		2			1		1					5		
Western	251	13	Stanford	Joseph	1		1			1		1					4		
Western	251	14	Baxter	Stephen Revd		1	1	1	1		1		2				7		
Western	251	15	Greenleaf	William	1		2			1	1	1	1	1			8		
Western	252	1	Munroe	Samuel			1			1			1	1			4		
Western	252	2	Allen	Joseph		1	1					1	1				4		
Western	252	3	Bascom	Samuel	1	1			1			1					4		
Western	252	4	Newport	Dan											8		8		
Western	252	5	Bellows	Jotham				1			1		1				3		
Western	252	6	Ramsdel	Joseph		1	2			1		1					5		
Western	252	7	Stone	Joseph	3	1		1		1			1				7		
Western	252	8	Shepherd	Moses		1		1			1		1				4		
Western	252	9	Blackmore	Willard	1			1				1					3		
Western	252	10	Rood	Sarah			2						1				3		
Western	252	11	Bugbee	Ebenz			1					1					2		
Western	252	12	Farley	Samuel		1			1	2	1		1				6		
Western	254	1	Rich	Ezra			1			2		1					4		
Western	254	2	Robbins	Samuel	1		1			1		1					4		
Western	254	3	Rice	Silas	3	1	1	1		1	1		1				9		
Western	254	4	Root	Mary						1		1		1			3		
Western	254	5	Shepherd	William	4		1	2	1	1	1		2	1			13		
Western	254	6	Shepherd	Amos	4		1			1			1		1		8		
Western	254	7	Stone	James		2		2	1			2		1	1		9		
Western	254	8	Sweetser	Henry	3			1	1			2	1				8		
Western	254	9	Smith	Ezra			1	1		1			1				4		
Western	254	10	Sweetser	Henry Jr	5	2		1					1				9		
Western	254	11	Smith	Benjm		2		1		1	1		1				6		
Western	254	12	Tenney	Amasa	1			1				1					3		
Western	255	1	Hatch	James	3		1	1				2					7		
Western	255	2	Hitchcock	Luke		1		2		2		1	2				8		
Western	255	3	Hill	John	1			1				1	1				4		
Western	255	4	Harmon	John				1		1			1				3		
Western	255	5	Haskall	John	1			1					1	1	1		5		
Western	255	6	Hathway	Nathan		1	1			1		1					4		
Western	255	7	Hitchcock	John	1			1					1				3		
Western	255	8	Johnson	John	2		1						1				4		
Western	255	9	Joslin	John R.		1		1		4	1	1	1				9		
Western	255	10	Knight	Samuel	2	1	1	1	1	1	2		1	1			11		
Western	255	11	Keyes	Danforth		3		1			2	2	1		1		10		
Western	256	1	Kellog	Medad		1	1		1	2		3		1			9		
Western	256	2	Lincoln	Seth	2	2		1		1	1	1					8		
Western	256	3	Sampson	David	3			1		2			1				7		
Western	256	4	Maynard	William		1		1		2	1		1				6		
Western	256	5	Marr	William		1		1	1	2	2		1				9		
Western	256	6	Mills	John	1			1		2			1				5		
Western	256	7	Mills	Abijah	1		1	1		3			2				8		
Western	256	8	Marsh	Marcus	1	1	1	1		1		1					6		
Western	256	9	Miller	Polly	1	2						1	1				5		
Western	256	10	Moor	Isaac	1	1	3		1	1	2	1	1				11		
Western	256	11	Makepeece	Elliot	1	1	2		1	1	1		2	1			10		
Western	256	12	Moor	William	1		1					1					3		
Western	256	13	Miles	Solomon	1	1		1		3			1				7		
Western	256	14	Nevens	Sarah	1					1	1		1				5		
Western	257	1	Crabtree	John Jur	1	1		2	1	2			1	1			9		
Western	257	2	Carpenter	Fredk	1		2	1		5			1				10		
Western	257	3	Chadwick	Solomon			1					1					2		
Western	257	4	Collester	Samuel				1			1		1				3		
Western	257	5	Chickering	Nathll	1	1	1	1		1	1	1	1				8		
Western	257	6	Dow	Isaiah				1			1		1				3		
Western	257	7	Dwight	Simeon	1	2	1	1		2		2	1				10		
Western	257	8	Day	Nathan	1		1	1		1		2					6		
Western	257	9	Damon	John	2			2					1				5		
Western	257	10	Damon	Jude	3	1	1		1	2	2			1			11		
Western	257	11	Davis	John				1					1				2		
Western	257	12	Field	Asa K.	1		4				1	1					7		
Western	257	13	Davis	Gideon		1		1				1		1			4		
Western	258	1	Foster	Nathan		1		1	1	3			1	1			8		
Western	258	2	Field	Joseph		1		1					1				3		
Western	258	3	Ferrey	Hezekiah	5			1		1			1				8		
Western	258	4	Chamberlain				1			2		1					4		First name left blank
Western	258	5	Gleason	Jonathan			1		1	1		1	1				5		
Western	258	6	Gleason	Isaac		1	1		1			1	1	3			8		
Western	258	7	Gleason	Hannah			1			1	1	2		1			6		

TOWN	PG#	LN#	LAST NAME	FIRST NAME	FREE WHITE MALES					FREE WHITE FEMALES					TOTAL ALL OTHER	TOTAL SLAVES	TOTALS	DISTRICT/ TOWNSHIP	NOTES
					under 10	10 to 16	16 to 26	26 to 45	45 and over	under 10	10 to 16	16 to 26	26 to 45	45 and over					
Western	258	8	Gray	Elizabeth	1			1						1			3		
Western	258	9	Gray	Samuel					1								1		
Western	258	10	Goulding	Joseph		2	1		1	2		1	1				8		
Western	258	11	Gray	Matthew		1			1					1			3		
Western	258	12	Gaba	George					1	1				1			3		
Western	258	13	Hodges	Daniel	1	2	1	1	1	2		2	1	2			13		
Western	259	1	Brooks	Benjamin			1						2				3		
Western	259	2	Brooks	Asa			1			2		1		1			5		
Western	259	3	Bell	John	1	2				1		1		1			7		
Western	259	4	Blair	James		3	1		2		1	1					9		
Western	259	5	Bridges	Timothy P.	2				1	2		1	1				7		
Western	259	6	Brown	James Jr	3	1	1		1			1	1		1		9		
Western	259	7	Brown	William		2			2	1		1	1		2		9		
Western	259	8	Blair	William	1	2		1	1	1			1	1			8		
Western	259	9	Blair	Samuel	2	2	2		1	1		2		1			11		
Western	259	10	Blodgit	Nathan	1	2		2		2	1			1			9		
Western	259	11	Blackmore	John	1		1	1		3	4	1		1			12		
Western	259	12	Bascom	Moses		1			1	1	1	2		1			7		
Western	259	13	Bliss	Isaac	2	2		1	1	3	1	1	1	1			13		
Western	260	1	Bellows	Joseph					1			1		1			3		
Western	260	2	Blair	Reuben	1	3	1		1	4		2	1				13		
Western	260	3	Bascom	Caleb					1	2			1				4		
Western	260	4	Cummings	Solomon	1	1	1		1			1	2		1		8		
Western	260	5	Cutler	Joseph		1	2		1	1	1			2			8		
Western	260	6	Combs	John Jr	1	1			2				1				5		
Western	260	7	Cutler	Joseph Jr	3	1	1	1		2	1	1	1				11		
Western	260	8	Cordee	William	1		1		1	1		1	1	1			7		
Western	260	9	Collister	William	2		2	1		2		1	1				9		
Western	260	10	Cutler	Ebenezer		1	1		1		1	1	1	1			7		
Western	260	11	Collis	John		1	1		1		1	2		1			7		
Western	260	12	Chadwick	Nathan					1					1			2		
Western	260	13	Chadwick	Nathan Jr	1			1		1			1				4		
Western	261	1	Arnold	Ezeck		1	1		1	2	1	2		1			9		
Western	261	2	Arnold	Joseph	1			1		2			1				5		
Western	261	3	Adams	George	1				1					1			3		
Western	261	4	Bond	Seth		1		1	1			1		1			5		
Western	261	5	Bliss	Noah	2	1				2	1		1				8		
Western	261	6	Bliss	Oliver	1		1	1					1	1			5		
Western	261	7	Bliss	Solomon	1	1	2		1	2	1	1		1			10		
Western	261	8	Bliss	Aaron	2	1	2	1	2	3	2	1	1	1			16		
Western	261	9	Bliss	Edwd Junr					1		1	1	1	1			5		
Western	261	10	Blair	Daniel		1		1				1	1				4		
Western	261	11	Burrough	David	1		1		1		1	2	1	1	1		9		
Western	261	12	Blackmore	James		1		1		4	1		1				8		
Western	261	13	Burrough	Tyler				1		1	1		1				4		

TOWN	PG#	LN#	LAST NAME	FIRST NAME	FREE WHITE MALES under 10	10 to 16	16 to 26	26 to 45	45 and over	FREE WHITE FEMALES under 10	10 to 16	16 to 26	26 to 45	45 and over	TOTAL ALL OTHER	TOTAL SLAVES	TOTALS	DISTRICT/ TOWNSHIP	NOTES
Westminster	441	1	Adams	John		1	2	1		2	1	1		1			9		
Westminster	441	2	Bigelow	Jabez			2		1					1			4		
Westminster	441	3	Bigelow	Ephraim	3	1		1		1	2		1				9		
Westminster	441	4	Bemis	William				1						1			2		
Westminster	441	5	Bigelow	Elisha	1		1		1					1			4		
Westminster	441	6	Bigelow	Elisha Jr	1			1		2		1					5		
Westminster	441	7	Baker	Nathan	2	1			1	2	1			1			8		
Westminster	441	8	Bartlett	Daniel			1	1				1	1				4		
Westminster	441	9	Bigelow	Luke	1			1		2			1				5		
Westminster	441	10	Bard	Joseph	1		1		1	2	2		1				8		
Westminster	441	11	Barns	Frances	3	1	1		1			2		1			9		
Westminster	441	12	Blodget	Isaac	3	2	1		1	2				1			10		
Westminster	441	13	Blanchard	Zilphar										1			1		
Westminster	441	14	Brun	Samuel			1					1					2		
Westminster	441	15	Bolton	Aaron				1		3	2	1		1			8		
Westminster	441	16	Bond	Thadeus		1		1		4	3		1				10		
Westminster	441	17	Bacon	Edward		1	1		1		1			1			5		
Westminster	441	18	Bemis	Zacheus				1						1			2		
Westminster	441	19	Bigelow	John		1		1			1		1				4		
Westminster	441	20	Bemis	William			2						1				3		
Westminster	443	1	Conant	Thomas Jr	2			1			1		1				5		
Westminster	443	2	Cones	James		1			1		1			1			4		
Westminster	443	3	Cates	Stephen		1			1					1			3		
Westminster	443	4	Cooper	Jedidiah		1		1	1	1		1		1			5		
Westminster	443	5	Drury	Elezar				1				1					2		
Westminster	443	6	Darby	Andrew		1	1	1	1		1			1			6		
Westminster	443	7	Damon	John				1		1	1		1				4		
Westminster	443	8	Darby	Joseph	1		1			2			1				5		
Westminster	443	9	Damon	Timothy			1		1			1					3		
Westminster	443	10	Darby	Abel	1		1					1					3		
Westminster	443	11	Damon	Timothy Jr	1			1		4			1				7		
Westminster	443	12	Darby	Ezra		1				1		1					3		
Westminster	443	13	Darby	Nathan		1		1				1		1			4		
Westminster	443	14	Dunn	John	3	1		1		1	1	1					8		
Westminster	443	15	Dale	Joseph		1				1		1					3		
Westminster	443	16	Darby	John Jr	2			1				1					4		
Westminster	443	17	Darby	John		1			1					2			4		
Westminster	443	18	Dime	Nicholas				1						1			2		
Westminster	444	1	Brooks	Ezra			1		1		1		1				4		
Westminster	444	2	Bemis	Edmund			1	1		1				1			4		
Westminster	444	3	Beamon	Joseph	3		1	1		1			1				7		
Westminster	444	4	Barnard	Edmund	1		2		1	1	1	1					7		
Westminster	444	5	Barker	Richard				1						1			2		
Westminster	444	6	Bigelow	Benjamin	2	2		1		1			1				7		
Westminster	444	7	Brooks	Samuel	1			1		2		1					5		
Westminster	444	8	Brooks	Isaac		1	1		2	1	1			2			8		
Westminster	444	9	Bemis	Thomas	3			1		2				1			7		
Westminster	444	10	Brown	Josiah	1			1		2			1				5		
Westminster	444	11	Brown	Jonathan		1		1			1		1				4		
Westminster	444	12	Brown	Benjamin	2			1					1				4		
Westminster	444	13	Barker	Joel	1		1					1					3		
Westminster	444	14	Bigelow	Ezekiel	1			1		2			1				5		
Westminster	444	15	Bemis	Stephen	2			1		1			1				5		
Westminster	444	16	Childs	David		1	1		1		2			1			6		
Westminster	444	17	Conant	Thomas	1				1					1			3		
Westminster	444	18	Childs	Joseph	1			1					1				3		
Westminster	445	1	Fesendon	John		1		1				1		1			4		
Westminster	445	2	Fesendon	Jonas	1		1					1					3		
Westminster	445	3	Farnsworth	Asa		1			1	2	1		1				6		
Westminster	445	4	Fesendon	Timothy Jr			1					1					2		
Westminster	445	5	Gates	Phinihas	1				1					1			3		
Westminster	445	6	Graves	Jonathan	1	2	1		1	2		2	1				10		
Westminster	445	7	Gates	Amos	1				1	1				1			4		
Westminster	445	8	Graves	Levi	1	1			1	1	1	1	1				7		
Westminster	445	9	Gager	Jeremiah					1		2		1				4		
Westminster	445	10	Garish	Ruth		1							1	1			3		
Westminster	445	11	Gibbs	Elisabeth										1			1		
Westminster	445	12	Goodall	John				1						3			4		
Westminster	445	13	Holden	Rebeckah									1	1			2		
Westminster	445	14	Hart	David	2			1					1				4		
Westminster	445	15	Hoar	Samuel	2	1		1		2			1				7		
Westminster	445	16	Hoar	Stephen	2	1	2	1		2		2	1				11		
Westminster	446	1	Dime	Nicholas Jr	2	1				3	1		1				9		
Westminster	446	2	Dunster	Thomas	1				1		1	1		1			5		
Westminster	446	3	Dupee	John			1			1		1					3		
Westminster	446	4	Dunster	Shubael		2	1	1				1		1			6		
Westminster	446	5	Eaton	Nathan	1			1		2			1				5		
Westminster	446	6	Eaton	Mary		1							3	1			5		
Westminster	446	7	Easterbrook	John		1	2		1	1	1		1				7		

TOWN	PG#	LN#	LAST NAME	FIRST NAME	FREE WHITE MALES					FREE WHITE FEMALES					TOTAL ALL OTHER	TOTAL SLAVES	TOTALS	DISTRICT/ TOWNSHIP	NOTES
					under 10	10 to 16	16 to 26	26 to 45	45 and over	under 10	10 to 16	16 to 26	26 to 45	45 and over					
Westminster	446	8	Easterbrook	John Jr				1						1			2		
Westminster	446	9	Easterbrook	Thomas			1			1	1		1				4		
Westminster	446	10	Edgell	William		1			1		1			1			4		
Westminster	446	11	Edgell	William Jr				1		2			1				4		
Westminster	446	12	Everett	Pelitiah	3	1			1	1	1	1					8		
Westminster	446	13	Fesenden	Samuel	3				1		1			1			6		
Westminster	446	14	Foskett	Daniel	1	1		1				1		1			5		
Westminster	446	15	Fesenden	Timothy				1						1			2		
Westminster	446	16	Jones	Farrwell			2										2		
Westminster	446	17	Johnson	Oliver	2	1		1		2	1		1				8		
Westminster	446	18	Jackson	Edward		1	2						1	1			5		
Westminster	446	19	Jackson	Sebin				1					3	1			5		
Westminster	446	20	Johnston	Thomas				1					1	1			3		
Westminster	446	21	Johnson	John				1		4				1			6		
Westminster	446	22	Knower	Thomas	1			1		1		2	1	1			7		
Westminster	446	23	Lewis	Thomas			1	1		1			1	1			5		
Westminster	446	24	Lincoln	Heamon			2		1	2	3	1		1			10		
Westminster	446	25	Leonard	Enoch			2					1					3		
Westminster	446	26	Luis	Abijah		1						1					2		
Westminster	446	27	Laws	James				1		1	1		1				4		
Westminster	446	28	Laws	James Jr	2			1				1					4		
Westminster	446	29	Laws	Thomas Jr	1		1	1		1			2				6		
Westminster	446	30	Miles	Noah		1		1						1			3		
Westminster	446	31	Millin	Joshua		1		1		1	1	2		1			7		
Westminster	446	32	Maynard	David		1	1	1		2				1			6		
Westminster	448	1	Hoar	John		1	1	1		1	2			1			7		
Westminster	448	2	Holden	Stephen		1	2	1		4	2		1				11		
Westminster	448	3	Haywood	Benjn			1	1		1			1				4		
Westminster	448	4	Holden	Abner				1						1			2		
Westminster	448	5	Holden	Abner Jr		1		1					1				3		
Westminster	448	6	Holden	Ezra	3			1		2	1		1				8		
Westminster	448	7	Hager	Jonathan			1	1	1			1		1			5		
Westminster	448	8	Harrington	Seth	1			2		1			1	1			6		
Westminster	448	9	Holden	Elias	2	2		1		1			1				7		
Westminster	448	10	Hadley	John	2			1					1				4		
Westminster	448	11	Holden	Levi	1		1	1		1			1	1			6		
Westminster	448	12	Haywood	Nathan	2		1	1	1	1			1	2			9		
Westminster	448	13	How	Daniel			1										1		
Westminster	448	14	Hall	Elisha			1			1							2		
Westminster	448	15	Haywood	Timothy		3	2		1	1		2		1			10		
Westminster	448	16	Hoar	Timothy	2	1		1		2		2	1				9		
Westminster	448	17	Harrington	Benjn	3			1					1				5		
Westminster	449	1	Merraim	Samuel Jr	1	1			1	1	1		1				6		
Westminster	449	2	Miller	Ephraim				1				2		1			4		
Westminster	449	3	Miller	Asa	1			1		1			1				4		
Westminster	449	4	Mathews	Paul		1			1			1		1			4		
Westminster	449	5	Miller	Ezra	3			1					1				5		
Westminster	449	6	Miles	John				1						1			2		
Westminster	449	7	Morman	Abel				1						1			2		
Westminster	449	8	Miles	Thomas				1		3			1				5		
Westminster	449	9	Munjoy	Daniel				1		1			1				3		
Westminster	449	10	Martin	John	1		1	1	1	1		3		1			9		
Westminster	449	11	Morman	Ezra	1			1		2	1		1				6		
Westminster	449	12	Miles	Polly								1					1		
Westminster	449	13	Nichols	Benjamin		1	1		1	2	1		1				7		
Westminster	449	14	Tabor	Joseph			1										1		
Westminster	449	15	Pennemon	William		2	3	1				1	1				8		
Westminster	449	16	Peirce	Jarvis				1		2	1		1				5		
Westminster	449	17	Philips	Jonathan	1	2	1			2		1	1				9		
Westminster	450	1	Maynard	John				1		1		1					3		
Westminster	450	2	Minot	Jonathan	4		1		1	3		1					10		
Westminster	450	3	Miles	Stephen		1			1	1				1			4		
Westminster	450	4	Miller	Samuel	1	1	2		1	2	1	1	1				10		
Westminster	450	5	Miles	Margrett		1							1	1			3		
Westminster	450	6	Morman	Samuel	1			2	2	1	4			2			12		
Westminster	450	7	Miles	Isaac	1			1		3			1				6		
Westminster	450	8	Miles	Asa	1			1									2		
Westminster	450	9	Miles	Jonas	3		1	1		2			2				9		
Westminster	450	10	Merraim	Thomas			1		1					2			4		
Westminster	450	11	Mordock	William	1			1	1	2	1	1		1			8		
Westminster	450	12	Merraim	Jonas	1	1		1		3			1				7		
Westminster	450	13	Merraim	Asa	1			1		1			1				4		
Westminster	450	14	Miller	Joseph	1	1	1	1	1	1	1	1		1			9		
Westminster	450	15	Miller	John 2d				1				1					2		
Westminster	450	16	Miller	Isaac	1	1	1		1	2	2	1		2			11		
Westminster	450	17	Mudge	Joseph				1			1		1				3		
Westminster	450	18	Merraim	Samuel				1						1			2		
Westminster	451	1	Sampson	Abraham	1		1	1			1		1	1			6		
Westminster	451	2	Sawin	Joseph	1	1	1			3		2		1			9		

147

TOWN	PG#	LN#	LAST NAME	FIRST NAME	under 10	10 to 16	16 to 26	26 to 45	45 and over	under 10	10 to 16	16 to 26	26 to 45	45 and over	TOTAL ALL OTHER	TOTAL SLAVES	TOTALS	DISTRICT/ TOWNSHIP	NOTES
					FREE WHITE MALES					FREE WHITE FEMALES									
Westminster	451	3	Sawin	Jonathan		1			1			1		1			5		
Westminster	451	4	Sawin	James	1	1		1					1				4		
Westminster	451	5	Sawyer	Calvin	1		1		1		1			1			5		
Westminster	451	6	Sawin	Samuel	1	1	2		1	1		1	2	1			10		
Westminster	451	7	Spaulding	Merari	3			1		2			1				7		
Westminster	451	8	Spaulding	Joseph	2		1	1				2					6		
Westminster	451	9	Spaulding	Zebina	1			1		1			1				4		
Westminster	451	10	Severs	Benjn	2	1		1		2	2		1	1			10		
Westminster	451	11	Smith	Joseph	2	1				1	1		1				7		
Westminster	451	12	Shatock	Stephen										1			1		
Westminster	451	13	Sawin	David				1	1	1			1	2			6		
Westminster	451	14	Sawyer	Eli	1		1	1		4		1	1	1			10		
Westminster	451	15	Sawyer	Jonathan			2	2	1		1	2		1			9		
Westminster	451	16	Smith	Jonathan		1		1		1	1			1			5		
Westminster	451	17	Sawyer	Amos	1	1		1		2		1					6		
Westminster	452	1	Peirce	John			1	1	1	1			1	1			6		
Westminster	452	2	Puffer	Jonas	2			1		1	1		1				6		
Westminster	452	3	Puffer	Josiah			1	1	1	1	1			1			6		
Westminster	452	4	Rice	Revd Asaph			2		1			2	1				6		
Westminster	452	5	Fenno	Ephraim	1			1		2	1		1				6		
Westminster	452	6	Ray	Heamon	3			1		1			1				6		
Westminster	452	7	Rand	Zachariah	1	1	1		1	3	2		1				10		
Westminster	452	8	Raymond	Jonathan	1		1	1		1			1	1			6		
Westminster	452	9	Robens	Ephraim		1	1	1					1				4		
Westminster	452	10	Raymond	John				1					1				2		
Westminster	452	11	Sawin	Daniel	3			1		1			1				6		
Westminster	452	12	Smith	Silas	2			1		1	1		1				6		
Westminster	452	13	Sawin	William				1		1			1				3		
Westminster	452	14	Smith	Charles				1		1		1					3		
Westminster	452	15	Shumway	Abishun	1			1			1		1				4		
Westminster	452	16	Sawin	Abner		1		1					1				3		
Westminster	453	1	Woodward	Abel	2			1		1			1				5		
Westminster	453	2	Wetherbee	Caleb	1		1						2				4		
Westminster	453	3	White	Jonas	2			1		2			1				7		
Westminster	453	4	Wetherbee	Thomas	1		1		1	1	1	1		1			7		
Westminster	453	5	Wilder	Joel	1			1		1			1				4		
Westminster	453	6	Whitcomb	Jorge M.				1					1				2		
Westminster	453	7	Whitcomb	Oliver					1	1	1	2		1			6		
Westminster	453	8	Wetherbee	Ephraim		2	1	1		1				1			6		
Westminster	453	9	Whitman	Zachn		1	2		1	2	3	2		1			12		
Westminster	453	10	Warren	Jeduthan	3	1	1	1		1		1	1				9		
Westminster	453	11	Winchip	Jonas				1						2			3		
Westminster	453	12	Wood	Nathan		1			1	2			1				5		
Westminster	453	13	Woodward	Rebeckah								1	1	1			3		
Westminster	453	14	Wheeler	Hamon	1	1		1		3	1		1				8		
Westminster	453	15	Wetherbee	Caleb	2		1	1		2	1	1	1				9		
Westminster	453	16	Wiswell	John	2		1						1				4		
Westminster	453	17	White	John		2	1		1	2	1	1		1			9		
Westminster	453	18	Ward	John	1		2		1	1	1		1				7		
Westminster	454	1	Taft	Asa		1	1		1	1		2		1			7		
Westminster	454	2	Thurston	Moses	2				1	2	1	1	1				8		
Westminster	454	3	Thurston	Gilman			1			1		1					3		
Westminster	454	4	Taylor	Asa	2		2	1	1					1			7		
Westminster	454	5	Taylor	Samuel	1		1	1		2		1					6		
Westminster	454	6	Taylor	Joseph			2		1			1		1			5		
Westminster	454	7	Tottingham	Nathll		1	1					1		1			4		
Westminster	454	8	Taylor	Joseph Jr	1			1		3			1				6		
Westminster	454	9	Tayor	Elizabth										2			2		
Westminster	454	10	Taylor	Rebeckah								1					1		
Westminster	454	11	Trane	Elisha	2				1	2			1				6		
Westminster	454	12	Talor	Ezra	1			1					1				3		
Westminster	454	13	Whiting	William	2			1		1	2		1				7		
Westminster	454	14	White	James	2			1		1			1				5		
Westminster	454	15	Wynon	David	2	1		1		1	2		1				8		
Westminster	454	16	Whitney	Nathan Jr	2			1		1	2		1				7		
Westminster	454	17	Woodward	Nathll			1		1			1		1			4		
Westminster	455	1	Whitney	Phenias	3			1		2	1		1				8		
Westminster	455	2	Whitney	Samuel		3			1	2				1			7		
Westminster	455	3	Walker	Paul	1		2		1			1		1			6		
Westminster	455	4	Wheeler	Josiah	1	2			1			2	2				9		
Westminster	455	5	Rand	Thomas			1										1		
Westminster	455	6	Houghton	Abel	3	1	1		1	1	1	1					9		
Westminster	455	7	Haywood	Michar	3	2			1	1	1	1					9		
Westminster	455	8	Rice	Elijah	2	1		1		2	1		1	1			9		
Westminster	456	1	Whitney	Susanna	2									1			3		
Westminster	456	2	Winchip	Cyrus			1			2			1				4		
Westminster	456	3	Wheeler	Nathll	1			1		2	1		1				6		
Westminster	456	4	Winchip	Jonas Jr	2			1		2		2					7		
Westminster	456	5	Wood	Susanna										1			1		

TOWN	PG#	LN#	HEADS OF HOUSEHOLD		FREE WHITE MALES					FREE WHITE FEMALES					TOTAL ALL OTHER	TOTAL SLAVES	TOTALS	DISTRICT/ TOWNSHIP	NOTES
			LAST NAME	FIRST NAME	under 10	10 to 16	16 to 26	26 to 45	45 and over	under 10	10 to 16	16 to 26	26 to 45	45 and over					
Westminster	456	6	Williams	Isaac		1	1		2		1		1	1			7		
Westminster	456	7	Walker	James					1					1			2		
Westminster	456	8	Wood	Abijah	1	1	1		1	3	1	1	1				10		
Westminster	456	9	Wood	Abel	2	2	2	1		2			2				11		
Westminster	456	10	Wyman	David 2d	2			1		2			1				6		
Westminster	456	11	Wiswell	Noah	1	1	1		1	2	1	1	1	1			10		
Westminster	456	12	Whitney	Joel	2	1		1		3			1				8		
Westminster	456	13	Whitney	Elisha	1	1		1			2	1		1			7		
Westminster	456	14	Whitney	Jonas	2		1	1		2	1		1	1			9		
Westminster	456	15	Whitney	Nathan				1						1			2		
Westminster	456	16	Whitney	Abner	1		2		2	1	1			1			8		
Westminster	456	17	Whitney	David	2	1		1		1	1	1	1				8		
Westminster	456	18	Whitney	John	1	1		1		1			1				5		
Westminster	456	19	Whitney	Alpohus				1					1				2		

TOWN	PG#	LN#	HEADS OF HOUSEHOLD LAST NAME	FIRST NAME	FREE WHITE MALES under 10	10 to 16	16 to 26	26 to 45	45 and over	FREE WHITE FEMALES under 10	10 to 16	16 to 26	26 to 45	45 and over	TOTAL ALL OTHER	TOTAL SLAVES	TOTALS	DISTRICT/ TOWNSHIP	NOTES
Winchendon	223	1	Adams	Benjamin	1		2	1		2	1		1				8		
Winchendon	223	2	Arnold	Eber	2			1		2			1				6		
Winchendon	223	3	Alger	Abiel	2			1		4	1		1				9		
Winchendon	223	4	Alger	David	2			1		1			1				5		
Winchendon	223	5	Boynton	Joseph			1		1			1		1			4		
Winchendon	223	6	Boynton	Danll				1		1		1					3		
Winchendon	223	7	Boynton	Paul	2				1	1	1	1	1	1			8		
Winchendon	223	8	Brown	Amasa	1	1		1		3			1				7		
Winchendon	223	9	Brown	Benjamin		1	1						1				3		
Winchendon	223	10	Brown	Samll	1	2	1		1	1	1	2		1			10		
Winchendon	223	11	Brown	Levi			1		1			1	1				4		
Winchendon	223	12	Brown	Hezekiah		1	1		1	1		1	2	1			8		
Winchendon	223	13	Brown	Joseph				1				1		1			3		
Winchendon	223	14	Bixby	Levi			1		1		1	3	1	1			8		
Winchendon	223	15	Biglow	Elishahell	2			1		1			1				5		
Winchendon	223	16	Biglow	Roger	1	2	1		1			1	3		1		10		
Winchendon	223	17	Burr	Sarah		1	1						1				3		
Winchendon	225	1	Buckland	Oliver			1		1			1	3		1		7		
Winchendon	225	2	Bradish	Robert	1			1		3			1				6		
Winchendon	225	3	Bradish	Jonas	2			1		1		1	1				6		
Winchendon	225	4	Crosby	Samuel				1					1				2		
Winchendon	225	5	Crosby	Flavel	2	1	1	1		1			1				7		
Winchendon	225	6	Curtiss	Abner				1					1	1			3		
Winchendon	225	7	Curtiss	Abner Junr	3			1		2			1				7		
Winchendon	225	8	Curtiss	Moses			1			1			1				3		
Winchendon	225	9	Coffin	George	2			1		2	1		1				7		
Winchendon	225	10	Chase	Charles	1			1		2			1				5		
Winchendon	225	11	Crooks	Henry	2		1	1		1	2	1		1			9		
Winchendon	225	12	Cook	John			1			2			1				4		
Winchendon	225	13	Darling	John				1						1			2		
Winchendon	225	14	Darling	Jewett			1			2		1	1				5		
Winchendon	225	15	Darling	Luther			1			1			1				3		
Winchendon	225	16	Davis	Phinehas			1						1				2		
Winchendon	225	17	Day	Joseph		1						1					2		
Winchendon	225	18	Dunham	Alexr		1				1		1					3		
Winchendon	225	19	Day	Danll		1	1			1		2		1			6		
Winchendon	225	20	Edmunds	Amos		1		1				2	1				5		
Winchendon	225	21	Evans	Jona	2	1	1	1		1	1			1			8		
Winchendon	225	22	Emory	Stephen		1	2			1		2		1			8		
Winchendon	225	23	Emory	Francis			1			2			1				4		
Winchendon	225	24	Fisk	Jonathan	2		1	1		2	1	1		1			9		
Winchendon	225	25	Flint	Nathan	2	2			1	3	1	1	1				11		
Winchendon	225	26	Flint	John				1									1		
Winchendon	225	27	Flint	Thomas	3	1		1		2			1				8		
Winchendon	225	28	Farrar	Daniel		1		1				2		1			5		
Winchendon	225	29	Fairbank	Moses				1						1			2		
Winchendon	225	30	Flagg	John	3			1		1			1				6		
Winchendon	225	31	Fry	Job	2			1		2			1				6		
Winchendon	225	32	Freeman	Joseph			1			1	1						3		
Winchendon	226	1	Fessenden	John	2			1			1	1	1				6		
Winchendon	226	2	Gooderidge	Eliphalet		1		1				1	2				5		
Winchendon	226	3	Gooderidge	Danll		2	1	1				2					6		
Winchendon	226	4	Gooderidge	David	1	1		1		1	1						5		
Winchendon	226	5	Gooderidge	Samll	2			1		1			1				5		
Winchendon	226	6	Goodhue	John	2	1		1		2			1				7		
Winchendon	226	7	Goodhue	Amos			1						1				2		
Winchendon	226	8	Grout	Isaac	2	1		1		2			2				8		
Winchendon	226	9	Greenwood	Thos	2	1	2		1	1	1	1		1			10		
Winchendon	226	10	Graton	Thomas	2			1		3	1		1				8		
Winchendon	226	11	Goss	Calvin				1						1			2		
Winchendon	226	12	How	Peter	2		1			2		2	1				8		
Winchendon	226	13	Hale	Moses		2		1			1	2		1			7		
Winchendon	226	14	Hale	Jacob		2						1		1			5		
Winchendon	226	15	Hale	Amos	3	1	1		1	1		1	1				9		
Winchendon	226	16	Heywood	Amos	1	1	1	1				2					6		
Winchendon	226	17	Heywood	*				1		1		2					4		
Winchendon	226	18	Benjamin	Andrew		1								1			2		
Winchendon	226	19	Brooks	John	2			1		1	1		1				6		
Winchendon	226	20	Brooks	Levi		1		1		2		1	1				6		
Winchendon	226	21	Beal	Stover			1			2			1				4		
Winchendon	226	22	Baldwin	Samll				1					1	1			3		
Winchendon	226	23	Baldwin	Wm			1						1				2		
Winchendon	226	24	Buttrick	Abiel	2	1	1			2	1	1		1			10		
Winchendon	226	25	Buttrick	Daniel	3	1	1			1	1		1				8		
Winchendon	226	26	Battles	Noah	2	1		1		3	1		1	1			10		
Winchendon	226	27	Beaman	David	1	2	1			1		1					6		
Winchendon	226	28	Bruce	Jonas		1	1	1			2	1	1				7		
Winchendon	226	29	Bosworth	Walsm		1				2			1				4		
Winchendon	226	30	Brown	Esther							1	1					3		

TOWN	PG#	LN#	HEADS OF HOUSEHOLD		FREE WHITE MALES					FREE WHITE FEMALES					TOTAL ALL OTHER	TOTAL SLAVES	TOTALS	DISTRICT/ TOWNSHIP	NOTES
			LAST NAME	FIRST NAME	under 10	10 to 16	16 to 26	26 to 45	45 and over	under 10	10 to 16	16 to 26	26 to 45	45 and over					
Winchendon	226	31	Balcom	Daniel				1		1				1			3		
Winchendon	226	32	Balcom	Gideon	1			1		1			1				4		
Winchendon	226	33	Bemis	John			1	1				1	1	1			5		
Winchendon	227	1	Murdock	James				1						1			2		
Winchendon	227	2	Murdock	James Jr	1			1		3			1				6		
Winchendon	227	3	Murdock	Ephrm	1		2	1		1		1					6		
Winchendon	227	4	Maynard	Nathan		1		1					1				3		
Winchendon	227	5	Moar	Levi		1	1	1				1	1				5		
Winchendon	227	6	Miles	James				1					1	1			3		
Winchendon	227	7	McElwain	James		2	3	1	1			1	1	1			10		
Winchendon	227	8	Massey	Aaron				1		4			1				6		
Winchendon	227	9	Nurse	Asa		2	2	1				1		1			7		
Winchendon	227	10	Nutting	Benja				1		2		1					4		
Winchendon	227	11	Noyce	Samll			1	1				1		1			4		
Winchendon	227	12	Noyce	James	1	1	2	1			1	1	1				8		
Winchendon	227	13	Noyce	Isaac	3			1		1			1	1			7		
Winchendon	227	14	Prentiss	Samll				1						1			2		
Winchendon	227	15	Prentiss	Samll Jr	2			1		2			1				6		
Winchendon	227	16	Prentiss	Luke	1			1		1			1				4		
Winchendon	227	17	Partridge	Jairus	1			1		3			1				6		
Winchendon	227	18	Poor	David	1	1			1	1		2	1	1			8		
Winchendon	227	19	Poor	Daniel	1			1			1		1				4		
Winchendon	227	20	Perley	Dudley		1	1	1	1			1		1			6		
Winchendon	227	21	Perley	John	1			1		1	1		1				5		
Winchendon	227	22	Peyson	James				1		1			1	1			4		
Winchendon	227	23	Payson	Elliot			1			1		2					4		
Winchendon	227	24	Parks	Jacob	2			1		1		1		1			6		
Winchendon	227	25	Parks	Phino	2		1	1		1			1				6		
Winchendon	227	26	Parks	Eleazer			1	1				1					3		
Winchendon	227	27	Poland	William		3		1		4	2	1	1				12		
Winchendon	227	28	Parmenter	Ephrm	1		2		1	1	1	1		1			8		
Winchendon	227	29	Prouty	Seth	3			1				1					5		
Winchendon	227	30	Putnam	Danll	2	2	3	1		4			1				13		
Winchendon	227	31	Petts	John	2			1		1			1				5		
Winchendon	227	32	Wilder	Anna								1		1			2		
Winchendon	228	1	Richardson	Ebenz			1		1					1			3		
Winchendon	228	2	Robbins	William	1			1		1		1	1				5		
Winchendon	228	3	Raymond	Paul	2	1	2	1	1	2	2	1	1	1			14		
Winchendon	228	4	Raymond	James	2	1		1		3		1	1				9		
Winchendon	228	5	Raymond	Jesse	4			1		1			1				7		
Winchendon	228	6	Roberts	David			1			1			1				3		
Winchendon	228	7	Rice	Benja	1			1		2	1	1					6		
Winchendon	228	8	Rice	David	2	1	1	1		2	1	1	1				10		
Winchendon	228	9	Rice	Amos	1		1						1				3		
Winchendon	228	10	Russell	Peter	2			1		2		1					6		
Winchendon	228	11	Stimson	Isaac				1						1			2		
Winchendon	228	12	Stimson	Luther	3			1		1			1				6		
Winchendon	228	13	Sterns	Barthw		1	1	1				1		1			5		
Winchendon	228	14	Smith	Isaac		2		1						1			4		
Winchendon	228	15	Smith	David				1			1			1			3		
Winchendon	228	16	Stuart	Paul	2			1		1			1				5		
Winchendon	228	17	Sergeant	Samll	3			1		3			1				8		
Winchendon	228	18	Sylvester	Nathl	2	1		1		3	1	2	1				11		
Winchendon	228	19	Heywood	Lemuel				1									1		
Winchendon	228	20	Hyde	Ezra	1		3	1		1	1	1		1			9		
Winchendon	228	21	Hyde	Job	2	2		1		1	1	1	1				9		
Winchendon	228	22	Houghton	Robert	4	1		1		1			1				8		
Winchendon	228	23	Hubbard	Benja		1		1			1		1				4		
Winchendon	228	24	Hancock	Timo	4	1		1					1				7		
Winchendon	228	25	Hartwell	Samll	2			1		5		1	1				10		
Winchendon	228	26	Hall	Benja	2			1		1			1				5		
Winchendon	228	27	Hunt	David	1			1		2			1				5		
Winchendon	228	28	Hancock	Thos	2			1		2			1				6		
Winchendon	228	29	Jones	Abel		1	1	1		2			1				6		
Winchendon	228	30	Kidder	Benja			2		1	1		1	1	1			7		
Winchendon	228	31	Kidder	Heywood	2			1		1	1		1				6		
Winchendon	228	32	Knight	Matthew				1						1			2		
Winchendon	228	33	Knight	Nathan		1	2	1		1				1			6		
Winchendon	228	34	Keith	Appolus	1			1					1				3		
Winchendon	228	35	Litch	Thos			1	1					2	1			5		
Winchendon	228	36	May	Benjamin	2	2		1		1			1				7		
Winchendon	229	1	Wilder	Gardner	1	1		1		1			1				5		
Winchendon	229	2	Wilder	John			1			1		1					3		
Winchendon	229	3	Weston	Stephen	2	1		1				1	1				6		
Winchendon	229	4	Willard	Isaac	1	1	1			1			1				5		
Winchendon	229	5	Whitney	Wm	1		2		1			1		1			6		
Winchendon	229	6	Whitney	Phins	1			1		2		2					6		
Winchendon	229	7	Whitney	Joseph			1					1					2		
Winchendon	229	8	Wilder	Joseph	1	2	2			1				1			7		

151

TOWN	PG#	LN#	LAST NAME	FIRST NAME	under 10	10 to 16	16 to 26	26 to 45	45 and over	under 10	10 to 16	16 to 26	26 to 45	45 and over	TOTAL ALL OTHER	TOTAL SLAVES	TOTALS	DISTRICT/ TOWNSHIP	NOTES
Winchendon	229	9	Wilder	Abel	5	1		1					1				8		
Winchendon	229	10	Whitcomb	Israel	1		4		1	2		2		1			11		
Winchendon	229	11	Whiton	Israel	2	1			1		1		1				6		
Winchendon	229	12	Wyman	Thos	2	2	1		1	1	1			1			9		
Winchendon	229	13	Wyman	Thomas Jr			1					1					2		
Winchendon	229	14	Wales	Jacob		1			1	2	1	1		1			7		
Winchendon	229	15	Woodbury	Jacob B.	2	2	1	1		2	1		1				10		
Winchendon	229	16	Wilson	Nathaniel	2	1			1	1		2	1				8		
Winchendon	229	17	Stone	Edmund	1		1		1	2	1	1		1			8		
Winchendon	229	18	Stow	Molly										1			1		
Winchendon	229	19	Tufts	Benjamin	1		1					1					3		
Winchendon	230	1	Sherwin	Ebenzr	3		1	1	1	1	1		1				9		
Winchendon	230	2	Sherwin	Ebenzr Jr	1		1			1			1				4		
Winchendon	230	3	Stoddard	James	1		1		1	1		1		1			6		
Winchendon	230	4	Stoddard	David					1		1			1			3		
Winchendon	230	5	Stoddard	Levitt	2	1		1		1			1				6		
Winchendon	230	6	Stephens	Amos	1			1		1			1				4		
Winchendon	230	7	Tolman	Desire	2	1	2		1		1	1		1			9		
Winchendon	230	8	Tucker	Seth	2	1		1		1		1	1				7		
Winchendon	230	9	Tucker	Elisha	1		1			3	1		1				7		
Winchendon	230	10	Tuttle	Jedidiah	2			1		1	1		1				6		
Winchendon	230	11	Tuttle	Simon	2			1		2			1				6		
Winchendon	230	12	Taylor	Isaac	2	1		1		2			1				7		
Winchendon	230	13	Winch	David					1								1		
Winchendon	230	14	Walker	Samll			1	1		3		1					6		
Winchendon	230	15	Wilder	Benja	4			1		2	2		1				10		
Winchendon	230	16	Whitney	Hanariah	3	1		1		1			1				7		
Winchendon	230	17	Whitney	Jacob	2			1		1			1				5		

TOWN	PG#	LN#	HEADS OF HOUSEHOLD		FREE WHITE MALES					FREE WHITE FEMALES					TOTAL ALL OTHER	TOTAL SLAVES	TOTALS	DISTRICT/ TOWNSHIP	NOTES
			LAST NAME	FIRST NAME	under 10	10 to 16	16 to 26	26 to 45	45 and over	under 10	10 to 16	16 to 26	26 to 45	45 and over					
Worcester	171	1	Alford	James	2	1	1	1	1	1	1	1			1		10		
Worcester	171	2	Andrews	David		1	2	2			2	1	1				9		
Worcester	171	3	Andrews	Benjamin			2		1	2			1				6		
Worcester	171	4	Andrews	Samuel	1		1	1				1	1				5		
Worcester	171	5	Austin	Samuel	1		1	2		1			1				6		
Worcester	171	6	Annam	Hager											1		1		
Worcester	171	7	Allen	Ahbel			1					1					2		
Worcester	171	8	Allen	Mary										1			1		
Worcester	171	9	Boyter	David	2			1				1					4		
Worcester	171	10	Bancroft	Aaron	3	2		2		3		1	1		1		13		
Worcester	171	11	Bigbee	Solomon				1					1				2		
Worcester	172	1	Bigbee	Joel	3		1	1		1			1				7		
Worcester	172	2	Burbank	Elijah	1	2	8	1		2		5	1				20		
Worcester	172	3	Blackman	Nathan	2			1		2	1		3				9		
Worcester	172	4	Bangs	Edward	1			1		1	1	1	1	1			7		
Worcester	172	5	Bigelow	Anna								2		1			3		
Worcester	172	6	Blake	Jason	2	1		1		2			1				7		
Worcester	172	7	Baird	Daniel			2		1		1	2		1			7		
Worcester	172	8	Brazer	Samuel	1	2	1			1		1	2				9		
Worcester	172	9	Blair	Joseph				1		1			1				3		
Worcester	173	1	Barker	William	1	3			1	1		4		1	1		12		
Worcester	173	2	Butman	Benjamin	3	3		1		1	1		1				10		
Worcester	173	3	Brown	David			2			1		1					4		
Worcester	173	4	Ballard	Joseph			1					1					2		
Worcester	173	5	Brant	Henry		1		1					1				3		
Worcester	173	6	Curtis	Samuel	1		1	1	1			1	1	1			7		
Worcester	173	7	Curtis	Samuel Junr	3			1		1	2		1				8		
Worcester	173	8	Chamberlain	Willm	2		1	1		3			2				9		
Worcester	173	9	Chapin	Elijah	1		1	1		3	1	1	1				9		
Worcester	173	10	Chapin	Thads	1		2	1		3			1				8		
Worcester	173	11	Chandler	Samuel			3	1				1					5		
Worcester	173	12	Chamberlain	John		2	1		1	1		1		1	2		9		
Worcester	173	13	Caldwell	William	1	1	1	1	1		1	1	2	1	1		11		
Worcester	173	14	Cooledge	Nathaniel	3	2	1	1		3			2				12		
Worcester	173	15	Chamberlain	Thads			1		1					3	1		6		
Worcester	173	16	Craige	Jesse	2	2		2			1	1	1				9		
Worcester	173	17	Cook	George	2	1		1			1		1				6		
Worcester	173	18	Chadwick	Daniel	2		1	1		3	1	1	1				10		
Worcester	174	1	Blair	Robert	1	2			1	3	1		1				9		
Worcester	174	2	Barber	Ebenezer	1	3	2		2	2		1	1	1			13		
Worcester	174	3	Barrel	James		1		1		1			1				4		
Worcester	174	4	Barber	Joseph		3	1		1		1	1		1			8		
Worcester	174	5	Brooks	Nathaniel		1	3	1	1					1			7		
Worcester	174	6	Barber	James		1	2	1		1	1			1			7		
Worcester	174	7	Bigelow	David		1			1				1	1			4		
Worcester	174	8	Bigelow	Silas	2			1		2			1				6		
Worcester	174	9	Brown	William				1					1				2		
Worcester	174	10	Barnard	John			1		1					2	1		6		
Worcester	174	11	Brooks	Samuel			1		1				1	1			4		
Worcester	174	12	Boyden	Alven		1	5			1		2			1		10		
Worcester	174	13	Baird	Daniel Jr	1			1		2			1				5		
Worcester	174	14	Bigelow	Walter		1	1	1				1					4		
Worcester	174	15	Bigelow	David Junr	1	1			1	2	1	1	1				8		
Worcester	174	16	Butler	Smith	2			1		1		1					5		
Worcester	175	1	Duncan	Simeon	2	1	1	1		2	1	1	1				10		
Worcester	175	2	Denny	Daniel	2		1	1		1	1	2	1				9		
Worcester	175	3	Denny	Samuel			1	1					1				3		
Worcester	175	4	Elder	John				1				1					2		
Worcester	175	5	Elder	John Junr	1	1				2			1				6		
Worcester	175	6	Elder	William	5			1		1	1	1	1				10		
Worcester	175	7	Eaton	Amherst	3		2	1		1	1	1	1				10		
Worcester	175	8	Eaton	William	2		4		1	1	1		1	1			11		
Worcester	175	9	Eaton	Alpheus		1		1		1	1		1	1			6		
Worcester	175	10	Elder	Thomas				1									1		
Worcester	175	11	Farrar	John	1		1	2	1			2			2		9		
Worcester	175	12	Flagg	Benjamin					1								1		
Worcester	175	13	Flagg	Benjamin Jun	1		1		1			2	1				6		
Worcester	175	14	Flagg	John		1	2					1					4		
Worcester	175	15	Flagg	Aaron		1	1	1		1			1				5		
Worcester	175	16	Flagg	Samuel		1	2	1	1					2			7		
Worcester	176	1	Chadwick	Dolly	1				1	1			1				4		
Worcester	176	2	Chadwick	Lydia			1						1	1			3		
Worcester	176	3	Curtis	Tyler	2		2	2	1	1	1	1	1	1			12		
Worcester	176	4	Curtis	David	2		2	1		1	2		1				9		
Worcester	176	5	Coes	John	3			1		1	1			1			7		
Worcester	176	6	Cambell	James	2	1		1		1	1	1	1				8		
Worcester	176	7	Child	Benjamin				1				1		1			3		
Worcester	176	8	Chase	Matilda						1	1		1				3		
Worcester	176	9	Cleveland	Thomas	1		1						1				4		

TOWN	PG#	LN#	LAST NAME	FIRST NAME	under 10	10 to 16	16 to 26	26 to 45	45 and over	under 10	10 to 16	16 to 26	26 to 45	45 and over	TOTAL ALL OTHER	TOTAL SLAVES	TOTALS	DISTRICT/ TOWNSHIP	NOTES
			HEADS OF HOUSEHOLD		FREE WHITE MALES					FREE WHITE FEMALES									
Worcester	176	10	Chadwick	Isaac	2		1	1				1					5		
Worcester	176	11	Conner	Edward	1			1		1		1					4		
Worcester	176	12	Child	Moses	2			1				1					4		
Worcester	176	13	Chapman	Abel			1					1					2		
Worcester	176	14	Chandler	Sarah			1			1		1	1				4		
Worcester	176	15	Donohoe	Philip											1		1		
Worcester	177	1	Griggs	David			1	1				1					3		
Worcester	177	2	Gates	Paul	1		1	1		1			1		1		6		
Worcester	177	3	Goddard	Samuel		3			1	1		2	2	1			10		
Worcester	177	4	Grout	Jonathan			1	1	1			2		1			6		
Worcester	177	5	Grosvenor	Elizah	2							3		2			7		
Worcester	177	6	Gray	Reuben	2	2			1		1	2		1			9		
Worcester	177	7	Goulding	William	2		1	1		3		1	1				9		
Worcester	177	8	Gates	Jonathan									1	1			3		
Worcester	177	9	Gates	Thomas	3			1	1	1		1	1				8		
Worcester	177	10	Gates	William		1		1	1	1		1	1	1			7		
Worcester	177	11	Gates	Samuel	2	1	1		1			3	2				10		
Worcester	177	12	Green	John	2		4	1			3	1	2				13		
Worcester	177	13	Green	Mary		1	1	1					1	2			6		
Worcester	177	14	Gleason	Silas	2			1		1		1	1				6		
Worcester	177	15	Goulding	Daniel		1	2		1			1					5		
Worcester	177	16	Gates	Simon	2	1	1	1		2	2		1	1			11		
Worcester	177	17	Gates	Jonathan 2d		2			1			2		2			7		
Worcester	177	18	Goulding	Clark	1			1		2		1					5		
Worcester	177	19	Gray	Thomas	1	1	1	1		2		1	1				8		
Worcester	178	1	Flagg	Francis		1	1		1	1		1	1	1			7		
Worcester	178	2	Fullerton	Samuel					1	3		1					5		
Worcester	178	3	Fiske	Oliver	2	2		1				1		1	2		9		
Worcester	178	4	Flagg	Levi	2	2	1	1		1	1		1				9		
Worcester	178	5	Flagg	Elisha	2	1	1	1		2	2	1	1	1			12		
Worcester	178	6	Fiske	Samuel		1	2	1		3	1		1				9		
Worcester	178	7	Flagg	Nathaniel	4		1	1			1		1				8		
Worcester	178	8	Flagg	David		1		1					1				3		
Worcester	178	9	Flagg	Benjamin				2						1			3		
Worcester	178	10	Flagg	Asa	1												1		
Worcester	178	11	Flagg	Amos			1			3			1				5		
Worcester	178	12	Follet	Walter	1		1			1			1				4		
Worcester	178	13	Fay	Lucretia							1		1				2		
Worcester	178	14	Fowler	Ezekiel		2		1	1	1			1				6		
Worcester	178	15	Flagg	Eli	2		1			2			1				6		
Worcester	178	16	Femo	Sally	2		3						2				7		
Worcester	179	1	Heywood	Phine				1			2		1				4		
Worcester	179	2	Heywood	Benja	2	1	2		1	1	2	1		1			11		
Worcester	179	3	Heywood	Daniel	2		1		2	1	1	1	1		2		11		
Worcester	179	4	Heywood	Abel	1	1	1	1			1	1	1				7		
Worcester	179	5	Heywood	Daniel 2d	1	1		1		1			1				5		
Worcester	179	6	Heard	Nathn		2	3	1	1		1	2	1	1			12		
Worcester	179	7	Howe	Joel		1		1					1				3		
Worcester	179	8	Harrington	Joshua	1			1		2	1	2	1				9		
Worcester	179	9	Hayward	Stephen		1		1					1				3		
Worcester	179	10	Hayward	James	1			1		2			1				5		
Worcester	179	11	Harrington	Silas		1	1		1		1	1		1			6		
Worcester	179	12	Harrington	Elijah		1	1		1	1	1	1		1			7		
Worcester	179	13	Harrington	Saml	2	1	1		1	1	1	1	1	1			11		
Worcester	179	14	Harrington	Noah	1	2		1		2	1		1				8		
Worcester	179	15	Hastings	Ebenz	1	3		1	1			1	2				9		
Worcester	179	16	Hamilton	Asa		1	1	1				1	1				5		
Worcester	179	17	Hemminway	James	1			1		1		1	1				5		
Worcester	179	18	Hemminway	Jacob		1	1	1						1	2		7		
Worcester	180	1	Gleason	Jonathan		1	2	1	1	2	2	1		1			11		
Worcester	180	2	Gleason	Jonathan 2d		1		1		1				1			4		
Worcester	180	3	Gleason	Phinehas	2	1	1		1	2	3		1				11		
Worcester	180	4	Gleason	Isaac		1		1			1		1				4		
Worcester	180	5	Gates	Nathaniel	1			1		1			1				4		
Worcester	180	6	Goulding	Lucy		1						1	1				3		
Worcester	180	7	Gleason	Jonathan Jun	3		1				1		1				6		
Worcester	180	8	Gould	Stephen	1	1		1				1	1				5		
Worcester	180	9	Green	Bristol											3		3		
Worcester	180	10	Gould	Ebenezer		3	1					1					5		
Worcester	180	11	Gay	John				1					1				2		
Worcester	180	12	Glasgow	Prudence											1		1		
Worcester	180	13	Greenleaf	Daniel		2	2					1	1				6		
Worcester	180	14	Hearsey	David	3	1		1		2	1	1	1				10		
Worcester	180	15	Healey	Jeddh			1		2	1	2		2	1			9		
Worcester	180	16	Harris	Noah			1	1					1				3		
Worcester	181	1	Johnson	William	2	2		1		2			1	1			9		
Worcester	181	2	Johnson	Daniel			1		1		1		1	1			5		
Worcester	181	3	Johnson	Benja			1			1		1					3		
Worcester	181	4	Johnson	Clark							3						5		

TOWN	PG#	LN#	LAST NAME	FIRST NAME	FREE WHITE MALES under 10	10 to 16	16 to 26	26 to 45	45 and over	FREE WHITE FEMALES under 10	10 to 16	16 to 26	26 to 45	45 and over	TOTAL ALL OTHER	TOTAL SLAVES	TOTALS	DISTRICT/ TOWNSHIP	NOTES
Worcester	181	5	Johnson	Timothy	1			2		3		1		1			8		
Worcester	181	6	Johnson	John	1	1		1		3	1		1				8		
Worcester	181	7	Jennison	Samuel			2	1	1			3	1		2		10		
Worcester	181	8	Johnson	Samuel	3	1	4	3				1		1			13		
Worcester	181	9	Johnson	Gardner			1			4			1				6		
Worcester	181	10	Jennings	Mary						2			1				3		
Worcester	181	11	Johnson	Amos				1			1			1			3		
Worcester	181	12	Knower	John				1						1			2		
Worcester	181	13	Kingston	Saml	2			1		1	1		1				7		
Worcester	181	14	Kingsbury	Joseph	1	1	2		1	2	1	1		1			10		
Worcester	181	15	Knight	Isaac	3			1			1		1				6		
Worcester	181	16	Knight	Edward	1	1	2		1			1	1				7		
Worcester	181	17	Knight	William	3	1	1	1	1	1	2	1	1				12		
Worcester	181	18	Webb	Adams	1		1	1		4	1		1				9		
Worcester	181	19	Young	Mary									1				1		
Worcester	181	20	Young	James	2	1		1		1			1				6		
Worcester	182	1	Holbrook	Joseph			2		1	1	2	2		1			9		
Worcester	182	2	Harris	Rezinah									1				1		
Worcester	182	3	Hemminway	Jeffrey											6		6		
Worcester	182	4	Holbrook	Phine	2			1					1				4		
Worcester	182	5	Harris	Leml	1			1		1			1				4		
Worcester	182	6	Howe	Abel	1		1		1	2	1		1				7		
Worcester	182	7	Holmes	Anna						2			1				3		
Worcester	182	8	Hardy	Levi	1		1			1		1					4		
Worcester	182	9	Hais	John	1			1		1		1					4		
Worcester	182	10	Hopkins	Esuck	1		1			2		1					5		
Worcester	182	11	Hill	Jacob											2		2		
Worcester	182	12	Harrington	Nathl		1	2		1	1	1		2				8		
Worcester	182	13	Jones	Phinehas		1	2			1	1		1				7		
Worcester	182	14	Johnson	Thomas	2	1		1		1		1	1				7		
Worcester	182	15	Johnson	Joshua			1	1				1		1			4		
Worcester	182	16	Johnson	Micah				1					1				2		
Worcester	182	17	Johnson	Micah Junr	2	2	1		1	3		1	1				11		
Worcester	183	1	Livermore	Reuben	1			1		1			1				4		
Worcester	183	2	Medra	Jack											3		3		
Worcester	183	3	Mixer	Daniel			2	1		2		2					7		
Worcester	183	4	Mower	Thomas		1	2		1	1	1	1		1			8		
Worcester	183	5	Moore	Calvin			1						1				2		
Worcester	183	6	Moore	Luther	1	1		1					1				4		
Worcester	183	7	Mower	Ephraim			3		1				1		2		8		
Worcester	183	8	Morse	Willard		1	1	1		3			1				7		
Worcester	183	9	Meriam	George	1	1	3	1				2		1			9		
Worcester	183	10	Miller	Jacob	1			1		3			1				6		
Worcester	183	11	Moore	William		1	1	1		3	1		2				9		
Worcester	183	12	Moore	John		1	1		1			1		1			5		
Worcester	183	13	Mills	Thomas		1			1			1		1			4		
Worcester	183	14	Mower	Ebenz	5		1	1					2				9		
Worcester	183	15	Moore	David			1	1		2		1					5		
Worcester	183	16	Moore	Jesse	1			1		2			2				6		
Worcester	183	17	White	Nathan	3	2				1	2	2	1				12		
Worcester	183	18	Whitney	Joshua		1	1		1	1		2		1			7		
Worcester	183	19	Willard	Isaac				1				1		1			3		
Worcester	183	20	Willard	Isaac Junr	1		1	1		4			1				8		
Worcester	183	21	Ward	Phinehas				1					1				2		
Worcester	183	22	Willard	Clark	1		1			2		1					5		
Worcester	183	23	Waters	Kezia						1		1	3	1			6		
Worcester	183	24	Wheeler	Theophilus	3			1		2		1	1				8		
Worcester	183	25	Wheeler	Margaret								1		1			2		
Worcester	183	26	Wheeler	Danl G.		1	1										2		
Worcester	183	27	Woodburn	Saml Junr			2	1	1				1	1	1		8		
Worcester	183	28	Ward	Elisha			1				1		1				3		
Worcester	183	29	Ward	Asa			2	1	1		1			1			6		
Worcester	183	30	Wheeler	Amos					1		1	2		1			5		
Worcester	183	31	Walker	John	3	1	1	1		1		2	1				10		
Worcester	183	32	Willington	Ebenz Jun	2	1	1			1	1	1	1				9		
Worcester	183	33	Willington	Ebenz 3d	1		2	1				1					5		
Worcester	183	34	Willington	Daniel		2	2		2	2		1					9		
Worcester	184	1	Waldo	Daniel		1	2	1	1		1	2	3	2			13		
Worcester	184	2	Wilson	James	2			1		1	2		1				7		
Worcester	184	3	Warren	John	1			1		2	1		1				6		
Worcester	184	4	Whitney	Benja Jr			1	1	1					1			4		
Worcester	184	5	Whitney	Amos	1	1		1	1					1			5		
Worcester	184	6	Whitten	Abel	2		1		1			1		1			6		
Worcester	184	7	Walker	Joseph	2				1	1		1	1				6		
Worcester	184	8	Williams	James	1		1	1		2		1					6		
Worcester	184	9	Warden	Saml				1					2				3		
Worcester	184	10	Warden	Samuel Jr	2			1			1	1					5		
Worcester	184	11	Wheelock	Joseph	1			1		2	1		1				6		
Worcester	184	12	Wiswall	Henry	1		2			2		1		1			7		

TOWN	PG#	LN#	LAST NAME	FIRST NAME	Males under 10	Males 10 to 16	Males 16 to 26	Males 26 to 45	Males 45 and over	Females under 10	Females 10 to 16	Females 16 to 26	Females 26 to 45	Females 45 and over	TOTAL ALL OTHER	TOTAL SLAVES	TOTALS	DISTRICT/ TOWNSHIP	NOTES
Worcester	184	13	Wright	Samuel					1					1			2		
Worcester	184	14	Walker	Cato											2		2		
Worcester	184	15	Willard	Thomson	4	1		1		1	1		1				9		
Worcester	184	16	Wheeler	Amos Jr	2	2	1	1		1	1		1				9		
Worcester	184	17	Whitney	Ebenz				1		2		1	1				5		
Worcester	184	18	Williams	Ebenz	1			1		3			1	1			7		
Worcester	184	19	Knight	Reuben	3	1		1		2			1				8		
Worcester	184	20	Kendall	Ezekiel	2	1		1					1				5		
Worcester	184	21	Knight	Jonah	1		1						1				3		
Worcester	184	22	Kelly	Thomas	1			1					1	2			5		
Worcester	184	23	Kennedy	John				1				1	1	2			5		
Worcester	184	24	Lincoln	Levi	2	2	3	1	1			2	3				14		
Worcester	184	25	Lincoln	Abrm		1	1			2	2	1					7		
Worcester	184	26	Lynde	George											2		2		
Worcester	184	27	Lovell	Ebenz				1		1		1	1	1			5		
Worcester	184	28	Lovell	Jona	1	1	2	1				2		1			8		
Worcester	184	29	Lovell	Jona Jun		1	2			2		1					6		
Worcester	184	30	Lyon	Abigail		1				2	2	1					6		
Worcester	184	31	Lamson	Ebenz	1		1				1	1	1				5		
Worcester	184	32	Legg	Reuben	2	1	4	1		1		1		1			11		
Worcester	184	33	Lewis	Thomas											3		3		
Worcester	185	1	Newton	Benjamin	1		1	1		2	1		1				7		
Worcester	185	2	Newton	Lucy	1		1			1							3		
Worcester	185	3	Nazro	John		1		1		1	2	1	1				7		
Worcester	185	4	Nichols	Thomas	1			2					1	2	1		7		
Worcester	185	5	Nelson	John	1	1	1	1		2			1				7		
Worcester	185	6	Nelson	Abijah		1	2					1	1				5		
Worcester	185	7	Peck	Robert M.	2	1	1	2				2					8		
Worcester	185	8	Putnam	Amos				1			1	1	1				4		
Worcester	185	9	Parker	William			1							1			2		
Worcester	185	10	Parker	William Jr	1	1		1	1	2	1		1				8		
Worcester	185	11	Patch	Henry	1		2	1	1	1	3	1	1				11		
Worcester	185	12	Berry	Nathan		1		1				1		1			4		
Worcester	185	13	Perry	Moses	5		1	1			1		1				9		
Worcester	185	14	Perry	Josiah		1		1		1			1				4		
Worcester	185	15	Patch	Nathan		1		1		1		1		1			5		
Worcester	185	16	Porter	Saml	2		1	1		3		1	1				9		
Worcester	185	17	Patch	Joseph	4	1		1		1	1	1	1				10		
Worcester	185	18	Southworth	Simeon	1			1		1	1		1				5		
Worcester	185	19	Sprague	Miles	3		1						1				5		
Worcester	185	20	Stratton	James	1			1		3			1				6		
Worcester	185	21	Slaid	Jack											5		5		
Worcester	185	22	Smith	Ithamar	1	1			1	4	2		1				10		
Worcester	185	23	Torrey	Joseph	1			1		1	1		1				5		
Worcester	185	24	Trowbridge	James				1				1	1				3		
Worcester	185	25	Torrey	Willm	3		1		1	2	1	2	1				11		
Worcester	185	26	Tracy	Thomas	1			1		3	2	2	1				10		
Worcester	185	27	Taft	Timothy	1	1	1	1				2		1			7		
Worcester	185	28	Tufts	Walter	1			1		2			1				5		
Worcester	185	29	Taylor	Stephen			1	1			1		1				4		
Worcester	185	30	Thomas	Isaiah			1	1		1	1		2		2		8		
Worcester	185	31	Thomas	Isaiah Jr		1	6	1		1	1	1	1				12		
Worcester	186	1	Tradwell	Mary		1				2	1	2					7		
Worcester	186	2	Taylor	Othniel		2	4	1					1				8		
Worcester	186	3	Taylor	William				2		3		1	1	1			8		
Worcester	186	4	Tufts	Andrew	1			1		2			1		1		6		
Worcester	186	5	Totman	John	3	1	1	1					1				7		
Worcester	186	6	Totman	Jabez				1									1		
Worcester	186	7	Terrey	Geer			3					1	1				5		
Worcester	186	8	Tucker	Enos	1		1	1		1		1	1				6		
Worcester	186	9	Thaxter	Benja	2	1	1	1		2			1				8		
Worcester	186	10	Taft	Jesse				1						1			2		
Worcester	186	11	Taft	Josiah	2			1		1	1		1				6		
Worcester	186	12	Tucker	Benja				1						1			2		
Worcester	186	13	Tower	Mary								1	1				2		
Worcester	186	14	Taft	John	1			1		1		1					4		
Worcester	186	15	Wight	Oliver		1		1		1			1				4		
Worcester	186	16	Winslow	Worcester											3		3		
Worcester	186	17	Wiswall	Ebenz Jun		1	1	1	2				1				6		
Worcester	186	18	Whittemore	Clark	2	1		1		1		1	1		1		8		
Worcester	186	19	Moore	Zerviah								1		1			2		
Worcester	186	20	Mower	John			1	1						1	1		4		
Worcester	186	21	Moore	Willard		1				1		1					3		
Worcester	186	22	Mann	Joseph	3	3		1				2	1				10		
Worcester	186	23	Moore	Nathl				1			1		1				3		
Worcester	186	24	McFarland	Willm				1					1				2		
Worcester	186	25	McFarland	Willm Jun		1	1					2					4		
Worcester	186	26	Moore	Saml		1		1					1	1			4		
Worcester	186	27	McFarland	James	2		1	1		1	1		1	1			8		
Worcester	186	28	Miller	Moses		1	1		2		1			2			7		

156

TOWN	PG#	LN#	HEADS OF HOUSEHOLD		FREE WHITE MALES					FREE WHITE FEMALES					TOTAL ALL OTHER	TOTAL SLAVES	TOTALS	DISTRICT/ TOWNSHIP	NOTES
			LAST NAME	FIRST NAME	under 10	10 to 16	16 to 26	26 to 45	45 and over	under 10	10 to 16	16 to 26	26 to 45	45 and over					
Worcester	186	29	Morse	Joseph			1		1	1				2			5		
Worcester	186	30	Mansfield	John M			3	1		1	1	1					7		
Worcester	186	31	Merrifield	Timothy			1		1				1				3		
Worcester	186	32	Merrifield	Penude	1			1		1			1				4		
Worcester	186	33	Moore	Sewell	2	1		1		3			1				8		
Worcester	186	34	Mahon	William	1			1				1					3		
Worcester	187	1	Rice	Eunice								1		1			2		
Worcester	187	2	Rice	Jonas	1	1	1					1					4		
Worcester	187	3	Rice	Thomas	1		1		1	1	1	2		1			8		
Worcester	187	4	Rice	Judith			1							1			2		
Worcester	187	5	Rand	Daniel	2	1	2	1		2	2	1		2			13		
Worcester	187	6	Read	Ebenezer		1	4		1	1		2	2	1			12		
Worcester	187	7	Rice	Leml				1	1			1		1			4		
Worcester	187	8	Rice	Samuel				1					1				2		
Worcester	187	9	Rockwood	Frost	3					1		1	1	1			7		
Worcester	187	10	Parks	Christopher		1	1	1		1		1	2				7		
Worcester	187	11	Rice	Luke		1		1					1				3		
Worcester	187	12	Rowland	Willm	2			1		2	1	1	1				8		
Worcester	187	13	Rich	Peter											6		6		
Worcester	187	14	Seaver	Nathan	2			1		1			1				5		
Worcester	187	15	Snow	Pete											3		3		
Worcester	187	16	Seaver	Edward	2			1		2			1				6		
Worcester	187	17	Stearns	Mary	1	1				2		2		2			8		
Worcester	187	18	Smith	Ezekiel			1			4			1				6		
Worcester	187	19	Shepard	John	2			1		2	1	1	1				8		
Worcester	187	20	Slater	Peter	3	2		1		3			1				10		
Worcester	187	21	Stowell	Elias	3		1	1		2	1		1				9		
Worcester	187	22	Stowell	Cornelias				1					1				2		
Worcester	187	23	Stearns	Willm J			1	1	1			1	1				5		
Worcester	187	24	Stowell	Peter		5	3	2		4	1	1	1				17		
Worcester	187	25	Stowell	Abel	3	2	1		1	1	1	1		1			11		
Worcester	187	26	Stearns	Elizabeth										1			1		
Worcester	187	27	Stowell	Anna	2	2	1				1	2		1			9		
Worcester	187	28	Stowell	Benja		1		1					1	3			6		
Worcester	187	29	Stowell	Nathl	1			1		2			1				5		
Worcester	187	30	Stowell	David	1		1	1		1	1	1					6		
Worcester	187	31	Stanton	Sarah	2	2	1	1				2	1	2			11		
Worcester	187	32	Seaver	Mary	1				2		2		1				6		
Worcester	188	1	Smith	Jacob	2			1		2	1		1				7		
Worcester	188	2	Stearns	Daniel	2	1	1	1		1			1				7		
Worcester	188	3	Stearns	John Junr				1				1		1			3		
Worcester	188	4	Stearns	Willm				1		2				1			4		
Worcester	188	5	Salisbury	Stephen	1	1	1	1	1	1	1	1	1				9		
Worcester	188	6	Shepard	Thomas	3		1	1		1			1				7		
Worcester	188	7	Stearns	Charles		1	2	1	1	1	1	1	1				9		
Worcester	188	8	Stair	Samuel		2		1				1		1			5		
Worcester	188	9	Smith	Elisha Jun	3		1		1	1		2		2			10		
Worcester	188	10	Smith	Daniel	1		1			1	1	1					5		
Worcester	188	11	Smith	Robert M.				1						1			2		
Worcester	188	12	Stow	John	1	1		1		2			1	1			7		
Worcester	188	13	Smith	Elizabeth			1			2		1	1				5		
Worcester	188	14	Stiles	Jeremiah	2	1		1					1				5		
Worcester	188	15	Stearns	Bezahiel				1					1				2		
Worcester	188	16	Scott	Reuben			1					1					2		
Worcester	188	17	Sturtevant	Saml	2			1		1			1				5		
Worcester	188	18	Paine	Sarah									1	1			2		
Worcester	188	19	Paine	Nathl	2			2		1	2		2		2		11		
Worcester	188	20	Paine	Rufus	2	2	1	1		1			1				8		
Worcester	188	21	Paine	William	2	1	2		1	1	1	2	1		1		12		
Worcester	188	22	Peirce	Josiah				1				1		1			3		
Worcester	188	23	Peirce	Abijah	1	1		1		1	1	1					6		
Worcester	188	24	Peirce	John				1		1	1	1		1			5		
Worcester	188	25	Peirce	Byfield	1					1	1		1				5		
Worcester	188	26	Potter	John		1		1					1				3		
Worcester	188	27	Peirce	Seth				1		2			1				4		
Worcester	188	28	Prince	Libbey											5		5		
Worcester	188	29	Parker	John	2			1		2		1					7		
Worcester	188	30	Putnam	Isaac	4	2		1	1		1		1				10		
Worcester	188	31	Phillips	Rufus	1		1			1	1	1					5		
Worcester	188	32	Rice	Silas	1			1					1				3		
Worcester	188	33	Rice	Luther	3		1	1	1	1	2		1				10		

TOWN	PG#	LN#	HEADS OF HOUSEHOLD		FREE WHITE MALES					FREE WHITE FEMALES					TOTAL ALL OTHER	TOTAL SLAVES	TOTALS	DISTRICT/ TOWNSHIP	NOTES
			LAST NAME	FIRST NAME	under 10	10 to 16	16 to 26	26 to 45	45 and over	under 10	10 to 16	16 to 26	26 to 45	45 and over					
Bolton	207	1	*	*		1	1		1				1	1			5		Name is obscured by tape mark
Rutland	505	23	*	*	2			1					1	1			5		Name illegible due to fading
Rutland	505	24	*	*		1				1		1					3		Name illegible due to fading
Grafton	196	4	Aaron	Joseph											2		2		
Dudley	339	8	Abbit	Daniel	1		1			1	1	1					5		
Paxton	499	2	Abbot	Abijah		1		1		2	1	2	1				8		
Grafton	196	12	Abbot	Abner	3		1	1		1		1	1				8		
Boylston	375	6	Abbot	Jason		1		1		2	1	1	1	1			8		
Brookfield	265	1	Abbot	Jesse		1	1		1		1	2		1			7	Third Parish	
Brookfield	265	5	Abbot	Joel		2	2		1			2	2	1			10	Third Parish	
Petersham	271	6	Abbot	Lewis	1			1		2			1				5		
Brookfield	245	5	Abbot	Moses		1	1	1		1		1					5	First Parish	
Charlton	325	9	Abbot	Zebina			1			1	1		1				4		
Brookfield	265	2	Abbot	Zephaniah	2		1		1	1		1					6	Third Parish	
Brookfield	245	4	Abbot	John		1		1		4		2	1		1		10	First Parish	
Holden	515	3	Abbott	John	2	2		1		2	1		1				9		
Brookfield	245	3	Abbott	Jonathan		1			1	1	1	1		1			6	First Parish	
Holden	515	2	Abbott	Samuel	4		3	2		1		1	1	1			13		
Lunenberg	421	1	Adams	*iel		1	1		1		4	1	1				9		
Northbridge	478	6	Adams	Aaron	3	1	1		1	1		1		1			9		
Spencer	502	6	Adams	Abigail									1				1		
Sutton	149	12	Adams	Abner	3			1			2	1	1				8		
Brookfield	265	6	Adams	Amos		2		1		2	1	1	2				9	Third Parish	
Grafton	196	16	Adams	Andrew	2	1	2	1		2	2		1				11		
Northbridge	478	13	Adams	Andrew	3		1	1		1		1	1				8		
Rutland	505	2	Adams	Asa	2	1	1	1		1	1	1					8		
Brookfield	245	7	Adams	Benjamin		1						1					2	First Parish	
Brookfield	253	6	Adams	Benjamin	1	2	3		1		1			2			10	Second Parish	
Uxbridge	461	15	Adams	Benjamin	3	1		1	1			1	1		1		9		
Winchendon	223	1	Adams	Benjamin	1		2	1		2	1	1					8		
Northbridge	478	16	Adams	Clark	2		1					1					4		
Barre	399	1	Adams	Daniel	1	1		1		1			1				6		
Rutland	505	1	Adams	Daniel	2	2		1					1				6		
Barre	399	14	Adams	Daniel 2d	1	1		1		1			1				6		
Barre	400	2	Adams	Daniel 2d		1		1		1	1			1			5		
Spencer	502	5	Adams	David		2		1		1	2			1			7		
Hubbardston	415	5	Adams	Eben			1						1				2		
Leicester	485	4	Adams	Ebenezer	1	4	4	1		2	2	3	1				18		
Ashburnham	458	22	Adams	Ebezn Thoms	1	2		1		3		1	1				9		
Lunenberg	421	4	Adams	Edward	3		1			1	1		1				7		
Brookfield	265	13	Adams	Eleazer		1			1		1	1	?				5	Third Parish	
Spencer	502	2	Adams	Elias	2	1		1					1				5		
Hubbardston	415	3	Adams	Elijah		1				1	1	1	1	1			6		
Milford	393	11	Adams	Enoch Deac			1					1	1				3		
Brookfield	245	2	Adams	Ephraim	2		1	1	1	2		1	3	1			12	First Parish	
Northbridge	478	1	Adams	Francis	1			1		1	2	1					6		
Western	261	3	Adams	George	1			1						1			3		
Oakham	315	4	Adams	Hannah						2	1		1				4		
Westborough	191	23	Adams	Isaac		1		1			1			1			4		
Hubbardston	415	4	Adams	Isachar	2		1	1	2	2	2		1				11		
Sutton	149	7	Adams	Israel	2			1		2		1	1				7		
Oakham	315	1	Adams	Jacob			1				1		1				3		
Barre	399	17	Adams	James	3	1		1		1			1				7		
Brookfield	265	15	Adams	James	1			1		1			1				4	Third Parish	
New Braintree	308	7	Adams	James	2		2		1	2	2		1				10		
Sutton	149	3	Adams	James			1				1						2		
Barre	399	12	Adams	Jesse	1			1		1			1				4		
Brookfield	265	11	Adams	Jesse	2	2	1		1	2	1		1				10	Third Parish	
New Braintree	308	6	Adams	Jno	2		1	1		2		1	1				8		
Ashburnham	458	20	Adams	John			2		1		2	1		1			7		
Barre	399	15	Adams	John		1		1	2			1					5		
Brookfield	265	10	Adams	John				1						2			3	Third Parish	
Leicester	485	5	Adams	John			1						1	1			3		
New Braintree	308	2	Adams	John	1	1			1	1	2	1	1				8		
Northbridge	478	2	Adams	John	1	1	1		1	1	1		1				7		
Westminster	441	1	Adams	John		1	2	1		2	1	1		1			9		
Ashburnham	458	21	Adams	John Jr	1		1					1					3		
Lunenberg	421	3	Adams	Jona Jun	1	1	2	1		2	1	1					9		
Lunenberg	421	2	Adams	Jonathan		1				1		1	1				4		
Shrewsbury	361	1	Adams	Jonathan			1	1				1	1				4		
Uxbridge	461	1	Adams	Joseph			1						2				3		
Mendon	379	5	Adams	Joseph Dr.	2	1				1	1	2	1	1			9	1st Parish	
Uxbridge	461	3	Adams	Joseph Jun	1		1			1			1				4		
Mendon	379	4	Adams	Josiah Deac.			1						1				2	1st Parish	
Brookfield	265	9	Adams	Jude		2	1	1		1		1		1			7	Third Parish	
Brookfield	265	17	Adams	Jude Junr	1		1			1	1						4	Third Parish	
Brookfield	265	16	Adams	Lemuel	1			1		1	1		1				5	Third Parish	
Ashburnham	458	23	Adams	Levi		1		1		1		1					4		
Barre	399	7	Adams	Luther	2	2	1	1	1	1		1	1	1			11		
Brookfield	265	7	Adams	Moses			1	1		2	1	1					6	Third Parish	
Grafton	198	12	Adams	Moses		1		1					1				3		
Barre	399	2	Adams	Nathan					1	1			1	1			4		
Ashburnham	458	24	Adams	Nathaniel		1			1	1	1		1				5		
Grafton	196	13	Adams	Nathll	4	1	3	1		1	2	1	1				14		
Northbridge	478	5	Adams	Nathll		1		1		3		2		1			8		
Northbridge	478	3	Adams	Nehemiah	1	1		1	1	3	1	1		1			10		
Bolton	207	2	Adams	Oliver	1	1	1	1					1				5		
Milford	393	12	Adams	Oliver			2				1		1				4		
Northbridge	478	4	Adams	Oliver	1			1				1	1				4		
Mendon	379	3	Adams	Polly Wd.		1						1	1				3	1st Parish	
Rutland	505	3	Adams	Reuben	1	1		1		3	1	1	1				9		
Grafton	196	7	Adams	Samuel				1			1		1				3		
Uxbridge	461	2	Adams	Samuel	1		1	2		3		1	1				9		

158

TOWN	PG#	LN#	LAST NAME	FIRST NAME	FREE WHITE MALES under 10	10 to 16	16 to 26	26 to 45	45 and over	FREE WHITE FEMALES under 10	10 to 16	16 to 26	26 to 45	45 and over	TOTAL ALL OTHER	TOTAL SLAVES	TOTALS	DISTRICT/ TOWNSHIP	NOTES
Hubbardston	415	7	Adams	Titus	1	1		1		2	1		1				7		
Brookfield	265	8	Adams	William	1			1		2			1				5	Third Parish	
Charlton	325	10	Addams	Emerson			1			2		1					4		
Hardwick	293	2	Aikin	David			1		1		2		1				5		
Brookfield	265	3	Ainsworth	Daniel				1		1			1				3	Third Parish	
Brookfield	265	4	Ainsworth	Eunice	1		1				2		1				5	Third Parish	
Brookfield	265	12	Ainsworth	Hannah									1				1	Third Parish	
Petersham	271	10	Ainsworth	Jacob	1		2			1	1		1				7		
Barre	399	19	Ainsworth	Moss	1			1		1			1	1			5		
Petersham	271	5	Ainsworth	Samuel	1		1						1				3		
Milford	393	3	Albee	Abel	2		1	1		2		1	1				8		
Charlton	325	7	Albee	Benja	1	2		1		1	2	2		1			10		
Charlton	325	8	Albee	Benja Jun		1				2		1					4		
Milford	393	6	Albee	Caleb	1			1		3		1					6		
Milford	393	1	Albee	Elijah	2			3		1		1	1	1			9		
Uxbridge	461	7	Albee	James	1		2		1	2	2		1				9		
Dudley	339	4	Albee	John		1	1		1	1		1	1				6		
Mendon	382	3	Albee	Levi				1		2	2		1				6	1st Parish	
Milford	393	7	Albee	Mary Wd									1	1			2		
Mendon	382	4	Albee	Samuel	1		1		1	2	1		1				7	1st Parish	
Milford	393	2	Albee	Seth			2			1			4	2			9		
Charlton	325	4	Albee	Silas	1		1			1		1					4		
Mendon	379	16	Albee	Simeon	2	1		1		4			1				9	1st Parish	
Milford	393	8	Albee	Thomas	2	1		1		1		1					6		
Harvard	217	34	Albertson	Jacob				1		1	2		1				5		
Douglas	475	3	Aldrich	Aaron		1	3		1		1		1				7		
Uxbridge	461	4	Aldrich	Abel	4	2	2		1	1		1	2				13		
Northbridge	478	17	Aldrich	Ahaz	1		2			2		1	1				7		
Northbridge	478	14	Aldrich	Alexander	2		1	1		1		1	1				7		
Douglas	475	9	Aldrich	Amariah		1	1			1		1					4		
Douglas	475	6	Aldrich	Amos	3		1			1		1					6		
Douglas	475	10	Aldrich	Ananias			1			4		1					6		
Charlton	325	3	Aldrich	Barlow	3		1					1					5		
Northbridge	478	15	Aldrich	Barnebus		1			1		1		1				4		
Uxbridge	461	8	Aldrich	Benjamin		1			1		1			2			5		
Mendon	379	7	Aldrich	Benoni	1			1		1		1					4	1st Parish	
Milford	393	10	Aldrich	Caleb	2	1		1		2	1		1				8		
Douglas	475	8	Aldrich	Calvin		1		1		1		1					4		
Mendon	387	2	Aldrich	Calvin	1	1	1	1		1			1				6	2d Parish	
Mendon	379	9	Aldrich	Charles			1			2		1	1				5	1st Parish	
Mendon	387	4	Aldrich	Dan				1					1				2	2d Parish	
Douglas	475	2	Aldrich	Daniel		1		1			3		1				6		
Uxbridge	464	2	Aldrich	Daniel			1			2	1		1				5		
Northbridge	478	10	Aldrich	David	2	1	1	1		1	1		1				8		
Douglas	475	12	Aldrich	Ebenezer	1		1			1		1					4		
Mendon	382	2	Aldrich	Ebenezer			1	1		1	1		1				5	1st Parish	
Uxbridge	461	10	Aldrich	Enoch	2	2	1		1	2			2				11		
Uxbridge	464	1	Aldrich	Enoch 2d	1			1				1					3		
Uxbridge	461	12	Aldrich	Ephraim		1		1		1		1					4		
Mendon	379	10	Aldrich	George	3		1			1	2		1				8	1st Parish	
Uxbridge	461	17	Aldrich	George	1		1			2		1					5		
Douglas	475	4	Aldrich	Israel	2	1		1		2		1	1				8		
Uxbridge	461	16	Aldrich	Israel			3	1		2	3		1				10		
Douglas	475	7	Aldrich	Jacob		1		1			1	2		1			6		
Mendon	379	11	Aldrich	Jacob				1									1	1st Parish	
Mendon	379	8	Aldrich	Jasan	1			1		2		1					5	1st Parish	
Douglas	475	11	Aldrich	Jesse	1		1			2		1					5		
Northbridge	478	11	Aldrich	Jesse		2				1		1	1	1			6		
Uxbridge	464	3	Aldrich	Jesse	2		1			1		1			1		6		
Northbridge	478	7	Aldrich	John	1	1	1			2		1					6		
Mendon	379	15	Aldrich	Luke		1	1	1			1			2			6	1st Parish	
Mendon	382	1	Aldrich	Luke 2d	3	1	1	1		1	1	1	1				10	1st Parish	
Mendon	387	1	Aldrich	Luther	1	1					1	1	1				6	2d Parish	
Northbridge	478	9	Aldrich	Lyman	1		1	1	1	4			3	1			12		
Uxbridge	461	5	Aldrich	Nathl		2		1		1	1		1				7		
Uxbridge	461	13	Aldrich	Nehemiah	1	2	2		1	1	1	2		1			11		
Douglas	475	5	Aldrich	Noah	4	1		1				1					7		
Uxbridge	461	9	Aldrich	Obadiah	2		1			1	1		1				6		
Mendon	379	17	Aldrich	Pardon	2		1						1				4	1st Parish	
Northbridge	478	12	Aldrich	Paul	2	1		1		2	2	1	1				10		
Mendon	387	3	Aldrich	Phinehas Capt		1	1	2			1		2				7	2d Parish	
Mendon	387	6	Aldrich	Rufas Majr		1		1			1		1	1			5	2d Parish	
Northbridge	478	8	Aldrich	Samuel Jun	1	1		1		2	1		1				7		
Douglas	475	13	Aldrich	Seth			1					1					2		
Uxbridge	461	11	Aldrich	Seth	1		1	1		1	1		1				7		
Uxbridge	461	14	Aldrich	Seth Junr		1	2		1		1			1			6		
Mendon	379	12	Aldrich	Silas		1		1			1		1				4	1st Parish	
Petersham	271	1	Aldrich	Simeon		1		1			1	1					4		
Upton	390	1	Aldrich	Stephen			1			1		1					3		
Upton	390	2	Aldrich	Timothy	2		1				1						4		
Uxbridge	461	6	Aldrich	William	2	1		1		1		1					6		
Mendon	387	5	Aldrich	Willm		1	2			1			1				5	2d Parish	
Mendon	379	1	Alexander	Caleb	1	1	1	1		3	2	2	1				12	1st Parish	
Charlton	325	2	Alexander	Daniel		1			1		1	1	1				5		
Dudley	339	3	Alexander	Daniel	1			1		1		1					4		
Dudley	339	7	Alexander	Israel		1	1			1							3		
Shrewsbury	361	4	Alexander	James	1			1		1	1		1				5		
Petersham	271	9	Alexander	Jesse	1		1			2	1		1				6		

TOWN	PG#	LN#	LAST NAME	FIRST NAME	FREE WHITE MALES under 10	10 to 16	16 to 26	26 to 45	45 and over	FREE WHITE FEMALES under 10	10 to 16	16 to 26	26 to 45	45 and over	TOTAL ALL OTHER	TOTAL SLAVES	TOTALS	DISTRICT/ TOWNSHIP	NOTES
Western	251	12	Alexander	Joseph	1		2			1		1					5		
Mendon	387	7	Alexander	Timothy	1		1	1		1	2	1	1				8		2d Parish
Upton	390	3	Alexander	Willm			1	1					1				3		
Worcester	171	1	Alford	James	2	1	1	1	1	1	1	1			1		10		
Winchendon	223	3	Alger	Abiel	2			1		4	1		1				9		
Winchendon	223	4	Alger	David	2			1		1			1				5		
Garry	279	3	Allard	Isaac	2			1				1					4		
Sturbridge	339	2	Allen	Aaron			2		1	1	1	1	2				8		
Sturbridge	339	9	Allen	Abel	1	1			1	1			1				5		
Oakham	315	2	Allen	Abia		1	2			1			1				5		
Charlton	325	5	Allen	Abner	2	1		1		1			1				6		
Sturbridge	339	8	Allen	Abner	2	1	2		1		2	1		1			10		
Sturbridge	339	10	Allen	Abner 2d	1	1	1		1	1			1				6		
Mendon	379	18	Allen	Ahaz	1	1		1		1			2				6		1st Parish
Worcester	171	7	Allen	Ahbel		1					1						2		
Mendon	379	19	Allen	Alvan	1	1		1		1			1				5		1st Parish
Shrewsbury	361	5	Allen	Ashel			1				1						2		
Lunenberg	421	8	Allen	Benjamin			1				1						2		
Lancaster	345	5	Allen	Daniel	1	1		1		1	1	1	1				7		
Sturbridge	339	1	Allen	Daniel			1										1		
Barre	400	1	Allen	David		1		1				1					3		
Hardwick	293	3	Allen	David	1			1				2		1			5		
Petersham	271	4	Allen	David	2	1		1		3			1				8		
Dudley	339	5	Allen	Eleazer	1	2		1				1	1				6		
Petersham	271	8	Allen	Elijah	1	1		1		1	1		1				6		
Sturbridge	339	4	Allen	Elijah	1	2		1		1	2		1				8		
Shrewsbury	361	2	Allen	Elnathan		1	1		1				1	1			5		
Holden	515	4	Allen	Ephraim			1	1	1	2		3	1	1			10		
Hubbardston	415	2	Allen	Ephraim	2	1		1		1	1		1				7		
Mendon	379	13	Allen	Ezra	1			1					1				3		1st Parish
Mendon	379	14	Allen	Ezra Junr			1					1					2		1st Parish
Paxton	499	1	Allen	Ichabod			1					1					2		
Sterling	357	1	Allen	Israel		1	1	2			1						5		
Spencer	502	3	Allen	Israil		1	1		1		2		1				6		
Sturbridge	339	7	Allen	Jacob Jun		3	1	1	3	2		1	1				12		
Oakham	315	3	Allen	Jesse	1		1	1	1	2	2	1	1				10		
Barre	399	9	Allen	John	2	1		1		2		1	1				8		
Brookfield	265	14	Allen	John		1	3		1		1		2	1			9		Third Parish
Sturbridge	339	6	Allen	John		1	1		1		1	2		1			7		
Hardwick	293	10	Allen	Jonas	2	2	1		1	2			1				9		
Royalston	242	6	Allen	Jonas		1	1	1		1	1	1	1				7		
Barre	399	4	Allen	Jonathan	1		1	1				1	1	1			6		
Barre	399	11	Allen	Joseph	1			1		1			1				4		
Hardwick	293	6	Allen	Joseph		1		1	1			1					4		
Mendon	379	20	Allen	Joseph				1						1			2		1st Parish
Western	252	2	Allen	Joseph		1	1				1	1					4		
Hardwick	293	4	Allen	Keziah	1			1		3	1	1	1				8		
Worcester	171	8	Allen	Mary									1				1		
Brookfield	245	6	Allen	Molly								2		1			3		First Parish
Barre	399	16	Allen	Moses	1	1		1		1			1				5		
Hardwick	293	5	Allen	Moses			1	1		1	1						4		
Barre	399	6	Allen	Nathan	1		1			2	1		1				6		
Brookfield	245	1	Allen	Nathan	2	2		1		1		1		1			8		First Parish
Barre	399	3	Allen	Nehem	1			1	2				2				6		
Sturbridge	339	14	Allen	Nehemiah			1		1				1				3		
Holden	515	5	Allen	Peletiah				1		1		1	1				4		
Lancaster	345	7	Allen	Phillemon	1	1			1	1	1		1				6		
Leominster	433	33	Allen	Phinehas	3	1		1		2	1	1					9		
Sturbridge	339	11	Allen	Sabin	1			1		2		1	1				6		
Barre	399	8	Allen	Saml	4	2		1					1				8		
Lancaster	345	4	Allen	Samuel	2	1		1	1	1	1		1	2			10		
Northborough	370	1	Allen	Samuel	2	1	2	1		1		2	1	2			12		
Mendon	379	6	Allen	Samuel Capt.	2	1		1			1		1				6		1st Parish
Milford	393	4	Allen	Seth		1	1	1	1		1		1				6		
Leominster	431	1	Allen	Silas	1			1		2		1					5		
Shrewsbury	361	3	Allen	Silas		1		1					1				3		
Spencer	502	4	Allen	Silas			1	1		2		1					5		
Sturbridge	339	3	Allen	Simeon			1	1					1				3		
Hubbardston	415	1	Allen	Simon		1		1	1	2		3		1			9		
Sturbridge	339	5	Allen	Timothy	1	1	1	1	1				2				7		
Sutton	149	11	Allen	Timothy				1									1		
Sturbridge	339	15	Allen	Willard	2			1					1				4		
Barre	399	10	Allen	Zeb		1		1		1	1		1				5		
Lunenberg	421	5	Allexander	John		1		1					1				3		
Charlton	325	6	Alton	Moses	2	1						1	1				5		
Oxford	164	3	Alverson	George		1		1	1			1	1				5		
Sutton	149	10	Ambler	Christopher				1					1				2		
Oxford	164	1	Amedown	Jeremiah				1			1		1				3		
Grafton	200	6	Ames	Jack											6		6		
Barre	399	5	Ames	John			1	1					1	1			4		
Hubbardston	415	6	Ames	Jonathan	1			1				1					3		
Hardwick	293	7	Amesden	Joel			1	1		1		1					4		
Hardwick	293	9	Amesdenn	John		1	1	1		1	1	1					6		
Hardwick	293	8	Amesdenn	Rhoda							3	1					4		
Sturbridge	339	13	Amidown	Cyrus	2			1	2	3			1				9		
Charlton	325	1	Ammidon	Calvin	1			1		5		1	1				9		
Douglas	475	1	Ammidon	John				1		2	1	1					5		
Mendon	379	2	Ammidon	Philip Esq		1	1	1			1	1	1	2			8		1st Parish
Dudley	339	2	Ammidown	Ebenz		1	1		1			1		1			5		
Dudley	339	1	Ammidown	John	2	3	1	1		2		1					10		

			HEADS OF HOUSEHOLD		FREE WHITE MALES					FREE WHITE FEMALES					TOTAL ALL OTHER	TOTAL SLAVES			
TOWN	PG#	LN#	LAST NAME	FIRST NAME	under 10	10 to 16	16 to 26	26 to 45	45 and over	under 10	10 to 16	16 to 26	26 to 45	45 and over			TOTALS	DISTRICT/ TOWNSHIP	NOTES
Sturbridge	339	12	Ammidown	Joseph	1			1		1		2		1			6		
Petersham	271	7	Amsbury	Jesse	2			1		1		4	1				9		
Petersham	271	12	Amsden	Bozaleel	1		1	1		1	1		1				6		
Southborough	205	32	Amsden	David	1			1		2			1				5		
Petersham	271	11	Amsden	Ephm	3			1		1	2		2	1			10		
Southborough	202	1	Amsden	Ephraim					1	2			1				4		
Petersham	271	3	Amsden	Jacob	3	1	1			1		2	1				9		
Southborough	202	7	Amsden	John	1	2		1		2			1				7		
Petersham	271	2	Amsden	Thomas	1			1		1	1		1				5		
Boylston	375	7	Anderson	Allen			1					1	1				3		
Templeton	231	1	Anderson	James		2		1		1	2	2		1			9		
New Braintree	308	4	Anderson	John	5		1					1	2				9		
Westborough	198	133	Andrew	George Jun	1		1			3	1		2				8		
Westborough	197	110	Andrew	Nathll		1	1	1		3	1		1	1			9		
Westborough	196	101	Andrew	Thomas		1	1	1		1	1		1				6		
Worcester	171	3	Andrews	Benjamin		2		1		2			1				6		
Boylston	375	2	Andrews	Daniel		1	1	1		1		1	1				6		
Leominster	433	34	Andrews	Daniel	4	2	1	1			1		1				10		
Worcester	171	2	Andrews	David		1	2	2			2	1	1				9		
Royalston	241	1	Andrews	Ebenz							1	1	1				3		
Templeton	231	2	Andrews	Elisha	3			1		1		1	1				7		
Boylston	375	1	Andrews	John	1		2	1	1	2		1	1	1	1		11		
Boylston	375	8	Andrews	Jotham			1					1					2		
Boylston	375	4	Andrews	Robert	1	1	2		1	1		1		1			7		
Boylston	375	5	Andrews	Robert Jr	1		1			1		1					4		
Boylston	375	3	Andrews	Samuel			1										1		
Worcester	171	4	Andrews	Samuel	1		1	1				1	1				5		
Milford	393	9	Andrews	William			2						1				3		
Southborough	202	12	Angeir	Charles	2	1		1		3	1		1				9		
Ashburnham	458	19	Anger	Timothy				1					1	1			3		
Southborough	203	13	Angier	Calvin	1			1		2			1				5		
Southborough	203	14	Angier	Mary									1				1		
Worcester	171	6	Annam	Hager											1		1		
Sutton	149	4	Armsby	Enos				1			1	1					3		
Sutton	149	9	Armsby	Joshua	1		1	1			2	1		1			7		
Sutton	149	5	Armsby	Silas			1			3	1		1	1			7		
Leicester	485	1	Arnold	*has			1	1		2		1	1				6	First name obscured by tape mark
Leicester	485	3	Arnold	Ahab		3		1		1			1				6		
Winchendon	223	2	Arnold	Eber	2			1		2			1				6		
Western	261	1	Arnold	Ezeck		1	1	1		2	1	2	1				9		
Dudley	339	6	Arnold	Joseph		2		1		1	1	1	1				7		
Western	261	2	Arnold	Joseph	1			1		2			1				5		
Lancaster	345	1	Arnold	Nathaniel		2	1			3			1				7		
Leicester	485	2	Arnold	Oliver		1						1					2		
Lancaster	345	2	Arnold	William		1		1		3	1	1		2			9		
Bolton	207	3	Atherton	Benjamin			1			2			1				4		
Harvard	219	1	Atherton	David	3	1		1		1	1		1				8		
Lancaster	345	3	Atherton	Israel			1	1	1		1	4	1	2	1		12		
Harvard	219	13	Atherton	Oliver		1	1	1				1	2	1			7		
Lancaster	345	6	Atherton	Peter				1		1	1	1	1				5		
Harvard	220	32	Atherton	Sarah									1				1		
Hardwick	293	1	Atkins	John		1	1	1		3	2		1				9		
Oxford	164	2	Atwood	Abial				1		2			1				4		
Spencer	502	1	Atwood	Daniel	1	1		1					1	1			5		
Milford	393	5	Atwood	Eldad				1			1		1				3		
Sutton	149	8	Atwood	Elkanah	1		1					1					3		
Templeton	240	12	Atwood	James				1			1	1	1				4		
Garry	279	1	Atwood	Martha		1		1		1		2	1	1			7		
Barre	399	18	Atwood	Wait		1		1					1				3		
Barre	399	13	Atwood	Zack		2	2	1		1	1		1				8		
Hardwick	293	11	Atwood	Zechh		1		1				1					3		
Lunenberg	421	7	Austin	John				3			1		1				5		
Worcester	171	5	Austin	Samuel	1		1	2		1			1				6		
Lunenberg	421	6	Austin	Timothy	3	1	1	1		1			1	1	1		9		
Holden	515	1	Avery	Joseph		1	1		1		1	2	1				7		
Grafton	196	6	Axtel	Mary							1		3				4		
Grafton	196	5	Axtell	Thomas		1		1		1	2		1				6		
Sutton	149	6	Axtell	Thomas	1	2	1	1		2	1	1	1				10		
Sutton	149	1	Axtell	William	1			1	2					1			5		
Sutton	149	2	Axtell	William Junr			1			2		1					4		
Brookfield	253	10	Ayres	Cyrus			1	1				1					3	Second Parish
Brookfield	253	5	Ayres	Eli	1			1		6			1				9	Second Parish
Brookfield	253	3	Ayres	Increase	2	1		1		1			1	1			7	Second Parish
Brookfield	253	8	Ayres	Jabez	1		1	1		1			1				5	Second Parish
Garry	279	2	Ayres	Jason	2			1		2			1				6		
New Braintree	308	1	Ayres	Joseph		1		1		1				1			4		
Brookfield	253	2	Ayres	Jude		1		1		1	2		1				6	Second Parish
Brookfield	253	4	Ayres	Moses		2	1	1		1		2	1				8	Second Parish
New Braintree	308	3	Ayres	Moses	1	1		1		2	1	1	1				8		
Brookfield	253	7	Ayres	Onesephorus				1		1		1	1				4	Second Parish
Brookfield	253	9	Ayres	William			1	1		1		1	2	1			7	Second Parish
Brookfield	253	1	Ayres	William 2d	1	1		1		2		1	1				7	Second Parish
New Braintree	308	5	Ayrez	Jabez	3			1	1	2			1				8		
Lunenberg	421	25	Ba*	Josiah				1						1			2		
Petersham	271	19	Babbit	Abner			1	1		1	1		1				5		
Brookfield	256	17	Babbit	Elkanah				1			1	1		1			4	Second Parish
Barre	401	14	Babbit	Erasmus			1			2		1	1				5		
Brookfield	245	9	Babbit	Seth	2	1		1		1	1	1	1				8	First Parish
Petersham	274	4	Babbit	Silas	2		1			1	1		1				6		

TOWN	PG#	LN#	LAST NAME	FIRST NAME	FREE WHITE MALES					FREE WHITE FEMALES					TOTAL ALL OTHER	TOTAL SLAVES	TOTALS	DISTRICT/ TOWNSHIP	NOTES
					under 10	10 to 16	16 to 26	26 to 45	45 and over	under 10	10 to 16	16 to 26	26 to 45	45 and over					
Princeton	513	2	Babcock	Amos	2	2		1		1			1				7		
Petersham	274	3	Babcock	Enoch		1						2	1				5		
Petersham	271	16	Babcock	James	1			1		2			1				5		
Milford	396	23	Babcock	Stephen			2			1		1					4		
Charlton	328	13	Babit	Erasmus	1	1		1		1			2				6		
Sturbridge	339	18	Babit	Thomas	3	1	2	1				1	1	1	1		11		
Upton	390	9	Bachellor	Enoch	2	2		2		1			2	1			10		
Upton	390	17	Bachellor	Jont		1	1		1				2		1		6		
Charlton	328	9	Bachelor	Elijah			1		1	3	1			1			7		
Charlton	325	12	Bachelor	Perin				1						1			2		
Charlton	325	11	Bacon	Asa	1		2	1					1	1			6		
Dudley	339	9	Bacon	Cyrel	1		1	1		1			1	1			6		
Charlton	325	25	Bacon	Daniel		1		1					1	1			4		
Charlton	325	28	Bacon	Daniel Jun	3		1	1		3	3	1	1				13		
Charlton	328	1	Bacon	David		1							1				2		
Charlton	328	2	Bacon	Ebenezer	1			1		1			1				4		
Westminster	441	17	Bacon	Edward		1	1	1			1			1			5		
Sturbridge	340	12	Bacon	Enoch	2		1			1	1		1				6		
Barre	401	7	Bacon	Ephm	1		1			3		1		1			7		
Sturbridge	340	1	Bacon	Ephraim				1						1			2		
Uxbridge	464	4	Bacon	George			1			2			1				4		
Barre	401	10	Bacon	John	4	2		1		1			1				9		
Charlton	328	6	Bacon	John	3	1		1		1	1		1				9		
Barre	401	1	Bacon	John 2d	2			2					1	1	1		6		
Dudley	339	21	Bacon	Jonathan		1		1	1		1		1	1			6		
Dudley	339	15	Bacon	Jonathan 2d				1		1	1	1	1	1			6		
Barre	400	15	Bacon	Joseph				1				2		1			4		
Gardner	451	1	Bacon	Joseph	1	1		1		1		2		1			7		
Barre	401	13	Bacon	Josiah	2			1		2			1				6		
Spencer	499	4	Bacon	Noah	1			1		2	2		1				7		
Charlton	328	21	Bacon	Rufus	1					2	1	1	1				6		
Berlin	214	4	Badcock	Ephraim	2		1			1		1					5		
Northborough	367	2	Badcock	Jonas		1		1		1		1		1			5		
Bolton	211	4	Badcock	Josiah		1				1			1				3		
Leominster	431	19	Badcock	Malicai	1		1			1		1	1				5		
Fitchburg	430	13	Badcock	Nathan		1		1		2	2		1				7		
Fitchburg	430	15	Badcock	Nathan Jun		1				1		1					3		
Northborough	367	6	Badcock	Reuben	1	2		1		4	1		1				11		
Berlin	214	7	Badcock	William		2	1	1		2		1					7		
Northborough	367	7	Badcock	William				1					1				2		
Petersham	274	19	Bagg	Solomon	1			1		2	1	1	1				7		
Leominster	431	3	Bagwell	James	1		1						1				3		
Lunenberg	421	16	Bailey	Benja		1		1				2		1			5		
Brookfield	245	19	Bailey	Ephraim	2		1	1		3		1	1				9	First Parish	
Lunenberg	421	22	Bailey	Jedidiah	1		1	1		1			1	1			6		
Sterling	358	13	Bailey	Jonas	1	1		1					2	1			6		
Sterling	358	18	Bailey	Jonathan				1				1	1	1			4		
Sterling	357	5	Bailey	Jonathan 3d	1		1					1					3		
Sterling	358	14	Bailey	Jonathan Jr	2	1		1	1	3		1	2				11		
Sterling	357	17	Bailey	Joseph	1			1		1			1				4		
Lunenberg	424	1	Bailey	Josiah Jun	2	1		1				2					6		
Sterling	355	2	Bailey	Nathaniel		1		1		1			1				4		
Sterling	358	21	Bailey	Paul	2			1	1	3		1	2				10		
Sterling	357	11	Bailey	Shuball		1		1		2			1				5		
Northborough	367	1	Bailey	Silas	2	2	2	1		1	1	1	1				11		
Sterling	357	4	Bailey	William		1	1	1		3	1		1				8		
Worcester	172	7	Baird	Daniel			2		1		1	2		1			7		
Worcester	174	13	Baird	Daniel Jr	1			1		2			1				5		
Garry	279	7	Baits	Asa			1					1					2		
Garry	279	10	Baits	Noah	2	2		1		1		1	1				8		
Royalston	234	4	Baker	Amos			1						1				2		
Berlin	212	12	Baker	Benjamin			1						1				2		
Garry	279	4	Baker	Charles Esq			1					1	1				3		
Garry	279	14	Baker	Charles Jr		3	1	1		2		1	1				9		
Petersham	274	13	Baker	Cyprian			1				1		1				4		
Shrewsbury	361	9	Baker	Daniel	1	2	1	1				2	1				8		
Petersham	274	12	Baker	Edwd				1			1			2			4		
Douglas	478	14	Baker	John	1	1	2	1		3		3		1			13		
Shrewsbury	361	8	Baker	John			1			2			1				4		
Berlin	214	14	Baker	Jonathan	1			1		1			1				4		
Garry	279	15	Baker	Joseph	2			1		1	1		1				6		
Princeton	513	10	Baker	Joseph		1	1	1					1				4		
Charlton	325	23	Baker	Joseph C.		3	2	1		1		1		1			9		
Garry	279	5	Baker	Levi		1	1	1		1		1	1				6		
Princeton	516	2	Baker	Luke			1						1				2		
Athol	290	25	Baker	Marshall	1		1			2	1	1					6		
Uxbridge	464	14	Baker	Menasseh	1	1		1		2			1				6		
Westminster	441	7	Baker	Nathan	2	1		1		2	1		1				8		
Berlin	213	8	Baker	Obediah	1			1		2			1				5		
Shrewsbury	361	7	Baker	Reuben	1		1	1		2		1	1				7		
Berlin	211	6	Baker	Samuel	3	2	1	1		1		1	1				10		
Sterling	357	3	Baker	Samuel	1			1		4		1	1				8		
Garry	280	2	Baker	Silas			2		1	2	1		1				7		
Berlin	212	13	Baker	Stephen	1			1		1			1				4		
Upton	390	7	Baker	Thos Capt.				1		1	1	1	1				5		
Upton	390	8	Baker	Ward		1		1				1	1	1			6		
Winchendon	226	31	Balcom	Daniel				1		1			1				3		
Winchendon	226	32	Balcom	Gideon	1		1			1		1					4		
Templeton	239	10	Balcom	Joseph	3			1		1			1				8		
Fitchburg	430	2	Baldwin	Abel				1					1				2		

TOWN	PG#	LN#	LAST NAME	FIRST NAME	FREE WHITE MALES under 10	10 to 16	16 to 26	26 to 45	45 and over	FREE WHITE FEMALES under 10	10 to 16	16 to 26	26 to 45	45 and over	TOTAL ALL OTHER	TOTAL SLAVES	TOTALS	DISTRICT/ TOWNSHIP	NOTES
Spencer	502	16	Baldwin	Asa				1						1			2		
Shrewsbury	361	10	Baldwin	Azubah	1	1					1		1				4		
Leicester	488	1	Baldwin	Benja			1	1				2	1	1			6		
Leicester	488	11	Baldwin	Benja Jun			1						1				2		
Fitchburg	430	3	Baldwin	David	3		1	1		1			1				7		
Leicester	488	2	Baldwin	David			1					1		1			4		
Leicester	485	20	Baldwin	Ebenz				1						1			2		
Templeton	240	8	Baldwin	Eden	2	1	2	1		1			1	1			9		
Leicester	485	19	Baldwin	James				1			1			1			3		
Templeton	231	9	Baldwin	Jona		1				1		1					5		
Spencer	500	6	Baldwin	Levi	1		1		1	1				1			5		
Brookfield	248	19	Baldwin	Luke	3			1		1	1	1	1				8	First Parish	
Lancaster	348	3	Baldwin	Oliver			1			1		1					3		
Winchendon	226	22	Baldwin	Samll			1					1	1				3		
Spencer	502	10	Baldwin	Samuel	1		1					1					3		
Leicester	488	4	Baldwin	Steph Jun		1											1		
Leicester	488	3	Baldwin	Stephen			2	1				2	2	1			8		
Garry	279	9	Baldwin	Thadeus	1	3	1	1		3		1	1				11		
Winchendon	226	23	Baldwin	Wm			1					1					2		
Spencer	502	11	Baldwin	Zerubl			1	1				1					3		
Berlin	213	17	Baley	Amhurst	2		1	1		2	1	1		1			9		
Berlin	212	5	Baley	Ebenezar				1						1			2		
Bolton	209	23	Baley	Elizabeth									1				1		
Berlin	211	11	Baley	Jedediah		1					1						2		
Bolton	209	21	Baley	Libella							1		1				2		
Berlin	211	3	Baley	Stephen	2		2		1	2	1			1			9		
Douglas	478	7	Balkcom	Aaron			1		1	1			1				3		
Douglas	478	15	Balkcom	Bezaleel	2	1	1	1		1	1	1	1				9		
Douglas	478	6	Balkcom	David		1	1		1	3	2	1	1				10		
Douglas	475	15	Balkcom	Ellis	1		1					1					3		
Douglas	478	5	Balkcom	John	2	1			1	3	1	1	1				10		
Douglas	477	3	Balkcom	Luke	1				1	1		1					4		
Douglas	475	14	Balkcom	Mark	3		1						1				5		
Princeton	513	3	Ball	Aaron	1		1	1		1	2	1	1				8		
Athol	290	29	Ball	Adanijah	3	1		1				1	1				7		
Barre	400	4	Ball	Adonijah		1						1					2		
Boylston	378	25	Ball	Amaziah	1		1			1	1						4		
Spencer	499	2	Ball	Daniel		1	1		1			2		1			6		
Rutland	505	12	Ball	Eleazer	1	3		1		3			2				10		
Boylston	378	24	Ball	Elijah	1	2			1	1	1	1		1			8		
Boylston	378	31	Ball	Elijah Jun	2		1	1		2			1				7		
Southborough	203	12	Ball	Isaac		1				1			1				4		
Boylston	378	28	Ball	John			1	1		1		1			1		5		
Northborough	370	11	Ball	John	1	1	2		1			2		1			8		
Westborough	191	21	Ball	John	1		1		1	1	1		1				6		
Holden	515	16	Ball	Jonah	2							1					4		
Northborough	367	8	Ball	Jonas	1		2		1	1	1	1					7		
Southborough	202	13	Ball	Jonas		1	1	1	1				1	1			6		
Southborough	201	7	Ball	Jonas Junr		1		1		1			1				4		
Berlin	214	37	Ball	Jonathan	1			1		3		1					6		
Milford	393	17	Ball	Josiah			2		1	1		1	2	1			8		
Holden	515	15	Ball	Jotham	1	1		1		3	1		1				8		
Milford	393	15	Ball	Lazarus	1			1			1	1					4		
Westborough	191	24	Ball	Lucy			1			1	1		1				4		
Athol	290	28	Ball	Moses	1		2		1			1		1			6		
Berlin	214	29	Ball	Nathan	1				2	1				2			6		
Northborough	370	12	Ball	Nathan	3		1	1		2		1	1	1			10		
Holden	515	13	Ball	Phinehas	1			1		3	2		1	1			9		
Northborough	367	4	Ball	Stephen		1	2				1	1					5		
Brookfield	256	4	Ball	Thomas		4		1		1			1	1			8	Second Parish	
Boylston	377	1	Ball	William	1			2	1				1	1			6		
Athol	290	27	Ball	Nathan	2		1		3			1					7		
Lancaster	345	12	Ballard	Jeremiah		2		1	1		2	1					7		
Lancaster	345	14	Ballard	John	1	2		1		2		2	1				9		
Oxford	164	13	Ballard	John				1					1				2		
Oxford	164	14	Ballard	John Junr	1		1					1					3		
Worcester	173	4	Ballard	Joseph		1						1					2		
Athol	290	19	Ballard	Joseph	3	2	1		2	1		1		1			12		
Princeton	516	4	Ballard	Martha	2		1			1	2		1				7		
Lancaster	345	11	Ballard	Samuel	1			1		1	1		1				5		
Lancaster	345	9	Ballard	Thomas	1			1			1	2	2				7		
Brookfield	256	12	Ballch	Wyman				1		4		2	1	1			9	Second Parish	
Mendon	382	6	Ballou	Hepzibah Wd	1						1	1	1				4	1st Parish	
Worcester	171	10	Bancroft	Aaron	3	2		2		3		1	1		1		13		
Petersham	274	18	Bancroft	Benja			1			2	2	1	1				7		
Sutton	152	18	Bancroft	Benja				1		1	1		1				3		
Lunenberg	424	2	Bancroft	Edmand	1		1	1	1	1			1				6		
Gardner	454	3	Bancroft	Jonathan		1					2	3		1			8		
Gardner	454	5	Bancroft	Jonathan Jr		1			1		1						3		
Lunenberg	424	5	Bancroft	Joseph	3		1		1			1					6		
Sutton	152	16	Bancroft	Joseph	3	1		1				1	1	2			9		
Garry	279	13	Bancroft	Nathll	1			1					1				3		
Petersham	273	1	Bancroft	Willm		1	2	1		1	1						7		
Ashburnham	458	30	Banding	Barnard	1		1			2		1					5		
Barre	401	12	Bangs	Edmand		2	1				2		1				6		
Worcester	172	4	Bangs	Edward	1		1		1	1	1	1	1				7		
Hardwick	295	7	Bangs	Elijah	2	2	1	1		2		1	1				10		
Barre	400	14	Bangs	Want		1		1		1				1	1		5		
Brookfield	268	33	Banister	Aaron	1				1		2		1	1			6	Third Parish	
Gardner	451	2	Banister	Daniel		1					1						2		

TOWN	PG#	LN#	LAST NAME	FIRST NAME	FREE WHITE MALES under 10	10 to 16	16 to 26	26 to 45	45 and over	FREE WHITE FEMALES under 10	10 to 16	16 to 26	26 to 45	45 and over	TOTAL ALL OTHER	TOTAL SLAVES	TOTALS	DISTRICT/ TOWNSHIP	NOTES
Brookfield	245	8	Banister	Jesse	2	2			1			1	1	1			8	First Parish	
Spencer	500	7	Banister	Liberty			1			1		1					3		
Boylston	378	20	Banister	Nathan	1	1	1		1		1			2			7		
Brookfield	268	29	Banister	Seth		1	3		1			1		1			7	Third Parish	
Brookfield	268	34	Banister	Solomon				1		1			1				3	Third Parish	
Worcester	174	2	Barber	Ebenezer	1	3	2		2	2		1	1	1			13		
Milford	393	14	Barber	Hamlet	2	1	2		1	3	2	1	1				13		
Worcester	174	6	Barber	James		1		2	1		1	1		1			7		
Worcester	174	4	Barber	Joseph		3	1		1		1	1		1			8		
Barre	401	16	Barber	Nathan	3		1	1		1	1		1				8		
Berlin	211	4	Barber	Nathan		1								1			3		
Brookfield	245	11	Barbro	Isaac	3			1	1	1			1	1			8	First Parish	
Westminster	441	10	Bard	Joseph	1		1		1		2	2		1			8		
Northbridge	475	10	Bardeen	Samuel					1		3		1				5		
Gardner	451	3	Barker	Artimas			1					1					2		
Gardner	454	14	Barker	George	1	1			1	1		1	1				6		
Westminster	444	13	Barker	Joel	1		1					1					3		
Gardner	454	15	Barker	John		1			1			1		1			4		
Westminster	444	5	Barker	Richard					1				1				2		
Gardner	454	12	Barker	Thomas	2	1		1		1			1				6		
Worcester	173	1	Barker	William	1	3			1	1		4		1	1		12		
Hardwick	293	21	Barlow	Wyat		2	1		1	1	1	3		1			10		
Barre	401	15	Barnaby	Joseph	1			1		4			1				7		
Harvard	215	12	Barnard	Abigail									1				1		
Harvard	218	12	Barnard	Benjamin			1	1		1		1		1			5		
Harvard	218	11	Barnard	David			1						1				2		
Oakham	318	4	Barnard	David	2	1	2	1				1					7		
Westminster	444	4	Barnard	Edmund	1		2		1	1	1	1					7		
Northborough	367	11	Barnard	Ephraim		1			1		1	2		1			6		
Lunenberg	424	4	Barnard	Jacob	1			1		1		1					4		
Harvard	215	5	Barnard	Jesse	1			1		3		1					6		
Sterling	358	16	Barnard	John	1		1	1	1	2	2	1	1				11		
Worcester	174	10	Barnard	John			1		1		1		2	1			6		
Lancaster	348	1	Barnard	Jonathan	1	1		1	1	2			1				7		
Hardwick	295	11	Barnard	Joseph			1	1		2	1		1				5		
Berlin	213	14	Barnard	Josiah			1						1				2		
Harvard	218	18	Barnard	Jotham	2	1	1		1		1	2		2			10		
Berlin	211	12	Barnard	Martha	1							1		1			3		
Bolton	212	14	Barnard	Mary							1	1	1	1			4		
Harvard	221	5	Barnard	Phineas		1						1					2		
Harvard	217	33	Barnard	Samuel	2	2		1					1	1			7		
Paxton	499	11	Barnes	Abijah	2	1	1		1	3			1				9		
Hubbardston	415	8	Barnes	Daniel	1			1				1	1				4		
Spencer	499	3	Barnes	David			1		1		1	2					5		
New Braintree	308	14	Barnes	Joseph		1	2		1			2		1			7		
Brookfield	245	14	Barnett	Benjamin	1	1	1		1	1			1	1			7	First Parish	
Brookfield	248	22	Barnett	Rufus	2			1		2	1		1		1		8	First Parish	
Hardwick	295	4	Barns	Adonijah	2			1		3		1					7		
Berlin	213	19	Barns	David	2		1	1					1				5		
Hardwick	293	19	Barns	Eli	4			1		2	1		1				9		
Berlin	213	20	Barns	Fortenatus		1		1				1		1			4		
Westminster	441	11	Barns	Frances	3	1	1		1			2		1			9		
Grafton	202	3	Barns	Francis	1	1			1	1		2		1			7		
Hardwick	293	17	Barns	Jesse				1			1	2		1			5		
Boylston	377	5	Barns	John		1	1			2		1					5		
Hardwick	293	18	Barns	Jonas		1		1		2		1					5		
Boylston	378	17	Barns	Oliver		1		1			1		3				6		
Boylston	378	19	Barns	Oliver Jun	1		1					1					3		
Boylston	375	15	Barns	Peter	1		1	1				1					4		
Westborough	195	75	Barns	Richard	1		3		1	1		1					7		
Boylston	378	18	Barns	Thd. B	1			1		1	1	1					5		
Berlin	214	1	Barns	William	1			1		1			1				4		
Brookfield	245	18	Barns	Aaron	2			1		2	2		2	1			10	First Parish	
Brookfield	245	17	Barns	Asa		1	2		1	1			1				6	First Parish	
Brookfield	253	13	Barns	Dorothy							1			1			2	Second Parish	
Brookfield	255	5	Barns	Mary									1				1	Second Parish	
Brookfield	255	3	Barns	Moses				2				1		1			4	Second Parish	
Brookfield	245	10	Barns	Moses Jr			2		1	1		1		1			6	First Parish	
Brookfield	255	6	Barns	Nathan				1					1				2	Second Parish	
Brookfield	245	15	Barns	Samuel		1		1		1	1		1	1			6	First Parish	
Brookfield	255	4	Barns	Samuel	1			1		1	1	2	1				8	Second Parish	
Brookfield	253	11	Barns	Solomon		2	1		2		1	1	1	1			9	Second Parish	
Brookfield	248	23	Barns	Thomas	1	1			1	1	2	1		1			8	First Parish	
Brookfield	253	12	Barns	Thomas 2d	2			1		1			2				6	Second Parish	
Brookfield	255	2	Barns	William	3	1			1	1		2	1				10	Second Parish	
Sturbridge	340	4	Barnum	George	1		1		1	1							4		
Barre	401	19	Barol	Isaac	2	1	1		1	1	1		1				8		
New Braintree	308	13	Barr	Davidson	2			1		2			1				6		
New Braintree	308	17	Barr	George		1	1	1	1	1	2	2	1	1			11		
New Braintree	308	10	Barr	James		2			1					1			4		
New Braintree	308	15	Barr	John			1	1				2	1				5		
New Braintree	308	12	Barr	Joseph	1	1	1	1	1	1	1	1	1	1			9		
Worcester	174	3	Barrel	James		1		1		1		1					4		
Royalston	241	29	Barret	Benja	2		1	1				2					6		
Oxford	164	7	Barret	Jacob				1						2			3		
Athol	290	21	Barret	John	1	1		1		2			1	1			7		
Sturbridge	339	24	Barret	Joseph				1				1	1				3		
Sturbridge	339	17	Barret	Joseph Jr		1		1				1			1		4		
Templeton	236	5	Barret	Zaccheus								1	1				3		
Barre	401	2	Barrett	Joseph	2		1	1		1		1	1				7		

TOWN	PG#	LN#	LAST NAME	FIRST NAME	M under 10	M 10 to 16	M 16 to 26	M 26 to 45	M 45 and over	F under 10	F 10 to 16	F 16 to 26	F 26 to 45	F 45 and over	TOTAL ALL OTHER	TOTAL SLAVES	TOTALS	DISTRICT/ TOWNSHIP	NOTES
Bolton	210	7	Barrett	Oliver		1	1		1			1		1			5		
Barre	401	6	Barrows	Thomas		1								1			2		
Brookfield	256	1	Barstow	Jeremiah	1	1	1	1		3	1		1				9	Second Parish	
Uxbridge	464	5	Barstow	Job			1	1				1		1			4		
Fitchburg	430	10	Bartell	David	2					2	1	2	1				10		
Fitchburg	430	1	Bartell	Kendall Jun		1	2	1		3	1	2					10		
Rutland	505	19	Bartlet	Adonijah	1	1		1		1	2		2				8		
Rutland	505	7	Bartlet	Daniel				1				1	1	1			4		
Rutland	505	8	Bartlet	Daniel Junr	2			1		2	1		1				7		
Brookfield	255	1	Bartlet	Eli		1	1	1	1	3	2	2		2			13	Second Parish	
Brookfield	245	16	Bartlet	Elijah		1				1	1		1	1			6	First Parish	
Brookfield	268	32	Bartlet	Ezra	1			1			1	1					6	Third Parish	
Royalston	241	16	Bartlet	Ira	1	1	2	1					1				6		
Royalston	238	16	Bartlet	Jonas	1		1			1	1						4		
Royalston	241	9	Bartlet	Josiah	3		1			1				1			6		
Rutland	505	9	Bartlet	Levi	1		1							1			3		
Royalston	232	11	Bartlet	Nathan	1	1			1		1	1					6		
Sutton	151	6	Bartlet	Stephen	2	1	1	1		1		1	1	1			9		
Dudley	342	15	Bartlet	Zepheniah	1	1		1				1					4		
Berlin	211	17	Bartlett	Adam	3			1		2			1				7		
Northborough	367	3	Bartlett	Antiphas		1	2			1	1	1		2			9		
Holden	515	8	Bartlett	Artimas	1	1	1			1	1	1		2			8		
Hardwick	295	17	Bartlett	Bethuel	2		1	1		2			1				7		
Westminster	441	8	Bartlett	Daniel			1	1				1	1				4		
Northborough	367	10	Bartlett	Gill	1			1				1		1			4		
Holden	515	7	Bartlett	John	1			1		2			1				5		
Princeton	516	1	Bartlett	John	4	2	1	1		1			1				10		
Sutton	152	7	Bartlett	John				1									1		
Northborough	367	5	Bartlett	Jonas	1	1		1		2			1				6		
Northborough	370	8	Bartlett	Jonathan		1		1		3		1	1	1			8		
Northborough	370	7	Bartlett	Jotham	3		1	1		2		1	1				9		
Fitchburg	430	9	Bartlett	Nathaniel			1	1		3			1				5		
Boylston	378	32	Bartlett	Phinehas	4	1		1		2	2		1				11		
Hubbardston	413	2	Bartlett	Saml	2		1			1	1		1	1			7		
Spencer	502	14	Barton	Abia	3		1	1		2			1				7		
Leicester	488	5	Barton	Caleb	2			1		2	1		1				7		
Sutton	152	14	Barton	Jedidiah	2	2	1	1				2	1				9		
Leicester	488	6	Barton	Joshua	1	1	1			1		1	1				6		
Spencer	502	15	Barton	Nathl	3			1						2			6		
Leicester	488	8	Barton	Phinehas	2			1		2		2		1			8		
Sutton	152	12	Barton	Reuben	1	1		1		2	1		1				7		
Sutton	152	13	Barton	Reuben Junr			1	1				1					3		
Charlton	328	18	Barton	Sibley	3			1		2			1	1			8		
Charlton	328	15	Barttlet	Roger		2		1			1						4		
Western	260	3	Bascom	Caleb				1		2			1				4		
Western	259	12	Bascom	Moses		1		1		1	1	2		1			7		
Western	252	3	Bascom	Samuel	1	1		1					1				4		
Leominster	431	11	Bass	John	1		1	1		3	2		1				9		
Sutton	152	4	Basset	Alwan	1		1	1		2			1				6		
Sutton	151	12	Basset	Benja	1		1			1		1					4		
Sutton	152	9	Basset	Jacob	1	1	1			1		1					5		
Uxbridge	464	8	Basset	Joseph		1		1		4	1		1				8		
Sutton	152	8	Basset	Joshua				1						1			2		
Hardwick	295	1	Basset	Wm		2		1									3		
Hardwick	295	2	Basset	Wm Jr			1					1					2		
Northbridge	475	9	Bassett	Benjamin				1			2			1			4		
Northbridge	475	8	Bassett	Simeon	2		2			3		1					8		
Fitchburg	430	19	Batchelder	Timothy	1			1		2	3	1		1			9		
Sutton	149	21	Batcheller	Abner			1				1		1				3		
Sutton	149	20	Batcheller	Abram & Amos	2		1	1		1			1				6		
Sutton	149	22	Batcheller	Benja	1		1	1				1	1				5		
Sutton	152	2	Batcheller	Daniel			1										1		
Sutton	149	23	Batcheller	Ezra	3	1	1						1				6		
Sutton	151	13	Batcheller	Jonas	1		1						1				3		
Sutton	149	24	Batcheller	Mark		2		1			2	1	1				7		
Grafton	204	11	Batcheller	Nathll	3	1	1			2	2	1					11		
Grafton	204	16	Batcheller	Pearly		2		1				1		1			5		
Sutton	149	18	Batcheller	William		2		1	1			1		1			6		
Sutton	149	19	Batcheller	William Jr		2	1					2	1				6		
Northbridge	475	2	Batchellor	David		1		1						1			3		
Northbridge	475	3	Batchellor	Joel	1			1		2			1				5		
Northbridge	475	7	Batchellor	Simeon	1			1		2			1				5		
Royalston	235	3	Batchelor	John	1			1						1			3		
Royalston	241	13	Batchelor	John Jr	1			1		1			1				4		
Royalston	241	11	Batchelor	Stephen	2		1	1		2		2		2			8		
Royalston	235	2	Batchelor	Thomas			1	1		2	1						4		
Harvard	222	18	Bateman	Jonas	2			1		3	1			1			8		
Dudley	342	11	Bates	Alanson	3		1	1		2			1				8		
Charlton	325	13	Bates	David		1	1	1					2				5		
Charlton	328	5	Bates	David 2d	4	1							1				6		
Mendon	382	9	Bates	Martha Wd		1						1		1			3	1st Parish	
Mendon	382	8	Bates	Nahum	2		1	1			1	1					6	1st Parish	
Charlton	325	26	Bates	Obediah			1	1				1		1			4		
Leicester	488	10	Bates	Robert	1			1				1					3		
Westborough	196	104	Batherick	Jonathan	1	2	2		1	1	1	1		1			10		
Westborough	195	72	Batherick	Levi	1			1		1			1				4		
Westborough	195	71	Batherick	Solomon	1		1	1						2			6		
Upton	390	10	Bathrick	Jasan			1	1				1		1			4		
Lunenberg	421	9	Bathrick	Reuben		2		1						1			4		
Lunenberg	421	10	Bathrick	Samuel	1		1			2							5		

TOWN	PG#	LN#	LAST NAME	FIRST NAME	FREE WHITE MALES					FREE WHITE FEMALES					TOTAL ALL OTHER	TOTAL SLAVES	TOTALS	DISTRICT/TOWNSHIP	NOTES
					under 10	10 to 16	16 to 26	26 to 45	45 and over	under 10	10 to 16	16 to 26	26 to 45	45 and over					
Charlton	328	11	Batten	Mehitable Wid	1	1				2			1				5		
Uxbridge	464	13	Battey	Nicholas	3	2		1	1	1	1		1	1			11		
Leominster	431	21	Battle	David			1			2			1	1			5		
Milford	393	16	Battle	James				1		1				1			3		
Fitchburg	430	7	Battle	John	4	1		1		1	1		1				9		
Fitchburg	430	5	Battle	Joseph			1					2		1			4		
Fitchburg	430	6	Battle	Joseph Jun	1			1		2			1				5		
Fitchburg	430	11	Battle	Nathan			1			1		1					3		
Winchendon	226	26	Battles	Noah	2	1		1		3	1		1	1			10		
Spencer	499	5	Baxter	Ezekiel	2	2	6	1		1			1	1			14		
Princeton	513	8	Baxter	Joseph				1					2	1			4		
Rutland	505	10	Baxter	Moses		1		1					1	1			4		
Princeton	513	9	Baxter	Richard				1					1	1			3		
Western	251	14	Baxter	Stephen Revd		1	1	1	1		1		2				7		
Uxbridge	464	10	Baylis	Alpheus	2	1		1			1	1					6		
Uxbridge	464	9	Baylis	Nicholas		1	1	1		2	1						6		
Royalston	240	12	Beal	John	1			1					1				3		
Upton	390	6	Beal	Nehemiah		1		1		1	1	1					5		
Hardwick	293	12	Beal	Saml			2			1			1				5		
Templeton	242	1	Beal	Samuel	2	2		1		2	1		1				9		
Winchendon	226	21	Beal	Stover			1			2			1				4		
Royalston	242	3	Beal	Thomas		1		1					1	2			5		
Milford	396	26	Beall	Asa	1			1		5			1				8		
Milford	396	25	Beall	Daniel		1				1		1					3		
Charlton	325	16	Beals	Enos	2	1		1		1	1		1				7		
Winchendon	226	27	Beaman	David	1	2		1		1			1				6		
Sterling	358	19	Beaman	Elisha	3	1		1		1			1	1			8		
Sterling	357	16	Beaman	Gideon		1	1	1		4	1	1	1				10		
Leominster	431	16	Beaman	John	1			1						1			3		
Princeton	513	13	Beaman	Jonas	1	1	1	1		2	1	1	2	1			11		
Lancaster	345	17	Beaman	Joseph				1				1	1	2			5		
Sterling	357	10	Beaman	Josiah	2	1		1		1			1	1			7		
Princeton	513	12	Beaman	Phinehas		2		1		1	1	1	1				7		
Sterling	358	2	Beaman	Phinehas				1					1	1			3		
Boylston	375	13	Beaman	Ephraim	1		1	1	1	2	2		1	1			10		
Boylston	375	9	Beaman	Ezra Esq		1	1	3	1		1	3	1	1	1		13		
Westminster	444	3	Beamon	Joseph	3		1	1		1			1				7		
Brookfield	248	21	Beard	Daniel	1			2		1	1						5	First Parish	
Westborough	189	11	Beaton	John	1	1	3		1	1			1				8		
Westborough	189	12	Beaton	Martha									3				3		
Brookfield	268	20	Beemis	Moses			1			1		1					3	Third Parish	
Leicester	488	7	Beers	Nathan			1	1		1	1		1				5		
Spencer	500	5	Beers	Richard Jun			1	1	1	2		1	3				9		
Leominster	431	2	Belcher	Elizabeth	1	1				1	1		1				5		
Sturbridge	340	8	Belknap	Chester			1			1		1	1				4		
Sterling	357	15	Belknap	Cyrus	1	1		1		2			1				6		
Westborough	195	85	Belknap	Joseph		1	3		2		1	4		2			13		
Sturbridge	339	23	Belknap	Peter		1	1	1					1	1			5		
Charlton	328	19	Belknap	Stephen	3	1		1		1			1				7		
Westborough	194	67	Belknap	Stephen	3	1		1		1	1	1	1				9		
Oakham	315	15	Bell	James			1	4					1				6		
Spencer	502	8	Bell	John	3			1		2			1				7		
Brookfield	256	8	Bell	Simpson		1		1					1				3	Second Parish	
Western	259	3	Bell	John	1	2		1		1			1	1			7		
Hubbardston	415	9	Bellows	Asaph	3			1		1			1				6		
Southborough	201	8	Bellows	Ebenz	2	1		1		2	1	1	1	1			10		
Paxton	499	5	Bellows	Ezekiel	1	1		1			2		1				6		
Hubbardston	415	16	Bellows	Isaac	1			1		1			1				4		
Southborough	205	2	Bellows	James			1	1						2			4		
Paxton	499	6	Bellows	John	1		1	1		2			1				6		
Shrewsbury	361	12	Bellows	John		1	2	1				1	1				6		
Sterling	355	8	Bellows	Jonas	2			1		1			1				5		
Western	260	1	Bellows	Joseph				1			1		1				3		
Southborough	206	10	Bellows	Jotham		1		1				1	1				4		
Western	252	5	Bellows	Jotham				1				1	1				3		
Westborough	195	86	Bellows	Reuben	1			1		1	1		1				5		
Westborough	198	129	Bellows	Samuel	1	1		1		1	1		1	1			7		
Westborough	198	136	Bellows	Simeon		1	2		1			1	1	2			8		
Southborough	206	9	Bellows	Stephen	1			1		2	3		1				8		
Southborough	206	11	Bellows	Timothy	2		2	1		1			1	1			8		
Hardwick	295	18	Beluo	Hosea	1			1		1	1	1					5		
Westborough	198	124	Beman	Abraham				1						1			2		
Westborough	195	82	Beman	John				1		3			1				5		
Westborough	198	125	Beman	Levi				1					1				2		
Southborough	204	16	Bemas	Elisa Jun	1	3	2		1	2			1				10		
Westminster	444	2	Bemis	Edmund			1	1		1		1		1			4		
Royalston	241	26	Bemis	Jason	1	1	1			2			1	1			7		
Winchendon	226	33	Bemis	John			1	1				1	1	1			5		
Royalston	241	2	Bemis	Jonas	1	1		1		2			1	1			7		
Westminster	444	15	Bemis	Stephen	2			1		1			1				5		
Westminster	444	9	Bemis	Thomas	3			1		2			1				7		
Westminster	441	4	Bemis	William				1						1			2		
Westminster	441	20	Bemis	William		2						1					3		
Westminster	441	18	Bemis	Zacheus				1					1				2		
Spencer	499	8	Bemiss	Amasa	3	1	2	1		1	3						11		
Spencer	499	7	Bemiss	David	3	2		1		1	1	1					9		
Spencer	502	12	Bemiss	Jesse			1	1			1		1				4		
Spencer	499	13	Bemiss	John	1			1		2			1	1			6		
Spencer	500	4	Bemiss	Jonas	2	1	2	1		1		1	1				9		
Spencer	500	3	Bemiss	Joseph	2	1	1		1	2	2	1	1				11		

TOWN	PG#	LN#	LAST NAME	FIRST NAME	M under 10	M 10 to 16	M 16 to 26	M 26 to 45	M 45 and over	F under 10	F 10 to 16	F 16 to 26	F 26 to 45	F 45 and over	TOTAL ALL OTHER	TOTAL SLAVES	TOTALS	DISTRICT/ TOWNSHIP	NOTES
Spencer	500	2	Bemiss	Joshua	2	1		1		2			1	1			8		
Spencer	499	15	Bemiss	Nathan	3			1		2	1	1	1	1			10		
Spencer	500	1	Bemiss	Nathl	3		1			1			1				6		
Spencer	502	13	Bemiss	Silas	1					1	1	1					5		
Spencer	499	9	Bemiss	William			1	1	1		1	1		1			6		
Southborough	205	18	Bemos	Elisha				1					1				2		
Southborough	205	19	Bemos	Josiah	3		1										4		
Southborough	205	20	Bemos	Phinehas	1		3		1	2	1			1			9		
Winchendon	226	18	Benjamin	Andrew		1							1				2		
Ashburnham	458	34	Benjamin	Daniel	1	1	1	1		2	2	2	1				11		
Princeton	513	1	Bennet	Abner			1			3		1					5		
Fitchburg	430	17	Bennet	Abraham		1	1			1			1				4		
Boylston	375	11	Bennet	Asa	2	1		1		2	1		1				8		
Hubbardston	415	15	Bennet	David	1	1	1		1	2	1		1				8		
Boylston	377	2	Bennet	Elias	1	1		1		3		1		1			8		
Boylston	375	12	Bennet	Ephraim	2	1		1		2	1		1				8		
Leominster	431	12	Bennet	Jacob	1		1		2	2		2	1	1			10		
Grafton	201	8	Bennet	John	1			1		1		1					4		
Leominster	431	22	Bennet	John				1									1		
Boylston	377	4	Bennet	Mary									1				1		
Northbridge	475	5	Bennet	Robert			1	1				1		1			4		
Ashburnham	458	28	Bennet	Thomas	1			1		2		1					5		
Gardner	454	16	Bennet	Thomas	1			1					1	1			4		
Lunenberg	424	3	Bennett	David	2	1	1	1		4	1	3	1				14		
Lancaster	345	19	Bennett	Elisha Junr			1					1					2		
Spencer	500	8	Bennett	Ezra	5	1	1		1			1		1			10		
Mendon	387	18	Bennett	Hosea		1			1			1	1				4	2d Parish	
Lunenberg	421	14	Bennett	James			2		1	3	3		1				10		
Lancaster	345	16	Bennett	Jonathan	1	1			1			2	1				7		
Spencer	499	6	Bennett	Joseph	1		1		2	2	1	3		1			11		
Lancaster	348	5	Bennitt	Elisha Junr			1				1		1				3		
Lancaster	348	6	Bennitt	Nathan			1			1		1					3		
Lancaster	348	4	Bennitt	Thomas Jun	1			1	1	2		1	1	1			8		
Douglas	478	10	Benson	Aaron	1	1	1		1	1	1		1				7		
Hubbardston	415	14	Benson	Abner						1	1		1	1			4		
Mendon	387	12	Benson	Amasa	1			1				1					3	2d Parish	
Northbridge	475	6	Benson	Benjamin	1	1	1		1	1	1	3		1			10		
Mendon	387	11	Benson	Benoni		1			1				1				3	2d Parish	
Sturbridge	340	10	Benson	David	4	2		1		2	1	2	1				13		
Mendon	387	13	Benson	Henry	1			1		2			1				5	2d Parish	
Mendon	387	10	Benson	John Lt.	2	1	2		1	2	2		2				12	2d Parish	
Sturbridge	340	7	Benson	Joseph		1	1	1			1	1		1			6		
Rutland	505	17	Bent	Darius			2	1		2	1		1				7		
Barre	401	8	Bent	Joel Capt.			1		1			1	1	2	1		7		
Rutland	505	16	Bent	Martha		1	1				1		1				4		
Rutland	505	18	Bent	Phinehas	1		2			1		1		1			6		
Barre	401	3	Bent	Thaddeus	2			1		1			1				5		
Fitchburg	431	1	Berns	Edmund				1				1					2		
Worcester	185	12	Berry	Nathan		1			1			1		1			4		
Fitchburg	430	18	Berry	Samuel	1	2		1		1	1		1				7		
Lunenberg	421	18	Bicknell	Daniel	2	1	1	1		1	2	1	1				10		
Lunenberg	421	21	Bicknell	James	1		1			1			1				3		
Lunenberg	421	19	Bicknell	Joseph	1	2			2	1		2	1	1			10		
Worcester	172	1	Bigbee	Joel	3		1	1		1			1				7		
Worcester	171	11	Bigbee	Solomon					1				1				2		
Boylston	378	27	Bigelow	Abel	2	1	1	1	1		1	1		1			9		
New Braintree	308	8	Bigelow	Abijah	3	1	4	1	1	2	1	2	1				16		
Sterling	357	2	Bigelow	Abraham	1			1		2		1					5		
Berlin	216	9	Bigelow	Agustus		1	1			1		1	1				5		
Boylston	375	14	Bigelow	Andrew	3			1		1	2		1				8		
Worcester	172	5	Bigelow	Anna								2		1			3		
Westborough	192	42	Bigelow	Arnisa	2	1		1	1	1			1	1			8		
Brookfield	268	28	Bigelow	Asa			2	1	1	1	1		1	1			8	Third Parish	
Berlin	211	10	Bigelow	Banister			1			1	3		1				6		
Westminster	444	6	Bigelow	Benjamin	2	2		1		1			1				7		
Petersham	274	14	Bigelow	Daniel Esq		2	2		1	1	1	1	1	1	1		11		
Athol	290	22	Bigelow	David	1	2	1		1	1	1	2	1				10		
Worcester	174	7	Bigelow	David		1						1		1			4		
Worcester	174	15	Bigelow	David Junr	1	1			1	2	1		1				8		
Sterling	355	4	Bigelow	Elias	1	1	1		1	1	1	1		1			8		
Westminster	441	5	Bigelow	Elisha	1		1		1				1				4		
Westminster	441	6	Bigelow	Elisha Jr	1			1		2		1					5		
Westminster	441	3	Bigelow	Ephraim	3	1		1		1	2		1				9		
Westminster	444	14	Bigelow	Ezekiel	1			1		2			1				5		
Paxton	499	4	Bigelow	Ithamar		1	2		1			1		1			6		
Westminster	441	2	Bigelow	Jabez			2		1			1					4		
Brookfield	256	13	Bigelow	Jason	2		2		1	1	1	2		2			11	Second Parish	
Sutton	151	10	Bigelow	John	1		1	1		1			1				5		
Westminster	441	19	Bigelow	John		1		1			1		1				4		
Brookfield	253	15	Bigelow	Jonas			1	1					1				3	Second Parish	
Boylston	378	26	Bigelow	Joseph				1				1		1			3		
Rutland	505	15	Bigelow	Joseph	2			1		1	1		1				6		
Garry	279	6	Bigelow	Jotham					1		2	2		1			6		
Westminster	441	9	Bigelow	Luke	1			1		2			1				5		
Leominster	434	1	Bigelow	Nathal	3	2		1	1	1			1				9		
Charlton	328	14	Bigelow	Phillip			1			1			1	1			4		
Harvard	222	27	Bigelow	Roger	2	1		1						1			5		
Brookfield	268	31	Bigelow	Samuel	1			1		1			1				4	Third Parish	
Worcester	174	8	Bigelow	Silas	2			1		2			1				6		
Holden	515	17	Bigelow	Stephen	1					4			1	1			7		
Rutland	505	14	Bigelow	Thaddeus		1			1				1	1			4		

TOWN	PG#	LN#	LAST NAME	FIRST NAME	M <10	M 10–16	M 16–26	M 26–45	M 45+	F <10	F 10–16	F 16–26	F 26–45	F 45+	TOTAL ALL OTHER	TOTAL SLAVES	TOTALS	DISTRICT/ TOWNSHIP	NOTES
Douglas	475	17	Bigelow	Thomas	2	2	2		1			1		1			9		
Paxton	499	3	Bigelow	Timothy				1		1			1				3		
Worcester	174	14	Bigelow	Walter		1	1	1				1					4		
Bolton	209	7	Bigelow	William				1	1	2			1				5		
Athol	290	23	Bigelow	Willm				1						1			2		
Gardner	454	9	Bigford	William		1	1	1				1		1			5		
Gardner	454	8	Bigford	William Jr			1					1					2		
Barre	401	11	Biglow	David	3			1		1			1				6		
Winchendon	223	15	Biglow	Elishahell	2			1		1		1					5		
Royalston	232	1	Biglow	Gershom				1				1		1			3		
Shrewsbury	366	1	Biglow	Humphrey	1	1	1	1		3			1				8		
Winchendon	223	16	Biglow	Roger	1	2	1			1	3	1	1				10		
Barre	401	18	Biglow	Saml Capt.	3		2	1		3			1				10		
Douglas	478	12	Billing	Erastus			1			2			1				4		
Hardwick	293	13	Billings	Asael		1	2	1		1	2		1				8		
Hardwick	293	16	Billings	Asael Jr			1				1		1				3		
Hardwick	295	6	Billings	Daniel			1	2	1				1	1			6		
Hardwick	293	15	Billings	Elijah	2	1		1		1		1					6		
Hardwick	293	14	Billings	Elisha	1		1			1		1		2			6		
Lunenberg	421	12	Billings	John	1	2	1	1		4	1	1	1				12		
Ashburnham	458	31	Billings	Joshua	1		1	1		1	1		1				6		
Sutton	152	1	Billings	Robert	1			1					1				3		
Lunenberg	421	11	Billings	Samuel		1	2	1		2	1	1		2			10		
Shrewsbury	366	2	Billings	Silvanus	2	2	2	1			1	1		2			11		
Hardwick	293	20	Billings	Timothy	1		2				1	1		1			6		
Charlton	325	21	Billings	William		1	1	1					1				4		
Spencer	499	11	Bisco	Jacob	1		2	1		1		1		1			7		
Spencer	499	10	Bisco	John				1				1		1			3		
Oxford	164	5	Bixby	Jonathan				1			1		1				3		
Winchendon	223	14	Bixby	Levi		1		1			1	3	1	1			8		
Barre	400	6	Bixby	Saml	1	1		1		1	1		1	1			7		
Sutton	152	10	Bixby	Samuel		1	1	1	1	1	1	1					7		
Sutton	152	11	Bixby	Samuel Junr		1	1	1		1	1	1					6		
Holden	515	9	Black	Daniel				1					1				2		
Barre	401	5	Black	Elizabeth Wid		1							1				2		
Barre	400	7	Black	James	1	1		1		1			1		1		6		
Barre	400	18	Black	James Lt.		1		1	1	1	3	1	1		1		10		
Barre	401	4	Black	John			1	1									2		
Worcester	172	3	Blackman	Nathan	2			1		2	1		3				9		
Dudley	339	14	Blackmore	Adonijah				1			1	1		1			4		
Western	261	12	Blackmore	James		1		1		4	1	1					8		
Western	259	11	Blackmore	John	1		1	1		3	4	1		1			12		
Dudley	339	13	Blackmore	Joseph	2		1			1			1				5		
Petersham	273	4	Blackmore	Solo	2	2		1		1	1		1				8		
Western	252	9	Blackmore	Willard	1			1				1					3		
Western	261	10	Blair	Daniel		1		1				1	1				4		
Oakham	315	12	Blair	James	1	2	1	1				1		1			7		
Western	259	4	Blair	James		3	1	2		1	1		1				9		
Rutland	505	4	Blair	James Junr	2	4		2			1			2			11		
Brookfield	245	13	Blair	Joseph		1	1		1			2		1			6	First Parish	
Worcester	172	9	Blair	Joseph				1			1		1				3		
Brookfield	248	24	Blair	Mary									1				1	First Parish	
Western	260	2	Blair	Reuben	1	3	1		1	4		2	1				13		
Worcester	174	1	Blair	Robert	1	2		1		3	1		1				9		
Western	259	9	Blair	Samuel	2	2	2	1		1		2		1			11		
Western	259	8	Blair	William	1	2		1	1	1			1	1			8		
Mendon	387	14	Blake	Asa	1			1	1			1		1			5	2d Parish	
Mendon	387	15	Blake	Benjamin			1							1			2	2d Parish	
Westborough	191	33	Blake	Braman	2		1	1		1	1		1				7		
Westborough	194	59	Blake	Elisha	4		2	1		1		1	1				10		
Rutland	505	20	Blake	Francis	2	1	1	2		1	1	1					9		
Oakham	315	10	Blake	George		1		1			1			1			4		
Worcester	172	6	Blake	Jason	2	1		1		2			1				7		
Holden	515	11	Blake	Jeremiah	1	2		1		1		2		1			8		
Uxbridge	464	11	Blake	Joseph				1				1					2		
Mendon	387	16	Blake	Reuben	1		1			1	2	1					6	2d Parish	
Oakham	315	13	Blake	Sarah		1		2				1	2	1			7		
Athol	290	24	Blake	Timothy	1		1	1		2			1				6		
Mendon	387	17	Blake	Zacheus	2		1			2	1		1				7	2d Parish	
Harvard	222	8	Blanchard	Abel		1		1			1	1					4		
Brookfield	268	26	Blanchard	Amasa		1		1		1	1						4	Third Parish	
Sturbridge	339	16	Blanchard	Benj	2		1			2	1		1				7		
Athol	290	26	Blanchard	Benja			1	1				1	1				4		
Brookfield	268	30	Blanchard	Isaac	2		2				1	1					6	Third Parish	
Charlton	328	4	Blanchard	James Junr	2		1					1					4		
Sturbridge	340	11	Blanchard	John			1							1			2		
Charlton	328	3	Blanchard	Joseph		1		2	1				1				5		
Harvard	222	3	Blanchard	Lycias				1			1	1					3		
Charlton	328	12	Blanchard	Moses	1		1				2		1				5		
Oxford	164	12	Blanchard	Saml	1	1	1	1		1	1		1				7		
Petersham	271	20	Blanchard	Seth	2	1		1				2	1				7		
Harvard	222	11	Blanchard	Simon	2	1		1		1	2		1				8		
Brookfield	268	25	Blanchard	William		2		1				1		1			5	Third Parish	
Westminster	441	13	Blanchard	Zilphar									1				1		
Sutton	149	17	Blanden	Elisha			1				1	1					3		
Oxford	164	18	Blandin	Francis	3		1	1		2		1		1			8		
Royalston	236	10	Blanding	Ebenz	2		1	1		3			1				8		
Royalston	236	12	Blanding	Ebenz Jr		1					1		1				3		
Royalston	234	16	Blending	Shubael	1		1	1		2	1	2		1			9		
Royalston	234	5	Bliss	Aaron	2	1	1	1			4	1					10		
Western	261	8	Bliss	Aaron	2	1	2	1	2	3	2	1	1	1			16		

168

TOWN	PG#	LN#	LAST NAME	FIRST NAME	FREE WHITE MALES					FREE WHITE FEMALES					TOTAL ALL OTHER	TOTAL SLAVES	TOTALS	DISTRICT/ TOWNSHIP	NOTES
					under 10	10 to 16	16 to 26	26 to 45	45 and over	under 10	10 to 16	16 to 26	26 to 45	45 and over					
Brookfield	267	1	Bliss	David				1									1	Third Parish	
Western	261	9	Bliss	Edwd Junr				1									5		
Western	259	13	Bliss	Isaac	2	2		1	1	3	1	1	1	1			13		
Royalston	233	11	Bliss	Israel	2	2		1				1					8		
Petersham	273	5	Bliss	Moses				1		2			1				4		
Royalston	233	12	Bliss	Nathan		1		1		1	1		1				5		
Western	261	5	Bliss	Noah	2	1		1		2	1		1				8		
Western	261	6	Bliss	Oliver	1		1	1					1	1			5		
Brookfield	245	12	Bliss	Samuel	2	1		1		1	1		1				7	First Parish	
Western	261	7	Bliss	Solomon	1	1	2		1	2	1	1		1			10		
Royalston	231	2	Bliss	Sylvanus			1			3		1					5		
Royalston	233	9	Bliss	Timothy				1			1		1				3		
Royalston	233	10	Bliss	Timothy Junr	2		2	1		2		2	1				10		
Sturbridge	340	3	Blodget	Edward	2		1	1		1		1	1				7		
Westminster	441	12	Blodget	Isaac	3	2	1		1	2				1			10		
Fitchburg	430	14	Blodget	Thomas	1			1	1	1	1			1			5		
Western	259	10	Blodgit	Nathan	1		2		2	2	1		1				9		
Charlton	325	20	Blood	Joseph	1	2		1		1		2		1			8		
Charlton	325	19	Blood	Nathl	3	1	1		2	2		2	1	1			13		
Sterling	358	6	Blood	Reuben	1		1	1		2			1				6		
Charlton	325	18	Blood	Richard		2	2		2					2			8		
Bolton	211	11	Blood	Samuel	2	1	3	3	1	1		2	2	1			18		
Bolton	211	12	Blood	Thomas	2	1		2					1				6		
Charlton	328	20	Blood	William	2			1				1					4		
Hubbardston	413	4	Boardman	Ebenezer			1			1		1			3		6		
Rutland	505	27	Boice	John			1		1			1		1			4		
Rutland	505	29	Boice	John Junr	2			2		1			1				6		
Rutland	505	28	Boice	Thomas	3			2		1	1		1				8		
Oakham	315	9	Boid	James	1	1	1	1		2	1	1	1				9		
Oakham	315	8	Boid	John	2	1	1		1	2	1		1	1			10		
Douglas	478	16	Bolster	Richard		1	2		1	1	2	1		1			9		
Westminster	441	15	Bolton	Aaron				1		3	2	1		1			8		
Gardner	454	13	Bolton	Ebezr			1					1					4		
Fitchburg	430	4	Bolton	William	1	1		1					1				4		
Westborough	195	74	Bond	Abraham	4			1		1			1	1			8		
Brookfield	256	15	Bond	Amos			2					1	1				4	Second Parish	
Gardner	454	2	Bond	Andrew			2		1	3	1		1				8		
Gardner	454	10	Bond	Andrew Jr	1			1					1				3		
Leicester	485	7	Bond	Benja		1		1				2		1			5		
Leicester	485	12	Bond	Benja		1		1				2		1			5		
Southborough	205	10	Bond	John				1				1					2		
Leicester	485	17	Bond	Jona		2	1			1		1	1	1			7		
Sutton	151	1	Bond	Jonas				1					1				2		
Sutton	151	2	Bond	Jonas Junr	1			1		1		1	1				5		
Boylston	378	22	Bond	Jonathan	2	1		1		1	1		1	1			8		
Sutton	151	3	Bond	Josiah				1					1				2		
Sutton	151	4	Bond	Oliver	2	2	3	1				1	1				10		
Leicester	485	10	Bond	Richard		1	1		1			1	2	1			7		
Leicester	485	15	Bond	Richard		1	1		1			1	2	1			7		
Leicester	485	16	Bond	Richard Jun		2				1		1	1	1			6		
Western	261	4	Bond	Seth		1		1	1				1	1			5		
Westminster	441	16	Bond	Thadeus			1		1	4	3		1				10		
Brookfield	256	14	Bond	Thomas		1	2		1		1	1	1	1			8	Second Parish	
Leicester	485	18	Bond	Thomas	2	1		1		2			1				7		
Sutton	151	5	Bond	William	2			1		1			1				5		
Petersham	274	15	Bond	Willm	1			1		1			1				4		
Boylston	378	21	Bond	John	1	1	1	1		1		2					7		
Boylston	377	3	Bondman	Cato											6		6		
Grafton	204	3	Boney	Sarah											1		1		
Hardwick	295	5	Bonney	Job		2	1		1	1		1		1			7		
Leominster	433	38	Bontell	Asaph	1			1		2			1				5		
Leominster	431	6	Bontell	James		1		1		2	2		1				7		
Leominster	431	8	Bontell	John	2		1	1		1	1		2	1			9		
Leominster	433	37	Bontell	Kendall		1			1	1		2	1	1			7		
Leominster	431	7	Bontell	Timothy			4		1			1		2			8		
Oxford	164	17	Bonzey	Peter A	2		1			1	2	2					9		
Northborough	370	13	Booker	Josiah			1	1				1		2			5		
Sturbridge	339	22	Borden	Isaac		1		1		1			1				4		
Hardwick	295	20	Borden	Luba				2			1		1				4		
Rutland	505	13	Borman	John	1			1		1		1					4		
Lunenberg	424	8	Boston	Phillip											5		5		
Petersham	273	2	Bosworth	Benja	1	2	1		1	1			1				7		
Petersham	273	3	Bosworth	George	3		1	1		2		1	1	1			10		
Royalston	231	5	Bosworth	Ichabod	1			2			1		1				5		
Royalston	237	12	Bosworth	Jona	2	2	2		1	2	1			1			11		
Mendon	382	7	Bosworth	Joseph	3			1				1	1				6	1st Parish	
Winchendon	226	29	Bosworth	Walsm			1			2			1				4		
Oakham	315	11	Botherill	John	1	1			1			1	1	1			6		
Oakham	318	1	Boulton	Nathl		1			1			1		1			4		
Oxford	164	4	Bound	John					1			1		1			3		
Spencer	502	7	Bowen	Asa	2		1			1			1				5		
Douglas	477	1	Bowen	Eaner	1	1		1		3			1				7		
Brookfield	268	36	Bowen	Moses			1		1	1			1				3	Third Parish	
Brookfield	268	27	Bowen	Peter			1	1		1				1			4	Third Parish	
Hardwick	295	3	Bowen	Samll			1	1		4		1	1				8		
Northbridge	475	4	Bowen	Thomas		1	1	1				1					6		
Mendon	387	9	Bowen	Willm			1	1		1			1				4	2d Parish	
Dudley	342	13	Bowers	John	3	2		1		2	2		1				11		
Lancaster	345	13	Bowers	Jonah				1					1	1			3		
Leominster	431	4	Bowers	Mary							1	2	2	1			6		
Leominster	431	5	Bowers	Samuel	2	1	2		1	1		1	1	1			10		

TOWN	PG#	LN#	LAST NAME	FIRST NAME	FREE WHITE MALES under 10	10 to 16	16 to 26	26 to 45	45 and over	FREE WHITE FEMALES under 10	10 to 16	16 to 26	26 to 45	45 and over	TOTAL ALL OTHER	TOTAL SLAVES	TOTALS	DISTRICT/ TOWNSHIP	NOTES
Milford	396	19	Bowker	Edmond	1		1	1		1	1	1		1			7		
Petersham	274	8	Bowker	Ezekel	1			1			1			1			4		
New Braintree	308	9	Bowker	Jerusha	1			1		1				1			4		
Garry	279	16	Bowker	Jona	2			1		2			1				6		
Petersham	274	9	Bowker	Jotham	3		2	1		2			1				9		
Rutland	505	32	Bowker	Oliver	1	1		1		3	1	1	1				9		
Royalston	237	16	Bowker	Samll W.	2		1					1					4		
Royalston	242	9	Bowker	Silas				1				1	1				3		
Royalston	242	8	Bowker	Stephen	1		1					1					3		
Garry	280	1	Bowker	Susannah	2		2			2	3		1				10		
Westborough	194	55	Bowman	Benjm	3	1		1		3			1				9		
Westborough	191	25	Bowman	James			2	1			1			1			5		
New Braintree	308	11	Bowman	Joseph	2	1		1				1	1	1			7		
New Braintree	308	18	Bowman	Joseph Jr	1	1		1		1	1	1					6		
Westborough	192	48	Bowman	Levi		1				1	1						3		
Westborough	197	121	Bowman	Nathaniel		1		1			1		1				4		
Berlin	211	7	Bowman	Simeon			1			2			1				4		
Worcester	174	12	Boyden	Alven		1	5			1		2			1		10		
Mendon	387	19	Boyden	Amos	1			1		3				1			6	2d Parish	
Holden	515	14	Boyden	Daniel	1		3		1		2	2		1			10		
Sturbridge	339	20	Boyden	John			1	1		2		2					6		
Sturbridge	339	21	Boyden	Joseph			1	1						2			4		
Sturbridge	339	19	Boyden	Justice			1	1					1				3		
Sturbridge	340	6	Boyden	Paul			1			3			1				5		
Barre	400	8	Boydon	Moses			1	1					1				3		
Rutland	505	30	Boynes	Philip				1		1	1	1		1			5		
Sterling	355	7	Boynton	Abial	1	2	1		1	4	1		1				11		
Winchendon	223	6	Boynton	Danll				1		1		1					3		
Lunenberg	421	24	Boynton	David		1		1			1		1				4		
Holden	515	12	Boynton	Ebenezer	2	2	2		1			2		2			11		
Hubbardston	413	3	Boynton	Edward		1		1		2			1				5		
Sterling	358	11	Boynton	Ephraim		1		1		1			1				4		
Lunenberg	421	23	Boynton	Jona				1				2	1				4		
Leominster	433	40	Boynton	Jonathan	1	1	1		1		1	1	1				7		
Winchendon	223	5	Boynton	Joseph		1		1				1		1			4		
Winchendon	223	7	Boynton	Paul	2			1		1	1	1	1	1			8		
Lunenberg	421	15	Boynton	Wm	4		2			1			2				9		
Worcester	171	9	Boyter	David	2		1				1						4		
Sturbridge	340	9	Bracket	Aaren			1				1		1				3		
Dudley	339	19	Bracket	Ebenz	1		1		4	1		1					8		
Dudley	342	12	Bracket	John		2		1					2				5		
Dudley	339	10	Bracket	Moses	1	3	1			2	2	1					10		
Upton	390	13	Bradish	Amos	3		1	1		2		1	1				9		
Upton	390	14	Bradish	Elisha	1	1	1		1		3		1				8		
Upton	390	12	Bradish	James				1					1				2		
Brookfield	248	20	Bradish	John	2	2		1	1		1		1				8	First Parish	
Winchendon	225	3	Bradish	Jonas	2			1		1		1	1				6		
Winchendon	225	2	Bradish	Robert	1		1			3			1				6		
Brookfield	256	3	Bradshaw	Eleazer				2			1	1					4	Second Parish	
Shrewsbury	361	6	Bragg	John	1	1		1		1	1		1				6		
Royalston	242	17	Bragg	Nathl	1	1	1	1				2	1				7		
Charlton	328	10	Bragg	William	1		1		1	3	2		1				9		
Sutton	151	7	Braman	Amasa	1			1		2		1	1				6		
Holden	515	6	Brannan	Daniel	2	1	2		1	1	1		1				10		
Worcester	173	5	Brant	Henry		1		1				1					3		
Mendon	387	8	Brayley	Solomon	1	1		1		2	1			1			7	2d Parish	
Worcester	172	8	Brazer	Samuel	1	2	1	1		1		1	2				9		
Paxton	499	7	Brewer	Eliab	1	1		1	1	2	1	2	1				10		
Boylston	377	6	Brewer	James	2	2	1		1	2			1				9		
Southborough	203	1	Brewer	Joel	3	1	2		1		1	1	1				10		
Spencer	499	12	Brewer	John	2	1		1			2		1				7		
Brookfield	256	10	Brewer	Jonas		1	2		2			2		1			8	Second Parish	
Royalston	234	7	Brewer	Jonas	1		1		1	2		3		3			11		
Brookfield	256	11	Brewer	Jonas Jun			1			2		1					4	Second Parish	
Spencer	499	14	Brewer	Samuel			1						1				2		
Northbridge	475	11	Briant	Asa	5	1		1					1				8		
Rutland	505	6	Briant	Isaac	2			1		1	1		1				6		
Templeton	240	13	Briant	Nathan	3	1		1		2	2	1	1				13		
Barre	401	17	Brick	John			1				1	1					3		
Gardner	454	1	Brick	Jonas	2			1		1	2		1				7		
Petersham	271	14	Bridge	Nancy	1	1				1		2	1		1		7		
Lancaster	345	10	Bridge	William	2			1		3		1	1				8		
Rutland	505	5	Bridge	William		1	1	1			1	2	1				7		
Brookfield	268	24	Bridger	Silas		1		1				1	1				4	Third Parish	
Spencer	502	9	Bridges	Caleb		1		1					1				3		
Southborough	205	25	Bridges	Hacklisah		1		1		2			1				5		
Hardwick	295	12	Bridges	Isaac		2		1					1				4		
Hardwick	295	13	Bridges	Isaac Jr	3		1			1			1				6		
Southborough	205	28	Bridges	James				1			1		1				3		
Harvard	221	31	Bridges	Jonathan			2	3			3	2	10				20		
Southborough	205	30	Bridges	Josiah	1			1		2			1				5		
Southborough	201	6	Bridges	Nathan	1			1			1		1				4		
Southborough	205	29	Bridges	Nathan Jr		1		1				1					3		
Brookfield	253	14	Bridges	Stephen	1			1		3		1					6	Second Parish	
Western	259	5	Bridges	Timothy P.	2			1		2	1	1					7		
Douglas	478	9	Briggs	Abraham			1		1			1					3		
Oxford	164	10	Briggs	Abraham	1	1	1		1		2			1			7		
Petersham	274	5	Briggs	Amos	1		1			2	1		1				7		
Sutton	152	3	Briggs	Elijah				1			1	1		1			4		
Douglas	477	2	Briggs	Greenlief			1	1				1					3		

170

TOWN	PG#	LN#	LAST NAME	FIRST NAME	FREE WHITE MALES					FREE WHITE FEMALES					TOTAL ALL OTHER	TOTAL SLAVES	TOTALS	DISTRICT/ TOWNSHIP	NOTES
					under 10	10 to 16	16 to 26	26 to 45	45 and over	under 10	10 to 16	16 to 26	26 to 45	45 over					
Athol	290	20	Briggs	Isaac	2	1		2		4	2		1				12		
Royalston	234	1	Briggs	Jacob					1					1			2		
Petersham	271	18	Briggs	Job	1			1					1				3		
Petersham	271	17	Briggs	Job Jur	1			1		2			1				5		
Sutton	151	8	Brigham	Amariah		1		1			1			2			5		
Northborough	370	2	Brigham	Antiphas	1		1	1		2	2	1	1				9		
Northborough	370	3	Brigham	Artemas		1	1	1				2	1				6		
Brookfield	256	9	Brigham	Barnabas	2			1		1			1				5	Second Parish	
Westborough	196	97	Brigham	Benajah	1	1	2		1					1			6		
Grafton	197	13	Brigham	Charles	1		1	1				1					4		
Berlin	213	2	Brigham	Daniel	1	1		1		1		1	1				6		
Shrewsbury	361	13	Brigham	David		2	1		1			2		2			8		
Westborough	195	76	Brigham	David	2	1	1	1		2			1				8		
Westborough	197	117	Brigham	Ebenz		1		1		1			1				4		
Boylston	378	30	Brigham	Edmond			1			2	1						4		
Templeton	236	8	Brigham	Edmund	1	1	1	1		2	1	1	1	1			10		
Westborough	198	130	Brigham	Edmund		2	1		1	1		2		1			8		
Petersham	274	11	Brigham	Edwd	1	1		1		3			1	1			8		
Southborough	200	1	Brigham	Elijah	1		2		1		2	1		1			8		
Westborough	189	1	Brigham	Elijah	1	1	1	1	1	3	1	1	2				12		
Brookfield	268	21	Brigham	Elisha		1	1			1		1	1				5	Third Parish	
Grafton	200	13	Brigham	Elisha				1				1	1				3		
Grafton	197	4	Brigham	Ezekiel	2	1		1		1	2		1				8		
Northborough	370	9	Brigham	Gardner		1	1	1			1	1					5		
Southborough	206	14	Brigham	George			1	1	1		1		1				5		
Barre	401	9	Brigham	Henry	1	1	1		1	1	1	1	1				8		
Northborough	367	9	Brigham	Henry	1			1			1	1					4		
Hubbardston	415	11	Brigham	Hosea		1	2		1	1		1		1			7		
Milford	396	21	Brigham	Isaac Dr	1	1		2				1	1				6		
Leominster	431	10	Brigham	Joel	2	2			1	3	2		1				11		
Garry	279	12	Brigham	John		1	1		1			1	1				5		
Grafton	197	2	Brigham	John		1	1	1									3		
Paxton	499	8	Brigham	John	1			1		4			1		1		8		
Rutland	505	33	Brigham	John	3	1	1	1		1	1		1				9		
Northborough	370	15	Brigham	Jonah		1			1			1	1				4		
Brookfield	268	23	Brigham	Jonathan	1		1		1		3		1				7	Third Parish	
Westborough	192	52	Brigham	Joseph	1	1		1		1			1				5		
Brookfield	268	35	Brigham	Lot			1			2			1				4	Third Parish	
Brookfield	268	19	Brigham	Michael	2		2	1		1		2					8	Third Parish	
Grafton	197	3	Brigham	Millitent								1		1			2		
Northborough	370	10	Brigham	Moses	1			1		1	1		2				6		
Southborough	201	5	Brigham	Nathan		1		1	1			2		2			7		
Shrewsbury	361	14	Brigham	Nathl			1					1					2		
Southborough	206	15	Brigham	Phinehas	1	2		1		2	1	1	1				9		
Boylston	378	23	Brigham	Samuel	2		1	1		3	2		1				10		
Shrewsbury	361	11	Brigham	Samuel		1	1		2					2			6		
Gardner	454	4	Brigham	Seth	1	2		1		1			1				6		
Southborough	200	4	Brigham	Silas	1			2				1	1				5		
Southborough	200	2	Brigham	Silvester	2			1			1		1				5		
Grafton	197	14	Brigham	Solomon				1				1					2		
Boylston	378	29	Brigham	Stephen		1	1		1	1		1		2			7		
Princeton	513	7	Brigham	Stephen	1	1	1	1	1	4			2				11		
Berlin	212	7	Brigham	Thomas	2			1		1			1				5		
Brookfield	268	22	Brigham	Tilley		2	1	2	1	3	1	1	1				12	Third Parish	
Westborough	197	115	Brigham	Trowbridge			1					1					2		
Berlin	211	9	Brigham	Willard			1			1		1					3		
Grafton	197	12	Brigham	William	1	1	2		1		1	2		1			9		
Southborough	206	6	Brigham	William	1			1			1	1					4		
Westborough	199	140	Brigham	William	1			1			1	1					4		
Northborough	370	6	Brigham	Winslow	2	2	1	1		3	2		1	1			13		
Barre	400	5	Brimball	Sylvanus	4	2		1		1			1				9		
Oakham	315	17	Brimhall	Saml	3	1	1	1		1	1	1	3				12		
Barre	400	10	Brimstall	Peter			1	1					1	1			4		
Barre	400	12	Brimstall	Phinas 2d	1	2	1	1		4			1				10		
Barre	400	11	Brimstall	Phins				1						1			2		
Uxbridge	464	16	Brister	Abigail								2	1				3		
Barre	400	16	Broad	Elisah	1		1		2					3			7		
Barre	400	17	Broad	Joseph	3			1		1		1					6		
Holden	515	10	Broad	Josiah	1	1	2	1	1	2	1	4		1			14		
Harvard	221	1	Bromfield	Hennery					1		1			1	1		4		
Lunenberg	424	6	Brooks	Aaron	1	1			1				1				4		
Petersham	274	17	Brooks	Aaron	2	1		1		2	1		1				8		
Sterling	355	1	Brooks	Ami	4			1			1	1	1				7		
Western	259	2	Brooks	Asa			1			2		1	1				5		
Western	259	1	Brooks	Benjamin			1					2					3		
Princeton	513	6	Brooks	David	3	2	1		1	2	1	3		1			14		
Sterling	357	14	Brooks	Ebenezer			1	1			2						4		
Grafton	195	7	Brooks	Elijah		1	1	1		2		1	1				7		
Princeton	513	14	Brooks	Enoch		1	2		1		1		1				6		
Barre	400	13	Brooks	Eph Dr.	1		1	1	1	1			1	1			7		
Grafton	200	7	Brooks	Ephr		1		1				1					3		
Westminster	444	1	Brooks	Ezra			1			1		1		1			4		
Sterling	357	6	Brooks	Helan	1		1	1		2		1					6		
Fitchburg	430	21	Brooks	Isaac	1			1		1		1					4		
Westminster	444	8	Brooks	Isaac		1	1		2		1	1		2			8		
Northborough	370	14	Brooks	Jacob	1		1			3		1					6		
Gardner	454	6	Brooks	Joel	2	1		1		3			1				8		
Grafton	195	6	Brooks	Joel					1					1			2		
Petersham	274	16	Brooks	Joel	4	1		1			1		1				8		
Sterling	358	22	Brooks	John					1	1				1			3		

TOWN	PG#	LN#	LAST NAME	FIRST NAME	FREE WHITE MALES					FREE WHITE FEMALES					TOTAL ALL OTHER	TOTAL SLAVES	TOTALS	DISTRICT/ TOWNSHIP	NOTES
					under 10	10 to 16	16 to 26	26 to 45	45 and over	under 10	10 to 16	16 to 26	26 to 45	45 and over					
Western	249	1	Brooks	John	3	1	3			3	2	2	1				15		
Winchendon	226	19	Brooks	John	2				1	1	1		1				6		
Sterling	357	8	Brooks	John 2d				1	1				1				3		
Princeton	513	5	Brooks	Jonas	2		1	1				1					5		
Ashburnham	458	32	Brooks	Jonathan	4				1	1			1				7		
Upton	390	15	Brooks	Joseph	2		1			2		1					6		
Sterling	357	12	Brooks	Joshua		1			1	1	1	1	1				6		
Winchendon	226	20	Brooks	Levi		1		1		2	1		1				6		
Ashburnham	458	33	Brooks	Luther		1		1			1			1			4		
Princeton	513	4	Brooks	Mary		1	1				1			1			4		
Worcester	174	5	Brooks	Nathaniel		1	3	1	1					1			7		
Grafton	195	12	Brooks	Noah									1	1			2		
Upton	390	11	Brooks	Peter	1		2					2					5		
Harvard	221	24	Brooks	Samuel				1		4		2	1				8		
Westminster	444	7	Brooks	Samuel	1			1		2		1					5		
Worcester	174	11	Brooks	Samuel			1		1			1		1			4		
Ashburnham	458	27	Brooks	Simeon	2	2		1		1	1			1			8		
Templeton	236	2	Brooks	Stephen	4	2	2	1		2	1	1					13		
Ashburnham	458	29	Brooks	Thadus	2	1		1		1			1				6		
Lancaster	348	8	Brooks	Thomas				1					1				2		
Leicester	485	6	Brooks	Thomas				1					1				2		
Leicester	485	11	Brooks	Thomas				1					1				2		
Ashburnham	458	25	Broughton	Wait	2	2	1		1	1			1				8		
Mendon	382	5	Brown	Aaron		1	1		1	1				1			5	1st Parish	
Paxton	499	10	Brown	Abel		1		1			1	1	1				5		
Charlton	328	16	Brown	Abijah	1		1	1		2		2	1				8		
Sutton	149	15	Brown	Abram	1			1					3				5		
Charlton	325	24	Brown	Alexander		1		1						1			3		
Spencer	499	1	Brown	Alpheus	1	1	1		1	2		2		1			9		
Winchendon	223	8	Brown	Amasa	1	1		1		3			1				7		
Hubbardston	415	13	Brown	Asa			2		1		1		1				5		
Sterling	357	9	Brown	Benjamin	1	1			1	3	1		1	1			9		
Westminster	444	12	Brown	Benjamin	2			1				1					4		
Winchendon	223	9	Brown	Benjamin		1	1					1					3		
Dudley	339	20	Brown	Chad		1	1					1					3		
Dudley	339	16	Brown	Charles 1st	2	2		1					1				6		
Dudley	339	17	Brown	Charles 2d	4	1	1	1					1				8		
Templeton	233	11	Brown	Cyrus				1					1				2		
Charlton	325	14	Brown	David	1	1		1		1			1				5		
Worcester	173	3	Brown	David			2			1		1					4		
Charlton	325	27	Brown	David Jun	2		1			1		1					5		
Hubbardston	415	17	Brown	Eben	4	2		1		1		1	1				10		
Dudley	339	18	Brown	Ebenz	3	1		1	1	1	1		1				9		
Uxbridge	464	15	Brown	Elihu	1		1			3		1					6		
Douglas	478	8	Brown	Elijah	2			1		1		1	1				6		
Winchendon	226	30	Brown	Esther						1	1		1				3		
Dudley	339	11	Brown	Ezekiel	1		2		1	1	3		1				9		
Petersham	274	6	Brown	Frederick F	4	1		1		1	2		1		1		11		
Shrewsbury	361	15	Brown	George				1					1				2		
Winchendon	223	12	Brown	Hezekiah		1	1		1	1		1	2	1			8		
Oakham	315	18	Brown	James			1	1					2	1			5		
Oxford	164	11	Brown	James	1		1	1			1		1				5		
Princeton	513	11	Brown	James	2	2		1					1				6		
Western	259	6	Brown	James Jr	3	1	1		1	1	1		1				9		
Princeton	513	15	Brown	Jesse	1			1		1		1					4		
Bolton	216	9	Brown	John				1		1	3		1				6		
Douglas	475	16	Brown	John		1	1		2	1	3		1				9		
Hubbardston	413	5	Brown	John			1					1					2		
Upton	390	18	Brown	John				1		4	2			2			9		
Western	249	2	Brown	John	2			1		1			1				5		
Douglas	478	1	Brown	John 2d	1	2		1		1	1	3		1			10		
Sterling	355	6	Brown	John 2d	1			1		1			1	1			5		
Grafton	199	10	Brown	Jonas		1	1			3	2		1				8		
Gardner	454	7	Brown	Jonathan	4			1					1				6		
Westminster	444	11	Brown	Jonathan		1		1			1		1				4		
Oxford	164	9	Brown	Joseph	1			1		1			1				4		
Petersham	271	15	Brown	Joseph		1	2	1		1	1		1	1			8		
Sutton	152	20	Brown	Joseph	2			1		1			1	1			6		
Winchendon	223	13	Brown	Joseph				1				1		1			3		
Ashburnham	458	26	Brown	Josiah	2			1					1				4		
Oxford	164	8	Brown	Josiah		1		1		3			1				6		
Rutland	505	31	Brown	Josiah			1	1		2			1				5		
Southborough	206	5	Brown	Josiah				1					1				2		
Sutton	152	19	Brown	Josiah				1				2		1			7		
Westminster	444	10	Brown	Josiah	1			1		2			1				5		
Winchendon	223	11	Brown	Levi			1		1			1	1				4		
Hardwick	295	9	Brown	Luke			1			2			1				4		
Charlton	325	15	Brown	Nathan	4			1					1				6		
Garry	280	3	Brown	Nathan	1	1		1		2		1	1				7		
Sturbridge	340	2	Brown	Nathan	3	1		1		2		1					8		
Douglas	478	2	Brown	Nathl				1						2			3		
Douglas	478	3	Brown	Nathl Jun	1			1		3			1				6		
Hubbardston	415	18	Brown	Oliver	1		1					1					3		
Leominster	433	35	Brown	Oliver	2	2	1		1	1	1	1	1				10		
Leominster	433	36	Brown	Pearson	3	2		1	1	1			1	1			10		
Lunenberg	421	20	Brown	Peter	2	2	1		1	2		1	1				11		
Milford	396	20	Brown	Peter		1			1			1		1			4		
Milford	396	24	Brown	Peter Junr	1			1		1			1				4		
Lunenberg	421	13	Brown	Philemon			1		1			2		1			5		
Oxford	164	6	Brown	Philip	1	2	2		1		1	1		1			9		

172

TOWN	PG#	LN#	LAST NAME	FIRST NAME	FREE WHITE MALES under 10	10 to 16	16 to 26	26 to 45	45 and over	FREE WHITE FEMALES under 10	10 to 16	16 to 26	26 to 45	45 and over	TOTAL ALL OTHER	TOTAL SLAVES	TOTALS	DISTRICT/ TOWNSHIP	NOTES
Fitchburg	430	8	Brown	Phinehas		2	2		1		1	1		1			8		
Charlton	328	8	Brown	Rufus	6			1		2	1	1		1			12		
Templeton	238	6	Brown	Samll	2	1			1	1	1	1					7		
Winchendon	223	10	Brown	Samll	1	2	1		1	1	1	2		1			10		
Douglas	478	4	Brown	Samuel				1		1	1	1	1				5		
Paxton	499	9	Brown	Samuel			1	2					1				4		
Sterling	358	1	Brown	Samuel		1		1		1		1		1			5		
Sterling	358	3	Brown	Samuel 2d	3		2	1		2	1		1				10		
Rutland	505	11	Brown	Solomon	2		1	1		2	1		1	1			9		
Garry	279	17	Brown	Thadeus	1		1	1	1	2	1		1				8		
Petersham	274	10	Brown	Thomas	1		1			1		1					4		
Fitchburg	430	12	Brown	William		1		1		1		2					5		
Sterling	355	3	Brown	William	1		1			1		1		1			5		
Sutton	152	21	Brown	William		1		1				1		1			4		
Western	259	7	Brown	William		2		2		1	1	1		2			9		
Worcester	174	9	Brown	William				1					1				2		
Royalston	239	2	Brown	William 2d	1	1		1		2	1		1				7		
Dudley	342	18	Brown	Wm	1		2		1	2	1	1	1				9		
Dudley	342	16	Brown	Wm 2d			1		1	1		1					4		
Dudley	342	17	Brown	Zepheniah	1	1				1		2					5		
Grafton	199	9	Brown	Clark	1	1	1	1		1		1					6		
Rutland	505	22	Browning	Ephraim		1	1			1			1	1			5		
Rutland	505	25	Browning	James	3	1	1			3	3		1	1			13		
Rutland	505	26	Browning	James 2d	1	1	1	1		1			1				6		
Grafton	199	3	Browning	John	3	1			1	1	2	1	1				10		
Hubbardston	415	12	Browning	John Lt.	3	2		1		2	1		2				11		
Rutland	505	21	Browning	William				1						1			2		
Milford	396	22	Bruce	Abijah	1	1	1			2			1				6		
Berlin	214	13	Bruce	Benjamin		1		1				1		1			4		
Berlin	212	2	Bruce	Calvin	1		1			1		1					4		
Westborough	197	112	Bruce	Eli	2			1		1			1				5		
Templeton	240	5	Bruce	Eli	3		1	1				1					6		
Grafton	201	5	Bruce	Ellis									1				1		
Grafton	201	11	Bruce	Eunice								2					2		
Berlin	214	2	Bruce	Hugh	1		1			1		1					4		
Lancaster	348	2	Bruce	Joel	2		1		1	1		2					7		
Berlin	212	15	Bruce	John	1	1	1		1	1	2	1		1			9		
Hardwick	295	8	Bruce	John	1		2	1	1	1			1				7		
Winchendon	226	28	Bruce	Jonas		1	1	1		2	1	1					7		
Northborough	370	4	Bruce	Jonathan				1			1	1	1				4		
Shrewsbury	366	3	Bruce	Jonathan			1	1		1			1				4		
Templeton	239	3	Bruce	Josiah	2		1	1		1		1					6		
Hardwick	293	22	Bruce	Josph	1		1			1							3		
Westborough	197	108	Bruce	Mary									1				1		
Brookfield	256	5	Bruce	Roger				1					1				2	Second Parish	
Petersham	274	2	Bruce	Rueben	1			2		1			2				6		
Grafton	201	6	Bruce	Sarah		1				2			1				4		
Northborough	370	5	Bruce	Silas		1	2			2			1				6		
Garry	279	11	Bruce	Simeon	1		1		1	1	2		1				7		
Berlin	216	1	Bruce	Timothy				1	1	3	2		1				7		
Garry	279	8	Brumdell	Willm	1	1	1		1	1		1		2			8		
Westminster	441	14	Brun	Samuel			1					1					2		
Lunenberg	421	17	Bryant	Amos	1		1		1	2	1		1				7		
Hardwick	295	15	Bryant	Calvin	2		1			2	1		1				7		
Leicester	485	9	Bryant	David		1		1				1		1	1		5		
Leicester	485	14	Bryant	David		1		1				1	1	1			5		
Petersham	274	7	Bryant	Joel	2	1	1	1	1	2		1		1			10		
Leicester	485	8	Bryant	Jona	2		1		1			1		1			6		
Leicester	485	13	Bryant	Jona	2	1		1		1			1				6		
Hardwick	295	14	Bryant	Wm		1	1		1	1	1	1	1	1			8		
Upton	390	16	Buck	Ebenezer	1	2		1		1	3		1				9		
Sutton	152	15	Buck	Samuel			1							1	1		3		
Winchendon	225	1	Buckland	Oliver		1		1		1	3		1				7		
Douglas	478	13	Bucklin	Lonnon											2		2		
Sutton	151	9	Buckman	Russell		2						1					3		
Petersham	274	1	Buckwith	Eliot		1	1			1		1	1				5		
Royalston	241	4	Bud	Nathan	1	1	1	1		3		1	1				9		
Douglas	478	11	Buffam	Benjamin		1	1			2	2	2	1				10		
Western	252	11	Bugbee	Ebenz			1					1					2		
Milford	393	13	Bullard	Aaron	1			1		1			1				4		
Northbridge	475	1	Bullard	Artemus		1		1		1		1					4		
Uxbridge	464	7	Bullard	Baruch	2	2		1				1		1			7		
Sturbridge	340	5	Bullard	Elijah	1		2					1					4		
Hubbardston	413	1	Bullard	Isekiah		1		1					1				3		
Oakham	315	6	Bullard	Jno	4	1	1	1				2		1			10		
Westborough	199	147	Bullard	Joseph	2		1					1					4		
Dudley	342	14	Bullard	Lynde	1		2			2		2					7		
Oakham	318	3	Bullard	Moses		1	1	1		1			2	1			7		
Oakham	315	14	Bullard	Phinehas	3			1				2	1				7		
Brookfield	256	16	Bullard	Rachel	1		1	1		1	1		1				6	Second Parish	
Barre	400	9	Bullard	Saml		1			1	1		1		2			6		
Oakham	315	5	Bullard	Silas	2	1	2		1	1	1	1		1			10		
Oakham	318	2	Bullard	Vonentine	2			1		3	1		1				8		
Charlton	325	17	Bullen	Samuel	2		1			1		1					5		
Charlton	325	22	Bullen	Stephen Jun	3		1			2			1	4			11		
Royalston	236	15	Bullock	Christopher		1			1		1		1	1			5		
Royalston	236	16	Bullock	Christopher Jr	1	2		1		1		2		1			8		
Royalston	233	2	Bullock	Ebenz			1	1		2		1	1				6		
Royalston	234	13	Bullock	Hugh	1	1	2		1	1	1		1				8		
Royalston	234	14	Bullock	Molten	1		1		1	1	1		1	1			7		

TOWN	PG#	LN#	LAST NAME	FIRST NAME	FREE WHITE MALES					FREE WHITE FEMALES					TOTAL ALL OTHER	TOTAL SLAVES	TOTALS	DISTRICT/ TOWNSHIP	NOTES
					under 10	10 to 16	16 to 26	26 to 45	45 and over	under 10	10 to 16	16 to 26	26 to 45	45 and over					
Royalston	239	15	Bullock	Molton	1		1		1	1	1		1	1			7		
Royalston	233	3	Bullock	Nathan	1				1				2	1			5		
Sutton	152	17	Burbank	Caleb		2	2	1		1		4	1				11		
Worcester	172	2	Burbank	Elijah	1	2	8	1		2		5	1				20		
Oakham	315	7	Burbank	John	1		1	1	1	1			1				6		
Royalston	237	6	Burbank	John	1			1				1	1				4		
Lancaster	345	15	Burbank	Nathaniel	4	1				1	2	1			2		11		
Leominster	433	39	Burbank	Samuel	4	1					1	1	1				9		
Harvard	222	6	Burdeen	Thomas			1		1			1	1	1			5		
Sutton	152	6	Burden	John			2		1			1	1	1			6		
Sutton	149	16	Burden	Jonathan	2	2		1		2	1	1	1	1			11		
Charlton	328	7	Burden	Nathl			1		1			3	1		3		10		
Leominster	431	9	Burdit	John	2	1	1		1			2		1			8		
Hubbardston	415	10	Burditt	Jesse		1	4		1	1	2			1			10		
Ashburnham	458	35	Burges	Ebenezar		1		1			2			1			5		
Harvard	217	16	Burges	Ebenz				1						1			2		
Ashburnham	458	36	Burges	Joseph	1		1					1					3		
Harvard	217	15	Burges	Loammi	2			1		2			1				6		
Hardwick	295	10	Burges	Luther	2			1					1				4		
Harvard	217	14	Burges	Marritt	3			1		2	1		1				8		
New Braintree	308	16	Burk	James				1		3			1	1	4		10		
Uxbridge	464	6	Burk	Joseph				1						1			2		
Sutton	151	11	Burnap	Abijah	1	1						1	1	2			7		
Fitchburg	430	20	Burnap	Edward	2			1		2	2		1				8		
Fitchburg	430	16	Burnap	Jacob	3			1		2	1		1				8		
Sutton	152	5	Burnap	Timothy	4	2			2		1	1	1				11		
Southborough	205	14	Burnet	Charles R.	2	1		1		2	2		1	1			10		
Bolton	211	17	Burnham	Benjamin		1		1		1	1		1	1			6		
Bolton	211	16	Burnham	Hannah									1				1		
Bolton	207	6	Burnham	Lemuel			1			1		1					3		
Dudley	339	12	Burns	Josiah	2	1	1	1		1	1	1	1				9		
Templeton	231	8	Burpee	Samll		1							1				2		
Sterling	358	8	Burphee	Ebenezer		3	1	1		1		1	1				8		
Sterling	358	20	Burphee	Elijah	3	2		1		1			1				8		
Sterling	358	5	Burphee	Jeremiah	2	2		1	1	2			1	1			10		
Sterling	358	4	Burphee	Moses	1		2		1	1	1	1	1				8		
Sterling	355	5	Burphee	Nathan	2			1					1				4		
Sterling	358	12	Burphee	Samuel	1			1					1	1			4		
Sterling	358	15	Burphee	Thomas			1						2	2			5		
Oxford	164	16	Burr	Daniel	1	1		1		2			1				6		
Leicester	488	9	Burr	Luther	2	2		1			1		1				7		
Winchendon	223	17	Burr	Sarah		1	1						1				3		
Templeton	231	5	Burrage	Thomas		1	1	1		4			1				8		
Lunenberg	424	7	Burridge	Jonathan				1	1	1	1	1					5		
Leominster	431	14	Burridge	Josiah				1				1					2		
Leominster	431	13	Burridge	Wm				1	1	1	2	1	1				7		
Leominster	431	17	Burridge	Wm Jun	1		2	1		2			1				7		
Western	261	11	Burrough	David	1		1		1		1	2	1	1	1		9		
Western	261	13	Burrough	Tyler			1			1	1		1				4		
Petersham	271	13	Burroughs	Wellsworth	1							1					3		
Sterling	358	9	Burrs	Benjam	3	1		1		1			1				7		
Sterling	357	7	Burrs	Ebenezer				1				3	1				5		
Sterling	358	10	Burrs	Ebenezer Jun	1	1		1		2	2		1				8		
Sterling	358	7	Burrs	John	2	1		1		1			1				6		
Sterling	357	13	Burrs	Silas	1	1		1		1			1				5		
Barre	400	3	Bursley	Barnabas				1					1				2		
Petersham	274	20	Burt	Alven	2	1	1	1				1	1				7		
Leominster	431	20	Burt	Daniel	2	1		1				1	1				6		
Hardwick	295	19	Burt	Ebenz	1			1		4			1				7		
Harvard	222	7	Burt	William		1		1					1	1			4		
Bolton	207	5	Bush	Calvin	1		2	2				1	2	1			9		
Templeton	235	6	Bush	Ephraim			1			3			1				5		
Templeton	240	2	Bush	Jabez	1	3		1					1	1			7		
Templeton	237	19	Bush	Jessee		1	1	1					2				5		
Bolton	207	4	Bush	Jonathan			1			3	1		1				6		
Brookfield	256	2	Bush	Joseph	1	1		1		1	1		1				6	Second Parish	
Brookfield	256	7	Bush	Joseph W.			1										1	Second Parish	
Brookfield	256	6	Bush	Josiah	3			1		1			1				6	Second Parish	
Boylston	375	10	Bush	Jotham Cap		1	1	2		4	1	1	1	1			12		
Templeton	240	1	Bush	Stephen	2	1		1		2		1	1				8		
Sterling	358	17	Buterick	Jonathan		1	3	1				2		1			8		
Bolton	213	2	Butlar	Joseph	2			1		4			1				8		
Lancaster	345	18	Butler	Ebenezer	1	1		1			1				1		5		
Upton	390	5	Butler	Ebenezer		1	1	1				1		1			5		
Hardwick	295	21	Butler	Isaac	1	1	2	1			1		1				7		
Lancaster	348	7	Butler	Israel		1		1					1				3		
Oakham	315	16	Butler	John	2		1	1		1	2		1				8		
Upton	390	4	Butler	Peter				1					1				2		
Lancaster	345	8	Butler	Simon	2		1	1		1	1	1	1				8		
Worcester	174	16	Butler	Smith	2			1		1			1				5		
Charlton	328	17	Butler	Stephen		1		1					1				3		
Worcester	173	2	Butman	Benjamin	3	3		1		1	1		1				10		
Leominster	431	15	Butter	Abijah	1		2		1	2	2	1	2				11		
Oxford	164	15	Butter	James	1		2		1	1		2		1			8		
Leominster	431	18	Butter	Phino				1					1				2		
Hardwick	295	16	Butterfield	Aaron	2			1					1				4		
Winchendon	226	24	Buttrick	Abiel	2	1	1		1	2	1	1		1			10		
Winchendon	226	25	Buttrick	Daniel	3	1		1		1	1		1				8		
Sutton	149	13	Buxton	Enos				1					2				3		

TOWN	PG#	LN#	LAST NAME	FIRST NAME	FREE WHITE MALES					FREE WHITE FEMALES					TOTAL ALL OTHER	TOTAL SLAVES	TOTALS	DISTRICT/ TOWNSHIP	NOTES
					under 10	10 to 16	16 to 26	26 to 45	45 and over	under 10	10 to 16	16 to 26	26 to 45	45 and over					
Sutton	149	14	Buxton	Enos Junr	1	1	1		1	2	2		1				9		
Uxbridge	464	12	Buxton	Samuel			1	1	1		1	1	1				7		
Templeton	238	13	Byam	Phinehas	1				1		1			1			4		
Templeton	233	8	Byam	Samll Junr	1		1					1					3		
Templeton	233	7	Byam	Samuel				1				1	1				3		
Barre	402	1	Caldwell	David Dr.			2		1		1	1		1			6		
Sutton	156	3	Caldwell	Eliza Wd							1	1	1				3		
Lunenberg	424	12	Caldwell	Jacob		1	1		1		1	1		1			6		
Barre	402	12	Caldwell	James Maj				1									1		
Barre	402	8	Caldwell	John & Benj			3										3		
Barre	404	1	Caldwell	Moses		1	1		1		1		1	1			6		
Barre	402	10	Caldwell	Saml	1			1					1				3		
Barre	402	11	Caldwell	Seth Maj	3	2	1	3	1	2	2	1	1	2			18		
Worcester	173	13	Caldwell	William	1	1	1	1	1		1	1	2	1	1		11		
Barre	402	4	Caldwell	Wm	3		2	1	1	1		1	1				10		
Oakham	318	14	Caldwell	Wm			1			2	1		1				5		
Barre	402	5	Caldwell	Wm 3d	3	1		1	1	1			1				8		
Petersham	276	18	Calhoon	James	3			1		2			1				7		
Petersham	276	20	Calhoon	John				1									1		
Mendon	390	18	Callum	Caleb	2			1		2			1				6	2d Parish	
Mendon	390	12	Callum	Ebenezer				1					1				2	2d Parish	
Worcester	176	6	Cambell	James	2	1		1		1	1	1	1				8		
Templeton	233	12	Cambridge	Edwd				1			1			1			3		
Oxford	161	3	Campbell	Archibald			2				1		1				4		
Hardwick	296	12	Campbell	Jeremiah	1			1		1	2		1				6		
Oxford	164	20	Campbell	Saml	1	2	3		1	2	1	1	1	1	3		16		
Sutton	153	22	Cane	John			1			3			1	1			6		
Petersham	276	5	Canning	Reuben				1			1		1				3		
Grafton	197	16	Cannon	James			1			1		1					3		
Leominster	434	14	Capen	James	2	1		1		1	1		1				7		
Rutland	505	45	Capen	Lemuel		1	1			2		1					5		
Spencer	500	9	Capen	Timothy Jun		1	1		2		2	1	1	2			10		
Spencer	497	5	Capon	James Jun	1	1		1	1	1	1		2	1			9		
Athol	289	4	Capran	Ephm	1	1		1		2			1				6		
Uxbridge	463	8	Capron	Charles	2	1	2		1	1	1	1		1			10		
Uxbridge	463	2	Capron	John	3		3	1		4	2		1	1			15		
Mendon	390	15	Capron	Nathl	2			1		2			1				6	2d Parish	
Sterling	355	9	Carey	Ezra	2	2		1				2		1			8		
Oxford	161	2	Carey	William	2	1		1		1	1	1		1			8		
Ward	179	69	Cariel	Daniel			1			1				1			3		
Sutton	153	13	Carleton	Benja		1	1		1	2		1					6		
Lunenberg	424	17	Carleton	Calvin	1	1		1				1		1			4		
Sutton	154	14	Carleton	Joshua	2		1					1					4		
Fitchburg	431	12	Carlisle	Silas			1	1			1		1				4		
Garry	280	10	Carliss	Thomas	1		1						1				3		
Lunenberg	424	13	Carlton	Asahel	1	1	1	1			1	1	1				8		
Fitchburg	431	2	Carlton	Solomon		1		1				2		1			5		
Uxbridge	463	1	Carpenter	Daniel	2			2		1		1	1				7		
Douglas	477	7	Carpenter	Edmund		1	1				1		1				4		
Hardwick	296	16	Carpenter	Elijah	1			1		3	1		1				7		
Sturbridge	337	2	Carpenter	Elijah	1			1	1	1		2		1			7		
Western	257	2	Carpenter	Fredk	1		2	1		5			1				10		
Hardwick	296	14	Carpenter	Gideon	1			1	1				1	1			5		
Dudley	341	5	Carpenter	Harvey				1					1				2		
Sutton	154	15	Carpenter	John	1	1		1		1			1				5		
Uxbridge	463	12	Carpenter	Joseph	1	2			1	1		2		1			8		
Douglas	477	10	Carpenter	Nathl			1	1		4	1		1				8		
Brookfield	267	15	Carpenter	Oliver			1			3			1				5	Third Parish	
Mendon	382	14	Carpenter	Oliver			2		1	2	2		1				8	1st Parish	
Upton	387	2	Carpenter	Reuben	2	2		1		1		1	1				8		
Sutton	154	5	Carpenter	Simeon	3	1		1		1	1		1	2			10		
Sutton	153	14	Carpenter	Widos S			2					1		1			4		
Uxbridge	463	13	Carpenter	William				1		1			1				3		
Rutland	505	41	Carrell	Benjamin	1	1		1					1				4		
Garry	280	9	Carreth	James		2	2		1			1	1	1			8		
Sutton	151	15	Carriel	Aaron	1		1	1	1	2	2		1				9		
Sutton	151	18	Carriel	Henry	1		1				1	1					4		
Sutton	154	7	Carriel	Jednathan			1			2			1				4		
Sutton	151	17	Carriel	John	1	1	1	1					1				5		
Sutton	154	13	Carriel	Joseph				1						1			2		
Sutton	151	14	Carriel	Nathaniel	1			1			1	1		1			6		
Sutton	151	16	Carriel	Timothy			1			2			1				4		
Royalston	238	6	Carrol	Anna		1	2			2	1	2		2			10		
Paxton	499	12	Carruth	Ephraim			1			3			1				5		
Petersham	273	17	Carruth	Jonas			1	1			1		1				4		
Barre	402	13	Carruth	Saml	2	2	1		1	1		1	2	1			11		
Leominster	434	4	Carter	Asa		1							1	1			3		
Ward	179	67	Carter	Benjamin			1							2			3		
Berlin	214	18	Carter	Daniel	2	3		1		3			1				10		
Milford	395	4	Carter	Daniel			1		1					2			4		
Fitchburg	431	9	Carter	Elijah	1	1	2		1	1		1		1			8		
Leominster	434	7	Carter	Ephm	1		4		1			3		2			11		
Leominster	433	7	Carter	Ephm Jun	2			1		1			1	1			6		
Lancaster	348	15	Carter	Ephraim	1	3	1			1	1	2		2			11		
Dudley	341	8	Carter	Esborn	2		1	2		2		2	1	1			11		
Brookfield	255	17	Carter	Jacob											4		4	Second Parish	
Leominster	433	2	Carter	Jacob	2			1			1	1					5		
Lancaster	348	11	Carter	James	1	1	7		1	1	1	2	2				16		
Fitchburg	431	10	Carter	John		1	1	1	1	1				2			8		
Lancaster	348	13	Carter	John		1	1		1	1				2			6		

TOWN	PG#	LN#	HEADS OF HOUSEHOLD		FREE WHITE MALES					FREE WHITE FEMALES					TOTAL ALL OTHER	TOTAL SLAVES	TOTALS	DISTRICT/ TOWNSHIP	NOTES
			LAST NAME	FIRST NAME	under 10	10 to 16	16 to 26	26 to 45	45 and over	under 10	10 to 16	16 to 26	26 to 45	45 and over					
Leominster	434	5	Carter	John		1	1		1	2		2		1			8		
Petersham	273	11	Carter	John	6			1					1				8		
Leominster	434	11	Carter	Jonathan		1		1	1	1	1	1	1				7		
Lancaster	348	12	Carter	Joseph	1	1	3		1		3	2		1			12		
Sutton	153	21	Carter	Joshua	2	1		1		1	1		1				7		
Leominster	434	6	Carter	Josiah	1		1	1	1	2		2	1				9		
Leominster	434	8	Carter	Josiah Jun	5			1		1	1	1					10		
Leominster	433	8	Carter	Nathl Jun		1		1				1	1				4		
Leominster	433	9	Carter	Nathl Jun				1		2			1				4		
Lancaster	348	10	Carter	Oliver	3	1		1				1	1	1			8		
Leominster	434	17	Carter	Phinehas		1		1				2	1	1			6		
Lunenberg	424	19	Carter	Phinehas	1	2	3	1		3			1				11		
Berlin	211	1	Carter	Sanderson		1		1		2		1	1				6		
Leominster	434	10	Carter	Silas		1		1					1				3		
Leominster	434	18	Carter	Silas Jun		1						1					2		
Lancaster	348	14	Carter	Thomas	5	2		1		2			2				12		
Lunenberg	424	18	Carter	Thomas	1	2	3	1					1				8		
Leominster	433	4	Carter	Warren	1		1			1		1					4		
Dudley	341	1	Carter	William	1			1		1				1			4		
Sturbridge	337	19	Carter	William		1	1							1			4		
Shrewsbury	366	8	Cary	Peter	2		1	1		1			1				6		
Ward	179	61	Cary	Recompence	1	1	1	1		1	1		1				7		
Brookfield	255	14	Casey	Josiah	3	1		1		1	2		1				9	Second Parish	
Mendon	390	11	Cass	John	3	1		1		2			1				8	2d Parish	
Paxton	502	1	Cass	Jonathan				1					1				2		
Douglas	480	11	Caswell	Nathan	3			1		2	1		1				8		
Fitchburg	431	3	Caswell	Samuel		1	1		1			2	1				6		
Westminster	443	3	Cates	Stephen		1		1					1				3		
Mendon	390	8	Chace	Anthony				1					2				3	2d Parish	
Mendon	390	6	Chace	Coggsall		1	2		1			1	1				6	2d Parish	
Barre	402	9	Chace	Elias	1			1					1				3		
Dudley	342	32	Chace	Isaac				1					1				2		
Mendon	390	7	Chace	Timothy	1			1		1			1				4	2d Parish	
Charlton	327	28	Chace	Waite	1							2	1	1			5		
Oakham	318	5	Chadwick	Bowman	2		1	1		1	1		1				7		
Worcester	173	18	Chadwick	Daniel	2		1	1		3	1	1	1				10		
Worcester	176	1	Chadwick	Dolly	1			1		1			1				4		
Worcester	176	10	Chadwick	Isaac	2		1	1					1				5		
Brookfield	267	6	Chadwick	Joseph	2		1	1		2		1	1				8	Third Parish	
Oakham	318	13	Chadwick	Joseph		1		1		1				1			4		
Western	249	6	Chadwick	Lucy			1						2	2			5		
Worcester	176	2	Chadwick	Lydia		1							1	1			3		
Western	260	12	Chadwick	Nathan				1						1			2		
Western	260	13	Chadwick	Nathan Jr	1			1		1			1				4		
Western	257	3	Chadwick	Solomon			1					1					2		
Brookfield	267	14	Chaffee	Nathan		2		1				1	1	1			6	Third Parish	
Harvard	222	26	Chaffin	Elias				1			1						2		
Harvard	219	19	Chaffin	Gladwin	1		1	1		3	2		1				9		
Holden	515	23	Chaffin	Nathan	3	1		1		3			1				9		
Holden	515	21	Chaffin	Samuel		1	2	1				1	1	1			8		
Holden	515	22	Chaffin	Tilly	3		1	1			2		1				8		
Royalston	237	1	Chamberain	Josiah	1			1		2	1		1				6		
Southborough	205	24	Chamberlain	Abel		1		1		1	2		1				6		
Dudley	342	31	Chamberlain	Calvin	1			1		2			1				6		
Westborough	197	119	Chamberlain	Daniel		2	2	1		2	1	1	1				10		
Westborough	195	83	Chamberlain	Ebenz		1	1	1				1	1				5		
Southborough	205	1	Chamberlain	Edmind Jun		1	2	1				1	1				7		
Dudley	342	22	Chamberlain	Edward			2					1	1	1			6		
Southborough	205	26	Chamberlain	Edward				1						1			2		
Southborough	202	4	Chamberlain	Edward Junr		1				1		1					3		
Charlton	328	25	Chamberlain	Eliakim	2	2	1		1	1	1	2	1				11		
Fitchburg	431	11	Chamberlain	Elisha	2			1		2	2		1				8		
Sturbridge	337	16	Chamberlain	Ezra			1	1		3			1				6		
Dudley	342	23	Chamberlain	John	1	1	1	1		3	1	2	1				11		
Royalston	235	15	Chamberlain	John	2		1	1				1	1	1			7		
Worcester	173	12	Chamberlain	John		2	1	1		1			1	1	2		9		
Dudley	342	26	Chamberlain	Joshua		2											2		
Southborough	205	27	Chamberlain	Lemuel	2	1		1		1		1		1			11		
Dudley	342	24	Chamberlain	Luther	2	1		1				1		1			6		
Hardwick	296	9	Chamberlain	Moses		1		1	1	1					1		5		
Worcester	173	15	Chamberlain	Thads		1		1					3		1		6		
Charlton	328	23	Chamberlain	Timothy				1			1		1				3		
Worcester	173	8	Chamberlain	Willm	2		1	1		3			2				9		
Western	258	4	Chamberlain					1		2		1					4		First name left blank
Petersham	276	13	Chamberlin	Caleb	2			1					1				4		
Sutton	153	17	Chamberlin	Jacob	1	2		1		1	1	1	1				7		
Petersham	273	16	Chamberlin	Joshua	1	1		1		2			1				6		
Petersham	273	15	Chamberlin	Saml		2		1				1	1	2	1		8		
Petersham	273	8	Chamberlin	Saml Jr	3			1					1				7		
Lancaster	347	4	Chambers	David	2			1				1		1			5		
Southborough	206	13	Champney	Benjm		1	2	2					1				6		
Southborough	206	12	Champney	Jonathan		1		1	1	1			1				5		
Petersham	273	10	Chandler	Benja	2	1	1						1	1			7		
Princeton	516	6	Chandler	John			2	1		1			1				5		
Petersham	276	3	Chandler	John Esq			3	2				2	2	1			10		
Hardwick	297	7	Chandler	Josiah	1		1	1				1					5		
Worcester	173	11	Chandler	Samuel		3	1						1				5		
Worcester	176	14	Chandler	Sarah		1				1		1	1				4		
Petersham	273	14	Chandler	Willm	3			1		1	1		1				7		

176

TOWN	PG#	LN#	LAST NAME	FIRST NAME	FREE WHITE MALES under 10	10 to 16	16 to 26	26 to 45	45 and over	FREE WHITE FEMALES under 10	10 to 16	16 to 26	26 to 45	45 and over	TOTAL ALL OTHER	TOTAL SLAVES	TOTALS	DISTRICT/ TOWNSHIP	NOTES
Milford	396	34	Chapin	Adam	1	2	2		1	1		1	1				9		
Uxbridge	463	3	Chapin	Amariah	2	1		1		2			1				7		
Bolton	215	9	Chapin	Coffin	2		1			1			1				5		
Upton	387	1	Chapin	David	2		2	1		1	2		1				9		
Mendon	382	11	Chapin	Ebenezer				1						1			2	1st Parish	
Mendon	382	12	Chapin	Ebenezer Jr	1	1		1		2	1	2		1			10	1st Parish	
Worcester	173	9	Chapin	Elijah	1		1		1	3	1	1	1				9		
Milford	396	28	Chapin	Ephm Lt.			2		1			1		1			5		
Uxbridge	463	6	Chapin	Gershom			2		1		1	2		1			7		
Northbridge	475	16	Chapin	Henry	3		4	1					1				9		
Milford	395	9	Chapin	Joel	1		2			1		1	1				6		
Milford	395	7	Chapin	John Deac		1		1	1	1		1	1	1			6		
Uxbridge	463	9	Chapin	Joseph			1	1						1			3		
Milford	396	29	Chapin	Levi	1	1		1		2		1	1				7		
Milford	395	5	Chapin	Marvel	1			1		2			1				5		
Milford	395	3	Chapin	Mary Wd										1			1		
Milford	395	11	Chapin	Moses			2		1			1		1			5		
Uxbridge	463	10	Chapin	Moses	2		1	1					1				5		
Milford	395	12	Chapin	Nathan Lt	2			1			1	1		1			6		
Uxbridge	463	7	Chapin	Phinehas			1		1	3		2					6		
Mendon	382	10	Chapin	Seth Deac		1	1		1	2	1	1		1			8	1st Parish	
Milford	395	10	Chapin	Stephen		1	1	1						1			4		
Worcester	173	10	Chapin	Thads	1		2	1			3		1				8		
Lancaster	347	6	Chaplin	Joseph	1	1		1					1				4		
Lunenberg	424	11	Chaplin	Joseph				1			1			1			3		
Sutton	153	16	Chaplin	Revd Ebenza		1	1		1					1			4		
Worcester	176	13	Chapman	Abel			1					1					2		
Gardner	451	17	Chappell	William				1			2			1			4		
Sutton	153	6	Chase	Abel	1	1		1		1				1			5		
Sutton	153	7	Chase	Abel 3rd	3			1		1			1				6		
Sutton	153	20	Chase	Abel Junr			1		1		2	1	1				7		
Douglas	477	17	Chase	Amasa	1		2		1		2		1	1			8		
Sutton	153	1	Chase	Ambrose		1	1			1		1					4		
Royalston	241	19	Chase	Archebald	1	1	1	1	1	3		1	1				10		
Douglas	477	13	Chase	Asa	1			1		2	1		1				6		
Sutton	154	17	Chase	Caleb				1						1			2		
Lancaster	348	9	Chase	Charles	2	1		1		1			1				6		
Winchendon	225	10	Chase	Charles	1			1		2		1					5		
Douglas	477	5	Chase	David		1	1	2		1				1			6		
Royalston	238	1	Chase	David	2	2		1		2	1		1				9		
Sutton	153	18	Chase	David P.		1	1		1				1				4		
Athol	289	6	Chase	Ebenz			1					1					2		
Leominster	434	9	Chase	John	3		2	2		1	3	1	1				13		
Paxton	499	15	Chase	Jonathan	1	1	1		1		1	1	2	1			9		
Douglas	477	16	Chase	Joseph		3		1		3			1				8		
Sutton	153	4	Chase	Joshua	1	1		1		2	1		1				7		
Sutton	153	3	Chase	March				1		1			1				3		
Worcester	176	8	Chase	Matilda						1	1		1				3		
Leominster	433	3	Chase	Metaphor	2	1	2	1		2	1	2	1				12		
Athol	290	30	Chase	Moses	1		1				1						3		
Sutton	154	19	Chase	Moses	2		1						1				4		
Sutton	153	5	Chase	Nathan	1	1		1		2	1		1				7		
Sutton	154	18	Chase	Nehemiah	1	2	1		1	1		1	1				8		
Petersham	273	20	Chase	Peter	1	1		1		1		2	1				7		
Royalston	241	32	Chase	Roger		1							2	1			5		
Sutton	153	2	Chase	Samuel			1						1				2		
Royalston	242	15	Chase	Silas	1	1		1		1	1		1				6		
Leominster	433	1	Chase	Stephen		1			1					1			3		
Sutton	153	19	Chase	Thaddeus	1			1		1			1				4		
Sutton	151	19	Chase	Thomas F.	2		1	1		3	1	1	1	1			11		
Fitchburg	431	4	Chase	Warren			1			4			1	1			7		
Douglas	480	10	Chase	William	2			1			1		1				5		
Royalston	238	2	Chase	William	1		1	1		2		1	1				7		
Barre	404	2	Chattock	Ezekiel		1		1			2		1				5		
Ward	179	66	Cheeney	Aquilla			1				1		1				3		
Ward	179	62	Cheeney	Ephm		1		1	1	1	2	1	1				7		
Holden	516	7	Cheeney	Isaac	2	1	1		1		1	1	1	1			9		
Ward	179	65	Cheeney	Joseph		1		1			1		1				4		
Holden	515	19	Cheeney	Josephus			1					1					2		
Holden	515	18	Cheeney	Josiah			1						1				2		
Holden	516	1	Cheeney	S Clark		2		1		2			1				6		
Princeton	516	7	Cheever	Daniel	3			1		2	2		1				9		
Brookfield	255	15	Cheever	Samuel	2	2			1		1	3	1				10	Second Parish	
Milford	396	30	Cheney	Caleb	2			1					1				4		
Milford	395	13	Cheney	Calvin			1			1		1					3		
Milford	396	32	Cheney	Charles			1			2		1					4		
Royalston	235	8	Cheney	Elisha	3	1			1	1	2	1	2				11		
Milford	396	31	Cheney	Mary Wd			1				1	1	1				4		
Sutton	153	12	Cheney	Nathaniel		1	1		1	2	2			1			8		
Dudley	342	25	Cheney	Thomas		2	2		1	1	2		1				10		
Milford	396	35	Cheney	Wales			1	1		1		1					4		
Sturbridge	340	19	Cheny	Joseph			2	1				2		1			6		
Sturbridge	340	20	Cheny	Nathan	1		2	1		1	1	1	1				8		
Hardwick	297	6	Chess	Luther			1				3		1				5		
Western	257	5	Chickering	Nathll	1	1	1	1		1	1	1	1				8		
Rutland	505	40	Chickering	Oliver		1			1					1			3		
Shrewsbury	366	9	Chickering	Oliver			1			1			1				3		
Holden	516	2	Chickering	Samuel	2	1	1		1			1	1				7		
Rutland	505	36	Child	Abiathar	1		2		1	2	1			1			8		

177

TOWN	PG#	LN#	LAST NAME	FIRST NAME	FWM under 10	FWM 10 to 16	FWM 16 to 26	FWM 26 to 45	FWM 45 and over	FWF under 10	FWF 10 to 16	FWF 16 to 26	FWF 26 to 45	FWF 45 and over	TOTAL ALL OTHER	TOTAL SLAVES	TOTALS	DISTRICT/ TOWNSHIP	NOTES
Sturbridge	337	3	Child	Abijah	4	1		1	1		1	1		1			10		
Rutland	505	37	Child	Amherst	5			1		1			3				10		
Boylston	377	10	Child	Amos			1			4	1		1				7		
Worcester	176	7	Child	Benjamin				1			1		1				3		
Boylston	377	9	Child	David				1					2				3		
Hardwick	296	19	Child	Ebenz	3	1	2		1			2		2			11		
Grafton	206	8	Child	Elizabeth				1					1				2		
Sturbridge	337	13	Child	Ephraim			1			3			1				5		
Sturbridge	337	4	Child	Isaac	2			1					1				4		
Charlton	327	23	Child	John			2	1			1		1				5		
Sturbridge	337	5	Child	Joseph		1	1					2		1			5		
Worcester	176	12	Child	Moses	2			1					1				4		
Sturbridge	337	7	Child	Rufus		1		1		2	1		1				6		
Rutland	505	35	Child	Thomas	1			1					1	2			5		
Templeton	239	17	Child	William	1	1		1		2	1		1				7		
Boylston	377	15	Child	Zechariah	3	1		1		2	3		1				11		
Upton	390	20	Childs	Asa Lt.	2	1		1	1	2		2		1			10		
Gardner	451	11	Childs	Daniel	1	2	1		1	4	1		1				11		
Sutton	156	2	Childs	Daniel				1					2				3		
Westminster	444	16	Childs	David		1	1				2		1				6		
Upton	390	21	Childs	John	1	2	1	1	1	1			1				8		
Barre	402	7	Childs	Jona	3	1		1		1	3		2	2			13		
Westminster	444	18	Childs	Joseph	1			1					1				3		
Princeton	516	3	Chillenden	Isaac	1	1		1		1	2	1		2			9		
Brookfield	267	11	Chillson	Levi	3	2		1		1	1		1				9	Third Parish	
Uxbridge	463	15	Chilson	Israel	4			1					1				6		
Uxbridge	463	4	Chilson	Jeremiah				1				1	1				3		
Boylston	377	8	Chinnery	Thaddeus	3			1		1	1						6		
Barre	402	3	Chipman	Perez			1	1				1					3		
Barre	402	2	Chipman	Stephen	2		2	1					1				6		
Lunenberg	424	20	Choate	Robert	2	1		1		2			1				7		
Royalston	237	10	Chubb	Silas	1	1	1		1	1	2	1	1				9		
Holden	516	3	Church	Alexander		1		1		2			1				5		
Hubbardston	415	33	Church	Asa Capt.	3	2	1		1			2		1			10		
Templeton	234	15	Church	Nathan		1		1		1	1	1		1			6		
Athol	289	2	Church	Paul	1			1		2			1				5		
Templeton	234	4	Church	Silas		2	3	1		1	1			2			10		
Sterling	355	12	Churchell	Samuel		1	1	1		1	1			1			6		
Lunenberg	423	8	Chute	George W.			1						1				2		
Lunenberg	423	7	Chute	Paul G.	2			1		1			1	1			6		
Milford	395	6	Claflin	John			3						2				5		
Douglas	477	6	Claflin	Oliver	3			1		1		1	1				7		
Rutland	505	42	Clap	Asahel			1	1			1	1	1				5		
Uxbridge	463	11	Clap	Eleazer	1	2		1				1		1			6		
Brookfield	248	31	Clap	Elijah		2	1	1			3		2				9	First Parish	
Lunenberg	423	6	Clap	Ezra				1					1				2		
Grafton	204	13	Clap	Jeremiah	1		1			1	1						4		
Templeton	238	10	Clap	Jonas	3	1		1		2			1				8		
Charlton	327	20	Clap	Mathew S.	2			1		2		1	1				7		
Royalston	241	27	Clap	Nehemiah	1	1	2	1					3	1			9		
Petersham	276	11	Clap	Samuel	1			1		1			1				4		
Holden	516	4	Clap	Seth	2		1		1	2	1			1			8		
Gardner	451	8	Clap	Stephen			1			1			1				3		
Hubbardston	415	36	Clark	Aaron R.	1	1		1		1		1					5		
Hubbardston	415	41	Clark	Amos	1			1		1	1	1			5		10		
Athol	289	7	Clark	Benja	2	2			1	1	1			1			8		
Princeton	516	8	Clark	Benjamin	3	2		1			1	1	1				9		
Petersham	273	21	Clark	David		1		1					1	1			4		
Ashburnham	457	15	Clark	David Jr	2			1		4			1				8		
Sturbridge	340	17	Clark	Ebenzr	2	1	2	1			1	1	1				9		
Hardwick	296	20	Clark	Edward		1	1	1			1		1				5		
Petersham	273	12	Clark	Edwd		1	1					1					3		
Hubbardston	415	28	Clark	Eli Lt.		2	1	1		2		1		1			9		
Sutton	154	12	Clark	Erasmus		1							1				2		
Hubbardston	415	20	Clark	Ezra	3	1		1		1		1	1				8		
Brookfield	267	3	Clark	Francis		2	3	1		1				2			9	Third Parish	
Brookfield	267	4	Clark	Francis O	2			1					1				4	Third Parish	
Petersham	276	1	Clark	Hardin	3			1		1		1					6		
Sturbridge	340	16	Clark	Henry		1	1	1	1	4			1	1			10		
Hardwick	296	15	Clark	Isaac		1	1	1			1	1		1			6		
Hubbardston	415	23	Clark	Isaac	4	1		1			2						8		
Sturbridge	340	13	Clark	Isaac	1			1		2			1				5		
Hardwick	297	3	Clark	Isaac Jr	1	1		1		1	1		1				7		
Brookfield	255	7	Clark	James			1	1			3		1				6	Second Parish	
Hubbardston	415	27	Clark	Jenny Wid								1	1		2		4		
Sturbridge	340	15	Clark	Jepthed		2		1		4		1	1				9		
Barre	404	3	Clark	John		1				2		1					4		
Charlton	327	18	Clark	John		1	1			3			1				6		
Ward	179	59	Clark	John	1	1		1				1	1				5		
Hubbardston	415	35	Clark	John Capt.				1				2					3		
Hubbardston	415	19	Clark	John Jr		2	1	1		1	3			1			9		
Petersham	276	2	Clark	Jonah		1		1		1		1		1			5		
Harvard	221	8	Clark	Jonathan			1	1					2				4		
Hubbardston	415	24	Clark	Joseph	2	2	1	1		1		2	1				10		
Ward	179	57	Clark	Joseph				1						1	1		3		
Milford	395	14	Clark	Lovell	2			1		2			1				6		
Hubbardston	415	37	Clark	Luther	2	1		1		1		1					6		
Harvard	217	23	Clark	Matthew	1			1		1	1	1					5		
Hubbardston	415	22	Clark	Moses	2	1	2	1			2	1	2				12		
Sturbridge	340	14	Clark	Moses	1			1					1	1			4		
Petersham	273	13	Clark	Nathl	2	1	1	1		2			2				9		

178

TOWN	PG#	LN#	LAST NAME	FIRST NAME	FREE WHITE MALES under 10	10 to 16	16 to 26	26 to 45	45 and over	FREE WHITE FEMALES under 10	10 to 16	16 to 26	26 to 45	45 and over	TOTAL ALL OTHER	TOTAL SLAVES	TOTALS	DISTRICT/ TOWNSHIP	NOTES
Princeton	516	5	Clark	Norman	1	1		1	1		3		1				8		
Bolton	216	1	Clark	Peter	1			1				1					3		
Hubbardston	415	26	Clark	Peter	3			1			2		1		1		8		
Sturbridge	337	8	Clark	Rufus				1						2			3		
Hubbardston	415	25	Clark	Saml	1		2		1	2	1		1				8		
Ward	179	60	Clark	Samuel			1			1		1					3		
Hardwick	297	8	Clark	Simeon	3			1		1		1					6		
Sturbridge	340	18	Clark	Solomon	2		2					1					5		
Oxford	161	7	Clark	Thomas				1					1				2		
Hubbardston	415	29	Clark	Thos	2			1		1	1		1				6		
Barre	402	6	Clark	Wm		2		1	2				3	2			10		
Lunenberg	424	15	Clark	Wm				1						3			4		
Hubbardston	415	21	Clark	Wm.	1	3		1		1	1	1		1			9		
Paxton	499	14	Clarke	Amos	1	1		1		3	1	1	1				9		
Westborough	194	63	Clarke	Benjm		1		1				2					4		
Lancaster	348	17	Clarke	James			1		1				1				3		
Spencer	500	10	Clarke	John			1			3			1				5		
Sterling	355	11	Clarke	Samuel			2		1		2		1				6		
Paxton	499	13	Clarke	Simeon	1	2		1	1			3	1	1			10		
Charlton	327	26	Cleavland	Edward		1		1		1		1					4		
Petersham	276	14	Clements	John	1	2	1		1	1	1		1				8		
Petersham	276	9	Clements	John Jr			1					1					2		
Petersham	276	7	Clements	Mary			1			1			1				3		
Petersham	276	4	Clements	Saml		1		1			1		1				4		
Petersham	276	8	Clements	Thomas				1			1						2		
Royalston	238	4	Clements	Widow								1	1				2		
Royalston	242	5	Clements	Wm		1	1	1		2	1	2	1				9		
Sturbridge	337	14	Clemons	Aaron	1		2			1	1	1					6		
Charlton	328	27	Clemons	Asa	3	1		1		2		1	1				9		
Charlton	327	1	Clemons	Benjm				1					1				2		
Charlton	327	2	Clemons	Benjm Jun		1						1					2		
Charlton	327	3	Clemons	Ebenzr	1	1	1			1		1					5		
Charlton	327	8	Clemons	Jacob	1			1		1		1					4		
Charlton	328	29	Clemons	Jonathan		1		1					1				3		
Charlton	328	28	Clemons	Jonathan Junr		1		1		4		1	1				8		
Charlton	328	26	Clemons	Phillip		1		1			2	2	1				7		
Charlton	327	24	Clemons	Reuben		1		1		2			1				5		
Sturbridge	337	12	Clemons	Richard	3		1		1		1	1		1			8		
Gardner	451	6	Clerk	Benjamin	1			1		4	1		1				8		
Ashburnham	457	16	Clerk	Daniel		1		1		3	1		1				7		
Ashburnham	457	7	Clerk	David				1					1				2		
Gardner	451	5	Clerk	Joseph		1		1					1				3		
Hardwick	296	4	Cleveland	Ebenz	3			1		1			1				6		
Hardwick	296	13	Cleveland	Elijah	3			1		3		1	1				9		
Hardwick	296	8	Cleveland	Ephraim	2		1	1		3	1		1	1			10		
Hardwick	297	2	Cleveland	Joseph		3		1			2	1		1			8		
Worcester	176	9	Cleveland	Thomas	1		1			1		1					4		
Lancaster	347	1	Cleverly	John				1					1				2		
Hubbardston	415	32	Clifford	Jonath	2		1		1	2	1	2	1				10		
Charlton	327	27	Clough	Obediah				1					1				2		
Shrewsbury	366	4	Cloyes	Eunice	1					1		1					3		
Garry	280	4	Cluney	James		1	1		1			2	1	1			7		
Hardwick	296	6	Cobb	Ebenz	1	1		1					1				4		
Westborough	189	4	Cobb	Edward	3	2	1		1	1			1				9		
Hardwick	296	5	Cobb	Gershom	3	1		1			1			1			7		
Garry	280	13	Cobb	Jacob	2			1		2	1		1				7		
Hardwick	296	10	Cobb	Lemll		1		1		1	1		1				5		
Milford	395	1	Cobb	Lewis	3			1				1					5		
New Braintree	308	19	Cobb	Perez	2			1	1		1			1			6		
Hardwick	295	22	Cobb	Sherabiah		2		1			1	1	1				6		
Hardwick	297	1	Cobb	Sylvanus		3		1		2	2	1	1				10		
Ashburnham	457	6	Cobleigh	Ephraim		1		1					1				3		
Templeton	236	1	Cobley	David				1		1			1				3		
Templeton	233	19	Cobley	John	1	1	1	1				1	1	1			7		
Dudley	341	4	Coburn	Edward					1	1	1		1				4		
Sturbridge	337	10	Coburn	Edward	1			1		1			1				4		
Charlton	328	24	Coburn	Jacob	1			1		1		1					4		
Charlton	327	4	Coburn	John	1	1		1		1			1				5		
Sturbridge	340	21	Coburn	John	1	1		1		3	1		1				8		
Charlton	327	7	Coburn	John Junr	3		1	1		1			1				7		
Charlton	327	9	Coburn	Joseph	1		1			2		1					5		
Oxford	161	1	Coburn	Richard		1			2			1		1			5		
Oxford	161	4	Coburn	Samuel	1		1						1				3		
Sturbridge	337	15	Coburn	Zacheus	1			1				1		1			4		
Dudley	341	7	Cody	John	1	1		1	1	2			1	1			9		
Worcester	176	5	Coes	John	3			1	1	1	1		1				7		
Winchendon	225	9	Coffin	George	2			1		2	1		1				7		
Rutland	505	43	Coggswell	Stephen	1	1		1		2	2		1				8		
Paxton	502	2	Coggswell	Aaron			1			2			1				4		
Paxton	499	17	Coggswell	Ebenn				1						2			3		
Lunenberg	424	22	Coggswell	Wm	2	1		1		1	1	2		2			10		
Holden	516	5	Colburn	Alpheus			1						1				2		
Leominster	434	3	Colburn	Ebenz	3		1			1	1	1					7		
Lancaster	347	3	Colburn	Eijah	2		1			1		1					5		
Leominster	434	15	Colburn	Elisha	2		1						1				4		
Leominster	434	16	Colburn	John	1	1	1		1	1		2		1			8		
Leominster	434	12	Colburn	Jona		1		1				2		1			5		
Leominster	434	13	Colburn	Nathan	2		1		1	1		2	3	1			11		
Leominster	433	5	Colburn	Nathaniel	1				1	1		1	1				5		

TOWN	PG#	LN#	LAST NAME	FIRST NAME	FREE WHITE MALES under 10	10 to 16	16 to 26	26 to 45	45 and over	FREE WHITE FEMALES under 10	10 to 16	16 to 26	26 to 45	45 and over	TOTAL ALL OTHER	TOTAL SLAVES	TOTALS	DISTRICT/ TOWNSHIP	NOTES
Sterling	355	14	Colburn	Paul	2			1		2			1				6		
Leominster	434	2	Colburn	Pliny	3			1					1				5		
Holden	516	6	Colburn	Thaddeus	1			1	1	3			1				7		
Sutton	154	11	Cole	Abel		1		1				1					3		
Sutton	154	9	Cole	David	1			1		1		2					5		
Garry	280	8	Cole	Elkanah	1	1			1	2	1	1	1	1			9		
Gardner	451	7	Cole	John	2			1		1			1				5		
Sutton	154	8	Cole	John				2			1		1				4		
Sutton	154	3	Cole	Stephen	2	2		1		2			1				8		
Oxford	164	21	Collar	James	3	2	1	1	1	1	2	1	1	1			14		
Douglas	477	4	Collar	Jonas				1			1		1				3		
Charlton	327	22	Coller	Ezra	1			1				1					3		
Charlton	327	21	Coller	John	1			1		2			1				5		
Western	257	4	Collester	Samuel				1		1			1				3		
Hardwick	296	7	Collings	Jonah			1			1		1					3		
Hardwick	296	1	Collings	Rachel		1	1					1		1			4		
Southborough	205	5	Collins	Aaron	3			1				1					5		
Sutton	154	10	Collins	Benjamin		1	1	1				1					4		
Southborough	205	8	Collins	John	2			1				1					4		
Southborough	205	4	Collins	Mark				1					1				2		
Southborough	206	24	Collins	Mark	1	1	1		1	1			1				6		
Southborough	206	23	Collins	William				1					1				2		
Southborough	206	25	Collins	William Jun			1					1					2		
Western	260	11	Collis	John		1	1		1		1	2		1			7		
Western	260	9	Collister	William	2		2	1		2	1	1					9		
Brookfield	248	28	Combs	Jacob	1		2		1	2	2	1					9	First Parish	
Western	260	6	Combs	John Jr	1	1			2			1					5		
Northbridge	475	15	Combs	Reuben	2			1				1					4		
Gardner	451	12	Comee	David		1		1		3	1	1	1				8		
Gardner	451	13	Comee	David Jr			3					1					4		
Sutton	153	11	Comings	Allen				1		3		1					5		
Sutton	153	10	Comings	Asa		1		1		1	1	1					5		
Sutton	153	8	Comings	Jacob				1			1	1					3		
Sutton	154	1	Comings	Jacon Junr	2	1	2		1	1	1	1		2			11		
Sutton	153	9	Comings	Jesse		1	2		1		1			1			6		
Sutton	154	2	Comings	Jonathan				1				1					2		
Sutton	154	4	Comings	P. Widow						2		1					3		
Charlton	327	19	Comins	Barnabas			1	1		3		1					6		
Ward	179	64	Comins	Daniel	2	2		1		2		1					8		
Charlton	327	5	Comins	Free	2	1	1		1	1		1	1				8		
Charlton	327	14	Comins	James	2	1		1		1			1				6		
Ward	179	70	Comins	Rachel							1		1				2		
Charlton	327	16	Comins	Reuben				1					1				2		
Charlton	327	17	Comins	Reuben Junr		1		1		1		1	1				5		
Charlton	327	13	Comins	Wm	2	1		1		3		1					8		
Charlton	327	12	Commins	Cooledge				1		1		1					3		
Leicester	488	12	Comstock	George			1		1			1		1			4		
Northborough	367	12	Con	Polly								1					1		
Oxford	161	5	Conant	Asa				1		1			1				3		
Charlton	328	22	Conant	Harvey			1				1						2		
Oakham	318	15	Conant	James	2	1	1	1		3	1	1	1				11		
Sturbridge	337	17	Conant	Jonathan				1				1	1				3		
Dudley	341	11	Conant	Josiah	1		1	1		1			1				5		
Gardner	451	16	Conant	Josiah	2	1		1		3	2		1				10		
Harvard	219	29	Conant	Levi	1	1		1		2			1				6		
Oakham	318	11	Conant	Luther		2		1		3	1		1				8		
Oakham	318	6	Conant	Oliver	1		1			1		1					4		
Dudley	341	12	Conant	Rufus	2			1		2	1		1				7		
Sterling	355	10	Conant	Samuel			2		1	2	2		2				9		
Lunenberg	423	4	Conant	Simeon	4			1		2	1		1				9		
Westminster	444	17	Conant	Thomas	1			1						1			3		
Westminster	443	1	Conant	Thomas Jr	2			1			1		1				5		
Oakham	318	10	Conant	Thos	5			1					1				7		
Harvard	219	30	Conant	William			1							1			2		
Harvard	220	12	Cond	George			1		1		1			1			4		
Fitchburg	431	5	Condin	Hannah			1			1	2	1	1	1			7		
Fitchburg	431	13	Condin	James	1	1		1		1	1						6		
Fitchburg	431	6	Condin	Thomas	1	1	2		1	1	1	2		1			10		
Westminster	443	2	Cones	James		1		1		1		1					4		
Brookfield	248	26	Coney	Daniel	3		1	1				1					6	First Parish	
Northbridge	475	14	Congdon	Joshua	4		1					1					6		
Templeton	235	13	Conlin	Benja	1			1		1		1					4		
Ashburnham	457	10	Conn	John				1					1				2		
Ashburnham	457	14	Conn	John Jr	1			1			1		1				4		
Worcester	176	11	Conner	Edward	1			1		1			1				4		
Petersham	276	6	Conner	Joseph											2		2		
Ashburnham	457	17	Constantine	Jacob	1	1	1		1		2	1					7		
Spencer	497	4	Convers	Daniel		2	2	1			1	2		1			9		
Leicester	488	13	Convers	Joshua		1		1				1		2			5		
Leicester	487	1	Convers	Reuben	2			1		2			1				6		
Brookfield	255	11	Converse	James		1			2				2	1			6	Second Parish	
Charlton	327	11	Converse	Luke			1		1	1		1		1			5		
Brookfield	255	12	Converse	Samuel	1			1		2		1					5	Second Parish	
Brookfield	248	27	Cony	William			1		1		1						4	First Parish	
Lancaster	348	16	Cook	Aaron	1		1		2			2					6		
Mendon	390	9	Cook	Adanis	3		1		1			1					6	2d Parish	
Mendon	390	3	Cook	Arthur	1			2		2			2				7	2d Parish	
Templeton	242	2	Cook	Cyrus		1					1	1					4		

TOWN	PG#	LN#	LAST NAME	FIRST NAME	FREE WHITE MALES					FREE WHITE FEMALES					TOTAL ALL OTHER	TOTAL SLAVES	TOTALS	DISTRICT/ TOWNSHIP	NOTES
					under 10	10 to 16	16 to 26	26 to 45	45 and over	under 10	10 to 16	16 to 26	26 to 45	45 and over					
Mendon	390	16	Cook	Daniel				1						1			2	2d Parish	
Douglas	480	13	Cook	Ebenezer	2		1			1		1					5		
Garry	280	11	Cook	Elisha	1		1	1		2		1	1				7		
Lunenberg	424	14	Cook	Enoch	1	2		1		2		1		1			8		
Mendon	390	1	Cook	Ezekiel	1			1		1			1				4	2d Parish	
Lancaster	347	2	Cook	Finnis			1										1		
Worcester	173	17	Cook	George	2	1		1			1		1				6		
Mendon	390	4	Cook	Ichabod	1	1	2		1			2		1			8	2d Parish	
Douglas	480	15	Cook	Jesse			1			2		1					4		
Mendon	390	14	Cook	John	1			1					1				3	2d Parish	
Winchendon	225	12	Cook	John			1			2			1				4		
Westborough	195	80	Cook	Jonathan				1						1			2		
Mendon	390	10	Cook	Joseph	2			1		2		1					6	2d Parish	
Mendon	390	17	Cook	Margaret								2	1				3	2d Parish	
Mendon	390	13	Cook	Pasco	2			1		1			1				5	2d Parish	
Templeton	238	12	Cook	Samll		1	1	1				2		1			6		
Mendon	390	5	Cook	Stephen	1			1	1	1	2			1			8	2d Parish	
Mendon	390	2	Cook	Thaddeus	2	1		1		1		2	1				8	2d Parish	
Bolton	215	14	Cooledge	Isaiah	1		1						1				3		
Gardner	451	10	Cooledge	James		2		1				1		1			5		
Worcester	173	14	Cooledge	Nathaniel	3	2	1	1		3			2				12		
Bolton	213	13	Cooledge	Phillip			1						1				2		
Bolton	216	19	Cooledge	Silas		2		1		1	1	1					6		
Brookfield	267	9	Cooley	Ephraim	1		1		1		1		1				5	Third Parish	
Brookfield	267	13	Cooley	Moses			1					1					2	Third Parish	
Brookfield	267	10	Cooley	Obadiah		1		1				2					4	Third Parish	
Brookfield	267	5	Cooley	Obadiah Junr	2		1	1		1	1	1	1				8	Third Parish	
Berlin	213	18	Coolidge	Stephen	3	1		1		1	1	1	1				9		
Barre	404	4	Coolidge	Thoms				1		2		1					4		
Westminster	443	4	Cooper	Jedidiah		1		1		1		1		1			5		
Northbridge	476	1	Cooper	John		2	1		1	1		2	1				8		
Northbridge	475	13	Cooper	Nathll		2	2	1		1		1		1			8		
Sturbridge	337	18	Copeland	Daniel	1		1	1		2			1				6		
Princeton	516	10	Copeland	Eliphalet	3			1		1	1		1				7		
Leicester	488	15	Copeland	Ephraim	2			1		1			1				5		
Westborough	192	47	Corbet	Elisha	3	1	1	1		1		1	1				9		
Milford	396	27	Corbett	Ichabod	1	2		1		2	1	1					9		
Milford	395	2	Corbett	John	1	2		1		3			1				8		
Dudley	341	14	Corbin	Ephraim				1						1			2		
Dudley	342	30	Corbin	Hannah						2			1	1			4		
Dudley	342	27	Corbin	Jedediah	3	1	2		1	2	1	1	1				12		
Dudley	341	13	Corbin	Joshua	3	1		1		1	1	2	1				10		
Dudley	342	29	Corbin	Leml Junr	1			1		1	1	1					5		
Dudley	342	28	Corbin	Lemuel			1		1	1	1		1				5		
Dudley	341	15	Corbin	Rufus			1						1				2		
Dudley	341	6	Corbin	Timothy	2			1		2	1	1		1			8		
Douglas	480	14	Corbit	Edward			1							1			2		
Western	260	8	Cordee	William	1		1	1		1	1	1	1				7		
Holden	516	8	Cordwell	Martha	2					1			1				4		
Ashburnham	457	3	Corey	Hezekiah			1	1		1	1	1	1	1			7		
Ashburnham	457	5	Corey	Hezekiah Jr	1		1			4		1					7		
Ashburnham	457	12	Corey	John	3		1			1		1					6		
Gardner	454	11	Corey	Stephen	1		1			2		1					5		
Milford	395	8	Cornell	Philip		1	1	1	1			1	1				6		
Douglas	477	8	Corrary	Benja				2						1			3		
Northborough	367	14	Corruth	John				1						1			2		
Northborough	367	13	Corruth	Joseph			2				1	1					4		
Brookfield	255	8	Corruth	Nathan		1	1		1			1		1			5	Second Parish	
Sturbridge	337	1	Cory	David	1			1		3	2	1	1	1			10		
Sturbridge	340	22	Cory	Jacob		2		1		2		2		1			8		
Dudley	342	33	Cotril	Benja			2	1	1			1	1				6		
Dudley	342	21	Cotril	Thomas	3			1				1	1				6		
Harvard	221	18	Cotton	Edward			1							1			2		
Harvard	221	20	Cotton	John	1	1	1		1		1						6		
Harvard	221	35	Cotton	Josiah	1	1		1		2			1				6		
Boylston	377	14	Cotton	Ward Revd			1						2		1		4		
Sterling	355	13	Coulton	William	1			1						1			3		
Hardwick	297	4	Covel	Philip	4		1				1		1				7		
Rutland	505	34	Cowden	James	1	1		1	1	2		1	1				8		
Lunenberg	423	2	Cowdry	Ezra	3			1		1	1		1				7		
Gardner	451	15	Cower	David	1	1		1					1				4		
Gardner	451	14	Cower	James	2	1		1		4		1	1				10		
Hardwick	296	18	Cox	Elizabeth		1						1		1			3		
Western	257	1	Crabtree	John Jur	1	1		2	1	2			1	1			9		
Oakham	318	9	Crafford	Alexander			1			3	1		1				6		
Oakham	318	7	Crafford	Calvin	3		1						1				5		
Oakham	318	8	Crafford	John		1			1	4	2		1				9		
Oakham	318	12	Crafford	Wm	1	1	2		1	1	1	2		1			10		
Douglas	477	9	Craggin	Benjamin		1	1			2		1					5		
Mendon	382	13	Craggin	John		1		1	1		1	2		1			7	1st Parish	
Douglas	477	14	Craggin	Timothy			1			1		2					4		
Fitchburg	431	7	Crague	William	1		1			1		1	1				5		
Ward	179	58	Craige	Abijah	1	1		1			1		1				5		
Leicester	487	2	Craige	Amos		1		1		1			1				4		
Charlton	327	6	Craige	David		1				4		1	1				8		
Rutland	505	44	Craige	David	1			1		2			1				5		
Worcester	173	16	Craige	Jesse	2	2		2			1	1	1				9		
Spencer	497	3	Craige	Nathan	1		1			1	1	1	1				6		
Leicester	487	3	Craige	Robert	1			1						1			3		
Brookfield	248	25	Crandal	Caleb	1		1			1			1				4	First Parish	

TOWN	PG#	LN#	LAST NAME	FIRST NAME	M under 10	M 10 to 16	M 16 to 26	M 26 to 45	M 45 and over	F under 10	F 10 to 16	F 16 to 26	F 26 to 45	F 45 and over	TOTAL ALL OTHER	TOTAL SLAVES	TOTALS	DISTRICT/ TOWNSHIP	NOTES
Oxford	161	8	Crane	Gilbert				2		1			2				5		
Northbridge	475	17	Crane	John	2	2	4	1			2		1				12		
Oxford	161	6	Crane	Lemuel	1	1	1		1			2		1			7		
Northborough	367	15	Crawford	John	1		1	2		2	1	1	1				9		
Ashburnham	457	11	Crehore	Timothy	1	1	2		1		1		1				7		
Paxton	499	16	Crocker	Nathl	2	3		1	1	1			1	1			10		
Lunenberg	424	10	Crocker	Paul				1					1	1	1		3		
Northbridge	475	12	Croney	John		1			1	1		1		1			5		
Leominster	433	6	Crooker	Samuel			1					1					2		
Winchendon	225	11	Crooks	Henry	2		1		1	1	2	1		1			9		
Brookfield	267	12	Crosby	Amos	2			1		1			1				5	Third Parish	
Ashburnham	457	8	Crosby	Fitch	1			1				1					3		
Winchendon	225	5	Crosby	Flavel	2	1	1		1	1			1				7		
Ashburnham	457	9	Crosby	Fredrick	1	3		1		3			1				9		
Brookfield	267	7	Crosby	Jabez				1			1		1				3	Third Parish	
Sturbridge	337	11	Crosby	Jeremiah	2			1	1	1			1	1			7		
Athol	289	3	Crosby	John		1		1		1			1				4		
Athol	289	1	Crosby	Jona	2	1	1	1		1	1		1				8		
Athol	290	31	Crosby	Joseph	1		1	1		3		1					8		
Brookfield	267	8	Crosby	Oliver		1		1	1	1		1	2	1			8	Third Parish	
Shrewsbury	366	7	Crosby	Philip	3		1	1					1				6		
Winchendon	225	4	Crosby	Samuel			1						1				2		
Holden	515	20	Crosby	Sparrow	3	2		1		3		2	1				12		
Athol	290	32	Crosby	Willm	1	1		1		1		1					5		
Boylston	377	16	Crosman	Abisha	1			1		1	1						4		
Athol	289	5	Crosman	Danl	1		2	1		2	1		1				8		
Petersham	273	6	Cross	Silas	1			1		1	1		1				5		
Petersham	276	10	Crosset	Susannah		1							1				2		
Berlin	212	4	Crossman	Elizabeth									1				1		
Sutton	154	16	Crossman	Ezra	1		1					1					3		
Sutton	154	6	Crossman	Noah	3		1		1	2	1		1				9		
Sutton	153	15	Crossman	Samuel	2		1	1		2	1		1				8		
Douglas	480	12	Crowd	William											7		7		
Hardwick	296	3	Crowell	Joshua			1	1					1				3		
Hardwick	297	5	Crowell	Joshua Jr	2		2	1		2			1	1			9		
Brookfield	248	32	Crowell	Mary	1	1	4				1	1		1			9	First Parish	
Brookfield	248	33	Crowell	Paul		1	1		1	3	2	2		1			11	First Parish	
Petersham	276	15	Crowl	Alpheus			1			1			1				3		
Petersham	273	9	Crowl	Artimus	?		1						1				4		
Petersham	276	17	Crowl	Cyrus	1			1		3			1				6		
Petersham	276	16	Crowl	John				1					3	1			5		
Uxbridge	463	14	Crowney	Daniel	2			1		1			1				5		
Upton	390	19	Croxford	Willm	2				1	1	1		1				6		
Ward	179	63	Cudworth	Abigail		1				1	2		1				5		
Oxford	164	19	Cudworth	James			1	1		1		1					4		
Dudley	341	2	Cudworth	Lemuel	1			1		1		2		1			6		
Oxford	161	9	Cudworth	Warren	1		1			2		1					5		
Petersham	276	19	Cuming	Nathan	1	1		1		2		1					6		
Garry	274	14	Cuming	Samuel	1		1						1				3		
Ashburnham	457	13	Cumings	Abraham	4	1			1	1			1				8		
Garry	280	6	Cumings	Joseph				1					1				2		
Garry	280	7	Cumings	Stephen	1		1	1		4			1				8		
Douglas	477	15	Cummings	Abel	2	1		1		1	1		1				7		
Spencer	500	11	Cummings	Gershom	1			1		3	2	1	1				9		
Hardwick	296	11	Cummings	Isaac	2	1	3		1	3	1		1				12		
Fitchburg	431	8	Cummings	Jonathan		1			1				1				3		
Douglas	477	11	Cummings	Samuel				1					1				2		
Western	260	4	Cummings	Solomon	1	1	1			1	2		1				8		
Lunenberg	424	16	Cummings	Thaddeus	1			1		1	1		1				5		
Uxbridge	463	5	Cumstock	Laban	1		1		1			1					4		
Lunenberg	423	5	Cuningham	Nath	1			1		1		1	1				5		
Brookfield	255	10	Cunningham	Hugh			1	1		1			1	2			5	Second Parish	
Spencer	500	14	Cunningham	Jona		1		1			1	1					4		
Rutland	505	39	Cunningham	Mary		1	1	1					1				4		
Spencer	500	13	Cunningham	Nathl	4			1		1	2		1				9		
Barre	402	14	Cunningham	Robert	1	1		1		3		1					7		
Spencer	500	12	Cunningham	Robt			1	1			2		1				6		
Lunenberg	424	21	Cunningham	Wm	1		1	1			1		1				5		
Gardner	451	9	Currier	Jonathan			1			1		1		1			4		
Gardner	451	4	Currier	Nathll	1		1					1					3		
Dudley	342	19	Curtis	Asa		1		1				2		1			5		
Dudley	341	10	Curtis	Bethiah									2				2		
Charlton	327	10	Curtis	Caleb			1	1		1			2				4		
Dudley	341	3	Curtis	Charles	2	1		1		1	1		1				7		
Petersham	273	18	Curtis	David				1					1				2		
Worcester	176	4	Curtis	David	2		2	1		2	1		1				9		
Douglas	477	12	Curtis	Ebenezer	1			2		3			1	1			9		
Petersham	276	12	Curtis	Ebenz	2			1		2	1	1		1			8		
Dudley	341	9	Curtis	Edward		4			1	1	1		1				8		
Dudley	342	20	Curtis	John	2	2	1		2	1		2	1	1			12		
Charlton	327	15	Curtis	Jonathan	2			1		1			1				6		
Lunenberg	424	9	Curtis	Joseph				1				1					2		
Charlton	327	25	Curtis	Mary Wd						1			1				2		
Sutton	156	1	Curtis	Oliver	1	1	1		1	1	2	1					9		
Worcester	173	6	Curtis	Samuel	1	1	1			1	1	1					7		
Worcester	173	7	Curtis	Samuel Junr	3		1			1	2	1					8		
Sturbridge	337	6	Curtis	Silvanus	1		2			2	1						6		
Petersham	273	19	Curtis	Thomas	3	2		1		3	1	1	1				12		
Lancaster	347	5	Curtis	Timothy				1					2				3		
Worcester	176	3	Curtis	Tyler	2		2	2	1	1		1	1	1			12		

			HEADS OF HOUSEHOLD		FREE WHITE MALES					FREE WHITE FEMALES					TOTAL ALL OTHER	TOTAL SLAVES			
TOWN	PG#	LN#	LAST NAME	FIRST NAME	under 10	10 to 16	16 to 26	26 to 45	45 and over	under 10	10 to 16	16 to 26	26 to 45	45 and over			TOTALS	DISTRICT/TOWNSHIP	NOTES
Winchendon	225	6	Curtiss	Abner				1					1	1			3		
Winchendon	225	7	Curtiss	Abner Junr	3			1		2			1				7		
Winchendon	225	8	Curtiss	Moses			1			1		1					3		
Lunenberg	423	1	Cushing	Charles		1		1			1	1		1			5		
Shrewsbury	366	5	Cushing	Col Job				1						2			3		
Ashburnham	457	2	Cushing	David	2	1		1		2	1	1	1				9		
Lunenberg	423	3	Cushing	Edmund			3					1	1				5		
Harvard	219	20	Cushing	James			1							1			2		
Ashburnham	457	1	Cushing	John Revd		1	1		1	1		2		1			7		
Barre	402	15	Cushing	William	1	1	1	1		1	1		1				7		
Brookfield	255	9	Cutler	Abijah	2		1			2			1				7	Second Parish	
Ward	179	68	Cutler	Amos	3		1			1			1				6		
Brookfield	248	30	Cutler	Asa		2	1			1		1	1				6	First Parish	
Hardwick	296	2	Cutler	Convers	2		1			1	1	1					6		
Western	260	10	Cutler	Ebenezer		1	1		1	1	1	1	1				7		
Grafton	195	8	Cutler	Ebenz			1						1				2		
Royalston	232	13	Cutler	Ebenz	1		1			2	2		2	1			9		
Grafton	195	9	Cutler	Ebenz Jun	2	1	1	1					1				6		
Templeton	233	1	Cutler	Ephraim	1		1						1				3		
Brookfield	255	16	Cutler	Jesse			1				1		1				3	Second Parish	
Brookfield	267	2	Cutler	John		3		1		2		3		1			10	Third Parish	
Royalston	240	8	Cutler	Jonathan			1	1		2		2		1			7		
Shrewsbury	366	6	Cutler	Jonathan		1	2	1					2	1			7		
Brookfield	248	29	Cutler	Joseph		1	1		1	1		2	1	1			8	First Parish	
Western	260	5	Cutler	Joseph		1	2			1	1			2			8		
Western	260	7	Cutler	Joseph Jr	3	1	1	1		2	1	1	1				11		
Milford	396	33	Cutler	Moses			1						1				2		
Grafton	195	11	Cutler	Moses		1	1					1	1				4		
Grafton	195	10	Cutler	Moses Jun	1		1					1					3		
Brookfield	255	13	Cutler	Robert	3	1		2		2			1	1			10	Second Parish	
Petersham	273	7	Cutler	Samuel	1	3	1			4	1		1		1		12		
Templeton	234	17	Cutler	Silas			1						1				3		
Brookfield	247	1	Cutler	Thomas B.	1		1						1				3	First Parish	
Templeton	233	4	Cutler	William	1	1		1		3	1		1				8		
Hardwick	296	17	Cutler	Wm	2		2	1	1	2		1	1		1		11		
Spencer	497	1	Cutter	Isaac				1					1	1			3		
Spencer	497	2	Cutter	Jedediah			1	1		2	1		1				6		
Hubbardston	415	34	Cutting	Abraham	1	1		1		2			1				6		
Templeton	242	12	Cutting	Asa	1		1			2			1				5		
Leicester	488	14	Cutting	Darius	2	2	5	1		2	2		1				15		
Boylston	377	7	Cutting	David	2			1		1			1	1			6		
Garry	280	5	Cutting	Earl	1	1		1		1	1		1	1			8		
Sturbridge	337	9	Cutting	Ebenze	1	1		1	1	2			1	1			8		
Ashburnham	457	4	Cutting	Eunis		1		1			1	2		1			6		
Templeton	234	14	Cutting	Jona Jr		2	1				1		1				5		
Hubbardston	415	38	Cutting	Jonathan			1						1				2		
Templeton	234	13	Cutting	Jonathan		2	2	1				2		1			8		
Bolton	215	10	Cutting	Joseph	2	1							1				4		
Boylston	377	12	Cutting	Josiah	1			1				3	1	1			7		
Princeton	516	9	Cutting	Josiah	1	2		1		3			1				8		
Rutland	505	38	Cutting	Keziah									1	1			2		
Westborough	199	148	Cutting	Merrick	1			1		1			1				4		
Royalston	242	10	Cutting	Nathan				1		2	1			1			5		
Royalston	242	12	Cutting	Nathan Jr				1		1			1				3		
Garry	280	12	Cutting	Saml		1	1		1	1				1			5		
Boylston	377	11	Cutting	Silas	2			1			1		1				5		
Boylston	377	13	Cutting	Thannel		1		1				1					3		
Harvard	217	17	Daby	Asa	2		1				1	1					6		
Princeton	516	12	Dadnum	Samuel	2			1		1	1	1					6		
Dudley	344	30	Dagget	Ebenzr	1		1			1			1				4		
Sturbridge	338	4	Dagget	Ebenzr	3	1							1				5		
Sutton	156	13	Daggett	Lydia Wd							2	1	1				4		
Boylston	377	23	Daken	David	1	1		1					1				4		
Boylston	377	22	Daken	Oliver			1	2					1	1			5		
Princeton	516	20	Dale	David	2			1		1			1				5		
Westminster	443	15	Dale	Joseph			1			1			1				3		
Sterling	355	15	Dale	Samuel	1	1	1	2		2	1		1				9		
Dudley	344	27	Dalrimple	John	1		1						1				3		
Dudley	344	26	Dalrimple	Robert	2		1	1		1			1				6		
Northborough	368	5	Dalrymple	Samuel	1	1		1		3			1				7		
Bolton	209	11	Dammon	Ebenezer			1						1				2		
Western	257	9	Damon	John	2			2					1				5		
Westminster	443	7	Damon	John			1			1	1		1				4		
Western	257	10	Damon	Jude	3	1	1		1	2	2			1			11		
Holden	513	1	Damon	Samuel		1	4	1	1			2		1			10		
Holden	513	2	Damon	Stephen	2	1		2		2			1	1			9		
Lunenberg	423	13	Damon	Thomas	2	1	1		1		1		1				7		
Westminster	443	9	Damon	Timothy		1	1					1					3		
Westminster	443	11	Damon	Timothy Jr	1			1		4			1				7		
Sterling	355	18	Dana	Jesse	1	1	3	1		1	1	1	1				10		
Princeton	516	15	Dana	John	2	1		1		3			1				8		
Barre	404	5	Dana	Josiah				1		1	1	1	2		1		7		
Brookfield	247	4	Dane	Joseph			1					2	1	1			6	First Parish	
Brookfield	258	6	Dane	William			1				1			1			3	Second Parish	
Brookfield	258	7	Dane	William Jun	2	1		1					1	1			6	Second Parish	
Sutton	155	15	Danforth	Elijah	1			1		2			1				5		
Templeton	240	14	Danforth	Jesse	1	1		1	1			2			1		7		
Hardwick	297	15	Danforth	Jno	2	1	4		1	2	2	1	1		1		17		
Athol	289	8	Danforth	John	3			1		2			1				7		
Leominster	433	16	Daniel	Elias	1		1										3		

TOWN	PG#	LN#	LAST NAME	FIRST NAME	FREE WHITE MALES					FREE WHITE FEMALES					TOTAL ALL OTHER	TOTAL SLAVES	TOTALS	DISTRICT/ TOWNSHIP	NOTES
					under 10	10 to 16	16 to 26	26 to 45	45 and over	under 10	10 to 16	16 to 26	26 to 45	45 and over					
Southborough	203	24	Daniels	Abigail										1			1		
Mendon	381	5	Daniels	Adams	1			1		1	1						4	1st Parish	
Mendon	381	1	Daniels	Darius			1	1	1			1		1			5	1st Parish	
Mendon	390	19	Daniels	David	1	1	3		1	2		1		1			10	2d Parish	
Holden	516	9	Daniels	Joseph		2	1	1				1	1				6		
Mendon	381	2	Daniels	Joseph				1			2		2				5	1st Parish	
Brookfield	270	18	Daniels	Levi		2				1	1		1				6	Third Parish	
Mendon	390	20	Daniels	Moses	2	1	1	1	1	1		2	1	2			12	2d Parish	
Mendon	381	3	Daniels	Nathan	1			1		1		2	2				6	1st Parish	
Milford	395	15	Daniels	Oliver			2		1			1		1			5		
Grafton	200	12	Daniels	Zebulon	2	1	1	1		1	1	1	1				9		
Charlton	329	10	Danilson	Lothario				1		2		1					4		
Lancaster	347	11	Danson	Samuel			1		1	2		1		1			5		
Barre	404	14	Danton	George Wasn	1		1					1					3		
Boylston	377	21	Danton	Reuben		2		1	1	1		1		1			6		
Fitchburg	431	17	Darby	Aaron	3	1		1		2			1				8		
Westminster	443	10	Darby	Abel	1		1					1					3		
Westminster	443	6	Darby	Andrew		1	1	1	1		1		1				6		
Leominster	436	23	Darby	Benjamin		1	3		1	2	1	1	1				10		
Leominster	433	13	Darby	Deliverance				1				1	1				3		
Westminster	443	12	Darby	Ezra			1			1		1					3		
Harvard	217	25	Darby	John				1					1				2		
Westminster	443	17	Darby	John		1		1					2				4		
Westminster	443	16	Darby	John Jr	2			1				1					4		
Fitchburg	432	1	Darby	Jonathan	1		1		1	3	2	1		1			10		
Leominster	433	11	Darby	Joseph				1			2		1				4		
Westminster	443	8	Darby	Joseph	1		1			2			1				5		
Leominster	436	21	Darby	Joseph Jun	1			1		3			1				5		
Leominster	433	20	Darby	Joshua	1		1					1					3		
Westminster	443	13	Darby	Nathan		1		1				1	1				4		
Leominster	433	12	Darby	Nathan	4			1					1				6		
Leominster	433	10	Darby	Simon		1		1				1	1				4		
Mendon	389	6	Darling	Abigail	1	1							1	1			4	2d Parish	
Mendon	389	3	Darling	Benson			1		2			1	1				5	2d Parish	
Mendon	389	1	Darling	Jesse			1					1					2	2d Parish	
Winchendon	225	14	Darling	Jewett			1		2		1	1					5		
Mendon	389	7	Darling	Job		1		1		4	2		1				9	2d Parish	
Mendon	389	4	Darling	John		1	1			1	1	1	1				7	2d Parish	
Winchendon	225	13	Darling	John				1					1				2		
Mendon	381	6	Darling	John Jr	3			1					1				5	1st Parish	
Uxbridge	463	17	Darling	Joshua	3	1		1		1	2		1				9		
Winchendon	225	15	Darling	Luther				1		1			1				3		
Mendon	389	2	Darling	Matthew			1		1	1	1	1	1	2			8	2d Parish	
Grafton	201	4	Darling	Nathan	1			1		1			1	1			5		
Uxbridge	463	18	Darling	Pelitiah	2			1		2			1		1		7		
Mendon	389	5	Darling	Phinehas			1						3				4	2d Parish	
Sutton	156	6	Darling	William				1					1				2		
Sutton	156	7	Darling	Zeleck	4	2		1					1				8		
Spencer	498	4	Darling	Zenas	1			1		3			1				6		
Sutton	156	10	Davenport	Aaron				1				1					2		
Mendon	382	17	Davenport	David	2		3	1					2				8	1st Parish	
Oxford	161	13	Davenport	Richard		1		1		1		1	1				5		
Mendon	382	16	Davenport	Seth	2	1		2				2	1				8	1st Parish	
Mendon	382	15	Davenport	Seth Jr	2		1						2		1		6	1st Parish	
Sutton	156	11	Davenport	William		1	1	1				3	1				7		
Douglas	480	20	Davidson	Douglas	1			1	4			1					7		
Douglas	480	19	Davidson	Samuel	1	1		1					3				6		
Harvard	220	14	Davis	Aaron Junr			1		1		1		1				4		
Oxford	161	15	Davis	Abijah		1	1					1					3		
Royalston	237	15	Davis	Alexander P.		1		1	2		1		1				6		
Rutland	505	47	Davis	Alpheus	1	1	1	1		2			1	1			8		
Charlton	329	7	Davis	Amasa	2	1	1	1		2	1		1				9		
Grafton	206	3	Davis	Amos	1		1		1	1	1		1				6		
Charlton	329	12	Davis	Asa		1	1	1				1	1				5		
Rutland	506	4	Davis	Asa			1			2			1				4		
Royalston	234	12	Davis	Asahel	1							1	1				3		
Douglas	480	18	Davis	Benja				1					1				2		
Brookfield	258	1	Davis	Benjamin			1			1	1	1					4	Second Parish	
Oxford	161	10	Davis	Benjamin	3			1		1	2	1	1				9		
Hubbardston	415	40	Davis	Benjm	1		1			1			1				4		
Oxford	162	5	Davis	Craft	2	1		1				1	1				7		
Paxton	502	3	Davis	David		2		1		2		1					6		
Paxton	502	4	Davis	David Junr		1	1			2		1					5		
Ashburnham	460	19	Davis	Eben & Benj	3	1		1		2	1		1				9		
Holden	516	18	Davis	Edmund	1	1		1		3		1	1				8		
Dudley	341	18	Davis	Edward		1	1	1		4	1	1	1				10		
Templeton	235	8	Davis	Eleazer	2	1				1	1	2	2	1	1		11		
Rutland	506	2	Davis	Eliakim	2		1	1		3	2	1	1	1			12		
Oxford	162	1	Davis	Elijah		1		1	1		2		1				6		
Leominster	433	14	Davis	Elisha				1			1		1				3		
Holden	516	19	Davis	Elnathan		1		1		3		2					7		
Holden	516	20	Davis	Ethan	2		1	1		2			1				7		
Oxford	161	12	Davis	Ezekiel	1	1		1		3	1	1	1				9		
Harvard	219	11	Davis	Flint		1		1				1					4		
Lancaster	347	13	Davis	Francis											4		4		
Western	257	13	Davis	Gideon		1		1			1		1				4		
Northborough	368	1	Davis	Isaac		1	2		1	1		1	3				10		
Harvard	221	25	Davis	Isaiah	1		1	1		1		1					5		
Holden	516	22	Davis	Israel		1	1		1		1	1		1			6		

TOWN	PG#	LN#	LAST NAME	FIRST NAME	FREE WHITE MALES					FREE WHITE FEMALES					TOTAL ALL OTHER	TOTAL SLAVES	TOTALS	DISTRICT/ TOWNSHIP	NOTES
					under 10	10 to 16	16 to 26	26 to 45	45 and over	under 10	10 to 16	16 to 26	26 to 45	45 and over					
Hubbardston	415	39	Davis	Israel		1		1					1				3		
Holden	516	17	Davis	James			1	1					1				3		
Oxford	162	6	Davis	James	1		1						1				3		
Holden	516	21	Davis	James 2d			1	1		1			1				4		
Oxford	161	14	Davis	Jeremiah			3	1				2	1	1			8		
Rutland	506	1	Davis	Jesse			1	1					1	1			4		
Royalston	234	11	Davis	Joanna			1					1	1	1			4		
Holden	516	23	Davis	John			2		1	1			1				5		
Oxford	162	7	Davis	John	1	1	1	1	1			1	1	1			8		
Oxford	162	8	Davis	John		1	1	1	1	1			2	1			8		
Western	257	11	Davis	John				1					1				2		
Princeton	516	17	Davis	John P.	1		1	1		4	1		1				9		
Oxford	162	3	Davis	Jonathan	2	2		1				1	2	1			9		
Dudley	341	21	Davis	Joseph				1					1	1			3		
Northborough	368	2	Davis	Joseph	1		2	1				1					5		
Oxford	162	4	Davis	Joseph	1	2	1		2				1	4			11		
Royalston	231	12	Davis	Joseph	1		1			1							3		
Dudley	341	16	Davis	Joseph Jun	1		1			2			1		1		6		
Dudley	341	17	Davis	Joshua	1		1					1					3		
Harvard	222	15	Davis	Josiah			1	1					1				3		
Princeton	516	13	Davis	Josiah Junr			1	1		2			1				5		
Oxford	162	2	Davis	Learned	1	1	1	1		1	1		1				7		
Holden	516	10	Davis	Lemuel	1	1	1	1		3	1		1	1			10		
Charlton	329	11	Davis	Levi		1	2		1	1	1	1		1			8		
Fitchburg	431	14	Davis	Levi			1			2		1					4		
Athol	289	17	Davis	Mary	2							2	1				5		
Harvard	222	16	Davis	Mary			1			1			1				3		
Rutland	506	3	Davis	Mary			1						2				3		
Oxford	161	11	Davis	Mary Wd		2	2			2			1				7		
Charlton	329	20	Davis	Moses	1			1		2			1				5		
Milford	395	21	Davis	Moses	1			1		2			1				5		
Bolton	211	1	Davis	Nathan	1	2	1		1		1	2		1			9		
Oxford	161	17	Davis	Nehemiah		2	1						1				4		
Leominster	436	22	Davis	Oliver	1	1	1		1		1		1				6		
Princeton	516	18	Davis	Oliver			1		1		1		1				4		
Holden	516	12	Davis	Paul		2		1				1	1	1			6		
Royalston	241	33	Davis	Peter	1			1		4		1	1				8		
Milford	395	20	Davis	Phinehas			1	1		1		1	1	1			6		
Northborough	368	3	Davis	Phinehas	2		2	1		1	1		1				8		
Winchendon	225	16	Davis	Phinehas			1						1				2		
Rutland	506	7	Davis	Rebeckah		1	1				1	1		1			5		
Dudley	341	20	Davis	Saml	2			1		3			1				7		
Oakham	318	19	Davis	Samll			1		1	2	2		1				7		
Oxford	161	18	Davis	Samuel		1		1				2	1				5		
Princeton	516	14	Davis	Samuel			1		1	1	2	1		1			7		
Boylston	377	19	Davis	Simon		1	2	1			1						5		
Princeton	516	19	Davis	Simon	2	1		1			1		1				6		
Princeton	516	16	Davis	Solomon	1	1		1		2	2	1	1				9		
Templeton	235	12	Davis	Solomon	3		1		1				1				6		
Royalston	236	6	Davis	Squire	2	2		1		1	1		1				8		
Rutland	505	46	Davis	Thaddeus	1		1	1					1	1			5		
Holden	516	14	Davis	Thomas	2	2	1		1		1		1				8		
Oxford	161	16	Davis	Thomas	1		1	1		1			1				5		
Brookfield	247	2	Davis	Timothy	2			1		2			1				6	First Parish	
Sutton	156	8	Davis	Timothy		1		1		2		2					6		
Douglas	480	17	Davis	William			1	1				1	1	1			5		
Rutland	506	5	Davis	William	2			1		1			1				5		
Spencer	498	1	Davison	Benja				1					1				2		
Spencer	498	2	Davison	Benja Jun	2		1	1		1	2		1				8		
Charlton	329	9	Davison	Ebenzr				1				2	1	1			5		
Spencer	497	6	Davison	John	2			1		2	1		1				7		
Harvard	219	9	Dawes	Robert	2		1	1		3			1				8		
Rutland	506	10	Daws	Cato											5		5		
Sutton	155	6	Day	Aaron	1			1	1				1				4		
Mendon	390	21	Day	Daniel	3		1	1		1	1		2				9	2d Parish	
Winchendon	225	19	Day	Danll		1		1		1		2	1				6		
Oxford	162	9	Day	David		1	1						1				3		
Dudley	344	29	Day	Jabez	1	1	1			1		2					6		
Milford	395	18	Day	Joel			1			1		1					3		
Templeton	231	3	Day	John	3			1					1				5		
Dudley	341	19	Day	Jonathan		1	2		1			2	1				7		
Paxton	502	5	Day	Joseph		2		1					2				5		
Winchendon	225	17	Day	Joseph			1						1				2		
Milford	395	17	Day	Mordecai				1				1	1	1			3		
Sutton	155	5	Day	Moses	2			1		2			2				7		
Western	257	8	Day	Nathan	1		1	1		1		2					6		
Boylston	377	20	Day	Solomon		2		1	1	1		1	1				7		
Brookfield	258	4	Dean	Abiel			2	1					1				4	Second Parish	
Oakham	317	2	Dean	Isaiah	1		1			1		1					4		
Oakham	318	16	Dean	James	1	2		1		1			1				6		
Petersham	275	9	Dean	Jereh	1		1	1				2					5		
Royalston	231	4	Dean	Joshua	1	1	1	1			2		1				7		
Rutland	506	9	Dean	Lavery	1			1		3			2				7		
Hardwick	297	13	Dean	Paul	3	1	2	1			1	1	1				10		
Oakham	318	17	Dean	Samll	1			1			1	1	1				5		
Templeton	239	4	Dean	Seth			1					2	1				4		
Rutland	506	6	Dean	William	2			1		1		1					5		
Oakham	318	18	Dean	Zebulon			1	1					1				3		
Shrewsbury	366	15	Deane	Ebenezer			1			2			1				4		
Upton	387	3	Deane	Josiah Esq.					1					1			2		

TOWN	PG#	LN#	LAST NAME	FIRST NAME	FREE WHITE MALES					FREE WHITE FEMALES					TOTAL ALL OTHER	TOTAL SLAVES	TOTALS	DISTRICT/ TOWNSHIP	NOTES
					under 10	10 to 16	16 to 26	26 to 45	45 and over	under 10	10 to 16	16 to 26	26 to 45	45 and over					
Shrewsbury	365	1	Deane	Nathaniel	1		1			1			1				4		
Upton	387	4	Deane	Saml		1	1			2		1					5		
Sutton	155	7	Deane	William		1	1	1					1	1			5		
Royalston	234	2	Deck	Danll Junr	2		1			2		1					6		
Royalston	233	7	Deck	John				1				1		1			3		
Royalston	233	8	Deck	Squire	1		1			1		1					4		
Brookfield	258	9	Deland	Charles	1		1			2			1				5	Second Parish	
Brookfield	258	11	Deland	Jedidiah	2	2		1		1			1				7	Second Parish	
Brookfield	258	8	Deland	Philip		1	1	1					1	1			5	Second Parish	
Northborough	368	4	Delane	Partrick			1			2			1				4		
New Braintree	308	22	Delano	Abisha				1						1			2		
New Braintree	309	1	Delano	Gideon	1	1		2			1	1	1				7		
New Braintree	309	2	Delano	Philip	4								1				6		
Ashburnham	455	4	Demster	Samuel		1		1					1				3		
Petersham	275	4	Demula	Jesse		1		1					1				3		
Charlton	329	13	Denis	Isaac	2		1						1				4		
Charlton	329	4	Denis	Jonathan		1	2	1		1	1			1			7		
Charlton	329	15	Denis	Nathan				1						1			2		
Charlton	329	14	Denis	Silas	1	1	2	1					1				6		
Hardwick	297	11	Dennis	Adonijah		1	2	1		1	1	1	1				8		
Barre	404	10	Dennis	Isaac	1		1			1		1					4		
Barre	404	6	Dennis	Thomas	1	1	1					1	1				5		
Western	249	3	Dennison	David		1	1	1		2		2	1				8		
Worcester	175	2	Denny	Daniel	2		1	1		1	1	2	1				9		
New Braintree	308	20	Denny	Isaac		1	1			3		1	1				7		
Leicester	487	4	Denny	Joseph	1		1					1					3		
Leicester	487	6	Denny	Samuel		1		1						2			4		
Worcester	175	3	Denny	Samuel			1	1					1				3		
Leicester	487	7	Denny	Thomas	1		3	1	1	3		3	1	1			14		
Leicester	487	5	Denny	Thomas 2d				1			1		1				3		
Spencer	497	7	Denny	William	3		1			2	1		1				8		
Boylston	377	18	Densmore	John		1		1		1							4		
Boylston	377	24	Densmore	Silvanus	2			1		1		1					5		
Barre	404	7	Denton	Gershom		1		1						1			3		
Southborough	204	2	Denton	James	2			1					1				4		
Lancaster	347	14	Deputson	William				1				1		1			3		
Lancaster	347	8	Deputson	William Jun		1				1		1	1				4		
Royalston	235	9	Derry	Thaddeus	1	1		1		2	1		1				7		
Rutland	506	8	Desmond	Daniel	3		1	1					1				6		
Brookfield	258	14	Deuing	Solomon	1	1	1	1		2			1	1			8	Second Parish	
Boylston	377	17	Devenport	Mathew	1	2	3	1		1		2	1	1			12		
Mendon	381	4	Dexter	Andrew	1	1	2	1				1	1				7	1st Parish	
Athol	289	16	Dexter	Benja		1	1					1					3		
Hardwick	297	16	Dexter	Ebenz	2			1		5			1		1		10		
Royalston	231	13	Dexter	James	2	1		1		1	1		1				7		
Hardwick	297	10	Dexter	Job	1	2	1	1						1			7		
Berlin	216	20	Dexter	John	2	1		1				1	1				6		
Hardwick	297	12	Dexter	Samll	3	2	2	1		1		2		1			12		
Petersham	275	5	Dickerson	David		1	1					1		1			4		
Lancaster	347	15	Dickerson	Moses		1		1					1				3		
Harvard	219	27	Dickinson	David		2							1				3		
Harvard	217	11	Dickinson	Francis		1	1	1		1	1	1					7		
Harvard	217	24	Dickinson	Samuel		1		1				1	1				4		
Ashburnham	460	18	Dickson	Elizabeth		1					1			1			3		
Sutton	156	5	Dike	Anthony		2	2	1						1			6		
Athol	289	10	Dike	David	1			1		2			1				5		
Athol	289	9	Dike	John				1						1			2		
Westminster	443	18	Dime	Nicholas				1						1			2		
Westminster	446	1	Dime	Nicholas Jr	2	1		1		3	1		1				9		
Barre	404	8	Dimmond	Israel	2	1		1		2	1		1				8		
Grafton	198	16	Disau	Joseph	1		1			1		1					4		
Milford	395	16	Disper	Edward				1		1	1			1			4		
Lunenberg	423	9	Divol	Asahel	4		1						1				6		
Lancaster	347	9	Divol	Ephraim				1				2	1	1			5		
Lancaster	347	12	Divol	Menasseh		1	1	1				1	2	2			8		
Lunenberg	423	11	Divol	Phinehas	1			2				2	1	1			7		
Lunenberg	423	10	Divol	Sarah		1							1	1			3		
Lancaster	347	16	Divol	Thomas	1		1			2		1	1				6		
Leominster	433	17	Divoll	John				1				1		1			3		
Leominster	433	15	Divoll	John Jun		1	1			1			1				4		
Leominster	433	19	Divoll	Luke	3		1			2			1				7		
Leominster	433	18	Divoll	Oliver	1	1	1			3	1		1				8		
Sturbridge	337	20	Dix	David		1	1						1				3		
Milford	395	22	Dixen	Marvel											5		5		
Douglas	480	24	Dixon	Polladore											4		4		
Petersham	275	3	Doan	Edwd	1		1					1					3		
Petersham	275	2	Doan	Noah				1						1			2		
Brookfield	258	5	Doane	Benjamin			1	1		1		1	1				5	Second Parish	
Brookfield	258	2	Doane	David	2	1		1				2	2	1			9	Second Parish	
Brookfield	270	20	Doane	Elisha	1		1	1		1		1					5	Third Parish	
Brookfield	270	22	Doane	Eunice			1							3			4	Third Parish	
Brookfield	267	17	Doane	Nathan	5	1		1				1	1				9	Third Parish	
Hardwick	297	9	Doane	Uriah	3	1		1		1	1		1				8		
Holden	516	13	Dodds	James		2		1			1	2		1			7		
Holden	516	11	Dodds	John			1					1	1				6		
Princeton	516	11	Dodds	William		2		1		1			1				7		
Brookfield	258	12	Dodge	Artemas	2			1		2			1				6	Second Parish	
Ward	180	74	Dodge	Daniel		1		1		2			1				5		
Charlton	329	23	Dodge	David	2		1					1					4		
Sturbridge	338	2	Dodge	Ebenzr	2		1						1				4		

TOWN	PG#	LN#	LAST NAME	FIRST NAME	M under 10	M 10 to 16	M 16 to 26	M 26 to 45	M 45 and over	F under 10	F 10 to 16	F 16 to 26	F 26 to 45	F 45 and over	TOTAL ALL OTHER	TOTAL SLAVES	TOTALS	DISTRICT/ TOWNSHIP	NOTES
Lunenberg	423	17	Dodge	Elijah	1				1		1			1			4		
Sutton	156	4	Dodge	Isaac		1	2	1	1				2	1			8		
Lunenberg	423	18	Dodge	James	2		1			1		1					5		
Sutton	155	4	Dodge	Josiah	1	1	1			1		1					5		
Dudley	344	24	Dodge	Mark		1		1					1				4		
Charlton	329	21	Dodge	Moses	1	1	1						1				4		
Brookfield	258	3	Dodge	Nath Jun		1	1						1				3	Second Parish	
Brookfield	258	10	Dodge	Nathll		1	1	1					2	1			6	Second Parish	
Brookfield	258	13	Dodge	Nathll 2d	2	2	1					1	1				7	Second Parish	
Dudley	344	28	Dodge	Paul	2		1						1				4		
Sutton	155	3	Dodge	Richard H.		1	1	1					1	1			5		
Brookfield	247	5	Dodge	Thaddeus	1	1	1		1	3	2	1	1	1			12	First Parish	
Templeton	234	7	Dolbear	Benja			1	1				1	1	1			5		
Templeton	236	7	Dolbear	Benja			1	1				1	1	1			5		
Templeton	236	6	Dolbear	James	4	1		1		1	1	1	1				10		
Lunenberg	423	16	Dole	John		1		1					1				4		
Lancaster	347	10	Dollison	John	2	1	1	1		3	1	1	1	1			12		
Worcester	176	15	Donohoe	Philip											1		1		
Petersham	275	8	Doolittle	Joel		2	3	1				2	1	1			10		
Sterling	355	17	Dorchester	Ishmael												8	8		
Brookfield	247	3	Dorr	Joseph		1	1	1	1	1		2	1	1			9	First Parish	
Brookfield	247	6	Dorr	Moses	2	1		1		1			1	1			7	First Parish	
Charlton	330	4	Doskett	Samuel		2	1		1				1	2			7		
Charlton	330	3	Doskett	Thomas	1	1	1		1			2	2	1			9		
Hardwick	297	14	Doty	John		1	1	1		2	2	1	1				9		
Charlton	329	18	Douty	Benjm		1		1					1	1			4		
Charlton	329	19	Douty	Benjm Junr	1		1						1				3		
Western	257	6	Dow	Isaiah				1				1		1			3		
Western	249	4	Dow	Jonathan		2	1						1				4		
New Braintree	308	21	Dow	Joseph	2	2		1					1	1			8		
Fitchburg	431	15	Downe	Joseph		1	3	1				2		2			9		
Fitchburg	431	16	Downe	Joseph Jun	1		1	1					1				4		
Westborough	197	120	Downs	Farris											2		2		
Grafton	204	15	Drak	Francis	2			1		1		1					5		
Spencer	498	3	Drake	Elisha		1	1	2				1		1			6		
Douglas	480	23	Drake	Stephen	2	1	1	1				2		1			8		
Shrewsbury	366	10	Drane	Jonathan		1	1	1		1		2		1			6		
Spencer	498	5	Draper	David			1					1					2		
Uxbridge	463	16	Draper	David	2			1				2		1			6		
Brookfield	267	18	Draper	Ellis	2	1		1		2	1		1				8	Third Parish	
Sturbridge	338	5	Draper	Jacob			1			3			1		1		6		
Spencer	497	9	Draper	James	1		2	1		3	1		1				9		
Spencer	497	8	Draper	John	1	1		1		1	2		1				8		
Bolton	216	14	Draper	Samuel	1			1		3			1				6		
Brookfield	267	16	Draper	Simeon	3		1	1		1	1	1	1				9	Third Parish	
Sturbridge	337	23	Draper	Stephen				1						1			2		
Spencer	497	10	Draper	Zenas	1		1						1				3		
Holden	513	4	Dreary	William	4	1	1	1		1	2		1				11		
Charlton	329	1	Dresser	Aaron	3			1				1	1	1			7		
Sturbridge	337	21	Dresser	Anna									1	1			2		
Charlton	329	8	Dresser	Asa		1	1	1					2	1			6		
Sturbridge	338	1	Dresser	Caleb	2			1		1			1				5		
Sterling	355	16	Dresser	Elijah	1			1		1		1					4		
Sturbridge	338	8	Dresser	Meriam				1		1				1			3		
Charlton	329	3	Dresser	Moses	1	2	1	1		1	1	2					9		
Charlton	329	2	Dresser	Richard				1		1	1	1					4		
Lunenberg	423	12	Dressor	Ama		1	1	1					2	1			6		
Grafton	198	4	Drewry	Luke			2	1	1				1	1			6		
Grafton	198	13	Drewry	Sarah										1			1		
Shrewsbury	366	13	Drury	Abijah	1		1	1		2			1				6		
Spencer	497	11	Drury	Benja	2	1	1	1		1	2		1				9		
Shrewsbury	366	11	Drury	Caleb				1				1		1			3		
Shrewsbury	366	14	Drury	Ebenezer	3		1	1	1	2		1	1				10		
Spencer	497	12	Drury	Ebenz			2	1						1			4		
Spencer	497	13	Drury	Ebenz Jun	1	1		1		2		1	1				7		
Westminster	443	5	Drury	Elezar				1					1				2		
Garry	280	15	Drury	Huldah				1				1	1				3		
Athol	289	15	Drury	Joel	1			1		3			1				6		
Shrewsbury	366	12	Drury	Joel	1	1		1		2		1	1				7		
Athol	289	11	Drury	John			2	1		1	1			1			6		
Athol	289	12	Drury	Saml	2		1						1				4		
Ward	180	75	Drury	Thomas		1		1						2			4		
Ward	180	76	Drury	Thomas Junr	2	1	1						1				5		
Brookfield	270	19	Drury	Winsor	1			1		4				1			7	Third Parish	
Holden	513	3	Dryden	Artimas	2	2		1		1				2			8		
Sutton	156	12	Dudley	Abel		1	1	1					1	1			5		
Douglas	480	16	Dudley	Benja		2		1		3	1	1	2				10		
Sutton	155	8	Dudley	David	1	1		1				1	1	1			9		
Petersham	275	6	Dudley	Francis			2	1		1		1	1	1			7		
Sutton	156	16	Dudley	Jemima Wd						2	2			1			5		
Sutton	156	15	Dudley	John	1		1	1		3			1				7		
Sutton	155	1	Dudley	Jonathan	1	1		1		2			1				6		
Douglas	480	22	Dudley	Lemuel	1		1			1			1				4		
Sutton	155	2	Dudley	Nabby Wd	2							1	1	1			5		
Douglas	480	21	Dudley	Paul	3	1	5	2					1	1			13		
Sutton	156	14	Dudley	Peter		1	1	1				1	1	1			6		
Harvard	220	31	Dudley	Samuel	1		2	1		1				1			6		
Sutton	155	14	Dudley	Samuel	3		1	1						1			6		
Harvard	219	23	Dudley	Zacheus			1		1					1			3		
Charlton	329	5	Dugor	Charles		1	2		1		1	1					6		

TOWN	PG#	LN#	LAST NAME	FIRST NAME	FWM under 10	FWM 10 to 16	FWM 16 to 26	FWM 26 to 45	FWM 45 and over	FWF under 10	FWF 10 to 16	FWF 16 to 26	FWF 26 to 45	FWF 45 and over	TOTAL ALL OTHER	TOTAL SLAVES	TOTALS	DISTRICT/ TOWNSHIP	NOTES
Charlton	329	6	Dugor	Charles Junr				1		2		1					4		
Charlton	329	22	Dugor	Gload			2			1		1		2			6		
Leicester	487	8	Dunbar	Abnor	1		1	1	1	1			1	1			7		
Oakham	317	1	Dunbar	Benson	1	1		1		2	1	1	1	1			9		
Charlton	329	16	Dunbar	David	1		1		1			1	1				5		
Leicester	487	9	Dunbar	Lucretia	1							1	1	1			4		
Charlton	329	17	Dunbar	Samuel	1	1		1		4	2		1				10		
Barre	404	9	Duncan	John	1			1		2		3		1			8		
Petersham	275	1	Duncan	John				1									1		
Worcester	175	1	Duncan	Simeon	2	1	1	1		2	1	1	1				10		
Petersham	275	7	Duncan	Willm				1		5			1				7		
Dudley	341	22	Duncan	Wm		1		1		1				1			4		
Winchendon	225	18	Dunham	Alexr			1			1		1					3		
Lancaster	347	7	Dunlap	Samuel	2			1		1			1				5		
Brookfield	270	21	Dunn	Anna						1				2			3	Third Parish	
Northbridge	476	2	Dunn	Henry		2	1		1	1		1	1	1			8		
Westminster	443	14	Dunn	John	3	1		1		1	1		1				8		
Gardner	451	18	Dunn	Lewis				1					1	1			3		
Milford	395	19	Duno	Andrew											6		6		
Lunenberg	423	15	Dunsmoor	Ebenezer	2	3	2	1				1		2			11		
Lunenberg	423	14	Dunsmoor	Phinehas	1	2			1			3		1			8		
Holden	513	6	Dunsmore	Reuben	1	1		1					1				4		
Hubbardston	415	42	Dunster	David				1					1				2		
Gardner	452	1	Dunster	Hubard	1			1		1			1				4		
Westminster	446	4	Dunster	Shubael			2	1	1				1	1			6		
Westminster	446	2	Dunster	Thomas	1			1				1	1	1			5		
Holden	513	5	Dunton	Beulah		1				1	1		1				4		
Garry	280	14	Dunton	Eben	1		2		1	1	1		1				7		
Sturbridge	338	6	Dunton	Ebenzr				1						1			2		
Sturbridge	338	7	Dunton	Jesse				1						1			2		
Southborough	204	15	Dunton	Levi	2			1		2	1		1				7		
Southborough	205	6	Dunton	Samuel				1						1			2		
Sturbridge	337	22	Dunton	Silas	1			1		2	2		1	1			9		
Westminster	446	3	Dupee	John				1		1		1					3		
Fitchburg	431	18	Durant	Edward	2	2	3	2		2		1	1				13		
Fitchburg	432	2	Durant	Jackson	2			1		2			1				6		
Holden	516	15	Dwelly	Joseph				1						1			2		
Holden	516	16	Dwelly	Joseph Junr	1			1					1				3		
Western	257	7	Dwight	Simeon	1	2	1	1		2		2	1				10		
Sutton	155	13	Dwinnel	Abram	1			1					1				3		
Harvard	221	10	Dwinnel	Elijah	1		2	1		1			1	1			7		
Sutton	155	9	Dwinnel	Henry			1	1				1		1			4		
Sutton	155	12	Dwinnel	Henry Junr	1			1		3			1				6		
Sutton	155	11	Dwinnel	Moses	1			1					1				3		
Sutton	156	9	Dwinnel	Saml	2			1		1			1				5		
Sutton	155	10	Dwinnel	Solomon	2	1		1	1					1			6		
Sturbridge	337	24	Dyer	James	2	1	2	1		2	2	1	1		2		14		
Dudley	344	31	Dyer	Thomas	2			1		3	3		1				10		
Sturbridge	338	3	Dyer	Thos	2			1		3	2		1				9		
Dudley	344	25	Dyre	John				1		1			1				3		
Athol	289	13	Dyre	Shubnow	2			1		1	2		1				7		
Athol	289	14	Dyre	Shubnow Jr	2			1		1	2		1				7		
Berlin	211	20	E*	J				1									1		Name covered by tape mark
Lancaster	347	19	Eager	Aaron				1						1			2		
Northborough	368	9	Eager	Ephron	3		1					1					5		
Sterling	355	19	Eager	Fortunatus		1	1	1				1	1	1			7		
Northborough	368	6	Eager	Francis		1		1			1	1		2			6		
Gardner	452	4	Eager	Jonathan	1	1		1		3	1		1				8		
Boylston	377	27	Eager	Joseph	1	1	1	1				1		1			6		
Shrewsbury	365	3	Eager	Lewis	2	1		1		2		2	1				10		
Northborough	368	7	Eager	Oliver	1	1	1	1		1	1		1				7		
Hardwick	297	22	Eager	Paul				1			1			1			3		
New Braintree	309	3	Eager	Paul				1			1			1			3		
Royalston	239	7	Eager	Solomon	1	1		1				1	1				5		
Sutton	158	1	Eager	Stephen			1	1	1					1			4		
Northborough	368	8	Eager	William	1		1	1		1			1				5		
Petersham	275	11	Eager	Winslow	2			1				1	1				5		
Boylston	377	26	Eames	Gershom	1	1			1	1	2		1				7		
Mendon	381	7	Eames	John				1				2	1				4	1st Parish	
Upton	387	5	Eames	Moses		2		1		3			1				7		
Petersham	275	10	Eames	Peter	2			1		2			1				6		
Milford	395	23	Eames	Phinehas		1		1		5			1				8		
Boylston	377	25	Eames	William	1	1	1		1	1	1	1		1			8		
Milford	395	24	Earl	Elizabeth Wd									1				1		
Hardwick	297	21	Earl	Jacob				1		1		1					3		
Hardwick	298	2	Earl	John	1	1		1		1	1	1					6		
Garry	277	3	Earl	Stephen	1		3		1	2	2			1			10		
Leicester	487	10	Earle	Antipas			2	1	1	1		1		2			8		
Leicester	490	1	Earle	Asahel	1			1		2	1		1				6		
Paxton	502	8	Earle	Clark		1	1		2		1	1					6		
Leicester	490	3	Earle	Henry			1			1			1				3		
Leicester	487	15	Earle	James	4	1	1		1			1	1				9		
Leicester	487	11	Earle	John			1			1			1				3		
Leicester	487	12	Earle	Jonah	3		1	1		1		2		1	1		10		
Paxton	502	10	Earle	Marmaduke	2	1			1	3	1		1				9		
Paxton	502	9	Earle	Oliver		1	3		1			1	2	1			9		
Leicester	487	14	Earle	Pliny	2	1	1	1		2		1	1				9		
Leicester	487	13	Earle	Robert		2		1						1			5		

TOWN	PG#	LN#	LAST NAME	FIRST NAME	FREE WHITE MALES					FREE WHITE FEMALES					TOTAL ALL OTHER	TOTAL SLAVES	TOTALS	DISTRICT/ TOWNSHIP	NOTES
					under 10	10 to 16	16 to 26	26 to 45	45 and over	under 10	10 to 16	16 to 26	26 to 45	45 and over					
Leicester	490	2	Earle	Silas	1		2	1		2		3					9		
Leicester	490	6	Earle	Thomas				1			1	1					3		
Leicester	490	4	Earle	William				1				1	1				3		
Leicester	490	5	Earle	Winthrop		2	2			1	1	1					7		
Boylston	377	28	Earls	Jacob				1						1			2		
Hardwick	297	18	Easterbrook	Benn				1			2	1		1			5		
Westminster	446	7	Easterbrook	John		1	2	1			1	1		1			7		
Westminster	446	8	Easterbrook	John Jr			1							1			2		
Westminster	446	9	Easterbrook	Thomas			1			1	1		1				4		
Mendon	389	9	Easty	Abijah	1		1		1	1		2	1				7	2d Parish	
Fitchburg	432	5	Eaton	Aaron	1	1	3		1		1	1	1	1			10		
Worcester	175	9	Eaton	Alpheus		1		1		1	1		1	1			6		
Worcester	175	7	Eaton	Amherst	3		2	1		1	1	1	1				10		
Southborough	204	17	Eaton	Benjm		1		1		2			1				5		
Gardner	452	2	Eaton	Joanna		1						1					2		
Gardner	452	7	Eaton	John	2	1		1		1	1	1	1				8		
Dudley	344	34	Eaton	John S.			2	1		3		2	1				9		
Garry	277	2	Eaton	Jonas		1											1		
Ward	180	71	Eaton	Jonas	3		1	1		1		1	1	1			9		
Barre	404	11	Eaton	Jonas Deac		1	1	1			1	1	1				6		
Gardner	452	5	Eaton	Jonathan	1			1		1			1				4		
Sterling	355	20	Eaton	Joseph	2		1					1					4		
Garry	277	1	Eaton	Maltiah		1	1	1		1	1		1				6		
Westminster	446	6	Eaton	Mary		1						3	1				5		
Westminster	446	5	Eaton	Nathan	1		1		2		1						5		
Lancaster	347	18	Eaton	Nathaniel		1		1	2			1					5		
Lunenberg	423	19	Eaton	Pearson			1										1		
Sutton	158	2	Eaton	Reuben	2			1		1		2	1				7		
Gardner	452	3	Eaton	Sally							1						1		
Sutton	158	3	Eaton	Samuel			1				1						2		
Brookfield	270	31	Eaton	Thomas		1		1		1		1					3	Third Parish	
Fitchburg	432	3	Eaton	Thomas		1	1			1		1					4		
Fitchburg	432	4	Eaton	Thomas 3d		1				1							2		
Holden	513	11	Eaton	Uriah			1										1		
Worcester	175	8	Eaton	William	2		4	1		1	1		1	1			11		
Barre	404	12	Eaton	James Jr	1		3	1		3			1				9		
Dudley	344	35	Eddy	Augustus			4	1				1					6		
Leicester	490	8	Eddy	Azariah	1			1				1	1				4		
Royalston	235	6	Eddy	Benja	1	1	1	1				2		2			8		
Shrewsbury	365	2	Eddy	Benjamin			1		1	1	1		1	4		9		
Charlton	330	1	Eddy	Edmund	2		1	1		2		1					7		
Northbridge	476	4	Eddy	Jesse	1		1	1	1	2			1	1			8		
Brookfield	247	10	Eddy	John			1		1	1				2			5	First Parish	
Dudley	344	33	Eddy	John	4	1	2		1		1	1	1				11		
Leicester	490	9	Eddy	John	3			1					1				5		
Oxford	162	13	Eddy	Jonas			2		1		1		1	1			6		
Sterling	356	1	Eddy	Joshua	1	2			1	4			1				9		
Sturbridge	338	10	Eddy	Josiah	2			1	1		2	1					7		
Ward	180	72	Eddy	Levi	2	2	2		1	1			1				9		
Oxford	162	14	Eddy	Parley	1	1		1			1		1				5		
Oxford	162	12	Eddy	Reuben	1	2			1	2		1	1				8		
Ward	180	73	Eddy	Samuel	2			1		1			1	1			7		
Brookfield	247	11	Eddy	Seth	1			1		2			1				5	First Parish	
Oxford	162	10	Eddy	Silas	2		2		1		1			1			7		
Oxford	162	11	Eddy	William				1						2			3		
Gardner	452	6	Edgell	Benjamin	1	1		1		3			1				7		
Gardner	452	9	Edgell	Joseph	1			1		2			1				5		
Gardner	452	8	Edgell	Samuel	3			1		2	2		1				9		
Westminster	446	10	Edgell	William		1		1		1			1				4		
Westminster	446	11	Edgell	William Jr			1			2			1				4		
Brookfield	258	15	Edmands	John	1		1	1		1		1	1				6	Second Parish	
Brookfield	258	16	Edmands	Samll			1			1		2	1	1			6	Second Parish	
Winchendon	225	20	Edmunds	Amos		1		1				2	1				5		
Sturbridge	338	11	Edmunds	Ebenzr	3	1	1	1					1				7		
Dudley	344	32	Edmunds	John	4	1		1		2	2		1				11		
Oakham	317	3	Edson	Calvin			1			1		1					3		
New Braintree	309	4	Edson	Elijah		2		1		1	2			1			8		
Hardwick	297	17	Edson	Oliver		1	1	1					1				4		
Oxford	162	15	Edson	Rhodolphus		1		1				1	1				4		
Charlton	329	24	Edwards	John		1			1	1	2	2	1	1			9		
Charlton	330	2	Edwards	Joseph				1			1	1					3		
Charlton	329	26	Edwards	Robert		1		1		2	2		1				7		
Bolton	216	3	Edwards	Susannah	1						1		1				3		
Charlton	329	25	Edwards	Thomas	2	1		1					1				6		
Hardwick	297	20	Egery	Daniel		1		1				2		1			5		
Hardwick	298	1	Egery	Thos	1			1			1	1	1				5		
Lancaster	347	17	Elder	James	1			1						1			3		
Worcester	175	4	Elder	John				1				1					2		
Worcester	175	5	Elder	John Junr	1			1		2			1				6		
Worcester	175	10	Elder	Thomas			1										1		
Worcester	175	6	Elder	William	5			1		1	1	1	1				10		
Princeton	516	21	Eldridge	Hezekiah	1			1			1	1					4		
Barre	404	13	Elit	Wm	1			1		1			1	1	5		10		
Sutton	155	16	Elliot	Aaron		1	1		1		1	1		1			6		
Sutton	155	17	Elliot	Aaron Junr	1			1		3			1				6		
Sutton	155	20	Elliot	Andrew			4	1	1			1		2			9		
Sutton	155	19	Elliot	Jonathan	1	2			1	1			1				6		
Leicester	490	7	Elliot	Joseph		1	2		1	1	2		1				8		

Heads of household census table. Columns under "FREE WHITE MALES" and "FREE WHITE FEMALES" are each split into age ranges: under 10 / 10 to 16 / 16 to 26 / 26 to 45 / 45 and over.

TOWN	PG#	LN#	LAST NAME	FIRST NAME	FWM under 10	FWM 10 to 16	FWM 16 to 26	FWM 26 to 45	FWM 45 and over	FWF under 10	FWF 10 to 16	FWF 16 to 26	FWF 26 to 45	FWF 45 and over	TOTAL ALL OTHER	TOTAL SLAVES	TOTALS	DISTRICT/ TOWNSHIP	NOTES
Uxbridge	465	17	Elliot	Mehitable	1	1				3			1				6		
Sutton	155	18	Ellis	Abel		1	1	1		1	1		1				6		
Royalston	240	2	Ellis	Adams			1	1		2			1	1			6		
Southborough	203	32	Ellis	Amos	2		1	1		1	1		1				7		
Brookfield	247	7	Ellis	Asa				1						1			2	First Parish	
Brookfield	247	8	Ellis	Asa Junior		1		1		1	1	1	1				6	First Parish	
Royalston	240	4	Ellis	Ezekiel	2	1	1	1		1	1		1				8		
Princeton	515	3	Ellis	James	1	1		1		1	1		1				6		
Sturbridge	338	12	Ellis	Jedediah	1	2	1	1		3		2	1				11		
Ashburnham	460	20	Ellis	Jesse		1		1				2		1			5		
Brookfield	247	9	Ellis	Nathan B.	2	1	1	1		1	1		3				10	First Parish	
Sturbridge	338	9	Ellis	Saml				1						1			2		
Northbridge	476	5	Ellison	Eliab	1		1					1					3		
Uxbridge	465	21	Ellison	Joseph		1				1	1	1					4		
Northbridge	476	3	Ellison	Thomas	1			1		2	1	1	1				7		
Hardwick	297	19	Ellwell	David	3		1			1			1	1			7		
Athol	289	18	Elmwood	Daniel		2					1	1	1	1			6		
Bolton	215	8	Elmwood	Nathan	2		1			1			1				5		
Uxbridge	465	18	Emerson	Jonathan		1		1				2		1			5		
Douglas	480	25	Emerson	Joseph		1		1		1	1		1				5		
Royalston	239	5	Emerson	Joseph	1			1			1	3		1			7		
Uxbridge	465	19	Emerson	Nathl			2	1		2		2	1				8		
Uxbridge	465	20	Emerson	Nathl Jur	1		1	1		1		1					5		
Sterling	355	21	Emes	Patty						2			1				3		
Harvard	218	10	Emmerson	Peter	1	1	1	1	1			1		1			7		
Winchendon	225	23	Emory	Francis			1				2		1				4		
Winchendon	225	22	Emory	Stephen		1	2	1			1	2	1				8		
Mendon	389	8	Engly	Timothy	2			1		3			1				7	2d Parish	
Rutland	506	13	Estabrook	Daniel		1		1		1			1				4		
Rutland	506	14	Estabrook	Daniel Jr		1	1					1					3		
Holden	513	7	Estabrook	Ebenezer	1		2	1				1		1			6		
Paxton	502	14	Estabrook	Ebenz	2	1		1		2	1		1				8		
Holden	513	9	Estabrook	James	2	1	1			1		1					7		
Rutland	506	15	Estabrook	Jedediah	5		1					1	1				8		
Paxton	502	6	Estabrook	Jonah	1	1		1		2		1					6		
Holden	513	8	Estabrook	Jonathan	2		2	1				2					9		
Holden	513	10	Estabrook	Samuel		1			1			1		1			4		
Paxton	502	7	Estabrook	Thads	2	1		1			1	2	1				8		
Athol	289	19	Estabrooks	Joseph Revd	2	1	2	1		2			2	1			11		
Westborough	198	123	Estee	John	3			1					2				6		
Westborough	199	153	Estee	Nathaniel	1			1		2			1				5		
Southborough	206	17	Estee	Solomon	2			1				1	1	1			6		
Oakham	317	4	Esterbrook	Joel	3			1				1					5		
Charlton	329	27	Eustice	Thomas		1	1			3	1						6		
Rutland	506	11	Eustis	Chamberlain		1	1	1		1			2				6		
Rutland	506	12	Eustis	Joseph	1	1	1			2		1					6		
Winchendon	225	21	Evans	Jona	2	1	1			1	1		1				8		
Leominster	436	24	Evans	Samuel		1	1	1		1		2	1				7		
Princeton	516	22	Eveleth	Abishai			1			2		1	1	1			6		
Princeton	516	23	Eveleth	Joshua Junr	1		1			4		2					8		
New Braintree	309	5	Evens	Robert	1		1					1					3		
Princeton	516	24	Everett	Joshua		1	1						1	2			5		
Princeton	515	1	Everett	Joshua Junr	2		1						1				4		
Westminster	446	12	Everett	Pelitiah	3	1		1		1	1	1					8		
Rutland	506	16	Everett	Phinehas		1	1					2	1	1			7		
Princeton	515	2	Everett	William	1	1		1					1				4		
Lancaster	347	20	Everton	Benjamin	3	1		1					1				6		
Sterling	356	10	Fairbank	Abijah		1		1				1		1			4		
Sterling	356	2	Fairbank	Alpheus	1		1			2	1		1				6		
Harvard	217	18	Fairbank	Amos		1		1				1		1			4		
Athol	289	20	Fairbank	Benja	2	2		1		1			1				7		
Berlin	216	11	Fairbank	Caleb	2	1		1		2			1				7		
Lancaster	350	8	Fairbank	Cyrus	2	1		1		2	1		1		1		9		
Lancaster	350	1	Fairbank	Cyrus Jun			1						1				2		
Leominster	436	28	Fairbank	Elijah		1	1	1		1	1	1	1				7		
Leominster	436	29	Fairbank	Elizabeth	1					2			1				4		
Harvard	217	6	Fairbank	Ephraim	2		1			3	2		1				9		
Grafton	196	2	Fairbank	Isaiah	1		1	1				2	1				8		
Harvard	217	5	Fairbank	Jabez	1			1		2			1				5		
Sterling	356	5	Fairbank	Jabez	1			1	1	1			1	1			6		
Harvard	220	20	Fairbank	Jacob		1	1			2			1				5		
Athol	289	27	Fairbank	John			1	1			1			1			4		
Athol	289	24	Fairbank	John Capt	1	1	1			3			1				8		
Lancaster	350	9	Fairbank	Jonas		1	2	1		1	1		1				8		
Berlin	213	13	Fairbank	Jonathan		1				4			1				6		
Harvard	217	9	Fairbank	Jonathan	2		1			1			1				5		
Westborough	194	58	Fairbank	Jonathan	1		1						1	1			4		
Harvard	217	10	Fairbank	Joseph					1			1					2		
Sterling	356	9	Fairbank	Joseph	1		1	1				2		1			6		
Bolton	209	12	Fairbank	Jotham		1						1	1				4		
Sterling	356	4	Fairbank	Lemuel			1	1				2		1			5		
Berlin	216	13	Fairbank	Manassah	2			1		2	2		1	2			10		
Winchendon	225	29	Fairbank	Moses				1						1			2		
Harvard	217	19	Fairbank	Noah		1		1		1			1				4		
Sterling	356	8	Fairbank	Oliver	1	2	2	1				1	1	1			9		
Bolton	213	18	Fairbank	Phineas		2						1	2				5		
Harvard	217	12	Fairbank	Phineas				1						1			2		
Sterling	356	6	Fairbank	Seth	3		1	1		1		2	2	1			11		
Harvard	218	19	Fairbank	Thomas	2	1		1		2			1	1			8		

TOWN	PG#	LN#	LAST NAME	FIRST NAME	M under 10	M 10 to 16	M 16 to 26	M 26 to 45	M 45 and over	F under 10	F 10 to 16	F 16 to 26	F 26 to 45	F 45 and over	TOTAL ALL OTHER	TOTAL SLAVES	TOTALS	DISTRICT/TOWNSHIP	NOTES
Athol	289	26	Fairbank	Thos				1				1		1			3		
Sterling	356	7	Fairbank	William			1			3	1	1	1				7		
Douglas	479	2	Fairbanks	Amos		1	1	1		1	1		1				6		
Harvard	221	9	Fairbanks	Amos Junr	2		1					1	1				5		
Ashburnham	460	28	Fairbanks	Cyrus	1	1		1		1	2	1	1				8		
Ashburnham	460	27	Fairbanks	Ithamer	1		1			3	1		1				7		
Douglas	479	4	Fairbanks	Joshua	2	1		1		1	1		2				8		
Gardner	452	12	Fairbanks	Levi	1	2	2			1	2		1				9		
Mendon	381	11	Fairbanks	Nancy Wd.	2					2	1	1	1				7	1st Parish	
Lunenberg	426	2	Fairchild	Elijah	2	1		1				1					5		
Harvard	222	39	Fairfield	John				1					2		1		4		
Harvard	221	26	Fairwell	Edmund	1	1	3	1		1	1		1				9		
Spencer	498	7	Fales	James		1	1	1		1	1	1	1				7		
Lancaster	350	7	Fales	Jeremiah		1	1	1		3	2		1				9		
Holden	513	18	Fales	Lemuel	2	1	1			1		1	1				7		
Hubbardston	417	19	Falis	John H.	1		2	1		1		1	1				7		
Bolton	207	7	Fallass	William								1		1			2		
Bolton	216	20	Fallass	William								1		1			2		
Western	252	12	Farley	Samuel		1		1		2	1		1				6		
Lunenberg	426	1	Farmer	John								1		1			2		
Dudley	344	43	Farnam	Calvin	1		1			1	1	1					5		
Harvard	220	9	Farnsworth	Abel		1		1				2	1				5		
Westminster	445	3	Farnsworth	Asa		1		1		2	1		1				6		
Lancaster	350	2	Farnsworth	Benjamin	1		1			1			1				4		
Leominster	436	33	Farnsworth	Elias	2	1	2	1		2	2		1				11		
Petersham	275	16	Farnsworth	Ephm		1	1	1		1		1		1			6		
Fitchburg	429	1	Farnsworth	Joseph	1		1	1		3	3		1				10		
Sutton	158	11	Farnsworth	Joseph		3					1						4		
Harvard	221	33	Farnsworth	Mathias				1					1				2		
Harvard	222	10	Farnsworth	Nathl	1		1	1			1		1				5		
Templeton	235	9	Farnsworth	Oliver	1	1	1	1		3	1	1	1				10		
Garry	277	5	Farnsworth	Phinehas						1	2		1				4		
Uxbridge	465	27	Farnum	Caleb	2		3	1		1		1	1				9		
Uxbridge	465	29	Farnum	David	2	2		1		1		1	1				8		
Uxbridge	465	22	Farnum	David Junr	2	1		1				2					6		
Uxbridge	465	30	Farnum	George			2	1		1			1				5		
Douglas	479	1	Farnum	John	2	1		1	1	3	1		1	1			11		
Charlton	330	11	Farnum	Joshua			1	1					1				3		
Uxbridge	465	25	Farnum	Moses	2			1		1			2				6		
Uxbridge	465	26	Farnum	Peter	3	1		1		1			1				7		
Uxbridge	465	24	Farnum	Royal	2	2		1		2			1				8		
Charlton	330	7	Farnum	Thomas	1		1	1		1		1		1			6		
Harvard	215	4	Farr	Francis	2	1		1		3	1	1	1				10		
Holden	513	12	Farr	Simeon								1		1			2		
Winchendon	225	28	Farrar	Daniel		1		1			2		1				5		
Worcester	175	11	Farrar	John	1		1	2	1		2				2		9		
Petersham	278	2	Farrar	Joseph	1	1	1	1		2	1		1				8		
Barre	403	5	Farrar	Joseph Maj			3			1	3	2	2	1			12		
Barre	403	15	Farrar	Saml	2	1		1					1				5		
Sutton	158	4	Farrar	Seth	1			1		1	1		1				5		
Upton	387	12	Farrer	Benjm Maj				1					2	1			4		
Upton	387	7	Farrer	Ezra	2		1	1					1				5		
Harvard	222	1	Farrer	Stephen			1	1					1				3		
Northbridge	476	12	Farrow	Benjamin	2		1	1			1		1				6		
Fitchburg	432	10	Farwell	Abraham		2		1		1	1		1				6		
Lancaster	350	18	Farwell	Amsa						1	1						2		
Fitchburg	432	19	Farwell	Asa	1		1			1			1				4		
Fitchburg	432	15	Farwell	Daniel	1	1	1	1		1		1	1				7		
Fitchburg	432	21	Farwell	John		1		1					1				3		
Harvard	219	18	Farwell	John				1					1	1			3		
Lancaster	350	4	Farwell	Joseph	1		1	1		1	1		1				6		
Lancaster	350	12	Farwell	Leonard	2	1	3	1		1	1	1	1				11		
Fitchburg	432	17	Farwell	Simeon	3		1	1		1			1				7		
Fitchburg	432	11	Farwell	Zacheus	3	1	1	1		2	1	1	1	1			12		
Royalston	241	35	Faulkner	Ammi R*	2		1	1			1		1				6		
Sturbridge	338	19	Faulkner	Daniel	1		1				1	1	1				5		
Boylston	378	7	Faulkner	Paul				1					1				2		
Lancaster	350	14	Faulkner	Paul	2		1						1				4		
Sturbridge	338	18	Faulkner	Peter				1				1		1			3		
Berlin	212	19	Faulkner	William	1		1						1				3		
Northborough	365	1	Fay	Abigail						2	1		1				4		
Barre	403	13	Fay	Adam	3		1						1				5		
Northborough	368	10	Fay	Adam			3	1					2				6		
Northborough	368	13	Fay	Asa	2			1			1		1	1			6		
Westborough	196	88	Fay	Benjm	1	3		2	1	1		3		1			12		
Southborough	200	9	Fay	Brigham	1	1		1		1		1		1			6		
Westborough	192	44	Fay	Catharine									1				1		
Shrewsbury	365	4	Fay	Charles	2	1		1		1		1	1				7		
Sturbridge	338	20	Fay	Cyrus	1	2		1		2		1	1				8		
Westborough	197	118	Fay	Daniel			3				1						4		
Northborough	368	14	Fay	David				1					1				2		
Southborough	205	17	Fay	David	2	1	2	1		2	1	1	1				11		
Westborough	196	93	Fay	David	4	1	2	1		1	1	1	1	1			13		
Westborough	199	146	Fay	Elisha		1	2			1	2		1				8		
Southborough	205	35	Fay	Francis	2		1	1					1				5		
Southborough	202	9	Fay	Heman	1	1	1	1		3	1	1	1				10		
Southborough	200	7	Fay	Hezekiah	4	1	1	1		2	1	1	1				12		
Grafton	193	4	Fay	Jedithen	2			2		3		1		3			11		
Southborough	205	34	Fay	Jeremiah	1		1			1			1	1			5		

TOWN	PG#	LN#	LAST NAME	FIRST NAME	FREE WHITE MALES					FREE WHITE FEMALES					TOTAL ALL OTHER	TOTAL SLAVES	TOTALS	DISTRICT/ TOWNSHIP	NOTES
					under 10	10 to 16	16 to 26	26 to 45	45 and over	under 10	10 to 16	16 to 26	26 to 45	45 and over					
Bolton	213	9	Fay	John	1	1	1		1	2		1		1			8		
Bolton	213	10	Fay	John Junr		1		1	1	1	1						6		
Athol	289	22	Fay	Joseph	1		2		1	2	2			1			9		
Athol	289	23	Fay	Josiah			1			1			1				3		
Worcester	178	13	Fay	Lucretia								1		1			2		
Southborough	206	1	Fay	Mary			1						1				2		
Northborough	368	15	Fay	Nahum Esq		1	1	1		1		1	1				6		
Southborough	202	2	Fay	Nathan	1	2	1		1	1		2	1				9		
Southborough	202	16	Fay	Nathl	1		2		1		3		2				9		
Southborough	205	36	Fay	Peter	1			1		3	3		1				9		
Hardwick	298	9	Fay	Reuben			1		1	1	2	1					6		
Southborough	204	6	Fay	Reuben	1	1				1	1	1	1				7		
Southborough	203	6	Fay	Robert Jun	3	2		1	1	2	1	1	1				12		
Princeton	515	5	Fay	Silas		2	3	1	1	1	1	1		1			10		
Westborough	196	89	Fay	Silas	1		3	1		2			2				9		
Athol	289	25	Fay	Solomon		1		1		1	1		1				5		
Southborough	204	7	Fay	Solomon	1		2					1					4		
New Braintree	309	6	Fay	Stephan		1	1		1	1	1	1					6		
Charlton	330	10	Fay	Stephen		1		1	1		2		1				6		
Northborough	368	12	Fay	Thaddeus	1		2	1	1	1		2	1				9		
Hardwick	298	7	Fay	Timothy	3	2	1		1	1		1	1	1			11		
Northborough	368	11	Fay	Timothy	2		1	1			1		1	1			7		
Uxbridge	465	31	Feechum	Samuel	2			1		1			1				5		
Royalston	235	7	Felch	Caleb	3	1		1		1	3		1				9		
Royalston	239	3	Felch	Samll				1				1	1				3		
Royalston	239	4	Felch	Samll Junr		2		1				1	1				5		
Barre	403	7	Fellows	John			1	1			2		1				5		
Brookfield	270	24	Felton	Benjamin	1	2	2		1	1	1	1		1			10	Third Parish	
Holden	513	13	Felton	John	1			1		1			1				4		
Barre	403	8	Felton	Shelton	2	3		1	1	1		3	1	1			13		
Worcester	178	16	Femo	Sally	2		3						2				7		
Brookfield	270	27	Fenner	Sion			1			3		1	1				6	Third Parish	
Westminster	452	5	Fenno	Ephraim	1		1			2	1		1				6		
Ashburnham	460	29	Fenno	Joseph	2	2		1		1	1		1				8		
Gardner	452	11	Fenno	William	3			1			1		1				6		
Western	258	3	Ferrey	Hezekiah	5			1		1			1				8		
Westminster	446	13	Fesenden	Samuel	3			1			1			1			6		
Westminster	446	15	Fesenden	Timothy				1						1			2		
Westborough	189	8	Fesendon	John				1			1	1	1				4		
Westminster	445	1	Fesendon	John		1		1				1		1			4		
Westminster	445	2	Fesendon	Jonas	1		1					1					3		
Barre	403	18	Fesendon	Mary Wid							1	2		1			4		
Barre	403	2	Fesendon	Peter	1	2		1		3			1				8		
Westminster	445	4	Fesendon	Timothy Jr			1				1						2		
Rutland	510	1	Fessenden	Elizabeth		1	1				1		1	1			5		
Rutland	510	2	Fessenden	Inman			1						1				2		
Winchendon	226	1	Fessenden	John	2			1		1	1	1					6		
Southborough	201	13	Fessendon	Benjm				1					1				2		
Westborough	194	56	Feywether	John		1	1	1									4		
Western	257	12	Field	Asa K.	1		4				1	1					7		
New Braintree	312	2	Field	Benm		1	1		1		2		1				6		
New Braintree	312	1	Field	Ebenz	1	1	2	1	1	2		2	1	1			12		
Hardwick	298	3	Field	George		1	2		1	1	1		1				7		
Western	258	2	Field	Joseph		1		1					1				3		
Brookfield	247	14	Field	Seth	1	1		1		3			2				8	First Parish	
Oakham	317	6	Field	Spencer			6	1	1	1	1	3	1				13		
Berlin	214	36	Fife	William		3		1		3		1	1	1			10		
Athol	289	29	Fish	Ezra	1			1				1					3		
Hardwick	298	5	Fish	Henry	1			1		1	2		1				6		
Athol	289	21	Fish	Samuel	2			1		1		1					5		
Athol	289	28	Fish	Simeon		1		1		1	2		1				6		
Dudley	344	40	Fishel	Wm		1		1	1	1		1	1				5		
Dudley	344	41	Fishel	Wm Jun	1		1				1		1				4		
Sutton	158	8	Fisher	Aaron	2		1	1		1	1		1				7		
Royalston	233	4	Fisher	David	2			1		3			1				7		
Upton	387	13	Fisher	Elias	2	2		1				1	1				8		
Princeton	515	4	Fisher	Ichabod		2		1		2			1				6		
Lancaster	350	3	Fisher	Jacob	2	1	1	1		3		3					11		
Southborough	204	3	Fisher	Joshua	2			2		1	1		1				7		
Mendon	389	10	Fisher	Nathan	1			1					1				3	2d Parish	
Templeton	236	11	Fisher	Nathan				1						2			3		
Westborough	194	53	Fisher	Nathan	2			1		1	2	1		1			8		
Templeton	235	18	Fisher	Samll		1		1			1		1	1			5		
Westborough	189	15	Fisher	Samuel	2	1		1			1		1				6		
Templeton	236	12	Fisher	Thomas	2	1	1	1		3	1		1				10		
Southborough	203	31	Fisher	Timothy				1				1		1			3		
Rutland	506	21	Fisk	Asa	2			1	1	1		1	1				8		
Upton	387	17	Fisk	Benjamin				1							1		2		
Upton	387	6	Fisk	Benjamin Jr	4	3	1		1	1	1	2	1				15		
Oxford	162	19	Fisk	Daniel	1		3	1		2	1	2			1		12		
Sturbridge	338	14	Fisk	Daniel	2	2	1	1		2	2						12		
Upton	387	16	Fisk	Daniel		1		1		4		1	1				8		
Sturbridge	335	3	Fisk	David	2	2	1	1		2		2	1	1	1		13		
Barre	403	6	Fisk	David Col		2	1		1			1		1	1		7		
Petersham	275	12	Fisk	Ebenz			1						1				2		
Sturbridge	338	13	Fisk	Henry	1		3		1	2	3		2				12		
Barre	403	3	Fisk	Jason	2		1	1		1			1				6		
New Braintree	309	12	Fisk	John	1	2		1				1	1		2		9		
Petersham	275	14	Fisk	John	1	1		1		4		1	1				9		
Westborough	189	6	Fisk	John	2	2		1				1	1				8		

TOWN	PG#	LN#	LAST NAME	FIRST NAME	FREE WHITE MALES under 10	10 to 16	16 to 26	26 to 45	45 and over	FREE WHITE FEMALES under 10	10 to 16	16 to 26	26 to 45	45 and over	TOTAL ALL OTHER	TOTAL SLAVES	TOTALS	DISTRICT/ TOWNSHIP	NOTES
Leominster	436	30	Fisk	Jonas			1			1		1	1	1			5		
Holden	513	16	Fisk	Jonathan		1	1	1			1	1	1				6		
Winchendon	225	24	Fisk	Jonathan	2		1		1		2	1	1	1			9		
Upton	387	18	Fisk	Josiah	1	1		2	1	1		2		1			9		
Holden	513	17	Fisk	Lemuel		1		1				1	1	1			5		
Holden	513	15	Fisk	Nahum	3	1				1	2		1	1			9		
Sturbridge	338	17	Fisk	Nathan	2		1	1		2		1	1				8		
Uxbridge	465	23	Fisk	Nathl	2	1		1		2	2	1	1				10		
Upton	387	19	Fisk	Robert		2		1					1	1			5		
Barre	403	4	Fisk	Saml	4		1					1	1	1			8		
Sturbridge	338	16	Fisk	Saml			1										1		
Sturbridge	338	15	Fisk	Simeon		1		1				1		1			4		
Rutland	506	19	Fisk	William	1						2		1	1			5		
Upton	387	20	Fisk	William	1		2	1	1	1		2		1			9		
Petersham	275	15	Fiske	Abigail								1		1			2		
Brookfield	247	12	Fiske	Abner	1	2	1	1						1			6	First Parish	
Brookfield	257	1	Fiske	Frances	1		1			1		1	1				5	Second Parish	
Worcester	178	3	Fiske	Oliver	2	2		1				1		1	2		9		
Worcester	178	6	Fiske	Samuel		1	2	1		3	1	1					9		
Shrewsbury	365	6	Fitch	Charles M.		1	1			2		2					6		
Sterling	356	11	Fitch	Ebenezer	3	2	1				1	3	1	1			12		
Oxford	159	1	Fith	Benja Junr	2		1						1				4		
Royalston	238	3	Fith	Isaac	1		1			3		1					6		
Royalston	238	15	Fith	Robert	2		1						1				4		
Templeton	235	14	Fith	Robert		1			1		1	1		1			5		
Oxford	162	17	Fitts	Bena & Andrew		2		1				1		1			5		
Charlton	330	8	Fitts	Caleb	1		1	1		3		1	1	4			12		
Oxford	162	21	Fitts	Daniel	2	1		1		2		1	1				8		
Oxford	162	18	Fitts	David	1		1			1			1				4		
Charlton	330	5	Fitts	John	1	1	2		1	2	1	1	1				10		
Oakham	317	5	Fitts	Peter	3		1	1			1	1	1	3			11		
Charlton	330	12	Fitts	Robert	2	1	1	1		1	1	1	1				9		
Ward	180	77	Fitts	Walter	2			1		2	1		1				7		
Fitchburg	432	13	Fitzgerald	Elizabeth		1								1			2		
Worcester	175	15	Flagg	Aaron		1	1	1		1			1				5		
Worcester	178	11	Flagg	Amos			1			3			1				5		
Worcester	178	10	Flagg	Asa	1												1		
Boylston	378	8	Flagg	Benjamin	3	1		1	1	2	1		1				10		
Holden	513	14	Flagg	Benjamin		1	1	1		1		2		2			8		
Worcester	175	12	Flagg	Benjamin				1									1		
Worcester	178	9	Flagg	Benjamin				2						1			3		
Worcester	175	13	Flagg	Benjamin Jun	1		1					2	1	1			6		
Worcester	178	8	Flagg	David		1		1					1				3		
Barre	403	9	Flagg	Earle	1	3	1		1	1			4	1			12		
Barre	403	16	Flagg	Earle Jr			1						1				2		
Boylston	378	2	Flagg	Ebenezer				1						1			2		
Northbridge	476	11	Flagg	Eleazer	2			1			2		1				6		
Worcester	178	15	Flagg	Eli	2			1		2			1				6		
Petersham	275	13	Flagg	Elisha	1		1		1		1			1			5		
Worcester	178	5	Flagg	Elisha	2		1	1	1	2	2	1	1	1			12		
Worcester	178	1	Flagg	Francis		1	1		1	1		1	1	1			7		
Boylston	378	6	Flagg	Gershom	3		2	1		1			1				8		
Winchendon	225	30	Flagg	John	3		1			1			1				6		
Worcester	175	14	Flagg	John		1	2					1					4		
Holden	513	19	Flagg	Jonathan	3	2	1	1		1			1				9		
Brookfield	270	28	Flagg	Josiah		1							1				3	Third Parish	
Lancaster	350	5	Flagg	Josiah	1	1	1	1		3	1		1				9		
Fitchburg	432	8	Flagg	Levi	3		5			2			1				11		
Worcester	178	4	Flagg	Levi	2	2	1	1		1	1		1				9		
Upton	388	1	Flagg	Nathaniel	2	1		1		4	1	1	1				11		
Worcester	178	7	Flagg	Nathaniel	4		1	1			1		1				8		
Lancaster	350	10	Flagg	Rebeca	5					1			3	1			10		
Boylston	378	11	Flagg	Rebeckah						3			1				4		
Grafton	198	14	Flagg	Robartus	3	1			1	4			1				10		
Boylston	378	12	Flagg	Rufus	1				1	1			1				4		
Spencer	498	6	Flagg	Saml				1						1			2		
Grafton	204	4	Flagg	Samuel		1	3	1					1	1			7		
Worcester	175	16	Flagg	Samuel		1	2	1					1	2			7		
Holden	513	20	Flagg	Silas	2			1		1	1		1				6		
Boylston	378	5	Flagg	Stephen			1	1					1	1			4		
Boylston	378	9	Flagg	Stephen Jun	2	2		1		2	2	1	1				11		
Mendon	381	12	Fletcher	Asa		1		1					1	2			5	1st Parish	
Templeton	242	10	Fletcher	Caleb		1	3	1				1	1				7		
Sutton	158	10	Fletcher	Ebenz	1		1	1		2		1	1				7		
Northbridge	476	6	Fletcher	James	2		3	1		1		2	1	1			11		
Templeton	233	9	Fletcher	Joel		1		1				1		1			4		
Bolton	216	17	Fletcher	Joseph	2		1			1				1			5		
Lancaster	350	6	Fletcher	Joshua			1	1			1		1				4		
Ashburnham	460	23	Fletcher	Josiah	4			1		1			1				7		
Charlton	330	6	Fletcher	Nathan	1			1					1	1			4		
Garry	277	7	Fletcher	Peter	2		2	1		3			1	1			10		
Leominster	436	32	Fletcher	Rebeckah										2			2		
Lancaster	347	21	Fletcher	Rufus	2			1		2	1		1				7		
Lancaster	350	11	Fletcher	Timothy	2			1		1		1	1				6		
Templeton	233	10	Fletcher	William	2		1			3	1		1				8		
Leicester	490	10	Flint	Austin	2	5	3	2		2		1	1				16		
Fitchburg	432	6	Flint	Benjamin	1	1		1		1		1	3	1			9		
Shrewsbury	365	5	Flint	Edward Doct.	1		3	1		1			1				7		
Gardner	452	13	Flint	Ezekiel		1				1		1	1				4		

TOWN	PG#	LN#	LAST NAME	FIRST NAME	FREE WHITE MALES					FREE WHITE FEMALES					TOTAL ALL OTHER	TOTAL SLAVES	TOTALS	DISTRICT/ TOWNSHIP	NOTES
					under 10	10 to 16	16 to 26	26 to 45	45 and over	under 10	10 to 16	16 to 26	26 to 45	45 and over					
Oakham	317	10	Flint	John	1	1	1		1	1	1			1			7		
Winchendon	225	26	Flint	John				1									1		
Fitchburg	432	9	Flint	Jonathan	1		2	1						1			5		
Winchendon	225	25	Flint	Nathan	2	2		1		3	1	1	1				11		
Winchendon	225	27	Flint	Thomas	3	1		1		2			1				8		
Rutland	510	3	Flint	Tilly	1		1	1	1	1			1	1			7		
Lancaster	350	15	Flood	William	3			1		2			1				7		
Oakham	317	8	Fobes	Jno		1		1		1			1				4		
Oakham	317	15	Fobes	Joseph	1		1	1			2		1	1			7		
Leominster	436	27	Folinsbee	Edward	3			1		2			1	1			8		
Worcester	178	12	Follet	Walter	1			1		1			1				4		
Leominster	436	25	Folliensbee	Francis	1	1	1		1	1	1	1	1				8		
Hubbardston	417	18	Follit	Saml	2	1		4		1	1	1	1				11		
Brookfield	270	26	Forbes	Aaron		2		1		2	1	1	1				8	Third Parish	
Barre	403	14	Forbes	Charles	3		1	1		1			1				6		
Brookfield	263	12	Forbes	Daniel	2	1	2		1	1	1	1					9	Second Parish	
Royalston	236	7	Forbes	James	1	1	1	1		3	1	1	1				10		
Rutland	506	20	Forbes	John		1	1	1		2	1		1				7		
Barre	403	12	Forbes	Martha Wid									1	1			2		
Upton	387	9	Forbes	Susannah Wd	1	1	1			2		1	1	1			8		
Oxford	162	20	Forbes	William			3	1				1	1				6		
Oakham	317	16	Forbs	Elenor	2		1			2			1				6		
Westborough	191	32	Forbs	Elisha	1		3		1		1	2		1			9		
Westborough	197	116	Forbs	Jonath		2	2	1		1	2	1		1			10		
Westborough	196	91	Forbs	Moses			1			1		2					4		
Westborough	192	49	Forbs	Phinehas		1	1	1		2	1	2	1				9		
Westborough	198	126	Forbush	Asa	1	2		1		2	2		1				9		
Westborough	194	70	Forbush	Colledge	1		1	1		4			1				8		
Harvard	221	21	Forbush	Daniel	1		1	1			1	1	1				6		
Westborough	196	100	Forbush	Ebenz				1					1				2		
Southborough	203	27	Forbush	Elizabeth						3	1		2				6		
Southborough	203	33	Forbush	Enoch			1			1			1				3		
Westborough	189	3	Forbush	Isaac		1	2	2		2		1	1				9		
Harvard	221	3	Forbush	John			1							3			4		
Westborough	191	27	Forbush	Rufus	2	2	1	1		1		1	1				9		
Harvard	221	2	Forbush	Samuel		2	1		1	1	1		1	1			8		
Westborough	196	102	Forbush	Samuel				1					1	1			3		
Westborough	196	103	Forbush	Samuel Jun	2			1					1				4		
Harvard	217	36	Forbush	Sarah										1			1		
Southborough	203	26	Forbush	Silas	2			1		3	1		2				9		
Brookfield	270	23	Force	Ebenezer	2	1		1			1		1				6	Third Parish	
New Braintree	309	11	Force	Jno	1			1						1			3		
New Braintree	309	8	Force	Jno Jr	1		2	1		2	1		1				8		
Berlin	214	5	Fosgate	Joel		2	3	1		4	1		1				12		
Westminster	446	14	Foskett	Daniel	1	1		1				1		1			5		
Boylston	378	1	Fosset	Abel	3			1		1			1				6		
Boylston	378	3	Fosset	Jonathan		1	1	1		1	2		1				7		
Boylston	378	4	Fosset	Jonathan Jun	3		1	1		2			2	1			10		
Dudley	344	39	Foster	Abel	1	1		1		2			1				6		
Garry	277	6	Foster	Abner	1		1	1	1	1			1	1			7		
Ashburnham	460	24	Foster	Abram	1			1		3			1				6		
New Braintree	309	9	Foster	Betsey						1		1	1				3		
Gardner	452	10	Foster	David		1		1		1		1	1				5		
Brookfield	247	13	Foster	Dwight	1	1		2		1	1	2	1	1			10	First Parish	
Dudley	344	37	Foster	Ebenze	1		1							1			4		
Oakham	317	7	Foster	Ebenzr	1		1	1		1	1		1				6		
Sturbridge	338	21	Foster	Fletcher	2	2	2	1			1	1		2			11		
Lunenberg	423	20	Foster	Isaac Jun		1	1	1				1	1				5		
Ashburnham	460	21	Foster	James			1	1		4	1	1					7		
Royalston	233	5	Foster	John			1	1		1	1						4		
Barre	403	11	Foster	Laml Capt	1			1		2		1	1	1			7		
Barre	403	17	Foster	Leml	1	1		1					1				4		
Dudley	344	42	Foster	Mary						1		1		1			3		
Western	258	1	Foster	Nathan		1		1	1	3		1	1				8		
Ashburnham	460	22	Foster	Nathanll	1		1	1		2	2		1				8		
New Braintree	309	10	Foster	Nathl	3		1		2	3	3		1	1			14		
Ashburnham	460	25	Foster	Nathll Jr	1	1		1		2			1				6		
Oakham	317	14	Foster	Samll	1			1			1		1				4		
Lunenberg	423	23	Foster	Samuel				1						1			2		
Ashburnham	460	26	Foster	Susanna			1			1	1		1				4		
Royalston	241	7	Foster	Tammy	4	1	1			2	1		1				10		
Dudley	344	36	Foster	Timothy		2	1				1	1		1			6		
Brookfield	257	2	Foster	William		1	1	1				2					5	Second Parish	
Northbridge	476	9	Fowler	Barnard	2			1		2			1				6		
Worcester	178	14	Fowler	Ezekiel		2		1		1	1		1				6		
Northbridge	476	8	Fowler	John		1		1		3		1					6		
Northbridge	476	7	Fowler	Jonathan			1	1		1			1				3		
Northbridge	476	10	Fowler	Samuel			1	1		1			3	1			7		
Fitchburg	432	7	Fox	Joseph	1		2	1	1	1	1	4					11		
Mendon	381	8	Fox	Joseph	1			1		1			1				4	1st Parish	
Brookfield	270	25	Foxcoft	Francis		2		1				3	2	1			9	Third Parish	
Lunenberg	423	22	France	Hannah	1		1							1			3		
Sterling	356	3	Francis	Caleb		1		1		3	1	1	1				8		
Sutton	158	9	Freeland	James		1						1					2		
Rutland	506	17	Freelove	Samuel		1				2	1	1					5		
Sturbridge	338	22	Freeman	benj				1				1		2			4		
Sturbridge	335	4	Freeman	Chester	1		1	1		2		1	1				7		
Sturbridge	338	23	Freeman	Comfort		1	1	1		2	1		1				7		
Dudley	344	38	Freeman	David		1							1				2		
Hardwick	298	8	Freeman	Eli			1	2		1	1		1				6		

TOWN	PG#	LN#	LAST NAME	FIRST NAME	M under 10	M 10 to 16	M 16 to 26	M 26 to 45	M 45 and over	F under 10	F 10 to 16	F 16 to 26	F 26 to 45	F 45 and over	TOTAL ALL OTHER	TOTAL SLAVES	TOTALS	DISTRICT/ TOWNSHIP	NOTES
Oakham	317	11	Freeman	Elijah			1					1					2		
Barre	403	10	Freeman	Haskell Capt	1		2		1	2	1	1		1			9		
Winchendon	225	32	Freeman	Joseph			1			1		1					3		
Hardwick	298	6	Freeman	Nathan	4		1	1		1	1		1				9		
Upton	387	8	Freeman	Prince											7		7		
Mendon	381	10	Freeman	Ralph			1			2			1				4	1st Parish	
Sturbridge	335	2	Freeman	Saml	1	1	1					1					4		
Mendon	381	15	Freeman	William	3		1		1	1	1		1				8	1st Parish	
Oakham	317	12	French	Asa		1	1	1				1	1	1			7		
Templeton	235	2	French	Ebenz		1	1		1		1	1	1				7		
Templeton	235	1	French	Ebenz Jr	2			1		1			1				5		
Oakham	317	9	French	John	1		1		1			3	1	1			8		
Barre	403	1	French	Leml	3		1		1				1				7		
Templeton	242	4	French	Lypha	1	1		1	1	2			1				7		
Mendon	381	14	French	Royal	1		1			3	2	1	1				9	1st Parish	
Fitchburg	432	20	French	Thomas	4		1			1			1				7		
Royalston	242	7	French	Widow	1	1				1			1				4		
Mendon	381	13	French	William	1			1					1	1			4	1st Parish	
Rutland	506	22	Frink	John	1	1	1	2	1		2	1	1	1			11		
Uxbridge	465	28	Frost	Gideon			1			1			1		1		4		
Paxton	502	13	Frost	Jonathan		1		1		4			2	1			9		
Rutland	506	18	Frost	Ruth										1			1		
New Braintree	309	7	Frost	Seth	1	1		1		2			1				6		
Hubbardston	417	20	Frost	Stephen		2	1	1		3			1				8		
Royalston	238	10	Fry	David		1		1					1				3		
Royalston	241	24	Fry	Ebenz	2	1	1	1		1	1						7		
Royalston	237	14	Fry	James	1			1		2			1				5		
Winchendon	225	31	Fry	Job	2			1		2			1				6		
Royalston	241	25	Fry	John					1			1		1			3		
Berlin	214	35	Fry	William	1			1		3			1				6		
Lancaster	350	17	Frye	Obediah	1			1		3			1				6		
Harvard	218	7	Fullam	Elisha			1	1						1			3		
Fitchburg	432	16	Fullam	Jacob	4	1		1	1		2		1	1			11		
Leominster	436	31	Fullam	Jacob	1	1	1		1		2	3		1			10		
Fitchburg	432	14	Fullam	Oliver	1			1		4	1		1				8		
Boylston	377	29	Fuller	Amasa		1		1					1				3		
Boylston	378	10	Fuller	Amos	1			1	1			3	1				7		
Sutton	158	7	Fuller	Amos	2		1	1				1					5		
Paxton	502	11	Fuller	Azariah	2	1		1		2			1				7		
Mendon	381	9	Fuller	Charlotte Mrs.	1								1				2	1st Parish	
Oxford	162	16	Fuller	Daniel	3	1		1		2			1				8		
Lancaster	350	16	Fuller	Edward		2	1						1				4		
Leominster	436	26	Fuller	Edward	3	2		1		1	1		1				9		
Garry	277	4	Fuller	Elisha	1			2		1		1	1				6		
Royalston	236	14	Fuller	George			1			1		1					3		
Lancaster	350	13	Fuller	James				1				2		1			4		
Sutton	158	6	Fuller	Jeduthun	1	2		1			2			1			7		
Douglas	479	3	Fuller	John		1		1				3		1			6		
Lunenberg	423	21	Fuller	John	1		1	1		1			1	1			6		
Charlton	330	9	Fuller	Jonathn				1					1	1			3		
Athol	289	30	Fuller	Joseph	1		1					2					4		
Fitchburg	432	18	Fuller	Joseph	2	2		1		2	1	1	1				10		
Paxton	502	12	Fuller	Josiah		1		1				1		1			4		
Oxford	159	2	Fuller	Lemuel				1		1	1		1				5		
Sutton	158	5	Fuller	Levi	1	1	1	1		2		1		1			8		
Mendon	383	3	Fuller	Miller	2	1		2		1		1	2				9	1st Parish	
Fitchburg	432	12	Fuller	Nehemiah			1	1		1	1	1	1	1			7		
Fitchburg	429	2	Fuller	Nehemiah Jun	5			1		1			1				8		
Athol	289	31	Fuller	Sarah	1									1			2		
Worcester	178	2	Fullerton	Samuel				1		3			1				5		
Petersham	278	1	Fulton	George	3	1		1		1	2		1				9		
Brookfield	270	29	Furbush	Benja Junr	4	1		1					1				7	Third Parish	
Brookfield	270	30	Furbush	Benjamin			1	1			1		1	1			5	Third Parish	
Royalston	239	12	Furbush	David	1	1	1		1	1	1			1			7		
Upton	387	15	Furbush	Elijah	1		1					1					3		
Hardwick	298	4	Furbush	Moses		1		1	1	1			1	1			6		
Sturbridge	335	1	Furbush	Noah	1						1	1	1				4		
Upton	387	14	Furbush	Peter		1		1				1		1			4		
Upton	387	10	Furbush	Saml		1		1		1		1		1			5		
Upton	387	11	Furbush	Saml Jr	1		1					1					3		
Petersham	278	3	Furness	Benja	1			1		2			1				5		
Berlin	211	18	G*	Aaron	2		1			1			1				5		Name covered by tape mark
Western	258	12	Gaba	George			1			1				1			3		
Hubbardston	417	22	Gage	Abraham			1			1			1				3		
Hubbardston	417	25	Gage	Daniel	1		2	1			1	1	1	1			8		
Milford	395	28	Gage	David	1		2				3		1				7		
Leicester	490	13	Gage	Jonathan	2	1		1		1			1				6		
Milford	395	29	Gage	Moses				1				1		1			3		
Westminster	445	9	Gager	Jeremiah				1			2			1			4		
Oxford	159	9	Gale	Abijah				1					1	1			3		
Westborough	198	131	Gale	Abijah		1		1	1	1			1				7		
Petersham	277	1	Gale	Daniel	1	1	3		1	1			1	1			9		
Holden	514	5	Gale	Isaac	1	1		1		2			1				6		
Royalston	240	11	Gale	Isaac	2			1		1		1	1				6		
Sutton	157	5	Gale	Jonas				1						1			2		
Sutton	157	7	Gale	Jonas Junr	1		1	1		2	1		1				7		
Boylston	375	18	Gale	Jonathan	1			1		1	1		1				5		
Royalston	234	3	Gale	Jonathan		1		1		2	1		1				6		
Holden	514	4	Gale	Mary			1			1	1			1			4		
Westborough	198	132	Gale	Nahum	3	1	1	1		1			1				8		

TOWN	PG#	LN#	LAST NAME	FIRST NAME	FWM under 10	FWM 10 to 16	FWM 16 to 26	FWM 26 to 45	FWM 45 and over	FWF under 10	FWF 10 to 16	FWF 16 to 26	FWF 26 to 45	FWF 45 and over	TOTAL ALL OTHER	TOTAL SLAVES	TOTALS	DISTRICT/ TOWNSHIP	NOTES
Sutton	157	6	Gale	Nehemiah					1			1	1	1			4		
Holden	514	6	Gale	Oliver		1		2					1				4		
Petersham	278	9	Gardenor	Jesse	1	2	2		1		1		1				8		
Lunenberg	426	12	Gardner	Daniel	3			1		1			1	1			7		
Southborough	203	5	Gardner	David	2			1		2	2	1	1				9		
Leominster	436	38	Gardner	Francis	1	1			1	1	1	6	2	1			14		
Leominster	436	37	Gardner	John	1			1		4			1		1		8		
Bolton	212	16	Gardner	Stephen P.		1	1			1		1	1				5		
Shrewsbury	365	11	Garfield	Abijah	2	1		1		3			1	1		1	10		
Fitchburg	429	19	Garfield	Jane								1	1	1			3		
Spencer	498	8	Garfield	Joseph	2			1					1				4		
Royalston	234	8	Garfield	Joshua		1	1		1	2	1	2	1				9		
Northborough	365	6	Garfield	Mary								1	1				2		
Princeton	515	14	Garfield	Moses	2		1			1			1				5		
Harvard	220	1	Garfield	Reubin		1		1				1	1				4		
Westborough	197	106	Garfield	Susannah		1					1		1	1			4		
Fitchburg	429	9	Garfield	Timothy	2	1	1	1					1	1			7		
Sterling	356	16	Garish	Paul	2			1		2				1			6		
Westminster	445	10	Garish	Ruth			1						1	1			3		
Ashburnham	460	33	Garter	John	1	1		1		1	1	2	1				9		
Royalston	238	17	Gary	Aaron			1			2	1						4		
Leominster	436	36	Gary	David	1		1			1	1	2					6		
Harvard	217	29	Gary	John	1		1					1					3		
Leominster	436	34	Gary	Thomas	2		1		1	2		2	1	1			10		
Uxbridge	465	2	Gaskill	Benja			2	1		1	1	1	1				7		
Uxbridge	465	32	Gaskill	Ezekiel	2	1						1	1				5		
Mendon	389	11	Gaskill	George			1	1				2	1				5	2d Parish	
Mendon	389	12	Gaskill	Peter	2		1	1		3			1				8	2d Parish	
Northborough	365	4	Gasset	Henry	1		1	1			2		1				6		
Northborough	365	7	Gasset	Winslow	1			1					1				3		
Barre	406	14	Gates	Aaron	1		3	1			1		1	1			8		
Bolton	207	15	Gates	Abraham	2		1	1				1					5		
Sterling	356	20	Gates	Amos	2	1		1		2	1	1	1				9		
Westminster	445	7	Gates	Amos	1		1			1			1				4		
Hubbardston	417	31	Gates	Benj	2		1			2		1					6		
Bolton	211	6	Gates	Calvin			1				1	1					3		
Barre	406	13	Gates	Exp Wid		1	1			1		1		1	1		6		
Ashburnham	460	34	Gates	Henery		1	1	1						1			4		
Ashburnham	459	1	Gates	Henery Jr	1		1			1		1					4		
Hubbardston	417	30	Gates	Henry	2		1	1		4	1		1				10		
Petersham	277	5	Gates	John		1	1	1		1		1	2	1			8		
Hardwick	298	15	Gates	Jonah	2	1			1	3			1				8		
Leominster	436	40	Gates	Jonas	3	1		2					3				9		
Barre	406	21	Gates	Jonathan	1		1			1	1						4		
Gardner	449	5	Gates	Jonathan	4			1			1		1				7		
Hubbardston	417	29	Gates	Jonathan		1	1			1		2	1				6		
Worcester	177	8	Gates	Jonathan				1					1	1			3		
Worcester	177	17	Gates	Jonathan 2d		2		1			2		2				7		
Rutland	510	4	Gates	Joseph	2		1	1		2		1	1	1			9		
Bolton	211	7	Gates	Joseph			1						1				2		
Templeton	239	16	Gates	Laban	2		1						1				4		
Ashburnham	460	30	Gates	Levi		1						1					2		
Charlton	330	15	Gates	Levi	1		1			4		1					7		
Barre	406	12	Gates	Makw	1	1	2	1	1	1	2		1				10		
Gardner	449	4	Gates	Nathan	5							1					5		
Worcester	180	5	Gates	Nathaniel	1		1			1			1				4		
Worcester	177	2	Gates	Paul	1		1	1		1			1		1		6		
Westminster	445	5	Gates	Phinihas	1		1							1			3		
Leominster	436	39	Gates	Reuben	2		2	1		2	2		1				10		
Petersham	278	14	Gates	Saml	3		1	1		2			1				8		
Ashburnham	459	13	Gates	Samuel	1		1			1		1					4		
Worcester	177	11	Gates	Samuel	2	1	1		1			3	2				10		
Rutland	510	12	Gates	Sarah	1							2	1				4		
Petersham	278	8	Gates	Silas	2	2		1		1		1	1				8		
Spencer	498	9	Gates	Silvanus	2		1		1	2	1	2	1	1			11		
Gardner	449	6	Gates	Simon	1	2	2	1					1	1			8		
Worcester	177	16	Gates	Simon	2	1	1	1		2	2		1	1			11		
Harvard	218	31	Gates	Submit								1	1	1			3		
Lancaster	350	21	Gates	Thomas		1		1				1	1	1			5		
Worcester	177	9	Gates	Thomas	3		1	1		1		1	1				8		
Worcester	177	10	Gates	William		1		1	1	1		1	1	1			7		
Rutland	510	7	Gates	Zadock			3	1		1		1	1				7		
Oakham	317	17	Gault	Matthew	3		1	1				1	1				7		
Hubbardston	417	38	Gay	Abner	1		1					1					3		
Templeton	237	10	Gay	Amos	2		1						1				4		
Worcester	180	11	Gay	John				1						1			2		
Boylston	378	15	Gay	William	2		1						1				4		
Petersham	278	15	Geningson	John	1		1	1				1	1				5		
Charlton	330	25	George	John	1		1	1				1	1				5		
Sturbridge	335	6	Gerrold	Stephen	2		1		1	2	1	1		1			9		
Westminster	445	11	Gibbs	Elisabeth									1				1		
Sutton	157	11	Gibbs	Jacob	2		1			1		1					5		
Charlton	330	21	Gibbs	John	2		1			3	1		1				8		
Sturbridge	335	9	Gibbs	Jonathan		1	2		1	3		1		1			9		
Ashburnham	460	31	Gibbs	Joseph	2	2		1		1			1				7		
Charlton	330	19	Gibbs	Joseph			1					1					2		
Milford	395	27	Gibbs	Joseph Lt				1						1			2		
Charlton	330	20	Gibbs	Nathl	1	1	3	1						1			7		
Sterling	356	14	Gibbs	William	2	1		2		1		1	1				8		
Sturbridge	335	7	Gibbs	Zephr	2		1		1	1	1	1	1				8		
Boylston	378	14	Gibs	Jonathan	1		1					1					3		

TOWN	PG#	LN#	LAST NAME	FIRST NAME	FREE WHITE MALES under 10	10 to 16	16 to 26	26 to 45	45 and over	FREE WHITE FEMALES under 10	10 to 16	16 to 26	26 to 45	45 and over	TOTAL ALL OTHER	TOTAL SLAVES	TOTALS	DISTRICT/ TOWNSHIP	NOTES
Fitchburg	429	18	Gibson	Armington		2		1				1		1			5		
Fitchburg	429	11	Gibson	Ephraim	1			1		2			1				5		
Fitchburg	429	10	Gibson	Jacob	1	1	1		1		1	2		1			8		
Harvard	220	8	Gibson	John	2			1		1			1				5		
Fitchburg	429	13	Gibson	Reuben		1	1		1	2	3	2		1			11		
Fitchburg	429	16	Gibson	Samiel Jun	1	1	1		1				1				5		
Fitchburg	429	8	Gibson	Samuel			1		1			1		1			4		
Fitchburg	429	14	Gibson	Solomon	2			1		2	2		1				8		
Ashburnham	460	32	Gibson	Thomas	2		1		1	1	2			1			8		
Fitchburg	429	3	Gibson	Thomas	2		1	1		3			1				8		
Lunenberg	426	14	Gibson	Timothy	1		1		1			1		1			5		
Lunenberg	426	13	Giddings	Mehitable								1	1	1			3		
Fitchburg	429	12	Giddings	William	2			1		1				1			5		
Hardwick	298	12	Giffen	John	3	2	3	1	1	3	2		2				17		
Uxbridge	465	1	Gifford	Seth	2	1	2		2	1	1		2				11		
Brookfield	247	27	Gilbert	Aaron		1	1		1					1			4	First Parish	
Brookfield	247	31	Gilbert	Benjamin			1			2			1				4	First Parish	
Brookfield	247	33	Gilbert	Bernard	2		1					1					4	First Parish	
Brookfield	257	3	Gilbert	Daniel		1		1						1			3	Second Parish	
Brookfield	247	30	Gilbert	David		1	1	1				2		1			6	First Parish	
Brookfield	247	29	Gilbert	Estes	1	2	1					1		1			6	First Parish	
Brookfield	247	25	Gilbert	Gershom				1						1			2	First Parish	
Brookfield	257	6	Gilbert	Hannah		1							1	1			3	Second Parish	
Brookfield	247	32	Gilbert	Henry	1		2		1				1	1			6	First Parish	
Brookfield	257	4	Gilbert	Humphrey	4		1	1		1			1				8	Second Parish	
Brookfield	247	23	Gilbert	Joel	1	1		1				1	1				5	First Parish	
Brookfield	247	21	Gilbert	John				1						1			2	First Parish	
Brookfield	247	28	Gilbert	John 2			1	1	1	2	1		1				7	First Parish	
Brookfield	247	22	Gilbert	Jonas	1		1	1		2			1				6	First Parish	
New Braintree	309	13	Gilbert	Josiah			1			1			1				3		
Brookfield	247	24	Gilbert	Lemuel	2		2		1		1	2		1			9	First Parish	
Brookfield	247	18	Gilbert	Levi		1	1		1	1		1		1			6	First Parish	
Brookfield	247	17	Gilbert	Nathan	1		2		1	1	2			1			8	First Parish	
Brookfield	247	20	Gilbert	Pearley	2			1		3		1					7	First Parish	
Brookfield	247	19	Gilbert	Pelatiah	1		3		1	2	1	1		1			10	First Parish	
Brookfield	247	26	Gilbert	Philip			1		1			1		1			4	First Parish	
Brookfield	257	7	Gilbert	Reuben			1	1		3	1		1	1			8	Second Parish	
Hardwick	298	10	Gilbert	Samll	1			1		1			1				4		
Brookfield	247	16	Gilbert	Solomon Jr	2		1	1					1	2			7	First Parish	
Hardwick	298	11	Gilbert	Timothy	1	1	1	1	1			2		1			8		
Lunenberg	426	10	Gilchrist	James	2	1		1		3	1		2	1			11		
Sutton	158	15	Giles	James				1						1			2		
Spencer	498	11	Gilford	John		3		1	1					1			6		
Spencer	498	12	Gilford	Jonas	2	3		1		3		1	1				11		
Princeton	515	8	Gill	John		1		1	1	2	2	1	1				10		
Princeton	515	7	Gill	Michael	2	1	2		1	1	1	1	1				10		
Princeton	515	6	Gill	Moses	1	3	3	2		2	2	3	2				18		
Leicester	490	14	Gilmore	Adam		1		1						1			3		
Grafton	197	5	Gimbe	Lucy											4		4		
Northbridge	476	16	Glasco	Jacob											4		4		
Worcester	180	12	Glasgow	Prudence											1		1		
Brookfield	257	5	Glass	John	1			1		1				1			4	Second Parish	
Boylston	375	16	Glazier	Jason	2		1			1			1				5		
New Braintree	309	16	Glazier	Jotham	1	1			1	2	2	2	1	1			11		
Boylston	375	23	Glazier	Oliver	3		2				1		1				7		
Gardner	452	14	Glazor	John				1				1		1			3		
Gardner	452	15	Glazor	Levi	1		1					1					3		
Gardner	449	2	Glazor	Smarna	1		1				1		1				4		
Spencer	495	1	Gleason	Benja		1	2		1				3	1			8		
Ward	180	79	Gleason	David	1		2		1				2	1			7		
Ward	180	80	Gleason	David Junr	2		1			3			1				7		
Western	258	7	Gleason	Hannah		1				1	1	2		1			6		
Western	258	6	Gleason	Isaac		1	1		1			1	1	3			8		
Worcester	180	4	Gleason	Isaac		1		1					1	1			4		
Oxford	159	7	Gleason	James	1		1			1	1	1	1				6		
Oxford	159	6	Gleason	James Junr		2	1	1	1	1	1	1		1			9		
Brookfield	247	15	Gleason	John		1	2	1	1		1	2		1			9	First Parish	
Oxford	159	5	Gleason	Jona & Jesse	1		1	1		1		1	1	1			7		
Western	258	5	Gleason	Jonathan			1	1				1	1	1			5		
Worcester	180	1	Gleason	Jonathan		1	2	1	1	2	2	1		1			11		
Worcester	180	2	Gleason	Jonathan 2d		1		1		1				1			4		
Worcester	180	7	Gleason	Jonathan Jun	3		1				1		1				6		
Oxford	159	8	Gleason	Josiah	1			1		1			1	1			5		
Hardwick	298	13	Gleason	Nathaniel		2	2	1				1	1	1			8		
Worcester	180	3	Gleason	Phinehas	2	1	1		1	2	3		1				11		
Worcester	177	14	Gleason	Silas	2		1			1		1	1				6		
Fitchburg	429	17	Gleason	William	1		1				1	1					4		
Hubbardston	417	39	Gleazon	Barzeleel			1							1			2		
Hubbardston	417	40	Gleazon	Clark	1		1	1		1		1					5		
Petersham	277	3	Gleson	Joseph		1	2	1		1	1	3			1		10		
Holden	513	21	Glezen	Jason				1				1					2		
Holden	513	22	Glezen	Jason Junr		1	1					1	1				4		
Holden	513	23	Glezen	Joel	1		2					1	1	1			6		
Princeton	515	11	Glezon	John	1			1					1	1			4		
Princeton	515	13	Glezon	Thomas	2	3		1	1			1		1			9		
Leominster	436	35	Glover	John	1	3			1			2		1			8		
Grafton	193	1	Goddard	Benj		1							1	1			3		
Shrewsbury	365	7	Goddard	Benja	1	1	1	1	1	1		1	1	3			11		
Shrewsbury	365	8	Goddard	Daniel			1		1			1		1			4		

TOWN	PG#	LN#	LAST NAME	FIRST NAME	FREE WHITE MALES under 10	10 to 16	16 to 26	26 to 45	45 and over	FREE WHITE FEMALES under 10	10 to 16	16 to 26	26 to 45	45 and over	TOTAL ALL OTHER	TOTAL SLAVES	TOTALS	DISTRICT/ TOWNSHIP	NOTES
Petersham	277	2	Goddard	David	2		1	1						1			5		
Athol	290	8	Goddard	Ebenz			1		1			1		1			4		
Berlin	213	16	Goddard	Eber	2			1		2			1				6		
Athol	290	7	Goddard	Edwd	1		1		1		2	2		1			8		
Athol	290	6	Goddard	Elijah	4	1						1		1			8		
Athol	290	10	Goddard	Ephm			1			1			1				3		
Boylston	375	21	Goddard	Gardner	2			1		1	1		1				6		
Royalston	241	15	Goddard	Henry			1					1					2		
Athol	290	5	Goddard	James			1	1	1			3		1			7		
Berlin	212	8	Goddard	James		1	1		1					1			4		
Berlin	216	6	Goddard	James Junr	3	2		1			1		1	1			9		
Petersham	278	5	Goddard	Joel	4	1		1		1	1	1					9		
Athol	290	9	Goddard	Joseph			1			2			1				4		
Grafton	197	9	Goddard	Joseph			1		1	1		1					3		
Athol	290	4	Goddard	Josiah Esq	2	2	1		1	2		2		1			11		
Grafton	193	2	Goddard	Levi	1			1				1					3		
Shrewsbury	365	9	Goddard	Luther	1	2	1	1		4	1		2				12		
Petersham	278	4	Goddard	Nathl	3	1		1		2	1		1				9		
Petersham	278	6	Goddard	Robert	1		1	1	1			1					8		
Sutton	158	17	Goddard	Robert	1	1		1		1	1	1	1				8		
Royalston	234	6	Goddard	Samll	2	1	2		1	1	1		1				9		
Royalston	241	14	Goddard	Samll	2		1	1				1					5		
Worcester	177	3	Goddard	Samuel		3		1		1		2	2	1			10		
Garry	277	8	Goddard	Simeon	2	1	2		1			2		1			9		
Northborough	365	5	Goddard	Solomon				1					1				2		
Milford	395	25	Godfrey	Benjm Capt	1	2	2	1	1	3		3	1	1			15		
Fitchburg	429	15	Godfrey	Daniel		1		1		1		1	1	1			5		
Harvard	222	29	Godfrey	Lucy	1									1			2		
Lancaster	349	6	Godfrey	Salmon	1		1		1			1	1	1			6		
Grafton	200	9	Godward	Pearly			1		1		1		1				4		
Sutton	157	4	Goffe	Joseph Revd	1			1				1	1				4		
Lunenberg	426	8	Going	Jonathan	1	1	2		1	1			1	1			8		
Grafton	193	3	Golding	Ephraim	2		2	1		2		1	1				9		
Harvard	221	6	Goldsmith	Richard	1	1		1	1	1		1		1			7		
Harvard	221	15	Goldsmith	Theodore		2				1							3		
Northbridge	476	14	Goldthwait	Jacob	1		1		1	2		1					6		
Northbridge	476	13	Goldthwait	Stephen		2		1	1	1				1			5		
Sutton	158	12	Goldthwait	Stephen	1			1		3	1		1				7		
Northbridge	476	15	Goldthwait	Thomas	2	1		1		1			1	1			7		
Petersham	278	11	Gollund	Jereh			2		1			2	1	1			7		
Petersham	278	12	Gollund	Joseph	1		1	1			1		1				5		
Sterling	356	19	Goney	Jonathan	4				1			1	1				7		
Sterling	356	18	Goney	Nathan			1	1	1					1			4		
Sterling	356	13	Goney	Rheuben	1		2	1	1	2	1	2	1	2			13		
Sterling	356	15	Goney	Thomas	2	2		1		1			1		1		8		
Templeton	231	15	Goodah	William	3			1	1	2			1				8		
Boylston	375	20	Goodale	Aaron		2			1		1	1	1				6		
Sturbridge	335	5	Goodale	Benj	1	2	1	1			3	1					9		
Petersham	278	7	Goodale	Enoch	1	1		1		3			1				7		
Mendon	381	16	Goodale	Ephm	1	3	2	1		3	1	1	1				13	1st Parish	
Sturbridge	335	8	Goodale	John		1	1	1			1		1	1			5		
Charlton	330	26	Goodale	Jonathan	3			1		1			1				6		
Petersham	278	10	Goodale	Joseph	2	1	1		2	1	1	1		1			10		
Brookfield	257	8	Goodale	Josiah	3	1			2	2		1	1				10	Second Parish	
Boylston	378	13	Goodale	Moses			1		1					1			3		
Charlton	330	13	Goodale	Nathl	1	1	1					1	2	2			9		
Charlton	330	14	Goodale	Nathl Junr	2			1		1			2				6		
Holden	514	1	Goodale	Paul		2	2	1		1		1		1			8		
Boylston	375	17	Goodale	Peter		2	3	1		1		1		3			11		
Charlton	330	22	Goodale	Zacheriah			1	1			1		1				4		
Westminster	445	12	Goodall	John				1						3			4		
Sutton	157	8	Goodell	Asa	3	1	1		1		3		1				10		
Rutland	510	8	Goodell	John	1	1		2				1	1				6		
Sutton	158	16	Goodell	John				1						1			2		
Sutton	157	9	Goodell	Relief Wd	2						2		2				6		
Paxton	501	2	Goodenough	David	1			1	1	1	2	1	1	1			9		
Northborough	365	3	Goodenow	Asa				1						2			3		
Rutland	510	9	Goodenow	Asa	1			1		1			1				4		
Rutland	510	5	Goodenow	Daniel		1		1		3			1				6		
Boylston	375	19	Goodenow	Elijah	3		2	1		2			1	1			10		
Boylston	375	22	Goodenow	Jonas	2	1			1	1			1				6		
Princeton	515	12	Goodenow	Lois	1	3	1					1					6		
Winchendon	226	3	Gooderidge	Danll		2		1	1			2					6		
Winchendon	226	4	Gooderidge	David	1	1			1		1	1					5		
Winchendon	226	2	Gooderidge	Eliphalet		1		1				1	2				5		
Winchendon	226	5	Gooderidge	Samll	2			1		1			1				5		
Winchendon	226	7	Goodhue	Amos			1						1				2		
Winchendon	226	6	Goodhue	John	2	1		1		2			1				7		
Boylston	378	16	Goodman	Abel	2		1	1		2			1				7		
Rutland	510	11	Goodrich	Hezekiah	1	1		1				1	1				5		
Fitchburg	429	7	Goodridge	Abijah	2	1			1	2	1	2		2			11		
Fitchburg	429	5	Goodridge	Asaph		2			1	1		1		1			6		
Lunenberg	426	3	Goodridge	Benja	1		2		1	1		1					6		
Templeton	233	15	Goodridge	Ebenz		1	2		1	3	1	1					10		
Lunenberg	426	11	Goodridge	Ezekiel		1		1		3	1	1	1	1			9		
Fitchburg	429	6	Goodridge	John		1		1		1	2	1	2				8		
Lunenberg	426	4	Goodridge	Oliver		1	2		1	2		1					7		
Lunenberg	426	6	Goodridge	Phinehas	2	1		1		1			2	1			8		
Lunenberg	426	9	Goodridge	Simon	1			1		1			1	1			5		

TOWN	PG#	LN#	LAST NAME	FIRST NAME	FREE WHITE MALES					FREE WHITE FEMALES					TOTAL ALL OTHER	TOTAL SLAVES	TOTALS	DISTRICT/ TOWNSHIP	NOTES
					under 10	10 to 16	16 to 26	26 to 45	45 and over	under 10	10 to 16	16 to 26	26 to 45	45 and over					
Hubbardston	417	21	Goodspeed	Ann Wid	1								1	1			3		
Hubbardston	417	36	Goodspeed	Elijah	3		1						1				5		
Hubbardston	417	37	Goodspeed	Heman	1			1	1	1			1				5		
Hubbardston	417	23	Goodspeed	Isaac	1		1	1		2	1		1				7		
Hubbardston	417	35	Goodspeed	Luther				1		2			1				4		
Lancaster	349	1	Goodwin	Edward	1	1		1		1		2		1			7		
Lancaster	349	5	Goodwin	James					1			3		1			5		
Lancaster	349	2	Goodwin	James Junr	1		1	1		1			1				5		
Lancaster	349	8	Goodwin	John	1		1	1					1				4		
Lancaster	350	19	Goold	Benjamin	1	1			1	1	1	1		1			7		
Lancaster	350	20	Goold	William			2		1	1	2			1			7		
Upton	388	2	Gore	Ebenezer	1			1						1			3		
Dudley	344	44	Gore	John		1		1		2		1	3	1			9		
Petersham	278	13	Gore	Peter											3		3		
Sterling	356	17	Gorey	Ichabod		1		1						1			3		
Barre	406	17	Gorham	David	1			1		2			1				5		
Barre	406	16	Gorham	John	1	1		1	1	1	1		1	1			8		
Barre	406	20	Gorham	Joseph	1			1					1				3		
Hardwick	298	14	Gorham	Stephen	1			1	1				1	1			5		
Charlton	330	24	Gorton	John	3	1		1		2	1		1				9		
Sutton	158	13	Gorton	William	2	1		1		2	1		1				8		
Winchendon	226	11	Goss	Calvin				1						1			2		
Lancaster	349	3	Goss	Daniel		1		1		1	1			1			5		
Lancaster	349	7	Goss	Daniel Jun	1			1		1				1			4		
Lancaster	349	4	Goss	John	2			1						1			4		
Sterling	356	12	Goss	Joseph			1	1		1	1	1	1				6		
Garry	277	11	Goss	Stephen	1	1		1		2			1	1			7		
Mendon	381	17	Goss	Zebulon			1	1		1	1			2			6	1st Parish	
Sturbridge	335	11	Gould	Amos	2	1	2			1		1	1	1			9		
Princeton	515	15	Gould	Benjamin			1			1			1				3		
Petersham	277	4	Gould	Daniel		1		1		2			1				5		
Douglas	479	5	Gould	Ebenezer	1	2		1		3	1		1	1			10		
Worcester	180	10	Gould	Ebenezer			3	1					1				5		
Oxford	159	4	Gould	Ebenz				1	1	1				1			3		
Douglas	479	6	Gould	Eleazer		1	2		1	1	1			1			7		
Garry	277	9	Gould	Elijah	4	1		2				1	1				9		
New Braintree	309	15	Gould	George	2		1	1		3			2				9		
Westborough	194	66	Gould	James		1		1						1			3		
Douglas	479	7	Gould	Jedidiah	1			1	1	1	1		1	1			7		
New Braintree	309	14	Gould	Jno		1	1	2				1		1			6		
Charlton	330	18	Gould	Jonathan				1		2			1				4		
Sutton	157	10	Gould	Jonathan	1	1		1				2		1			6		
Harvard	219	37	Gould	Joseph		1		1						1			3		
Oxford	159	3	Gould	Lyman	1		1			1		1					4		
Lunenberg	426	5	Gould	Sampson			1			2			1				4		
Charlton	330	17	Gould	Thomas	2	2	1	1		2	1		1	1			11		
Lunenberg	426	7	Gould	Thomas		1			1	1				1			4		
Worcester	180	8	Gould	Stephen	1	1		1				1	1				5		
Garry	277	10	Goulding	Abel	1	1	1	1						1			5		
Worcester	177	18	Goulding	Clark	1			1		2			1				5		
Worcester	177	15	Goulding	Daniel		1	2	1					1				5		
Holden	513	24	Goulding	Ignatius			1	1	1			1	1	1			6		
Holden	514	3	Goulding	John M.	2	2		1			1		1				7		
Ward	180	78	Goulding	Jonah		1	1				1	3		1			8		
Western	258	10	Goulding	Joseph	2	1		1		2		1	1				8		
Worcester	180	6	Goulding	Lucy	1								1	1			3		
Worcester	177	7	Goulding	William	2		1	1		3			1	1			9		
Holden	514	2	Goulding	Winsor			2	1	1								5		
Rutland	510	6	Graham	William			1					1	1	1			4		
New Braintree	309	17	Granger	Noah	2	1	1	1		2	1		2	1			11		
Royalston	236	3	Grant	Aaron		1	1	1		1				1			5		
Barre	406	19	Grant	Phillip	3	1		1			1	1	1				8		
Holden	514	7	Grant	Samuel				1			1		1				3		
Winchendon	226	10	Graton	Thomas	2					3	1		1	1			8		
Athol	290	3	Graves	Abner		1	2	1	1		1	2	1				9		
Athol	290	1	Graves	Eliazer	1	1		1	1	3	1	1	2	2			13		
Westminster	445	6	Graves	Jonathan	1	2	1		1	2		2	1				10		
Westminster	445	8	Graves	Levi	1	1		1		1	1	1	1				7		
Athol	290	2	Graves	Nathl	1	1	1			2		2		1			8		
Princeton	515	9	Graves	Richard				1					1				2		
Southborough	202	6	Graves	Thomas			1			3			1				5		
Western	258	8	Gray	Elizabeth	1		1							1			3		
Rutland	510	10	Gray	John			1			3	1		1				6		
Fitchburg	429	4	Gray	Joseph	1		1	1	1	2	2		2				10		
Western	258	11	Gray	Matthew		1		1						1			3		
Worcester	177	6	Gray	Reuben	2	2		1			1	2		1			9		
Western	258	9	Gray	Samuel				1									1		
Worcester	177	19	Gray	Thomas	1	1	1	1		2		1	1				8		
Leicester	489	6	Greaton	John				1					1				2		
Leicester	489	2	Greaton	John Jun	1		2	1			1	3		1			9		
Leicester	490	12	Green	Abel		1		1		2		1		1			6		
Spencer	495	3	Green	Benja	3	1		1		2		1		1			9		
Upton	388	5	Green	Benjamin	2				1				1	1			5		
Uxbridge	465	33	Green	Benjamin		2	1	1			1	3	3	1			12		
Worcester	180	9	Green	Bristol											3		3		
Uxbridge	465	3	Green	David	2		1	1		1	1	2	1	1			10		
Leicester	489	1	Green	Isaac	2	1	1	1		1		1	1	1			9		
Lunenberg	426	15	Green	Jabez	2		1	1						1			5		
Leicester	489	3	Green	Jabez Jun	4			1				2		1			9		
Leicester	490	11	Green	Jabez Jun				1					1				2		

199

TOWN	PG#	LN#	LAST NAME	FIRST NAME	M under 10	M 10 to 16	M 16 to 26	M 26 to 45	M 45 & over	F under 10	F 10 to 16	F 16 to 26	F 26 to 45	F 45 & over	TOTAL ALL OTHER	TOTAL SLAVES	TOTALS	DISTRICT/ TOWNSHIP	NOTES
Barre	406	15	Green	Jedn	1	1			1			2		1			6		
Mendon	389	13	Green	Job	2			1		3		1	1				8	2d Parish	
Shrewsbury	365	12	Green	John	2		1	1				1					5		
Upton	388	3	Green	John				1		1				2			4		
Worcester	177	12	Green	John	2		4	1		3	1	2					13		
Hubbardston	417	24	Green	Joseph	1		2		1	3		2		1			10		
Barre	406	18	Green	Keziah Wid							1	1		1			3		
Hardwick	298	16	Green	Larkin			1	1	1					1			4		
Spencer	495	2	Green	Lemuel	2	1			1		1	1		1			7		
Spencer	498	10	Green	Lydia			2				1	1		1			5		
Worcester	177	13	Green	Mary		1	1	1					1	2			6		
Milford	395	26	Green	Moses	4		1	1		1			1				8		
Gardner	449	3	Green	Nathan		1		1						2			4		
Northborough	365	2	Green	Nathan		2	3	1			2			1			9		
Shrewsbury	365	10	Green	Nathaniel	3			1		1			1				6		
Hubbardston	417	41	Green	Robert			1	1		1		1					4		
Leicester	489	4	Green	Samuel	1		1	1		1	1		1				6		
Royalston	237	13	Green	Samuel	1			1		2		1					5		
Leicester	489	5	Green	Samuel Jun		2	1	1		1	1	1		1			8		
Charlton	330	16	Green	Thomas				1			1			1			3		
Ward	180	81	Green	Thomas		1	1	1		2		1	1				7		
Shrewsbury	365	13	Green	Zacheus	1			1				1					3		
Upton	388	4	Green	Zalmon	2		1	1		1		1	1				7		
Bolton	213	6	Greenleaf	Calvin		1	1	1									3		
Worcester	180	13	Greenleaf	Daniel		2	2					1	1				6		
Templeton	234	2	Greenleaf	Danll	1	1		1		2			1				6		
Templeton	234	3	Greenleaf	John	1			1		4	2	1	1				10		
Western	251	15	Greenleaf	William	1		2			1	1	1	1	1			8		
Gardner	452	16	Greenwood	Aaron		1		1		1			1				4		
Hubbardston	417	32	Greenwood	Abijah		1	2		1	1	2		1	1			9		
Holden	514	8	Greenwood	Asa			1						1				2		
Sutton	157	3	Greenwood	Daniel				1						1			2		
Sutton	157	12	Greenwood	Danl Junr			1			3			1				5		
Grafton	197	15	Greenwood	Enoch	2		1			2			1				6		
Sutton	157	1	Greenwood	James				1						1			2		
Sutton	157	2	Greenwood	Jas Junr	1		1			1			1				5		
Gardner	452	17	Greenwood	Jonathan		2	1	1		1	1		1				7		
Hubbardston	417	34	Greenwood	Levi			1			1	1		1				4		
Hubbardston	417	33	Greenwood	Moses Mj	1	1	3		2	2	1		1	1			12		
Winchendon	226	9	Greenwood	Thos	2	1	2		1	1	1	1		1			10		
Royalston	238	11	Gregory	Amasa	1		1					1					3		
Royalston	232	9	Gregory	Isaac	2	2		1				1	1				7		
Princeton	515	10	Gregory	Phinehas			2		2	2		1	1	1			9		
Royalston	237	17	Gregory	Samll			2	1			1		1				5		
Worcester	177	1	Griggs	David			1	1				1					3		
Sturbridge	335	10	Griggs	Ichabod	2			1		3	1		1				8		
Sutton	158	14	Griggs	Mary Wd	1	2						1		1			5		
Hubbardston	417	26	Grimes	Bill		2		1	1	1	1	1					7		
Hubbardston	417	28	Grimes	Ephraim	3			1	1			1					6		
Hubbardston	417	27	Grimes	Joseph			1		1	1	2						5		
Petersham	278	16	Gross	Thomas				1									1		
Paxton	501	1	Grosvenor	Daniel	2		4		1		2	1	1				11		
Worcester	177	5	Grosvenor	Elizah	2							3		2			7		
Winchendon	226	8	Grout	Isaac	2	1		1		2		2					8		
Spencer	498	13	Grout	Jona	4	1				2	1	1	1				10		
Petersham	278	17	Grout	Jona Esq	1	1	4		1		2	1	2				12		
Westborough	196	92	Grout	Jonathan		1		1	1		3	1	1				8		
Worcester	177	4	Grout	Jonathan			1	1	1		2		1				6		
Uxbridge	465	4	Grout	Rhoda		2					1		1				4		
Westborough	196	94	Grout	Samuel	1	1		1		4		1	1				9		
Spencer	498	14	Grout	Thomas				1					1				2		
Grafton	204	14	Grover	Benjn		1		1				1					3		
Harvard	217	21	Grugg	Samuel	4			1	1	1	1		1				9		
Sturbridge	335	12	Grve	Peter	1		1				1						3		
Brookfield	270	32	Guilford	John	1			1		2		1					5	Third Parish	
Brookfield	270	33	Guilford	William	1	1	2	1		3	1	1	1				11	Third Parish	
Charlton	330	23	Gulley	William	1	3	2	1	1		1						9		
Southborough	203	30	Haden	Daniel		2		1			1		1				5		
Boylston	373	1	Hadley	Ephraim			1			1		1					3		
Westminster	448	10	Hadley	John	2		1					1					4		
Hubbardston	418	13	Hagar	David	2	2	2		2	1	1			2			12		
Bolton	216	12	Hagar	Lois									1				1		
Oxford	160	10	Hager	Benja	1		1	1		2		1	1				7		
Garry	277	13	Hager	John	2	1	1	1	1	2	1		1	1			11		
Westminster	448	7	Hager	Jonathan			1	1	1			1		1			5		
Brookfield	260	5	Hair	Mary		1								1			2	Second Parish	
Worcester	182	9	Hais	John	1			1		1		1					4		
Barre	406	25	Haistins	John	3							1					4		
Winchendon	226	15	Hale	Amos	3	1	1		1			1	1				9		
Leominster	435	10	Hale	Calvin	1	1	3	1		3	1	1	1	1			13		
Rutland	509	3	Hale	David	1			1		2			1				5		
Oakham	319	5	Hale	Dolly								1		2			3		
Douglas	479	13	Hale	Elisha		1	2		1			1		1			6		
Leominster	435	13	Hale	Ezra	2		1		1					2			6		
Royalston	241	3	Hale	Jacob	2			1			1		1				5		
Winchendon	226	14	Hale	Jacob		2			1	1			1				5		
Hardwick	298	17	Hale	Joseph	3			2		2		1	1				9		
Winchendon	226	13	Hale	Moses			2		1		1	2		1			7		
Templeton	237	9	Hale	Oliver			1		1				3	1			6		
Leominster	435	4	Hale	Samuel Jun	2	2			2	2	1	1					10		
Garry	277	12	Hale	Silas		1	1		1		1			1			5		

200

TOWN	PG#	LN#	HEADS OF HOUSEHOLD LAST NAME	FIRST NAME	FREE WHITE MALES under 10	10 to 16	16 to 26	26 to 45	45 and over	FREE WHITE FEMALES under 10	10 to 16	16 to 26	26 to 45	45 and over	TOTAL ALL OTHER	TOTAL SLAVES	TOTALS	DISTRICT/ TOWNSHIP	NOTES
Brookfield	257	12	Hale	Thomas			3		1		1	2	1	2			10	Second Parish	
Leominster	435	11	Hale	Thomas	2		2	1		2	2	1	1	1			12		
Upton	388	7	Hall	Abijah Capt.		1	1		1	4			1				8		
Winchendon	228	26	Hall	Benja	2			1		1			1				5		
Uxbridge	465	12	Hall	Deborah	1		1			1	3		1				7		
Gardner	449	18	Hall	Edward			1						1				2		
Brookfield	260	3	Hall	Eli		1		1		3		2	1				8	Second Parish	
New Braintree	310	5	Hall	Elias	1			2	1		2	3	1	3			13		
Westminster	448	14	Hall	Elisha			1			1							2		
Ashburnham	459	11	Hall	Henary				1		1	1	1					4		
Leominster	435	7	Hall	Jacob	2		1	1			1		1				6		
Uxbridge	465	15	Hall	James W				1			1		2				4		
Sutton	160	5	Hall	John	1	1	1		1	2	1			1			8		
Uxbridge	465	14	Hall	Jonathan	1	1	1	1		2		2	1				9		
Sutton	160	7	Hall	Joseph	2	2		1		1		1	1				8		
Sutton	160	8	Hall	Joseph Junr	1	1		1		2			1				6		
Sutton	160	6	Hall	Josiah		1		1		3	1		1				7		
Ashburnham	459	18	Hall	Mary									1				1		
New Braintree	310	8	Hall	Nathan	2			1		2			1				6		
Oxford	159	11	Hall	Nathan	2	2			1			1	1				7		
Uxbridge	465	13	Hall	Nehemiah	3	1		1		1	1		1				8		
Oakham	319	1	Hall	Percivil	1			2		2			1	1			7		
Spencer	495	7	Hall	Saml Jun	1			1				1					3		
Spencer	495	4	Hall	Samuel	1	1	3		1		1	2		1			10		
Milford	393	18	Hall	Sarah Wd										1			1		
Sutton	160	4	Hall	Stephen		1	1		1	1	1		1				6		
Sutton	160	19	Hall	Stephen Junr	1			1		1		1					4		
Uxbridge	465	16	Hall	William	3	1		1		1			1				7		
Spencer	496	11	Hallowell	David			1	1			1		1				4		
Spencer	496	10	Hallowell	Joseph				1					1				2		
Brookfield	269	11	Hamilton	Amos	1			1				1					3	Third Parish	
Worcester	179	16	Hamilton	Asa		1	1	1				1	1				5		
Brookfield	270	1	Hamilton	Beemis	1			1		3			1				6	Third Parish	
Brookfield	269	27	Hamilton	Erastus			2	1	1			1		1			6	Third Parish	
Brookfield	260	2	Hamilton	Israel	3		1	1		2		1	1				9	Second Parish	
Barre	405	18	Hamilton	James			1	1						1			3		
Brookfield	269	23	Hamilton	Joseph	2	2		1		3	2		1				11	Third Parish	
Brookfield	269	8	Hamilton	Josiah		1	5		1			1	1				9	Third Parish	
Brookfield	269	32	Hamilton	Levi	2			1		1		1					5	Third Parish	
Brookfield	269	34	Hamilton	Lydia								1	1				2	Third Parish	
Barre	405	16	Hamilton	Micah Lt	1		1							1			3		
Barre	405	15	Hamilton	Michael				1				1	1				3		
New Braintree	310	6	Hamilton	Moses			1		2			1		1			5		
Brookfield	270	2	Hamilton	Polly				2					1				3	Third Parish	
Brookfield	269	20	Hamilton	Rhoda	1					3			1				5	Third Parish	
Brookfield	257	14	Hamilton	Rufus	2	2	2	1		3	1	2	2				15	Second Parish	
Brookfield	269	30	Hamilton	Seth	1	1		1		2			1	1			7	Third Parish	
Brookfield	269	19	Hamilton	William		2	2		1	2		1	1				9	Third Parish	
Harvard	219	26	Hammon	Thomas			1			1			1				3		
Charlton	332	11	Hammond	Aaron	2	2		1		3	2		1				11		
Lancaster	352	3	Hammond	Casar											5		5		
Charlton	332	12	Hammond	David		1		1					1				3		
Charlton	332	13	Hammond	David Junr	1		1					1					3		
Oakham	319	3	Hammond	Elijah		1		1		2	1		1	1			7		
Petersham	277	10	Hammond	Elisha		3	1		1	1	4	1	1				12		
Petersham	280	3	Hammond	Enoch				1	1	1	1		1				4		
Petersham	280	2	Hammond	Enoch Junr	2		1	1		2			1				7		
Hardwick	299	10	Hammond	Gideon				1						1			2		
Sturbridge	336	10	Hammond	Job	2			1		1	1	1					6		
Sturbridge	336	1	Hammond	Job Junr	2		1			1			1				5		
Charlton	332	10	Hammond	Moses	3	2		1		1		1	1				9		
Sturbridge	336	11	Hammond	Saml		1	2		1			2		1			7		
Sturbridge	335	23	Hammond	Seth	1			1				1					3		
Rutland	510	24	Hammond	Stephen	2	1	1	1		2			1				8		
Dudley	343	7	Hancock	Allen	2		1	1		1		1	1				7		
Templeton	236	15	Hancock	Hezekiah	2	1		1		2	1		1				8		
Templeton	240	6	Hancock	John	1		1					1					3		
Milford	396	14	Hancock	Joseph	1			1		1	1	1		1			6		
Winchendon	228	28	Hancock	Thos	2			1		2			1				6		
Winchendon	228	24	Hancock	Timo	4	1		1					1				7		
Uxbridge	465	8	Handy	Benja		1	1			1	1		1	1			6		
Uxbridge	465	9	Handy	Caleb	3		1						1				5		
Mendon	389	15	Handy	David	3			1					1				5	2d Parish	
Petersham	277	16	Handy	Ebenz	2		1	1		1		1					6		
Mendon	389	19	Handy	Mary Wd		1				1		1		1			4	2d Parish	
Barre	405	3	Hanes	Dan Capt		2		1		1	1	1					6		
Barre	408	15	Hanes	Jason	3		1			1	1	1					7		
Boylston	373	3	Hannah	John	1			1		1	1	1		1			6		
Barre	405	2	Hapgood	Artemas	1	1		1				2					5		
Shrewsbury	368	7	Hapgood	Ephraim			1			1			1				3		
Petersham	277	13	Hapgood	Hutchins	2		2	1		2			2				9		
Shrewsbury	368	6	Hapgood	Joab			1	1				1	1				4		
Harvard	219	32	Hapgood	John	1			1				1					3		
Petersham	280	1	Hapgood	Seth		1		1	1				1	1			5		
Harvard	219	33	Hapgood	Shadrack	1	1	1		1			2		1			7		
Hubbardston	418	11	Hapgood	Thomas Esq		1		1	1				1	1			5		
Barre	405	1	Hapgood	Winsor		1		1				1					3		
Sutton	160	11	Harbach	Daniel	3	1		1		2	1		1				9		
Sutton	160	9	Harbach	John			1	1		1		1	1				5		
Sutton	160	10	Harbach	Thomas			2	1		1	2	2	1				9		
Oxford	160	17	Hardin	Amos	2			1		1	2		1				7		

TOWN	PG#	LN#	LAST NAME	FIRST NAME	FREE WHITE MALES under 10	10 to 16	16 to 26	26 to 45	45 and over	FREE WHITE FEMALES under 10	10 to 16	16 to 26	26 to 45	45 and over	TOTAL ALL OTHER	TOTAL SLAVES	TOTALS	DISTRICT/ TOWNSHIP	NOTES
Barre	405	7	Harding	Abijah Capt	2	1	2	1	1			1	2	1			11		
Sturbridge	336	6	Harding	Jabez		1		1			1		1				4		
Sturbridge	336	4	Harding	Joshua	4	1	1		1	1	1		1				10		
Sturbridge	336	21	Harding	Meriam										2			2		
Sturbridge	336	5	Harding	Ralph	2	1		1		1		1	1				7		
Sturbridge	336	7	Harding	Stephen	1	1	1		1	2	1	1	1	2			11		
Upton	388	16	Hardy	Constant	1	1		1		4			2				9		
Westborough	196	95	Hardy	Elijah		3		1			2	1					7		
Worcester	182	8	Hardy	Levi	1		1			1		1					4		
Milford	396	1	Hardy	Nathan			1	1			1		1				4		
Westborough	191	26	Hardy	Phinehas	1	1		1			1		1				5		
Upton	388	14	Hardy	Silas	1	1		1					1	1			5		
Brookfield	257	17	Hardy	Thomas		1		1		1			1				4	Second Parish	
Sturbridge	336	18	Haris	Wm	1		1	1		1			1				4		
Mendon	389	14	Harkness	Samuel	3		1			2	1		1				8	2d Parish	
Lunenberg	426	19	Harkness	Thomas	1		1		1	2	4	1	2				12		
Shrewsbury	367	6	Harlow	Arunah		1		1			1						3		
Harvard	222	9	Harlow	Ellis	2	2		1		1	1		1				8		
Shrewsbury	367	7	Harlow	Thomas	1		1	1				1					4		
Harvard	219	36	Harlow	William	1		1					1	1	1	1		6		
Hardwick	299	7	Harmon	Elijah	2	1		1		1		1					6		
Western	255	4	Harmon	John				1		1		1					3		
Grafton	197	8	Harmon	Timothy				1		2	2		1				6		
Lunenberg	425	6	Harrad	Noah	2	1		1		2	2		1				9		
Princeton	515	22	Harrington	Abijah			1	1		1	1		1				5		
Brookfield	269	12	Harrington	Amos			1		1	1		2		1			5	Third Parish	
Brookfield	269	35	Harrington	Amos			1										1	Third Parish	
Grafton	197	11	Harrington	Anna										1			1		
Westminster	448	17	Harrington	Benjn	3		1					1					5		
Northborough	365	8	Harrington	Caleb	2	2	1		1		1		1				8		
Shrewsbury	368	16	Harrington	Daniel	1	1		1		2		1	1				7		
Spencer	496	3	Harrington	Eliha	3	1	2	1		3			2				12		
Shrewsbury	368	17	Harrington	Elijah		1	1		1	1	1	1	1				7		
Worcester	179	12	Harrington	Elijah		1	1		1	1	1	1	1				7		
Grafton	201	9	Harrington	Ephraim		3	3		4	1	2	1					14		
Holden	511	8	Harrington	Ephraim			1					2					3		
Shrewsbury	368	14	Harrington	Fortunatas	1		1		1	1		1	1				5		
Shrewsbury	368	13	Harrington	Isaac		1	1	1					1	1			5		
Grafton	201	10	Harrington	Jacob	1		1			1		1					4		
Westborough	191	30	Harrington	John		2		1	2			1	1				7		
Shrewsbury	367	1	Harrington	Jonathan	3		1	1		1		1					7		
Westborough	191	29	Harrington	Joseph		1	3		1	1			3				9		
Grafton	197	10	Harrington	Joshua	1	1	1	1				1					5		
Worcester	179	8	Harrington	Joshua	1		1		1	2	1	2		1			9		
Grafton	193	9	Harrington	Mary							1		1				2		
Holden	511	7	Harrington	Micah			1	1	1			1					4		
Grafton	196	9	Harrington	Moses		1		2		2		1					6		
Holden	511	5	Harrington	Nathan				1				2	1				4		
Worcester	182	12	Harrington	Nathl		1	2		1	1	1		2				8		
Rutland	510	18	Harrington	Noah			1		1			1					3		
Worcester	179	14	Harrington	Noah	1	2			1	2		1		1			8		
Brookfield	269	13	Harrington	Rufus	1		1	1		1			1				5	Third Parish	
Worcester	179	13	Harrington	Saml	2	1	1		1	2	1	1	1	1			11		
New Braintree	310	1	Harrington	Samll	1		2	1		1	2						7		
Grafton	198	5	Harrington	Samuel	2					1		1	1				5		
Holden	511	6	Harrington	Samuel			2	1		2		1					6		
Westminster	448	8	Harrington	Seth	1			2	1	1			1	1			6		
Worcester	179	11	Harrington	Silas		1	1		1	1	1		1				6		
Grafton	200	8	Harrington	Solomon	1			1		2		1					5		
Shrewsbury	368	15	Harrington	Thomas		1		1		2		1					5		
Westborough	197	109	Harrington	Wentworth	1		1				1						3		
Southborough	202	3	Harrington	William	1		1			1		1					4		
Lunenberg	425	3	Harrington	Wm	1	1		1		1	1	3		2			11		
Oxford	160	6	Harris	Abijah				1					1				2		
Sterling	353	12	Harris	Amasiah	1		1				1						3		
Oxford	160	7	Harris	Asa			2	1		1		1					5		
Boylston	376	11	Harris	Daniel	2	1		1		1	1	1	1				8		
Uxbridge	468	5	Harris	Israel				1					1				2		
Ashburnham	459	7	Harris	Jacob		1				1	1		1				5		
Oxford	160	5	Harris	Jonathan	2	1	1	1		2	1	1	1	1			11		
Worcester	182	5	Harris	Leml	1			1		1			1				4		
Harvard	222	22	Harris	Lydia		1							1				2		
Worcester	180	16	Harris	Noah			1	1				1					3		
Worcester	182	2	Harris	Rezinah									1				1		
Sutton	160	20	Harris	Thomas			1	1			1		1				4		
Ashburnham	459	10	Harris	William	3		1		2	1	1						8		
Lunenberg	425	10	Harris	Wm		2		1		1		1					5		
Brookfield	248	11	Harrison	Mary		1					1	1					3	First Parish	
Lancaster	349	12	Harskell	Elias	1			1	1	2	1	1					7		
Lancaster	349	19	Harskell	Henry			1			1		1					3		
Sterling	353	7	Hart	Aaron	1		1	1		2		1					6		
Westminster	445	14	Hart	David	2			1			1						4		
Ward	180	83	Hart	James		1		1				1					3		
Ward	177	34	Hart	James Jur			1		2		1						4		
Ward	177	31	Hart	John	1		3		1			1	1	1			8		
Ward	180	82	Hart	Martha									1				1		
Sutton	160	18	Hart	Peter R.	1		1		1	4			1				8		
Ward	177	36	Hart	Thomas	3	1		1				1					6		
Harvard	220	34	Hartwell	Hannah							1		1				2		

TOWN	PG#	LN#	LAST NAME	FIRST NAME	FWM <10	FWM 10-16	FWM 16-26	FWM 26-45	FWM 45+	FWF <10	FWF 10-16	FWF 16-26	FWF 26-45	FWF 45+	TOTAL ALL OTHER	TOTAL SLAVES	TOTALS	DISTRICT/TOWNSHIP	NOTES
Lunenberg	426	20	Hartwell	Jacob	1		1			2		1					5		
Lunenberg	425	20	Hartwell	John	1		2	1		2		1					7		
Lunenberg	425	9	Hartwell	Jonathan		1		1			1	2	1				6		
Lunenberg	425	18	Hartwell	Joseph				1				1	1				3		
Lunenberg	425	8	Hartwell	Josiah			1		2			1		1			5		
Oxford	160	12	Hartwell	Saml	3	1	1	1		1	1		1				9		
Winchendon	228	25	Hartwell	Samll	2			1		5		1	1				10		
Holden	511	10	Harvy	James	3			1				1					5		
Brookfield	260	1	Harwood	Abel	1	1		1		1	1		1				6	Second Parish	
Charlton	332	4	Harwood	Daniel			1			2	2		1	1			7		
Sutton	157	13	Harwood	Daniel			2	2	1			1	1	2			9		
Douglas	482	25	Harwood	David	1			1				1		1			4		
Oxford	159	12	Harwood	David				1					1				2		
Oxford	159	13	Harwood	David Junr	1			1					1				3		
Oxford	159	15	Harwood	Elihu	2			1					1				4		
Charlton	332	5	Harwood	Ezra				1					1	1			3		
Charlton	332	3	Harwood	Ezra Junr			1			1		1					3		
Charlton	332	9	Harwood	Gershom	1	2		1		1	1		1				7		
Leicester	489	14	Harwood	James			2	1					2	1			6		
Sutton	159	14	Harwood	John	2			1		2			1				6		
Charlton	332	7	Harwood	Jonathan	1	1		1			3		1				7		
Sutton	157	18	Harwood	Jos & Jerusha				1			1			2			4		
Brookfield	259	1	Harwood	Katey	1					1		1					3	Second Parish	
Brookfield	269	2	Harwood	Nathaniel	1		1		1			1			1		5	Third Parish	
Charlton	332	1	Harwood	Nicholas		1		1		1	1	2	1				7		
Barre	406	22	Harwood	Peter			1	1		1	2	1					6		
Brookfield	260	7	Harwood	Peter		1		1		5		1	1				9	Second Parish	
Oxford	159	14	Harwood	Solomon	1		1	1		1			1				5		
Oxford	159	16	Harwood	Stephen		1	1	1	1			1	2	1			8		
Hubbardston	418	15	Hasey	Zanus				1					1				2		
Brookfield	260	15	Haskal	Silas	1		2			1	1						5	Second Parish	
Western	255	5	Haskall	John	1		1	1					1	1	1		5		
Brookfield	260	13	Haskall	Samuel	1	1	1	1		1			1	1			7	Second Parish	
Brookfield	257	10	Haskall	Simeon	4		1				1		1				7	Second Parish	
Hardwick	298	19	Haskel	Sheveriah	4	1	1			1			1				8		
Lunenberg	426	18	Haskell	Abraham		2	3	1			2	1	1				10		
Westborough	198	135	Haskell	Asa	1		1			2		1	1				6		
Holden	511	11	Haskell	Ebenezer				1		2	2	3	1				9		
Hardwick	298	22	Haskell	Ephraim		1	1			2			1				5		
Oakham	319	2	Haskell	George			1			2		1					4		
Harvard	219	3	Haskell	Jacob	2		1	1		2		1	1				8		
Harvard	221	23	Haskell	James			1	1			1	1		1			5		
Harvard	221	22	Haskell	James Junr	2						1	1					4		
Harvard	221	29	Haskell	Jonathan			1	1		2	2		1				7		
Templeton	238	8	Haskell	Joseph	1	1			1	1	1		1				6		
Harvard	219	2	Haskell	Josiah		1		1					1				3		
Harvard	219	12	Haskell	Josiah Jun			1			1			1				3		
Lancaster	352	2	Haskell	Louis						2	2		1	1			6		
Hardwick	299	6	Haskell	Micah	1		1				1						3		
Hardwick	299	1	Haskell	Nathl				1						1			2		
Templeton	238	9	Haskell	Oliver	1	2	1				1	1					6		
Westborough	198	134	Haskell	Phinh			1	1		1			1				4		
Oakham	319	4	Haskell	Roger		1	1	1					1				4		
Harvard	219	5	Haskell	Samuel	1		1	1		1	1	5		1			12		
Templeton	238	7	Haskell	Stephen				1				1		1			3		
Lancaster	352	1	Haskell	William	1		1	1		2	1	1	1				9		
Dudley	343	12	Haskil	James	1	1		1		1	1	1	1				7		
Dudley	343	8	Haskil	John		1					1			2			5		
Dudley	343	9	Haskil	John Junr	1	1	1	1	1	1	2		1				9		
Dudley	343	11	Haskil	Stephen	1	1		1		2			1				6		
Petersham	277	8	Haskins	Elkanah		1		1		2		1	1				6		
Hardwick	299	5	Haskins	Samll	2			1	1	3			2	1			10		
Hardwick	299	9	Haskins	Samll Jr	3	3	1	1		1		1	1				11		
Berlin	214	28	Hastings	Benjamin	1	1		1	1	3	1		1				9		
Boylston	376	1	Hastings	Benjamin			1						1				2		
Lunenberg	425	14	Hastings	Caleb				1		1			1				3		
Ashburnham	459	4	Hastings	Charles	2	2		1		2	1	1	1				10		
Boylston	375	28	Hastings	David			1		1			1		1			4		
Lunenberg	425	13	Hastings	David				1									1		
Boylston	375	29	Hastings	David Jn	3			1					1				5		
Worcester	179	15	Hastings	Ebenz	1	3		1	1			1	2				9		
Boylston	375	26	Hastings	Eliakim	3	2		1				2	1	1			10		
Ashburnham	459	17	Hastings	Ezra	2			1		1			1				5		
Holden	514	21	Hastings	Ezra	1	2	1	1		1	1		1				8		
Petersham	280	4	Hastings	Henry	1			1	1			1	1				7		
Bolton	212	12	Hastings	John				1		1	1			1			4		
Boylston	376	3	Hastings	John		1	1					1		1			4		
Hardwick	298	21	Hastings	John	1	2	2		1	1	1	1		1			10		
Shrewsbury	367	3	Hastings	Jonas	1	2	1	1		1			1				7		
Boylston	375	27	Hastings	Jonathan	1		2		1		1			1			6		
Lunenberg	425	17	Hastings	Jonathan	2			1		3			1				7		
Shrewsbury	367	2	Hastings	Joseph		1			1					1			3		
Brookfield	269	4	Hastings	Moses		1			1	2	1	1	1				7	Third Parish	
Boylston	376	2	Hastings	Nathan	1		1						1				3		
Berlin	212	11	Hastings	Nathaniel		1	1	1					1	1			5		
Brookfield	269	3	Hastings	Nevenson	1	1		1		3	1	2	1	1			11	Third Parish	
Mendon	384	1	Hastings	Seth Esq	1		2	2		1		1	1				8	1st Parish	
Boylston	376	6	Hastings	Silas	2	1	1		1	3	1	2	1				12		
Sterling	353	4	Hastings	Stephen	2	1		1					2				6		
Boylston	376	8	Hastings	Timothy F.			1	1		2			1				5		

203

TOWN	PG#	LN#	LAST NAME	FIRST NAME	FREE WHITE MALES under 10	10 to 16	16 to 26	26 to 45	45 and over	FREE WHITE FEMALES under 10	10 to 16	16 to 26	26 to 45	45 and over	TOTAL ALL OTHER	TOTAL SLAVES	TOTALS	DISTRICT/ TOWNSHIP	NOTES
Barre	408	16	Hastings	Timy Jr	1	1		1		4	1		1				9		
Berlin	214	38	Hastings	William	1			1		3	1		1				7		
Barre	407	1	Hastins	Theophs	2	1		1			2		1				7		
Barre	405	8	Hastins	Timy					1		1			1			3		
Spencer	495	5	Hatch	Elias	2			1		1			1				5		
Western	255	1	Hatch	James	3		1	1				2					7		
Spencer	495	8	Hatch	Joshua				1					1				2		
Spencer	495	9	Hatch	Stevens					1					1			2		
Spencer	495	6	Hatch	Thomas	2	1		1		2			1				7		
Spencer	495	11	Hathaway	Enos	3	1		1		2			1				8		
Spencer	495	10	Hathaway	James		1		1	2	1		1	1	2			9		
Hardwick	298	18	Hathaway	Jereh	1	1	1	1		2	1		1				8		
Petersham	277	9	Hathaway	Joel	2	2	1	1		2	1		1				10		
Sutton	160	17	Hathaway	Simeon	1	2	4		2	4	1	1	1				16		
Boylston	376	14	Hatherly	Thomas				1					1				2		
Boylston	376	7	Hathern	David	2	1		1		2		1	1				8		
Boylston	376	12	Hathern	Micah	1		1		1		1	2					6		
Hardwick	299	2	Hatheway	Timothy	2	2		1		2	1		1				9		
Brookfield	260	8	Hathway	Jonathan	3	1		1			1		1				7	Second Parish	
Brookfield	259	3	Hathway	Levi	1			1			1		1				4	Second Parish	
Western	255	6	Hathway	Nathan			1	1		1		1					4		
Brookfield	257	15	Hathway	Robert	1			1	1	3	4	1		1			12	Second Parish	
Brookfield	260	11	Hathway	Thomas		1		1		1				1			4	Second Parish	
Brookfield	260	10	Hathway	Wilson			1			1		1	1				4	Second Parish	
Petersham	280	12	Hatstall	George	2	3		1		3			1				10		
Lancaster	349	14	Haven	Ebenezer		1		1			1		1	2			6		
Leicester	489	15	Haven	Elkanah	2	1		1		1	1		1				7		
Leicester	489	16	Haven	Hannah									1	1			2		
Ashburnham	459	16	Haven	John				1									1		
Athol	290	16	Haven	John	1		2		1			1		1			6		
Leominster	435	12	Haven	John	1		1					1					3		
Sutton	157	15	Haven	John			1						3				4		
Charlton	332	8	Haven	John D.	1		1	1		2			1				6		
Athol	290	17	Haven	John Jur	2	1	3		1	3	1	1	1				13		
Ashburnham	459	8	Haven	Jonathan	1			1		1			1				4		
Lancaster	349	18	Haven	Richard	3		1	1		1		2					8		
Shrewsbury	367	9	Haven	Samuel	2		3		1	2	2		1	3			14		
Shrewsbury	367	10	Haven	Samuel Jr	2			1					1				4		
New Braintree	309	21	Hawes	Paul		1	2				1	1		1			6		
Leominster	435	5	Hawks	Benjm			4	1		4	1		2		2		14		
Lancaster	349	15	Hawks	John	1			1				3	1				6		
Lancaster	349	16	Hawks	John Jun	2			1		2		1					6		
Leominster	435	6	Haws	Benjm	2		1		1			1	1				6		
Westborough	196	98	Haws	James		1			1				1				3		
Westborough	196	99	Haws	James Jun			1			3		1					5		
Sutton	159	1	Hayden	Asa	1			1				1					3		
Sutton	160	21	Hayden	Elias				1					1				2		
Sutton	159	10	Hayden	Hezekiah		1		1					1				3		
Holden	514	10	Hayden	Jonathan			1					1					2		
Southborough	203	25	Hayden	Jonathan		1		1	1				1				4		
Grafton	206	5	Hayden	Moses	1	1		1		1			1				5		
Harvard	217	39	Hayden	Polly	3					1		1					5		
Grafton	202	14	Hayden	Solomon			1				1						2		
Sterling	353	18	Haydon	Benjamin	1			1		1		1					4		
Ashburnham	459	6	Haynes	James				1		3	1	2	1				8		
Templeton	234	5	Haynes	Jonas	2			1					1				4		
Rutland	509	11	Haynes	Jonathan			1	1				1		1			5		
Gardner	449	9	Haynes	Reuben			1		1	3	1	2	1				9		
Bolton	210	4	Haynes	Silas	3			1					1				5		
Leominster	435	9	Hayns	Samuel	3	2		1					1				7		
Milford	396	2	Hayward	Adam	5	1		1		2		2	1	1			13		
Northbridge	473	3	Hayward	Amasa	1			1		1			1				4		
Milford	396	10	Hayward	Amos			1			1		1					3		
Milford	395	30	Hayward	David				1					1				2		
Mendon	384	5	Hayward	Elijah		1	2	1					1				5	1st Parish	
Mendon	384	4	Hayward	Elisha	2		1	1		1	1		1				7	1st Parish	
Northbridge	476	17	Hayward	Elisha		1		1		1	1		1				4		
Milford	395	31	Hayward	Ephm			1	2					1				4		
Milford	396	4	Hayward	Hannah Wd	1	1					1	1		1			5		
Sutton	159	12	Hayward	Hartwell		1				1		1		1			4		
Mendon	384	6	Hayward	Ichabod			1						1				2	1st Parish	
Milford	396	12	Hayward	Jacob		1		1		1	2		1				6		
Sutton	157	17	Hayward	James	1			1		1	2	1	1				7		
Worcester	179	10	Hayward	James	1			1		2			1				5		
Milford	396	6	Hayward	Joel	1	1	1	1		2			1				7		
Mendon	384	7	Hayward	John		1	2		2			1	1	1			8	1st Parish	
Milford	396	3	Hayward	Jonathan	1	1		1		2		1	1				7		
Charlton	332	17	Hayward	Jonathn			1				1						2		
Upton	388	6	Hayward	Jont	1		2			3		2					8		
Upton	388	12	Hayward	Jont Lt.	2	1			1	1		1	1				7		
Sutton	159	11	Hayward	Joseph			1							1			2		
Milford	396	11	Hayward	Margaret Wd									2				2		
Milford	396	7	Hayward	Samuel			1			1			1				3		
Charlton	332	15	Hayward	Samuel Junr			1	1				1	1				4		
Sutton	159	9	Hayward	Simeon		1		1	1	1	2		1				6		
Worcester	179	9	Hayward	Stephen	1		1						1				3		
Milford	396	5	Hayward	Warfield				1			1	1	1				4		
Gardner	449	17	Haywood	Benje			1					1					2		
Westminster	448	3	Haywood	Benjn		1		1		1			1				4		
Barre	408	22	Haywood	Ezekiel				1				1		1			3		

TOWN	PG#	LN#	LAST NAME	FIRST NAME	FREE WHITE MALES					FREE WHITE FEMALES					TOTAL ALL OTHER	TOTAL SLAVES	TOTALS	DISTRICT/ TOWNSHIP	NOTES
					under 10	10 to 16	16 to 26	26 to 45	45 and over	under 10	10 to 16	16 to 26	26 to 45	45 and over					
Westminster	455	7	Haywood	Michar	3	2			1			1	1	1			9		
Westminster	448	12	Haywood	Nathan	2		1	1	1	1			1	2			9		
Gardner	449	16	Haywood	Seth			1		1			1		1			4		
Barre	406	23	Haywood	Stephen	1		2			1	1	1					6		
Westminster	448	15	Haywood	Timothy		3	2		1	1		2		1			10		
Sterling	353	9	Headley	John	1			1		4			1	1			8		
Sterling	353	2	Headley	Josiah	3	2		1			1			1			8		
Sterling	354	2	Headley	Josiah Jun			1				1						2		
Hubbardston	418	1	Heald	Ebenezer		1			1		1	1	1				5		
Hubbardston	418	4	Heald	Luther	3	1		1		2	1		1				9		
Hubbardston	418	2	Heald	Stephen Lt	2		1		1			1	1				6		
Hubbardston	418	3	Heald	Timy Capt	2	2		1	1	2	1		1	1			11		
Dudley	344	45	Healey	Hezekiah			1	1					1				3		
Worcester	180	15	Healey	Jeddh			1		2	1	2		2	1			9		
Dudley	343	13	Healey	John	2	1		1		1		1	1				7		
Dudley	343	5	Healey	Joseph		1			1	1	1		1				5		
Dudley	343	6	Healey	Leml	1		1	1		3			1	1			8		
Dudley	343	3	Healey	Moses	2	1		1		1		2	1				8		
Dudley	344	46	Healey	Nathl			1		1				1		1		4		
Dudley	343	1	Healey	Nathl Jun	1	1		1		3			1				7		
Dudley	343	4	Healey	Saml	1		1	1		1	1		1	1			7		
Dudley	343	2	Healey	Wm	2			1		3	1		1				8		
Oxford	160	8	Healy	Ruth Wd	1		2			1		1	1	1			7		
Lancaster	349	9	Heard	Edmund	2		1			1			1				5		
Rutland	509	4	Heard	Mark	2		1		1	1		3		1			9		
Worcester	179	6	Heard	Nathn		2	3	1	1		1	2	1	1			12		
Leicester	492	2	Hearkness	James	1		3	1			2		1				8		
Worcester	180	14	Hearsey	David	3	1		1		2	1	1	1				10		
Charlton	332	2	Heath	John	1			1		2	1	1		1			7		
Shrewsbury	368	9	Hemanway	Jonas		1		1			1	1		1			5		
Shrewsbury	368	8	Hemanway	Silas			2		1		1		1				5		
Shrewsbury	368	10	Hemanway	Vashni	2		3	1				1					7		
Barre	405	12	Hemenway	Daniel	1		2	2	1	1		1		1			9		
Barre	405	11	Hemenway	Jonathan				1		1		1					3		
Barre	405	13	Hemenway	Solomon	1	1	1		1		1		1				6		
Bolton	213	12	Heminway	Joshua			1			2	1		1				5		
Holden	514	9	Hemmenway	Daniel	4		1			1			1				7		
Worcester	179	18	Hemminway	Jacob		1	1	1	1				1		2		7		
Worcester	179	17	Hemminway	James	1			1		1		1	1				5		
Worcester	182	3	Hemminway	Jeffrey											6		6		
Leicester	489	7	Hemsey	Calvin	2	1		1	1	2	1	1					9		
Leominster	435	1	Henderson	John				1						2			3		
Northborough	365	11	Henderson	Nathan	1			1		1			1				4		
Northborough	365	12	Henderson	William			1	1					1				3		
Spencer	496	9	Henderson	William				1	1		1		1				4		
Harvard	222	38	Henney	Joseph				1			1	1	1				4		
Barre	406	26	Henry	Adam			1				2	1	1				5		
Rutland	509	7	Henry	David			1	1				2		1			5		
Lunenberg	425	19	Henry	George				1									1		
Lunenberg	425	12	Henry	George Jun	1			1		1	1			1			5		
Lunenberg	425	11	Henry	John	2	1		1		3	1		1				9		
Barre	408	24	Henry	Robert	2			1				1					4		
Barre	408	32	Henry	Saml			1	1			2						4		
Rutland	509	8	Henry	Samuel	1			1		1			1				4		
Rutland	509	9	Henry	Silas	1			1				1					3		
Rutland	509	10	Henry	William		1	1	1	1			1	1	1			7		
Barre	405	4	Henry	Wm Capt				1				1		1			3		
Leicester	492	1	Henshaw	David	2	1	2		1	1	1	2		1			11		
Ward	177	35	Henshaw	Joseph			1					1		1			3		
Leicester	489	8	Henshaw	William		1	3		1	1	1	1		1			9		
Shrewsbury	365	14	Henshaw	Joshua Esq		1			1			2		2			6		
Shrewsbury	367	5	Henshaw	Sarah			1	1			1	1		1	1		6		
Douglas	482	23	Herendeen	Simeon			3		1	1	1	1		1			8		
Uxbridge	468	1	Herendun	Asa		1			1	2		1	1				6		
Barre	408	26	Herington	David	3	1		1				1					6		
Barre	408	20	Herrick	Amos	2			1				1					4		
Fitchburg	429	20	Herrick	Benjamin	2				1								3		
Barre	407	2	Herrick	Saml			1	1			1		1				4		
Brookfield	269	22	Hersey	Elijah	1	3			1	3		1		1			10	Third Parish	
Royalston	239	6	Hewes	Joshua				1					1				2		
Sutton	159	4	Hewit	Daniel	1			1		1			1				4		
Sutton	159	2	Hewit	William	3	2	1		1	2	1		1	1			12		
Templeton	234	12	Heyward	Samll			1										1		
Winchendon	226	17	Heyward	*				1		1	2						4		
Worcester	179	4	Heyward	Abel	1	1	1	1			1	1	1				7		
Holden	511	4	Heyward	Alpheus			1		1			1					3		
Grafton	202	5	Heyward	Amasiah	1	1		1		3			1				7		
Winchendon	226	16	Heyward	Amos	1	1	1		1		2						6		
Worcester	179	2	Heyward	Benja	2	1	2		1	2	1		1	1			11		
Worcester	179	3	Heyward	Daniel	2		1		2	1	1	1	1		2		11		
Worcester	179	5	Heyward	Daniel 2d	1	1		1		1			1				5		
Lunenberg	425	4	Heyward	John T.	2	2	1		1	1			1	1			9		
Winchendon	228	19	Heyward	Lemuel			1										1		
Shrewsbury	367	4	Heyward	Nathaniel	1	2	3		1	1	1		1				10		
Worcester	179	1	Heyward	Phine				1			2		1				4		
Holden	511	2	Heyward	Samuel	1	1		1		2		1		1			7		
Royalston	239	9	Heyward	Silas	1	1	1		1				1	1			6		
Holden	511	3	Heyward	Thaddeus			1						1				2		
Sturbridge	335	22	Hibbard	Eleaser			1	1	1			1	1	1			6		
Sutton	160	12	Hicks	Benjamin		1			1		1	1		1			5		
Sutton	160	15	Hicks	Caleb	1		1				1	1					4		

TOWN	PG#	LN#	LAST NAME	FIRST NAME	FWM under 10	FWM 10 to 16	FWM 16 to 26	FWM 26 to 45	FWM 45 and over	FWF under 10	FWF 10 to 16	FWF 16 to 26	FWF 26 to 45	FWF 45 and over	TOTAL ALL OTHER	TOTAL SLAVES	TOTALS	DISTRICT/ TOWNSHIP	NOTES
Sutton	160	16	Hicks	Ebenz	1	2		1		1	1		1				7		
Sutton	160	13	Hicks	Eliza Wd	1		1						1	1			4		
Sutton	160	14	Hicks	Joseph		1	2	1				1	1	1			7		
Barre	408	23	Hicks	Joshua	3			1		2			1				7		
Westborough	191	35	Hide	Rachel		1				1			1				3		
Spencer	496	6	Hide	William	1			1					1				4		
Milford	395	32	Highland	Ruth						2			1				3		
Rutland	510	21	Hildreth	Ralph	1						2		1				5		
Boylston	376	15	Hildrick	Timothy	1	1	4	1		1		2	2				12		
Petersham	280	14	Hildruth	Elijah	1	1		1		1			1				5		
Petersham	280	13	Hildruth	John	1		2		1	1	2	2		1			10		
Petersham	280	15	Hildruth	John	1		1						1				3		
Douglas	479	14	Hill	Aaron		2	1	1				2	1				7		
Oxford	160	13	Hill	Aaron	3			1		1	1		1				7		
Gardner	449	12	Hill	Abigail						1			1				2		
Gardner	449	11	Hill	Barzelial	2			1		3	1		1				8		
Mendon	389	18	Hill	Daniel	2			1		2	1	2	1				9	2d Parish	
Spencer	496	7	Hill	Daniel			2		1				1				4		
Upton	388	8	Hill	Edmond	2	1		1					1	1			6		
Uxbridge	468	3	Hill	Elizabeth	2		1						1	1			5		
Mendon	384	3	Hill	Elizabeth Wd	1							1	1	1			4	1st Parish	
Royalston	231	9	Hill	Ephraim	1			1		3	1		1				7		
Ashburnham	459	19	Hill	Isaac		2		1		4		1					8		
Northbridge	473	1	Hill	Jacob			2	1	1			1	2	1			8		
Worcester	182	11	Hill	Jacob											2		2		
Gardner	449	7	Hill	Jesse	2		1	1		1	1		1				7		
Douglas	482	27	Hill	Job	1			1				1	1	2			6		
Mendon	384	8	Hill	Joel			1			3			1				5	1st Parish	
Athol	290	14	Hill	John	1		1			1		1					4		
Brookfield	269	18	Hill	John				1									1	Third Parish	
Charlton	332	16	Hill	John		1		1				1		1			4		
Harvard	217	27	Hill	John		1		1		1				1			4		
Leicester	492	4	Hill	John			1						1				2		
Mendon	381	18	Hill	John				1				1		1			3	1st Parish	
Western	255	3	Hill	John	1			1				1	1				4		
Mendon	389	17	Hill	John 2d	2			1		1			1				5	2d Parish	
Athol	287	3	Hill	John 2nd	1		2							1			4		
Royalston	241	20	Hill	Jonah				1						1			2		
Northbridge	473	2	Hill	Joseph				1				1	1				3		
Spencer	496	8	Hill	Joshua	3			1				1					5		
Harvard	218	6	Hill	Levi	2			1				2					5		
Athol	290	15	Hill	Moses		2	1	1						1			5		
Douglas	479	12	Hill	Moses	3	1	2	1			1		1	1			10		
Gardner	449	8	Hill	Moses	2	1	2	1		3	1	1	1				12		
Gardner	449	13	Hill	Nathll			1	1		4	1		1				8		
Douglas	482	26	Hill	Noah		1		1		1			1				4		
Harvard	222	24	Hill	Oliver	2		2	1				2					7		
Royalston	241	21	Hill	Oliver	2	1		1					2				6		
Harvard	217	28	Hill	Sarah						1	1		1				3		
Gardner	449	10	Hill	Silvanus	1	1							1				3		
Brookfield	257	13	Hill	Thomas		1	1		2	3	1	1		1			10	Second Parish	
Sturbridge	335	18	Hill	Ziba		1		1						1			3		
Dudley	343	14	Hillman	Ebenz	2			1					1				4		
Dudley	343	10	Hillman	James	1		1	1				1	1	1			6		
Leominster	435	8	Hills	John	2		3	1		1			1				8		
Leominster	435	15	Hills	Sarah									1				1		
Leominster	436	41	Hills	Silas	3	1	1	2		2		2	1				12		
Leominster	435	16	Hills	Smith	1		2	1		1			1	1			7		
Lunenberg	425	5	Hilton	Samuel		1		1						1			3		
Mendon	389	20	Himpton	John				1	1	1			3	1			6	2d Parish	
Brookfield	269	26	Hincher	Joshua	4			1			1		1				7	Third Parish	
Brookfield	248	4	Hincher	Josiah	2	2		2	1	2	2		1				12	First Parish	
Brookfield	269	24	Hincher	Thomas	1			1		1	1		1				5	Third Parish	
Brookfield	269	25	Hincher	William				1						1			2	Third Parish	
Hubbardston	418	14	Hinds	Abner			1	1					1	1			4		
Barre	405	9	Hinds	Corlis Jr				1		1			1				3		
Barre	405	5	Hinds	Corlis Lt				1						1			2		
Barre	405	10	Hinds	Eli	2		1	1		2			2				8		
Hubbardston	418	12	Hinds	Howard	3	1	1		1	1	1	1					10		
Boylston	375	24	Hinds	Jacob	1		2	1					1				6		
Brookfield	260	4	Hinds	John				1		1		1		1			4	Second Parish	
Brookfield	257	16	Hinds	Oliver	1		2		1	1		1	1				7	Second Parish	
Boylston	375	25	Hinds	Tabatha			2	1						1			4		
Barre	408	17	Hines	Forbes	2	1		1		2	2	1					10		
Barre	408	18	Hines	Jesse				1		2			1				4		
Hardwick	298	20	Hinkley	Barnabas	1		1	1					1	2			6		
Barre	405	17	Hinkley	Judah	3		1	1		1	1		1				7		
Hardwick	299	3	Hinkley	Samll	1		1	1		1	2		1	1			8		
Hardwick	299	4	Hinkley	Seth	1			1		1	3		1				7		
Royalston	233	6	Hinsley	Peleg	2		2	1		2		1	1				9		
Brookfield	248	3	Hitchcock	Caleb			2	1				2		1			6	First Parish	
Brookfield	248	5	Hitchcock	David		1	1	1	1		1	2	2	1			9	First Parish	
Western	255	7	Hitchcock	John	1			1					1				3		
Western	255	2	Hitchcock	Luke		1		2		2			1	2			8		
Brookfield	248	1	Hitchcock	Moses	1	2	5			1		1	1	1			13	First Parish	
Brookfield	248	6	Hitchcock	Peletiah	2			2		1			1	1			7	First Parish	
Uxbridge	465	10	Hix	David	1			1		3			1				6		
Royalston	236	9	Hix	Ephrm	1		1			2			1				5		
Upton	388	9	Hix	Joshua				1						1			2		
Royalston	236	8	Hix	Josiah		1				1		1	1	1			6		
Berlin	213	4	Hoar	David				1					1				2		

206

TOWN	PG#	LN#	LAST NAME	FIRST NAME	FREE WHITE MALES					FREE WHITE FEMALES					TOTAL ALL OTHER	TOTAL SLAVES	TOTALS	DISTRICT/ TOWNSHIP	NOTES
					under 10	10 to 16	16 to 26	26 to 45	45 and over	under 10	10 to 16	16 to 26	26 to 45	45 and over					
Westminster	448	1	Hoar	John		1	1		1		1	2		1			7		
Brookfield	260	9	Hoar	Samuel			2	1		2	2	1	1				9		Second Parish
Westminster	445	15	Hoar	Samuel	2		1	1		2			1				7		
Westminster	445	16	Hoar	Stephen	2	1	2	1		2		2	1				11		
Westminster	448	16	Hoar	Timothy	2	1		1		2		2	1				9		
Leicester	489	13	Hobart	John	2	1		2		1	1	1	1				9		
Ashburnham	459	3	Hobart	Shubiel		1		1					1				3		
Ashburnham	459	5	Hobart	Thomas	1			1				1					3		
Sturbridge	336	8	Hobbs	Benj				1			1		1				3		
Spencer	496	5	Hobbs	Daniel	4		1	1					1	1			8		
Princeton	515	23	Hobbs	Elisha			3	1				1		1			6		
Princeton	515	24	Hobbs	Elisha Junr	4		1			1		1					7		
Brookfield	269	17	Hobbs	Jesse	3	2		1		2	1	1	1				11		Third Parish
Brookfield	269	28	Hobbs	Josiah				1					1				2		Third Parish
Brookfield	269	29	Hobbs	Moses	1	1	1	1		4		1	1				10		Third Parish
Sturbridge	335	21	Hobbs	Nathan	1		4	1			1		2				9		
Sturbridge	336	12	Hobbs	Saml		3	3	1	1	1		2		1			12		
Brookfield	269	14	Hobbs	Silas	2	1		1		1	1		1				7		Third Parish
Petersham	280	11	Hodges	Abiel				1	1				2	1			5		
Western	258	13	Hodges	Daniel	1	2	1	1	1	2		2	1	2			13		
Rutland	510	13	Hodges	Job			1	1	1	1		2		1			7		
Southborough	204	4	Holaway	David	1			1		3	1		1				7		
Uxbridge	465	7	Holbrook	Amariah			1	1				1		1			4		
Milford	396	8	Holbrook	Calvin	2		1	1	1	2		2		1			10		
Northborough	365	13	Holbrook	Daniel	4	1		1		1			1				8		
Upton	388	11	Holbrook	Daniel	1		1					1					3		
Holden	514	22	Holbrook	David	1	1	1	1		1	1		1				7		
Brookfield	269	9	Holbrook	Elihu	1		1	1		3	1	1					8		Third Parish
Leominster	435	17	Holbrook	Elijah		1		1		3			1				6		
Brookfield	269	10	Holbrook	George	1		2	2					1				6		Third Parish
Sturbridge	336	16	Holbrook	Hannah	1							2		1			4		
Uxbridge	465	6	Holbrook	Henry			1						1	1			3		
Brookfield	269	21	Holbrook	Isaiah D.	1			1		1			1				4		Third Parish
Sturbridge	335	17	Holbrook	James		1	2		1	1	1		1				7		
Sturbridge	335	13	Holbrook	John				1	1	1			1				3		
Sturbridge	335	14	Holbrook	John 2d	2	1	2		1	1		2	1				10		
Sturbridge	335	20	Holbrook	John 3d	2	1	2		1	1		2	1				10		
Worcester	182	1	Holbrook	Joseph			2		1	1	2	2		1			9		
Charlton	332	6	Holbrook	Josiah		1		1		2	1		1				6		
Uxbridge	468	2	Holbrook	Moses	1		1	1		1			1				5		
Upton	388	13	Holbrook	Nathan			1			2			1				4		
Mendon	384	2	Holbrook	Peter Lt.	2		1	1					1				5		1st Parish
Worcester	182	4	Holbrook	Phine	2			1					1				4		
Upton	388	10	Holbrook	Simeon			1	1						1			3		
Sutton	157	16	Holbrook	Stephen	2	1		1		1			1				6		
Uxbridge	465	5	Holbrook	Stephen	3		1				1	2					7		
Douglas	482	24	Holbrook	Sylvanus			1	1		1			1				4		
Ashburnham	459	15	Holbrook	William	1	2	1		1	1			1				7		
Milford	396	9	Holbrook	Ziba	1			1		2	1	1					6		
Sterling	353	1	Holcomb	Rheuben		1		1	1	1		1	1		1		7		
Grafton	199	4	Holdbrook	Moses		1		1					1				3		
Grafton	193	5	Holdbrook	Moses Jun	2		1			3	1		1				8		
Grafton	200	15	Holdbrook	Sarah										1			1		
Grafton	200	14	Holdbrook	Stephen		1		1		1			2				5		
Barre	406	27	Holden	Aaron Capt			1		1				1	1			4		
Westminster	448	4	Holden	Abner				1						1			2		
Westminster	448	5	Holden	Abner Jr		1		1					1				3		
Rutland	510	20	Holden	Benjamin	2	1		1		1			1				6		
Shrewsbury	365	15	Holden	Daniel	1	1		2					1	1			6		
Westminster	448	9	Holden	Elias	2	2		1					1				7		
Westminster	448	6	Holden	Ezra	3			1		2	1		1				8		
Southborough	205	16	Holden	Isaac			2		1	1	1			2			7		
Ashburnham	459	12	Holden	James	1	1		1		1			1				5		
Barre	408	29	Holden	James	1				1	2	2			1			7		
Barre	408	30	Holden	James Jr			1	1		1			1				4		
Leicester	489	9	Holden	John	2			1		3			1				7		
Mendon	381	19	Holden	John Capt.		1		1					1				3		1st Parish
Templeton	240	11	Holden	Jonathan			1			4		1					6		
Ashburnham	459	9	Holden	Joshua	1			1					1				3		
Westminster	448	11	Holden	Levi	1		1	1				1		1			6		
Petersham	277	14	Holden	Nathan	1		1	1		3	3		1				10		
Hubbardston	418	5	Holden	Nathan	3	1	1	1		1		1	1				9		
Rutland	510	19	Holden	Phidelia	2	1	1			1	1		1				7		
Westminster	445	13	Holden	Rebeckah							1		1				2		
Templeton	240	10	Holden	Robert	1	1		1		1		1	1				6		
Westminster	448	2	Holden	Stephen		1	2	1		4	2		1				11		
Lunenberg	426	17	Holden	Sylvanus	4		1			1			1				7		
Berlin	212	10	Holder	Thomas	3	2		1				2		2			10		
Shrewsbury	368	12	Holding	Amasa			1	1		2			1				5		
Barre	405	14	Holdon	Moses Lt	1		1	1		3		1	2				9		
Petersham	277	6	Holland	John	2	3		1		2		2	1				11		
Sutton	159	13	Holland	Joseph	1	1		1		1		1	1	1	1		7		
Petersham	280	10	Holland	Luther	1		3			2	1		1				9		
Petersham	280	8	Holland	Wilder		1		1		1		1					3		
Barre	408	25	Holland	James Lt	3		1						1				5		
Barre	408	27	Holland	Joab	3	1	1			1	1	1	1				9		
Barre	408	28	Holland	Nathan	1		1					1	1				4		
Oxford	159	10	Holley	Joseph		2		1		1				1			5		
Ward	180	84	Holman	Abel				1						2			3		
Bolton	210	10	Holman	Abraham			4			2	1	1	2				11		
Bolton	213	5	Holman	Asa	1		1			1		1					4		

TOWN	PG#	LN#	LAST NAME	FIRST NAME	FREE WHITE MALES					FREE WHITE FEMALES					TOTAL ALL OTHER	TOTAL SLAVES	TOTALS	DISTRICT/ TOWNSHIP	NOTES
					under 10	10 to 16	16 to 26	26 to 45	45 and over	under 10	10 to 16	16 to 26	26 to 45	45 and over					
Sutton	159	6	Holman	David		1	1		1		1			1			5		
Athol	290	18	Holman	Edwd			1	1				1		1			4		
Ward	177	30	Holman	Eliphalet		1		1		1	1	1					5		
Sutton	159	8	Holman	Francis	3			1				1	1	1			7		
Ward	177	29	Holman	Hannah	1	1								1			3		
Athol	287	1	Holman	John	3			1		1	1		1				7		
Southborough	206	18	Holman	John	2		2	1		1			1	1			8		
Sterling	353	16	Holman	John	3			1		2	1		1				8		
Ward	177	32	Holman	John	1	1	1				1	1					5		
Petersham	280	9	Holman	Jona		1	1	1	1		1	2	1	1			9		
Templeton	236	3	Holman	Jona	5	2		1			2	1	1				12		
Sutton	159	5	Holman	Jonathan		1	2		1	1		2	1				8		
Bolton	207	19	Holman	Nathaniel		1		1						1			3		
Bolton	207	20	Holman	Nathaniel Junr	2			1					1				4		
Bolton	216	2	Holman	Oliver	1		2	1		1		1					6		
Sutton	159	7	Holman	Peter	1			1		1		1					4		
Sterling	354	3	Holman	Rufus	1		1					2					4		
Bolton	215	16	Holman	Silas	2	1		1		1	1	1	1				8		
Royalston	237	9	Holman	Smith	1			1		3			1				6		
Athol	287	2	Holman	Stephen	1	1							1				4		
Sterling	353	10	Holman	Stephen	2	1	2		1	1		2	1	1			11		
Brookfield	248	2	Holmes	Abraham	2	1	1		1		1			1			7	First Parish	
Worcester	182	7	Holmes	Anna								2		1			3		
Harvard	221	36	Holmes	William		1		1	1				1	1			5		
Sterling	353	6	Holmes	William		1		1						1			3		
New Braintree	310	4	Holms	James	1	1	2		1	1	3	1	1	1			12		
New Braintree	310	7	Holms	Wm	1		1			3	1	1					7		
Holden	514	12	Holt	Aaron			1					1					2		
Boylston	376	9	Holt	Abel	1	1	1		1			1		1			6		
Boylston	376	16	Holt	Abel Junr			1				1	1					3		
Sterling	354	4	Holt	Abial		1	1	1		4	1		1				9		
Lunenberg	426	16	Holt	Abiel	2			1		1			1				5		
Berlin	214	11	Holt	Amasa			2	1		1		1					5		
Holden	514	13	Holt	Amos			1			3		1					5		
Holden	514	11	Holt	Ephraim				1				1		2			4		
Sterling	353	20	Holt	James		1						1					2		
Lunenberg	425	15	Holt	Jonathan				1					1				2		
Fitchburg	429	21	Holt	Joseph		1		1	1	2	1		1				7		
Hardwick	299	8	Holt	Thos	1	1		1		2		1	1				7		
Garry	274	15	Homans	Jonas	1			1				1					3		
Rutland	509	1	Homer	Thomas	3	1	1		1			1	1	1			10		
Rutland	509	2	Homer	Thomas Junr			1					1					2		
Leicester	492	3	Hood	Daniel		1	1						1				3		
Sturbridge	336	22	Hooker	Henry	1			1		1		2		1			6		
Sturbridge	336	15	Hooker	Oliver	2		1	1				1					5		
Charlton	332	14	Hooker	Parker		1						1					2		
Sturbridge	336	19	Hooker	Parker	1		1	1			2		2				7		
Sturbridge	336	9	Hooker	Saml	2		1		1	1	1	1	1				8		
Rutland	510	23	Hooker	Samuel		1		1		1		1					4		
Bolton	215	19	Hooker	Silas	1	1		1		1		1	1				6		
New Braintree	313	15	Hooper	Isaac			1					1					2		
Worcester	182	10	Hopkins	Esuck	1		1			2		1					5		
Petersham	277	15	Hopkins	Saml			2		1	3	1		1				8		
Bolton	210	3	Hopping	John	2			1		1	3	1	1	1			10		
Southborough	201	9	Horn	Martha		1	1						1				3		
Brookfield	257	9	Horton	Andrew	1			1	1	4	1		2	1			11	Second Parish	
Templeton	238	3	Horton	Jona			2		1	1	1			1			6		
Lancaster	349	13	Hosley	David		1	2	1					1				6		
Templeton	240	16	Hosmer	Asa	3			1				1	1				6		
Templeton	240	15	Hosmer	Josiah	2	2		1		1		1	1				8		
Sterling	356	22	Hosmore	Timothy	1		1	1				1					4		
Bolton	211	3	Houghton	Abel	2			1		2	1		1				7		
Westminster	455	6	Houghton	Abel	3	1	1		1	1	1	1					9		
Leominster	435	14	Houghton	Abiathar			1				1	1	1				4		
Lancaster	349	11	Houghton	Abijah				1						2			3		
Harvard	220	22	Houghton	Asa				1					1				2		
Harvard	220	23	Houghton	Asa Junr	2	2	2	1		2		1	1				11		
Lunenberg	425	7	Houghton	Asahel	1		1					1	1				4		
Boylston	376	13	Houghton	Benja	2		1			4		1					8		
Bolton	215	17	Houghton	Benja				1				1					2		
Sterling	353	19	Houghton	Benjamin	2		2		1			2					7		
Lancaster	349	17	Houghton	Benjmn	3	1		1	1	1		1	1	1			10		
Berlin	211	14	Houghton	Cyrus	1		1		1			2		1			6		
Harvard	218	32	Houghton	Cyrus	1	1		1					1				4		
Leominster	435	3	Houghton	Ebenezer	1			1	1	3	1		2	2			10		
Lunenberg	426	23	Houghton	Eleazer				1			2	1	1				5		
Harvard	220	26	Houghton	Elijah				1		3			1				5		
Lancaster	349	21	Houghton	Elijah Jun	2			1	1				1	1			7		
Harvard	220	28	Houghton	Elijah Junr	2		2			2		1					7		
Bolton	207	9	Houghton	Henery	3		1					1					5		
Bolton	213	3	Houghton	Jaazariah		1						1					3		
Bolton	216	4	Houghton	Jacob Junr	2		1			1		1					5		
Bolton	207	13	Houghton	James	2		1			2		1					6		
Petersham	277	18	Houghton	Jemima			1				2	2		1			6		
Sterling	353	8	Houghton	Joel		1		1		1	1		1				5		
Bolton	207	12	Houghton	John				1						1			2		
Harvard	220	18	Houghton	John				1						1			2		
Sutton	159	3	Houghton	Jona				1		1		1					3		
Bolton	207	17	Houghton	Jona P				1			1		1				3		
Bolton	207	18	Houghton	Jona P. Junr		1	1					1					3		
Bolton	207	21	Houghton	Jonas		2		1		1	1						5		

TOWN	PG#	LN#	LAST NAME	FIRST NAME	FREE WHITE MALES					FREE WHITE FEMALES					TOTAL ALL OTHER	TOTAL SLAVES	TOTALS	DISTRICT/ TOWNSHIP	NOTES
					under 10	10 to 16	16 to 26	26 to 45	45 and over	under 10	10 to 16	16 to 26	26 to 45	45 and over					
Sterling	356	23	Houghton	Jonas	3	2		1		2	1		1	1			11		
Bolton	207	22	Houghton	Jonas Junr	2		*	*	*	2	2	1					7		Enumeration numbers obscured
Bolton	210	12	Houghton	Jonas Junr	1	1	1	1		3	1		1	1			10		
Bolton	207	10	Houghton	Jonathan				1						1			2		
Bolton	215	15	Houghton	Joseph				1		1			1				3		
Bolton	209	17	Houghton	Joseph 3d	1	1		1		1		1					5		
Sterling	353	3	Houghton	Joshua				1		1	1	1					4		
Sterling	353	21	Houghton	Josiah R.	2	1		1		1		1					6		
Petersham	280	16	Houghton	Levi				1				1					2		
Lunenberg	425	16	Houghton	Levi Jun		1	1	1				1					4		
Lunenberg	426	22	Houghton	Levi Jun		1			1			1	1				4		
Bolton	213	4	Houghton	Martin		1						1					2		
Sterling	353	11	Houghton	Nathanl		2		1				1	1				5		
Harvard	220	19	Houghton	Peter	3			1		2		1	1				8		
Winchendon	228	22	Houghton	Robert	4	1		1		1		1					8		
Bolton	207	11	Houghton	Rufus	2			1		1	1						5		
Sterling	353	14	Houghton	Saml			1	1					2				4		
Berlin	211	13	Houghton	Silas			1			3		1					5		
Bolton	210	1	Houghton	Silas	1		1					1					3		
Bolton	207	14	Houghton	Simon	1	2	1	1	1	1	1	2		1			11		
Lunenberg	425	1	Houghton	Stephen	2			1				1					4		
Sterling	353	15	Houghton	Stephen	2			1		1		1					5		
Bolton	207	8	Houghton	Susannah			2						1				3		
Princeton	515	21	Houghton	Thankful	1	1	1			1		1		1			6		
Harvard	220	27	Houghton	Thomas	4	3		1				1					9		
Bolton	215	20	Houghton	Timothy	1			1		1	1						4		
Petersham	277	17	Houghton	Zarah	1	2			1	1		1	1				7		
Sterling	353	22	Houhgton	Ephraim	1			1		2		1					5		
Sterling	353	17	Houhgton	Menasseh			1			1		1					3		
Sterling	356	21	House	Prudence									1				1		
Oxford	160	14	Hovey	Gideon	2			2	1		1		1				7		
Charlton	332	18	Hovey	Josiah		2	1		1	2	2		1				9		
Lunenberg	425	2	Hovey	Solomon	1	2	1		1	1		1		2			9		
Princeton	515	17	How	Abner			1	2	1			1	1				7		
Holden	514	18	How	Abraham		1			1				1				3		
Princeton	515	18	How	Adonijah			1	2	1			2		1			7		
Sterling	353	13	How	Alven	1	1			1	3		1	1				8		
Grafton	196	14	How	Anna	2			1				1	1	1			6		
Templeton	237	15	How	Artemas	1	1		1		1	2	2		1			10		
Princeton	515	20	How	Artimas				1		2	1	1					5		
Sterling	356	24	How	Asa	1	1			1				2				5		
Sterling	354	5	How	Asa Jun	1			1				1					3		
Northborough	366	1	How	Benjamin	1			1				1					3		
Westminster	448	13	How	Daniel		1											1		
Hubbardston	418	6	How	Daniel Capt		1		1			1	1					4		
Rutland	510	15	How	David	1	2		1	1	1	1	1	1				9		
Upton	388	15	How	Ebenezer	1	1	1	1		2			1				7		
Gardner	449	14	How	Elezer		1	1	1	1	1			1	1			7		
Spencer	495	13	How	Elijah		1	1		1		2	1					7		
Spencer	495	12	How	Elijah Jun	4			2				1	1				8		
Barre	405	6	How	Eliphalet	1	1		1	1	3	1		1	1			10		
Berlin	216	7	How	Ephraim	2	1		2		2		1	1				9		
Templeton	242	5	How	Fisk	1	1			1	1	1	1	1				7		
Barre	408	19	How	Francis Esq		1	1		1			1	1				6		
Spencer	496	1	How	Fredk	3			1		1	1		1				7		
Northborough	365	14	How	Isaac	1	1	2		1	4	1	1	1				12		
Princeton	515	16	How	Israel		2			1	1	1		1				6		
Petersham	280	6	How	John		1	1		1			1	1				5		
Rutland	510	14	How	Jonas		1		1	1		2	1					6		
Holden	514	20	How	Jonathan		1			1	2		3		1			8		
Templeton	238	15	How	Josiah	3			1	1			1	3	1			10		
Holden	514	19	How	Jotham	2	1	1		1		1			1			7		
Spencer	496	2	How	Kerly	2	1		1		2	1		1				8		
Rutland	510	16	How	Lucy		1	1			1	1	1					5		
Rutland	510	17	How	Matthias			1		1	1		1		1			5		
Gardner	449	15	How	Parley			1			1		1					3		
Princeton	515	19	How	Peabody			1	2					2				4		
Winchendon	226	12	How	Peter	2			1		2		2	1				8		
Barre	408	31	How	Saml	2		1	2	1	1	2		1				10		
Sterling	353	5	How	Silas	2		1	1		1		1	1	1			9		
Petersham	280	7	How	Silvanus	1		2	1	1			1	1	1			8		
Barre	406	24	How	Wm	1			1				1					3		
Petersham	280	5	How	Benja		1	1	2		3	1		1				9		
Sturbridge	336	23	Howard	Abijha			1					1					2		
Sturbridge	336	3	Howard	Abner		1				1		1					3		
Oxford	160	11	Howard	Asahel	3	3		1		1			1				9		
Brookfield	248	9	Howard	Barzela	1			1		1	1	1					5	First Parish	
Brookfield	248	7	Howard	Barzela 2d	1		1					1					3	First Parish	
Sturbridge	335	19	Howard	Benajah	1			1		1		1					4		
Sturbridge	336	20	Howard	Charles	1	1	3	2	1	1		1	2		1		13		
Ward	177	33	Howard	Daniel				1					1				2		
Sturbridge	336	13	Howard	Eleazer			2		1		1	1	1				6		
Brookfield	269	31	Howard	Hannah	1	1	1		1	1			1	2			9	Third Parish	
Sturbridge	335	15	Howard	Jacob	1			1		1			1				4		
Bolton	210	2	Howard	Job	1	1	1	1		1			1				7		
Leicester	489	10	Howard	John	2	1	1	1				1	1	1			8		
Oxford	159	17	Howard	John			1		1		1	1		1			5		
Petersham	277	12	Howard	John				1						1			2		
Oxford	160	1	Howard	John Junr			1			2			1				4		
Holden	514	23	Howard	Joseph		1	1	1	1			3		2			9		
Sturbridge	336	2	Howard	Josiah		1			1	1		1	1				5		

TOWN	PG#	LN#	LAST NAME	FIRST NAME	FREE WHITE MALES under 10	10 to 16	16 to 26	26 to 45	45 and over	FREE WHITE FEMALES under 10	10 to 16	16 to 26	26 to 45	45 and over	TOTAL ALL OTHER	TOTAL SLAVES	TOTALS	DISTRICT/ TOWNSHIP	NOTES
Grafton	199	12	Howard	Levi			2					1					3		
Sturbridge	335	16	Howard	Nathan			1										1		
Petersham	277	11	Howard	Nehemiah	1	1	1		1	2	2	2		1			11		
Oxford	160	3	Howard	Simeon	1		1					1					3		
Oxford	160	2	Howard	Stephen	3			1		1			1				6		
Boylston	373	4	Howard	Timothy			1					1					2		
Lunenberg	426	21	Howard	Timothy	3	1	1			2			1				8		
Shrewsbury	368	11	Howard	Timothy			1	1						1			3		
Paxton	501	5	Howard	William	1		1			1	1	1		1			7		
Worcester	182	6	Howe	Abel	1		1	1		2	1		1				7		
Brookfield	248	8	Howe	Amasa	2	1		1		2			1				7	First Parish	
Oakham	317	18	Howe	Artemas		2	3		1	1	2	1	1				11		
Shrewsbury	367	8	Howe	Daniel	3		1			1			1				6		
Shrewsbury	368	5	Howe	Dennis	2	1		1	1	2	1		1	1			10		
Brookfield	269	16	Howe	Ebenezer				1									1	Third Parish	
Brookfield	260	6	Howe	Eli		1	2	1		1	3			1			9	Second Parish	
Shrewsbury	368	2	Howe	Gideon				1			2		1				4		
Worcester	179	7	Howe	Joel		1		1						1			3		
Boylston	376	10	Howe	John	1			1		3	1		1				7		
Paxton	501	7	Howe	John	3		1	2		2		2	1	2			13		
Shrewsbury	368	3	Howe	John H.	1			1		1	2		1				6		
Paxton	501	3	Howe	Jonah		1		1		2	1			2			7		
Paxton	501	4	Howe	Jonah Jun		1				1	1						3		
Shrewsbury	368	4	Howe	Jonah Maj.		1		1			1		1				4		
Brookfield	269	5	Howe	Joseph				1			1			1			3	Third Parish	
Brookfield	269	6	Howe	Joseph Jun	1		1			1		1					4	Third Parish	
Brookfield	260	14	Howe	Josiah	2	1		1				1	2	1			8	Second Parish	
Boylston	376	4	Howe	Levi	2	1	1	2		1	1		1				9		
Shrewsbury	368	1	Howe	Nathan	2	1		1	1	2	1	1	1	2			12		
Boylston	376	5	Howe	Silas		2	3		2	1		2		1			11		
Brookfield	260	16	Howe	Silas				1									1	Second Parish	
Brookfield	269	15	Howe	William	4	2		1			1	1	2				11	Third Parish	
Douglas	479	10	Howell	Barnebus			1						1				2		
Douglas	479	11	Howell	Philip	1		1			2		1					5		
Douglas	479	9	Howell	Richard				1						1			2		
Barre	408	21	Howes	Edmond Capt	1	2	1	1	1	1	1	2		1			11		
Spencer	496	4	Howland	Abner	1		2	1		1	2	1					9		
Brookfield	269	33	Howland	John				1		1				1			3	Third Parish	
Douglas	482	22	Howland	Joseph	2			1		1		?	2				8		
Brookfield	247	34	Howland	Southwerth			4	4				1					9	First Parish	
Douglas	482	21	Howland	Thomas	1	1	1			1			1	1			7		
Brookfield	248	10	Hoyt	Robert	2	1		1					1	1			6	First Parish	
New Braintree	310	2	Hoyt	Wyman	1	1	1	1				1		1			6		
Winchendon	228	23	Hubbard	Benja		1		1			1		1				4		
Leicester	489	11	Hubbard	Daniel				1			1			1			3		
Leicester	489	12	Hubbard	Daniel Jun	1		1	1		3	2	2	1				11		
Holden	514	15	Hubbard	Elisha		1	2	1		1		2	1				8		
Holden	514	24	Hubbard	Isaac		1	2					2	1				6		
Royalston	241	8	Hubbard	James	2		1			1		1	1				6		
Rutland	509	6	Hubbard	Joel	4		1					2					7		
Holden	514	16	Hubbard	John	1		1			2		1					5		
Paxton	501	6	Hubbard	Jona		1		2						3			6		
Rutland	509	5	Hubbard	Jonathan		1		1		1	1	1		1			6		
Holden	514	14	Hubbard	Joseph	2	3	1	1		2							12		
Holden	514	17	Hubbard	Peter	1	1	2	1					1	1			7		
Holden	511	1	Hubbard	Samuel	1		1	1		1				1			5		
Holden	511	9	Hubbard	W. Moore			1			1		1					3		
Brookfield	260	12	Hubbard	William				1			1	1		1			4	Second Parish	
New Braintree	310	3	Hudson	Edward		1	1	1				2					5		
Oxford	160	16	Hudson	John	1		1			2		1	1				6		
Ashburnham	459	14	Hudson	Me*ar	2		1			2		1					6		
Lancaster	349	10	Hudson	Robert	1		1			2		1	1				6		
Southborough	202	8	Hudson	Samuel	4		1			2	1	1	1				10		
Bolton	209	22	Hudson	Wd								1	1				2		
Oxford	160	15	Hudson	William		1		2		1	1	1					7		
Uxbridge	465	11	Humes	Amos		1						1					2		
Douglas	479	15	Humes	David		1				2		1					4		
Douglas	479	8	Humes	Josiah		1		1				1	1				4		
Douglas	479	16	Humes	Moses	2	1		1		1		1	1				7		
Douglas	479	17	Humes	Nahum		1				1		1					3		
Brookfield	269	1	Humphrey	Asa				1						2			3	Third Parish	
Sturbridge	336	17	Humphrey	Benja				1			1		1				3		
Oxford	160	4	Humphrey	Ebenz	1	1		1		1	1	1	1	1			9		
Athol	290	13	Humphrey	James		2	1	1		1		2					7		
Athol	290	12	Humphrey	John			2	1		3	1	1	2				10		
Athol	290	11	Humphrey	Royal	2	1		1		1			1				6		
Paxton	501	8	Hunt	Aaron			2	1		1	1		1				6		
Templeton	239	1	Hunt	Abel			1				1						2		
Sterling	354	1	Hunt	Caleb	1		1	1		2	2		1				8		
Milford	396	17	Hunt	Daniel		3	1			1			1				7		
Sutton	160	2	Hunt	Daniel	1		2		1	4	1	2	1				12		
Winchendon	228	27	Hunt	David	1		1	1		2			1				5		
Douglas	482	18	Hunt	Ezekiel		1		1						1			3		
Northborough	365	10	Hunt	Jeremiah		1		1		1	2						6		
Lancaster	349	20	Hunt	John	1	2	2		1	4		1		1			12		
Mendon	389	16	Hunt	John				1			1	1	1				4	2d Parish	
Northborough	365	9	Hunt	John				1				1	1				3		
Douglas	482	19	Hunt	Joseph	1		1					1					3		
Milford	396	18	Hunt	Joseph			1			1		1					3		

TOWN	PG#	LN#	LAST NAME	FIRST NAME	FREE WHITE MALES					FREE WHITE FEMALES					TOTAL ALL OTHER	TOTAL SLAVES	TOTALS	DISTRICT/ TOWNSHIP	NOTES
					under 10	10 to 16	16 to 26	26 to 45	45 and over	under 10	10 to 16	16 to 26	26 to 45	45 and over					
Douglas	482	20	Hunt	Oliver	1		1						1				3		
Templeton	240	18	Hunt	Oliver	1	1		1			2		1				6		
Milford	396	13	Hunt	Pearley			1	1				1					3		
Templeton	240	17	Hunt	Rebecca				1				1		1			3		
Ashburnham	459	2	Hunt	Sheribiah		1		1		2		1	1				6		
Rutland	510	22	Hunt	Thomas				1		1	2		1				5		
Sutton	160	3	Hunt	Timothy Junr	2		1						1				4		
New Braintree	309	20	Hunter	Isaac		2	2		1		1	2		1			9		
New Braintree	310	9	Hunter	Isaac Jr		1	1	1				1	1				6		
New Braintree	309	18	Hunter	John	1		3		1	1	1		1	1			9		
Petersham	277	7	Hunter	Jona	1	1	1	1	1	2	1	1	1	1			11		
Boylston	373	2	Hunter	Uriah			1			1			1	1			4		
Brookfield	257	11	Hunter	William	1	1	1						1	1			6		Second Parish
New Braintree	309	19	Hunter	Wm	2	1		2	1	1		1	1	1			9		
Hubbardston	418	10	Hunting	Alexander	1			1		2			1				5		
Hubbardston	418	9	Hunting	Convas	2	3		1	1			1	1	1			10		
Milford	396	16	Hunting	Joseph				1						1			2		
Milford	396	15	Hunting	Joseph Jr	1			1					1				3		
Hubbardston	418	16	Hunting	Moses	3			1						1			5		
Hubbardston	418	7	Hunting	Stephen Jr				1		1	2		1				4		
Hubbardston	418	8	Hunting	Wm.		1	2		1		1		1				6		
Leicester	492	5	Huntington	Asahel			1			1			1				3		
Oxford	160	9	Hurd	Joseph			1	1				1	1	2			6		
Sutton	157	19	Hurst	Timothy	1		1		1	1	1	1		1			7		
Uxbridge	468	4	Huse	Alpheus	2			1		1			1				5		
Harvard	220	11	Huse	Enoch				1						1			2		
Brookfield	259	2	Hutchins	Pearly	1		2	1					1				5		Second Parish
Sutton	157	14	Hutchinson	Barthl		1	1		1		1	2		3			9		
Royalston	241	22	Hutchinson	Benja	1		1		1		1	1		1			6		
Templeton	233	3	Hyde	Aaron	3				1	1		1		1			7		
Winchendon	228	20	Hyde	Ezra	1		3		1	1	1	1		1			9		
Winchendon	228	21	Hyde	Job	2	2			1	1	1	1	1				9		
Harvard	219	10	Hyde	John	2			1		1			1				5		
Brookfield	269	7	Hyde	Joseph			1			4			1				6		Third Parish
Leominster	435	2	Hyde	Joseph				1						1			2		
Sturbridge	336	14	Hyde	Joshua	1		1			2		1					5		
Oxford	160	20	Ide	Liberty			1			1		1					3		
Oxford	160	19	Ide	Nathan			1					1					2		
Douglas	482	28	Ide	Reuben	1	1		1					1				3		
Oxford	160	18	Ide	Timothy	1	1		1		1	1			1			6		
Royalston	236	13	Ingolls	Ebenz	2	1	1		1	1			1				7		
Lunenberg	428	7	Jackman	Joseph			1			2			1				4		
Templeton	234	10	Jackson	Daniel			1					1					2		
Uxbridge	468	6	Jackson	David	1	1		1		3	2		1				9		
Westminster	446	18	Jackson	Edward		1	2					1		1			5		
Petersham	279	1	Jackson	James	1			1				1		1			4		
Petersham	279	2	Jackson	James Jur	2			1		1			1				5		
Templeton	234	11	Jackson	Jona			1			2		1					4		
Upton	388	19	Jackson	Joseph	3			1		1			1				6		
Leicester	492	6	Jackson	Marthew		1	3	1		2		1					8		
Petersham	279	3	Jackson	Nathan			2	1				1	1				5		
Upton	388	18	Jackson	Nathan			1					1					2		
Hardwick	299	11	Jackson	Nathll	2	1		1		4	2		1	1			12		
Westminster	446	19	Jackson	Sebin				1				3		1			5		
Athol	287	5	Jacobs	John	1	2	2			2		1		1			10		
Sutton	159	17	Jacobs	John		1	1	1		2		1	1				7		
Ward	177	37	Jacobs	John		1		1					1				3		
Royalston	235	13	Jacobs	Joseph			1			3			1				5		
Royalston	235	14	Jacobs	Simeon	1	1	1	1		2	2		1				9		
Royalston	235	12	Jacobs	Whitman			1	1		1			1				4		
Uxbridge	468	7	Jacobs	William	1	1	1	1		1			1				6		
Ward	177	40	Jacoby	Israel	2			1				1	1				5		
Ward	177	39	Jacoby	Samuel		1	1			1	1		1	1			6		
Barre	407	11	James	Eleazer Esq		1		1		2		1	1				6		
Lunenberg	428	2	Japson	Wm	2			1		1			1				5		
Ward	177	38	Jenison	Daniel	1		2	1		2		1					7		
Ward	177	41	Jenison	Joseph				1						1			2		
Shrewsbury	367	14	Jenison	Joseph B.	4		1	2		1		1	1				10		
Barre	407	5	Jenison	Nathl			1	1						2			4		
Ward	177	42	Jenison	Nethl	1		1						1				3		
Charlton	332	22	Jenison	Peter	2	1		1		1	1		1				9		
Charlton	332	23	Jenison	Peter Junr	1		1			2			1				5		
Southborough	204	11	Jenison	Samuel	3	2	1						1				7		
Shrewsbury	367	15	Jenison	William	2	2	1				1		1				7		
Holden	511	14	Jenkins	Lucy	1					1			1				3		
Barre	407	7	Jenkins	Benj Esq		1		1						1			3		
Barre	407	9	Jenkins	South		1	1	1		1	1			1			6		
Barre	407	8	Jenkins	Timith	2	1		1		2		3		1			11		
Brookfield	270	3	Jenks	Francis	2		1	1		1			1				6		Third Parish
Spencer	496	12	Jenks	Isaac		1	3	1	1		2	1		1			10		
Brookfield	259	4	Jenks	Lucy		1	2	1		1		1	1				7		Second Parish
Brookfield	259	5	Jenks	Nicholas		3	1	1		1			2				8		Second Parish
Brookfield	270	5	Jennings	Gershom		1		1		1		1	1				5		Third Parish
Brookfield	270	8	Jennings	Joel	1	1		1		1							5		Third Parish
Brookfield	248	15	Jennings	John	1			1					2	1			5		First Parish
Hardwick	299	12	Jennings	John	4	1			2		1		2	1	1		12		
Brookfield	270	4	Jennings	Jonathan	2	1		2			2		2				9		Third Parish
Worcester	181	10	Jennings	Mary						2			1				3		
Brookfield	270	6	Jennings	Moses		1			1					1			3		Third Parish
Brookfield	270	7	Jennings	Roswell	1							1		1			3		Third Parish
Brookfield	248	12	Jennison	Josiah					1					1			2		First Parish

211

TOWN	PG#	LN#	LAST NAME	FIRST NAME	FREE WHITE MALES under 10	10 to 16	16 to 26	26 to 45	45 and over	FREE WHITE FEMALES under 10	10 to 16	16 to 26	26 to 45	45 and over	TOTAL ALL OTHER	TOTAL SLAVES	TOTALS	DISTRICT/ TOWNSHIP	NOTES
Paxton	501	9	Jennison	Saml	3	1		1					1				6		
Sutton	159	18	Jennison	Saml					1				1				2		
Worcester	181	7	Jennison	Samuel			2	1	1			3	1		2		10		
Mendon	384	10	Jennison	Willm	1		1						1				3	1st Parish	
Douglas	482	33	Jepherson	Aaron	3	1		1		2	2		1				10		
Uxbridge	468	9	Jepherson	John	3			1					1				5		
Douglas	482	32	Jepherson	Reuben	3	2		1		1	1	2	1				11		
Douglas	482	31	Jepherson	Seth	1	1	1	1		1	1		1				7		
Douglas	482	29	Jepherson	William				1				1	1				3		
Douglas	482	30	Jepherson	Wm Junr			1	1									2		
Harvard	221	30	Jewett	Aaron			6	12	3			10	21	2			54		
Berlin	211	2	Jewett	Jesse	1		1	1		1	1	2					7		
Bolton	211	2	Jewett	John	1	1		1		1	1	1		1			7		
Ashburnham	459	21	Jewett	Joseph	2	2		1		1		1	1				8		
Dudley	343	15	Jewett	Moses		1	1	1		1	1		1				6		
Dudley	343	17	Jewett	Roger			1			2		1					4		
Sterling	354	7	Jewitt	David		1	2	1		1			1				6		
Sterling	354	11	Jewitt	Ebenezer			1			1			1				3		
Sturbridge	333	3	Jewitt	Jesse	3	2		1		2	1	1	1				11		
Sterling	354	8	Jewitt	Samuel	1		1	1				1		3			7		
Sterling	354	6	Jewitt	Solomon				1						1			2		
Lancaster	352	8	Johnson	Aaron	2		1	1	1			3		1			9		
Berlin	216	14	Johnson	Amos		1	2			1		1	1				7		
Worcester	181	11	Johnson	Amos				1		1			1				3		
Leominster	438	23	Johnson	Asa			2			1		1					4		
Sterling	354	12	Johnson	Asa				1					1				2		
Mendon	384	12	Johnson	Baxter	4	1		1		2		1	1				10	1st Parish	
Leominster	438	34	Johnson	Benja	1			1		2		1					5		
Lunenberg	428	3	Johnson	Benja	2	1		1		2		1	1	1			9		
Worcester	181	3	Johnson	Benja			1			1		1					3		
Worcester	181	4	Johnson	Clark			1			3		1					5		
Sturbridge	333	1	Johnson	Comfort		2	1	1		1		2	1				8		
Hardwick	299	14	Johnson	Daniel	2		1					1					4		
Lancaster	352	9	Johnson	Daniel			1			1	1	1					4		
Shrewsbury	367	11	Johnson	Daniel	2		1	1		1	2	1	1				9		
Westborough	199	143	Johnson	Daniel				1						1			2		
Worcester	181	2	Johnson	Daniel			1	1		1		1	1				5		
Southborough	203	10	Johnson	David			1					1					2		
Rutland	509	12	Johnson	Dillington		2		1	3				1				8		
Barre	407	6	Johnson	Ebenz	2	1		1	3			1	1				9		
Sterling	354	10	Johnson	Edward	1		1	1		1	2	1	1				9		
Brookfield	248	14	Johnson	Eli	1	1		2		1		1	1				7	First Parish	
Southborough	204	10	Johnson	Elijah	4			1		2		1					8		
Gardner	450	1	Johnson	Elisha		1	4	1		1	1		1				9		
Southborough	206	3	Johnson	Elisha			4		1	2			1				8		
Berlin	214	3	Johnson	Elizabeth									1				1		
Garry	278	1	Johnson	Elizabeth		1				2	1		1				5		
Templeton	237	4	Johnson	Enoch	3			1		2			1				7		
Leominster	438	21	Johnson	Ephraim		1		1		3			1				6		
Worcester	181	9	Johnson	Gardner			1			4			1				6		
Southborough	206	2	Johnson	Isaac				1									1		
Sturbridge	336	24	Johnson	James		1	2	1			1		1				6		
Templeton	240	19	Johnson	James	2		1	1		4			1				9		
Hardwick	299	16	Johnson	Joel				1		1			1				3		
Barre	407	13	Johnson	John				1				1	1				3		
Barre	407	14	Johnson	John	3			1		1	1		1				7		
Southborough	206	4	Johnson	John	1	1	2		1	2		2	1				10		
Western	255	8	Johnson	John	2			1					1				4		
Westminster	446	21	Johnson	John				1		4			1				6		
Worcester	181	6	Johnson	John	1	1		1		3	1		1				8		
Petersham	279	4	Johnson	Jona	1	2	1		1				1				6		
Sterling	354	9	Johnson	Jonas	1	2		1		1	1		1				7		
Leominster	438	22	Johnson	Joseph	2	1		1		2			1				7		
Milford	393	19	Johnson	Joseph	1	1		1		1			1				5		
Westborough	199	144	Johnson	Joseph		1		1		5	2		1				10		
Hardwick	299	20	Johnson	Joshua	2			1				1					4		
Worcester	182	15	Johnson	Joshua			1	1				1		1			4		
Leominster	438	25	Johnson	Jotham	1		1	2	1	2		1	1				9		
Berlin	216	10	Johnson	Laban	1	1		1		1	1		1				7		
Petersham	279	5	Johnson	Levi			2			2	1		1				6		
Leominster	438	31	Johnson	Luke	1			1		2			1	1			6		
Southborough	202	11	Johnson	Mary									1				1		
Worcester	182	16	Johnson	Micah				1					1				2		
Worcester	182	17	Johnson	Micah Junr	2	2	1		1	3		1	1				11		
Berlin	216	3	Johnson	Nathan	1	2	1		1	1	1	1		3			11		
Westminster	446	17	Johnson	Oliver	2	1		1		2	1		1				8		
Shrewsbury	367	13	Johnson	Philip		1		1	1					2			5		
Lancaster	352	11	Johnson	Ruth									1				1		
Lunenberg	428	1	Johnson	Samuel	1			1		1	3		1				7		
Westborough	197	111	Johnson	Samuel	1		1	1				1					4		
Worcester	181	8	Johnson	Samuel	3	1	4	3				1	1				13		
Hardwick	299	13	Johnson	Seth		1	1	1		1			1				5		
Hardwick	299	18	Johnson	Seth Jr				1									1		
Templeton	237	3	Johnson	Shubael		1		1						1			3		
Hardwick	299	17	Johnson	Silas	1	1		1	1			1	1				6		
Dudley	343	16	Johnson	Smith				1			1		1				3		
Mendon	384	9	Johnson	Solomon	2			1		3		1	1				8	1st Parish	
Leominster	435	19	Johnson	Stephen				1					1				2		
Mendon	384	11	Johnson	Stephen	1	1		1		1		2	2	1			9	1st Parish	

Town	PG#	LN#	Last Name	First Name	FWM <10	FWM 10-16	FWM 16-26	FWM 26-45	FWM 45+	FWF <10	FWF 10-16	FWF 16-26	FWF 26-45	FWF 45+	Total All Other	Total Slaves	Totals	District/Township	Notes
Shrewsbury	367	12	Johnson	Stephen	1		1	2		3			1				8		
Leominster	435	20	Johnson	Stephen Jun	2	1		1					1				5		
Worcester	182	14	Johnson	Thomas	2	1		1		1		1	1				7		
Grafton	198	9	Johnson	Timothy		1	1			1		1					4		
Sturbridge	333	2	Johnson	Timothy		1	2	1		1		1					6		
Worcester	181	5	Johnson	Timothy	1			2		3		1	1				8		
Grafton	198	10	Johnson	Widow								1	1				2		
Brookfield	270	9	Johnson	William	1	1		1		3			1				7	Third Parish	
Westborough	195	87	Johnson	William			1	1				1	1				4		
Worcester	181	1	Johnson	William	2	2		1		2			1	1			9		
Barre	407	10	Johnson	Zachr		1	1	1		1	1		1				6		
Hardwick	299	15	Johnson	Zebediah	1		1	1			1	1					5		
Westminster	446	20	Johnston	Thomas			1						1	1			3		
Lancaster	352	5	Jones	Aaron		1		1		1			1				4		
Leominster	438	33	Jones	Aaron	1			1					1				3		
Templeton	238	16	Jones	Aaron Jun	3	1		1	1	1	1		2				10		
Winchendon	228	29	Jones	Abel		1	1	1		2			1				6		
Leominster	438	24	Jones	Amasa		1		1					1	1			4		
Athol	287	6	Jones	Amos			2	1				3	1				7		
Athol	287	7	Jones	Amos Jr			1					1					2		
Templeton	236	16	Jones	Benja	2	2			2	2	1	1	1	2			13		
Milford	393	22	Jones	David	2			1		1			1				6		
Ashburnham	459	24	Jones	Edmund			1					1					2		
Charlton	332	19	Jones	Eli	1	2		1		3			1				8		
Sutton	159	15	Jones	Elnathan	1		1			1		1					4		
Ashburnham	459	22	Jones	Enos		1		1				3	1				6		
Milford	393	21	Jones	Ezekiel Lt.	1		1				2	1	1				6		
Barre	407	3	Jones	Ezra Capt				1					1				2		
Westminster	446	16	Jones	Farrwell		2											2		
Spencer	496	14	Jones	Francis				1					1				2		
Sutton	159	16	Jones	Jesse		2	1	1		1		1	1				7		
Hardwick	299	19	Jones	John	1			1					1				3		
Lunenberg	428	6	Jones	John	1		1			2		1					5		
Garry	278	2	Jones	Jona	2		1	1			2		1				8		
Berlin	214	8	Jones	Jonathan			1	1					1				3		
Lunenberg	428	8	Jones	Joseph			1	1					1				3		
Spencer	496	15	Jones	Josiah	1		1			2		1					5		
Charlton	332	21	Jones	Mary Wd									1				1		
Lancaster	352	4	Jones	Moses	2		1			3			1				7		
Berlin	212	1	Jones	Nathan		1							1				3		
Garry	278	3	Jones	Nathan			1					1					2		
Ashburnham	459	23	Jones	Nathan	2	1	1			1	1		1				8		
Barre	407	4	Jones	Nathl Lt		1		1		2	1		1		1		7		
Spencer	496	13	Jones	Phinehas	2	2		1		1			1				7		
Worcester	182	13	Jones	Phinehas		1	2	1			1	1	1				7		
Athol	287	4	Jones	Presket	1	1		1			1		1				5		
Milford	393	23	Jones	Ruth Wd.	1	1						4	1		1		8		
Barre	407	12	Jones	Saml											3		3		
Milford	393	20	Jones	Saml Esq				1						2			3		
Berlin	216	17	Jones	Samuel		1	3	1		2	2	2	1	1			13		
Lancaster	352	7	Jones	Samuel	2	1	2	1		2	1	1	1	1			12		
Leominster	435	18	Jones	Samuel	1	1		1			2	1	1				7		
Charlton	332	20	Jones	Seth		1		1		2		3	1				8		
Upton	388	17	Jones	Sylvanus			1					1					2		
Berlin	214	15	Jones	Timothy			1										1		
Lunenberg	428	4	Jones	Wm			1					1					2		
Lunenberg	428	5	Jones	Wm Jun	1	1		1		2		1					6		
Brookfield	259	6	Jordan	Bathsheba	1	1	1			3		2	1	3			12	Second Parish	
Brookfield	248	13	Jordan	Dudley		3		1				1					5	First Parish	
Ashburnham	459	20	Joslin	Abijah		1	1	1		1		2	1	1			8		
Mendon	392	1	Joslin	Abraham			1						1	1			3	2d Parish	
Leominster	438	20	Joslin	Elias	2	1	1			1	1	1	1				9		
Leominster	438	28	Joslin	James		2		1				1		1			5		
Leominster	438	26	Joslin	John		2		1						1			4		
Western	255	9	Joslin	John R.		1		1		4	1	1	1				9		
Leominster	438	30	Joslin	Joseph		1		1				1	1				4		
Leominster	438	27	Joslin	Luke		1	1	1				1					4		
Leominster	438	32	Joslin	Peter	1	1				1		1					5		
Charlton	332	24	Joslin	Saml	1			1			1		1				4		
Leominster	438	29	Joslin	Samuel	2		1			1		1					5		
Hubbardston	418	17	Josling	Ebenezer		1	2		2			1	1	1			8		
Hubbardston	418	18	Josling	Silas	1		1						1				3		
Hubbardston	418	19	Josling	Wm.			1			1			1				3		
New Braintree	310	11	Joslyn	Benm	1	1	1		1	1	2		1	1			9		
New Braintree	310	10	Joslyn	Henry	1		1			2			1				5		
Lancaster	352	6	Joslyn	Jonas	3		1	1	1	1			1				9		
New Braintree	310	13	Joslyn	Matthew	1	1		1		2			1				6		
New Braintree	310	12	Joslyn	Samll			1	1				2		1			5		
Lancaster	352	10	Joslyn	Samuel			1					1		2			6		
Uxbridge	468	8	Judson	Samuel	1			1			1		1				4		
Bolton	213	14	K*mings	John	1			1		1		1					4		
Uxbridge	468	12	Keith	Abijah	4			1					1				6		
Winchendon	228	34	Keith	Appolus	1			1					1				3		
Uxbridge	468	14	Keith	Chapin	4	2	1						1				8		
Uxbridge	468	13	Keith	Comfort	1	3	1		1			2		1			9		
Uxbridge	468	16	Keith	Gershom			1	1		1			1				4		
Uxbridge	468	15	Keith	James			2	1				2		1			3		
Uxbridge	468	10	Keith	Job		1							1				3		
Dudley	343	18	Keith	Joseph		1	2		1		2		1				7		
Mendon	384	13	Keith	Nathan Lt.		1	1	1	1		1	1	1				7	1st Parish	

TOWN	PG#	LN#	LAST NAME	FIRST NAME	FWM <10	10-16	16-26	26-45	45+	FWF <10	10-16	16-26	26-45	45+	TOTAL ALL OTHER	TOTAL SLAVES	TOTALS	DISTRICT/TOWNSHIP	NOTES
Sutton	162	5	Keith	Stephen	1			1		1			1				4		
Dudley	343	20	Keith	Thos	1			1		2			1				5		
Upton	388	20	Kelley	David Lt.			2	1			2	1		1			8		
Milford	393	25	Kelley	George	1	1		1	1	3	1		1				9		
Barre	410	20	Kelley	Joel			1										1		
Barre	410	19	Kelley	John	1	1			1	1	2	1	1	1			9		
Mendon	392	4	Kelley	John		1	2					2		2			7	2d Parish	
Milford	393	24	Kelley	Luke	1		1	1		2	1	1	1				8		
Bolton	215	3	Kelley	Micajah	1	2	1	1		2			1				8		
Harvard	217	37	Kelley	Morris				1			1		1				3		
Barre	410	21	Kelley	Robert		1				2		1					4		
Mendon	392	2	Kelley	Seth	4		1	1		1		1	1				9	2d Parish	
Mendon	392	3	Kelley	Wyllis	2		1	1		1			1				6	2d Parish	
Western	256	1	Kellog	Medad		1	1		1	2		3		1			9		
Lunenberg	428	15	Kelly	John				1									1		
Douglas	482	35	Kelly	Mercy	1	1					1		1				4		
Oakham	319	6	Kelly	Richard		2		1				2		1	1		7		
Worcester	184	22	Kelly	Thomas	1			1				1	2				5		
Athol	287	11	Kelton	Calvin			1				1						2		
Athol	288	3	Kelton	George				1			1	1	1				4		
Athol	287	14	Kelton	James	1		1			1		1					4		
Athol	287	12	Kelton	Jonah			1				1						2		
Athol	288	2	Kelton	Jonah			1				1		1				3		
Ashburnham	459	29	Kelton	Lemuel			1		1	1		1					3		
Royalston	236	4	Kelton	Lovell		1				1	1						3		
Uxbridge	467	1	Kempton	George	2		3	1				2	1				9		
Boylston	373	9	Kendal	Caleb	2		3	1		3	2		1				12		
Brookfield	259	12	Kendal	Lucy		1				1	1	1					4	Second Parish	
Brookfield	270	11	Kendal	Peter	1	1		1		1	1	1		1			7	Third Parish	
Gardner	450	5	Kendall	Abel	2		1			3			1				7		
Leominster	438	40	Kendall	Abel	1	1	2	1		1	1	1	2	1			11		
Leominster	438	41	Kendall	Asa	2	1	1	1		1	1	1	1				10		
Athol	287	8	Kendall	Calvin	1		1			2	1						6		
Leominster	438	35	Kendall	David	1	1	1		1	1	1	1		1			8		
Sterling	351	2	Kendall	Etham Junr	1			2					1				4		
Sterling	354	21	Kendall	Ethan		2	2		1	2		2	2	1			12		
Worcester	184	20	Kendall	Ezekiel	2	1		1					1				5		
Sterling	354	17	Kendall	Ezekiel Jun	3	2		1	1	1			1				9		
Sterling	354	14	Kendall	Ezra		1	1				1	1					4		
Sterling	354	20	Kendall	James	1			1			1	1		2			6		
Garry	278	9	Kendall	Jesse	2	1		1		2	3		1				10		
Athol	288	6	Kendall	Joel		1	1	1		4		2	1				10		
Athol	288	5	Kendall	John	1			1				1					3		
Leominster	438	37	Kendall	John		2	1	2			1		1	1			8		
Athol	288	4	Kendall	Jona		1			1			2		1			5		
Leominster	438	39	Kendall	Jonas	1	1	3	1		1		2	3	1			13		
Hubbardston	418	20	Kendall	Jonathan	3		1	1				1	1	1			8		
Sterling	354	19	Kendall	Joseph	1	1	2		1	1	2	2		1			11		
Sterling	354	13	Kendall	Josiah		1		1				1		1	1		5		
Sterling	354	16	Kendall	Josiah Jun	3		1	1		2	1		2				10		
Sterling	354	18	Kendall	Mary		1	2	1		1	1	2		1			9		
Barre	410	17	Kendall	Saml	2		1						1				4		
Petersham	279	11	Kendall	Samuel	1	1		1		3	1		1				8		
Athol	287	10	Kendall	Seth	1			1			1	1					5		
Sutton	159	19	Kendall	Thos Revd		1		1					1				3		
Ashburnham	459	27	Kendall	William	1			1			1		1				4		
Fitchburg	427	1	Kendall	William			1				1		2				4		
Garry	278	6	Kendall	Willm		1		1	2	1		1		1			7		
New Braintree	310	14	Kennada	Lemll	2			1		2	1	2	1				9		
Rutland	509	13	Kennan	Andrew	2	1			1	2	1		1				8		
Worcester	184	23	Kennedy	John				1		1	1	1	2				6		
Brookfield	270	10	Kenney	Isaac	1			1		2	1	1					6	Third Parish	
Royalston	240	15	Kenney	William	3	2	1		1	1	1						10		
Royalston	232	8	Kenny	Elizbath Widow			2					2	1	1			6		
Leicester	492	7	Kent	Ebenezer		1		1		1	1		1				5		
Brookfield	248	16	Kent	Jacob	2		2	1	1	2			1	1			10	First Parish	
Spencer	493	3	Kerny	Jeremiah			1						1				3		
Athol	287	13	Ketchum	Justus			1						1				2		
Athol	287	9	Ketchum	Roger	1		1					1					3		
Spencer	493	2	Ketridge	Elijah	1			1				1					4		
Boylston	373	11	Keyes	Amasa	1			1			1						3		
Boylston	373	10	Keyes	Benja Junr	2			1		1			1				5		
Boylston	373	7	Keyes	Benjamin				1						1			2		
Western	255	11	Keyes	Danforth			3	1				2	2	1	1		10		
Gardner	450	2	Keyes	Ebenzar	3	1		1		1			1				7		
Northborough	366	2	Keyes	James	1	2	1		1	2	1	1		1			10		
Boylston	373	8	Keyes	Reuben	1			1					1				3		
Northborough	366	3	Keyes	Silas	2	1		1		3			1				9		
Northborough	366	4	Keyes	Tho.	3	1		2			1	1	1	1			10		
Ashburnham	459	28	Keyes	Thomas	2		1			2			1				6		
Boylston	373	5	Keyes	Thomas		1					1		1				3		
Boylston	373	6	Keyes	Thomas Junr	1			1		3			1				6		
Uxbridge	468	11	Keys	Oren			1			3	2		1				7		
Lunenberg	428	13	Keys	Simon	3			1		1		1					6		
Ashburnham	459	26	Kiblinger	Henery			1				1		1				3		
Ashburnham	459	25	Kiblinger	Jacob	1	1	1		1	2	1	2	1	1			11		
Dudley	343	19	Kidder	Benja				1			1		1				3		
Winchendon	228	30	Kidder	Benja		2		1		1		1	1	1			7		
Winchendon	228	31	Kidder	Heywood	2			1		1	1		1				6		
Oxford	157	12	Kidder	Jesse			1						1				2		

TOWN	PG#	LN#	HEADS OF HOUSEHOLD LAST NAME	FIRST NAME	FREE WHITE MALES under 10	10 to 16	16 to 26	26 to 45	45 and over	FREE WHITE FEMALES under 10	10 to 16	16 to 26	26 to 45	45 and over	TOTAL ALL OTHER	TOTAL SLAVES	TOTALS	DISTRICT/ TOWNSHIP	NOTES
Oxford	157	11	Kidder	Jonathan		1	1		1			2		3			8		
Sterling	351	1	Kies	Asa	1	1		1					1				4		
Lancaster	352	12	Kies	Daniel	2		1	1		1	1	2	1				9		
Grafton	204	10	Kieth	Royal		1	3	1		2		2		1			10		
Sterling	351	6	Kilborn	John	2	1	1		1	1	1		1				8		
Sterling	351	4	Kilborn	Levi	1							2	1	1			5		
Sterling	354	15	Kilborn	Timothy	1	1	1	1			2	2	1	1			10		
Lunenberg	428	11	Kilburn	David	2			1		1			1				5		
Leominster	438	38	Kilburn	Jacob	2			1		1	1						5		
Lunenberg	428	10	Kilburn	Jona			1	1					1	1			4		
Lunenberg	428	12	Kilburn	Wm				1						1			2		
Lunenberg	428	14	Kilburn	Wm Jun	1			1		1		1	1				5		
Milford	393	26	Kilburne	Josiah				1					1				2		
Milford	393	27	Kilburne	Stephen	1		1	1		1	1	1	1				7		
Gardner	450	4	Kilton	Samuel		1	2		1	1		1		1			7		
Brookfield	259	9	Kimbal	Aaron	2		1		1	2	1	3	1				11	Second Parish	
Grafton	195	13	Kimball	Aaron		1		1					1				3		
Sterling	354	22	Kimball	Aaron		1	1			2	1		1				6		
Grafton	195	14	Kimball	Aaron Jun	2		1	1		1	2	2	1				10		
Harvard	222	32	Kimball	Benjamin		1		1	1	1	1	1	2	1			9		
Grafton	196	8	Kimball	Isaac			1				1		1				3		
Sutton	162	9	Kimball	Leonard	1		1	1		1			1				5		
Grafton	198	3	Kimball	Noah		1	2	1			2	2	1				9		
Lunenberg	428	16	Kimball	Saml				1		3	3			1			8		
Lunenberg	428	9	Kimball	Thomas	1		2		1	1	1	1	1				8		
Holden	511	12	Kimbel	David	1	1		1		1			2				6		
Templeton	242	6	Kindall	Abijah		1	4		1	1		2	1				10		
Templeton	231	7	Kindall	Noah		1			1		1		1				4		
Templeton	233	16	Kindall	Paul			1	2	1		2	2		1			9		
Templeton	231	11	Kindall	Pearson	1			1			1		2				5		
Brookfield	259	10	Kindrick	Thomas	2	2	2		1	2	1	1	1	1			13	Second Parish	
Charlton	332	25	King	Daniel	1			1		2			1				5		
Leicester	492	11	King	Henry		1	1		1		1			1			5		
Petersham	279	7	King	Henry	3		1			1		1					6		
Sutton	162	8	King	Isaac	3		1			1	1	1	1				8		
Ward	177	43	King	John		1		1			1	1					4		
Petersham	279	8	King	Jona				1						1			2		
Sutton	159	20	King	Jonathan	3		1			2	1		1				8		
Rutland	509	15	King	Joseph	2	2	3	1		1		1					10		
Barre	410	16	King	Saml	1	1											2		
Paxton	501	10	King	Samuel	2		1					1					4		
Rutland	509	14	King	Samuel		1	1					1	1	1			5		
Sutton	162	7	King	Samuel	1			1		2		1	1	1			7		
Petersham	279	6	King	Stephen	1	1		1		1		1					5		
Sutton	162	6	King	William			2	1									3		
Barre	410	18	King	Wm	1	1	1		1		1			1			6		
Sutton	162	4	King	Solomon			1					1		1			3		
Oxford	157	4	Kingsbury	Amasa				1		1			1				3		
Oxford	157	5	Kingsbury	Danl		1	2	1		4	1		1				10		
Spencer	493	1	Kingsbury	Ebenz	1	1	1	1					1				5		
Brookfield	270	12	Kingsbury	Edward			1							1			2	Third Parish	
Oxford	157	8	Kingsbury	Ephm			1			1		1					3		
Oxford	157	7	Kingsbury	Jacob	1		1		1	1		1	1	2			8		
Oxford	157	1	Kingsbury	Jer				1						1			2		
Oxford	157	2	Kingsbury	Jer Junr	2	1		1		1			1				6		
Brookfield	259	11	Kingsbury	John	1			1					1				3	Second Parish	
Sutton	160	1	Kingsbury	John	1		1						1				3		
Oxford	157	10	Kingsbury	Joseph			1						1				2		
Worcester	181	14	Kingsbury	Joseph	1	1	2		1	2	1	1		1			10		
Oxford	157	3	Kingsbury	Josiah	1		1			1			1				4		
Oxford	157	9	Kingsbury	Saml	1		1			2			1				5		
Oxford	157	6	Kingsbury	Simeon		1							1				2		
Worcester	181	13	Kingston	Saml	2		1			1	1		1	1			7		
Sutton	162	10	Kinney	Asa		1		1						1			3		
Sutton	162	3	Kinney	John	2	1		1		1			1				6		
Sutton	162	12	Kinney	Reuben				1						1			2		
Sutton	162	1	Kinney	Stephen		1	2	1				1		1			6		
Sutton	162	2	Kinney	Stephen Junr	1		1			1		1					4		
Royalston	233	1	Kinsley	Elisha	1	1		1		4	2		1				10		
Hubbardston	418	21	Kinsman	Daniel	1		4			1	1	2	1	1			11		
Brookfield	259	7	Kittredge	Jacob	2	1	6		1	1			1	1			13	Second Parish	
Sutton	162	11	Kittredge	Jacob				1				1					2		
Douglas	482	34	Knap	Job	2		1	1		2		2	1				9		
Spencer	493	7	Knapp	Enoch	2	2	1		1	3	1		1				11		
Petersham	279	10	Knapp	Jezneah			1			1			1				3		
Petersham	279	9	Knapp	John		1			1			1	3	1			7		
Spencer	493	6	Knapp	John		1		1		1		1		1			5		
Leicester	492	10	Knapp	Joseph		2			1	2	1		1				7		
Gardner	450	3	Kneeland	Timothy		1		1				1	1	2			6		
Bolton	216	18	Knight	Amaziah		1	1	1					1				4		
Bolton	210	20	Knight	Carter			1										1		
Garry	278	7	Knight	Daniel				1			1		1	1			4		
Harvard	218	3	Knight	Daniel				1					1				2		
Templeton	242	7	Knight	Daniel	4			1		1	1		1				8		
Athol	287	15	Knight	Ebenz				1						1			2		
Garry	278	4	Knight	Ebenz	3	2		1		1			1				8		
Worcester	181	16	Knight	Edward	1	1	2		1			1	1				7		
Oxford	154	14	Knight	Elisha			1						1				2		
Athol	288	1	Knight	Isaac	1	1		1		3	1	1		1			9		
Worcester	181	15	Knight	Isaac	3						1		1	1			6		

TOWN	PG#	LN#	HEADS OF HOUSEHOLD LAST NAME	FIRST NAME	FREE WHITE MALES under 10	10 to 16	16 to 26	26 to 45	45 and over	FREE WHITE FEMALES under 10	10 to 16	16 to 26	26 to 45	45 and over	TOTAL ALL OTHER	TOTAL SLAVES	TOTALS	DISTRICT/ TOWNSHIP	NOTES
Leicester	492	9	Knight	Jona Jun	1			1				1					3		
Worcester	184	21	Knight	Jonah	1		1						1				3		
Leicester	492	8	Knight	Jonathan				1		1				1			3		
Harvard	218	8	Knight	Joseph		2	1	2					1	1			7		
Spencer	493	8	Knight	Joshua			1						1	1			3		
Winchendon	228	32	Knight	Matthew				1						1			2		
Winchendon	228	33	Knight	Nathan		1	2		1	1				1			6		
Worcester	184	19	Knight	Reuben	3	1		1		2			1				8		
Western	255	10	Knight	Samuel	2	1	1	1	1	1	2		1	1			11		
Garry	278	8	Knight	Thadeus		1		1		1		1					4		
Leominster	438	36	Knight	William				1		3	2		1				7		
Spencer	493	4	Knight	William	4				1	3	2	1		1			12		
Worcester	181	17	Knight	William	3	1	1	1	1	1	2	1	1				12		
Spencer	493	5	Knight	William Jun			1			1		1					3		
Lancaster	352	13	Knights	Menasseh			1		1			2	1	1			6		
Garry	278	5	Knolton	Joseph		1		1		3		1	1				7		
Hardwick	299	22	Knoulton	Abm	2			1	1			1		2			7		
Worcester	181	12	Knower	John				1						1			2		
Westminster	446	22	Knower	Thomas	1		1			2	1		1				7		
Hardwick	299	21	Knowles	Simeon	3			1	1	1		1	1	1			8		
Ward	178	44	Knowls	Thomas		1	1	1				3		1			7		
Ward	178	45	Knowls	Thomas Junr			1			1				1			3		
Shrewsbury	370	4	Knowlton	Abraham		1	1			1	3		1				8		
Shrewsbury	370	6	Knowlton	Artemas	1			1					1				3		
Brookfield	259	8	Knowlton	Charles	1	1	2		1	1	2	1	1	2			12	Second Parish	
Berlin	211	16	Knowlton	Daniel	1	1		1			1		1				5		
Holden	511	13	Knowlton	Jesse	1			1		3			1				6		
Shrewsbury	370	1	Knowlton	Joseph	2			1		1	2		1				7		
Ward	178	46	Knowlton	Joseph			1							1			2		
Shrewsbury	370	2	Knowlton	Lucy	1		2				3			1			7		
Templeton	240	7	Knowlton	Lyman		1	1			2			1				5		
Templeton	237	2	Knowlton	Stephen	3		1						1				5		
Shrewsbury	370	3	Knowlton	Thomas	1	2		1		1	1	1		1			9		
Shrewsbury	370	5	Knowlton	William		2	1			1				1			5		
Templeton	237	1	Knowton	Ezekiel		1		1				2		1			5		
Grafton	202	1	Knox	John	1			1		2			1				5		
Sterling	351	5	Kowlton	Joseph	1			1		2			1				5		
Westborough	191	22	Lackey	Judith							1	1		1			3		
Sutton	162	20	Lackey	Matthew	1	2	2		1	1			1				8		
Upton	385	2	Lackey	Nathan			1		1	1				1			4		
Upton	385	1	Lackey	Samuel	1	2	1		1	1		1					7		
Charlton	331	1	Laflin	Parley	1			1		2			1				5		
Lunenberg	428	18	Lain	Eleazer	1	1		1		3			1	1			8		
Charlton	331	8	Lamb	Abijah			2		1		1	1		1			6		
Oxford	158	9	Lamb	Abijah	1	1		1					2				5		
Charlton	331	9	Lamb	Abijah Junr	1		1					1					3		
Garry	278	12	Lamb	Bezaleel			1	1				1	1				4		
Charlton	331	3	Lamb	David	1	2		1		2				1			8		
Spencer	494	8	Lamb	David		2	1		1	1				1			6		
Charlton	331	11	Lamb	Ebenzr		1	1	1				1		1			6		
Garry	278	11	Lamb	Isaac		2	3	1						1			7		
Spencer	493	9	Lamb	Isaac			1	1		3			1				6		
Templeton	239	6	Lamb	Israel			1		1	2	1			1			6		
Hubbardston	418	23	Lamb	James			2		1	1	1	1		1			7		
Charlton	331	12	Lamb	Jarvis	1			1		3			1				6		
Garry	278	14	Lamb	John	2		1	1		2	2	1	1				10		
Garry	278	16	Lamb	Jonas	3			1		1			1				6		
Spencer	494	5	Lamb	Jonas	2	1		1		1	1	2		2			11		
Templeton	239	7	Lamb	Joseph			1		1	1	1			1			6		
Garry	278	10	Lamb	Joshua				1		1	1			1			4		
Oxford	157	18	Lamb	Levi		1	1		2	1		1		2			8		
Charlton	331	14	Lamb	Nahum	2	1		1		2	1		1				8		
Charlton	331	13	Lamb	Reuben	2			1		1	1		1				6		
Oxford	158	8	Lamb	Reuben		2	1		1			1	1				6		
Charlton	331	2	Lamb	Richard	3			1		1			1				6		
Charlton	331	10	Lamb	Samuel		1	1		1		1	1		1			6		
Paxton	501	13	Lamb	Thomas	1	1	1		1		1	1	1				7		
Grafton	201	12	Lamb	William	2			1		2	1		1				7		
Garry	278	17	Lamb	Willm		1					1			1			4		
Garry	278	15	Lamb	Saml	2		2		1		2			1			8		
Brookfield	259	13	Lampron	John		1		2	1			3					7	Second Parish	
Charlton	331	6	Lampson	Ebenzr				1						1			2		
Charlton	331	5	Lampson	Isaac	3	1		1		2	1		1				9		
Boylston	373	12	Lampson	Nathll		1	2		1			1		1			6		
Worcester	184	31	Lamson	Ebenz	1			1		1	1	1					5		
Petersham	279	12	Lamson	Samuel	2			1		1	1		1				6		
Sutton	162	15	Lamson	Timothy		1		1		1		1		2			6		
Sturbridge	333	6	Lancaster	David	1		1	1		1			1				5		
Sutton	161	1	Landman	Thomas	2			1		1		1	1				6		
Ashburnham	459	30	Lane	Benjm	1		1		1	4	2		1				10		
Hardwick	300	7	Lane	Elijah	2			2				1					5		
Ashburnham	459	33	Lane	Frances	1	2			1		1	2					7		
Lancaster	352	22	Lane	Jonas	2	2		1				1	1				7		
Sturbridge	333	10	Lane	Otis			1										1		
Sturbridge	333	11	Lane	Robert				1	1	1			1				4		
Templeton	242	8	Langer	William	3			1		2		1					7		
Lancaster	351	4	Langley	Ezekiel	2	1				1		1		1			7		
Lancaster	351	5	Langley	William	2			1		1			1				5		
Boylston	374	1	Larkin	Edmond	1	1	1		1			1					5		

216

TOWN	PG#	LN#	LAST NAME	FIRST NAME	under 10	10 to 16	16 to 26	26 to 45	45 and over	under 10	10 to 16	16 to 26	26 to 45	45 and over	TOTAL ALL OTHER	TOTAL SLAVES	TOTALS	DISTRICT/ TOWNSHIP	NOTES
Berlin	216	18	Larkin	Ephraim	3			1		1			1				6		
Berlin	216	5	Larkin	John	1	1		1	1	2	2		1	1			10		
Sterling	351	3	Larkin	Seth	1			1					1				3		
Lancaster	352	14	Larkin	William				1					1				2		
Gardner	449	1	Larnard	Samuel	2		1	1		1			1				6		
Hardwick	300	6	Larned	James	2	1		1		5		1	1				11		
New Braintree	310	15	Larned	James	2	1		1		5		1	1				11		
Mendon	383	1	Lasall	Joshua	2		2		1		1		1				7	1st Parish	
Hardwick	299	23	Lathe	Asa				1					1				2		
Grafton	199	14	Lathe	Benjn		2	3	1	1		2	4		2			15		
Charlton	331	16	Lathe	Jabez		2			1	2	2			1			8		
Grafton	199	13	Lathe	Zephaniah	2				1		3			1			7		
Sutton	161	4	Lathe	Zephaniah			1					1					2		
Hardwick	300	4	Lathrop	Nathan	2				1	3	1			1			8		
Westborough	197	107	Lathrop	Thomas	1			1					1				3		
Lancaster	351	3	Laughton	Daniel	2	1	1		1	2	1			1			9		
Templeton	240	9	Lawater	Elias			1					1					2		
Templeton	231	4	Lawater	Sarah										1			1		
Harvard	221	7	Lawrance	Stephen		1		1					1				3		
Fitchburg	427	2	Lawrence	Amos		1	1		1		2	2		1			8		
Leominster	437	3	Lawrence	Bazalel		1	2	1		3		3	1	1			12		
Hardwick	300	5	Lawrence	Ebenz			3		1			3		1			8		
Ashburnham	459	34	Lawrence	Moses	1							1					3		
Hardwick	300	3	Lawrence	Moses	3	3	1	1	1	2	1		1				13		
Royalston	240	5	Lawrence	Samuel	1		1					1					3		
Ashburnham	459	32	Lawrence	Wm John			1					1					2		
Westminster	446	27	Laws	James				1			1	1		1			4		
Westminster	446	28	Laws	James Jr	2			1				1					4		
Westminster	446	29	Laws	Thomas Jr	1		1	1		1			2				6		
Lancaster	352	17	Lawson	James				1			2			1			4		
Hardwick	300	1	Lawton	James	1	2	1		1			3		1			9		
Dudley	343	21	Lawton	John	3		2		1	3	1	1	1				12		
Uxbridge	467	5	Lawton	William	2				1			2					5		
Sturbridge	333	7	Leach	Asa	2		1	1		1	1		1				7		
Lancaster	351	2	Leach	Joseph	1	1		1		2			1	1			7		
Grafton	204	8	Lealand	Benjn			1		1				1	1			4		
Leominster	437	2	Lealand	Caleb		1			1		1	1		1			5		
Grafton	204	9	Lealand	Daniel			1			1		1					3		
Grafton	199	8	Lealand	David W.	3	1		1		1	2	1	1				10		
Grafton	197	1	Lealand	Ebenz	1	1	2		1	1	2	1	1				10		
Upton	385	3	Lealand	Eli		1	1	1		1				1			5		
Grafton	199	5	Lealand	Phine	1	2		1	1	1	1	2		1			10		
Grafton	200	1	Lealand	Samuel	1	1			1		1	1	1				6		
Gardner	452	18	Lealand	Simeon	3	1		1				1	1				7		
Dudley	343	23	Learnard	Thomas		2		1		2			2				7		
Dudley	343	22	Learnard	Wm				1					1				2		
Oxford	157	13	Learned	Asa		1	1		1				1				4		
Douglas	481	2	Learned	Benja	3		2		1		1	1					8		
Oxford	158	4	Learned	Benja	3	1		1		2		1	1				9		
Charlton	331	17	Learned	David			1		2				1				4		
Oxford	157	20	Learned	Ebenz		1			1		1	1					4		
Oxford	157	14	Learned	Elijah			1	1	1	1				1			5		
Charlton	331	19	Learned	Erastus	1		1	1	1	3	1	2					10		
Douglas	481	1	Learned	Hezekiah			1	1				1	1				4		
Oxford	157	17	Learned	Jacob	1		1		2	1		1	1				8		
Oxford	158	3	Learned	Jeremiah	3	1		1		1			1				8		
Oxford	157	15	Learned	John		1	1	1				2		1			6		
Oxford	157	16	Learned	John Junr	1		1	1		4	3		1				11		
Oxford	158	5	Learned	Jona	3	1	1	1		1			1				8		
Oxford	158	2	Learned	Rufus		1		1		1			1				4		
Oxford	158	1	Learned	Silvanus		2	1	1		3	2	1	1				11		
Oxford	158	6	Learned	Simpson		1		1				1	1				4		
Templeton	235	15	Learned	Thomas	2		1	1		2	1		1	1			9		
Royalston	235	5	Leath	Benja	2	1			1	2				1			7		
Charlton	331	7	Leavens	Elijah			1		1	1	3			1			7		
Sutton	162	18	LeBarron	Lazarus		1	1		1			1	1				5		
Barre	409	9	Lee	Benj Esq	2	1		1		1	1		1				7		
Dudley	343	24	Lee	Benja			1	1			1		1				4		
Lancaster	352	21	Lee	Benjamin	1	1		1			1	3			1		8		
Charlton	331	4	Lee	Chartman			1										1		
Douglas	481	4	Lee	Comfort			1		1		2			1	1		6		
Douglas	481	3	Lee	Ephraim		1	1	1						1			4		
Barre	410	27	Lee	Ezekiel	1		1	1	1		1	1					7		
Barre	409	5	Lee	Henry	1			1		2		1	1				6		
Dudley	343	25	Lee	Isaac			1	2	1			1		2			7		
Douglas	481	6	Lee	James		1	1	1						1			4		
Douglas	481	7	Lee	John	2			1					1				4		
Royalston	239	11	Lee	Joseph		1		1	1	1	1	2		1			8		
Barre	410	24	Lee	Joshua			1		1			3		2			7		
Oakham	319	9	Lee	Philip				1			2			1			4		
Douglas	481	5	Lee	Richard	2	1	1	1		1			1	1			8		
Barre	410	25	Lee	Saml	1		1	1	1		1	1	1	1			7		
Barre	410	22	Lee	Saml 2d	1			1		2			1				5		
Barre	410	26	Lee	Saml Jr	3			1		2			1				7		
Barre	409	6	Lee	Seth	2		1	1		1		3		1			9		
Douglas	481	8	Lee	Simeon	1			1					1				3		
Brookfield	248	17	Leertourer	Maria W							1		1				2	First Parish	
Milford	393	30	Lefure	John	1				2				1				4		
Milford	393	31	Lefure	Simeon	1	1		1		2	2	1	1				9		

TOWN	PG#	LN#	LAST NAME	FIRST NAME	FREE WHITE MALES					FREE WHITE FEMALES					TOTAL ALL OTHER	TOTAL SLAVES	TOTALS	DISTRICT/ TOWNSHIP	NOTES
					under 10	10 to 16	16 to 26	26 to 45	45 and over	under 10	10 to 16	16 to 26	26 to 45	45 and over					
Leominster	437	6	Legate	Thomas		1	4		1		1	1	1				9		
Leominster	437	7	Legate	Thomas Jun	2	2	2	1	1		1	3	1	1			14		
Mendon	384	18	Legg	Benjamin		1			1	2	1	1	1				7	1st Parish	
Uxbridge	467	4	Legg	David	2		1		1	1	1	1	1				8		
Mendon	383	2	Legg	Joel	2	2		1		2			1				8	1st Parish	
Mendon	384	19	Legg	John				1						1			2	1st Parish	
Milford	393	29	Legg	Nathl		1			1			2		2			6		
Worcester	184	32	Legg	Reuben	2	1	4		1	1		1		1			11		
Mendon	392	5	Legg	Samuel		1		1				1					3	2d Parish	
Mendon	384	20	Legg	Susannah Wd						1		1		1			3	1st Parish	
Sutton	162	17	Leland	Jonathan			1			1			1				3		
Sutton	162	16	Leland	Solomon				1		1			1				3		
Sutton	162	19	Leland	Timothy	1		1			2	1		1				7		
Westborough	198	128	Lenard	Solomon				1					1				2		
Oakham	319	11	Leonard	Andrew				1					1				2		
Westminster	446	25	Leonard	Enoch			2				1						3		
Sturbridge	333	8	Leonard	Ezenas		1	1			1	1						4		
Oakham	319	8	Leonard	Ezra	1		1		1	4		1					8		
Sterling	351	10	Leonard	Linus											5		5		
Upton	388	21	Lesure	David		2					2		1				6		
Grafton	201	3	Lesure	Edward	2			1			1	1					5		
Uxbridge	467	3	Lesure	Gideon	2			1		2	1	1					7		
Mendon	392	6	Lesure	Levi		1	1		2	1	2		3				10	2d Parish	
Boylston	374	2	Lewis	Catherine									1		2		3		
Templeton	235	17	Lewis	Jacob	2			1		1		1					5		
Sterling	351	9	Lewis	Joseph	1	1	2		1	1	1		1				8		
Barre	409	4	Lewis	Peter											6		6		
Uxbridge	467	2	Lewis	Robert	3		1					1					5		
Athol	288	12	Lewis	Thomas	4	1		1				1					7		
Westminster	446	23	Lewis	Thomas			1	1		1		1	1				5		
Worcester	184	33	Lewis	Thomas											3		3		
Bolton	207	16	Lewis	Timothy				1		1		2					5		
Lancaster	351	6	Lewis	Timothy Jun	1		1					1					3		
Athol	288	13	Lewis	Willm	1	2	1	1	2	3		1	1	1			13		
Athol	288	11	Lilley	David	3		1					1					5		
Sutton	162	13	Lilley	David				1			1	1	1				4		
Oxford	157	19	Lilley	Ebenezer			1	1			1		1				4		
Sutton	162	14	Lilley	John	2		1			2	1	1					7		
Worcester	184	25	Lincoln	Abrm		1	1			2	2	1					7		
Lancaster	352	20	Lincoln	Caleb		1	1				1						3		
Petersham	279	13	Lincoln	Caleb	3	1		1				1	1				7		
Oxford	154	15	Lincoln	Collin	1		1					1					3		
Athol	288	9	Lincoln	Ebenz	1		2		1	1	1	1					8		
Petersham	279	15	Lincoln	Enos		2	1		1	3	1	1		1			10		
Leominster	437	4	Lincoln	Ephraim		2	1			3	1		1				8		
Westminster	446	24	Lincoln	Heamon		2		1		2	3	1		1			10		
Sutton	161	3	Lincoln	Isaac	3	1		1			1		1				7		
Lancaster	352	15	Lincoln	Jacob	2			1		2			1				6		
Lunenberg	427	2	Lincoln	Jeremiah		1	1	1				1	1				5		
Leominster	437	1	Lincoln	Jesse	2			1		2	1		1				7		
Worcester	184	24	Lincoln	Levi	2	2	3	1	1		2		3				14		
Rutland	509	17	Lincoln	Samuel	1	1		1		2	1	1	1				8		
Western	256	2	Lincoln	Seth	2	2		1			1	1	1				8		
Oakham	319	7	Lincoln	Stephan	3		2		1	2	1	2		1			12		
Leominster	437	11	Lincoln	Thomas		1	1			3	1		1				7		
Leominster	437	5	Lincoln	William				1				3		1			5		
Leominster	437	9	Lincoln	Wm Jun		1		1			1		1				4		
Gardner	450	6	Linds	William	2			1					1				4		
Rutland	509	16	Linkfield	John	2		1					1					4		
Sturbridge	333	5	Lion	Abner	1	1	1	1			3		1				9		
Lancaster	352	19	Liswell	James		1		1				2	1				5		
Lunenberg	428	20	Litch	John		1	1	1	1		2	1		1			8		
Winchendon	228	35	Litch	Thos		1		1				2	1				5		
Charlton	331	15	Litchfield	Comins	1		1				1						3		
Lancaster	352	16	Littayce	Noel	1	1		1		1	1	1					7		
New Braintree	310	16	Little	Benm		2					1	2					6		
Lunenberg	428	17	Little	John		1	1			1		1	1				6		
Brookfield	263	8	Little	Joseph			1		3				1				5	Second Parish	
Milford	393	28	Littlefield	Isaac		2		1	1				1	1			6		
Bolton	209	20	Littlejohn	Sarah									1				1		
Spencer	494	3	Livermore	Abijah			1					1	1				3		
Spencer	494	4	Livermore	Amos	2			1		4			1				8		
Paxton	501	12	Livermore	Bradl	2	2		1		1		2	1				10		
Spencer	494	7	Livermore	David		1	2		1	2	1		1				8		
Brookfield	248	18	Livermore	Elisha	2		2		1	2	2			1			10	First Parish	
Ward	178	47	Livermore	Elisha	1	1	2	1		3		1	1				10		
Leicester	491	1	Livermore	Isaac		1		1					1				3		
Spencer	493	11	Livermore	James	1	1		1				2					5		
Leicester	491	2	Livermore	Jonas				1				1	1				3		
Leicester	492	13	Livermore	Micah		1		1				1	1				4		
Spencer	494	2	Livermore	Moses	2	3	1	1			2		2	1			12		
Spencer	493	10	Livermore	Phins			1	1			1		1				3		
Worcester	183	1	Livermore	Reuben	1			1				1					4		
Leicester	491	3	Livermore	Salem		1	1			2		1					5		
Sturbridge	333	4	Lombard	Wm	2		1					1					4		
Douglas	481	10	Long	Elizabeth			1				1		1	2			4		
Oakham	319	10	Long	John		1		1			1		1				4		
Boylston	373	13	Longley	James	3	2		1		1	1		1				9		
Bolton	210	14	Longley	Nathaniel				1			1		1				3		

TOWN	PG#	LN#	LAST NAME	FIRST NAME	FREE WHITE MALES					FREE WHITE FEMALES					TOTAL ALL OTHER	TOTAL SLAVES	TOTALS	DISTRICT/ TOWNSHIP	NOTES
					under 10	10 to 16	16 to 26	26 to 45	45 and over	under 10	10 to 16	16 to 26	26 to 45	45 and over					
Bolton	210	9	Longley	Nathaniel Junr		1	1	1			1			1			5		
Bolton	212	9	Longley	Robert				1						1			2		
Bolton	212	10	Longley	Robert Junr		1		1		1		1					4		
Brookfield	264	4	Loomis	Caleb		1		1	1			2		1			6	Third Parish	
Athol	288	10	Lord	Thomas		2	2		1	1	1			1			8		
Mendon	384	17	Lord	Thomas		1				1		1					3	1st Parish	
Barre	409	2	Loring	Abel		1			1	1	1		1				5		
Petersham	279	14	Loring	Abel	2		1	1		2			1				7		
Sterling	351	7	Loring	John	1	1	1		1		1	1		1			7		
Sterling	351	8	Loring	Joseph	1		1	1					1				4		
Spencer	493	12	Loring	Nathl	2	1	2		1	3	1	1					12		
Barre	409	8	Loring	Reuben	2			1		2			1				6		
Holden	511	16	Lovell	Amos	1	1	1		2	1	2	2	1	1			12		
Holden	511	15	Lovell	Asa		1			1	2	1	2		2			9		
Worcester	184	27	Lovell	Ebenz				1		1		1	1	1			5		
Sutton	161	2	Lovell	Ezra		1	1		3	1		1		2			9		
Worcester	184	28	Lovell	Jona	1	1	2		1			2		1			8		
Worcester	184	29	Lovell	Jona Jun		1		2		2		1					6		
Holden	511	17	Lovering	Jesse			3		1	1							5		
Holden	511	18	Lovering	Jesse Junr	1	1		1		1			1				5		
Athol	288	7	Lovering	Levi		2						1					3		
Garry	278	13	Lovering	Rufus			1			4	1	1					7		
Mendon	384	14	Lovett	James				1					4	1			6	1st Parish	
Mendon	384	16	Lovett	James Jr			1					1					2	1st Parish	
Mendon	384	15	Lovett	Phinehas		1						1					2	1st Parish	
Ashburnham	459	31	Low	Abraham	1	1		1		2		1					6		
Barre	409	1	Low	Jenison	2			1		1	1		1				6		
Fitchburg	427	4	Low	Jonathan Jun	2	2	2		2	2	1	2		3			16		
Fitchburg	427	3	Low	Joseph Jun	4		1	1	1	1			2	1			11		
Lancaster	351	1	Low	Nathaniel Jun		1	1			2		1	1				6		
Leominster	437	10	Low	Nathl				1			1	1	1				4		
Leominster	437	8	Lowe	Edward		2		1			1	2	1				7		
Lunenberg	428	19	Lowe	Samuel				2			1		1				4		
Lunenberg	427	1	Lowe	Wm	2	2		2		1	1		1				9		
Upton	385	4	Lucas	Matthew			1			1		1					3		
Hardwick	300	2	Luce	Experience		1		1		1	1	3		1			8		
Barre	409	3	Luce	Reuben	4		1			3		1					9		
Athol	288	8	Lucus	James	1			1					1				3		
Spencer	494	1	Ludden	Enoch		1		1		2	2		1				7		
Westminster	446	26	Luis	Abijah		1					1						2		
Spencer	494	6	Luther	Robt			1	1		2			1				5		
Spencer	494	9	Luther	Thomas	1		1			1			1				4		
Douglas	481	9	Luther	William	1			1		2	1	1	1				7		
Worcester	184	26	Lynde	George											2		2		
Paxton	501	11	Lynde	Johnson	2	1		1				4	1				9		
Leicester	492	12	Lynde	Thomas	2		2	1		1	2		1				9		
Lancaster	352	18	Lyon	Aaron			4	10		3	4	5	22				48		
Worcester	184	30	Lyon	Abigail		1				2	2	1					6		
Charlton	331	18	Lyon	Abner Junr		1	1			4		1					7		
Hubbardston	418	22	Lyon	Asa	1		1				1	1					4		
Royalston	232	10	Lyon	David	4		1		1	3	1	1	1				12		
Shrewsbury	370	7	Lyon	Ephraim		1		1					1				3		
Shrewsbury	370	8	Lyon	Ephraim Jr			1			1	1						3		
Barre	410	23	Lyon	Josiah	2	1	1		1	1			1				7		
Hubbardston	418	24	Lyon	Mary Wid.						1			1				2		
Sturbridge	333	9	Lyon	Wm			3	1		1		2					7		
Brookfield	259	14	Lyscom	John				1					1				2	Second Parish	
Leicester	492	14	Lyscum	John	2			1		1	1	1	1				7		
Fitchburg	427	5	Mace	Abraham	2	1		1		3			1				8		
Fitchburg	427	15	Mace	James			1						1				2		
Oakham	319	13	Macumber	John	1	1		1		3		1					7		
Sturbridge	334	16	Macy	Daniel		2			1	1			1				5		
Sturbridge	334	20	Macy	Elijah	1	1		1		2			1				6		
Sturbridge	334	19	Macy	Theodore		1	2	1		1	1	2	1				9		
Milford	394	3	Madden	David	2	1		1			1	1					6		
Milford	393	32	Madden	Levi	2			2		1	1						6		
Milford	394	1	Madden	Michael			1					1	1				3		
Charlton	334	21	Madin	Edward				1					1				2		
Northborough	366	10	Mahan	David	4			1			1		1				7		
Petersham	282	6	Mahan	John	3	1	2	1			1	1	1				10		
Petersham	282	5	Mahan	Thomas				1				1	1				3		
Worcester	186	34	Mahon	William	1			1				1					3		
Western	256	11	Makepeece	Elliot	1	1	2		1	1	1		2	1			10		
Brookfield	259	18	Makepiece	Gershom	1	1	1		1			2		1			7	First Parish	
Brookfield	267	19	Makepiece	Jason		1			1	1			1	1			5	Third Parish	
Brookfield	259	19	Makepiece	Knights		1		1				1			1		4	First Parish	
Barre	412	33	Maldra	Moses	3			1		2	1		1		9		18		
Sturbridge	333	24	Mallens	Henry	2		1	1			1	1					6		
Lunenberg	427	14	Mallikin	Benja	3	1		1		2	2		1				10		
Hubbardston	417	13	Mandell	Daniel	1	1		1		1		1		1			6		
Hardwick	300	13	Manly	Josiah	3		1	1				1		1			7		
Sutton	164	10	Mann	Andrew	1		1			2	1		1				6		
Barre	412	24	Mann	Asa	1		1					1					3		
Ashburnham	460	1	Mann	Bela	2		1			3	2	1					9		
Mendon	392	7	Mann	Benedic	3	1		1		1	2	1	1	1			11	2d Parish	
Hubbardston	417	12	Mann	Ebenezer Capt.	2	1	1		1	2	1		1				9		
Barre	409	11	Mann	Elijah		1	1		1								3		
Ward	178	50	Mann	Elijah		1		1			1		1				4		
Petersham	282	10	Mann	Ensign		2	2		1	1		1	3	1			11		
Worcester	186	22	Mann	Joseph	3	3		1			2		1				10		
Sutton	164	11	Mann	Levi	2		1	1		3	1		1				9		

219

TOWN	PG#	LN#	LAST NAME	FIRST NAME	FREE WHITE MALES					FREE WHITE FEMALES					TOTAL ALL OTHER	TOTAL SLAVES	TOTALS	DISTRICT/ TOWNSHIP	NOTES
					under 10	10 to 16	16 to 26	26 to 45	45 and over	under 10	10 to 16	16 to 26	26 to 45	45 and over					
Holden	511	23	Mann	Nathan		1			2					1			4		
Paxton	501	14	Mann	Phinehas		2	1							1			5		
Sterling	351	22	Manning	Israel		1		1		2	1	3		1			9		
Spencer	491	8	Manning	Jacob	3			1		1			1	1			7		
Royalston	239	14	Manning	Joseph	1	1		1		1	1		1				6		
Ashburnham	460	7	Manning	Solomon	1				1	2			1				5		
Dudley	343	36	Mansfield	Daniel	3			1		4			1		1		10		
Worcester	186	30	Mansfield	John M			3	1		1	1	1					7		
Charlton	334	19	Marble	Aaron	1	2		1		2	1	1					8		
Sutton	164	4	Marble	Alpheus		2	1		1			2		1			7		
Sutton	164	3	Marble	Andrew	3	1		1		2	1		1				9		
Charlton	334	16	Marble	Daniel	2			1		1	1			1	1		7		
Hardwick	300	10	Marble	Daniel	3			1	1				1	1			7		
Sutton	161	8	Marble	Daniel	3	1	1		1				1				7		
Sutton	164	1	Marble	Enoch				1					1				2		
Ashburnham	460	9	Marble	Jabez	2	2		1		3	1	1	1				11		
Rutland	512	7	Marble	Jesse	1	1		1		4			1				8		
Sutton	164	2	Marble	Malachi	1	1	1		1			1	2	2			9		
Sutton	161	14	Marble	Nathan			1					1					2		
Ashburnham	460	2	Marble	Oliver	2	1		1		2	1	1	1				10		
Sutton	164	6	Marble	Rufus	1		1					1					3		
Sutton	164	5	Marble	Samuel			2			1		1					4		
Sutton	164	13	Marble	Solomon	4	1	2	1		1	2		1	1			13		
Sutton	161	7	Marble	Stephen	1	2	1	1	1	1	1	1	1				10		
Charlton	334	18	Marble	Thadeus	2	2		1		1		1					7		
Hubbardston	417	2	Marcan	Timy P.	1	1		1		1	1	1					6		
Hubbardston	417	1	Marcan	Wm. Maj.		1	1		1	1	1	1		1			7		
Brookfield	259	20	March	Ebenezer	2			1		2			1				6	First Parish	
Sutton	164	15	March	Jacob	1	4		1		3			1				10		
Sutton	164	14	March	Stephen	2	1			1	1	1		1				7		
Sutton	164	16	March	Tappan	2	1		1		2	1		1				8		
Dudley	343	33	Marcy	Daniel	4			1		1	2		1				10		
Brookfield	262	5	Marcy	Lemuel	1	1		1		1		1	2				7	Second Parish	
Dudley	343	30	Marcy	Theodore		1		1		2				1			5		
Sturbridge	333	13	Marey	Jedediah	1	2	2	1		3		2	1				12		
Western	256	5	Marr	William			1			2	2	2		1			9		
Templeton	235	3	Marret	Noah	1	1	1		1	1		1	2	1	1		10		
Templeton	235	4	Marret	Simeon	1			1					1				3		
Douglas	481	12	Marsh	Aaron	2	1		1	2	3	1		1	1			12		
Sutton	164	9	Marsh	Andrew	2		1						1				4		
Sutton	161	11	Marsh	Caleb			1				1	1	2				5		
Mendon	383	11	Marsh	Douglas	1	1		1					1	1			5	1st Parish	
Sturbridge	334	2	Marsh	Duty	3	1		1		1			1	1			8		
Douglas	481	21	Marsh	Ebenezer		1		1						1			3		
Sutton	164	12	Marsh	Ebenz		1		1		1	2		1				6		
Sturbridge	334	3	Marsh	Eli		1		1		1	1		2				6		
Oakham	319	14	Marsh	Elias	2	2	1		1			2	1				9		
Sturbridge	334	22	Marsh	Elisha	1			1			1	1					4		
Sturbridge	334	8	Marsh	Israel		1		1	1	2			1	1			7		
Hardwick	300	8	Marsh	Joel	1		1	1			2		1				6		
Douglas	481	20	Marsh	John	1		1				1						3		
Sturbridge	334	18	Marsh	John	2	2	3		1	3				2			13		
Charlton	331	25	Marsh	Jonathan				1						1			2		
Hubbardston	417	14	Marsh	Joseph	3			1			1	1					6		
Oxford	155	4	Marsh	Joshua	3			1		2	2	1					9		
Sutton	161	13	Marsh	Joshua		1		1		1			2				5		
Dudley	343	35	Marsh	Lot			2			2	1	2					8		
Western	256	8	Marsh	Marcus	1	1	1	1		1		1					6		
Petersham	282	4	Marsh	Moses	1	2	1	1		2	1	1	1				10		
Douglas	481	22	Marsh	Nahum	2		1					1					4		
Sutton	161	15	Marsh	Peter			1				2		1				4		
Sturbridge	334	1	Marsh	Silas		1			1	4	2	3	1				12		
Sutton	161	9	Marsh	Stephen			1							1			2		
Sutton	161	10	Marsh	Stephen Junr		1		1		2	2		1				7		
Spencer	491	9	Marsh	Tyler			1	1		4			1				7		
Sutton	161	12	Marsh	Tyler	1			1		3			1				6		
Holden	512	3	Marshall	Abel	1	1	1	1	1	2	2		2	1			12		
Fitchburg	427	13	Marshall	Benja				1				1					2		
Lunenberg	427	9	Marshall	David			2	1		4			1				8		
Lunenberg	427	11	Marshall	Jacob	1	1	3		1		2	1		1			10		
Fitchburg	427	6	Marshall	Jonas	1		3		1		1	1	1				9		
Fitchburg	427	12	Marshall	Jonas Jun	1		1	1		1	1	1					7		
Holden	512	4	Marshall	Mary						2		1	1				4		
Lunenberg	427	6	Marshall	Samuel		1	1			1		1		1			5		
Lunenberg	427	7	Marshall	Samuel Jun			1	1		3		1					6		
Holden	512	2	Marshall	Timothy		1		1				1	1				4		
Gardner	450	8	Martain	Jonathn			1		1	1	2		1	1			7		
Sutton	161	18	Martin	Abel	1	2	1			2	1						7		
Fitchburg	427	19	Martin	Barzilla								1					1		
Douglas	481	17	Martin	Comfort	1		1		1	3	2	1		1			10		
Lunenberg	427	13	Martin	Eunice										1			1		
Westminster	449	10	Martin	John	1		1	1	1	1			3	1			9		
Brookfield	259	22	Martin	Stephen	2			1	1	1			1				6	First Parish	
Sturbridge	334	9	Maryfield	Ithamer				1						1			2		
Sturbridge	333	21	Mason	Abel		2	1			2		2		1			8		
Templeton	237	11	Mason	Asa	2			1		1			1				5		
Mendon	383	9	Mason	Chad	3			1		1			1				6	1st Parish	
Barre	412	30	Mason	Daniel	1			1		2				1			5		
Spencer	491	11	Mason	Ebenz	1	1		1		3	1		1				8		
Spencer	494	10	Mason	Elliot		1	1	1			1	1		1			6		

220

TOWN	PG#	LN#	LAST NAME	FIRST NAME	FREE WHITE MALES under 10	10 to 16	16 to 26	26 to 45	45 and over	FREE WHITE FEMALES under 10	10 to 16	16 to 26	26 to 45	45 and over	TOTAL ALL OTHER	TOTAL SLAVES	TOTALS	DISTRICT/ TOWNSHIP	NOTES
Spencer	491	3	Mason	Enoch	3		1			1			1				6		
Spencer	494	11	Mason	Joseph		1											1		
Sturbridge	333	26	Mason	Joshua	1		1	1		1	1		1	1	1		8		
Sturbridge	333	22	Mason	Lemuel	2	1	1	1			1		1	1			8		
Barre	409	13	Mason	Lot	4		1						1				6		
Sturbridge	333	23	Mason	Moses			1			1		1					3		
Petersham	282	11	Mason	Newhall	1	1	1	1		1	1		1				7		
Princeton	517	1	Mason	Sadey			1					1	1				3		
Princeton	517	3	Mason	Silas	2	3	1			1			1				8		
Sturbridge	333	25	Mason	Simeon				1				1	1				3		
Sturbridge	334	15	Mason	Simeon				1			1			1			3		
Princeton	517	2	Mason	Thomas			1			1			2	1			6		
Winchendon	227	8	Massey	Aaron			1			4		1					6		
Lunenberg	427	10	Masson	Jona	4		1			1		1					7		
Leicester	491	4	Mathews	Asahel		1	1					1	1				4		
Gardner	450	11	Mathews	John		1		1			1		1				4		
Westminster	449	4	Mathews	Paul		1		1			1		1				4		
Brookfield	259	15	Mathews	Solomon	2			2		1			2	1			8	Second Parish	
Southborough	205	13	Matthews	Asahel				1					1				2		
New Braintree	310	17	Matthews	Elisha	4	1	2	1				2	1	2			13		
Royalston	234	9	Matthews	Jona			1	1		1	1	2		1			7		
Petersham	279	16	Maundry	Nathll		1	3	1			1		1	1			8		
Leominster	437	18	May	Aaron	3		1				1		1				6		
Sterling	351	13	May	Daniel	1		1			1		1					4		
Sturbridge	334	12	May	Eleazer	1	1	1			2		1	1				7		
Sterling	351	20	May	Ezra			1			1			1				3		
Leominster	437	13	May	Jacob			1			3			1				5		
Leominster	437	16	May	James				1				2	1				4		
Leominster	437	14	May	James Jun	2		1				1	1					5		
Sterling	351	12	May	Levi	3	1	1				1		1				7		
Leominster	437	17	May	Moses	1		1			4		1					7		
Dudley	343	26	May	Samuel	1	2	1		1	2	1	1		1			10		
Sterling	352	1	May	Thomas				1									1		
Spencer	494	12	May	William	5		1						1				7		
Winchendon	228	36	May	Benjamin	2	2		1		1			1				7		
Barre	409	7	Mayhew	Luce	4		1						1				6		
Barre	412	26	Mayhew	Sally Wd		2				1	1		1				5		
Berlin	211	19	Maynard	*				1		2				1			4		Name covered by tape mark
Garry	275	6	Maynard	Abner		1		1						1			3		
Garry	275	9	Maynard	Abraham	1		1					1					3		
Oakham	319	15	Maynard	Amasa	2			1		2		1	2	1			9		
Boylston	371	14	Maynard	Artemas				1						1			2		
Berlin	213	6	Maynard	Barnabas		1	1	1			1	1		1			7		
Shrewsbury	370	14	Maynard	Daniel	3	2	1		1	1	1	1	1	1			12		
Northborough	366	6	Maynard	David				1			1			1			3		
Westminster	446	32	Maynard	David		1	1	1		2				1			6		
Westborough	189	13	Maynard	Ebenz				1						1			2		
Garry	275	7	Maynard	Francis		1		1		3			1				6		
Garry	275	8	Maynard	Gardner		1	2		1		1	2		1			8		
Bolton	215	4	Maynard	John				1			2	2		1			6		
Lancaster	351	7	Maynard	John	1	1	1		1	3	2	1	1				11		
Leominster	437	15	Maynard	John	1		1					1					3		
Westminster	450	1	Maynard	John			1			1		1					3		
Berlin	213	1	Maynard	Levi	3		1			1		1					6		
Westborough	189	14	Maynard	Luther		1	1					1					3		
Rutland	509	21	Maynard	Moses	2	2	1			1	1		1	1			9		
Northborough	366	7	Maynard	Nathan		2	1	1			1	2	1				8		
Westborough	189	18	Maynard	Nathan		2	2	2		1				1			8		
Winchendon	227	4	Maynard	Nathan		1		1						1			3		
Ashburnham	460	5	Maynard	Nehemiah		1	3	1		1	1			1			8		
Northborough	366	12	Maynard	Reuben				1		4				1			6		
Westborough	195	73	Maynard	Solomon			1	1						1			3		
Westborough	195	81	Maynard	Stephen	1	1	2			1	1	1					7		
Northborough	366	13	Maynard	Taylor			1			2		1		1			5		
Bolton	215	13	Maynard	Uriah		1				2			1				4		
Western	256	4	Maynard	William		1		1		2	1			1			6		
Mendon	383	5	Maynard	Windsor	3		1					1	1				6	1st Parish	
Upton	385	6	Maynard	Winslow	2		1			1	2			1			7		
Barre	412	27	Mayo	Benj Capt.	1	1		1		2		1	1				7		
Oxford	158	10	Mayo	John	1			1	1	2	2	2		1			10		
Oxford	158	12	Mayo	John Junr			1						1				2		
Sturbridge	334	17	Mayon	Jacob		1	1						1				3		
Sterling	351	14	Mayson	Jonas		1		1				1		1			4		
Barre	412	23	Mayson	Thaddeus Lt	1		1	1		5	1		1	1			11		
Bolton	209	14	McBride	Abigail						2		1					3		
Berlin	211	5	McBride	James	2		1	1			1	1	1	1			9		
Berlin	216	12	McBride	Josiah	1		1			1		1					4		
Barre	412	25	McCallock	Joseph	2	1		1			1	1		1			7		
Petersham	282	9	McClallen	David		1	1				1	1		1			6		
Petersham	282	8	McClallen	Moses				1					1	2			4		
Petersham	279	17	McClallen	Reuben	1		1	2		1		1					6		
Garry	275	1	McClallen	Willm			1			2		1	1				5		
Hubbardston	415	30	McClanathan	John	2		1		1	1	2		1				8		
Hubbardston	415	31	McClanathan	Thoms	1	1	1			4	2		1				11		
Bolton	211	19	McClary	Hannah										1			1		
Sutton	164	8	McClellan	James		1		2		4	2		1				10		
Sutton	164	7	McClellan	Sarah Wd			1							1			2		
Brookfield	270	15	McClenathan	William	1		1			1	1		1				5	Third Parish	
Mendon	383	6	McClintock	Joseph	2	1	1			2	1		1		1		9	1st Parish	
Brookfield	270	17	McClure	Nicholas		2	3		1		1	1	1	2			11	Third Parish	
Rutland	512	9	McCuller	Matthew	1		1			1			1				4		

TOWN	PG#	LN#	LAST NAME	FIRST NAME	FREE WHITE MALES					FREE WHITE FEMALES					TOTAL ALL OTHER	TOTAL SLAVES	TOTALS	DISTRICT/ TOWNSHIP	NOTES
					under 10	10 to 16	16 to 26	26 to 45	45 and over	under 10	10 to 16	16 to 26	26 to 45	45 and over					
Paxton	504	9	McDonald	Archd			1	1						1			3		
Winchendon	227	7	McElwain	James		2	3	1				1	1	1			10		
Barre	409	12	McFarland	Andrew			1	1									2		
Milford	394	2	McFarland	Ebenz		1		1		1	1			1			5		
Worcester	186	27	McFarland	James	2		1	1		1	1		1	1			8		
Oakham	319	12	McFarland	Reuben	4	2		1			1	1	1				10		
Worcester	186	24	McFarland	Willm				1					1				2		
Worcester	186	25	McFarland	Willm Jun			1	1					2				4		
Charlton	334	14	McFarlen	Elijah				1			2			1			4		
Oxford	158	19	McFarling	Josiah	3		1			1			1				6		
Barre	409	10	McFarsan	Hugh	1			1		2	1	2	1				8		
Rutland	512	8	McGregory	Isaac											5		5		
Charlton	334	5	McIngtry	James	1	2	1		1		1	1		1			8		
Sturbridge	334	21	McInstry	Joseph			1					1					2		
Sturbridge	334	4	McInstry	Wm	2	1		1		1	2		1				8		
Charlton	333	9	McIntire	Alpheus			1						1				2		
Charlton	331	24	McIntire	Amos	1			2		2			1	1			7		
Fitchburg	427	8	McIntire	Daniel	2	2	1		1	1			1	1			9		
Charlton	333	6	McIntire	Deborah						1			1	1			3		
Charlton	333	1	McIntire	Ebenzr		1		1		2	2		1				7		
Charlton	333	2	McIntire	Elias	3			1					1				5		
Fitchburg	427	11	McIntire	Elias	2	1		1		2	1		1				8		
Charlton	334	22	McIntire	Elihu		2	2	1	1		1	1	1	1			10		
Charlton	331	23	McIntire	Elijah	1	1	1						1				4		
Fitchburg	427	10	McIntire	Elijah	1	1	1	1	1	1	1	1	1	1			10		
Charlton	333	8	McIntire	Elnathan	1			1	1	3	2	1	1				10		
Charlton	334	20	McIntire	Ephraim	1		1	1		3			1	1			8		
Charlton	331	22	McIntire	Ezra	2			1		3	1	1	1				9		
Dudley	343	27	McIntire	Gardner				1		2	1		3	1			8		
Fitchburg	427	9	McIntire	Gartrude				1				1	1		1		4		
Charlton	333	4	McIntire	Isaiah		1	1						1				3		
Fitchburg	427	14	McIntire	Jacob	1		1	1				1					4		
Charlton	334	15	McIntire	Joseph		1		1					1	2			5		
Charlton	334	23	McIntire	Nathan	1	3	2	1			1	1		1			10		
Charlton	333	11	McIntire	Nathl	2			1			1		1				5		
Charlton	334	10	McIntire	Nehemiah		1	1	1					1				4		
Charlton	334	3	McIntire	Robert				1						1			2		
Charlton	334	4	McIntire	Robert Junr			1						1				2		
Charlton	333	3	McIntire	Stephanus	2			1		1			1				5		
Charlton	334	2	McIntire	Zebulon		3	1	1			1		1				7		
Lancaster	351	8	McIntosh	Archabald	1			1						1			3		
Douglas	481	19	McKnight	James	3		1	1			1		1	1			8		
Northbridge	473	6	Mcnamara	Hugh	2	2		1		3	1		1	1			11		
Leominster	437	21	Mead	Abijah	3	1			2	4	1						11		
Rutland	512	2	Mead	Benjamin	1	1		1	1	3			1	1			9		
Harvard	222	25	Mead	John				1					1				2		
Petersham	282	1	Mead	John	2			1		1			1				5		
Lunenberg	427	5	Mead	Thomas	2			1		1		1	1	1			7		
Barre	412	21	Mead	Tilly Lt			2	1						1			4		
Holden	512	1	Mead	William	1		1	1					1				4		
Harvard	221	13	Mead	Samuel				1					1	1			3		
Harvard	219	21	Meads	Jason	1			1		2	1		1				6		
Harvard	222	33	Meads	Samuel		1	1	1				1		1			5		
Harvard	217	13	Meads	Samuel Junr	2			1	2				1				6		
Ashburnham	460	3	Medclif	Ezekiel		2	1		2	2	1			1			9		
Worcester	183	2	Medra	Jack											3		3		
Harvard	219	35	Meeds	Francis	1	1		1		2			1	1			7		
Brookfield	259	16	Mellen	David	2		1						1				4	Second Parish	
Mendon	383	10	Mellen	James Col.	1		2	1				1		2	4		11	1st Parish	
Charlton	334	9	Melody	James		2	1						1				4		
Hardwick	300	9	Mendal	Moses	2	4		1		2	2	1					12		
Hardwick	300	12	Mendall	Paul			1						1				2		
Barre	412	31	Mendall	Sylvester	3		1	1		4			1				10		
Brookfield	270	16	Menick	Pliny	3	1	1	1		2	1	1	1				11	Third Parish	
Leominster	437	12	Meriam	Amos	1			1	1	3	1	1	1				10		
Hubbardston	417	10	Meriam	David		1	1				1	2	1				8		
Oxford	155	2	Meriam	Ebenz	5	1	1						1				9		
Worcester	183	9	Meriam	George	1	1	3	1				2		1			9		
Oxford	158	23	Meriam	James		2				1	1	2					8		
Ward	178	51	Meriam	James			2										2		
Oxford	155	3	Meriam	Joel			2										2		
Oxford	155	1	Meriam	John	2		1	1		2		1					7		
Leominster	437	20	Meriam	Jonathan	1			1		3			1	1			7		
Oxford	158	22	Meriam	Joshua				1									1		
Oxford	158	20	Meriam	Sarah Wd	1	1	1					1	2	1			7		
Rutland	512	3	Merick	Silas	2			1					1				4		
Charlton	331	26	Merit	Amos			1			4	2	1	1				9		
Charlton	334	28	Merit	Amos	2			1		2			1				6		
Charlton	334	27	Merit	Benjm	1	1			1		1			1			5		
Charlton	334	25	Merit	Henry				1					2				3		
Charlton	334	26	Merit	Henry Junr	1			1		4			1				7		
Charlton	334	8	Merit	Jesse	1			1		4	1		1				8		
Charlton	331	21	Merit	Moses	3			1					1				5		
Charlton	331	20	Merit	Walter				1				2					3		
Westminster	450	13	Merraim	Asa	1		1			1			1				4		
Westminster	450	12	Merraim	Jonas	1	1		1		3			1				7		
Gardner	450	10	Merraim	Jonathan	2		1						1				4		
Ashburnham	460	8	Merraim	Joseph		2	1				1	1	1				7		
Westminster	450	18	Merraim	Samuel					1					1			2		

TOWN	PG#	LN#	HEADS OF HOUSEHOLD LAST NAME	FIRST NAME	FREE WHITE MALES under 10	10 to 16	16 to 26	26 to 45	45 and over	FREE WHITE FEMALES under 10	10 to 16	16 to 26	26 to 45	45 and over	TOTAL ALL OTHER	TOTAL SLAVES	TOTALS	DISTRICT/ TOWNSHIP	NOTES
Westminster	449	1	Merraim	Samuel Jr	1	1			1	1	1		1				6		
Westminster	450	10	Merraim	Thomas			1	1						2			4		
Ashburnham	460	6	Merraim	William	2	1		1		2			1				7		
Brookfield	259	24	Merriam	Ebenezer			5	1			1	1					8	First Parish	
Harvard	219	24	Merriam	Jonas			1					1					2		
Berlin	213	3	Merriam	Jonathan	1		1		1	1		1		1			6		
Southborough	203	19	Merriam	Joseph			2	1	1		1	1		1			7		
Berlin	211	15	Merriam	Levi	1	1	2	1		1	1	2	1				10		
Bolton	210	5	Merriam	Simon		1			1	3		1		1			7		
Southborough	203	21	Merriam	Timothy	1	1	2		1	2	1		1	1			10		
Hardwick	300	11	Merrick	Nathl		1											1		
Hubbardston	417	11	Merrick	Paul	1		1				1	1					4		
Holden	512	6	Merrifield	Asaph		1	1	1		3	2	1	1				10		
Upton	385	5	Merrifield	John	1	1	1		1	3		1	1				9		
Worcester	186	32	Merrifield	Penude	1		1			1		1					4		
Worcester	186	31	Merrifield	Timothy		1	1						1				3		
Rutland	509	18	Messenger	Pelitiah	1		1					1					3		
Rutland	512	6	Messenger	Wigglesworth		1	1	1		1	1		1				7		
Fitchburg	427	17	Messinger	Elias	1		1					1					3		
Fitchburg	427	7	Messinger	John	1		1			3	2	1					8		
Fitchburg	427	16	Messinger	Thomas	3		3		1	1	1	1		1			11		
Royalston	232	2	Metcalf	Enos	1	1		1		3	1	1					8		
Holden	512	5	Metcalf	Jabez		1		1		1	2		1				6		
Barre	409	14	Metcalf	John Lt	4	1		1		1	3	2	1				13		
Royalston	232	5	Metcalf	Michael		2		1		2	1	1					7		
Royalston	236	1	Metcalf	Pelatiah	1	1	1		1				1				5		
Paxton	504	15	Metcalf	Seth	1			1		1		1		1			5		
Barre	412	20	Metcalf	Simeon	2		1	1		2	1	1	1				9		
Rutland	509	19	Metcalf	Timothy	1		1	1		1		1	1	1			7		
Harvard	219	14	Mical	John			3	1		1	1	1		1			8		
Royalston	235	10	Michard	Eliphaley Jun	2	1		1		1	1		1				7		
Westminster	450	8	Miles	Asa	1		1										2		
Ashburnham	460	4	Miles	Asahel	1		1			1			1				4		
Rutland	509	24	Miles	Barzillas	1		1	1		3	1	1					8		
Petersham	282	7	Miles	Daniel			2		1		1	1	1	1			7		
Rutland	512	1	Miles	Ebenezer	2	1		1		2	1		1				8		
Westminster	450	7	Miles	Isaac	1		1			3		1					6		
Winchendon	227	6	Miles	James				1					1	1			3		
Petersham	282	3	Miles	Joab	2			1		2	1		1				7		
Grafton	201	7	Miles	John	1		1			1		1					4		
Westminster	449	6	Miles	John				1					1				2		
Westminster	450	9	Miles	Jonas	3		1	1		2			2				9		
Westminster	450	5	Miles	Margrett		1						1	1				3		
Westminster	446	30	Miles	Noah		1		1					1				3		
Gardner	450	7	Miles	Oliver	1		1	1		1		1					5		
Westminster	449	12	Miles	Polly							1						1		
Fitchburg	427	20	Miles	Richard		1					1	1					3		
Western	256	13	Miles	Solomon	1	1		1		3			1				7		
Westminster	450	3	Miles	Stephen		1		1		1			1				4		
Fitchburg	427	18	Miles	Thomas	1	1		1			2		1				6		
Shrewsbury	370	9	Miles	Thomas			1	1				2		1			5		
Westminster	449	8	Miles	Thomas			1			3		1					5		
Oxford	158	15	Millen	Abner		1		1				1		1			4		
Westminster	449	3	Miller	Asa	1		1			1		1					4		
Northborough	366	9	Miller	Caleb	1					1	1	1					5		
Upton	385	7	Miller	Elizabeth Wd							1			1			2		
Westminster	449	2	Miller	Ephraim				1				2		1			4		
Westminster	449	5	Miller	Ezra	3			1					1				5		
Westborough	196	96	Miller	Isaac		1		1					2	1			5		
Westminster	450	16	Miller	Isaac	1	1	1		1	2	2	1		2			11		
Worcester	183	10	Miller	Jacob	1		1			3		1					6		
Grafton	206	4	Miller	James	2	1	1				1	1					6		
Westborough	191	28	Miller	James				1				1	1				3		
Westminster	450	15	Miller	John 2d			1				1						2		
Westminster	450	14	Miller	Joseph	1	1	1	1	1	1	1	1		1			9		
Westborough	192	46	Miller	Joshua	1	2	1	1		2		2					9		
Mendon	383	4	Miller	Lewis			1										1	1st Parish	
Westborough	191	20	Miller	Moses			1			2			1				4		
Worcester	186	28	Miller	Moses		1	1		2	1				2			7		
Westborough	194	68	Miller	Nehemiah	1			1	1	2			1				6		
Uxbridge	467	6	Miller	Philip W			1					1					2		
Western	256	9	Miller	Polly	1	2				1			1				5		
Westminster	450	4	Miller	Samuel	1	1	2		1	2	1	1	1				10		
Westborough	192	40	Miller	Willard			1					1	1				3		
Westminster	446	31	Millin	Joshua		1		1		1	1	2		1			7		
Western	256	7	Mills	Abijah	1		1	1		3			2				8		
Garry	275	5	Mills	Brigham	1		1	1		1		1		1			6		
Leominster	437	22	Mills	Collins		1						1					2		
Sutton	161	5	Mills	Edmund Revd	2			1		2	1	1					7		
Lunenberg	427	8	Mills	James				1				1		1			3		
Western	256	6	Mills	John	1		1			2			1				5		
Barre	412	22	Mills	Richard Lt.	1		1	1			1	1					5		
Worcester	183	13	Mills	Thomas		1						1		1			4		
Charlton	334	6	Miner	Ezra		2	1		2					2			8		
Grafton	200	4	Minor	Samuel				1					1				2		
Westminster	450	2	Minot	Jonathan	4		1		1	3		1					10		
Holden	511	19	Mirick	Elisha				1				1	1				3		
Holden	511	20	Mirick	Tilly	1		1					1	1				4		
Lancaster	351	10	Mitchel	Abner											5		5		
Uxbridge	467	10	Mitchel	Hannah			1			2		1		1			5		

TOWN	PG#	LN#	LAST NAME	FIRST NAME	M under 10	M 10-16	M 16-26	M 26-45	M 45+	F under 10	F 10-16	F 16-26	F 26-45	F 45+	TOTAL ALL OTHER	TOTAL SLAVES	TOTALS	DISTRICT/TOWNSHIP	NOTES
Uxbridge	467	7	Mitchel	John			1						1	1			3		
Lunenberg	427	3	Mitchell	Andrew		2		1	1					1			5		
Shrewsbury	370	13	Mixer	Asa		1	1		1	2				1			6		
Southborough	206	19	Mixer	Bayman	1		1	1		3		1					7		
Worcester	183	3	Mixer	Daniel		2	1		2		2						7		
New Braintree	310	18	Mixter	Samll		1	1		1		2	1	1				7		
Winchendon	227	5	Moar	Levi		1	1	1			1	1					5		
Lunenberg	427	12	Moffett	Hannah							1		1				2		
Lunenberg	427	4	Moffett	Joseph		1			1			1	1				4		
Charlton	331	27	Moffit	Elihu	1		1					1					3		
Oxford	158	17	Moffit	Elihu	2		1		1			1					5		
Oxford	158	16	Moffit	Isaac				1	1		1		1				3		
Northbridge	473	7	Moffit	Jeremiah		2	1		2			1					6		
Oxford	158	18	Moffit	Lemuel	1		1		1			1					4		
Barre	412	28	Moolet	John	2		1		2			1					6		
Southborough	202	10	Moor	Abigail									1				1		
Brookfield	270	13	Moor	Daniel		1	1		1	2			1				6	Third Parish	
Templeton	242	3	Moor	Ebenz		1	1		1			1	1				5		
Southborough	206	21	Moor	Elisha			1		1		1						3		
Gardner	450	9	Moor	Ezra	1		1	1		1	1	1					6		
Brookfield	262	2	Moor	Holland		1											1	Second Parish	
Brookfield	262	3	Moor	Isaac	1	1		1		2		1	1				7	Second Parish	
Western	256	10	Moor	Isaac	1	1	3		1	1	2	1	1				11		
Boylston	371	15	Moor	Jacob				1	2			1					4		
Southborough	206	20	Moor	Joel			1		1	1		1	1				5		
Boylston	374	8	Moor	Molly	1		1		2			1					6		
Brookfield	262	4	Moor	Nathan	2		1	1		4	1	2	1				12	Second Parish	
Brookfield	262	1	Moor	Thomas				1					1				2	Second Parish	
Templeton	236	18	Moor	Uriah	1		1		2			1					5		
Western	256	12	Moor	William	1		1				1						3		
Brookfield	259	23	Moor	Elizebeth						1			1				2	First Parish	
Bolton	215	18	Moore	Abraham		2		1		1							4		
Sterling	351	15	Moore	Alvin	1		1		1	1	1	1					6		
Princeton	517	6	Moore	Boaz		1		1			1	1					4		
Bolton	210	15	Moore	Caleb	1		2	1		1	2				1		8		
Sterling	351	17	Moore	Calvin		1		1			1	1					4		
Worcester	183	5	Moore	Calvin			1						1				2		
Oxford	158	14	Moore	Collins	2		2		1	3		1					9		
Sterling	351	21	Moore	David	1		1		2			2					6		
Worcester	183	15	Moore	David			1	1		2		1					5		
Berlin	214	34	Moore	Desire			1						1				2		
Bolton	215	7	Moore	Ebenezer	2		1		1	1							5		
Douglas	481	11	Moore	Elijah	1	1	1		1	1			1				6		
Athol	285	10	Moore	Eliphalet				1					1				2		
Bolton	210	16	Moore	Henry	1		1	1		1							4		
Boylston	374	6	Moore	Hugh	2	2	2		1	1	2	3	2				15		
Berlin	212	20	Moore	Isaac	2		1	1		1	2	1	2				10		
Sterling	351	16	Moore	Israel		1	2		1				1	1			6		
Bolton	210	18	Moore	James			1				1						2		
Worcester	183	16	Moore	Jesse	1		1		2			2					6		
Lancaster	351	9	Moore	John				1				1					2		
Worcester	183	12	Moore	John		1	1			1		1	1				5		
Holden	511	22	Moore	Jonathan	1	1	1		1	1	1						6		
Sterling	351	18	Moore	Jonathan	1	2		2	1		1	1	2				10		
Athol	285	1	Moore	Joshua			1		1		1		1				4		
Bolton	210	17	Moore	Josiah				1			1	1					3		
Bolton	213	11	Moore	Levi	1	1				1	1						5		
Boylston	374	7	Moore	Levi		1	1		1			1	1				5		
Garry	275	4	Moore	Luther	3		1					1					5		
Worcester	183	6	Moore	Luther	1	1		1				1					4		
Oxford	158	21	Moore	Margaret Wd									1				1		
Oxford	158	13	Moore	Marvin	1	1	2		1	1		1	1				8		
Princeton	517	4	Moore	Molley		2					2	1					5		
Worcester	186	23	Moore	Nathl				1			1		1				3		
Garry	275	3	Moore	Peter				1			1	1					3		
Bolton	213	7	Moore	Phineas	1	1		1	1		2		2				8		
Paxton	504	13	Moore	Phins			1	1			1	1	1				5		
Paxton	504	14	Moore	Pliny		1	1		1		1						4		
Garry	275	2	Moore	Saml	2		2		1			1					6		
Worcester	186	26	Moore	Saml		1		1			1	1					4		
Worcester	186	33	Moore	Sewell	2	1		1		3		1					8		
Brookfield	259	17	Moore	Thomas Jun	1	1			1	1		2		1			7	Second Parish	
Berlin	214	39	Moore	Tille				1									1		
Princeton	517	5	Moore	Uriah	1	2		1		2	2	1	1				10		
Worcester	186	21	Moore	Willard		1			1	1							3		
Bolton	216	7	Moore	William	1	2		1		4		1					9		
Worcester	183	11	Moore	William		1	1	1		3	1		1				9		
Leicester	491	8	Moore	Zephl L.		2	4	1			2	1			1		11		
Worcester	186	19	Moore	Zerviah							1		1				2		
Barre	412	32	Moos	Ashbil	1		1		4			1					7		
Leicester	491	7	Moover	Samuel	1	1		1				1					4		
Westminster	450	11	Mordock	William	1		1		1	2	1	1		1			8		
Charlton	334	17	More	Jonathan				1					1				2		
Charlton	333	5	More	Marshal	1		1		3			1					6		
Grafton	204	2	Mores	Prince											4		4		
Charlton	333	7	Morey	Ephraim	1	2	2		1	1		2					10		
Charlton	334	24	Morey	Thomas	3		1		1	1	1	1					7		
Spencer	491	4	Morgan	Andrew	3	1		1		2	1	1	1				11		
Spencer	491	12	Morgan	Nicholas	1		1				1						3		
Spencer	491	5	Morgan	Robt			1	1		1		1					4		

| | | | HEADS OF HOUSEHOLD | | FREE WHITE MALES | | | | | FREE WHITE FEMALES | | | | | | | | | |
TOWN	PG#	LN#	LAST NAME	FIRST NAME	under 10	10 to 16	16 to 26	26 to 45	45 and over	under 10	10 to 16	16 to 26	26 to 45	45 and over	TOTAL ALL OTHER	TOTAL SLAVES	TOTALS	DISTRICT/ TOWNSHIP	NOTES
Dudley	343	29	Moris	Edward		2	2	1					1				6		
Charlton	334	11	Moris	Elijah G.	2			1		3			1				7		
Dudley	343	28	Moris	John				1						1			2		
Sturbridge	334	5	Moris	Jonathan				1				3		1			5		
Sturbridge	334	13	Moris	Jonathan Jr	2	2	1	1		2	1	1	1				11		
Sturbridge	334	14	Moris	Walter				1		1		1					3		
Charlton	334	12	Moris	Wm			1			1		1					3		
Dudley	343	34	Moris	Zebulon	1	1	1	2		1		1	1	1			9		
Westminster	449	7	Morman	Abel				1						1			2		
Westminster	449	11	Morman	Ezra	1			1		2	1		1				6		
Westminster	450	6	Morman	Samuel	1		2	2			1	4		2			12		
Sterling	351	11	Morris	William	1	2		1		3			1	1			9		
Paxton	504	12	Morse	Aaron		1					2	1	1				6		
Douglas	481	13	Morse	Abel	2		1	1		3	1		1				9		
Paxton	504	11	Morse	Abner		1			1					1			3		
Westborough	195	79	Morse	Abner W.	1		1	1					1				4		
Sturbridge	333	12	Morse	Alphans			1						1				2		
Sturbridge	334	6	Morse	Asa	3	1			1	3	2						10		
Sturbridge	334	7	Morse	Asa Junr	1			1		2		1	1				6		
Sutton	161	20	Morse	Benja			1			1	1		1	1			5		
Spencer	491	7	Morse	Caleb	1	1	1		1	1	1	1		1			8		
Sturbridge	334	11	Morse	Calvin	1		1						1				3		
Brookfield	259	21	Morse	Daniel		2	1	1					1	1			6	First Parish	
Sturbridge	333	16	Morse	Daniel	1		1	1				2	1	1			7		
Sturbridge	333	14	Morse	David		2		1		2	1		1				7		
Dudley	343	31	Morse	David 2d	2		1					1					4		
Boylston	374	3	Morse	Ebenezer		2		1					1		1		5		
Paxton	504	10	Morse	Elijah	2	1		1		2	1		1				8		
Rutland	509	20	Morse	Elisha	2			1		1	1		1				6		
Sutton	161	16	Morse	Ezekiel	2			1		1	1		2				7		
Uxbridge	467	14	Morse	Gideon		1		1					1				3		
Leicester	491	6	Morse	Hannah		1						1		1			3		
Northbridge	473	5	Morse	Henry	2	1		1		1	1		1				7		
Rutland	509	22	Morse	Isaac	2			1		2			1				6		
Southborough	200	8	Morse	Isaac			1		1		1		1				5		
Douglas	481	14	Morse	Jacob		1	1		1	2	1		1				7		
Northbridge	473	4	Morse	James				1		1		1		1			4		
Sturbridge	333	20	Morse	Jason	2	1		1	1	2			1	1			10		
Boylston	371	13	Morse	Jeremiah	2		1	1		1	2	1	1				9		
Sturbridge	333	17	Morse	Jeremiah		1	1	1				2		1			6		
Dudley	343	32	Morse	Jesse	1		1			2		1					5		
Uxbridge	467	11	Morse	Jesse	2		1	1					1	1			6		
Uxbridge	467	12	Morse	Jesse Jun			2	1		1	1	1		1			7		
Boylston	374	4	Morse	Joseph	2	3		1		1		1	1	1			10		
Holden	511	21	Morse	Joseph	4	2	1	1		2	1		1				12		
Leicester	491	5	Morse	Joseph	2	1		1		1	1	1	1				8		
Uxbridge	467	15	Morse	Joseph	1	1		1		4	2		1				10		
Worcester	186	29	Morse	Joseph			1		1	1				2			5		
Oxford	158	11	Morse	Joshua	1		1	1		2	2		1				8		
Douglas	481	16	Morse	Levi	2	1		1		1	1	1	1				8		
Boylston	374	5	Morse	Mary				1				2		1			4		
Sturbridge	334	10	Morse	Monasser	1	1	1				1	1					5		
Sutton	161	19	Morse	Moody & Fry	1	1		1	2	2	1	2		1			11		
Douglas	481	15	Morse	Obadiah	3	1	1	1		2			1				9		
Sturbridge	333	18	Morse	Oliver	2	1	1	1		2	1	1	1				10		
Sturbridge	333	19	Morse	Oliver 2d	2		1	1			1		1				6		
Charlton	334	13	Morse	Ruggles		1		1			1	1					4		
Sturbridge	333	15	Morse	Saml	1	2	1		1	1	2			1			9		
Northborough	366	8	Morse	Samuel		2		1			1			1			5		
Westborough	192	38	Morse	Seth		1	1	1		1				1			5		
Sutton	161	17	Morse	Simeon	3	1		1	1	1		2	1				10		
Uxbridge	467	13	Morse	Solomon	1		1						1				3		
Westborough	192	41	Morse	Thomas	2	1		1	2	1		1	2	1			11		
Charlton	334	1	Morse	Timothy		1	1		1	3	2	2	1	1			12		
Rutland	509	23	Morse	Timothy	2	1	1		1			1	1	1			8		
Worcester	183	8	Morse	Willard		1	1	1		3			1				7		
Berlin	213	7	Morse	William		1	1						1				3		
Upton	385	8	Morss	John		1		1						1			3		
Hubbardston	417	7	Morss	Katharine Wid.		1	1						1	1			4		
Hubbardston	417	8	Morss	Samuel	5	2	1	2		1			1	1			13		
Hubbardston	417	9	Morss	Wm.	2		1	1		2			1				7		
Athol	288	15	Morton	Daniel			1	1		2			1	1			6		
Athol	288	14	Morton	Joel			1						1				2		
Athol	285	5	Morton	Joshua	1	1		1		1		1	1				7		
Athol	285	3	Morton	Phinehas	1			1					1				3		
Athol	285	4	Morton	Reuben	1	1	1		1	2		2		1			9		
Athol	285	2	Morton	Samuel		1	3			1	3	2		1			12		
Charlton	334	7	Mory	Nathl	2			1					1	1			5		
Oxford	154	11	Moshier	Samuel	1			1		1			1	1			5		
Leominster	437	19	Mosman	Mark			1			2		1					4		
Athol	285	7	Moss	Samiel	1			1					1				3		
Petersham	282	2	Moss	Samuel				1						1			2		
Barre	412	29	Moss	Timothy		1			1		1		1	1			5		
Athol	285	8	Moss	Willm				1				2	1	1			5		
Athol	285	6	Moss	Willm Jur	2			1		1			1	1			6		
Spencer	494	13	Moulton	Daniel	1			1		2			1				5		
Worcester	183	14	Mower	Ebenz	5			1	1				2				9		
Worcester	183	7	Mower	Ephraim	3								1	1	2		8		
Worcester	186	20	Mower	John			1	1						1	1		4		

225

TOWN	PG#	LN#	LAST NAME	FIRST NAME	M<10	M10-16	M16-26	M26-45	M45+	F<10	F10-16	F16-26	F26-45	F45+	TOTAL ALL OTHER	TOTAL SLAVES	TOTALS	DISTRICT/ TOWNSHIP	NOTES
Worcester	183	4	Mower	Thomas		1	2		1	1	1	1		1			8		
Douglas	481	18	Mowry	David		1	1		1	1	1	1					6		
Mendon	383	8	Mowry	Henry	2			1		2			2				7		1st Parish
Mendon	383	7	Mowry	Isreal		1	1	1			1	2					7		1st Parish
Uxbridge	467	9	Mowry	Richard		1	1		1		2	3		1			9		
Uxbridge	467	8	Mowry	Wanton	1			1		4			1				7		
Westminster	450	17	Mudge	Joseph				1			1		1				3		
Oakham	319	16	Mullet	Abm	2			1		2			1				6		
Athol	285	9	Mundall	Paul		1	1	1			1	1		1			6		
Westminster	449	9	Munjoy	Daniel				1	1				1				3		
Shrewsbury	370	11	Munroe	Aaron	1		1	1		1			1				5		
Northborough	366	5	Munroe	Abraham	1	1	1	3	1		1	4		1			13		
Shrewsbury	370	12	Munroe	Abraham				1		2			1				4		
Spencer	494	14	Munroe	Amos	2	1	1	1						1			6		
Ashburnham	460	10	Munroe	Ebenzr	2	1	2	1		1			1	1			9		
Spencer	494	15	Munroe	Jona			1	1		1	2			1			6		
Charlton	333	10	Munroe	Lemuel	3	1		1		1			1				7		
Shrewsbury	370	10	Munroe	Nathaniel		3	3	1		1				1			9		
Northborough	366	11	Munroe	Oliver	1	1		1				1	1				5		
Western	252	1	Munroe	Samuel				1		1			1	1			4		
Sutton	161	6	Munroe	Stephen				1		4	1		1				7		
Bolton	212	15	Munroe	William	1		1					1					3		
Sterling	351	19	Munson	Samuel			2				1	1					4		
Hubbardston	417	5	Murdock	Abial	1	1	1		1			1		1			6		
Uxbridge	467	16	Murdock	Elisha	2	1		1	1	1			1	1	1		9		
Winchendon	227	3	Murdock	Ephrm	1		2	1		1		1					6		
Winchendon	227	1	Murdock	James				1						1			2		
Winchendon	227	2	Murdock	James Jr	1			1		3			1				6		
Hubbardston	417	4	Murdock	Joshua				1			1	1					3		
Hubbardston	417	3	Murdock	Robert Lt.		1	1	1					1				4		
Rutland	512	4	Murray	Alexander		1		1		2		2		1			7		
Rutland	512	5	Murray	Samuel	2	1						1					4		
Brookfield	270	14	Murry	John	2		1	1		2	1		1				8		Third Parish
Spencer	491	2	Muzzey	Edmund		1		1			1		1				4		
Spencer	491	10	Muzzey	Isaac			1			2		1					4		
Spencer	491	1	Muzzey	John	1	1	2	1					3	1			9		
Spencer	491	6	Muzzey	Jonas	3	1	2	1		3		1	2				13		
Ward	178	49	Muzzy	Jonathan	4		2	1		1		1					9		
Ward	178	48	Muzzy	Nathan	4		1	1		1		1	1	2			11		
Hubbardston	417	6	Muzzy	Wm. Lt				1				1	1				3		
Holden	512	10	Nash	Samuel	3	1		1		2			2	1			10		
Grafton	198	15	Nayson	Oliver	2		1			3	1		1				8		
Worcester	185	3	Nazro	John		1		1		1	2	1		1			7		
Paxton	504	20	Needham	Daniel		1		1		2		1	1				6		
Charlton	333	14	Needham	Thomas				1			1		1				3		
Charlton	333	15	Needham	Wm	2			1		4			1				8		
Petersham	282	12	Negus	Joel	2			1		3	1	2	1				10		
Petersham	282	14	Negus	John				1		4			1				6		
Petersham	282	13	Negus	Paul	1		1	1					1				4		
Worcester	185	6	Nelson	Abijah			1	2		1		1					5		
Milford	394	8	Nelson	Anna Wd										1			1		
Milford	394	10	Nelson	Ezra		1						1					2		
Milford	394	6	Nelson	Garshom Capt				1			1			1			3		
Upton	385	12	Nelson	Isaac		1	1	1		1	1	1	1				8		
Worcester	185	5	Nelson	John	1	1	1	1		2			1				7		
Sutton	164	17	Nelson	Joseph	2			1				1					4		
Upton	385	9	Nelson	Joseph	2		1	1		2		1	1	1			9		
Milford	394	9	Nelson	Josiah		1	1	1				1	1	1			6		
Sterling	352	5	Nelson	Michael	4	2	1	1		1		1	1				10		
Upton	385	13	Nelson	Paul Capt.	1		2	1		1	2	1	1				9		
Milford	394	7	Nelson	Saml Majr	2	1	1	1			1		2				8		
Milford	394	5	Nelson	Seth Deac			2	1					1	1			5		
Milford	394	4	Nelson	Simeon Lt.	1	1		1				1					5		
Upton	385	10	Nelson	Thomas			1	2				1	1				5		
Upton	385	11	Nelson	Thomas Jr	1		2	1		1	3		1				9		
Western	256	14	Nevens	Sarah	1	1				1	1		1				5		
Grafton	199	15	New	James	1					3	1		1	1			7		
Hardwick	300	19	Newcomb	Annis		1		1		3	1			1			7		
Holden	512	7	Newel	Aaron			1		1	1	1	3	1				8		
New Braintree	310	19	Newel	Jonas		1	1	1		1			1	1			6		
Holden	512	11	Newel	Rufus		1		1				1					3		
Sturbridge	331	1	Newel	Stephen	4	1		1		1	1	1	1	1			11		
Sturbridge	334	23	Newel	Timothy		1	1	1	1		2	3		1			10		
Charlton	333	20	Newell	Asa	3			1		1			1				6		
Brookfield	259	28	Newell	Joseph	2	1	2		1	2			1	1			10		First Parish
Charlton	333	13	Newell	Joseph			1	1		1				1			5		
Lunenberg	427	15	Newell	Thomas				1			1			2			4		
Leominster	437	28	Newhall	Daniel	2		1	1					1				5		
Sterling	352	3	Newhall	David	2	1	1	1		2	1	1	1				10		
Athol	285	12	Newhall	Hiram Esq	1	1	1		1	1		2	1		1		9		
Athol	285	11	Newhall	Jonah			1					1					2		
Paxton	504	19	Newhall	Joseph		1						1					3		
Athol	285	13	Newhall	Joshua	2		1			2			1				6		
Leicester	491	12	Newhall	Mary	1							2		1			4		
Leominster	437	26	Newhall	Michael				1						3			4		
Sterling	352	4	Newhall	Moses	1	1	2			2	1	1					9		
Leicester	491	9	Newhall	Phinehas		1	1	1		2			1				6		
Spencer	492	3	Newhall	Reuben	2	1	1	1		2	2	2	1				12		
Leicester	491	10	Newhall	Thomas									1				2		
Leicester	491	11	Newhall	Thomas 2d			2			1		1					4		

TOWN	PG#	LN#	LAST NAME	FIRST NAME	FREE WHITE MALES under 10	10 to 16	16 to 26	26 to 45	45 and over	FREE WHITE FEMALES under 10	10 to 16	16 to 26	26 to 45	45 and over	TOTAL ALL OTHER	TOTAL SLAVES	TOTALS	DISTRICT/ TOWNSHIP	NOTES
Lancaster	351	11	Newman	Gawen B.	2		1	1		1			2				7		
Lancaster	351	12	Newman	Joseph			1			1			1				3		
Garry	275	12	Newo	Iva			1	1			1		1				4		
Western	252	4	Newport	Dan											8		8		
Southborough	200	11	Newton	Aaron	1	1		1		2			1				6		
Southborough	203	11	Newton	Abel			1			1		1					3		
Southborough	204	12	Newton	Alven		1								1			2		
Southborough	203	7	Newton	Amos				1					1	1			3		
Rutland	512	11	Newton	Asa				1					1				2		
Westborough	194	61	Newton	Barnabas		2	1	1			2	2	1	1			10		
Southborough	200	10	Newton	Barzellel	2		1	1		1			1				6		
Worcester	185	1	Newton	Benjamin	1		1	1		2	1		1				7		
Southborough	201	14	Newton	Caleb	4			1				1	1				7		
Princeton	517	8	Newton	Charles			1	1				2		1			5		
Southborough	203	17	Newton	David				1						1			2		
Spencer	492	2	Newton	David		1	1	1		1	1			1			6		
Westborough	199	142	Newton	Ebenezer	1			1		1	1		1				5		
Hubbardston	419	15	Newton	Ebenr		1	2			1		2	1	1			8		
Southborough	206	22	Newton	Ebenz Jun	1			1				1	1				4		
Garry	275	11	Newton	Edmond	4	1	1	1		1			1				9		
Spencer	491	13	Newton	Edmund		2		1	1		1	1	1	2			9		
Southborough	201	16	Newton	Elijah				1				1		1			3		
Hubbardston	417	17	Newton	Emial		1		1		1			2				5		
Spencer	492	1	Newton	Ezekiel Jun	2	2		1		3	1	1	2				12		
Southborough	201	15	Newton	Ezra				1				1	1				3		
Bolton	209	4	Newton	Haven				1				2					3		
Rutland	512	12	Newton	Hezekiah	1	3		1		1				1			7		
Garry	275	10	Newton	Isaaac	1	1		1				1		1			5		
Southborough	205	15	Newton	Isaac	1	1	1	1		2		1	1				8		
Westborough	199	145	Newton	Jeremiah	2	1		1		1			2				7		
Hubbardston	417	16	Newton	Joel	1			1		2			1				5		
Brookfield	259	27	Newton	John	3			1		1	2		1				8	First Parish	
Southborough	203	9	Newton	John				1						1			2		
Sutton	164	18	Newton	John	1			1		2			1				5		
Paxton	504	18	Newton	Jonah	1			1					1	1			4		
Southborough	205	33	Newton	Josiah	2	1		2				2	1				8		
Sturbridge	331	4	Newton	Jotham		2	1	1		1				1			6		
Hardwick	300	14	Newton	Lemll		1		1		3	3	1	2				11		
Sutton	164	19	Newton	Levi	1		1			1		1					4		
Worcester	185	2	Newton	Lucy	1		1			1							3		
Northborough	361	1	Newton	Martin	1			1		3			1	1			7		
Southborough	201	1	Newton	Mary	1	1		1		1	1		1	1			7		
Paxton	504	17	Newton	Merriam		1								1			2		
Northborough	361	2	Newton	Moses		1		1		2	1		1				6		
Northborough	366	15	Newton	Nahum	2			1		1			1	1			6		
Paxton	504	21	Newton	Nahum	2	1		1		2		1		1			8		
Royalston	238	8	Newton	Nathan B.	2	2	2	1		3	1		1				12		
Southborough	206	8	Newton	Obediah	3			1					2	1			7		
Rutland	512	10	Newton	Peter				1						2			3		
Templeton	235	16	Newton	Peter	5			1				1	1				8		
Southborough	204	1	Newton	Reuben	2	2		1				1	1				7		
Southborough	200	14	Newton	Rhoda									1	1			2		
Rutland	512	13	Newton	Samuel			1						1				2		
Southborough	205	11	Newton	Seth		1	2	1				1		1			6		
Hardwick	300	16	Newton	Silas	2	1		1		3			1				8		
Paxton	504	16	Newton	Silas	1	3	1	1		1		3					10		
Sterling	352	2	Newton	Silas	2	1	1	1				1	1				7		
Westborough	199	141	Newton	Silas	3			1		2	2		1				9		
Southborough	200	12	Newton	Solomon						1	1			1			3		
Southborough	203	8	Newton	Stephen		1				1		1					3		
Hardwick	300	15	Newton	Timothy	1			1		1			2	1			7		
Hubbardston	419	16	Newton	Timothy		3	1	1				1		1			7		
Upton	385	15	Newton	Tyrus				1			1	3	1				6		
Princeton	517	7	Newton	Uriah		1	1	1		1		1	1				6		
Southborough	200	13	Newton	Willard	1		1	1		2			1				6		
Berlin	216	19	Newton	William	1		1					2					4		
Mendon	383	12	Nicholas	Mary Wd			1			1	1			2			5	1st Parish	
Brookfield	259	25	Nicholls	Asa		1	3	2				1	1				8	First Parish	
Brookfield	259	26	Nicholls	Isaac	1	2	1			1	1	2		1			9	First Parish	
Dudley	343	37	Nichols	Aaron		1		1			1		1				4		
Charlton	333	17	Nichols	Alexander		1		1		3			1				6		
Dudley	343	40	Nichols	Amasa			1	1				1	1				4		
Westminster	449	13	Nichols	Benjamin		1	1	1		2	1		1				7		
Sturbridge	331	3	Nichols	Caleb	2	1		1			1	2	1				8		
Oxford	155	8	Nichols	Daniel	1			1		1			1	1			5		
Gardner	450	15	Nichols	David	3			1		2	1		1				8		
Oxford	155	7	Nichols	David		1	2			3			1				7		
Royalston	240	7	Nichols	David	1			1		2	1		1				6		
Dudley	343	38	Nichols	David		1			1			2	1				5		
Dudley	343	39	Nichols	David Jun		2		1				1	1				5		
New Braintree	311	3	Nichols	Davidson		1	1	1				2	1				6		
Sturbridge	331	5	Nichols	Edmund		1	1	1		2		2		1			8		
Sturbridge	331	2	Nichols	Edmund Jr	2			1				1					4		
Royalston	239	1	Nichols	Elijah			1						1				2		
Westborough	189	10	Nichols	Fortunalus	1		1	1		2			1	1			7		
Royalston	242	13	Nichols	Henry		1		1				1		1			4		
Royalston	242	14	Nichols	Henry Junr			1						1				2		
Gardner	450	13	Nichols	Isaac	1		1					1					3		
Leominster	437	24	Nichols	Israel				1				1		1			3		
Leominster	437	23	Nichols	Israel Jun		1	1					1		1			4		

TOWN	PG#	LN#	LAST NAME	FIRST NAME	FREE WHITE MALES					FREE WHITE FEMALES					TOTAL ALL OTHER	TOTAL SLAVES	TOTALS	DISTRICT/ TOWNSHIP	NOTES
					under 10	10 to 16	16 to 26	26 to 45	45 and over	under 10	10 to 16	16 to 26	26 to 45	45 and over					
Sturbridge	331	6	Nichols	Jabez			1						1				2		
Charlton	333	18	Nichols	Jeremiah	3			1		1			1				6		
Charlton	333	16	Nichols	John	1	1		1		3			1				7		
Oxford	155	5	Nichols	John		1		1						1			3		
Royalston	241	12	Nichols	John		1		1		1		1	1	1			6		
Southborough	204	14	Nichols	John	2		1			3			1				7		
Oxford	155	6	Nichols	John Junr	1			1		1			1	1			5		
Holden	512	8	Nichols	Jonathan	1	2		1		3	1		1				9		
Hubbardston	419	17	Nichols	Jonathan	1	1		1			4		1				8		
Royalston	235	4	Nichols	Jonathan	2			1		2	1		1				7		
Charlton	333	19	Nichols	Jonathn		1		1		1			1				4		
Lancaster	351	13	Nichols	Joseph	1			1				1		1			4		
Westborough	189	9	Nichols	Joseph	1	1	1	1		1	1	2	1				9		
Gardner	450	14	Nichols	Kendal	2		1					1					4		
Leominster	437	27	Nichols	Levi	1	1		1		3		2	1				9		
Royalston	240	13	Nichols	Moses		1		1		2	2						6		
Gardner	450	12	Nichols	Rebeckah									1				1		
Royalston	238	14	Nichols	Robert	1			1		1		1					4		
Barre	412	37	Nichols	Robert Capt.		2		1	1	1	1		1				7		
Royalston	238	9	Nichols	Solomon	5		1					1					7		
Holden	512	9	Nichols	Thaddeus	2	1		1		1		2	1				8		
Worcester	185	4	Nichols	Thomas	1			2				1	2	1			7		
Leominster	437	25	Nichols	William		1	3	1			1	1					7		
Royalston	238	12	Nichols	William				1			1		1				3		
Royalston	238	13	Nichols	William Junr	1		1			2		1					5		
Charlton	333	12	Nichols	Wm	2	1		1		1			1				6		
Gardner	450	16	Nichols	Zachariah	3		1					1					5		
Garry	275	13	Nickerson	Nathan	2	1		1		3		1					8		
Hubbardston	417	15	Nightingale	Wm Capt.	3	1		1		3		1					9		
Barre	411	7	Nipton					1					1		2		4		First name blank
Southborough	204	13	Nixon	Thomas				1					2				3		
Upton	385	14	Nobles	Eunice Wd	1	1						1					3		
Templeton	231	18	Norcrop	Daniel		1	2		1		1	1		1			7		
Royalston	240	17	Norcross	Isaac				1					1				2		
Princeton	517	9	Norcross	Jacob				1	1	2	2	1					7		
Northborough	366	14	Norcross	Moses		2						1					3		
New Braintree	310	21	Norton	Burrows	4		1			2			1				8		
New Braintree	310	20	Norton	Elijah	3		1	1		1	1						7		
Royalston	235	1	Newton	John	1			1		3		1					6		
Brookfield	267	20	Nowell	John	3			1				1					5	Third Parish	
Winchendon	227	13	Noyce	Isaac	3			1		1		1	1				7		
Winchendon	227	12	Noyce	James	1	1	2			1	1	1	1				8		
Winchendon	227	11	Noyce	Samll			1		1		1		1				4		
Bolton	216	16	Nurse	Abigail									1				1		
Winchendon	227	9	Nurse	Asa		2	2		1		1		1				7		
Bolton	216	15	Nurse	Barnard	1		1	1		1		1					5		
Bolton	210	6	Nurse	David		1	1	1			2	3	1				9		
Harvard	215	1	Nurse	David	2		1	1			1	1					6		
Royalston	232	12	Nurse	Joel	2		3				1	1					7		
Bolton	210	19	Nurse	Jonathan	1	2	2	1			2		1				9		
Westborough	196	90	Nurse	Lydia								2					2		
Bolton	209	6	Nurse	Oliver	2			1		2	1		1				7		
Harvard	222	5	Nurse	Samuel		1		1		1	1	1					4		
Berlin	214	12	Nurse	Sibella						1		1	1				3		
Bolton	209	8	Nurse	Stephen	2	1		1		1			1				6		
Barre	411	5	Nurss	Caleb															No enumeration listed
Barre	411	4	Nurss	Daniel	3	2		1	1	1	1		1				9		
Barre	411	1	Nurss	Francis									1				1		
Barre	412	38	Nurss	Jane Wid	1			1		1			1	1	1		6		
Barre	411	2	Nurss	Jonathan Capt				1			1	1		1			4		
Barre	411	3	Nurss	Timothy	1	1	1		1	1	1	1					7		
Bolton	213	1	Nutlar	Isaac				1			1		1				3		
Winchendon	227	10	Nutting	Benja			1			2		1					4		
Barre	412	35	Nye	Benj Jr	1		1					1					3		
Barre	412	34	Nye	Benj Maj.				1		1			1				3		
Hardwick	300	21	Nye	Caleb				1				1	1				3		
Oakham	319	17	Nye	Crocker		1		2		1	1	1					6		
Brookfield	262	6	Nye	Ebenezer	2		1			2			1				6	Second Parish	
New Braintree	311	1	Nye	Jno	1	1		1	1	3	2	3	1				13		
Barre	412	36	Nye	John			1						1				2		
Hardwick	300	20	Nye	John R	1		1					1					3		
Hardwick	300	18	Nye	Joseph	1	2	2		1	2			1	1			10		
New Braintree	311	2	Nye	Philip	1	2	1	1			3	1	1	1			11		
Hardwick	300	17	Nye	Prince	2	2		1	2	1	1	1	1	1			12		
Barre	411	6	Nye	Simeon		1		2			2	1	2				8		
Oakham	319	18	Nye	Timothy				1		4	1						6		
Bolton	212	19	Oak	Abraham	1			1		1		1					4		
Bolton	212	18	Oak	James			1	1		1		1					4		
Bolton	212	17	Oak	Tabitha							2		1				3		
Athol	286	1	Oakes	Daniel		1					1	1					3		
Charlton	333	22	Oaks	Abijah		1	1		1	1			1	1			6		
Charlton	333	21	Oaks	Amos	2		1			2			1				6		
Holden	512	12	Obens	John				1									1		
Lunenberg	427	16	Oldham	Thomas				1					1				2		
Brookfield	267	27	Olds	Dorothy									1				1	Third Parish	
Brookfield	262	7	Olds	Ezekiel	2		1			2			1				6	Second Parish	
Brookfield	267	21	Olds	Jonathan			1										1	Third Parish	
Brookfield	267	25	Olds	Joseph	3	2		1		2	2		1				11	Third Parish	
Brookfield	267	29	Olds	Luke			1			1	1						3	Third Parish	
Brookfield	267	28	Olds	Nathan			2		2			2					6	Third Parish	
Brookfield	267	22	Olds	Reuben	2			1		2	2		1				8	Third Parish	
Brookfield	267	23	Olds	Silas	2	1	1		1	1	1	1	1				10	Third Parish	
Brookfield	267	26	Olds	Simion	1		2		1		1	1		1			7	Third Parish	

228

			HEADS OF HOUSEHOLD		FREE WHITE MALES					FREE WHITE FEMALES									
TOWN	PG#	LN#	LAST NAME	FIRST NAME	under 10	10 to 16	16 to 26	26 to 45	45 and over	under 10	10 to 16	16 to 26	26 to 45	45 and over	TOTAL ALL OTHER	TOTAL SLAVES	TOTALS	DISTRICT/ TOWNSHIP	NOTES
Brookfield	267	24	Olds	William		1		1				3		1			6	Third Parish	
Athol	285	14	Oliver	Aaron		2		2		1	1	1	1	1			9		
Barre	411	8	Oliver	Ana Wid	1	1						1		1			4		
Barre	411	12	Oliver	Crumwell											3		3		
Rutland	512	14	Oliver	David			1		1			1		1			4		
Athol	285	17	Oliver	George		2						2					4		
Athol	285	16	Oliver	John				1				1		1			3		
Athol	285	15	Oliver	John Jur	3		1			1			1				6		
Barre	411	11	Oliver	Simon											9		9		
Barre	411	13	Oliver	Thoms											4		4		
Southborough	203	3	Onthank	James	1		1		1	2	1		1				7		
Southborough	204	18	Onthank	Joseph		1		1		1	1		1				5		
Southborough	203	2	Onthank	William		1		1				1		1			4		
Southborough	203	18	Onthank	William Jun	3	2		1		2	2	1	1				12		
Templeton	236	17	Orcott	Jona	1	1	1	1		1	2	1	1	1			10		
Brookfield	259	29	Orcut	Sylvanus	2		1			3		1					7	First Parish	
Fitchburg	428	1	Ordway	Amos	1	1	1	1	1		2	1		1			9		
Spencer	492	5	Ormes	James		1				1	2	2		2			9		
Spencer	492	4	Ormes	James Jun			1			1			1				3		
Sterling	352	7	Osborn	Daniel	1		1						1				3		
Fitchburg	428	2	Osborn	Ephm	4	2					1	1	1				10		
Bolton	212	11	Osborn	Ephraim			1				1		1				3		
Fitchburg	428	4	Osborn	Jacob			1			2	2		1				6		
Fitchburg	428	3	Osborn	John	2			1		1	1		1				6		
Garry	275	14	Osborn	Mary			1							1			2		
Bolton	212	8	Osborn	Thomas		2		2		1	2	2	1	1			11		
Boylston	374	9	Osgood	Abel			1				1	2	1				5		
Boylston	374	10	Osgood	Abel Jun	1		1			2		1					5		
Barre	411	9	Osgood	Asahel		1	1	1		1			1				5		
Lancaster	351	14	Osgood	Ephraim	1		1			1	2		2	1			8		
Princeton	517	10	Osgood	Ephraim		1		1		1	1		1	1			5		
Princeton	517	11	Osgood	Houghton				1				1	1				4		
Lancaster	351	15	Osgood	Joel	4		1		1	1	2	3		4			16		
Lancaster	351	16	Osgood	Joel Jun	3		1						1				5		
Gardner	450	17	Osgood	Jonath Revd		2	1			2			2				7		
Fitchburg	428	5	Osgood	Joseph		3		1					1				5		
Templeton	237	7	Osgood	Joseph	1			1		1		1					4		
Templeton	237	8	Osgood	Joseph Jr	1	2		1		2		1		1			8		
Barre	411	10	Osgood	Manas	1		1		1	1	1	1		1			7		
Sterling	352	6	Osgood	Samuel		1	1	1			1	1		2			7		
Paxton	504	22	Osland	Jona	1	1		1		1	1	3	1				9		
Oakham	320	5	Packard	Caleb	1		1			1	1						4		
Grafton	197	17	Packard	Ephm	3		1		1			1					6		
Oakham	320	4	Packard	Ichabod				1				1	1				3		
Oakham	320	12	Packard	James		1	2			1	1	1					6		
Brookfield	262	16	Packard	Jonathan				1				1	1				3	Second Parish	
Oakham	320	2	Packard	Nehemh	1	1		1		1	1	2	1				8		
Brookfield	262	17	Packard	Samuel	1	1		1				1					4	Second Parish	
Brookfield	267	33	Paddock	Oliver			1				1	1	1				4	Third Parish	
Holden	512	15	Paddock	Reuben				1		1	1	1					4		
Holden	512	16	Paddock	Reuben Jr	1		1			1		1					4		
Lunenberg	430	14	Page	Abel	1	1		1		1	1		1				6		
Lunenberg	430	7	Page	Amos				1			1		1				3		
Fitchburg	428	19	Page	Jonathan		1	1	1			1		1				5		
Hardwick	301	8	Paige	Benm		1	1				1	1	1				5		
Hardwick	301	7	Paige	Charles	1		1			1		1	2				7		
Hardwick	301	14	Paige	David	2	1		1		2	1		1				8		
Hardwick	301	9	Paige	James		2	1				1			2	1		8		
Hardwick	301	4	Paige	Jesse	1	1	1		1	1	1	1		1			8		
Hardwick	301	11	Paige	John	1								1			2	5		
Hardwick	301	13	Paige	Luther		2	1	1				2		1			7		
Hardwick	301	3	Paige	Moses	2		1			2		1					6		
Hardwick	301	6	Paige	Nathl	3	1		1			2			2			9		
Hardwick	301	5	Paige	Paul	1	1		1		4		1	1				10		
Hardwick	301	10	Paige	Timt	1	3			3	1		3	1	1			13		
Athol	286	4	Paine	Barnabas	2	1		1		1			1				6		
Leicester	491	14	Paine	Jabez				1				1	1				3		
Athol	286	3	Paine	Joseph		1		1					1				3		
Uxbridge	470	5	Paine	Licester		1		1				2		1			5		
Sturbridge	331	24	Paine	Mary		1							1	1			3		
Worcester	188	19	Paine	Nathl	2			2			2	2		2		2	11		
Worcester	188	20	Paine	Rufus	2	2	1	1		1			1				8		
Worcester	188	18	Paine	Sarah									1	1			2		
Leicester	494	1	Paine	William		1		1				1	1	1			5		
Worcester	188	21	Paine	William	2	1	2		1	1	1	2	1		1		12		
Upton	385	16	Palmer	Abner		1		1	1			2		1			6		
Sterling	352	13	Palmer	John		1						2	2	1			7		
Dudley	343	45	Palmer	Joseph	1		1			1			1				4		
Sterling	352	18	Palmer	Joseph	1	1		1		3		1	1				8		
Sterling	352	14	Palmer	William			1			3			1				5		
Sutton	168	21	Park	Caleb		2		1		3	1	1	1				9		
Berlin	216	8	Park	James R.		1		1		1	1		2				6		
Sutton	168	23	Park	Joseph	2			1			1		1				5		
Sutton	168	22	Park	Samuel	3		1					1	1				6		
Harvard	221	37	Park	Thomas		1	3	1				1	1	1			8		
Brookfield	262	15	Park	William		1					2			1			4	Second Parish	
Harvard	222	2	Park	William	1			1			2		1				6		
Sutton	168	20	Park	Moses		2	1		1			1	1				6		
Charlton	336	15	Parker	Aaron	1	2		1		4	1		1				10		
Holden	512	18	Parker	Aaron	3		1	1									5		

229

TOWN	PG#	LN#	LAST NAME	FIRST NAME	FREE WHITE MALES					FREE WHITE FEMALES					TOTAL ALL OTHER	TOTAL SLAVES	TOTALS	DISTRICT/ TOWNSHIP	NOTES
					under 10	10 to 16	16 to 26	26 to 45	45 and over	under 10	10 to 16	16 to 26	26 to 45	45 and over					
Oxford	156	2	Parker	Aaron				1			1			1			3		
Northborough	361	3	Parker	Abigail							1		1				2		
Southborough	201	12	Parker	Abigail							1		1				2		
Westborough	199	150	Parker	Abner		1		1				1	1				4		
Hubbardston	419	27	Parker	Amos			3	1		1	1	1					7		
Douglas	481	26	Parker	Archilaus	1	1		1		1	1	2		1			9		
Southborough	201	10	Parker	Benjm	1		2			1		1					5		
Douglas	481	24	Parker	David			1	1		1		2					5		
Leicester	494	5	Parker	David			1			2		1					4		
Princeton	517	14	Parker	Ebenezer		1	1	1		1	2		3				10		
Garry	276	7	Parker	Elisha	2	2		1		1	1	3	1				11		
Lunenberg	427	18	Parker	Elisha		1		1	1				2				5		
Lunenberg	427	19	Parker	Elisha Jun	3		1					1					5		
Westborough	194	60	Parker	Gardner	1		1	1				1					4		
Northborough	361	4	Parker	Jabez M.		1				1		1					3		
Grafton	199	2	Parker	James	2	1		1		1			1	1			7		
Southborough	201	11	Parker	Jereboim			1			1		1					3		
Brookfield	267	31	Parker	Jesse			1			1			1				3	Third Parish	
Westborough	199	149	Parker	Jidediah		3		1					1				5		
Charlton	336	11	Parker	Joel			1					1	2				5		
Westborough	194	69	Parker	Joel			1			2	1						4		
Leicester	494	4	Parker	John		1				1	1						3		
Princeton	517	15	Parker	John	1	1	1		1	2	2	1	1				10		
Worcester	188	29	Parker	John	2			1		2		1		1			7		
Brookfield	262	10	Parker	Jonah	1			1		1		1	1				5	Second Parish	
Douglas	481	28	Parker	Joseph	2	1	1		1	1	1	1		1			9		
Southborough	206	25	Parker	Lois	1					1		1					3		
Westborough	192	37	Parker	Margen							1		1				2		
Garry	275	19	Parker	Moses				1					2				3		
Hubbardston	419	22	Parker	Nahl Rev			1	1		1			1				4		
Princeton	517	12	Parker	Nehemiah	2	2		1		2		1		1			9		
Westborough	192	36	Parker	Otis	2	1		1				1					5		
Princeton	517	13	Parker	Philemon	3	2	1			2	1	1	1				12		
Charlton	336	10	Parker	Saml		1		1				1					4		
Charlton	336	14	Parker	Saml Junr	1		1			3		1					6		
Douglas	481	23	Parker	Samuel		1		1			3		1				6		
Princeton	517	16	Parker	Solomon P.			1			1		1					3		
Leicester	494	3	Parker	Thomas				2			1		1				4		
Oxford	156	3	Parker	Thomas	2	1		1		1				1			6		
Sutton	163	15	Parker	Thomas				1			1	1	1				4		
Holden	512	17	Parker	Timothy		1	2	1	1		1	2					8		
Templeton	235	5	Parker	Timothy		1		1		1		1					4		
Leominster	438	6	Parker	Willard			1					1					2		
Leicester	494	2	Parker	William	1		1	1		3		1					7		
Worcester	185	9	Parker	William				1					1				2		
Worcester	185	10	Parker	William Jr	1	1		1	1	2	1		1				8		
Milford	391	2	Parkhurst	Amasa	1			1		1	1	1					5		
Milford	391	5	Parkhurst	Athiel	1			1		3			1				6		
Milford	391	7	Parkhurst	Elisha			1	1		1	1		1				5		
Fitchburg	428	8	Parkhurst	James	3	1		1					1				6		
Milford	391	8	Parkhurst	Jonas		1	2	1	1	2	1			1			9		
Milford	391	4	Parkhurst	Nathan	1		1	1				1	1				6		
Milford	391	6	Parkhurst	Nathl Capt.		1	3		1	4	2	1		1			13		
Harvard	222	31	Parkhurst	Silas		1			1			2		1			5		
Hubbardston	419	29	Parkis	Daniel Maj		1	2	1			1	2		1			8		
Brookfield	249	1	Parkis	James	1	1	1	1				2					8	First Parish	
Westborough	189	2	Parkman	Brick		1	3		2	3	1	2		2			14		
Brookfield	261	3	Parkman	Ebenz	1			1				1					3	Second Parish	
Milford	394	12	Parkman	Elias Lt.		3		1	1	1			1				7		
Brookfield	267	34	Parks	Bethiah				1				2	1				4	Third Parish	
Worcester	187	10	Parks	Christopher		1	1	1		1		1	2				7		
Winchendon	227	26	Parks	Eleazer		1		1				1					3		
Brookfield	262	9	Parks	Hannah	1						1		1				3	Second Parish	
Winchendon	227	24	Parks	Jacob	2		1			1		1		1			6		
Spencer	492	13	Parks	Jonathan	2		1	1		1	1	1					7		
Northbridge	473	10	Parks	Nathan				1					2				3		
Northbridge	473	11	Parks	Nathan Jun	2		1			1			1				5		
Winchendon	227	25	Parks	Phino	2		1	1		1			1				6		
Hardwick	301	1	Parkust	Jonathan				1					1				2		
Gardner	447	5	Parley	Allen	1	1	1		1		1	1					7		
Barre	411	20	Parling	Daniel	3	1		1		2		1					8		
Rutland	512	19	Parmenter	Abel		1		1		1	2		1	1			7		
Petersham	281	5	Parmenter	Abiel	2		1			3	1						9		
Oakham	320	11	Parmenter	Daniel	1	1	1	1			1	1	1	1			9		
Winchendon	227	28	Parmenter	Ephrm	1		2		1	1	1	1		1			8		
Ashburnham	460	14	Parmenter	Jacob	4	1	1				1		1				9		
Holden	509	1	Parmenter	John	1		1			2		1					5		
Petersham	281	4	Parmenter	John	1	1		1			3		1				7		
Rutland	512	18	Parmenter	Jonas	1		1	1		3		1					7		
Princeton	517	19	Parmenter	Luther		1		1		1		2					5		
Princeton	517	20	Parmenter	Reuben				1					1				2		
Oakham	320	8	Parmenter	Rufus	1		1	1		2			1				6		
Holden	512	23	Parmenter	Soloman		2		1		1		1					6		
Oakham	320	1	Parmenter	Wm		1		1		3	1		1				7		
Leominster	438	5	Parmeter	David		1	1			1		1	1	1			6		
Leominster	437	35	Parmeter	Silas		1	1			1		2		1			6		
Northborough	361	6	Parminter	Asa	2			1		1	1		1				6		
Northborough	361	5	Parminter	Joel		1		1		3	1		1				7		
Bolton	212	3	Parmiter	Asa			1	1					1				3		

TOWN	PG#	LN#	HEADS OF HOUSEHOLD		FREE WHITE MALES					FREE WHITE FEMALES					TOTAL ALL OTHER	TOTAL SLAVES	TOTALS	DISTRICT/ TOWNSHIP	NOTES
			LAST NAME	FIRST NAME	under 10	10 to 16	16 to 26	26 to 45	45 and over	under 10	10 to 16	16 to 26	26 to 45	45 and over					
Leicester	494	6	Parsons	Solomon	2			1	1		3		1				8		
Boylston	371	4	Partridge	Asel	2		1										3		
Gardner	447	3	Partridge	Jabez	1		1		1	2	2		1				8		
Winchendon	227	17	Partridge	Jairus	1			1		3			1				6		
Boylston	374	12	Partridge	James	1	1		1	1				2				6		
Holden	512	14	Partridge	Jesse		1	1		1	1			1	1			6		
Petersham	281	1	Partridge	John				1				1		1			3		
Hubbardston	419	18	Partridge	Liberty		1				1							2		
Sturbridge	331	22	Partridge	Malicha				1					1				2		
Boylston	374	13	Partridge	Ozias	1	1		1		1			1				5		
Gardner	447	9	Partridge	Reuben		1		1					1				3		
Paxton	503	6	Partridge	Samuel	2		1			2	1	1	1				8		
Barre	411	22	Partridge	John		1		1		1		1		1			5		
Barre	411	17	Partridge	John 2d	1	1		1				1	1				5		
Barre	411	21	Partridge	Thaddeus	1		1	1		1		2	1	1			8		
Templeton	234	6	Patch	Benja	1		1			3		1					6		
Templeton	239	8	Patch	Benja	1		1			3		1					6		
Worcester	185	11	Patch	Henry	1		2	1	1	1	3	1	1				11		
Templeton	234	1	Patch	Jonathan	1	1	1	1			1	1	1	1			8		
Templeton	239	9	Patch	Jonathan	1		1	1		1		1	1				7		
Worcester	185	17	Patch	Joseph	4	1		1		1	1	1	1				10		
Worcester	185	15	Patch	Nathan		1		1		1		1		1			5		
Brookfield	262	11	Patrick	Jacob											3		3	Second Parish	
Charlton	336	16	Patridge	Benjm		1					1						2		
Oakham	320	6	Patridge	Edward	1	1	1		1		1		1				6		
Oakham	320	9	Patridge	Silas		1		1		1			1				4		
Sturbridge	331	23	Patten	Thomas	1		2	1		1	1		1				7		
Harvard	219	22	Patterson	Abigail						1	1		1				3		
Petersham	281	10	Patterson	Andrew		1		1	1		1		1				5		
Northborough	361	7	Patterson	James				1		1	1						3		
Lunenberg	430	4	Patterson	John	2		1	1		2	3		2				11		
Harvard	217	38	Patterson	Lemue	1	2	1	1		1			1	1			8		
Barre	411	14	Pattrick	John Lt	1		1		1	2	1		1				7		
Brookfield	259	31	Paul	Edward		1	1		1			1	1	1			6	First Parish	
Winchendon	227	23	Payson	Elliot			1			1		2					4		
Fitchburg	428	15	Payson	John			2		1		1	1		1			6		
Gardner	447	7	Payson	Joseph			1		1			2					4		
Leominster	437	38	Payson	Sarah						3		1					4		
Lunenberg	430	12	Peabody	John	3	1		1		2			1				8		
Lunenberg	430	10	Peabody	Phinehas	2		1						1				4		
Upton	385	17	Pearce	Joshua	1			1		1			1				5		
Upton	385	22	Pease	Aaron	1		1	1		1	1		1				6		
Upton	385	21	Pease	Josiah			1			1					1		3		
Brookfield	259	32	Pease	Francis			1						1				2	First Parish	
Brookfield	259	33	Peasoe	William	3			1		1	1		1				7	First Parish	
Petersham	281	8	Pebody	Phinihas	3	1		1						1			6		
Royalston	233	13	Peck	Daniel			2		1	2	3		1				9		
Hubbardston	419	30	Peck	Ezra	1	1		1		1		2					6		
Worcester	185	7	Peck	Robert M.	2	1	1	2				2					8		
Royalston	234	10	Peck	Solomon	2		2	1		2	3		1				11		
Garry	275	17	Peckham	Mordica	2	1		1		1		1	1				7		
Petersham	281	12	Peekham	Elis	1			1		2			1				5		
Petersham	281	3	Peekham	John		1	1		1	1		1		1			6		
Petersham	282	16	Peekham	Robert		1				1			1				3		
Petersham	282	17	Peekham	Willm	1		1			1		1		1			6		
Berlin	214	19	Peiffer	Reubin Rev	2	1		1		1	2	1	1				9		
Paxton	503	9	Peirce	Aaron		1				3	1	1					6		
Sutton	168	18	Peirce	Aaron	1		1			3			1				6		
Grafton	199	7	Peirce	Abijah	1		1			1			1				4		
Worcester	188	23	Peirce	Abijah	1	1		1		1	1	1					6		
Ashburnham	460	15	Peirce	Amos	1		1			2		1					5		
Sutton	168	24	Peirce	Amos	1		1			1	3		1				7		
Sutton	168	8	Peirce	Amos Junr		1	1					1					3		
Ashburnham	460	12	Peirce	Asa			1						1				2		
Westborough	194	54	Peirce	Benjm		1				1		1					3		
Worcester	188	25	Peirce	Byfield	1		1			1	1	1					5		
Holden	512	13	Peirce	David Junr	2		1	1		1	2		1	1			9		
Sutton	168	16	Peirce	Ebenz				1						1			2		
Royalston	241	30	Peirce	Gad		1	1							1			4		
Royalston	240	1	Peirce	Gad Junr	2		1			2			1				7		
Westminster	449	16	Peirce	Jarvis			1			2	1		1				5		
Sutton	168	25	Peirce	Jesse	4		1			1	1		1				8		
Rutland	512	17	Peirce	Joel	3		1			1			1				6		
Gardner	447	10	Peirce	John	2	1		1		2			1				7		
Royalston	240	9	Peirce	John	2	1		1		2	1		1				8		
Spencer	492	10	Peirce	John	1		1			1			1				5		
Sutton	168	17	Peirce	John	1	1			1	1	1	1	1				7		
Westminster	452	1	Peirce	John		1	1	1		1			1	1			6		
Worcester	188	24	Peirce	John				1		1	1	1		1			5		
Sutton	163	21	Peirce	John Junr		1	1					1		1			4		
Royalston	241	31	Peirce	Jona	1		1	1					1				4		
Southborough	201	4	Peirce	Jonathan	1		2			3		2	1				10		
Boylston	374	14	Peirce	Josiah	2			1			1	1	1				6		
Worcester	188	22	Peirce	Josiah				1				1		1			3		
Boylston	371	3	Peirce	Levi	2	1		1					1				6		
Boylston	374	11	Peirce	Oliver		2		1		4		1		1			9		
Hardwick	301	16	Peirce	Seth		1		1		1			1				4		
Worcester	188	27	Peirce	Seth			1			2		1					4		
Spencer	492	6	Peirce	Shadrach				1					1				2		
Spencer	492	9	Peirce	Shadrach Jun		1	1			1		1	1				4		
Royalston	237	3	Peirce	William	2		1	1		4				1			9		
Sutton	168	7	Pek	John			1	1				1		1			4		

231

TOWN	PG#	LN#	LAST NAME	FIRST NAME	FREE WHITE MALES					FREE WHITE FEMALES					TOTAL ALL OTHER	TOTAL SLAVES	TOTALS	DISTRICT/ TOWNSHIP	NOTES
					under 10	10 to 16	16 to 26	26 to 45	45 and over	under 10	10 to 16	16 to 26	26 to 45	45 and over					
Brookfield	262	8	Pellel	Jonathan	2	1	1		1	3	3			1			12	Second Parish	
Brookfield	267	35	Pendleton	Ephrm				1				1					2	Third Parish	
Gardner	447	4	Pennamon	Ezra	1			1		3	1	1	1	1			9		
Westminster	449	15	Pennemon	William		2	3	1				1	1				8		
Mendon	383	14	Penniman	Andrew		1	1					2					4	1st Parish	
Mendon	383	16	Penniman	Baruch	2		1	2		2			1				8	1st Parish	
Hardwick	301	18	Penniman	Chiron			2			2		1					5		
New Braintree	311	8	Penniman	Henry		1	4		2	1	2	1	1				12		
Mendon	383	17	Penniman	John				1						1			2	1st Parish	
Paxton	503	2	Penniman	Joseph			1	1		1		1					5		
Mendon	383	19	Penniman	Josiah		1		1						1			3	1st Parish	
Mendon	383	18	Penniman	Josiah Jr	2		1	1		3		1					8	1st Parish	
Mendon	383	13	Penniman	Peter Esq				1					1				2	1st Parish	
Milford	394	14	Penniman	Saml				1					1				2		
Milford	394	13	Penniman	Saml Jr	1	1	1	1		1		1	1				7		
Paxton	503	4	Penniman	Sarrell	1			1		1		1					4		
Paxton	503	3	Penniman	Simeon				1				1					2		
New Braintree	311	6	Pepper	Ezra	1	1	2		1	1			1				7		
New Braintree	311	7	Pepper	Jacob	4	1		1	1	1	1	1	1				11		
Upton	385	19	Perham	Aaron	1		1			2		1					5		
Upton	385	18	Perham	Benjamin		1		1					1				3		
Upton	385	20	Perham	Benjm Jr			1	1		1	2		1				6		
Spencer	492	14	Perham	Jacob		2		1		1			1				5		
Grafton	206	7	Perham	Lemuel		1		1		1			1				4		
Upton	386	1	Perham	Sarah Wd	3						2		1				6		
Leominster	438	1	Perkins	Benja	2	2		1		1		3		1			10		
Lunenberg	427	20	Perkins	Frances				1					1				2		
Hardwick	301	12	Perkins	James	1			2				1	1				5		
Winchendon	227	20	Perley	Dudley		1	1	1	1			1		1			6		
Winchendon	227	21	Perley	John	1			1		1	1	1					5		
Fitchburg	425	2	Perly	Eliph	1		2		1	1	2	2	1				10		
Harvard	222	4	Perminan	Joseph				1		1	2		1				5		
Lunenberg	430	6	Perrin	Charles				1				1					2		
Sterling	352	20	Perris	Joseph	1			1					1				4		
Princeton	517	18	Perry	Aaron			1	1			1		1				4		
Holden	512	20	Perry	Abner	1	1		1		1		1					5		
Fitchburg	428	10	Perry	Asa	1	1	3	1			2	2	1				12		
Barre	411	16	Perry	Calvin			2	1		1			1				5		
Sturbridge	332	3	Perry	Calvin		1		1		2							4		
Dudley	343	44	Perry	Eliaphas	1	1		1	1	1	1	1	1				8		
Milford	391	9	Perry	Elihu	1			1		2	1		1				6		
Garry	276	8	Perry	Ezra			1			1		1					3		
Leominster	438	2	Perry	Ichabod	2	1		1		1	1	3	1				10		
Milford	394	15	Perry	James	1	1	1			1	1						5		
Holden	512	19	Perry	John				1					1				2		
Charlton	336	7	Perry	Jonathan	1	1		1		2	1		1				7		
Sturbridge	331	20	Perry	Jonathan	1	1		1	1			1	1				6		
Fitchburg	425	5	Perry	Joseph	1	2		1		1	1	1					8		
Worcester	185	14	Perry	Josiah			1	1		1	1		1				4		
Worcester	185	13	Perry	Moses	5		1	1			1		1				9		
Hardwick	301	15	Perry	Nathan			3	1					1				5		
Dudley	343	46	Perry	Rowland	1		1			1		1					4		
Barre	411	19	Perry	Seth		1		1			1	1	1				5		
Holden	512	21	Perry	Simeon	2		1			2		1					6		
Royalston	239	10	Perry	Thomas				1						1			2		
Grafton	199	16	Perry	Timothy	1	1		1		2	1		1				7		
Sterling	352	12	Person	Joseph	1	2		1	1	1	1		1	2			10		
Northbridge	473	8	Persons	George		1	1			5		1					8		
Uxbridge	470	2	Persons	James	1			1				1					3		
Uxbridge	470	3	Persons	John	4	2	1	1			1	1					10		
Hubbardston	419	19	Persons	Kendall				1		1	1						3		
Uxbridge	470	1	Persons	William				1			1	1					3		
Westborough	195	77	Peters	Andrew				1		1	1		1				4		
Mendon	383	15	Peters	Elinor Mrs.						1		1					2	1st Parish	
Westborough	195	78	Peters	Lovet	1	1	1	1		1	1						7		
Douglas	481	25	Pettefaw	Hosea	2			2		1	2		1				7		
Winchendon	227	31	Petts	John	2			1			1		1				5		
Winchendon	227	22	Peyson	James				1		1	1		1	1			4		
Leominster	438	3	Phelps	Abel	2	1		1					1				5		
Lancaster	354	7	Phelps	Abijah		1		1	1	1			2				6		
Sterling	352	16	Phelps	Abisha		1	2	1		1		2		1			8		
Lancaster	354	11	Phelps	Anson				1			1	1					3		
Sutton	168	19	Phelps	Azor	2		1	1		3		1	1				9		
Lancaster	351	17	Phelps	Calvin	1			1		1		1					4		
Sutton	163	17	Phelps	Ebenz	1		1			2		1					5		
Lancaster	354	3	Phelps	Elisha	1	1	1	1		1		1	1				7		
Lancaster	354	12	Phelps	Gardner	1			1		2	1		1				6		
Sutton	163	16	Phelps	Henry	3		1			1	1	1					8		
Lancaster	354	10	Phelps	Jacob			1			3	1	1					6		
Leominster	437	34	Phelps	John		1		1		1		2					4		
Fitchburg	425	7	Phelps	Joseph		1	4		2			1					8		
Hubbardston	419	26	Phelps	Moses Dr.	1	3	1		1			1		1			8		
Lancaster	354	13	Phelps	Robert			1	1		1	1	1					3		
Lancaster	351	19	Phelps	Ruth										2			2		
Fitchburg	425	1	Phelps	Samuel	1	1		1		2			2	1			8		
Spencer	492	11	Phelps	Simeon	1		1			1		1					4		
Lancaster	354	2	Phelps	Sylvester	2	1	1	1		1	1		1				10		
Mendon	392	8	Philips	Israel	2			1					1				4	2d Parish	
Westminster	449	17	Philips	Jonathan	1	2	1		1	2		1	1				9		

TOWN	PG#	LN#	HEADS OF HOUSEHOLD		FREE WHITE MALES					FREE WHITE FEMALES					TOTAL ALL OTHER	TOTAL SLAVES	TOTALS	DISTRICT/ TOWNSHIP	NOTES
			LAST NAME	FIRST NAME	under 10	10 to 16	16 to 26	26 to 45	45 and over	under 10	10 to 16	16 to 26	26 to 45	45 and over					
Athol	286	5	Philips	Nathl		1	1		1	1	2			1			7		
Garry	275	15	Philips	Saml				1						1			2		
Garry	275	16	Philips	Seth	2	1					1		1				6		
Fitchburg	428	12	Phillips	Blany			1		1			1	3	1			7		
Rutland	512	21	Phillips	Daniel	1		1			1		1					4		
Grafton	200	2	Phillips	Ebenz					1	4	1			1			7		
Charlton	336	9	Phillips	Ebenzr H.	1			1		1	1	1		1			6		
Charlton	336	13	Phillips	Edward	1			1		2		2	1				7		
Spencer	489	17	Phillips	John	1			1		1		1					4		
Sturbridge	331	8	Phillips	John	4		2	1					1	1			9		
Rutland	512	20	Phillips	Joshua	1		1		1	1	2	2		1			9		
Lancaster	354	8	Phillips	Micah	2		1	1		2	1	1		1			9		
Worcester	188	31	Phillips	Rufus	1		1			1	1	1					5		
Southborough	205	12	Phillips	Sarah	1								1	1			3		
Fitchburg	428	11	Phillips	Seth	2	2	1		1		1	1		1			9		
Ward	178	53	Phillips	Simon	1	1		1		1	1		2	1			8		
Hardwick	301	2	Phinney	Zenas	2	1		1		2	2			1			9		
Oxford	156	6	Phipps	Abigail Wd									1				1		
Leicester	491	13	Phipps	Moses	3	1	1			1	1	1					8		
Brookfield	259	30	Phips	Samuel		1	1	1	1		1	1		2			8	First Parish	
Mendon	392	13	Pickering	Asa	2	1	1	1		1			1				7	2d Parish	
Mendon	392	14	Pickering	Benjm	1	1			1		2			2			7	2d Parish	
Mendon	392	12	Pickering	Benjm Jr		1	1	1		1		1	1				6	2d Parish	
Mendon	392	9	Pickering	David	1			1		2			1				5	2d Parish	
Milford	394	11	Pickering	Ichabod			3		1	1	1			1			7		
Mendon	392	10	Pickering	Jona				1						1			2	2d Parish	
Mendon	392	11	Pickering	Willm	4	1		1		1			3	1			11	2d Parish	
Lunenberg	430	1	Pierce	Abraham	2		1			1		1	1	1			7		
Fitchburg	428	14	Pierce	Amos	4	2		1	1				1				9		
Lunenberg	430	8	Pierce	Benja		1	1			3		1					6		
Bolton	216	10	Pierce	Calvin	2	1		1		4	1		1				10		
Uxbridge	470	6	Pierce	Cuff											9		9		
Paxton	503	1	Pierce	David	1			1	1			1					4		
Lunenberg	430	3	Pierce	Ephraim			1	1					1	1			4		
Harvard	220	30	Pierce	John		1		1		1			1	1			5		
Petersham	281	13	Pierce	Jona	1	1		1		3			1				7		
Leominster	437	30	Pierce	Jonathan	1			1		2			1				5		
Lunenberg	430	5	Pierce	Jonathan		1	2	1						2			6		
Athol	286	2	Pierce	Joseph	1			1		2	1	1	1				7		
Fitchburg	428	6	Pierce	Joshua			1	1					1	2			5		
Leominster	437	33	Pierce	Joshua	1		1	2	1		1	1	1	1			9		
Hubbardston	419	20	Pierce	Moses H.	3			1		1			1				6		
Harvard	222	19	Pierce	Nathaniel				1						1			2		
Lunenberg	427	17	Pierce	Oliver		1		1		1		1					4		
Leominster	437	40	Pierce	Reuben		1	1	1				1		1			5		
Leominster	438	4	Pierce	Thomas	2			1		2			1				6		
Hubbardston	419	28	Pierce	Thoms				1					1	1			3		
Uxbridge	470	7	Pierce	Timothy	1		1						1				3		
Petersham	281	11	Pierce	Willm			1			2		1					4		
Garry	276	1	Pike	David	3	1		1		1	1		1				8		
Sterling	352	11	Pike	David			1						1				2		
Leominster	437	29	Pike	Ephraim	2	2		1		2		2	2				11		
Sturbridge	331	21	Pike	Ephram	2			1		1			2	1			7		
Paxton	503	5	Pike	Francis		1						1					3		
Charlton	336	2	Pike	George	1		1			2	3	2	1		1		11		
Sturbridge	332	4	Pike	James	1				1			1	1	1			5		
Paxton	503	7	Pike	John	2	2		1		1		1	1				8		
Brookfield	261	1	Pike	Jonas N				2		4	1		1				8	Second Parish	
Barre	411	15	Pike	Mary Wid										1			1		
Garry	276	5	Pike	Michal	2			1		2			1				6		
Charlton	336	1	Pike	Saml	1	1	1		1					1			5		
Petersham	281	6	Pike	Saml			1				1		1				3		
Charlton	336	3	Pike	Saml Junr	1		1	1					1		1		5		
Hardwick	301	17	Pike	Samll			1							1			2		
Westborough	192	43	Pike	Sarah		1				1			1				3		
Templeton	236	10	Pike	William			1										1		
Royalston	236	11	Pine	William	2		2						1				5		
Garry	276	2	Piper	Abel		1	2	1				3	1	2			10		
Garry	276	3	Piper	Amos	1			1		1			1				4		
Garry	276	4	Piper	Asa	3		1						1				5		
Royalston	237	2	Piper	Isaac			1			2		1					4		
Oakham	320	10	Piper	James	1	1		1		1	1		1				6		
Royalston	240	16	Piper	Josiah				1			1			1			3		
Royalston	242	11	Piper	Josiah Junr	1			1					1				3		
Lunenberg	430	2	Pirkins	Jonathan	3	1	1						1				6		
Fitchburg	425	6	Pirkins	Petmadus		1		1						1			3		
Sturbridge	331	7	Pitman	Benj			1										1		
Ward	178	52	Pitts	Ebenz					1			1	1	1			4		
Uxbridge	470	4	Pitts	Job	2			1	1			1	2	1			8		
Spencer	492	12	Pixley	Lot	1	1							1				3		
Leominster	437	31	Platts	Isaac	2		1					1	1	1			7		
Sturbridge	331	15	Plimton	Elias	1		1		1	3		1	1				8		
Sturbridge	331	12	Plimton	Elijah		1		1				1		1			4		
Sturbridge	331	13	Plimton	Elisha	1			1		1	1		1				5		
Sturbridge	331	10	Plimton	Fredric	3		1		1			2	2		1		10		
Sturbridge	331	9	Plimton	Gershom				1	1	2		1	1				6		
Sturbridge	332	1	Plimton	Gershom Jr	5		1	1		1			1	1			10		
Sturbridge	331	17	Plimton	James		1	2	1	1				2	1			8		
Sturbridge	331	18	Plimton	Joel	1			1		1			1				4		
Sturbridge	331	16	Plimton	John	4		2		1				1	1			9		

TOWN	PG#	LN#	LAST NAME	FIRST NAME	FREE WHITE MALES under 10	10 to 16	16 to 26	26 to 45	45 and over	FREE WHITE FEMALES under 10	10 to 16	16 to 26	26 to 45	45 and over	TOTAL ALL OTHER	TOTAL SLAVES	TOTALS	DISTRICT/ TOWNSHIP	NOTES
Sturbridge	331	11	Plimton	Oliver	1	1	1	2		3	3	2	1				14		
Sturbridge	331	14	Plimton	Raynolds	2	1		1		1			1				6		
Milford	394	16	Plumb	Samuel	1		1			1		1					4		
Barre	411	18	Plumer	Alphus		1		1		1		1					4		
Brookfield	262	14	Poland	Joseph	1	2			1	3		1	1				9	Second Parish	
Winchendon	227	27	Poland	William		3		1		4	2	1	1				12		
Berlin	214	21	Pollard	Aaron			1	2		1							4		
Berlin	214	32	Pollard	Abijah		2		1			1	1		1			6		
Lancaster	354	5	Pollard	Abner	1		1			4	1	1					8		
Bolton	211	13	Pollard	Armory		1	1	1		1			1	1			6		
Harvard	220	6	Pollard	David		1		1					1	1			4		
New Braintree	311	5	Pollard	Jno	2		1			3	1		1				8		
Hubbardston	419	25	Pollard	Joel	2		2		1	3	1	3	1				13		
Lancaster	354	4	Pollard	John			1	1			1		1				4		
Harvard	217	32	Pollard	Jonathan			1			1			1				3		
Harvard	222	35	Pollard	Luke		1		1		1	1	1					5		
Berlin	214	30	Pollard	Oliver		1	1	1		1			1				5		
Berlin	214	31	Pollard	Oliver Junr	1		1			2		1					5		
Bolton	209	2	Pollard	Thaddeus	1	1	1	1		1		2					7		
Harvard	217	30	Pollard	Thaddeus Junr	4	1		1		1	2	1	1				11		
Harvard	220	24	Pollard	Thaddeus Junr	1	1	2		1		2		1				8		
Berlin	216	2	Pollard	Thomas		2		1				1		1			5		
Ashburnham	460	11	Pollard	William		1		1				1		1			4		
Berlin	212	16	Pollard	William		1		1				1					3		
Harvard	218	20	Polley	Elnathan	1	1		1		3			1				7		
Fitchburg	428	16	Polley	Joseph	3	2	2	1		2		1	1	1			13		
Ashburnham	460	13	Polley	Peter	2	2		1		2	1		1				9		
Milford	391	1	Pond	Abner	1		1	1		1		1	1				6		
Northborough	361	8	Pond	Adam	2	1		1	1	1	1		1	1			9		
Petersham	282	15	Pond	Asa			3	1			2	1		2			9		
Paxton	503	8	Pond	Darius	2		1				1	1					5		
Hubbardston	419	23	Pond	Ezra Ens				1						1			2		
Hubbardston	419	24	Pond	Joseph	2	1		1		1	1		1				7		
Hubbardston	419	21	Pond	Levi	3	1		1		1	2		1				9		
Fitchburg	425	4	Pool	James				2					1	2			5		
Milford	391	3	Pool	William	1		1					1					3		
Winchendon	227	19	Poor	Daniel	1		1			1		1					4		
Winchendon	227	18	Poor	David	1	1		1		1		2	1	1			8		
Lancaster	351	20	Poor	Eunice										1			1		
New Braintree	311	4	Pope	Asa		1		1		1	1		1				5		
Sterling	349	1	Pope	Ebenezer	1		3			1	1	2	2	1			11		
Spencer	492	15	Pope	Joseph		1	2	1		1	1		1				7		
Sterling	352	19	Pope	Joseph			1	1					1				3		
Sterling	352	8	Porter	John	1	1		1		2	1	1					7		
Brookfield	267	30	Porter	Nathan				1			1	1	1				4	Third Parish	
Brookfield	267	32	Porter	Nathan Junr	1		1			1		1					4	Third Parish	
Worcester	185	16	Porter	Saml	2		1	1		3		1	1				9		
Douglas	481	27	Potter	Asa		2		1		1		1					5		
Leominster	437	39	Potter	Jacob	2		1			2	2		1				8		
Holden	512	22	Potter	James	3	1		1		2	1		1				9		
Brookfield	261	2	Potter	John	3	2		1		2		1		2			11	Second Parish	
Worcester	188	26	Potter	John		1	1							1			3		
Brookfield	262	13	Potter	Luke	1		1	1		3		1	1				8	Second Parish	
Brookfield	262	12	Potter	Silas	1	1	1		1	1		1		1			7	Second Parish	
Uxbridge	467	17	Pottle	Simon	2			1		2		1					6		
Garry	275	18	Powers	Edwd	1		1		1	2	1	1					7		
Berlin	216	15	Powers	Henry	1		1		1	2	1		1				7		
Petersham	281	7	Powers	Jacob	3		1	1		3	1	1	1	1			12		
Oakham	320	13	Powers	John	2	1		1		1	1	1	1				8		
Princeton	517	17	Powers	John	1		1			3		1					6		
Garry	276	6	Powers	Jonas	1		1			1		2					5		
Leominster	437	36	Powers	Levi	2		1			3	2		1				9		
Gardner	447	2	Pratt	Aaron	1		1			1							3		
Petersham	281	9	Pratt	Abigail						1		1					2		
Boylston	374	15	Pratt	Abijah				2			1		1				4		
Boylston	371	1	Pratt	Abijah Jun	2		1			2	1		1				7		
Oxford	156	4	Pratt	Benja		1		1		2		1					5		
Sutton	168	27	Pratt	Benja	2		1			2			1	2			8		
Fitchburg	428	13	Pratt	David	2	1	2		1			3		2			11		
Lunenberg	430	13	Pratt	Eleazer				1		1		1		2			4		
Oxford	155	16	Pratt	Elias		1	1			1		1		1			5		
Oxford	155	17	Pratt	Elijah	1	1	1	1				1	1				6		
Dudley	343	43	Pratt	Elisha	1		1			1		1					4		
Gardner	447	1	Pratt	Ephraim				1						1			2		
Sturbridge	332	2	Pratt	Freeman		1				1		1					3		
Sturbridge	331	19	Pratt	Henry	2	1	1		1	1	2	1	1				10		
Spencer	489	1	Pratt	Isaac		1		1				3			1		6		
Royalston	235	16	Pratt	Jabez	1		1						1				3		
Lancaster	354	9	Pratt	James	1		1			3			1				6		
Charlton	333	26	Pratt	Jesse				1	1	1	2		1				6		
Sterling	352	15	Pratt	Joel	1	1	1	1		1	1	1					7		
Fitchburg	425	3	Pratt	John	2		1			3	1		1	1			9		
Grafton	204	12	Pratt	John	3		1			1	1		1				7		
Oxford	156	1	Pratt	John	1		2	1	1	1	2			2			10		
Charlton	333	24	Pratt	Jonathan				1		2	1		1				5		
Oxford	155	19	Pratt	Jonathan				1		1	2	1					5		
Charlton	333	27	Pratt	Joseph		1	2		1	2	2		1				9		
Gardner	447	6	Pratt	Joseph	1	1		1		1		1		1			6		
Oxford	155	12	Pratt	Joseph		1	1	1				1	1	1			6		
Westborough	191	19	Pratt	Martin				1						1			2		

TOWN	PG#	LN#	LAST NAME	FIRST NAME	under 10	10 to 16	16 to 26	26 to 45	45 and over	under 10	10 to 16	16 to 26	26 to 45	45 and over	TOTAL ALL OTHER	TOTAL SLAVES	TOTALS	DISTRICT/ TOWNSHIP	NOTES
			HEADS OF HOUSEHOLD		FREE WHITE MALES					FREE WHITE FEMALES									
Oxford	155	18	Pratt	Nahum			1			2			1				4		
Charlton	333	23	Pratt	Nathan			1					1					2		
Spencer	492	16	Pratt	Othniel	2	1		1				2	1	1			8		
Royalston	241	17	Pratt	William	1		2						1	1			5		
Oxford	156	5	Pray	Ebenz	2		1			1	1			1			6		
Oxford	155	13	Pray	Jonathan	2		1			2			1	1			7		
Southborough	205	9	Prentice	John	1			1						4			6		
Ward	178	54	Prentice	John		1	2	1				1		1			6		
Mendon	392	15	Prentice	Saml	2		1	1		2	1		1				8	2d Parish	
Lunenberg	430	9	Prentice	Thaddeus		1		1		1	2			1			6		
Sutton	168	13	Prentiss	Calvin	2		1						1				4		
Princeton	517	21	Prentiss	Henry			1						1				2		
Sutton	168	12	Prentiss	James			2	1		1	1	1		1			7		
Lancaster	354	1	Prentiss	John	3	1		1		2		2	1				10		
Winchendon	227	16	Prentiss	Luke	1		1			1			1				4		
Petersham	281	2	Prentiss	Nathan	1		1			3			1				6		
Winchendon	227	14	Prentiss	Samll				1						1			2		
Winchendon	227	15	Prentiss	Samll Jr	2		1			2			1				6		
Sutton	163	13	Prentiss	Samuel				1						1			2		
Sutton	163	14	Prentiss	William	1	1		1		1	2		1				7		
Lancaster	354	6	Prescott	John				1			1	1					3		
Sterling	352	9	Prescott	Jonathan Jun	1	1	1		2		1		2	2			10		
Bolton	213	19	Prescott	Levi	1		4					1					6		
Templeton	234	8	Prescott	Ruthey	1					1		1	2				5		
Oakham	320	3	Presho	Isaac	2		1						1				4		
Oakham	320	7	Presho	James	1	1	1				1	1	1				6		
Athol	286	6	Presson	Pereicles	2		1			1			1				5		
Northbridge	473	9	Preston	Amariah		1	1	1			1	2		1			7		
Douglas	481	29	Preston	Ezekiel		1		1			1		1				4		
Charlton	335	2	Price	George R	1		1			1			1				4		
Harvard	220	17	Priest	Abel	2	2		1					1				6		
Berlin	211	8	Priest	Holman		1		1			1			2			5		
Harvard	218	22	Priest	Jacob	1	1		1				1	1				5		
Harvard	218	30	Priest	Jeremiah	2			1		2	1		1				7		
Berlin	214	22	Priest	John	1			1					1				3		
Harvard	217	20	Priest	John				1				1		1			3		
Leominster	437	32	Priest	Joseph				1					1				2		
Berlin	214	17	Priest	Luthar	1		1	1		1		1					5		
Leominster	437	37	Priest	Lydia						3	1	1	1	1			7		
Princeton	517	23	Priest	Nathan	1			1		1	1	1	1				7		
Harvard	215	9	Priest	Phillimon	3	2	1	1				2	1	2			12		
Oxford	155	15	Prince	David	1		1	1					1				4		
Oxford	155	14	Prince	Jonathan	3			1		2			1				7		
Worcester	188	28	Prince	Libbey											5		5		
Oxford	155	10	Prince	Stephen				1				1		1			3		
Oxford	155	11	Prince	Stephen Junr	1		2						1				4		
Grafton	200	10	Printice	Daniel	3	1	2	1		1	1		1				10		
Southborough	203	22	Printice	Joseph	2			1	1			1					5		
Princeton	517	22	Proctor	John	1			1	1	2			1	1			7		
Lunenberg	430	11	Proctor	Mary			1	1						1			3		
Spencer	489	14	Prouty	Anna		2							1				3		
Spencer	489	8	Prouty	Asa		1	3		1			1	1	1			8		
Spencer	489	6	Prouty	David		1		1					1	1			4		
Spencer	489	4	Prouty	David Jun				1					1				2		
Spencer	489	15	Prouty	Dolly							1		3	1			5		
Spencer	489	9	Prouty	Eli	1	1		1		1	1		1				6		
Boylston	371	2	Prouty	Elijah	1	2	1		1	1			1				7		
Spencer	489	11	Prouty	Elisha	1	1		1		2			1				6		
Spencer	489	3	Prouty	Isaac				1				2	1	1			5		
Spencer	489	5	Prouty	Isaac Junr			2	1		2	1			2			8		
Spencer	489	2	Prouty	James			1			1		1	1		1		5		
Spencer	489	13	Prouty	Jesse				1					1				2		
Spencer	489	7	Prouty	Johnson	3	1	1	1		2	1		1	1			11		
Spencer	489	12	Prouty	Joseph	3	1		1		2			1				8		
Spencer	489	10	Prouty	Joshua	2	1		1		2	1		1				8		
Spencer	492	7	Prouty	Nathan	3	2		1		2	2		1				11		
Winchendon	227	29	Prouty	Seth	3			1					1				5		
Spencer	492	8	Prouty	Thomas	3	1		1					1				6		
Spencer	489	16	Prouty	William			1			1			1				3		
Gardner	450	18	Pruett	Jonathan	2			1					1				4		
Westminster	452	2	Puffer	Jonas	2			1		1	1		1				6		
Westminster	452	3	Puffer	Josiah			1	1	1		1	1		1			6		
Lancaster	351	18	Puffer	Nathan	1			1		2			1				5		
Douglas	481	30	Pulsipher	Lovel				1			1	1	1				4		
Fitchburg	428	9	Putman	Amos			1	1		1	1		1	1			6		
Fitchburg	428	7	Putman	John				1				1		1			3		
Charlton	336	8	Putman	Simeon			1			2			1				4		
Sutton	163	7	Putnam	Aaron	3			1		1			1				6		
Sutton	163	20	Putnam	Abner			1			1			1				3		
Worcester	185	8	Putnam	Amos				1				1	1	1			4		
Rutland	512	22	Putnam	Andrew	1			1					1				3		
Sterling	352	10	Putnam	Andrew	4	1	2	1		1		1	1				11		
Sutton	168	10	Putnam	Archelaus	1			1		2			1				5		
Rutland	512	15	Putnam	Archilaus		1		1				2		1			5		
Sutton	163	11	Putnam	Asa	2		1	1		1	1		1				8		
Sutton	163	9	Putnam	Batho	1		1	1			1	1	1				6		
Sutton	163	12	Putnam	Benajah	1	1		1				1		1			5		
Rutland	512	16	Putnam	Benjamin	1	1	1			2			1	1			8		
Oxford	155	9	Putnam	Calvin			1						1				2		
Fitchburg	428	17	Putnam	Daniel		1	2	1				1		1			6		
Sutton	168	15	Putnam	Daniel	1			1		1			1				4		

235

TOWN	PG#	LN#	LAST NAME	FIRST NAME	FREE WHITE MALES under 10	10 to 16	16 to 26	26 to 45	45 and over	FREE WHITE FEMALES under 10	10 to 16	16 to 26	26 to 45	45 and over	TOTAL ALL OTHER	TOTAL SLAVES	TOTALS	DISTRICT/ TOWNSHIP	NOTES
Fitchburg	428	18	Putnam	Daniel Jun			1	1		2		4					8		
Winchendon	227	30	Putnam	Danll	2	2	3	1		4			1				13		
Sutton	168	9	Putnam	David		1	1		1		1	1		1			6		
Sutton	163	6	Putnam	Eliza Wd	1								1				2		
Sutton	163	19	Putnam	Francis	1	1		1		3	1		1				8		
Charlton	336	12	Putnam	Gideon	2				1		1			1			5		
Worcester	188	30	Putnam	Isaac	4	2		1	1		1		1				10		
Sutton	168	11	Putnam	Israel	1			1		1		2		1			6		
Gardner	447	8	Putnam	John	2			1		1			1				5		
Grafton	198	7	Putnam	John	1		1			1		1					4		
Upton	385	23	Putnam	John Dr.	1			1		1			1				4		
Sutton	163	18	Putnam	John Junr	3	1	1	1		1	3	2	2	2			16		
Sutton	168	14	Putnam	Jona F	1	1		1				1		1			5		
Sutton	168	26	Putnam	Luke	1			1				1	1				4		
Sutton	163	8	Putnam	Peter		1		1		1		1	1				5		
Sutton	163	10	Putnam	Tamar Wd	1						1		1	1			4		
Sterling	352	17	Putnam	William		1	1	1			1	1	1				6		
Grafton	198	6	Putnam	Zadock		3		1		1		1					6		
Dudley	343	41	Putney	Eleazer				1				1	1				3		
Dudley	343	42	Putney	Eleazer Junr	1	2	1	1		3		1					9		
Charlton	336	6	Putney	Ezra	1			1		2		1					5		
Charlton	336	4	Putney	Isaiah				1					1				2		
Charlton	336	5	Putney	Isaiah Jun		1				1		1					3		
Charlton	333	25	Putney	Jonathn		1		1		1	2	1		1			7		
Charlton	336	17	Putney	Saml	1			1		3			1				6		
Sutton	163	3	Putnum	Charles			1			3			1				5		
Sutton	163	2	Putnum	John	1			1				1	1	1			5		
Sutton	163	5	Putnum	Moses	1	2	2	1		2		2	1				11		
Sutton	163	1	Putnum	Nathan	1	1	1	1	1	1		2		1			9		
Sutton	163	4	Putnum	Nathll				2						1			3		
Barre	411	23	Quamens	Daniel											3		3		
Oxford	154	12	Radford	John	3					1	1		1				6		
Hardwick	301	21	Raimond	John		1	1			1		1	2				6		
Barre	412	18	Rainger	Amos Lt.	1		1	2		2			1				7		
Brookfield	261	10	Rainger	Joshua	1	1	2	1			1	1					7	Second Parish	
Brookfield	261	8	Rainger	William		1		1			1		2				5	Second Parish	
Mendon	386	2	Ramsdale	Saul	1	1		1	1	1			1				6	1st Parish	
Western	252	6	Ramsdel	Joseph		1	2			1		1					5		
Hardwick	302	2	Ramsdel	Sylvanus	1	1		1		1		1	1				6		
Harvard	221	34	Ramsdell	Nehemiah	1			1		1			1				4		
Lunenberg	430	18	Ramsdell	Seth	1			1		1			1				4		
Worcester	187	5	Rand	Daniel	2	1	2	1		2	2	1		2			13		
Lunenberg	430	16	Rand	Jonathan				1		4			1				6		
Harvard	221	16	Rand	Silas		1			1			1		1			4		
Harvard	221	17	Rand	Silas Junr			1			1		1					3		
Petersham	281	15	Rand	Solomon Revd	4		1		1	1	3	1	1				12		
Westminster	455	5	Rand	Thomas			1										1		
Westminster	452	7	Rand	Zachariah	1	1	1		1	3	2		1				10		
Petersham	281	19	Randall	Benja			1				1	1					3		
Ashburnham	457	26	Randall	Ephraim		1		1		2		1	1				6		
Rutland	511	12	Randall	Hannah	4					1		1					6		
Rutland	511	9	Randall	Joshua				1		1				1			3		
Sutton	167	14	Randall	Joshua	2			1				1	1				5		
Barre	409	16	Randall	Josiah	2	1		1	1					1			6		
Ashburnham	457	23	Randall	Phinihas		1		1			2	1	1				6		
Ashburnham	457	24	Randall	Stephen		1	1	1				1					4		
Ashburnham	457	20	Randall	Stephen Jr	2	2		1		1	1		1				8		
Brookfield	249	6	Ranger	Thomas	2			1	1	1	1	3	1				10	First Parish	
Uxbridge	470	14	Rawson	Charles	1			1		1			1				4		
Oxford	156	8	Rawson	Daniel		2		1		4	1	1	1				10		
Upton	386	8	Rawson	Dorcas Mrs.	2	1	1			2		1	1				8		
Sutton	167	8	Rawson	Ebenz	1		1	1	1		1	2		1			8		
Leicester	494	7	Rawson	Edward			1	1				1	1				4		
Uxbridge	470	11	Rawson	Grindal		1	2	1			1	1	1				7		
Uxbridge	470	9	Rawson	John	2	1		1		1			1				6		
Oxford	156	7	Rawson	Joseph			1		1			2		1			5		
Ward	175	8	Rawson	Joseph	2			1		1			1				5		
Upton	386	9	Rawson	Joshua	3	2			1		1	2	1				10		
Mendon	386	1	Rawson	Levi	1	2			1			2		2			10	1st Parish	
Uxbridge	470	16	Rawson	Nathan	2			1	1				1				5		
Milford	391	11	Rawson	Nathl Deac			2		1		2	2		1			8		
Mendon	386	5	Rawson	Parn	1	1	2		1			1	1				7	1st Parish	
Mendon	386	3	Rawson	Secretary	1			1		2		1	1				6	1st Parish	
Uxbridge	470	17	Rawson	Seth	3	1		1		2			1				8		
Uxbridge	470	13	Rawson	Silas			1		1			1	1	1			5		
Milford	391	12	Rawson	Thomas				1				1	1				3		
Brookfield	261	11	Rawson	Thomson	3	2		1		2	1	1	1				11	Second Parish	
Upton	386	2	Rawson	Wilson		1	1	1		1	1		2				7		
Westminster	452	6	Ray	Heamon	3			1		1			1				6		
Brookfield	261	7	Raymond	Barnabas			1			1	1		1				4	Second Parish	
Sterling	350	11	Raymond	David			1			3		1					5		
Sterling	349	6	Raymond	Edmund	1	1		1	2	1	1		1	2			10		
Athol	286	12	Raymond	Edwd	1			1		3	4		1				10		
Athol	286	8	Raymond	Freeborn	1	2		1		2	1		1	1			10		
Athol	286	9	Raymond	Freeborn Jur		1		1		2			1				5		
Winchendon	228	4	Raymond	James	2	1		1		3		1	1				9		
Winchendon	228	5	Raymond	Jesse	4			1		1			1				7		
Brookfield	261	12	Raymond	John	1		2	1			1	1	2	1			9	Second Parish	
Westminster	452	10	Raymond	John			1						1				2		
Westminster	452	8	Raymond	Jonathan	1		1	1		1			1	1			6		

TOWN	PG#	LN#	HEADS OF HOUSEHOLD		FREE WHITE MALES					FREE WHITE FEMALES					TOTAL ALL OTHER	TOTAL SLAVES	TOTALS	DISTRICT/ TOWNSHIP	NOTES
			LAST NAME	FIRST NAME	under 10	10 to 16	16 to 26	26 to 45	45 and over	under 10	10 to 16	16 to 26	26 to 45	45 and over					
Winchendon	228	3	Raymond	Paul	2	1	2	1	1	2	2	1	1	1			14		
Royalston	236	5	Raymond	Stephen	1			1		1		1					4		
Sterling	350	2	Raymond	William	3		3					1	1				8		
Royalston	241	18	Raymond	Wm	3	1	2	1		1	1		1	1			11		
Princeton	517	26	Raymore	Edward	1			1				1					3		
Princeton	517	24	Raymore	Thomas					1				1				2		
Princeton	517	25	Raymore	Thomas Jr			1			1		1					3		
Princeton	517	37	Raymore	Timson	1		1			2		1					5		
Lunenberg	429	2	Rea	Gideon	1	1		1	1	1	1	2		2			10		
Harvard	220	7	Read	Abijah	1		1					1	1				4		
Rutland	511	1	Read	Daniel		1	1	1		2		1	1	1			8		
Uxbridge	470	15	Read	Ebenezer				2					1				3		
Worcester	187	6	Read	Ebenezer		1	4		1	1		2	2	1			12		
Harvard	219	28	Read	Israel	3		1	1				1	1				7		
Rutland	512	24	Read	Jason	1		1					1	1				6		
Bolton	215	11	Read	John	1	2	6	1	1	2		2	1				16		
Holden	509	2	Read	John	1		1			1		1					4		
Harvard	220	15	Read	Jonathan	1		1			3	1		1				7		
Northbridge	473	12	Read	Mary			3					2		1	1		7		
Douglas	481	34	Read	Peter		1		1			1		1				4		
Uxbridge	470	12	Read	Samuel	1		2	1		3	1		1	1			10		
Rutland	512	23	Read	Thomas	1		1	1		2		3					8		
Oxford	156	12	Reading	Ebenz	2			1		1							4		
Oakham	321	2	Redding	Zachh	3	1			1	1		1					7		
Grafton	196	11	Reding	Zebede			1					1					2		
Grafton	196	10	Reding	Zebede Jun	1		1			2		1					5		
Templeton	233	14	Reed	Benja		2	1				1	2	1				7		
Princeton	517	36	Reed	Benjamin	3			1		1	1		1				7		
Mendon	386	7	Reed	Benjm Esq		1	1				1		1				5	1st Parish	
Brookfield	268	3	Reed	Cheney		2		2		2		1					7	Third Parish	
Sterling	350	13	Reed	Danford		1	1			2		1					5		
Gardner	447	12	Reed	David	2	1		1				1					5		
Rutland	511	10	Reed	Edmund		2	2	1		1	1	1					9		
Ashburnham	460	17	Reed	Isaac	1		1			3		1					6		
Athol	286	14	Reed	Israel	3	1		1		2		1					8		
Fitchburg	425	11	Reed	James	1		1			1		1					4		
New Braintree	311	12	Reed	Jeremiah	2		2	1	1	1		1	1	1			10		
Spencer	490	2	Reed	John		2	1						1				4		
Rutland	511	2	Reed	Jonas	2	1	2	1		1		1					10		
Brookfield	268	18	Reed	Joseph		1	1	2	1	1		1	1				8	Third Parish	
Sterling	350	5	Reed	Joshua	3	1	1	1		1		1					8		
Sterling	350	7	Reed	Levi	2		1					1					4		
New Braintree	311	10	Reed	Micah		1	1	1	1	1	1	2		1			9		
Sterling	349	18	Reed	Nathan	3	1		1		1		1					7		
Oakham	320	14	Reed	Silas	3	3		1		2		1					10		
Leicester	494	10	Reed	Simon	1		1			1		1					4		
Grafton	204	7	Reed	Thaddeus	1			1		2	1		3		1		9		
Sterling	349	4	Reed	William	1		1			2		1					5		
Mendon	392	16	Remmington	Benedic	2	1	1	1	1	1		1		1			9	2d Parish	
Dudley	343	47	Reynolds	Albro	1	1		1		2		1					6		
Dudley	344	1	Reynolds	Stephen	2		1			2		1					6		
Mendon	386	6	Rhodes	Zebulon	1		1	1		1		1					5	1st Parish	
Oxford	156	14	Riaford	Elijah	2		1	1		1	1						6		
Petersham	281	18	Rice	Abel	2		1			3		1					7		
Barre	412	7	Rice	Abel Capt.	3		1			1		1					6		
Hubbardston	420	2	Rice	Abigal Wid		1				1		1	2				5		
Brookfield	268	10	Rice	Amos	2		1	1		2		1					7	Third Parish	
Northborough	361	12	Rice	Amos	1		2		1	1	1	1	1				8		
Winchendon	228	9	Rice	Amos	1		1					1					3		
Hardwick	301	22	Rice	Antipah		2	1		2	3	1		1				10		
Princeton	517	33	Rice	Asa	1		2	1		1		1					6		
Northborough	361	15	Rice	Asaph	2	2	1	1				1					7		
Sturbridge	332	10	Rice	Asariah	2		1			2		1					6		
Sutton	167	5	Rice	Asel		1		1		1		1	1	1			6		
Hardwick	302	17	Rice	Ashbel	1	2		1		1		1					6		
Spencer	490	1	Rice	Ashur	1			1		2	1	1					6		
Northborough	361	13	Rice	Baxter		1		1		2		1					5		
Barre	412	6	Rice	Benj Esq		3		1		1		1	2				8		
Winchendon	228	7	Rice	Benja	1					2	1	1					6		
Sturbridge	332	8	Rice	Caleb	2	1	3		1	2	1	1		1			12		
Brookfield	261	5	Rice	Cheney	2	1		1		1		1					6	Second Parish	
Ward	178	56	Rice	Comfort	1			1				1					3		
Barre	412	4	Rice	Daniel		1	1							1			3		
Sutton	167	11	Rice	Daniel	2	1		1		1	1	1	1				8		
Holden	509	5	Rice	David	1		1			3		1					6		
Princeton	517	35	Rice	David	3	1	1	1		1		1					8		
Rutland	511	3	Rice	David		1	1	1			1	1					5		
Winchendon	228	8	Rice	David	2	1	1		1	2	1	1	1				10		
Barre	412	1	Rice	Ebenz Esq		2		1				1					4		
Ward	175	1	Rice	Edward		1	1			3		1					6		
Brookfield	268	14	Rice	Elijah	1	2	1	1		1	1		1				8	Third Parish	
Westminster	455	8	Rice	Elijah	2	1		1		2		1	1				9		
Brookfield	268	13	Rice	Elisha	1			1		4		1					7	Third Parish	
Barre	412	14	Rice	Eliza Wid		1		1				1					3		
Brookfield	265	22	Rice	Elnathan			1	1		1		1					4	Third Parish	
Brookfield	268	8	Rice	Ephraim				1					1				2	Third Parish	
Brookfield	268	9	Rice	Ephraim Junr	1		1					1					3	Third Parish	
Worcester	187	1	Rice	Eunice						1		1					2		
Barre	409	19	Rice	Ezekiel			1			1	1						3		
Northborough	361	11	Rice	Ezekiel		1		1		2		1					5		
Holden	509	7	Rice	Ezra	2		1			2		1					8		

TOWN	PG#	LN#	LAST NAME	FIRST NAME	FREE WHITE MALES under 10	10 to 16	16 to 26	26 to 45	45 and over	FREE WHITE FEMALES under 10	10 to 16	16 to 26	26 to 45	45 and over	TOTAL ALL OTHER	TOTAL SLAVES	TOTALS	DISTRICT/ TOWNSHIP	NOTES
Sterling	350	12	Rice	Ezra	2	1		1		2	1		1				8		
Ward	175	7	Rice	Gershom				1				1					2		
Barre	409	17	Rice	Henry	2	1		1	1	1	1	1	1				9		
Barre	412	5	Rice	James	1		2		1		1	1		1			7		
Brookfield	268	7	Rice	James	1			1		1		1	1				5	Third Parish	
Holden	509	4	Rice	Jasen				1		3			1				5		
Brookfield	265	20	Rice	Jesse	3	1		1			2	1	1				9	Third Parish	
Barre	412	17	Rice	John	1		1		1	2			1				5		
Brookfield	261	4	Rice	John	1	1			1	2			1				6	Second Parish	
Brookfield	265	21	Rice	John	2	2		1		1	1	1	2	1			11	Third Parish	
Holden	509	6	Rice	John	2			1		2	2		1				8		
Leominster	438	7	Rice	John	2			1					1				4		
Rutland	511	4	Rice	John	1		1		1	2		1	5	1	1		13		
Ashburnham	457	22	Rice	Jonah	3			1		1	1	1					7		
Ashburnham	460	16	Rice	Jonas	2	1		1		2	2	1					11		
Worcester	187	2	Rice	Jonas	1	1	1						1				4		
Bolton	215	2	Rice	Jonathan	1	1			1	2	1		1				7		
Holden	509	3	Rice	Jonathan				1				2	1				4		
Ward	175	2	Rice	Jonathan	2	2		1		1		1	1				8		
Lancaster	353	3	Rice	Joseph	1		1			1			1				4		
Northborough	361	14	Rice	Joseph	2	3		1		2	1	1	1				11		
Rutland	511	5	Rice	Josiah	3			1		2			1				7		
Barre	412	3	Rice	Jotham		2	2	1		1	1			2			9		
Worcester	187	4	Rice	Judith		1							1				2		
Worcester	187	7	Rice	Leml			1	1			1		1				4		
Southborough	205	3	Rice	Lot	3		1					1	1				6		
Worcester	187	11	Rice	Luke		1	1						1				3		
Boylston	371	5	Rice	Luther	1		1			1	1	1	1				6		
Worcester	188	33	Rice	Luther	3		1	1	1	1	2		1				10		
Petersham	281	14	Rice	Martin	4		1	1		2	1	1	1				11		
Brookfield	268	5	Rice	Mary		1	1				1		1				4	Third Parish	
Lancaster	354	18	Rice	Merrick			1				1		1	1			4		
Brookfield	265	19	Rice	Moses	3			1		1		1		2			8	Third Parish	
Northborough	362	1	Rice	Nathan	3			1		1	1		1				7		
Sutton	167	10	Rice	Noah			1				2		1				4		
Brookfield	268	11	Rice	Oliver				1					1				2	Third Parish	
Brookfield	268	15	Rice	Peter	2	1		1		1	2		1				8	Third Parish	
Ward	175	3	Rice	Peter		1		1		2			1				5		
Barre	409	23	Rice	Phineas		1						1		1			2		
Brookfield	268	12	Rice	Phinehas	2	1		1					1	1			6	Third Parish	
Ashburnham	457	21	Rice	Phinias			1					1					2		
Ashburnham	457	19	Rice	Reuben	2	1		1		2	1	1	1				9		
Garry	276	18	Rice	Reuben	1			1					1				3		
Westminster	452	4	Rice	Revd Asaph		2		1				2	1				6		
Brookfield	268	2	Rice	Rufus	4	1	1		1			2		1			10	Third Parish	
Sutton	167	7	Rice	Ruth & Mary Harwood									2				2		
Athol	286	7	Rice	Samuel			1			1			1				3		
Northborough	362	2	Rice	Samuel	2	2		1		1	1		1				8		
Worcester	187	8	Rice	Samuel				1				1					2		
Brookfield	268	6	Rice	Semion	2			1				1					4	Third Parish	
Northborough	361	9	Rice	Seth		1		1		1	1		1				5		
Western	254	3	Rice	Silas	3	1	1	1		1	1		1				9		
Worcester	188	32	Rice	Silas	1			1					1				3		
Sturbridge	332	9	Rice	Simeon	4	2		1		2			1				10		
Hardwick	301	19	Rice	Stephan	1		1	1			2	1	1				8		
Grafton	198	2	Rice	Stephen		1		1		1	1		1				5		
Grafton	198	1	Rice	Stephen Jun	1		1			1		1					4		
Worcester	187	3	Rice	Thomas	1		1			1	1	2		1			8		
Brookfield	249	8	Rice	Thomas 2d	1		2	2		1		1	1				8	First Parish	
Barre	412	2	Rice	Thomas Lt.		2	1	1				1					5		
Barre	412	16	Rice	Thoms Jr	1	1		1				1					4		
Brookfield	265	18	Rice	Tilley Jun	2	1	1	1		1	1	1		1	1		10	Third Parish	
Brookfield	249	9	Rice	Tilly	1		3	1		2	1		1		1		10	First Parish	
Brookfield	265	23	Rice	William	2			1		1	1		2				7	Third Parish	
Lancaster	353	6	Rice	William	1		1					1					3		
Northborough	361	10	Rice	William	1	1	2				1	1					6		
Templeton	233	13	Rice	William	1	1		1		2	1		1				7		
Barre	412	19	Rice	Willis	2			1		2			1				6		
Petersham	281	16	Rice	Willm		2				1		1					4		
Sutton	167	2	Rich	Amos	1	1		1		2	1	1	1	1			9		
Charlton	336	25	Rich	Benj Jun			1										1		
Garry	276	13	Rich	Benja			1	1		1		1					3		
Charlton	336	20	Rich	Benjm		1		1	1	1			1				5		
Sutton	167	4	Rich	Caleb			1				1	1					3		
Sutton	167	3	Rich	Ebenz	1	3		1			2		1				8		
Oxford	156	11	Rich	Elijah	1	1		1		2		1					6		
Western	254	1	Rich	Ezra			1			2		1					4		
Charlton	336	21	Rich	Jacob	2	1		1				1					6		
Charlton	336	27	Rich	Jonathan		3		1		1		1		1			7		
Garry	276	11	Rich	Joseph			1	1		3			1				6		
Garry	276	12	Rich	Joshua	1			1		3			1				6		
Worcester	187	13	Rich	Peter										6			6		
Ward	178	55	Rich	Reuben		1	2			1		1					5		
Brookfield	265	24	Rich	Salmon	2	2	2	1		2	2		1				12	Third Parish	
Sutton	167	1	Rich	Samuel	1	2		1			1		1				6		
Garry	276	15	Rich	Thacher	1	2		1		2	1	1	1	1			10		
Garry	276	10	Rich	Zacheus				1			2	1	1				5		
Garry	276	9	Rich	Zacheus Jr			1				1	1	1		1		5		
Athol	286	11	Rich	David	2	1		1		1	2	2	1				10		
Charlton	336	18	Rich	David	2	1	3		1	2		2	1				12		
Brookfield	249	10	Rich	John	1		1		1	1			1	1			6	First Parish	
Charlton	336	19	Rich	Paul		1			1		1		1				4		
Oakham	321	3	Rich	Reed	1			1				1					3		

TOWN	PG#	LN#	LAST NAME	FIRST NAME	FREE WHITE MALES under 10	10 to 16	16 to 26	26 to 45	45 and over	FREE WHITE FEMALES under 10	10 to 16	16 to 26	26 to 45	45 and over	TOTAL ALL OTHER	TOTAL SLAVES	TOTALS	DISTRICT/ TOWNSHIP	NOTES
Southborough	205	23	Richard	Ebenezer		2		1	1	1		2		1			7		
Ward	175	4	Richards	David				1					1				2		
Lunenberg	430	19	Richards	John	2		1			2	1						6		
Southborough	205	22	Richards	John			1			5	1	1	1				9		
Lunenberg	430	17	Richards	Mitchell			1						1				2		
Lunenberg	430	20	Richards	Mitchell Jun	2		1			2			1				6		
Hardwick	302	6	Richards	David	2	2	1	1	1	1		1					9		
Brookfield	261	13	Richards	Ephraim	4	1		1					1				7	Second Parish	
Sterling	349	16	Richardson	Abel	2	3		1		2		1	1				10		
Barre	409	21	Richardson	Abigal							1		1				2		
Athol	286	10	Richardson	Amos				1		2	1		1				5		
Garry	276	17	Richardson	Amos	4			1		2		1					8		
Templeton	239	14	Richardson	Amos				1					1				2		
Sutton	167	12	Richardson	Benja	3	1		1		2	1		1				9		
Sterling	349	14	Richardson	Benjamin		2	1	1	1		2	2		1			10		
Ward	175	5	Richardson	Charles		1	1	1			2		1	1			7		
Barre	409	15	Richardson	David		1		1		4			1				7		
Winchendon	228	1	Richardson	Ebenz			1	1					1				3		
Brookfield	268	17	Richardson	Ezekiel	2	1	1	1		2			2	1			10	Third Parish	
Oakham	320	15	Richardson	George		1		1		3	2	1					8		
Brookfield	249	2	Richardson	Harmon	1	1	2		1	1	2		1				9	First Parish	
Holden	509	9	Richardson	Heman	1		2			3		1					7		
Sterling	349	15	Richardson	James				1				1	1				3		
Hubbardston	420	1	Richardson	Job		1		1		1			1				4		
Leominster	438	11	Richardson	John	2	1	1	1	1		4	1	1				12		
Templeton	238	11	Richardson	John Junr	2	3		1		1		1					8		
Templeton	239	13	Richardson	John Junr	1	1		1		1	1	4		1			10		
Sutton	167	13	Richardson	Jona	2		1				1	1					5		
Gardner	447	11	Richardson	Jonas		1	1	1			1	1					5		
Brookfield	268	16	Richardson	Joseph	1	2	2		1	2		1	1				10	Third Parish	
Fitchburg	425	8	Richardson	Joseph			1			3		1					5		
Uxbridge	470	10	Richardson	Joseph	1	2	1			2		1	1				9		
Leominster	438	13	Richardson	Luke	2		2	1	1	1		2	1	1			11		
Leominster	438	15	Richardson	Luke Jun	1	1		1		2	1		1				7		
Sterling	350	9	Richardson	Menapah	3		2	1		1	1		1				9		
Brookfield	249	5	Richardson	Nathan	2		1	1					1				6	First Parish	
Brookfield	268	4	Richardson	Nathan	3	3	1		1	1		1		1			11	Third Parish	
Brookfield	249	3	Richardson	Nathaniel			1	1		1		2		1			6	First Parish	
Garry	276	14	Richardson	Person	2	1	1	1				1		2			8		
Ward	175	6	Richardson	Peter	1	1		1		1	1	1		1			8		
Brookfield	249	4	Richardson	Ralph	3	1	1		1	1	1	1		1			10	First Parish	
Sturbridge	332	11	Richardson	Saml	2		1			2			1				6		
Leicester	494	9	Richardson	Samuel	1		1	1		1		3	1				8		
Princeton	517	32	Richardson	Samuel	2	1		1		2	1	1	1				9		
Hardwick	302	5	Richardson	Silas	2		1				2		1				6		
Leominster	438	12	Richardson	Silas	1		1	1		1		1	1				6		
Holden	509	8	Richardson	Thomas		1		1		1		1		1			5		
Sterling	350	1	Richardson	Thomas		1		1			1		1				4		
Brookfield	265	25	Richardson	Thos	1			1		1			1				4	Third Parish	
Royalston	241	28	Richardson	Thos	2			1		3	1		1				8		
Royalston	242	16	Richardson	Timo	1	1	2		1		1	1		1			8		
Leicester	494	11	Richardson	William			1			1		1					3		
Princeton	517	31	Richardson	William				1			2		1				4		
Sturbridge	332	12	Richardson	Wm	2			1					1				4		
Charlton	335	3	Richardson	Zachriah				1					1				2		
New Braintree	311	14	Richmond	Desire							1		1				2		
Brookfield	261	6	Richmond	Ezra				1		2	1	3	1				8	Second Parish	
New Braintree	311	11	Richmond	Silvester	2	2	1	2	2	3		2	1				15		
Brookfield	261	9	Rickey	Robert	2	1		1		1	1	1					7	Second Parish	
Charlton	336	24	Rider	Eliezer		3	1		1	1		1		1			8		
Charlton	336	22	Rider	Mary Wdw	1	1	1					1		1			5		
Grafton	196	15	Rider	Samuel	3		1		1	1	1	1					8		
Fitchburg	425	9	Rider	William	1	1		1		1		2		1			7		
Charlton	336	23	Rider	Wm P.			2			1		1					4		
Douglas	481	31	Riedel	Polly	2	2	1			2	1	2		1			11		
Oakham	320	18	Ripley	Jepthah	2	1	1	1		1		3	2	1			12		
Oakham	320	17	Ripley	Zenas	1	1		1		1			1				5		
Uxbridge	470	8	Rist	Joseph		1	1	2				1		1			6		
Lunenberg	429	1	Ritter	David		1	1	1	1			1		2			7		
Fitchburg	425	10	Ritter	Ezra	1			1		3			1				6		
New Braintree	311	15	Rixford	Henry	1			1		3			1				6		
Westborough	194	62	Robartson	John			1	1		1		1	1				4		
Southborough	206	16	Robartson	Zacheus	3		1	1		1		1					7		
Douglas	481	33	Robbins	Abel	1			1					1				3		
Harvard	218	37	Robbins	Anna										1			1		
Douglas	481	32	Robbins	Benja	2	1		1		2			1				7		
Harvard	217	3	Robbins	Daniel			1				1	1					3		
Sterling	350	4	Robbins	Daniel				1			1			1			3		
Westborough	189	17	Robbins	Daniel			2	1		1		1	1				6		
Lancaster	354	16	Robbins	Eleazer			1	1		2		1					5		
Harvard	220	5	Robbins	Ephraim		3	1	1						1			6		
Lancaster	354	17	Robbins	John		1		1			1	1	1				5		
Sterling	349	7	Robbins	John		1		1			1	1	1				5		
Upton	386	4	Robbins	Joseph	2		1			2	1	1					7		
Sterling	349	5	Robbins	Jude			1				1						2		
Sterling	350	10	Robbins	Levi	1		1			3		1					6		
Athol	286	13	Robbins	Luke	1			1		1	1	2					6		
Paxton	503	10	Robbins	Nathl	2	1		1		2		1	1				8		
Western	254	2	Robbins	Samuel	1		1			1		1					4		

239

TOWN	PG#	LN#	LAST NAME	FIRST NAME	FREE WHITE MALES					FREE WHITE FEMALES					TOTAL ALL OTHER	TOTAL SLAVES	TOTALS	DISTRICT/ TOWNSHIP	NOTES
					under 10	10 to 16	16 to 26	26 to 45	45 and over	under 10	10 to 16	16 to 26	26 to 45	45 and over					
Leominster	438	9	Robbins	Thomas	1	1		1		1	2		1	1			8		
Winchendon	228	2	Robbins	William	1					1		1	1	1			5		
Westminster	452	9	Robens	Ephraim		1	1	1						1			4		
Dudley	344	2	Roberson	Asa	3		1		1	2				1			8		
Dudley	344	5	Roberson	Eliakim		2		1				2		1			6		
Dudley	344	4	Roberson	Saml	2		1	1		1			1				6		
Dudley	344	3	Roberson	William	3		1	1	1	1	1		1		1		10		
Sutton	167	9	Roberts	Amasa	1			1					1				3		
Winchendon	228	6	Roberts	David				1			1		1				3		
Grafton	200	5	Roberts	John			1	1		1	1			1			5		
Harvard	219	6	Robertson	George		2	1	1				3		1			8		
New Braintree	311	9	Robertson	Joseph	2		2	1		1	1	1					8		
Sturbridge	332	15	Robin	Asa	3			1					1				5		
Sturbridge	332	5	Robins	Ezekiel	1	1	1	1		2		1	1	1			9		
Sturbridge	332	13	Robins	Ichabod	1			1						1			3		
Harvard	218	36	Robins	Jacob	2			1		2			1				6		
Sturbridge	332	6	Robins	John	2			1		3	1		1				8		
Sturbridge	332	7	Robins	Saml	2		1	1		1	1		1	1			8		
Barre	412	10	Robinson	Benj			1				1						2		
Hardwick	302	19	Robinson	Danl		1		1		1			1				5		
Barre	412	8	Robinson	Deneson				1		1	1		1				4		
Barre	412	9	Robinson	Deneson Jr	2		1	1		1		1		1			7		
Barre	412	15	Robinson	Elijah	1	1		1		2	1		1				7		
Barre	409	22	Robinson	Hannah Wid	2	1	1				1		1				6		
Athol	284	18	Robinson	Jereh	1			1		3	1		1				7		
Petersham	284	4	Robinson	Jereh	1			1		3	1		1				7		
Oakham	320	16	Robinson	John	1	1	2	1		4	1	1	1				12		
Barre	412	11	Robinson	Joseph				1				1		1	1		4		
Hardwick	302	4	Robinson	Joseph		1						1	1				3		
Barre	412	13	Robinson	Leml	3	1		1		1	1		1				8		
Leicester	494	8	Robinson	Luther		1		1			1			1			4		
Hardwick	302	8	Robinson	Phebe		2						1	1				4		
Hardwick	302	18	Robinson	Sally			1	1	1		1	1					5		
Charlton	336	26	Robinson	Saml		2		2		1	2	1	2		1		11		
Barre	409	18	Robinson	Saml Lt.			1			3	2		1				7		
Hardwick	301	20	Robinson	Samll	1			1		3		1					6		
Rutland	511	11	Robinson	Samuel			1			2	2	1		1			7		
Grafton	204	5	Rocket	Benjn			1						1	1			3		
Grafton	204	6	Rocket	Moses	1		1	1		1				1			5		
Worcester	187	9	Rockwood	Frost	3			1		1		1		1			7		
Upton	386	5	Rockwood	Hezekiah	2	1		1		3	1	1	1				10		
Oxford	156	10	Rockwood	Joseph	2			1		2	2		1				8		
Milford	391	10	Rockwood	Saml	1	1		1		2	1		1	1			8		
Brookfield	268	1	Rockwood	Simeon	1	1		1		1		2		1			7	Third Parish	
Sturbridge	332	14	Rofee	Solomon				1		2	1			1			5		
Holden	509	11	Rogers	Aaron	2	1	1	1		1		1	1				8		
Athol	284	16	Rogers	Abel	1		1	1		1	2			1			7		
Petersham	284	2	Rogers	Abel	1		1	1		1	2			1			7		
Athol	284	17	Rogers	Abel Jr	2			1		3			1				7		
Petersham	284	3	Rogers	Abel Jr	2			1		3			1				7		
Leominster	438	8	Rogers	Benja				1					1				2		
Royalston	234	15	Rogers	Eliphalet	3	1	1		1		2		1				9		
Athol	284	15	Rogers	Jonah	1	2	2	1		1		2		1			10		
Holden	509	12	Rogers	Jonathan	5	1		1			1		1				9		
Lancaster	353	4	Rogers	Joseph				1		1		1	1				4		
Petersham	284	1	Rogers	Josiah	1	2	2	1	1		2						10		
Holden	509	10	Rogers	Nathan		2	1			1		1		1			6		
Spencer	490	3	Rogers	Stephen				1					1	1			3		
Hardwick	302	7	Roggers	Elkenah	4	3		1			1	1	1				11		
Hardwick	302	9	Roggers	James	1	1	1	1				1	1				6		
Princeton	517	34	Rolph	Solomon		1	3	1		3	1	1		2			12		
Western	252	10	Rood	Sarah			2							1			3		
Western	254	4	Root	Mary						1		1		1			3		
Upton	386	3	Rooth	Joseph	1			1		2			1				5		
Sterling	349	10	Roper	Asa	1	2		1				1	1				6		
Princeton	517	27	Roper	Benjamin	2			1			2			1			6		
Rutland	511	7	Roper	Daniel	1		1	1		1			1	1			6		
Rutland	511	8	Roper	Daniel Junr			1			2			1				4		
Sterling	349	13	Roper	Enoch			1										1		
Princeton	517	28	Roper	John	1			1		3			1	1			7		
Sterling	349	12	Roper	Monasseh	1	1	1	1		4			1	1			10		
Sterling	349	11	Roper	Silas		1	1	1		3			1				7		
Sterling	349	17	Roper	Sylvester	1	1	2						1				5		
Sterling	350	6	Ross	Ebenezer			1	1		1		1		1					
Brookfield	249	7	Ross	John		2		1	1	5		1	1				11	First Parish	
Brookfield	249	11	Ross	Lemuel	1					1		1	1				4	First Parish	
Sterling	349	9	Ross	Moses	2			1		2			1				6		
Sterling	350	3	Ross	Roger		2	2			1	1		1				9		
Petersham	281	17	Ross	Seth	3	1		1		2	1		1		1		10		
Garry	276	16	Ross	Simon		1		1					1				3		
Sterling	349	8	Ross	Thomas				1		1	1						3		
Berlin	214	23	Ross	William				1			1						2		
Sterling	349	19	Ross	William		1	1	1					1				4		
Holden	509	13	Rowe	Samuel	2			1		3	1		1				8		
Worcester	187	12	Rowland	Willm	2			1		1	1	1	1				8		
Leominster	438	14	Rugg	aaron			1	1		1		1	1				5		
Lancaster	354	20	Rugg	Abel	1		1		1	1			1	2			7		
Lancaster	353	2	Rugg	Abijah	3								1				6		
Sterling	350	8	Rugg	Asa	2			2	1	1			1				7		
Lancaster	354	15	Rugg	Daniel		2	1		1		2		1				7		

TOWN	PG#	LN#	LAST NAME	FIRST NAME	M under 10	M 10–16	M 16–26	M 26–45	M 45+	F under 10	F 10–16	F 16–26	F 26–45	F 45+	TOTAL ALL OTHER	TOTAL SLAVES	TOTALS	DISTRICT/TOWNSHIP	NOTES
Lancaster	354	21	Rugg	Elisha	2			2		1		1	1	1			8		
Lancaster	353	1	Rugg	Isaac	1	1		1		1		1	1	1			7		
Leominster	438	10	Rugg	Jacob	1			3				1	1				6		
Lancaster	354	14	Rugg	Jonph	2			1		2			1				6		
Sterling	349	20	Rugg	Luther			1					1					2		
Lancaster	354	19	Rugg	Samuel				1		2			1				4		
Hardwick	302	1	Ruggles	Benm			1	1		2	1	1					6		
Hardwick	302	10	Ruggles	Benm Jr	1		1	1		1	1	1		1			7		
Hardwick	302	11	Ruggles	Constant	2	1	1	1	1	2	1	1	1	1			12		
Hardwick	302	16	Ruggles	Daniel	1	1		2		1	3		1				10		
Hardwick	302	12	Ruggles	Edward	2	1	1		1	2	1	1		1			10		
Hardwick	302	3	Ruggles	Ephm			1	1		6	2		1				11		
Upton	386	7	Ruggles	Jeremiah	3	1	1	1		1	1		1				9		
Barre	412	12	Ruggles	John		2	1					2		1	2		8		
Hardwick	302	14	Ruggles	Lemll	1	1						1		1			4		
New Braintree	311	13	Ruggles	Lucy									1				1		
Bolton	215	12	Ruggles	Robert			1	2					2				5		
Hardwick	302	15	Ruggles	Seth	3		1			1		1	1				7		
Oakham	321	1	Ruggles	Thos	2		1	1		1	3	2	1				11		
Rutland	511	6	Ruggles	Timoth		1	2	1			1	1					7		
Hardwick	302	13	Ruggles	Welthy			1						1				2		
Westborough	194	64	Rugles	Isaac		2	1	2		1		1	1				8		
Princeton	517	30	Russel	Eunice	1	1				1	1		1				5		
Charlton	335	1	Russel	John	1			1		1			1				4		
Princeton	517	29	Russel	Joseph			1					1	1				3		
Sturbridge	332	16	Russel	Wm	1	1	1	1		1	1		1				7		
Mendon	386	4	Russell	Abigail Wd	2	1					2	2	1	1			9	1st Parish	
Brookfield	265	26	Russell	Asa	2		1					1		1			5	Third Parish	
Lancaster	353	7	Russell	Caleb	2			1		2			1				6		
Sutton	167	6	Russell	Darius		1	1						1				3		
Ashburnham	457	18	Russell	David	3		1			1			1				6		
Lancaster	353	5	Russell	Eleazer	1		1			1			1				4		
Lunenberg	430	15	Russell	Ephraim	2	1		1		1	2		1				8		
Oxford	156	9	Russell	Ephraim	1		1	1		1		1		1			6		
Winchendon	228	10	Russell	Peter	2		1			2		1					6		
Berlin	214	24	Russell	Thaddeus		1		1		1	1			1			5		
Ashburnham	457	25	Russell	Thomas	3	1	1	1		1	1	1					8		
Oxford	156	13	Russell	Thomas	1	1		1		2	1		1				7		
Sterling	349	3	Ruth	Samuel	1		1						1				3		
Sterling	349	2	Ruth	Solomon	1	1		1		3	1		1				8		
Upton	386	6	Rutter	Jesse				1			1		1				3		
Spencer	490	4	Ryan	Samuel	4	2		1		2	2		1	2			14		
Barre	409	20	Rypley	Noah	2		1	1		2	1	1					8		
Dudley	344	6	Sabin	Daniel	2	1	1	1		3	1	1		1			11		
Charlton	335	17	Sabin	Edmund	1	1		1		1	1		1				6		
Brookfield	264	9	Sabin	John			1										1	Second Parish	
Dudley	344	15	Sabin	Joseph		1	1						2				4		
Dudley	344	7	Sabin	Royal			1				1		2				4		
Upton	386	17	Sadler	Bial				1			1		1				3		
Grafton	199	1	Sadler	Ebenz		1	1	1					1				4		
Upton	386	12	Sadler	John	1		1			4		1	1				8		
Upton	386	11	Sadler	Joseph				1					1				2		
Upton	386	18	Sadler	Stephen Capt.				1					1				2		
Lancaster	353	13	Safford	Thomas	4	1	1	1		1		1	1	1			11		
Harvard	220	13	Safford	Ward		1		1						2			4		
Dudley	344	9	Sales	Royal	3	1		1	1				1	1			8		
Worcester	188	5	Salisbury	Stephen	1	1	1	1	1	1		1	1	1			9		
Uxbridge	469	7	Salsbury	David	1			1					1				3		
Charlton	335	27	Sampson	Aaron	1			1					1				3		
Westminster	451	1	Sampson	Abraham	1		1	1			1		1	1			6		
Brookfield	252	5	Sampson	Charles	4	1		1				1	1				8	First Parish	
Harvard	219	31	Sampson	David				1			1		1				3		
Western	256	3	Sampson	David	3		1			2			1				7		
Ashburnham	457	33	Sampson	Ephraim	3		1			1			1				6		
Ashburnham	457	28	Sampson	John		1							1				2		
Ashburnham	457	34	Sampson	Jonathan				1			1	1		1			4		
Boylston	371	11	Sampson	Jonathan	2	1		1		2	3	1	1				11		
Ashburnham	458	14	Sampson	Oliver	2		1			2			1				6		
Brookfield	249	12	Sampson	Perez		1		1		2	1		1				6	First Parish	
Fitchburg	426	5	Sampson	Robert	1	2		1		2			1				7		
Harvard	215	10	Sampson	Willis	1		1			1		1					4		
Oxford	158	7	Samson	William	2		1	1					1				5		
Westborough	194	65	Sandburn	John		1		1					2				4		
Rutland	511	24	Sanders	Daniel	1		1	2					2	1			7		
Sturbridge	332	21	Sanders	Thankful		2						1	1				4		
Royalston	237	5	Sanders	William	1		1					1					3		
Brookfield	249	17	Sanderson	David		1		1			1			1			4	First Parish	
Petersham	283	10	Sanderson	David				1					1				2		
Lancaster	356	13	Sanderson	Elisha	2	2		1		1	1		1				8		
Lunenberg	429	9	Sanderson	Isaac		1		1			1	3		1			7		
Lunenberg	429	14	Sanderson	Jacob				1				2	1				4		
Petersham	283	11	Sanderson	Jona		1		2	1				2	1			7		
Lunenberg	429	15	Sanderson	Jonan	3		1			2		1					7		
Ashburnham	458	6	Sanderson	Moses	2		2	1		1	1		1				8		
Gardner	448	1	Sanderson	Moses			1				2		1				4		
Petersham	283	18	Sanderson	Moses	2	1		1		2	1		1				8		
Petersham	283	9	Sanderson	Nathl			1				1	1		1			4		
Harvard	220	2	Sanderson	Oliver	1			1				1		1			5		
Lancaster	356	6	Sanderson	Samuel				1		2			1				4		
Gardner	447	18	Sandson	Samuel	1			1					1				3		

TOWN	PG#	LN#	LAST NAME	FIRST NAME	FREE WHITE MALES					FREE WHITE FEMALES					TOTAL ALL OTHER	TOTAL SLAVES	TOTALS	DISTRICT/ TOWNSHIP	NOTES
					under 10	10 to 16	16 to 26	26 to 45	45 and over	under 10	10 to 16	16 to 26	26 to 45	45 and over					
Brookfield	252	3	Sanford	Josiah			1			2		1					4	First Parish	
Brookfield	249	16	Sanford	Thomas			1	1						1			3	First Parish	
New Braintree	311	20	Sargant	Nathan		2	1			1		2		1			8		
Princeton	517	43	Sargeant	Amos			1			5			1	1			8		
Holden	510	1	Sargeant	Daniel	1	1	*	*	*	1				1			4		
Leicester	493	11	Sargeant	John	2		1	1		2	2		1	1			10		
Leicester	493	12	Sargeant	Joseph				1					2				3		
Princeton	517	44	Sargeant	Joseph	1			1		1		1					4		
Leicester	496	2	Sargeant	Mary		1						1	1				3		
Leicester	496	3	Sargeant	Samuel	4	1		1	1	3	1	1					12		
Leicester	493	13	Sargeant	Stephen	1	1		1					1				4		
Boylston	372	4	Sarvtell	Zechariah	1		1	1		3			1	1			8		
Milford	391	22	Saunders	John	2	1		1		2	1		1				8		
Milford	391	23	Saunders	Nathl	1	2		1				1	1				6		
Milford	391	21	Saunders	Robert Jr	2	1	2	1	1	1			2				10		
Rutland	514	6	Savage	Charlotte	2					1		1					4		
Princeton	517	41	Savage	Seth	2		1	1		2			2	1			9		
Rutland	514	5	Savage	Thankful				1			1			1			3		
Westminster	452	16	Sawin	Abner		1		1					1				3		
Ashburnham	458	5	Sawin	Asa			1			2			1				4		
Westminster	452	11	Sawin	Daniel	3			1					1				6		
Westminster	451	13	Sawin	David			1	1		1			1	2			6		
Princeton	517	46	Sawin	Ezekiel	3	2	1		1	2		1	1				11		
Westminster	451	4	Sawin	James	1	1		1					1				4		
Princeton	517	47	Sawin	Jesse	1	1		1		4			1				8		
Westminster	451	3	Sawin	Jonathan		1		1	1	1		1		1			5		
Westminster	451	2	Sawin	Joseph	1	1	1			3		2		1			9		
Westminster	451	6	Sawin	Samuel	1	1	2			1	1	2		1			10		
Fitchburg	426	11	Sawin	Stephen			1	1					1				3		
Westminster	452	13	Sawin	William			1			1			1				3		
Boylston	371	7	Sawyer	Aaron	2	2	1					2		2			10		
Berlin	212	6	Sawyer	Alvin	1			1		2			1				5		
Boylston	371	10	Sawyer	Amariah		1	1	1		3		1	1	1			9		
Berlin	213	5	Sawyer	Amos	2			2		3			1				8		
Lancaster	353	21	Sawyer	Amos	1			1					1				3		
Westminster	451	17	Sawyer	Amos	1	1		1		2		1					6		
Lancaster	356	11	Sawyer	Amos 2d	1			1		1			1				4		
Charlton	335	5	Sawyer	Bazaleel	1			1		1			1				4		
Bolton	211	15	Sawyer	Benjamin	2	2	1	1		2		1	1				10		
Harvard	218	13	Sawyer	Caleb				1						1			2		
Westminster	451	5	Sawyer	Calvin	1		1	1		1			1				5		
Templeton	236	4	Sawyer	Cooper		2	1					1					4		
Westminster	451	14	Sawyer	Eli	1		1	1		4		1	1	1			10		
Lancaster	356	8	Sawyer	Elias				1		1	1	1		1			5		
Templeton	234	16	Sawyer	Elias	2	4		1		2				1			10		
Bolton	211	5	Sawyer	Elijah		2	1			1	1	1					6		
Harvard	218	35	Sawyer	Elizabeth								1	1		1		3		
Bolton	209	18	Sawyer	Ezekah								1	1				2		
Sterling	350	15	Sawyer	Ezra		1		1				1	1	1			5		
Boylston	371	6	Sawyer	Hooker			1					1					2		
Lancaster	356	1	Sawyer	Israel	1		1	1		1			2	2			8		
Fitchburg	426	6	Sawyer	Jabez	4		1				1			1			7		
Bolton	216	11	Sawyer	John		1		1			2	1		1			6		
Templeton	231	16	Sawyer	John	3		1			1		1	1				7		
Bolton	216	13	Sawyer	Jonathan				1						1			2		
Harvard	218	14	Sawyer	Jonathan	2	1		1					2				6		
Westminster	451	15	Sawyer	Jonathan			2	2	1		1	2		1			9		
Bolton	212	13	Sawyer	Joseph	1	1		1		3	1	1	1	1			10		
Fitchburg	425	13	Sawyer	Joseph	3	2			1	1	1	3		1			12		
Bolton	212	1	Sawyer	Joshua				1						1			2		
Berlin	212	17	Sawyer	Josiah				1									1		
Berlin	214	33	Sawyer	Josiah		1		1		2				1			5		
Berlin	212	18	Sawyer	Josiah Junr	3	1		1		2		1	1	1			10		
Templeton	231	17	Sawyer	Jotham		1	1	1					1	1			5		
Gardner	447	14	Sawyer	Jude	1			1						1			3		
Bolton	216	5	Sawyer	Keziah		1						1		2			4		
Fitchburg	426	8	Sawyer	Luke	2		1			2			1				6		
Harvard	218	34	Sawyer	Luthar	1	1		1		1			1				6		
Hubbardston	420	15	Sawyer	Luther	1		1			1			1				4		
Lancaster	353	18	Sawyer	Luther	1	1		2		2	1	1	1				9		
Bolton	216	6	Sawyer	Lydia	2								1				3		
Harvard	217	35	Sawyer	Manasah Junr	2	1		1		1		1	1				7		
Harvard	218	33	Sawyer	Manassah				1				1		1			3		
Lancaster	356	3	Sawyer	Moses		1	2		1	2	1			1			8		
Templeton	238	14	Sawyer	Moses	1			1				1	1				4		
Lancaster	356	4	Sawyer	Moses Jun	2			1		1			1				5		
Rutland	514	3	Sawyer	Nathaniel	2	1		1		1	1		1				7		
Boylston	371	8	Sawyer	Oliver		2	1	1			1	1	2				9		
Bolton	212	2	Sawyer	Peter		1		1		1				1			4		
Harvard	218	27	Sawyer	Phineas	2		2	1	1		1		1	1			9		
Lancaster	356	7	Sawyer	Polly (or Calvin	2					1		1					5		
Berlin	214	9	Sawyer	Silas	2					3	1		1				8		
Berlin	214	10	Sawyer	William		2		1				2		1			6		
Northborough	362	7	Sawyer	William			1			1	1	1			1		5		
Milford	391	20	Scammel	Alexander	1	1						2					5		
Petersham	283	7	Schaal	Abraham				1		1			1				3		
Ashburnham	457	31	Scolley	Grover		2	1	1			1		1				6		
Ashburnham	458	3	Scolley	John			1						1				3		
Leicester	496	4	Scott	Andrew		2	1	1				1	1	1			7		
Fitchburg	425	16	Scott	Edward			1		1		1			1			4		

TOWN	PG#	LN#	LAST NAME	FIRST NAME	FREE WHITE MALES					FREE WHITE FEMALES					TOTAL ALL OTHER	TOTAL SLAVES	TOTALS	DISTRICT/ TOWNSHIP	NOTES
					under 10	10 to 16	16 to 26	26 to 45	45 and over	under 10	10 to 16	16 to 26	26 to 45	45 and over					
Fitchburg	426	13	Scott	John	2		1						1				4		
Harvard	220	29	Scott	Mary			1						1	1			3		
Mendon	391	1	Scott	Nathl	2			1		1		1		1			6	2d Parish	
Worcester	188	16	Scott	Reuben		1							1				2		
Ward	176	17	Scott	Thomas	1			1					3	1			6		
Ward	176	24	Scott	Thomas Junr			1						1				2		
Spencer	490	13	Seager	Ephraim	1	1		1		3			1				7		
Spencer	487	9	Seager	Oliver				1						2			3		
Hubbardston	420	11	Seargeant	Ebenezer	2	1		1		2			1				7		
Hubbardston	420	9	Seargeant	John	1	1	1	1		3	2	1	1	1			12		
Hubbardston	420	10	Seargeant	John Jr	1		1	1		1			1				5		
Leicester	493	10	Searle	Ambrose				1					1	1			3		
Charlton	335	23	Searles	Andrew	1			1		1			1				4		
Sutton	165	18	Searles	Curtis	2		1						1				4		
Mendon	386	11	Searles	James			1			3			1				5	1st Parish	
Lunenberg	429	8	Searls	Mary									2	1			3		
Barre	410	15	Sears	Elisha		1		1		1	1	1		1			6		
Oxford	153	1	Seary	Joseph			1			3			1				5		
Worcester	187	16	Seaver	Edward	2		1			2			1				6		
Worcester	187	32	Seaver	Mary	1			2			2			1			6		
Worcester	187	14	Seaver	Nathan	2		1			1			1				5		
Northborough	362	4	Segar	Caleb				1			2			2			5		
Uxbridge	469	1	Segraves	Bezaleel	1	1		1		3			1				7		
Uxbridge	469	2	Segraves	John	1	1	2	1		2		1	1				9		
Uxbridge	469	8	Segraves	Josiah			1	1		1			1	1			5		
Hubbardston	420	6	Selfredge	Edward			1		1			3	1		1		7		
Hardwick	303	8	Sellen	John	2	2			2	1		1		2			10		
Lancaster	353	20	Sergeant	Anson			1	1		1		1	1				5		
Lancaster	356	14	Sergeant	Ebenezer	1		1			1			1				4		
Lancaster	356	5	Sergeant	Richard			1		1	2	1	1	1				7		
Lancaster	353	12	Sergeant	Richard Junr	4			1					1				6		
Winchendon	228	17	Sergeant	Samll	3			1		3			1				8		
Lancaster	353	10	Sergeant	Seth		1			1	1			1				4		
Gardner	448	2	Sever	Eathan	2		1			1			1				5		
Northborough	362	5	Sever	Joseph	2			1						1			4		
Sterling	350	21	Sever	Joseph		1	1	1		2	2		1				9		
Boylston	372	3	Sever	Persis						1		2					3		
New Braintree	311	16	Severance	Benm		1	1			2	1	1		1			7		
Westminster	451	10	Severs	Benjn	2	1		1		2	2		1	1			10		
Sutton	166	34	Severy	Jacob				1			1	1	1				4		
Sutton	165	10	Severy	John				1						2			3		
Sutton	165	11	Severy	John Junr		1	1			2	1	1	1				7		
Ward	176	20	Severy	Joseph	1			1		1			1				4		
Sutton	166	35	Severy	Moody	3	1		1		1	1		1				8		
Uxbridge	469	3	Severy	Reuben	2			1		1			1				5		
Grafton	202	12	Sharman	David				1						1			2		
Grafton	202	9	Sharman	Ephm				1				1		1			3		
Grafton	202	11	Sharman	Ephm Jun	1		1	1		5	1		1				10		
Grafton	202	10	Sharman	Moses	3	2	1	1				2	1				10		
Westminster	451	12	Shatock	Stephen									1				1		
Hubbardston	420	7	Shattock	Abraham			2			1		1					4		
Sterling	350	14	Shattock	Walter			2	1						1			4		
Paxton	503	18	Shattuck	Caleb	1			2			1	1	1				6		
Fitchburg	425	17	Shattuck	Simon			2		1	1	1	1	1				7		
Ashburnham	458	4	Shaw	John				1						1			2		
New Braintree	311	18	Shaw	Joseph		1							1				3		
Brookfield	252	2	Shaw	William	1			1		3			1				6	First Parish	
Lunenberg	429	4	Shed	John		1		1					1				3		
Upton	386	13	Sheffield	Isaac				1						1			2		
Fitchburg	426	9	Sheldon	Amos	1			1		3	1		1				7		
Fitchburg	425	15	Sheldon	Benja	3		1			1			1				6		
Fitchburg	425	14	Sheldon	Zachh	2	1			1	2			1				7		
Sturbridge	332	25	Shepard	*		1		1					1				3		
Brookfield	252	1	Shepard	John	2	1	2		1	2	1			1			10	First Parish	
Worcester	187	19	Shepard	John	2			1		2	1	1	1				8		
Worcester	188	6	Shepard	Thomas	3		1	1		1			1				7		
Royalston	232	3	Shephardson	Isaac	1	1	1	1					1				5		
Royalston	232	4	Shephardson	Jonathan	1	1		1	1			2	1				7		
Western	254	6	Shepherd	Amos	4			1		1			1		1		8		
Western	252	8	Shepherd	Moses		1		1				1		1			4		
Holden	510	4	Shepherd	Paul		1							1				2		
Dudley	344	13	Shepherd	Simeon	1	1			1	2	1	1	1				8		
Western	254	5	Shepherd	William	4		1	2	1	1	1		2	1			13		
Barre	409	29	Sherman	Jason		1		2			1	4		1			9		
Winchendon	230	1	Sherwin	Ebenzr	3		1	1	1	1	1		1				9		
Winchendon	230	2	Sherwin	Ebenzr Jr		1		1		1			1				4		
Hardwick	304	3	Shirtlif	Jedediah	2	1		1					1				5		
Mendon	391	12	Shove	Josiah	1	2			1			2		1			7	2d Parish	
Uxbridge	469	9	Shove	Thomas B	4			1		1			1				7		
Sturbridge	332	18	Shumway	Abijah		1	3		1	2	1		1	1			10		
Westminster	452	15	Shumway	Abishun	1			1		1			1				4		
Oxford	156	20	Shumway	Amos				1									1		
Oxford	156	21	Shumway	Amos Junr	2		1		1	3	1		1				9		
Oxford	153	8	Shumway	David	2			1		1			1				5		
Oxford	153	4	Shumway	Ebenz	1	1		1				1		1			5		
Oxford	156	19	Shumway	Jacon Junr	2	2		1			1	1	1				8		
Sturbridge	332	20	Shumway	Jeremiah	2		1	1		2	1	1			1		9		
Oxford	153	10	Shumway	John				1						1			2		
Oxford	153	11	Shumway	Jonah	4			1		2			1				8		
Oxford	156	22	Shumway	Noah			1					1					2		

TOWN	PG#	LN#	LAST NAME	FIRST NAME	FREE WHITE MALES under 10	10 to 16	16 to 26	26 to 45	45 and over	FREE WHITE FEMALES under 10	10 to 16	16 to 26	26 to 45	45 and over	TOTAL ALL OTHER	TOTAL SLAVES	TOTALS	DISTRICT/ TOWNSHIP	NOTES
Athol	284	26	Shumway	Perez				1		1	1	1					4		
Petersham	284	12	Shumway	Perez				1		1	1	1					4		
Oxford	156	16	Shumway	Peter	1		1		1	1	2			1			7		
Sturbridge	332	19	Shumway	Saml	3	1			1	1		1	1				8		
Oxford	153	13	Sibley	Aaron			1		1	2			1				5		
Ward	176	22	Sibley	Aaron			2					1					3		
Douglas	482	9	Sibley	Abel	1			1		3			1				6		
Sutton	166	24	Sibley	Abel	1				1			2	1	2			7		
Hardwick	303	15	Sibley	Abijah	1			1		1	2	1					6		
Sutton	166	29	Sibley	Abner	1			1			1		1				4		
Sutton	165	15	Sibley	Archelaus	1			1		2			1				5		
Sutton	166	28	Sibley	Arthur	1			1				1					3		
Spencer	487	8	Sibley	Caleb	1			1		2			1				5		
Sutton	167	21	Sibley	Daniel		1		1		2		1	1				6		
Mendon	391	10	Sibley	David				1		3			1				5	2d Parish	
Sutton	165	14	Sibley	Ebenz	1	1	1		1			1		1			6		
Sutton	167	20	Sibley	Elijah				1				1	1	1			4		
Petersham	283	16	Sibley	Elisha	4	1	1	1		1	1		1				10		
Sutton	166	31	Sibley	Elisha		1		1		1		1					4		
Sutton	166	30	Sibley	Gibbs	3		1			2			1				7		
Oxford	156	18	Sibley	Gideon		3	1					1		1			6		
Sutton	167	19	Sibley	James			1	1		1			1				4		
Hardwick	303	12	Sibley	Jeremiah				1						1			2		
Barre	409	24	Sibley	Job	1	1		1		2	1	1					7		
Uxbridge	469	6	Sibley	Joel	2			1		2			2				7		
Sutton	166	27	Sibley	John			1		1					1			3		
Spencer	490	6	Sibley	Jona		1	1					1					3		
Sutton	165	1	Sibley	Jonas	2						1	1	1				5		
Oxford	153	2	Sibley	Jonathan		1		1		1		1	1				5		
Sutton	167	22	Sibley	Joseph		1		1						1			3		
Sutton	167	17	Sibley	Molley Wd		3				1		2	1	2			9		
Sutton	165	4	Sibley	Nathan	1	1	1	1	1	1	1	1	1	2			11		
Sutton	166	44	Sibley	Nathll				1						1			2		
Sutton	165	19	Sibley	Oliver				1			2	1					4		
Spencer	490	17	Sibley	Paul	1	1	1	1				3	1				8		
Spencer	487	7	Sibley	Paul Junr	3		1			1			2				7		
Athol	283	18	Sibley	Perley	1		1						1				3		
Sutton	166	42	Sibley	Peter	2	1		1			1	1	1				7		
Sutton	165	20	Sibley	Peter Junr	1			1			1	1	1				5		
Sutton	166	45	Sibley	Reuben		1	1	1				1		1			5		
Sutton	166	46	Sibley	Reuben Junr	1	1		1		1	1		1				6		
Barre	410	8	Sibley	Saml	1	2	1	1		1		1		1			8		
Hardwick	303	14	Sibley	Samll		1		1				1	1				4		
Sutton	165	6	Sibley	Simeon	1	1		1			1						4		
Ward	175	14	Sibley	Solomon	1		1		1			1					4		
Northborough	362	8	Sibley	Stephen	1	1	2	1		2	1	1	1				10		
Sutton	167	18	Sibley	Stephen	1	1						1					3		
Uxbridge	469	5	Sibley	Stephen			1	1				1		1			4		
Sutton	167	16	Sibley	Tarrant	4	2	1	1		1		1	1	1			12		
Sutton	167	15	Sibley	Timothy				1				1		1			3		
Grafton	204	1	Sibley	William	2	2		1		1		1	1				8		
Oxford	156	15	Sigourney	Andrew	2	1		2		4		1	1	1			12		
Brookfield	264	3	Simmonds	Job		1			1		1	1		1			5	Third Parish	
Petersham	283	15	Simmons	Benja	1	1	1	1				2	1	1			8		
Lunenberg	429	13	Simonds	daniel	1	2		1		3	1	1	1				10		
Gardner	447	13	Simonds	Elijah	1	1	3	1		2				1			9		
Leominster	438	18	Simonds	John	1	1	1	1		2	2	1		1			10		
Fitchburg	426	2	Simonds	Joseph	1			1		2			1				5		
Gardner	447	15	Simonds	Joseph			1			1				1			3		
Leominster	435	32	Simonds	Mehitable	1					1			1				3		
Harvard	222	37	Simons	Jonathan	1		1	1			1		1				5		
Sutton	166	26	Simpson	Lot	1			1		1			1				4		
Sutton	166	40	Simpson	William			1	1				1	1				4		
Sturbridge	332	17	Simpson	Wm	1			1			2		1				5		
Templeton	237	14	Simson	Joshua		1		1		1		1	1				5		
Sutton	165	7	Singletarry	Amos				1									1		
Ward	176	25	Singletary	Amos Jur	2	2	2	1		1	1		1				10		
Harvard	220	4	Sisson	George	1			1		2	1		1				6		
Sturbridge	332	22	Sith	Mary									1				1		
Rutland	514	4	Skinner	Israel	2			1					1				4		
Templeton	239	5	Skinner	Luther	1			1		2		1					5		
Paxton	503	23	Slade	Henry	1	1	2		1	1	1		1				8		
Worcester	185	21	Slaid	Jack											5		5		
Worcester	187	20	Slater	Peter	3	2		1		3			1				10		
Brookfield	265	27	Slayton	Isaac	1			1		1		1	1				5	Third Parish	
Brookfield	265	33	Slayton	Phinehas	1		2		1			1	1	1			7	Third Parish	
Brookfield	265	28	Slayton	Thomas				1						1			2	Third Parish	
Hardwick	304	1	Sloane	Ezekial	4			1			2			1			8		
Hubbardston	420	4	Slocomb	James	2	1	1	1		2	1		1				9		
Hubbardston	420	3	Slocomb	Saml Capt	1	1	2	1				1	1				7		
Northbridge	473	13	Slocum	Joshua	3	2		1		1	1		1				9		
Hubbardston	420	16	Slocumb	Peleg	1		1					1					3		
Sutton	166	43	Slocumb	William	3		1			1		2	1	1			9		
Dudley	344	16	Sly	Nathan	1	1	1	1		2	1	1					8		
Sutton	165	9	Small	Samuel	1	1			1	1	1	1		2			8		
Fitchburg	426	4	Small	William		1		1		1		1	1				4		
Athol	283	16	Smith	Aaron	2			1		3	3	2	1				12		
Hubbardston	420	17	Smith	Abel		1		1			1						3		
Holden	509	17	Smith	Amos		2		1		3	1	1					8		
Rutland	511	17	Smith	Andrew	1		1	1		1		1	2	1			8		
Athol	283	17	Smith	Asa			1	1			2	2	1				7		
Mendon	391	13	Smith	Asa			1		1		1	1		1			5	2d Parish	

244

TOWN	PG#	LN#	HEADS OF HOUSEHOLD LAST NAME	FIRST NAME	FREE WHITE MALES under 10	10 to 16	16 to 26	26 to 45	45 and over	FREE WHITE FEMALES under 10	10 to 16	16 to 26	26 to 45	45 and over	TOTAL ALL OTHER	TOTAL SLAVES	TOTALS	DISTRICT/ TOWNSHIP	NOTES
Fitchburg	426	1	Smith	Benja	2	2	1	1	1	1		1	1	1			11		
Western	254	11	Smith	Benjm		2		1		1	1			1			6		
Rutland	511	18	Smith	Benoni	2	1	2		1			1		1			8		
Athol	283	13	Smith	Caleb			1		1					1			3		
Mendon	386	14	Smith	Calvin Col.				1						1			2	1st Parish	
Westminster	452	14	Smith	Charles			1			1		1					3		
Worcester	188	10	Smith	Daniel	1		1			1	1	1					5		
Barre	410	6	Smith	David	1	2	1	1		1			2				8		
Bolton	211	14	Smith	David	1	1						1	1				4		
Holden	509	18	Smith	David	2	1	1	1				2	1	1			9		
Paxton	503	19	Smith	David	2			1		1	1		1	1			7		
Rutland	511	15	Smith	David	4		2	1				1	1				9		
Winchendon	228	15	Smith	David				1			1			1			3		
Douglas	482	6	Smith	Ebenezer				1		1			1	2			5		
Lunenberg	429	7	Smith	Ebenezer	4	2	1	1		1			1	1			11		
Athol	283	15	Smith	Elihu	1			1		1	1	1					5		
Douglas	481	35	Smith	Elijah	1	1	2		1		1			1			7		
Grafton	199	6	Smith	Eliphalet				1			1		1				3		
Worcester	188	9	Smith	Elisha Jun	3		1	1		1		2		2			10		
Worcester	188	13	Smith	Elizabeth			1				2	1	1				5		
Rutland	511	16	Smith	Enoch	1	1		1		3	1		1				8		
Southborough	205	31	Smith	Ephraim	1			1		2			1				5		
Worcester	187	18	Smith	Ezekiel			1			4		1					6		
Western	254	9	Smith	Ezra			1	1		1				1			4		
Barre	410	7	Smith	Francis				1									1		
Mendon	392	17	Smith	George	1	1	1	1		4	1			1			10	2d Parish	
Boylston	371	9	Smith	Isaac		2		1		1	1		1	1			7		
Winchendon	228	14	Smith	Isaac		2		1						1			4		
Worcester	185	22	Smith	Ithamar	1	1		1		4	2		1				10		
Northbridge	473	14	Smith	Jacob	1			1		1			1				4		
Worcester	188	1	Smith	Jacob	2			1		2	1		1				7		
Rutland	514	7	Smith	James	2	1	1		1	3	1	2	1				12		
Charlton	335	20	Smith	Jesse	1	1		1				1	1				5		
Paxton	503	16	Smith	Joel	2			1		1		1					5		
Barre	409	28	Smith	John	2	1	1	1		1		1	1	1			9		
Boylston	372	1	Smith	John	1		2	1		1			1	1			7		
Princeton	517	45	Smith	Jonas	2	2	2		1	1		1		1			10		
Rutland	511	19	Smith	Jonas	1			1		1			1				4		
Westminster	451	16	Smith	Jonathan		1		1		1	1			1			5		
Petersham	283	2	Smith	Joseph			1		1	2	2		1				7		
Westminster	451	11	Smith	Joseph	2			1		1	1		1	1			7		
Barre	409	26	Smith	Joseph Capt	1	1		1		1	1	1	1				7		
Ashburnham	458	13	Smith	Joshua		1		1			1	3		2			8		
Athol	283	14	Smith	Joshua		1	1			1			1				4		
Charlton	335	13	Smith	Joshua				1						1			2		
Brookfield	252	6	Smith	Levi	3			1		2	1		1				8	First Parish	
Westborough	192	45	Smith	Levi		1		1		1	1		1				5		
Rutland	511	13	Smith	Lockert	2	2		1		2	1		1	1			10		
Uxbridge	469	13	Smith	Luis			1			1	1		1				4		
Leominster	435	25	Smith	Lydia									1				1		
Leominster	435	26	Smith	Mary		1					1	1					3		
Leominster	438	16	Smith	Mary										2			2		
Holden	509	15	Smith	Moses			2	1				2	1	1			7		
Lancaster	353	19	Smith	Moses		1	2	1					1	2			7		
Sterling	350	18	Smith	Moses	1		1	1		3			1				7		
Holden	509	16	Smith	Moses 2d			1			2	3		1				7		
Barre	409	27	Smith	Moses Lt.		1		1				2		1			5		
Athol	284	24	Smith	Nathan	1			1		1	1		1	1			6		
Holden	510	3	Smith	Nathan	2		1							1			4		
Petersham	284	10	Smith	Nathan	1			1		1	1		1	1			6		
Princeton	517	39	Smith	Nathan				1		3		1	1	1			7		
Sturbridge	332	23	Smith	Nathan	2	1		1		1	1	1		1			8		
Hardwick	303	13	Smith	Nathl			1			2	1		1				5		
Barre	409	25	Smith	Nathl Lt.		1	2			1		1	1	1			8		
Charlton	335	15	Smith	Oliver			1	1			1		1	1			5		
Charlton	335	24	Smith	Reuben			1			2			1				4		
Fitchburg	426	7	Smith	Reuben	3		2	1				2	1				9		
Paxton	503	15	Smith	Reuben	2		1	1	1	3		1	1	1			11		
Sterling	350	19	Smith	Richard	2			1		3	1		1				8		
Athol	284	23	Smith	Robert	2			1		1			1				5		
Barre	407	15	Smith	Robert	1			1		2			1				5		
Douglas	481	36	Smith	Robert			1					1					2		
Petersham	284	9	Smith	Robert	2			1		1			1				5		
Worcester	188	11	Smith	Robert M.				1						1			2		
Barre	410	2	Smith	Saml	2	2	1	1	1		1			1			9		
Mendon	392	18	Smith	Saml	2		1	1	1	2		1	1	1			10	2d Parish	
Barre	410	3	Smith	Saml Dea.		4		1				2	2	1			10		
Mendon	391	4	Smith	Saml Jr	2			1		2			1				6	2d Parish	
Leominster	435	24	Smith	Samuel	1		1	1		1	2		1				7		
Barre	410	11	Smith	Sarah Wid								1	1				2		
Barre	410	9	Smith	Seth	2			1		1	1		1				6		
Westminster	452	12	Smith	Silas	2			1		1	1		1				6		
Barre	410	5	Smith	Stephen	3	1		1		2			1				8		
Sutton	166	38	Smith	Thomas	1	1		1		1		1					5		
Hardwick	303	7	Smith	Thos R	3			1					1				5		
Sutton	165	5	Smith	Timothy	2	3			1		1	1	1	1			10		
Hubbardston	420	5	Smith	Warren	1	1	1		1		1			1			6		
Charlton	335	25	Smith	William		2		1		3	1		1				8		
Rutland	511	14	Smith	William		1	1			1	1	1					6		
Barre	410	1	Smith	Wm		2		1				2		1			6		
Hardwick	303	6	Smith	Wm	1		1	1	1	1	1	3	2	1			12		

245

TOWN	PG#	LN#	LAST NAME	FIRST NAME	FREE WHITE MALES					FREE WHITE FEMALES					TOTAL ALL OTHER	TOTAL SLAVES	TOTALS	DISTRICT/ TOWNSHIP	NOTES
					under 10	10 to 16	16 to 26	26 to 45	45 and over	under 10	10 to 16	16 to 26	26 to 45	45 and over					
Dudley	344	12	Smith	Wm Jun	1		1			1		1			1		5		
Barre	410	4	Smith	Saml Jr	1			1		2			1				5		
Leicester	493	2	Snow	Abner	3	1		1		1	1		1				8		
Hardwick	303	5	Snow	Apollos	1			1		1			1				4		
Brookfield	249	14	Snow	David	2			1		3				1			7	First Parish	
Leicester	493	5	Snow	James	2			1		1	1	1					6		
Spencer	490	7	Snow	James	1	3		1		2			1				8		
Hardwick	303	3	Snow	Jesse	1		1		1				1	1			5		
Paxton	503	20	Snow	John			1		1		1			1			4		
Brookfield	249	15	Snow	Jonathan Jun	2			1	1	1		1	1	1			8	First Parish	
Brookfield	249	18	Snow	Joseph			1		1			1	1	1			5	First Parish	
Brookfield	261	14	Snow	Joseph	2	1		1						1			5	Second Parish	
Brookfield	252	4	Snow	Joseph Jun			1			2			1				4	First Parish	
Leominster	435	31	Snow	Moses	2			1		3				1			7		
Leicester	493	4	Snow	Nathan				1						1			2		
Paxton	503	13	Snow	Nathan				1									1		
Brookfield	261	15	Snow	Nathl				1						1			2	Second Parish	
Worcester	187	15	Snow	Pete											3		3		
Fitchburg	426	12	Snow	Peter	3		1	1				1	1				7		
Leominster	438	17	Snow	Samuel	2		1		1	1	2		1				8		
Paxton	503	22	Snow	Seth		1	1	1		1		1	1	1			7		
Spencer	490	8	Snow	Seth	2	1		1			1		1				6		
Lunenberg	429	10	Snow	Silas	1		1	1		1		1					5		
Lunenberg	429	12	Snow	Silas Jun	4		1			1			1				7		
Westborough	198	122	Snow	Susannah									1				1		
Leicester	493	3	Snow	Thomas				1						1			2		
Sutton	165	17	Snow	Warren	1		1						1				3		
Paxton	503	21	Snow	Willard	2		1			1	1	1					6		
Lancaster	356	10	Solendice	John			1		1					3			5		
Lancaster	353	15	Solenstine	Isaac				1						1			2		
Leicester	493	17	Southgate	Isaac				1				1		1			3		
Leicester	493	16	Southgate	John	1		1	1		1		1	1				6		
Leicester	493	9	Southgate	Susannah						1			1				2		
Berlin	213	9	Southick	David	2	2	1		1	2	1	2	1				12		
Berlin	213	10	Southick	Enoch	1	2			1	3	1	2	1				11		
Northborough	362	3	Southick	Nathl				1		2	1	1		1			6		
Upton	386	10	Southland	David	1			1		1			1				4		
Mendon	386	18	Southland	Joel			1					1					2	1st Parish	
Mendon	386	15	Southland	Willm	1			1		2		1					5	1st Parish	
Mendon	391	6	Southwick	Edward			1		1		1	1		1			5	2d Parish	
Uxbridge	469	12	Southwick	George	1	1	2		1	2	1	1	1				11		
Mendon	391	11	Southwick	Jacob	1			1		1			1				4	2d Parish	
Northbridge	474	1	Southwick	Jacob		3	1		1	4	1	2		1			13		
Mendon	391	15	Southwick	John	1		3	1	1	1	1	2		1			10	2d Parish	
Mendon	391	9	Southwick	John 2d		1			1	3	2		1				8	2d Parish	
Mendon	391	7	Southwick	John 3d	3			1		1			1				6	2d Parish	
Mendon	391	8	Southwick	Joseph			1		1			2		1			5	2d Parish	
Uxbridge	469	10	Southwick	Joseph	3	1	2		2	2	1	1			1		13		
Uxbridge	469	11	Southwick	Royal	2	1	1	1		2			1				8		
Mendon	391	5	Southwick	Seth	1		1	1		2			1				6	2d Parish	
Mendon	391	14	Southwick	Theophilus	1	1	2		1	1	1		1	1			9	2d Parish	
Ward	176	19	Southworth	Nethl	2		1	1		1		1	1				7		
Worcester	185	18	Southworth	Simeon	1		1			1	1		1				5		
Douglas	482	5	Southworth	Stephen	1		1	1		1	2	1		1			8		
Royalston	239	13	Soverein	Joseph	1		1			1							3		
Berlin	216	4	Spafford	Job	1		1		1	1		1	2	1			8		
Berlin	216	16	Spafford	Samuel	2			1		2	1		1				7		
Templeton	231	10	Sparhawk	Ebenz		2	2		1			3		2			10		
Oxford	153	12	Sparhawk	Ezra			1			1		1					3		
Oxford	153	7	Sparhawk	Joseph		1			1		1	1	1				5		
Oxford	153	6	Sparhawk	Timo	1	1			1	1	1	1	1				7		
Ashburnham	458	8	Spaulding	James	1	2	1	1		1	1		1				9		
Westminster	451	8	Spaulding	Joseph	2		1	1				2					6		
Westminster	451	7	Spaulding	Merari	3			1		2			1				7		
Oxford	156	23	Spaulding	Peter				1		2		1	1				5		
Westminster	451	9	Spaulding	Zebina	1		1						1				4		
Spencer	490	9	Spear	Daniel	2			1		2		1	1				7		
Templeton	235	11	Spear	Richard	2	2	1	1		1				2			11		
Princeton	517	38	Spence	Frederick	2		1	1		1	1		1				7		
Sterling	350	17	Spofford	John	1	1	2	1		1		1					8		
Oakham	321	6	Spooner	Benn			1	1		1	1		1				5		
Athol	284	21	Spooner	Clap	4	1	1	1		1	1		1				10		
Petersham	284	7	Spooner	Clap	4	1	1	1		1	1		1				10		
Oakham	321	5	Spooner	Eleazer	3	1	2	1	1			1	1	1			13		
Hardwick	303	19	Spooner	Jeduthan	3	1	1		1	1	2	1		1			11		
Brookfield	264	8	Spooner	Joshua				1			1	1					4	Second Parish	
Oakham	321	9	Spooner	Moses		1		1					1				3		
Petersham	283	14	Spooner	Philip	1		1	1			3		1				7		
Petersham	283	4	Spooner	Ruggles		1		1		1	1	1					5		
Hardwick	303	11	Spooner	Samll			1					1	1				3		
Hardwick	303	18	Spooner	Seth			1			2		1	2	1			7		
Athol	284	20	Spooner	Wing			1		1			2	1	1			6		
Petersham	284	6	Spooner	Wing			1		1			2	1	1			6		
Hardwick	303	9	Spooner	Zepheniah	3			1					1				5		
Spencer	490	14	Sprague	Caleb	4	3			1	1			1				10		
Spencer	490	15	Sprague	James	2	2			1	1	1		1				8		
Lancaster	356	9	Sprague	John	1	3			1	1	3			1			10		
Douglas	482	2	Sprague	Jonathan	3	2		1		1	2		1				10		
Petersham	283	12	Sprague	Joseph			1	1	1			2		1			6		

TOWN	PG#	LN#	LAST NAME	FIRST NAME	FREE WHITE MALES					FREE WHITE FEMALES					TOTAL ALL OTHER	TOTAL SLAVES	TOTALS	DISTRICT/ TOWNSHIP	NOTES
					under 10	10 to 16	16 to 26	26 to 45	45 and over	under 10	10 to 16	16 to 26	26 to 45	45 and over					
Athol	283	3	Sprague	Joshua	3			1		1		1	1				7		
Leicester	493	8	Sprague	Knight		2		1		1		1		1			6		
Douglas	482	1	Sprague	Mercy							1	1		1			3		
Worcester	185	19	Sprague	Miles	3		1						1				5		
Harvard	215	11	Sprague	Nathan			1	1					1				3		
Harvard	217	22	Sprague	Samuel			1	1		1		1		1			5		
Spencer	490	16	Sprague	Thomas		2		1					2				5		
Leicester	494	16	Sprague	Timothy		1	1		1		2	1	1		1		8		
Leicester	493	1	Sprague	William	2		1	1		1	3		1	1			10		
Templeton	238	1	Sprague	Wm	4		1	1		1	1	1					9		
Northbridge	473	15	Spring	Adolphus	2		3	2		2	1	1	1	2	1		15		
Uxbridge	469	4	Spring	Ephraim	2	2	1		1	3	1	1	1				12		
Holden	509	14	Spring	John	1		1			1		1					4		
Hubbardston	420	8	Springe	Saml	3	1		1		1	1	1					8		
Hardwick	303	2	Sprout	James	1	1		3		1	1		2				9		
Barre	410	14	Sprout	Leml			1										1		
Hardwick	303	4	Sprout	Nathan	1			1		2			1				5		
Hardwick	303	17	Sprout	Robert	1			1		1	1		1				5		
Charlton	335	8	Spurr	John	2		3	1				1	2				9		
Harvard	215	6	Stacy	John	2		1	1		1			1				6		
Worcester	188	8	Stair	Samuel			2		1			1		1			5		
Upton	386	16	Stanford	Jemime Mrs.								1		1			2		
Western	251	13	Stanford	Joseph	1		1			1		1					4		
Hardwick	303	20	Stanford	Polly							1		1				2		
Worcester	187	31	Stanton	Sarah	2	2	1	1			2	1	2				11		
Brookfield	265	30	Staples	Elias	3	1		1		2			1				8	Third Parish	
Brookfield	265	29	Staples	Elias Junr	2	1		1		1			1				6	Third Parish	
Mendon	386	17	Staples	George	1	2		1		2	1		1				8	1st Parish	
Mendon	386	16	Staples	Nahor	2	1	1	1		2	1	1	1				10	1st Parish	
Mendon	386	8	Staples	Simeon	3	2	1	1		1	1	2		1			12	1st Parish	
Mendon	386	12	Staples	Thomas				1					1				2	1st Parish	
Oakham	321	10	Starbuck	Uriah	1	2		1		2			2				8		
Ashburnham	458	9	Starnes	James	1	1	1	1		2	1		1				8		
Harvard	215	7	Steadman	Thomas	2	1		1	1	2	2	2	1				12		
Worcester	188	15	Stearns	Bezahiel				1					1				2		
Worcester	188	7	Stearns	Charles		1	2	1	1	1	1	1	1				9		
Lancaster	356	2	Stearns	Daniel				1			2		1				4		
Worcester	188	2	Stearns	Daniel	2	1	1	1		1			1				7		
Fitchburg	426	3	Stearns	Daniel M.	1	1	2			1	1		1	1			8		
Milford	391	17	Stearns	David			3		1	3		1	2				10		
Upton	386	15	Stearns	Ebenezer		1	1	1					1				4		
Lancaster	353	11	Stearns	Eli	1	2	3	1		4		1	1				13		
Rutland	514	2	Stearns	Elijah	1		1	1	1	1	1		1				7		
Hardwick	304	4	Stearns	Elizabeth	2	1					1	2	1				7		
Worcester	187	26	Stearns	Elizabeth									1				1		
Upton	386	14	Stearns	Increase	5	2		1			1		1				10		
Ashburnham	458	7	Stearns	Isaac	1	1	1		1	2	2	1		1			10		
Hardwick	304	5	Stearns	Jno		1		1			1	1		1			5		
Barre	410	10	Stearns	John	2	3	2	1		3	1		1				13		
Southborough	204	5	Stearns	John				1									1		
Worcester	188	3	Stearns	John Junr				1			1		1				3		
Princeton	517	42	Stearns	Jonas		2	1			2			1				6		
Rutland	514	1	Stearns	Jonathan			1	1					1	1			4		
Holden	510	2	Stearns	Joseph		2		1						1			4		
Leominster	435	29	Stearns	Josiah	1		1	1		2			1				6		
Lunenberg	429	11	Stearns	Josiah		1	1		1	2		3		1			9		
Lunenberg	429	16	Stearns	Levi	5		1			1		1	1	1			10		
Petersham	283	19	Stearns	Martha							1	1	1				3		
Worcester	187	17	Stearns	Mary	1	1				2		2	2				8		
Athol	283	2	Stearns	Saml	2		1			1		1					5		
Leominster	435	30	Stearns	Samuel				1		1		1		1			4		
Leominster	435	27	Stearns	Samuel Jun	2		1			2			1				6		
Leominster	435	28	Stearns	Thomas	1	1	1		1	2	1		1				8		
Ashburnham	458	10	Stearns	William	1	2			1	2	1		1				8		
Worcester	188	4	Stearns	Willm				1		2				1			4		
Worcester	187	23	Stearns	Willm J			1	1				1		1			5		
Petersham	283	3	Stears	Ephm			3	1			1	1		1			7		
Spencer	490	10	Stebbins	John			1	1						1			3		
Paxton	503	24	Stebbins	Peter	1	1		1		1	1	2	1				8		
Lancaster	353	16	Stedman	William	2	1		1		1		1	1				7		
Ashburnham	458	12	Steel	Joseph				1				1					2		
Leicester	494	12	Steel	Mary							1	1	1				3		
Hardwick	303	10	Stephans	Thos		1	2	1				2	1	1			8		
Charlton	335	11	Stephen	Saml	3		1				1						5		
Berlin	213	15	Stephens	Abel	2	1		1			1		1				6		
Winchendon	230	6	Stephens	Amos	1			1		1		1					4		
Sturbridge	332	24	Stephens	Cyprean		1	1		1		1	2		1			7		
Hardwick	304	2	Stephens	Jacob			1				2		1				4		
Northborough	362	6	Stephens	Jacob				1			1	1					3		
Western	249	5	Stephens	James			1			1		1					3		
Charlton	335	12	Stephens	John				1					1				2		
Charlton	335	16	Stephens	John Junr	1	1	3		1	3	1		1				11		
Barre	407	16	Stephens	Luther	2	1		1		1	1						6		
Charlton	335	9	Stephens	Moses			1										1		
Charlton	335	10	Stephens	Peter	1	1	1			4	1		1	1			10		
Brookfield	264	5	Stephens	Roger			1						1				2	Second Parish	
Brookfield	261	16	Stephens	Silas				1		1	1	1		1			5	Second Parish	
Winchendon	228	13	Sterns	Barthw		1	1		1			1		1			5		
Leicester	493	7	Stetson	Laban		1		1				3					5		
Petersham	283	5	Stevens	Gardner	4	2		1	1	1	1		1	1			12		
Brookfield	261	17	Stevens	Jeduthan	4		2	1		2		1	1				11	Second Parish	

TOWN	PG#	LN#	LAST NAME	FIRST NAME	M <10	M 10-16	M 16-26	M 26-45	M 45+	F <10	F 10-16	F 16-26	F 26-45	F 45+	TOTAL ALL OTHER	TOTAL SLAVES	TOTALS	DISTRICT/TOWNSHIP	NOTES
Brookfield	261	18	Stevens	Jude				1				1	1				3	Second Parish	
Brookfield	264	2	Stevens	Justus	2			1		3			1				7	Third Parish	
Ward	176	21	Stevens	Phins		1	1	1		1	1		1				7		
Lancaster	356	12	Stevens	Samuel	1			1		1	1		1				5		
Fitchburg	426	15	Steward	Daniel				1				1	1				3		
Leominster	435	23	Stewart	Alpheus	3			1		1			1				6		
Lunenberg	429	3	Stewart	Benja				1									1		
Leominster	438	19	Stewart	Huldah										1			1		
Leominster	435	22	Stewart	John		4		2				1	1				8		
Leominster	435	21	Stewart	Richard	1	2	1	1	1	1		2	2	1			12		
Sterling	350	16	Stewart	Samuel				1		2			1				4		
Leicester	493	6	Stickney	John			2	2					1	1			6		
Fitchburg	426	14	Stickney	Joshua			1						1				2		
Fitchburg	426	10	Stickney	Oliver			1	1						1			3		
Lunenberg	429	5	Stickney	Stephen		2		1					1	1			5		
Lunenberg	429	17	Stiles	Caleb	1			1		1		1	1				5		
Worcester	188	14	Stiles	Jeremiah	2	1	1						1				5		
Lunenberg	429	6	Stiles	Jonathan	4	1		1					1	1			9		
Boylston	371	12	Stiles	Joshua	1	1		1		3	1	1	1	1			11		
Sutton	165	8	Stiles	Josiah	2		1	1		1	1		2				8		
Lunenberg	429	20	Stiles	Levi	1			1	1			1	1	1			6		
Lunenberg	429	19	Stiles	Nahum	1			1		1			1				4		
Sutton	165	21	still	Freeman											3		3		
Hardwick	303	16	Stimpson	Thos	2			1		1		1					5		
Mendon	386	13	Stimson	Charles	2		1	1		1			1				6	1st Parish	
Winchendon	228	11	Stimson	Isaac				1						1			2		
Ashburnham	458	11	Stimson	Lemuel	2	1		1		2		1	1				8		
Winchendon	228	12	Stimson	Luther	3			1		1			1				6		
Ashburnham	457	32	Stimson	Phenihm	3			1			2		1				7		
Templeton	239	2	Stockwell	Abel	2			1		2			1				6		
Sutton	166	36	Stockwell	Amos		1		1		1			1				4		
Royalston	241	10	Stockwell	Asahel	1		1					1					3		
Douglas	481	37	Stockwell	Eli	2			1					1				4		
Sutton	165	16	Stockwell	Enoch	1		1	1		1		1					5		
Royalston	231	8	Stockwell	John	2	2		1		2			1	1			9		
Ward	175	16	Stockwell	John	1	1		1		4	1		1				9		
Royalston	240	6	Stockwell	Joseph		1		1					1	1			4		
Oxford	156	17	Stockwell	Joshua	1			1					1				3		
Royalston	240	3	Stockwell	Judah	3			1		3			1				8		
Sutton	165	2	Stockwell	Nathll		1		2		1	2		1				7		
Sutton	165	3	Stockwell	Nathll Junr	3			1		2			1				7		
Athol	283	1	Stockwell	Noah	1		1	1		1		1	1				6		
Athol	283	9	Stockwell	Peter			1				1						2		
Royalston	237	7	Stockwell	Simeon	2	1		1		1			1				6		
Sutton	166	41	Stockwell	Simeon	2			1		1		1					5		
Athol	284	1	Stockwell	Simon	1			1					1				3		
Sutton	166	37	Stockwell	Solomon		1	1	1		1	2	1	1				8		
Sutton	166	32	Stockwell	Stephen				1				2	1				4		
Sutton	166	33	Stockwell	Stephen Junr	1	1	1						1				4		
Milford	391	13	Stodard	Jeremiah				1					1				2		
Milford	391	14	Stodard	Sarah Wd	2					1	1						4		
Brookfield	264	7	Stoddard	Bela C.	2	1		1					1				5	Second Parish	
Winchendon	230	4	Stoddard	David				1		1			1				3		
Winchendon	230	3	Stoddard	James	1		1	1		1			1				6		
Winchendon	230	5	Stoddard	Levitt	2	1		1		1			1				6		
Brookfield	265	31	Stoddard	Samuel		2	1		1	1	2			1			8	Third Parish	
Upton	386	19	Stodder	Ezekiel	1	1		1		3	1	1					8		
Ashburnham	457	30	Stone	Adams	2	1		1		2	1	1					8		
Oakham	321	4	Stone	Alpheus	1	1	1	2	1		2	3	2	1			14		
Oxford	153	5	Stone	Ambrose		1		2			2		1				6		
Petersham	283	20	Stone	Amos	2		1	1		1	1		1				7		
Dudley	344	10	Stone	Benj				1				1	1				3		
Barre	407	17	Stone	Benj Esq	1		1						1				3		
Charlton	335	6	Stone	Benjm			1			2		1	1				5		
Oakham	317	13	Stone	Daniel	3	1		1				1	1				7		
Sterling	350	20	Stone	Daniel	2		1						1				4		
Sutton	166	39	Stone	Daniel	1			1		1				1			4		
Oxford	153	9	Stone	David	1		2					1	1				7		
Petersham	283	13	Stone	David				1					2	2			5		
Athol	284	19	Stone	David Jr		1		1		1	1		1				5		
Petersham	284	5	Stone	David Jr		1		1		1	1		1				5		
Hubbardston	420	14	Stone	Ebenezer	1		1	1		1			2				6		
Charlton	335	19	Stone	Ebenzr		1		1		1	1	1	1				6		
Winchendon	229	17	Stone	Edmund	1		1		1	2	1	1		1			8		
Barre	410	13	Stone	Elijah		1	2	1		2			1	1			8		
Rutland	511	22	Stone	Elijah	1	1			1			1	1	1			6		
Sutton	165	13	Stone	Elijah	2	1			1	2		1	1	1			9		
Hubbardston	420	13	Stone	Eliphalet	1			1				2					4		
Harvard	219	8	Stone	Ephraim			1					1	1				3		
Brookfield	264	6	Stone	Francis			1		1				2	2			6	Second Parish	
Oakham	321	7	Stone	Frederick	3	2		1				1		1			8		
Dudley	344	14	Stone	Henry			1			1			1				2		
Ashburnham	458	1	Stone	Hosea			1										1		
Douglas	482	8	Stone	Isaac	1		1	1			1	2		1			7		
Oakham	321	8	Stone	Isaac	1	1		1		1	1	1					6		
Ward	176	23	Stone	Isaac	3		1	1		1			1				7		
Ward	175	15	Stone	Israel	1	1			1	1				2			6		
Lancaster	353	14	Stone	Jacob	2			1	1			1		1			6		
Western	254	7	Stone	James		2		2	1			2		1	1		9		
Rutland	511	23	Stone	Jedithon		2		1			1	3		1			8		
Lancaster	353	8	Stone	Jemima	1					1			1				3		

| | | | HEADS OF HOUSEHOLD | | FREE WHITE MALES | | | | | FREE WHITE FEMALES | | | | | | | | | |
TOWN	PG#	LN#	LAST NAME	FIRST NAME	under 10	10 to 16	16 to 26	26 to 45	45 and over	under 10	10 to 16	16 to 26	26 to 45	45 and over	TOTAL ALL OTHER	TOTAL SLAVES	TOTALS	DISTRICT/ TOWNSHIP	NOTES
Rutland	514	10	Stone	Jerusha	1					1	1		1				4		
Petersham	283	1	Stone	Jesse		1		1		3	1	1		1			8		
Ward	176	18	Stone	Jesse				1					1				2		
Boylston	372	2	Stone	John				1					1				2		
Petersham	283	17	Stone	John	1		1					1					3		
Rutland	511	20	Stone	John			1	1	1	1		1	1	2			8		
Sutton	166	25	Stone	John				1					1				2		
Ward	175	13	Stone	John	1	2		1		1		1	1				7		
Petersham	283	8	Stone	Jona	1		2			1		1	1	1			7		
Ward	175	10	Stone	Jona Jr	2			1		1		1	1				6		
Leicester	496	6	Stone	Jonas	2	3	11	1		1	4	6	1				29		
Rutland	514	8	Stone	Jonas	1	1				3			1	1			8		
Ward	175	9	Stone	Jonathan		2	1	1				1	1				6		
Ashburnham	457	27	Stone	Joseph		1	1		1	1		1		1			6		
Harvard	219	25	Stone	Joseph			2	1				1		1			5		
Ward	175	11	Stone	Joseph		1		1					1				3		
Western	252	7	Stone	Joseph	3	1		1		1			1				7		
Charlton	335	21	Stone	Josiah				1									1		
Harvard	222	28	Stone	Lemuel				1				1					2		
Templeton	231	6	Stone	Leonard		1	2		2	1		1		2			9		
Sutton	165	12	Stone	Levi				1					1				2		
Oxford	153	3	Stone	Luther	1		3	2		1	1	1		1			10		
Southborough	204	9	Stone	Luther		1			1	2	2		1				7		
Harvard	220	21	Stone	Micah			2	1						1			4		
Douglas	482	7	Stone	Moses			1	1		1		1					4		
Grafton	198	8	Stone	Nahum		1		2	1			1					7		
Ashburnham	457	29	Stone	Nancy						1	1		1				3		
Hubbardston	420	12	Stone	Nathan Lt		2	1	1				1		1			6		
Ward	175	12	Stone	Nathl	2	1		1		3	1	2	1				11		
Charlton	335	18	Stone	Nehemiah	1		1	1		2	4	1	1	1			12		
Ashburnham	458	2	Stone	Oliver				1			1		1	1			4		
Dudley	344	11	Stone	Parley	2			1		1			1				5		
Harvard	222	36	Stone	Phineas	2		1	1		1			1	1			7		
Dudley	344	8	Stone	Reuben	3	1		1		2			1				8		
Athol	284	22	Stone	Saml	3	2	1		1	1	1	1	1				11		
Petersham	284	8	Stone	Saml	3	2	1		1	1	1	1	1				11		
Charlton	335	22	Stone	Sampson	2	1		1		2	1		1				8		
Gardner	447	17	Stone	Samuel	1	1	2		1	3	1	1					11		
Oxford	153	14	Stone	Samuel	2	1		1		1	1		1				7		
Hubbardston	420	18	Stone	Sary										1			1		
Barre	410	12	Stone	Seth	4			1			1		1				7		
Brookfield	249	13	Stone	Silas	1	1	2	1			1	1		1			8	First Parish	
New Braintree	311	17	Stone	Silas	3			1		1			1	1			7		
Templeton	240	3	Stone	Simeon		1	1		1	1	2	3		1			10		
Gardner	447	16	Stone	Simon	1			1		1							3		
Rutland	511	21	Stone	Stevens			1	1			1	2					6		
Mendon	386	10	Stone	Thomas	1	1				3			1				7	1st Parish	
Fitchburg	425	12	Storer	Solomon	3	1			1	3			1	2			11		
Harvard	215	8	Stow	Benjamin	2		1	1			1	1	1	1			8		
Grafton	201	15	Stow	Eliza									1				1		
Grafton	197	6	Stow	Ithimer	2		1	1		2			1	1			8		
Southborough	203	23	Stow	Jonathan		1	1		1			1		1			5		
Grafton	197	7	Stow	Lucy						1		1		1			3		
Petersham	283	6	Stow	Lydia	1								1				2		
Winchendon	229	18	Stow	Molly										1			1		
Southborough	202	15	Stow	William	2			1		1			1	1			6		
Worcester	188	12	Stow	John	1	1		1		2			1	1			7		
Athol	284	29	Stowell	Abel	3		1	1		1		1	1	1			9		
Petersham	284	15	Stowell	Abel	3		1	1		1		1	1	1			9		
Worcester	187	25	Stowell	Abel	3	2	1		1	1	1	1		1			11		
Worcester	187	27	Stowell	Anna	2	2	1					1	2	1			9		
Athol	284	28	Stowell	Asahel	1	1		1		2		2					7		
Petersham	284	14	Stowell	Asahel	1	1		1		2		2					7		
Worcester	187	28	Stowell	Benja		1		1					1	3			6		
Worcester	187	22	Stowell	Cornelias				1						1			2		
Athol	284	25	Stowell	David		1		1			1	1	1	1			6		
Petersham	284	11	Stowell	David		1		1			1	1	1	1			6		
Worcester	187	30	Stowell	David	1		1	1		1	1	1					6		
Worcester	187	21	Stowell	Elias	3		1	1		2	1		1				9		
Petersham	284	16	Stowell	Joab	1		1	1				1		1			5		
Athol	284	30	Stowell	Joal	1		1	1		1			1				5		
Athol	284	27	Stowell	John	3	2			1			1	1	1			9		
Petersham	284	13	Stowell	John	3	2			1			1	1	1			9		
Athol	284	31	Stowell	Lemuel		1	1	1		1			1				5		
Petersham	284	17	Stowell	Lemuel		1	1	1		1			1				5		
Worcester	187	29	Stowell	Nathl	1			1		2			1				5		
Worcester	187	24	Stowell	Peter		5	3	2		4	1	1	1				17		
Athol	286	15	Straton	Peleg	3	2	2	1	1			2		2			13		
Northborough	362	9	Stratten	Windsor	1			1		1			1				4		
Rutland	514	9	Stratton	Alpheus	2	1		1	1	3			1	1			10		
Bolton	215	5	Stratton	David			1		1	1	2	1		2			8		
Athol	283	8	Stratton	Eben	1	1		1		2			1	1			7		
Athol	283	6	Stratton	Elias				1				1		1			3		
Athol	283	7	Stratton	Elias Jur	4		1					1					7		
Holden	509	20	Stratton	Israel	2			1					1				4		
Athol	283	5	Stratton	Jabez				1					1				2		
Worcester	185	20	Stratton	James	1			1		3			1				6		
Athol	283	4	Stratton	Joseph	3			1		1			1				6		
Holden	509	19	Stratton	Josiah		1		1				1	1				4		
Athol	283	11	Stratton	Levi			1			1			1				3		

TOWN	PG#	LN#	LAST NAME	FIRST NAME	under 10	10 to 16	16 to 26	26 to 45	45 and over	under 10	10 to 16	16 to 26	26 to 45	45 and over	TOTAL ALL OTHER	TOTAL SLAVES	TOTALS	DISTRICT/ TOWNSHIP	NOTES
					FREE WHITE MALES					FREE WHITE FEMALES									
Princeton	517	40	Stratton	Samuel	2		1	1		3	3		1				11		
Brookfield	265	32	Stratton	Sarah						1	1	1		1			4	Third Parish	
Athol	283	10	Stratton	Stephen			2		1		1	1		1			6		
Holden	509	21	Stratton	Thomas	1			1		2		1					5		
Athol	283	12	Stratton	Willm		1	2		1	3	1			1			9		
Douglas	482	4	Streeter	Asa	3			1		2			1				7		
Charlton	335	7	Streeter	Daniel				1					2				3		
Brookfield	264	1	Streeter	Eunice									3				3	Third Parish	
Dudley	344	17	Streeter	John			1					1					2		
Charlton	335	14	Streeter	Mary									1				1		
Douglas	482	3	Streeter	Stephen				1					1				2		
Winchendon	228	16	Stuart	Paul	2			1		1			1				5		
Lancaster	353	9	Studley	Consider		2		1		2			1				7		
Leicester	493	14	Studly	Benj			1	1	1		1	1	1	1			7		
Leicester	493	15	Studly	Zenas			1					1					2		
Hardwick	303	1	Studson	Ezra				1			1		1				3		
Hardwick	302	20	Studson	Robert		2		2			1		1				6		
Worcester	188	17	Sturtevant	Saml	2		1			1		1					5		
Charlton	335	4	Stutson	Deborah						1		1					2		
Milford	391	16	Sumner	Darius	1	1	2		1	1	2		1				9		
Milford	391	18	Sumner	Ebenz				1			1						2		
Milford	391	19	Sumner	Ebenz Junr	2	2	1	1		1	1		1				9		
Spencer	490	11	Sumner	John	2	1	1		1	1	2		1				9		
Milford	391	15	Sumner	Joseph	1			1		1	2		2				7		
Westborough	199	151	Sumner	Samuel				1					1				2		
Spencer	490	12	Sumner	William			1				1	1					3		
Paxton	503	12	Swan	Nathan		1			1			1		1			4		
Leicester	496	5	Swan	Reuben			1	1		1	1		1	1	1		6		
Leicester	496	1	Swan	Reuben B			1				1	1					3		
Athol	286	16	Swatson	Samuel	2		1	2		2		1	2				10		
Royalston	242	4	Sweet		1	1		1		2	1		1				7		First name left blank
Mendon	386	9	Sweeting	Job	1		1		1			1					4	1st Parish	
Western	254	8	Sweetser	Henry	3			1	1			2	1				8		
Western	254	10	Sweetser	Henry Jr	5	2		1				1					9		
Lancaster	353	17	Sweetser	Jacob		1			1	2	2		1				7		
Paxton	503	14	Sweetzer	Benja		1	1	1		1		2		1			7		
Paxton	503	25	Sweetzer	Benja Jun			1				1	1					3		
Paxton	503	17	Sweetzer	Jacob		1	1	1					1				4		
Paxton	503	11	Sweetzer	Jacob F.			1						1				2		
New Braintree	311	19	Swetzer	John	2			1		4			1				8		
Mendon	391	3	Swift	Abraham			1					1					2	2d Parish	
Mendon	391	2	Swift	Joseph		1		1					1				3	2d Parish	
Spencer	490	5	Sylvester	Ichabod	2		1	1					1				5		
Leicester	494	14	Sylvester	John			2				1						3		
Leicester	494	13	Sylvester	Joshua	1		1		1	1		1					5		
Lunenberg	429	18	Sylvester	Lot			1	1				1	1				4		
Winchendon	228	18	Sylvester	Nathl	2	1		1		3	1	2	1				11		
Leicester	494	15	Sylvester	Peter Jun	1	1		1	1	1	1	1	1				8		
Princeton	517	48	Symonds	Isaac	1		1			2		1					5		
Templeton	233	5	Symonds	James		2	1	1			1	2	1				8		
Templeton	237	16	Symonds	James		1	1	1			1	1	1				6		
Holden	509	22	Symonds	John		1		1					1				3		
Templeton	237	17	Symonds	Samll	1			1					1				3		
Templeton	233	6	Symonds	Samuel	1			1					1				3		
Templeton	237	12	Symonds	Zebedia	3	1		1		2	2						9		
Westminster	449	14	Tabor	Joseph		1											1		
Hubbardston	420	22	Tabour	Joseph	1			1				1					3		
Boylston	372	15	Tacker	Jedediah	3			1				1					5		
Uxbridge	471	13	Taft	Aaron			1	1				1	1	1			5		
Uxbridge	472	7	Taft	Abner				1			1		1				3		
Mendon	385	11	Taft	Amasa	1		1				1						3	1st Parish	
Westminster	454	1	Taft	Asa		1	1	1		1		1					7		
Uxbridge	472	14	Taft	Bezeleel		2	2		1	1	1	2	2		1		12		
Uxbridge	472	12	Taft	Calvin	2	1		1		1			1				6		
Uxbridge	471	6	Taft	Cummings	3	1		1	1				1				7		
Uxbridge	472	9	Taft	Darias			1			2		1					4		
Royalston	232	14	Taft	David	1		1			3		1					6		
Uxbridge	471	12	Taft	Easmon	1		1	1		1			1				5		
Mendon	394	2	Taft	Ebenezer	2		1	1		2	3		1	1			11	2d Parish	
Upton	383	4	Taft	Eli	1			1		3		1	1				7		
Mendon	385	14	Taft	Elijah	1	1		1		2			1				6	1st Parish	
Upton	383	8	Taft	Elisha Lt.	3	1		1		1		1	1	1			8		
Mendon	385	6	Taft	Enos	1	1		1		1	1			1			7	1st Parish	
Mendon	394	1	Taft	Enos 2d			1					1					2	2d Parish	
Uxbridge	472	13	Taft	Ephraim		1			1	1	2	1	1	1			8		
Uxbridge	471	17	Taft	Frederic	1	1	1	1		3	2		2				11		
Mendon	385	15	Taft	George	2			1					1				4	1st Parish	
Uxbridge	474	3	Taft	Gerera	1			1		2		1					5		
Uxbridge	472	11	Taft	Gershom				1					1				2		
Northbridge	474	2	Taft	Israel	1	1		1		3	1	1	2				10		
Upton	386	20	Taft	Isreal			2			1		1					4		
Uxbridge	471	9	Taft	Jacob				1				1	1				3		
Uxbridge	471	11	Taft	Jacob Junr	2	1		1		1	2	1		1			9		
Uxbridge	471	10	Taft	James		1	1		1	1		1					6		
Mendon	394	11	Taft	Japheth	4			1		1	1		1	1			10	2d Parish	
Worcester	186	10	Taft	Jesse				1					1				2		
Royalston	241	5	Taft	Joel	3	1		1				1					6		
Upton	383	2	Taft	John	1			1			1		1				5		
Worcester	186	14	Taft	John	1			1		1		1					4		

250

TOWN	PG#	LN#	LAST NAME	FIRST NAME	FWM under 10	FWM 10 to 16	FWM 16 to 26	FWM 26 to 45	FWM 45 over	FWF under 10	FWF 10 to 16	FWF 16 to 26	FWF 26 to 45	FWF 45 over	TOTAL ALL OTHER	TOTAL SLAVES	TOTALS	DISTRICT/TOWNSHIP	NOTES
Upton	386	22	Taft	Joseph	1		1	1		3			1	1			8		
Uxbridge	472	10	Taft	Joseph Junr		1		1			1	1		1			5		
Uxbridge	474	5	Taft	Josiah	3		1	1		1		1		1			8		
Worcester	186	11	Taft	Josiah	2			1		1	1		1				6		
Mendon	385	12	Taft	Jotham		1	1		1			1		1			5	1st Parish	
Northbridge	474	3	Taft	Keith			1	1		1		1	1				5		
Uxbridge	471	5	Taft	Leonard	3			1				1					5		
Brookfield	266	3	Taft	Martha								1	1				2	Third Parish	
Northbridge	474	4	Taft	Marvel	3	3		1		1		1	1	1			11		
Upton	383	3	Taft	Matthew				1					1				2		
Uxbridge	472	5	Taft	Micajah		1		1		2		1					5		
Uxbridge	471	1	Taft	Mijaman			2		1			1		1			5		
Uxbridge	472	6	Taft	Moses	1			1		1	1	1					5		
Mendon	394	6	Taft	Nahum			1	1						2			4	2d Parish	
Uxbridge	472	15	Taft	Nathan				1			2		1				4		
Uxbridge	474	4	Taft	Nathan	1			1		2		1					5		
Uxbridge	472	16	Taft	Nathan Jun	1			1			1						3		
Mendon	385	9	Taft	Nathaniel	3	3		1	1	1		1	1	1			12	1st Parish	
Uxbridge	471	15	Taft	Noah	1			2	1	2			1	1			8		
Uxbridge	471	7	Taft	Paul					1				1				2		
Barre	407	24	Taft	Robert	1		1	1		1	2		1				7		
Upton	383	7	Taft	Robert Capt.	1			1				1	1				4		
Uxbridge	472	1	Taft	Samuel		2	1		1	2			1				7		
Mendon	385	8	Taft	Seth	3	1	1		1	2	1		1				10	1st Parish	
Upton	383	6	Taft	Solomon		1		1	3	1	1		1				8		
Upton	386	21	Taft	Stephen	1			1				1					3		
Uxbridge	474	1	Taft	Stephen	1	1		1		1	1		1				6		
Uxbridge	469	14	Taft	Sweeting	2	2		1		2	1		1				9		
Uxbridge	472	4	Taft	Thadeus	2	2		1		1		2	1				9		
Mendon	385	10	Taft	Thomas	3	1	1		1	2	1	3	1		2		15	1st Parish	
Worcester	185	27	Taft	Timothy	1	1	1		1		2		1				7		
Uxbridge	472	8	Taft	Webb	1			1		1		1					4		
Uxbridge	471	14	Taft	Willis	3	1		1		1	1		1				8		
Mendon	385	7	Taft	Zacheus	2	1		1		2			1				7	1st Parish	
Uxbridge	469	15	Taft	Amasa	1		1					1					3		
Hardwick	304	12	Tailor	Seth			2		1		1		1				5		
Hardwick	304	18	Tailor	Wm	2			1				1					4		
Sutton	165	36	Tainter	Abijah		1		1			1		1	1			4		
Sutton	165	41	Tainter	Abijah Junr	1	1					1						3		
Leominster	435	38	Tainter	Ayers	1		1	1			1						4		
Leominster	436	4	Tainter	Catherine		5	3		1	1	1	1					11		
Sutton	165	37	Tainter	Joel	1		1	1		2		1					6		
Sutton	165	40	Tainter	Stephen			1					1					2		
Leicester	496	11	Taintor	Nahum			1		1	2	2	1		1			8		
Westminster	454	12	Talor	Ezra	1			1				1					3		
Ashburnham	458	15	Talor	Jonathan	1	1		1		1		1					5		
Petersham	286	3	Tame	Joseph		2		1	2				1				6		
Westminster	454	4	Taylor	Asa	2		2	1	1				1				7		
Hardwick	304	19	Taylor	Benn	1			1		2		1					5		
Lunenberg	432	1	Taylor	Caleb		1		1	1		2	1					6		
Harvard	219	34	Taylor	Charles			1						1				2		
Douglas	482	12	Taylor	Daniel			2			2			2				6		
Ashburnham	458	16	Taylor	David			2	1					3	1			7		
Oxford	154	13	Taylor	Eliphalet			1						1				2		
Southborough	204	8	Taylor	Ezra			2		1	1	1	3	1				9		
Winchendon	230	12	Taylor	Isaac	2	1		1		2			1				7		
Lunenberg	432	5	Taylor	Isreal	2			1		2			1				6		
Sutton	165	33	Taylor	James	2	1		2					1				6		
Leominster	436	3	Taylor	John	1			1		1			1				4		
Hardwick	304	16	Taylor	Jonathan		1		1		1	1		1				5		
Westminster	454	6	Taylor	Joseph			2		1			1		1			5		
Westminster	454	8	Taylor	Joseph Jr	1			1		3			1				6		
Sutton	165	32	Taylor	Mary Wd	1	1	2					1		1			6		
Lunenberg	432	4	Taylor	Nathan			1			3			1				5		
Worcester	186	2	Taylor	Othniel		2	4		1					1			8		
Ashburnham	455	2	Taylor	Phenihas	2			1		2			1				6		
Westminster	454	10	Taylor	Rebeckah								1					1		
Hardwick	304	14	Taylor	Samll	2			1		3	2		1				9		
Fitchburg	423	3	Taylor	Samuel	2	1		1		1			1	1			7		
Westminster	454	5	Taylor	Samuel	1		1	1			2		1				6		
Harvard	222	21	Taylor	Solomon	1	2		1		1	2	2	1				10		
Worcester	185	29	Taylor	Stephen			1		1			1		1			4		
Hardwick	304	13	Taylor	Sylvanus		1											1		
Southborough	201	2	Taylor	Trowbridge		1		1		2		2	1				7		
Hardwick	304	15	Taylor	Uel		1		1				1					3		
Southborough	201	3	Taylor	William	2			1		2		1	1	1			8		
Worcester	186	3	Taylor	William				2		3		1	1	1			8		
Westminster	454	9	Tayor	Elizabth										2			2		
Boylston	372	11	Temple	Aaron	1			1				1	1				4		
Holden	510	7	Temple	Aaron			1		4				1				6		
Grafton	195	3	Temple	Abner		1		1				1					3		
Gardner	448	3	Temple	Ahio	1			1	3			1					6		
Boylston	372	14	Temple	Benja				1		2		1					4		
Boylston	372	13	Temple	Emary	1			1		1		1					4		
Gardner	448	4	Temple	Ephraim			1			1	1		1				4		
Northborough	362	11	Temple	Henry	2			1		2			1				6		
Boylston	372	7	Temple	John			3	2		2	2	1	1				11		
Boylston	372	6	Temple	Jonas		1	3	1						1			6		
Boylston	372	12	Temple	Joshua	2	1	1	1			1		1	1			8		

TOWN	PG#	LN#	LAST NAME	FIRST NAME	FWM under 10	FWM 10-16	FWM 16-26	FWM 26-45	FWM 45 & over	FWF under 10	FWF 10-16	FWF 16-26	FWF 26-45	FWF 45 & over	TOTAL ALL OTHER	TOTAL SLAVES	TOTALS	DISTRICT/TOWNSHIP	NOTES
Boylston	372	8	Temple	Timothy		1			1		1			1			4		
Grafton	200	3	Temple	Timothy			1		1			1					3		
Hubbardston	420	21	Tenney	Abel	4	3	1		1			1	2				12		
Western	254	12	Tenney	Amasa	1			1					1				3		
Upton	383	1	Tenney	Joshua					1					1			2		
Northborough	362	10	Tenny	Gideon	2	1		1		2	1		1				8		
Leominster	436	1	Tenny	Joseph	1	2	1		1	1	1	1		1			9		
Sutton	165	23	Terel	Gilbert			1	1			1		1				4		
Worcester	186	7	Terrey	Geer			3						1	1			5		
Hardwick	304	8	Terry	John	3	1	2	1					1	1			9		
Princeton	518	1	Thacher	John A.	4			1					2				7		
Princeton	517	49	Thacher	Obediah	1	3		1		2		1	1				9		
Worcester	186	9	Thaxter	Benja	2	1	1	1		2			1				8		
Mendon	385	20	Thayer	Aaron Capt.	3	1	3	1		2	1	2	1		1		15	1st Parish	
Douglas	482	14	Thayer	Abijah	1	1		1		2	1		1				7		
Mendon	385	17	Thayer	Alexander	1		1	1				2					5	1st Parish	
Mendon	385	18	Thayer	Amos	1		2					1					4	1st Parish	
Uxbridge	471	18	Thayer	Amos	1			1		1			1	1			5		
Mendon	394	4	Thayer	Artemas	2	1		1		1			2				7	2d Parish	
Uxbridge	472	3	Thayer	Asa	3	2	1			1	1	1	1				11		
Mendon	385	19	Thayer	Benjamin	2		2		1	2	1	1	2				11	1st Parish	
Mendon	391	19	Thayer	Benjamin 2d		1	1		1		1	1					5	2d Parish	
Mendon	394	5	Thayer	Caleb	1	1		1		3			1				7	2d Parish	
Uxbridge	474	2	Thayer	Denis	2			1					1				4		
Milford	391	28	Thayer	Elijah	2	1	2	1	1		1	1	1	1			11		
Douglas	482	13	Thayer	Elisha	2			1					1				4		
Hardwick	304	11	Thayer	Ephraim	1	2	1		1	1		2		1			9		
Douglas	482	10	Thayer	Gideon	1			1					1				3		
Uxbridge	472	17	Thayer	Grindale		1	1		2	1		1					6		
Mendon	394	9	Thayer	Ichabod	3			2		1			1	1			8	2d Parish	
Milford	391	29	Thayer	Ichabod Col.		1	3		1		1	2		1			9		
Mendon	385	16	Thayer	Increase Lt.		1	1			1	1		1				6	1st Parish	
Douglas	479	20	Thayer	Israel	1		1	1		3	2		3	1			12		
Hardwick	304	9	Thayer	James	3			1		1			1				6		
Douglas	482	17	Thayer	John	1	1	1			1	1		1				7		
Hardwick	304	10	Thayer	John				1			1		1				3		
Hardwick	306	14	Thayer	John Jr			1						1				2		
Douglas	482	16	Thayer	Joseph		1		1						1			3		
Mendon	391	18	Thayer	Joseph		2	2	1				1		2			8	2d Parish	
Douglas	479	21	Thayer	Moses	1		1			4			1				7		
Mendon	391	21	Thayer	Nahum	2		1			3		1	1				8	2d Parish	
Lancaster	356	21	Thayer	Nathaniel		2	1			3	1	1	1				9		
Mendon	391	20	Thayer	Nicholas		2	1			3		1	1				8	2d Parish	
Mendon	394	3	Thayer	Robert			1				1						2	2d Parish	
Milford	391	24	Thayer	Seth				1					1				2		
Milford	391	25	Thayer	Seth Junr	2			1		3			1				7		
Mendon	385	5	Thayer	Smith	1	1	1	1		2	1	1					9	1st Parish	
Douglas	479	18	Thayer	Thadeus		2	3		1	4	2		1				13		
Mendon	391	17	Thayer	Thomas	2			1		1		1					5	2d Parish	
Petersham	286	7	Thayne	Ephm	3	1			1	2	1	2	1				11		
Hardwick	304	17	Thomas	Daniel	1			1			1	1					4		
Worcester	185	30	Thomas	Isaiah			1		1		1	1		2	2		8		
Worcester	185	31	Thomas	Isaiah Jr		1	6	1		1	1	1	1				12		
Lancaster	356	22	Thomas	Joshua				1			1	1		1			4		
Brookfield	252	11	Thomas	Naaman	3		1	1		2			1				8	First Parish	
Barre	407	18	Thomas	Robert	3		1	1					1				6		
Brookfield	252	12	Thomas	Silas	2			1				1					4	First Parish	
Lancaster	355	3	Thomas	Thompson			1	1		1			1				3		
Brookfield	252	9	Thomas	William			2	1	1				1				5	First Parish	
Leicester	496	14	Thompson	Abner	3	2		1		2			1				9		
Barre	407	20	Thompson	Andrew	1		1	1			1	1	1	1	1		7		
Leominster	436	6	Thompson	Benja	1		1			3			1				6		
Uxbridge	471	2	Thompson	Benjamin	5		1			1			1				8		
Leicester	496	15	Thompson	Edward				1		2				1			4		
Charlton	338	20	Thompson	Elijah 1st	1		1			3			1				6		
Charlton	338	17	Thompson	Elijah 2d	2	1						1					4		
Charlton	338	16	Thompson	Elisha		1		1		2	1		1				6		
Douglas	482	11	Thompson	Elisha	2	1		1		1	1						7		
New Braintree	312	13	Thompson	Hugh	2			1		3			1				7		
Hubbardston	420	19	Thompson	James	2	1	1		1		2	2	1				10		
Paxton	503	26	Thompson	James		1			1				2				4		
Sutton	165	31	Thompson	Jeremiah			1						1				2		
Uxbridge	471	4	Thompson	Joel	1		1	2			1	1					6		
Mendon	391	16	Thompson	John			2				1	1	2				6	2d Parish	
New Braintree	312	3	Thompson	John				1			1	1	1				4		
New Braintree	312	9	Thompson	John	2	1		1		2	1		1				8		
New Braintree	312	5	Thompson	Nathan	1	1	1		1	1	1	2	1				9		
Barre	407	25	Thompson	Richard				1	1	1		1		1	5		10		
Hubbardston	420	20	Thompson	Saml	2			1		2			1				6		
Paxton	503	27	Thompson	William	2	1		1		3			1				10		
New Braintree	313	14	Thompson	Wm	1	1	1					1	1				5		
Templeton	233	2	Thomson	Abel			2					1					3		
Princeton	518	3	Thomson	Isaac		1		1			1		1				4		
Princeton	518	4	Thomson	John	1	1		1		1			1				5		
Royalston	238	7	Thomson	Jonas	1	2	2		1		1	2	1	2			12		
Royalston	238	5	Thomson	Margaret		1								2			3		
Princeton	518	2	Thomson	William	2			1		2			1	2			8		
New Braintree	312	8	Thrasher	Samll	1	2			1	3			1				8		
New Braintree	312	4	Thrasher	Stephan	2			2	1		1	3		1			10		

TOWN	PG#	LN#	LAST NAME	FIRST NAME	under 10	10 to 16	16 to 26	26 to 45	45 and over	under 10	10 to 16	16 to 26	26 to 45	45 and over	TOTAL ALL OTHER	TOTAL SLAVES	TOTALS	DISTRICT/ TOWNSHIP	NOTES
New Braintree	312	7	Thrasher	Wm			1		1			2		1			5		
Mendon	385	21	Thurber	Daniel Dr.		1		1					1				3	1st Parish	
Brookfield	266	1	Thurber	Lakan			1					1					2	Third Parish	
Fitchburg	423	2	Thurlo	Rhoda	1				3				1				5		
Royalston	232	7	Thurstin	Lewis	1	2	1		1		1	1	1				8		
Sutton	165	42	Thurstin	Nathan	1		1	1		4	1	1	1	1			11		
Mendon	385	13	Thurston	Daniel	1			1					1				3	1st Parish	
Southborough	203	29	Thurston	Daniel		1						1					2		
Fitchburg	423	7	Thurston	Ebenz		1		1			1		1				4		
Lancaster	356	18	Thurston	Gates	4		1		1	1	1					8		
Westminster	454	3	Thurston	Gilman		1			1	1		1					3		
Fitchburg	423	4	Thurston	John			1		1					1			3		
Grafton	193	8	Thurston	John		1		1			1	1				4		
Lancaster	355	4	Thurston	John	2	1	1		1	2	2	1					10		
Fitchburg	423	5	Thurston	John Jun	1	2		1		2	1	1	1				9		
Brookfield	264	12	Thurston	Joseph	2		1					1					4	Second Parish	
Leominster	436	5	Thurston	Mehitable									1				1		
Westminster	454	2	Thurston	Moses	2			1		2	1	1	1				8		
Upton	383	5	Thurston	Pardius		1			1								3		
Lancaster	355	1	Thurston	Peter				1					2				3		
Lancaster	356	17	Thurston	Peter Junr		1	1		2	1	1					6		
Lancaster	356	19	Thurston	Samuel			1		1	1	1	1				5		
Westborough	191	31	Thurston	Samuel	1	1	1			2		2				7		
Lancaster	356	20	Thurston	Silas	2	1		1		3	1		1				9		
Fitchburg	423	8	Thurston	Stephen	2	1		1	1	1			1	1			8		
Fitchburg	423	6	Thurston	Thomas	1	1	1	1		2		1	1				8		
Southborough	203	28	Thurston	Timothy	3	1		1		2	1	1					9		
Uxbridge	471	8	Thwing	Benja	1		1		1			2		1			6		
New Braintree	312	11	Tidd	Wm	1			1		3	1	1	1				8		
Douglas	479	19	Tiffany	Lemuel	3			1		1			1				6		
Uxbridge	472	2	Tillinghart	Daniel		1		1	1		1		1		2		7		
Uxbridge	471	16	Tillinghart	Sylvanus			3	1		1			2		2		9		
Douglas	482	15	Tilly	James			2		1	1	1		1				6		
Boylston	372	5	Tilton	Joseph	1	2		1		2		1	1				8		
Sutton	165	25	Tinney	Daniel					1				1				2		
Sutton	165	35	Tinney	Danl Junr	1		1	1		1	1	1					6		
Lancaster	355	6	Tinney	Jonathan		1		1		1			1	1			5		
Lancaster	355	7	Tinney	Oliver	1			1		2	1		1				6		
Sutton	165	34	Tinney	Simon		1			1			1		1			4		
Sutton	165	24	Tisdale	Rachel	1					2		1	1				5		
Sutton	165	30	Titus	John	2	1		1		1	1	1					7		
Sutton	165	29	Titus	Jonah	4			1	1	1			1				8		
Athol	284	13	Tolbert	George	3			1		2			1				7		
Winchendon	230	7	Tolman	Desire	2	1	2		1		1	1		1			9		
Petersham	286	1	Tolman	Willm	1		2		1	1	2		1				8		
Boylston	372	10	Tombs	Lydia		1					1			1			3		
Oakham	321	11	Tomlinson	Daniel	1	1		2		1		1	1				7		
Athol	284	11	Toney	Abram											3		3		
Athol	284	10	Toney	Caesar											6		6		
Athol	284	14	Toney	Calvin				1									1		
Sutton	165	26	Torrey	Caleb			1	2		2		1	1				7		
Lancaster	356	16	Torrey	Ebenezer		1	1		1		1		2	1			7		
Worcester	185	23	Torrey	Joseph	1			1		1	1		1				5		
Mendon	385	2	Torrey	Joseph Capt.	4			1					1				6	1st Parish	
Sutton	165	27	Torrey	Keziah Wd	1								2	1			4		
Sutton	165	28	Torrey	Samuel		1		1		2		1	1				6		
Mendon	385	3	Torrey	Stephen	1				2		1			1			5	1st Parish	
Worcester	185	25	Torrey	Willm	3		1		1	2	1	2	1				11		
Mendon	385	1	Torrey	Willm Capt.	2	1		1	1	1			1				7	1st Parish	
Barre	407	22	Totman	Ebenezer	1				1		1	1	2	1			7		
Worcester	186	6	Totman	Jabez					1								1		
Worcester	186	5	Totman	John	3	1	1						1				7		
Barre	407	21	Totman	Martha Wid					1					1			2		
Barre	407	19	Totman	Nathl					1				1	1			3		
Athol	284	2	Totman	Saml		2	1	1		2	1	1					8		
Ashburnham	455	3	Tottingham	Moses	3			1		2			1				7		
Westminster	454	7	Tottingham	Nathll		1	1					1	1				4		
Mendon	394	10	Tourtellotte	Asahel	1		2			1			1				5	2d Parish	
Mendon	394	7	Tourtellotte	Jesse	1		3		1	2				1			8	2d Parish	
Mendon	394	8	Tourtellotte	Stephen			1			1		1					3	2d Parish	
Harvard	219	17	Tousant	Joseph			1		1		1			1			4		
Lancaster	355	5	Tower	Asahel	2	1		1		1	2		1				8		
Rutland	514	12	Tower	John	2			1		1			1				5		
Petersham	286	2	Tower	Jonas	2		1	1		1		1	1	1			8		
Rutland	514	11	Tower	Jonathan	1			1					1				3		
Worcester	186	13	Tower	Mary								1	1				2		
Petersham	286	6	Town	Amos		1		1					1				3		
Sutton	165	22	Town	Asa		1			1					1			3		
Charlton	338	4	Town	Daniel			1		1		1						3		
Charlton	338	3	Town	Elisha	1		1		1			1					4		
Leicester	496	10	Town	Elisha		1		1		3			1				6		
Western	251	5	Town	Elisha			1		1			1					3		
Petersham	286	5	Town	Jedadiah	5	1		1		1			1				9		
Dudley	344	20	Town	Joel		2											2		
Dudley	344	19	Town	John	1		1			1		1					4		
Charlton	338	5	Town	Josiah				1						1			2		
Charlton	338	6	Town	Josiah Junr		1	1			2	1		1				6		
Oxford	153	18	Town	Moses				2						3			5		
Ward	176	26	Town	Phinehas		1	1			3			1				6		
Charlton	338	1	Town	Richard Jr	1			1		1		1	1				5		

253

TOWN	PG#	LN#	LAST NAME	FIRST NAME	FREE WHITE MALES					FREE WHITE FEMALES					TOTAL ALL OTHER	TOTAL SLAVES	TOTALS	DISTRICT/ TOWNSHIP	NOTES
					under 10	10 to 16	16 to 26	26 to 45	45 and over	under 10	10 to 16	16 to 26	26 to 45	45 and over					
Charlton	338	13	Town	Salem		2	1		1	1	1	1		2			9		
Oxford	153	17	Town	Silvanus	1	1		1		1		1					5		
Dudley	344	18	Town	Simon	1	1	1		1		1	2		1	1		9		
Charlton	338	18	Town	Thomas			1	1		1			1				3		
Royalston	241	34	Town	William		1		1			2	1	1				6		
Lancaster	356	15	Townsand	Robert	1		1	1		2		1	1		1		8		
Ashburnham	458	17	Townsend	Abraham	2			1		3	1	1					8		
Holden	510	8	Townsend	Jacob				1					1				2		
Berlin	214	25	Townsend	James		3		1		2		1		1			8		
Ashburnham	455	1	Townsend	Joshua				1						1			2		
Berlin	214	26	Townsend	Joshua				1						1			2		
Berlin	214	27	Townsend	Joshua Junr			1			2		1					4		
Ashburnham	458	18	Townsend	Reuben	2	1		1		1	1	1	1				8		
Athol	284	3	Townsend	Thomas	3		2	1				1	1				8		
Brookfield	264	15	Townshend	George				1			1			2			4	Second Parish	
Southborough	203	15	Tozer	Josiah		1		1		4	1		1				8		
Worcester	185	26	Tracy	Thomas	1			1		3	1	2	1				10		
Worcester	186	1	Tradwell	Mary		1				2	1	2		1			7		
Westminster	454	11	Trane	Elisha	2			1		2			1				6		
Leicester	496	7	Trask	David			1	1		1	1		2				6		
Uxbridge	469	16	Trask	Frederic			1			4	1		1				7		
Mendon	394	12	Trask	Jonathan	1	2	1		1	1		2		1			9	2d Parish	
Sutton	165	38	Trask	Jonathan	1	1		1		1		1	2				7		
Sutton	165	39	Trask	Peter			5	1			1	2					9		
Leicester	496	12	Trask	Saml Junr	1		1						1				3		
Leicester	496	9	Trask	Samuel	1	2	2		1	1	1			1			9		
Templeton	238	4	Trask	William	1			1				1		1			4		
Templeton	238	5	Trask	William Jr	2			1		1			1				5		
Hardwick	304	6	Trask	Israel	3		1	1	1	1		1		1			9		
New Braintree	312	10	Trow	Israel			1	1					1	1			4		
Worcester	185	24	Trowbridge	James				1					1	1			3		
Petersham	286	4	Trumball	Joseph	1			1				1	1	1			5		
Oxford	153	19	Trumbull	Ebenz	3			1		3			1				8		
Oxford	153	16	Trumbull	James	2			1		2	1		1				7		
Leicester	496	13	Trumbull	Peter	1	1	1	1		3			1				8		
Uxbridge	471	3	Tucker	Benja	4	1		1			1		1				8		
Worcester	186	12	Tucker	Benja				1						1			2		
Winchendon	230	9	Tucker	Elisha	1			1		3	1		1				7		
Worcester	186	8	Tucker	Enos	1		1	1		1		1	1				6		
Spencer	487	10	Tucker	Ezekiel		1	1	1		2		1	1				7		
Brookfield	264	13	Tucker	Ezra	1	1	2	1		1	2		1				9	Second Parish	
Boylston	372	9	Tucker	Jedediah				1					1				2		
Charlton	338	10	Tucker	Jonathan			2	1		1	1		1				6		
Leicester	496	8	Tucker	Joseph		2	4	1		1	1	1	1				11		
Templeton	237	13	Tucker	Joshua	1	1		1				1					4		
Charlton	338	12	Tucker	Loas									1				1		
Charlton	338	8	Tucker	Lucy	1								1				2		
Hardwick	304	7	Tucker	Seth		1	1	1		1	1		1				6		
Winchendon	230	8	Tucker	Seth	2	1		1		1		1	1				7		
Charlton	338	15	Tucker	Tamerson	1	2				2	1	1					7		
Charlton	338	7	Tucker	Wm	1	2		1		1	1		1				7		
Charlton	338	9	Tucker	Wm Junr	2	1		1		1			1				6		
Hubbardston	420	23	Tucker		1			1		1		1					4		First name blank
Brookfield	252	10	Tuffs	John	1	1	2	1			2		1				8	First Parish	
Dudley	344	21	Tufts	Aaron	1	1		1				1	1				5		
Worcester	186	4	Tufts	Andrew	1			1		2			1		1		6		
Winchendon	229	19	Tufts	Benjamin	1		1					1					3	Third Parish	
Brookfield	266	2	Tufts	John	1		1					1					3		
New Braintree	312	6	Tufts	John			1	1									2		
Worcester	185	28	Tufts	Walter	1			1		2			1				5		
New Braintree	312	12	Tufts	Wm	1			1			2		1				5		
Leominster	436	2	Tulip	Peter											6		6		
Grafton	195	2	Turner	Asa	3			1		1			1				6		
Templeton	240	4	Turner	Asa	2	1		1		2		1	1	1			9		
Holden	510	5	Turner	Bezaleel		1		1						1			3		
Holden	510	6	Turner	Bezaleel Junr			1			2		1					4		
Fitchburg	423	1	Turner	Consider		2		2	2	1				2			9		
Fitchburg	426	16	Turner	Israel		2		1	1	2	1		1				8		
Lunenberg	429	21	Turner	Joseph	2	2		1		3	1		1				10		
Lancaster	355	2	Turner	Joshua			1	1				1					3		
Oxford	153	15	Turner	Joshua			1	1				3	1				6		
Harvard	215	2	Turner	Luthar		1		1		1		1		1			6		
Leominster	435	33	Turner	Nathl		1		1			1		1				4		
Harvard	215	3	Turner	Rebeckah	1					2	2	1					6		
Royalston	231	7	Turner	Samll	1	2	1		1	3		1	1				10		
Harvard	218	9	Turner	Simeon		2		1				1		1			5		
Winchendon	230	10	Tuttle	Jedidiah	2			1		1	1		1				6		
Holden	510	9	Tuttle	Joseph		1	1		1	3	1	1	1	1			10		
Winchendon	230	11	Tuttle	Simon	2			1		2			1				6		
Charlton	338	2	Twhichell	Benjm	3			1				1					5		
Westborough	197	113	Twichel	Thomas				1					1	1			3		
Westborough	197	114	Twichel	Thomas Jun		1		1		1	1	1					6		
Athol	284	5	Twichell	Abner	2			1		1			2				6		
Athol	284	9	Twichell	Bailey	1		1			2		1					5		
Athol	284	8	Twichell	Benonah		1				1			1				3		
Athol	284	6	Twichell	Enos	2		1			1			1				5		
Athol	284	7	Twichell	Jereh			1	1			1	1	1				5		
Athol	284	4	Twichell	Josiah	1		1			4			1				7		
Athol	284	12	Twichell	Seth	3	1	2	1		1			1				9		
Charlton	338	11	Twiss	James	1	1				3			1	1			8		
Charlton	338	14	Twiss	Moses	1		1	1		3			1	1			8		

TOWN	PG#	LN#	LAST NAME	FIRST NAME	FREE WHITE MALES					FREE WHITE FEMALES					TOTAL ALL OTHER	TOTAL SLAVES	TOTALS	DISTRICT/ TOWNSHIP	NOTES
					under 10	10 to 16	16 to 26	26 to 45	45 and over	under 10	10 to 16	16 to 26	26 to 45	45 and over					
Charlton	338	19	Twiss	Stephen	1			1						1			3		
Charlton	335	26	Twist	Ebenzr		1			1					1			3		
Barre	407	23	Twitchel	Timy			3	1	1		1	1	2	1			10		
Milford	391	27	Twitchell	Ephm				1				2					3		
Milford	391	26	Twitchell	Garshom	1		2		1	1	1		1				7		
Western	251	3	Tyler	Abner	2	2	2		1	1	1	2		1			12		
Brookfield	252	7	Tyler	Gideon			1	1			1	1		1			5	First Parish	
Douglas	479	22	Tyler	Henry			1		2			1					4		
Western	251	1	Tyler	Isaac		1	1	1		1		1					5		
Western	251	2	Tyler	Isaac 2d	2		1	1		1	1	1	1				8		
Brookfield	264	10	Tyler	John		1	3		1			1		1			7	Second Parish	
Brookfield	252	8	Tyler	Moses	1	2		1	1	2		1	2	1			11	First Parish	
Western	251	4	Tyler	Moses	1	1	1		1	1	1	1	1				8		
Brookfield	264	14	Tyler	Phinehas	2	1		1					1				5	Second Parish	
Brookfield	264	11	Tyler	Royal	3		1		1	1	1	1	1				8	Second Parish	
Uxbridge	469	17	Tyler	Solomon	4	1	1	1				1	1	1			10		
Mendon	385	4	Tyler	Urana Wd		1	2			1	1	1	1				7	1st Parish	
Leominster	435	36	Tylor	Joshua		1			1	3	2	1	1				9		
Lunenberg	432	2	Tylor	Moses	1	1			1			2		1			6		
Lunenberg	432	3	Tylor	Nathan			1			2			1				4		
Leominster	435	39	Tylor	Parker	2	1		1	1	3	2		1				11		
Leominster	435	34	Tylor	Phinehas	1			1			1	2		1			6		
Leominster	435	35	Tylor	Phinehas Jun	3	1		1		1			1				7		
Leominster	435	37	Tylor	Simeon	2			1		1			1				5		
Barre	408	1	Underwood	David	1		1	1					2	1			6		
Hubbardston	419	3	Underwood	Israel		1		1		4			1				7		
Barre	408	3	Underwood	Ithamar			1	1		2		1					5		
Barre	408	2	Underwood	Jonas	1			1		2	1		1				6		
Fitchburg	423	9	Underwood	Mary							1	1	1				3		
Spencer	487	11	Underwood	Reuben	1		1		1	2			1				6		
Hubbardston	419	2	Underwood	Timothy	2	1		1		1	1	1					7		
Northborough	362	12	Underwood	Timothy		1	1		5			2					9		
Petersham	286	8	Underwood	Timothy	2			1		1			1				5		
Barre	408	4	Underwood	Thomas	2		1	1		1		1			4		10		
Dudley	344	23	Upham	Benj		1	2	1						1			5		
Garry	274	1	Upham	Benj		2	2					1					5		
Hubbardston	419	4	Upham	Calven	1			1		1		2					5		
Brookfield	266	5	Upham	Daniel	1	2		1		3			1	2			10	Third Parish	
Templeton	242	9	Upham	Daniel		2	2		1	1		1		1			8		
Leicester	496	17	Upham	Ebenz				1					1				2		
Leicester	495	1	Upham	Ebenz Jun	2		1	1		1		1	1				7		
Dudley	341	25	Upham	Ephraim	1		1	1		2			1	1			7		
Dudley	341	24	Upham	Eunice								1	1				2		
Sturbridge	329	5	Upham	Isaac Jr	1			1				1					3		
Brookfield	252	13	Upham	Jabez	1	1	2	1		2			2				9	First Parish	
Spencer	487	12	Upham	Jesse	2	1	1	1					1	1			7		
Spencer	487	13	Upham	John			1			2			1	1			5		
Sturbridge	329	6	Upham	Jonathan				1					1	1			3		
Sturbridge	329	1	Upham	Lenard	3		1	1		2			2	1			8		
Brookfield	266	4	Upham	Nathan		2	1	1					2	1			7	Third Parish	
Dudley	341	26	Upham	Nathan	3	1		1			1		1				7		
Sturbridge	329	3	Upham	Nathl		1	1		1		1	2		1			7		
Hubbardston	419	1	Upham	Nathl		2		1	1	1			1	1			7		
Sturbridge	329	2	Upham	Pease				2	1				1	1			5		
Brookfield	266	6	Upham	Phinehas		1	2		1			2	1	1	1		9	Third Parish	
Douglas	479	23	Upham	Samuel				1						1			2		
Leicester	495	2	Upham	Samuel	3		1	1			1		1				7		
Dudley	341	23	Upham	Simeon	2			1			2		1				6		
Leicester	496	16	Upham	Thaddeus	2		5	1		1				1			10		
Dudley	344	22	Upham	Thomas	2		1		1	1	1	1					7		
Sturbridge	329	4	Upham	Thomas	1		1	1		1	1	1	1		1		8		
Royalston	239	8	Upham	Willard			2			1		1					4		
Fitchburg	423	11	Upton	Jacob			2	1	1			1		1	2		8		
Fitchburg	423	10	Upton	John	1	1	1	1		2	1		1				8		
Hardwick	304	20	Utley	James	2	2		1	2	2			1				10		
Upton	383	11	Vaile	Edward			1	1		1	1			1			5		
Barre	408	7	Varney	Dennis	2			1		1			1				5		
Barre	408	5	Varney	John Jr		1		2	1			1	1	1			7		
Barre	408	6	Varney	Sirus	1			1		1				1			4		
Charlton	338	24	Vassal	Benjm		1	1				1		1	1			6		
Mendon	394	14	Verry	Nathan		1	1			1		1	1	1			6	2d Parish	
Mendon	394	13	Verry	Nathan Jr			2	1		3	1	1	1				9	2d Parish	
Leicester	495	3	Very	Isaac	3			1		1	1	1	1				8		
Upton	383	10	Vial	Caleb				1						1			2		
Upton	383	9	Vial	James	1			1		2	2		1				8		
Northbridge	474	5	Vilas	Samuel		1		1		1			1				4		
Holden	510	10	Viner	John	1	1			1	3			1				7		
Athol	281	1	Vining	Levet	1		1	1		2			1				6		
Charlton	338	23	Vinton	John					1		1	1		1			4		
Dudley	341	27	Vinton	Joseph	4	1	1	1				2		1			10		
Charlton	338	21	Vinton	Joshua			1			3			1				5		
Charlton	338	22	Vinton	Lyman			1			3			1				5		
Dudley	341	29	Vinton	Ralph	2	1	1		1			1	1	1			8		
Dudley	341	28	Vinton	Wm	3	1	1	1			1	1	2				10		
Barre	408	8	Vokes	Robert	2			1		2			1				6		
Dudley	341	30	Vorse	Olive	1						1		1				3		
Grafton	202	15	Wadsworth	David				1						1			2		
Grafton	195	5	Wadsworth	Ebenz	1	1	2	1		1	1	1	1	1			10		
Grafton	202	13	Wadsworth	Jonath			1	1		3		1	1				7		
Grafton	202	16	Wadsworth	Samuel			2						1				3		
New Braintree	313	7	Wait	David		1	1	1	1	2		2					9		
Hubbardston	419	12	Wait	Jacob	1							1	1				3		

TOWN	PG#	LN#	LAST NAME	FIRST NAME	under 10	10 to 16	16 to 26	26 to 45	45 and over	under 10	10 to 16	16 to 26	26 to 45	45 and over	TOTAL ALL OTHER	TOTAL SLAVES	TOTALS	DISTRICT/ TOWNSHIP	NOTES
					FREE WHITE MALES					**FREE WHITE FEMALES**									
Brookfield	263	1	Wait	John				2	1	1				2			6	Second Parish	
Athol	281	7	Wait	Joseph		1			1				1	1			4		
Brookfield	263	3	Wait	Joseph	2		1		1	1	1	1		1			8	Second Parish	
Hubbardston	419	10	Wait	Joseph	1	1	1		1	3	2	2	1				12		
Brookfield	263	4	Wait	Nathaniel					1				1				2	Second Parish	
Brookfield	263	5	Wait	Nathaniel 2d		1		1		2	1		1				6	Second Parish	
Hubbardston	419	11	Wait	Nathl			1		1	1		1	1	1			6		
Hubbardston	416	9	Wait	Nathl Jr.			2						1				3		
Sterling	348	20	Wait	Richard	1	1		1		1		1	1				6		
Brookfield	263	9	Wait	Samuel			1			1		1					3	Second Parish	
Grafton	195	4	Wait	Simon			1	1			2	1	1				6		
New Braintree	313	17	Wait	Wm		1			1	1		1		1			5		
Leicester	498	2	Waite	Asa			1			1		1					3		
Paxton	504	3	Waite	Ebenezer		2	1		1			4		1			9		
Sturbridge	327	1	Waite	John		2				1		1					4		
Leicester	498	4	Waite	Nathan		3	1	1				2		1	1		9		
Leicester	498	3	Waite	Phinehas				1			1	1					3		
Leicester	495	5	Waite	Samuel	4		1		1			1	1				8		
Paxton	504	4	Waite	Samuel	1		1		1	1	1	1					5		
Sutton	167	41	Waite	William Junr	4	1			1		2		1				9		
Oxford	153	20	Wakefield	Aaron	2		1		1	2	1		1				8		
Sutton	166	17	Wakefield	Amasa	1				1			1	1				4		
Charlton	340	16	Wakefield	Amos	2	2		1		2	2		1	1			11		
Sutton	167	26	Wakefield	Bariah Junr	1		1					1					3		
Oxford	154	1	Wakefield	Beza			1		1	1		1					3		
Sutton	166	18	Wakefield	Isaiah				1		1			1				3		
Dudley	341	44	Wakefield	Joel	2			1		2			1				6		
Sutton	167	28	Wakefield	Joseph				1					1				2		
Charlton	337	2	Wakefield	Luther		1	1		1	1			1				5		
Dudley	341	34	Wakefield	Simeon	3		1	1	1	1		1					8		
Dudley	341	33	Wakefield	Solomon	1	1		1		3	1		1				8		
Oxford	154	2	Wakefield	Timo	5		1					1					7		
Charlton	340	9	Walcot	James	1	1		1			2	1					6		
Bolton	211	8	Walcutt	Mary	1								1				2		
Bolton	211	10	Walcutt	Rebeckah		1	1	1		1	2		1				7		
Dudley	341	35	Walden	Nathan	3	2		1				1	1				8		
Worcester	184	1	Waldo	Daniel		1	2	1	1	1	2	3	2				13		
Sterling	348	19	Waldren	Edward				1				2	1				4		
Charlton	340	3	Wale	Abel	2			1		2		1					6		
Winchendon	229	14	Wales	Jacob		1		1		2	1	1		1			7		
Milford	389	14	Wales	John	2	1		1		3		1					8		
Hardwick	305	13	Walker	Abel	1	2	1	1			2		1				8		
Brookfield	263	13	Walker	Adoniram		1	1		1	1				2			6	Third Parish	
Charlton	338	26	Walker	Asa	2	1		1			1		1				6		
Sutton	166	23	Walker	Asa	1	1		1		3	1	1	1				10		
Barre	405	35	Walker	Asa Dr.		1	1	3		3		1	1				10		
Southborough	200	5	Walker	Barzellel				1					1				2		
Douglas	480	6	Walker	Benja		2	2	1		1			1				7		
Brookfield	266	11	Walker	Benjamin	1	1	1	1		1	1	1					8	Third Parish	
Worcester	184	14	Walker	Cato											2		2		
Athol	281	6	Walker	Daniel	1			1				1					3		
Brookfield	266	10	Walker	Daniel	1	1		1		1			1				5	Third Parish	
Rutland	514	19	Walker	Daniel	3		1	1		2	2	1	1	1			12		
Southborough	200	6	Walker	Daniel	2			1					1				4		
Upton	384	12	Walker	Ebenezer	1			1	1			1	1				5		
Upton	384	13	Walker	Ebenezer Jr	4	1		1					1				7		
Royalston	231	10	Walker	Elijah	2	2	1	1		1		1	1				9		
Brookfield	266	9	Walker	Ezekiel		2	2					2		1			7	Third Parish	
Sturbridge	327	5	Walker	Ezra		1	1		1	1	1		1				6		
Holden	510	11	Walker	Hezekiah	1	1	1		1	3	2	1		1			11		
Westminster	456	7	Walker	James				1					1				2		
Brookfield	263	18	Walker	Jason	1	1		1		3	2		1				9	Third Parish	
Leominster	433	28	Walker	John	1			1		1	1		1				5		
Worcester	183	31	Walker	John	3	1	1	1		1		2	1				10		
Brookfield	266	16	Walker	Joseph		1		1				1	1				4	Third Parish	
Worcester	184	7	Walker	Joseph	2			1		1		1	1				6		
Brookfield	263	21	Walker	Joseph Jun	2			1					1				4	Third Parish	
Petersham	287	5	Walker	Josiah	1	1		1		3	1		1				8		
Sturbridge	329	19	Walker	Josiah	1				1		2	1		3			8		
Petersham	285	7	Walker	Jotham		1	1	1			1		1	1			6		
Brookfield	263	24	Walker	Moses				1		2			1				4	Third Parish	
Royalston	231	14	Walker	Moses	2			1		4			1				8		
Brookfield	266	7	Walker	Nathan		1		1		2			1				5	Third Parish	
Sturbridge	329	15	Walker	Nathl	1		1		1	1		1		1			6		
Royalston	236	2	Walker	Obadiah		2			1	1		1	1	1			7		
Sturbridge	329	16	Walker	Obed			1		1	1		1	1				4		
Brookfield	263	15	Walker	Oliver		1		1						1			3	Third Parish	
Brookfield	263	25	Walker	Oliver Jun	1		1			1		1					4	Third Parish	
Westminster	455	3	Walker	Paul	1		2		1			1					6		
Sturbridge	329	24	Walker	Perez	1	1	1			1	1	1					6		
Barre	406	10	Walker	Prince											4		4		
Petersham	287	10	Walker	Reuben	1			1		1	1		1				5		
Royalston	231	6	Walker	Reuben			1			1				1			3		
Winchendon	230	14	Walker	Samll		1	1			3		1					6		
Leominster	433	23	Walker	Samuel	1			1		1				1			4		
Oxford	154	4	Walker	Solomon		1	1		1			1					4		
Sutton	166	19	Walker	Timothy	3			1				1					5		
Brookfield	263	10	Walker	Walter	2		1	1				2					6	Second Parish	
Brookfield	263	14	Walker	William			1			3		1					5	Third Parish	
Petersham	285	6	Walker	Willm		1			1	2	2	1	1				8		
Mendon	394	15	Walkup	Henderson				2		3	1			1			7	2d Parish	

TOWN	PG#	LN#	LAST NAME	FIRST NAME	FREE WHITE MALES					FREE WHITE FEMALES					TOTAL ALL OTHER	TOTAL SLAVES	TOTALS	DISTRICT/ TOWNSHIP	NOTES
					under 10	10 to 16	16 to 26	26 to 45	45 and over	under 10	10 to 16	16 to 26	26 to 45	45 and over					
Uxbridge	473	10	Wall	Phebe		1				1		1		1			4		
Templeton	237	5	Wallace	Abel			1			1			1				3		
Douglas	479	27	Wallis	Aaron	2		1	1		2			1				7		
Douglas	479	26	Wallis	Benja				1					1				2		
Douglas	480	1	Wallis	Benja Junr	2	1	2		1		1	1	1				9		
Douglas	479	33	Wallis	David		2	1	1		1		1	1				7		
Lunenberg	432	22	Wallis	Ebenezer	2	1		1		1			1				6		
Douglas	479	34	Wallis	James		1	2	1		1	1		1				7		
Barre	406	7	Wallis	Margaret Wid		1		1					1				3		
Douglas	479	31	Wallis	Samuel	1	1	2	1		3	1		1				10		
Rutland	514	14	Walton	John				1			1		1				3		
Rutland	514	15	Walton	Samuel		1	4	1		1			1	1			9		
Hardwick	306	11	Waner	Jno Jr	4	1		1				1		1			8		
Southborough	203	16	Ward	Abner		1		1					1				3		
Athol	281	3	Ward	Alphus		2	2	1		2		1	1	2			11		
Charlton	337	23	Ward	Artemas	1					2	1		1				6		
Worcester	183	29	Ward	Asa			2	1	1	1			1				6		
Charlton	337	16	Ward	Benj			1	1						2			4		
Charlton	337	17	Ward	Benj Junr	3			1					1				5		
Ashburnham	456	9	Ward	Caleb		1	3		1	1	1	1		1			9		
Paxton	503	29	Ward	Calvin	1	1		1					2	1			6		
Petersham	285	10	Ward	Daniel	1	1	1		1	2	1	1		1			9		
Charlton	337	18	Ward	David				1		4	1		1				7		
Charlton	337	15	Ward	Elijah	1		1		1	1	1	2		1			8		
Petersham	285	15	Ward	Elisha				1					1	1			3		
Worcester	183	28	Ward	Elisha			1				1	1					3		
Brookfield	252	14	Ward	Ephm Revd	1	1	1		1			2		1	1		8	First Parish	
Southborough	200	3	Ward	Erasmus	3	2			1		1		1				8		
Paxton	503	28	Ward	Hezekiah				1						1			2		
Garry	274	2	Ward	Jabez	1	1		1		3			1	1			8		
Westminster	453	18	Ward	John	1		2	1		1	1	1					7		
Brookfield	263	23	Ward	John Junr	2		1						1				4	Third Parish	
Charlton	337	19	Ward	Jonas		1	2		1			1		1			6		
Upton	384	16	Ward	Jonathan		1	1			2			1				5		
Southborough	205	7	Ward	Josiah	1	1		1		2			1				6		
Charlton	337	20	Ward	Levi		1		1			1		1				4		
Leicester	495	6	Ward	Luther	2			1		2	2		1				8		
Petersham	285	14	Ward	Nahum		1	1			1		1	1				5		
Upton	384	14	Ward	Nahum Capt.			1	1		1	1			1			5		
Worcester	183	21	Ward	Phinehas				1						1			2		
Lancaster	358	14	Ward	Samuel	1	1	2	1	1		1	2	2	1			12		
Charlton	337	21	Ward	Simon	2			1		1		1					5		
Westborough	199	154	Ward	Solomon				1					1				2		
Brookfield	266	15	Ward	Thomas	2	3	1			1	2	1	1				11	Third Parish	
Garry	274	3	Ward	Thomas	2	2		1		2		2	1				10		
Ashburnham	455	6	Ward	William	3	1		1			1		1				7		
Worcester	184	9	Warden	Saml				1					2				3		
Worcester	184	10	Warden	Samuel Jr	2			1			1	1					5		
Petersham	287	7	Wardin	Thomas		1		1		4		1					8		
Barre	405	33	Wardsworth	David Capt.	3	2	2			2	1		1	1			12		
Barre	405	34	Wardsworth	John		1	1	1		1	1	1					6		
Paxton	504	5	Ware	Amos	2	2		1	1				1				7		
Oakham	321	14	Ware	Archabald	4			1		1	1		1				8		
Fitchburg	424	6	Ware	Jonathan	1		2	1	1				2	1			8		
New Braintree	313	1	Ware	Pelatiah			1	1						1			3		
Westborough	189	5	Wares	Bariah	1			1			1		1				4		
Harvard	219	38	Wares	Moses	1			1					1				3		
Milford	389	20	Warfield	Abijah	2	1		1		3	2		1				10		
Mendon	388	9	Warfield	John	1		1		1			1	1				5	1st Parish	
Mendon	394	19	Warfield	Samuel Lt.		2	1	1		3	1	1					10	2d Parish	
Sturbridge	329	25	Warner	*		1	2			1		1		1			6		
Lancaster	358	12	Warner	Asa	1	1	1		1		1	1	1				7		
Harvard	218	21	Warner	Calvin	2	1		1	1	3			1				9		
Hardwick	304	21	Warner	Daniel		1		1					2	1			5		
Hardwick	305	5	Warner	Daniel		1		1					2	1			5		
Lancaster	357	6	Warner	Ebenezer	3	1					1	1					8		
Harvard	218	24	Warner	Elias	1	1	1	2		1			1				7		
Hardwick	305	8	Warner	Elijah	1		3		2	1	1	3		2			13		
Harvard	218	26	Warner	Ephraim	1		2			1			1				5		
Hardwick	305	6	Warner	Jno	1		2	2		1	2	3					14		
Harvard	218	23	Warner	John				1						1			2		
Barre	405	23	Warner	Leml	3	1		1		1			1	1			8		
Leominster	436	7	Warner	Levi	1		2		1	2				1			7		
New Braintree	313	10	Warner	Meriba	2	1						1		1			2		
Harvard	218	25	Warner	Phineas				1						1			2		
Leominster	436	9	Warner	Phinehas				1						1			2		
New Braintree	313	16	Warner	Phinehas		2	1	1		2		1	1				8		
Rutland	514	20	Warner	Thomas W			1	2					2				5		
Westborough	192	51	Warren	Aaron				1						1			2		
Westborough	197	105	Warren	Abner	1					3	1	1	1				8		
Westborough	189	7	Warren	Benjm	2	3	3		1	1	1	1	1	2			15		
Upton	384	5	Warren	Daniel Ens	1	1		1		2		2		1			9		
Westborough	192	50	Warren	David			1	1		1			1				3		
Hubbardston	419	13	Warren	Ebenz	4	2		1		1	1	1	1	1			12		
Leicester	495	16	Warren	Elijah		2	1	1		1	3						8		
Northborough	363	2	Warren	Elipatet		1	2		1		1	1		1			7		
New Braintree	313	13	Warren	Elisha	4		4	1			1	3	2				15		
Upton	383	21	Warren	Elisha				1			1	2	1				7		
Upton	383	18	Warren	Hepzibah Wid	1					2			1	1			5		

257

TOWN	PG#	LN#	LAST NAME	FIRST NAME	FREE WHITE MALES					FREE WHITE FEMALES					TOTAL ALL OTHER	TOTAL SLAVES	TOTALS	DISTRICT/ TOWNSHIP	NOTES
					under 10	10 to 16	16 to 26	26 to 45	45 and over	under 10	10 to 16	16 to 26	26 to 45	45 and over					
Hardwick	305	1	Warren	Isaac	1			1	1			1		1			5		
Dudley	341	43	Warren	Jacob				1						1			2		
Dudley	342	9	Warren	Jacob 2d			1					1					2		
Westminster	453	10	Warren	Jeduthan	3	1	1	1		1		1	1				9		
Dudley	341	42	Warren	John			2	1		1	1		2				7		
Grafton	201	17	Warren	John			2			1	1	1					5		
Paxton	504	1	Warren	John				1		1	1	1	1				5		
Westborough	198	138	Warren	John		2		1		1	1	2	1				8		
Worcester	184	3	Warren	John	1			1		2	1		1				6		
Upton	384	6	Warren	Jonas				1						1			2		
Grafton	206	6	Warren	Jonathan	3		2	2		2	1		2				12		
Leicester	495	15	Warren	Jonathan	1		2	1		1	1		1				7		
Upton	383	19	Warren	Jonathan			1	2				2	1	1			8		
Grafton	201	1	Warren	Joseph				1		1				1			3		
Hubbardston	416	6	Warren	Luke	2	1		1		1	1		1				7		
Dudley	341	41	Warren	Mansir	1			1		1	1		1				5		
Leominster	433	30	Warren	Oliver	2		2	2		3		2					11		
Grafton	201	2	Warren	Samuel	1			1					1				5		
Upton	383	22	Warren	Silas	1	1	1		1			2	1	1			8		
Westborough	198	137	Warren	Timothy				1									1		
New Braintree	313	4	Warren	Warham	1		2	1			1		1				6		
Leominster	433	24	Warren	William				1						1			2		
Paxton	504	2	Warren	William	1		1			1			1				4		
Sutton	167	27	Warren	William	2			1		1	1		1				6		
Leicester	498	10	Washburn	Asahel		1		1		2			1				5		
Hardwick	305	7	Washburn	Eliphalet		1		1	1	1	2		1	1			8		
Leicester	495	12	Washburn	Francis	1	1		1					1				4		
Leicester	495	11	Washburn	Jacob				1						1			2		
Leicester	495	7	Washburn	Joseph	4	3		1		2		1	2				13		
Brookfield	264	17	Washburn	Peter		2	2		1	2		2		1			10		Second Parish
Hardwick	306	12	Washburn	Siris			1					1					2		
Oakham	322	9	Waterman	Calvin			1			3		1	1				6		
Brookfield	251	4	Waterman	Jonathan			1		1	1	1	2	1				7		First Parish
Oakham	322	7	Waterman	Perez			1		1	1			3	1			7		
Brookfield	251	3	Waterman	Theophilus	2		1		1	2		2	1				9		First Parish
Sutton	166	4	Waters	Amos	1			1		1			1	1			5		
Sutton	167	30	Waters	Asa		1		1				1		1			4		
Sutton	168	4	Waters	Asa Junr			2	2				1					5		
Sutton	167	29	Waters	Ebenz				1									1		
Sutton	167	34	Waters	Elijah	1	5	1			3	1		2				13		
Sutton	167	32	Waters	John		1	1	1		1	1	1	1				7		
Sutton	166	2	Waters	John Junr	2	1		1		4		1	1				10		
Sutton	167	35	Waters	Jonathan		1	1	1				1		1			6		
Sutton	167	33	Waters	Joseph	1	2	3		1					2			9		
Ward	176	27	Waters	Judah	3	1	2	1		2	1		1				11		
Worcester	183	23	Waters	Kezia						1		1	3	1			6		
Sutton	166	5	Waters	Reuben	2		1	1		1		1					6		
Sutton	167	36	Waters	Salmon	1	1	3					2					7		
Leominster	436	8	Waters	Samel	2	1		1		2	1		1				10		
Sutton	167	31	Waters	Saml Junr	1		1	1				1					4		
Sutton	166	3	Waters	Samuel	1		2		1	1	2	2		1			10		
Sutton	166	6	Waters	Simeon			1					1					2		
Sutton	168	5	Waters	Simeon Junr		1						1		1			3		
Sutton	166	1	Waters	Stephen	1			1				1	1	1			5		
Leicester	495	10	Waters	Thomas	2			1		1	1						6		
Sturbridge	329	17	Watkins	Deliverance									1				1		
Sturbridge	329	18	Watkins	Hannah									1				1		
Leicester	498	12	Watson	Benjamin		1		1		2	1	1		1			8		
Brookfield	263	11	Watson	David	2	2	1		1	2				1			9		Second Parish
Lunenberg	432	18	Watson	Elizabeth			2						2	1			5		
Spencer	488	7	Watson	Jacob	1		1	1		1	1	2	1	1			9		
Spencer	488	9	Watson	James	2		1		1			2	2	1			9		
Princeton	518	10	Watson	John	1	1	1		1	2		1					7		
Leicester	498	11	Watson	Matthew			2	1				3	1	1			8		
Spencer	487	16	Watson	Oliver				1						1			2		
Spencer	488	8	Watson	Oliver Junr	1		2		1	2	3	1	1				11		
Spencer	487	17	Watson	Robert	1	2	2		1	3	1	1		1			12		
Leicester	495	9	Watson	Samuel	1		2		1	1	2	4	1				12		
Bolton	216	8	Watson	Thomas	1	1			1	1	1	1		1			7		
Leicester	498	5	Watson	William	1		1		1		1		2	1	2		9		
Spencer	487	18	Watson	William	1	2	1	1		1		2		1			10		
Charlton	337	12	Watters	Israel	1	1	2		1		1	1					8		
Charlton	340	4	Watters	Phillip	2			1		2			1				6		
Charlton	337	26	Watters	Simeon		2			1		1		1				5		
Oakham	321	18	Weaks	Nathl	1		1		1				1				4		
Fitchburg	424	10	Weatherbee	Daniel	3	3		1		2	1		1				11		
Lunenberg	432	10	Weatherbee	David	1			1		3	3	1					10		
Lunenberg	432	7	Weatherbee	Ephrm		2	1				1			1			6		
Fitchburg	424	9	Weatherbee	Paul		1	2		1	2				1			8		
Dudley	341	37	Weatheril	Joshua				1						1			2		
Dudley	342	4	Weatherly	Hannah	1	1	1							1			4		
Dudley	342	7	Weatherly	Joseph				1						1			2		
Dudley	342	8	Weaver	William				1	1				1				3		
Worcester	181	18	Webb	Adams	1		1	1		4	1		1				9		
Holden	510	18	Webb	Barnabas		1						1					2		
Uxbridge	473	15	Webb	Daniel	2		1			2		1					6		
Holden	510	17	Webb	George				1				3		1			5		
Hardwick	305	14	Webb	John	1	2	2		1		1	2	1				10		
Dudley	342	6	Webster	Coburn	1			1		2			1				5		
Dudley	342	2	Webster	John			1			2			1				4		
Upton	383	16	Webster	Thomas			1								8		9		

TOWN	PG#	LN#	LAST NAME	FIRST NAME	FW Males under 10	M 10-16	M 16-26	M 26-45	M 45+	FW Females under 10	F 10-16	F 16-26	F 26-45	F 45+	TOTAL ALL OTHER	TOTAL SLAVES	TOTALS	DISTRICT/TOWNSHIP	NOTES
Dudley	342	3	Webster	Wm	1			1		2			1	1			6		
Milford	389	5	Wedge	Daniel	1			1						1			3		
Milford	389	7	Wedge	Eli			1						1				2		
Milford	389	6	Wedge	Jepthah				1			1		1				3		
Hardwick	306	7	Weeks	David	3		1						1				5		
Petersham	287	9	Weeks	John	1		1			1			1				4		
Hardwick	305	3	Weeks	Joseph	1	2	2	1			1		1				8		
Petersham	287	8	Weeks	Roland	3	1	1	1		1			1				8		
Sturbridge	327	7	Welch	Thomas	2								1	1	8		12		
Sturbridge	329	9	Weld	Aaron			1			1			1				3		
Charlton	338	25	Weld	Asa			1										1		
Sturbridge	327	4	Weld	Caleb	3	1		1		2		1					8		
Charlton	340	2	Weld	Esquire	1	1		1		1	2		1	1	1		9		
Charlton	340	1	Weld	Mary		1							1				2		
Sturbridge	329	10	Weld	Pennal		1	1	1				1	1	1			6		
Sturbridge	329	7	Weld	Timothy	1	1	1	1	1			1	1	1			8		
Sturbridge	329	8	Weld	Warham	2		1	1		1			1				6		
Charlton	340	17	Weld	William			1			1			1	1			4		
Spencer	485	6	Weld	Josiah	3		1			1			1				6		
Bolton	211	18	Welsh	John				1						1			2		
Berlin	214	6	Welsh	Jonas				1				1					2		
Bolton	209	13	Welsh	Thomas	4		2	2					1	1			10		
Uxbridge	473	16	Were	Robert				1									1		
Grafton	193	6	Wesson	Abel	1	1	2		1	2	1	1	1				10		
Templeton	236	9	Wesson	James	1	1		1		3		1					7		
Grafton	193	7	Wesson	Joel		2	1	1	1	2		1	1				9		
Sutton	168	2	Wesson	Joel	1		1			1		1					4		
Templeton	242	11	Wesson	John	1	1		1		3	1		1				8		
Princeton	518	16	West	Amos				1		1		1		1			4		
Petersham	287	4	West	Charles			1			1		1					3		
Mendon	388	8	Westcott	Reuben			1			1		1					3	1st Parish	
Brookfield	263	20	Westers	James		1			1			1	2	1			6	Third Parish	
Barre	406	1	Weston	Abner	1		1		1	1			1				5		
New Braintree	313	5	Weston	Joshua	3		1			1		1	1				7		
New Braintree	313	9	Weston	Paul	2	2		1			1		1				7		
Winchendon	229	3	Weston	Stephen	2	1		1			1		1				6		
Harvard	220	10	Wetherbee	Abel	1		1			1		1					4		
Ashburnham	456	11	Wetherbee	Amos	2	1		1		3		1					8		
Westminster	453	2	Wetherbee	Caleb	1	1						2					4		
Westminster	453	15	Wetherbee	Caleb	2		1	1		2	1	1	1				9		
Brookfield	263	19	Wetherbee	Calvin	3		1	1				1	1				7	Third Parish	
Brookfield	264	20	Wetherbee	Charles		1		1						1			3	Second Parish	
Westminster	453	8	Wetherbee	Ephraim		2	1	1		1			1				6		
Harvard	222	34	Wetherbee	Ezra				2				2					4		
Brookfield	263	2	Wetherbee	Jonathan		1		1		2	1	2		1			8	Second Parish	
Harvard	220	3	Wetherbee	Joseph		1		1				1	1	1			5		
Southborough	203	4	Wetherbee	Joseph				1						1			2		
Bolton	212	20	Wetherbee	Reuben		1						1					2		
Southborough	205	21	Wetherbee	Sarah	1	1	2					2	1				7		
Ashburnham	456	6	Wetherbee	Thomas		1	1						1				3		
Westminster	453	4	Wetherbee	Thomas	1		1		1	1	1	1		1			7		
Barre	405	22	Wetherel	Jacob	2	2	1		1			2		1			9		
New Braintree	312	14	Wetherill	Jno	1		2	2					1				6		
New Braintree	313	8	Wetherill	Mehitable		1	1							1			3		
Barre	406	6	Wetherly	Ephraim	2	1		1						1			5		
Barre	406	5	Wetherly	George	2	1							1	1			5		
Charlton	340	10	Weto	Daniel				1						1			2		
Spencer	488	16	Wheat	Joseph		2	1		1	3	1		1				9		
Leicester	495	13	Wheaton	Abigail	1		1	1		1		2		1			7		
Fitchburg	424	5	Wheeler	Aaron	2		1	1		3			1	1			9		
Charlton	340	14	Wheeler	Abel				1		1			1				3		
Barre	405	31	Wheeler	Abial			1			4			1	1			7		
Barre	406	9	Wheeler	Abigal	1					1			1				3		
Bolton	213	16	Wheeler	Abraham	1	1	1		1	3		1	1	1			10		
Rutland	514	17	Wheeler	Abraham		1	2			1			1				5		
Hubbardston	419	5	Wheeler	Adam Capt		1		1						1			3		
Fitchburg	424	7	Wheeler	Amos	1		1					1	1				4		
Worcester	183	30	Wheeler	Amos				1			1	2		1			5		
Worcester	184	16	Wheeler	Amos Jr	2	2	1			1	1	1		1			9		
Bolton	213	15	Wheeler	Asa	2	1		1		2			1				7		
Rutland	507	3	Wheeler	Asa	2		1			4			1	1			9		
Hubbardston	419	7	Wheeler	Asa Lt.	4		1						1				6		
Berlin	213	11	Wheeler	Daniel	1	1	1				1	2	1	1			8		
Hardwick	305	19	Wheeler	Daniel	1	1	1	1	1			1		1			7		
Worcester	183	26	Wheeler	Danl G.		1	1										2		
Petersham	287	1	Wheeler	David	1		1			1			1				4		
Southborough	203	35	Wheeler	Ebenezer				1				1	1				3		
Westminster	453	14	Wheeler	Hamon	1	1		1		3			1	1			8		
Rutland	514	16	Wheeler	Isaac			1	1				1	1	1			5		
Rutland	513	2	Wheeler	Jacob	1		1					1					3		
Rutland	514	22	Wheeler	James				1					1				2		
Southborough	203	34	Wheeler	James	3	1	1	1		2	1	1	1				11		
Gardner	448	12	Wheeler	Joel	1		1			2	1	1	1				7		
Petersham	285	21	Wheeler	Joel				1			1		1				3		
Barre	405	25	Wheeler	John			1			5			1				7		
Boylston	369	7	Wheeler	John				1		1			1				3		
Gardner	448	15	Wheeler	John B.	3		1			1			1				6		
Boylston	369	8	Wheeler	John Jr		1						1					2		
Grafton	195	1	Wheeler	Jonathan	1	1	3	1	2			1	2				11		
Grafton	202	2	Wheeler	Jonathan Jun			1					1	1				3		
Petersham	285	2	Wheeler	Jonus	1	1		1		3	1	1	1	1			10		

259

TOWN	PG#	LN#	LAST NAME	FIRST NAME	FREE WHITE MALES					FREE WHITE FEMALES					TOTAL ALL OTHER	TOTAL SLAVES	TOTALS	DISTRICT/ TOWNSHIP	NOTES
					under 10	10 to 16	16 to 26	26 to 45	45 and over	under 10	10 to 16	16 to 26	26 to 45	45 and over					
Fitchburg	424	8	Wheeler	Joseph	3	1			1	1		1	1				8		
Princeton	518	11	Wheeler	Joseph			1	1		3	1		1				7		
Bolton	215	1	Wheeler	Joshua	3			1		1	1		1				7		
Gardner	448	14	Wheeler	Josiah		1	2	1				1		1			6		
Westminster	455	4	Wheeler	Josiah	1	2		1		2	2		1				9		
Lunenberg	432	6	Wheeler	Josiah G.	1		3	1		1			1				7		
Hardwick	306	4	Wheeler	Leml				1					1	1			3		
Berlin	212	9	Wheeler	Levi	2		1		2			1					6		
Petersham	285	11	Wheeler	Margaret									1	1			2		
Worcester	183	25	Wheeler	Margaret									1	1			2		
Bolton	213	17	Wheeler	Moses	1	1			1	1	1		1				6		
Holden	510	15	Wheeler	Moses				1					1	2			6		
Hardwick	306	16	Wheeler	Nathan				1						1			2		
Petersham	285	9	Wheeler	Nathan	3	1		1		1			1				7		
Westminster	456	3	Wheeler	Nathll	1			1		2	1		1				6		
Northborough	363	7	Wheeler	Obadiah	2	2	1			1	1	2		1			11		
Hubbardston	416	13	Wheeler	Oliver				1				1	1				3		
Athol	281	8	Wheeler	Paul	1			1		1		2					5		
Berlin	213	12	Wheeler	Perigrine								1					1		
Western	251	7	Wheeler	Rice		1		2		1	1	3		2			10		
Bolton	209	16	Wheeler	Samuel	1	2		1		1			1				6		
Hubbardston	419	6	Wheeler	Silas	1	3		1		1	1		1				8		
Berlin	212	3	Wheeler	Stephen	1	1	2		1	1	1		1				8		
Bolton	209	1	Wheeler	Thankful									1				1		
Worcester	183	24	Wheeler	Theophilus	3			1		2		1	1				8		
Garry	274	6	Wheeler	Thomas			1	1		1		1					4		
Holden	510	16	Wheeler	Thomas	2			1			1	2					6		
Hardwick	305	2	Wheeler	Thos				1						1			2		
Hardwick	305	4	Wheeler	Thos Jr	1	1		1		1		1					5		
Charlton	337	8	Wheelock	Aaron	2	1		1		1		1		1			7		
Charlton	337	14	Wheelock	Abner	1	1		1		1	1	1		1			7		
Charlton	340	12	Wheelock	Addams		1	1	1				1					4		
Charlton	337	13	Wheelock	Amos	3	1	1	1		1			1				8		
Charlton	337	10	Wheelock	Benj	1		2		1	2	1			1			8		
Lancaster	358	24	Wheelock	Benjamin	2	1		3		2	1	1	1				11		
Mendon	388	5	Wheelock	Calvin	1	1		1				2	1				6	1st Parish	
Milford	391	32	Wheelock	Cyrus	1	1		1		2			1				6		
Hardwick	305	15	Wheelock	David				1						1			2		
Uxbridge	474	10	Wheelock	Deborah		1					1		1				3		
Sturbridge	329	13	Wheelock	Denison		1	1		1	1	1		1				6		
Milford	391	31	Wheelock	Ebenz		1		2						2			5		
Sturbridge	329	11	Wheelock	Eleazer	1			1		1		1	1				5		
Northborough	363	6	Wheelock	Eliab	1	1		1		1		1	1				6		
Sturbridge	329	14	Wheelock	Ephraim	1			1		1		1					3		
Sturbridge	327	2	Wheelock	James			1										1		
Charlton	337	11	Wheelock	John		2		1		1		1	1				6		
Sutton	168	3	Wheelock	John	1	1	1	1		1		1	1				7		
Sutton	166	16	Wheelock	Jonah			1	1				1					3		
Worcester	184	11	Wheelock	Joseph	1			1		2	1		1				6		
Upton	383	17	Wheelock	Lucretia Mrs.	1						1		1				3		
Milford	389	1	Wheelock	Luther	1		1	1			1	1	1				6		
Westborough	194	57	Wheelock	Moses				1			1		1	1			3		
Barre	408	9	Wheelock	Moses B.	3			1		1			1	1			7		
Mendon	388	10	Wheelock	Nahum	3	2		1		2	2		1				11	1st Parish	
Milford	389	4	Wheelock	Obadiah	1	2		1		1		1	2	2			10		
Spencer	485	5	Wheelock	Paul	1	2	1	1		1			1				7		
Sutton	167	43	Wheelock	Paul				1						1			2		
Sutton	168	1	Wheelock	Paul	2	2	1		1	3			1				10		
Uxbridge	474	13	Wheelock	Paul	2			1	1	1	1		1	1			8		
Mendon	388	11	Wheelock	Peter									1	1			2	1st Parish	
Sturbridge	329	12	Wheelock	Ralph			2	1			1	1	2		1		9		
Charlton	337	9	Wheelock	Seth		2		1	1			1	1				6		
Mendon	388	12	Wheelock	Seth Lt.	1	1		1		1		1		2			6	1st Parish	
Royalston	231	3	Wheelor	Russell	3			1		1			1				6		
Templeton	236	14	Whelor	Abel	1		1					1					3		
Templeton	237	18	Whelor	Beulah	1			1				2		1			5		
Templeton	236	13	Whelor	Thos			2		1			1	1	1			6		
Barre	405	32	Whetherel	Sampson				1						1			2		
Brookfield	266	12	Whettemore	James	3			1		1			1				5	Third Parish	
Grafton	202	6	Whiple	James	1			1				2		1			7		
Southborough	203	20	Whiple	James Jun	1			1				1					3		
Grafton	202	7	Whiple	John				1						1			2		
Petersham	285	16	Whiple	John		1	1	1				2		1			6		
Grafton	202	8	Whiple	John Jun	2		1	1					1				5		
Grafton	202	4	Whiple	Joseph				1	1			1	1				4		
Grafton	198	11	Whiple	Pearle	1		2	1		1		1					6		
Petersham	285	18	Whiple	Richard	2			1		2			1	1	1		8		
Grafton	201	14	Whiple	Thads	2		1	1			1	1					6		
Petersham	285	17	Whiple	William	2			1			1		1				5		
Hardwick	305	21	Whipple	David	4			1		1	1		1				8		
New Braintree	312	15	Whipple	Francis		1	1	1				1		1			5		
Hardwick	306	2	Whipple	Jacob	1		1	1				1	1				5		
Hardwick	305	9	Whipple	James	2	1		1		3	1		1				9		
Boylston	369	6	Whipple	John	1	1	1	1			1	1		1			7		
Sutton	166	15	Whipple	John	1			1		2			2	1			7		
Uxbridge	473	5	Whipple	Jona	1	1	3	1	1	3		3	1				14		
Hardwick	305	16	Whipple	Samll		2	2			1	1	1		1			8		
Hardwick	306	3	Whipple	Simon			1	1				1	1				4		
Sutton	167	24	Whipple	Solomon			1	1		1		2		2			8		
New Braintree	312	16	Whipple	Thos				1					1				2		

260

TOWN	PG#	LN#	LAST NAME	FIRST NAME	FWM under 10	FWM 10-16	FWM 16-26	FWM 26-45	FWM 45+	FWF under 10	FWF 10-16	FWF 16-26	FWF 26-45	FWF 45+	TOTAL ALL OTHER	TOTAL SLAVES	TOTALS	DISTRICT/TOWNSHIP	NOTES
Oakham	321	15	Whitaker	Wm	1		1		1	2	1	1					7		
Sturbridge	329	26	Whitcomb	*	1		3						1				5		
Bolton	209	19	Whitcomb	Abel	1		1	1		1		1					5		
Bolton	210	8	Whitcomb	Asa	1	1	1	2	1	2	1	1	2	1			13		
Princeton	518	9	Whitcomb	Asa			1						1				2		
Bolton	212	7	Whitcomb	Azubah						2	1		1				4		
Lancaster	358	11	Whitcomb	Chapman	1			1		1			1				4		
Berlin	212	14	Whitcomb	Enoch	2	2		1		2		1	1				9		
Bolton	209	15	Whitcomb	Ephraim	3		2		1	3	1	1					11		
Winchendon	229	10	Whitcomb	Israel	1		4		1	2		2		1			11		
Templeton	237	6	Whitcomb	Job			1		1			1	2	1			6		
Bolton	212	5	Whitcomb	Joel		1						1	1				4		
Berlin	214	20	Whitcomb	John			1	1		2		1					5		
Princeton	518	17	Whitcomb	John			1	1		3		1	1				7		
Templeton	231	13	Whitcomb	Jona Jr	1		1			3			1				6		
Bolton	212	6	Whitcomb	Jonas			1			1			1				3		
Westminster	453	6	Whitcomb	Jorge M.			1						1				2		
Bolton	215	6	Whitcomb	Joseph	2		1			2			1				6		
Lancaster	357	5	Whitcomb	Leonard	1		1					1	1				4		
Bolton	211	9	Whitcomb	Molley											1		1		
Leominster	433	31	Whitcomb	Nathan			1			1			1				3		
Westminster	453	7	Whitcomb	Oliver				1		1	1	2		1			6		
Bolton	210	13	Whitcomb	Paul		1	1		1			1		2			6		
Harvard	218	29	Whitcomb	Phineas	2		1				1		1				5		
Harvard	220	16	Whitcomb	Reubin	1		1						1				3		
Bolton	212	4	Whitcomb	Richard			1						1				2		
Bolton	210	11	Whitcomb	Silas			1			4	1	1	1				8		
Boylston	369	1	White	Aaron	1		2	1					2				6		
Garry	274	8	White	Abel	1		1						1				3		
Lancaster	358	23	White	Abijah	1		1	1					1				4		
Northbridge	474	14	White	Abisha			1						1				2		
Uxbridge	473	12	White	Alpheus				1					1				2		
Uxbridge	474	12	White	Amariah		1		1		1		1					4		
Brookfield	252	15	White	Asa		1			2			2		2			7	First Parish	
Grafton	200	11	White	Benjn	4	1	1	1					1				8		
Douglas	480	4	White	Chloe			1				1			1			3		
Milford	389	15	White	Daniel		1	1	1					1				4		
Upton	383	23	White	Daniel		2		1		2			1				6		
Douglas	479	29	White	David	1	1		1		3			1				7		
Sturbridge	329	20	White	David			1	1		1				1			4		
Westborough	199	139	White	Dix			1			1			1				3		
Mendon	388	6	White	Ebenezer						1			1	1			3	1st Parish	
Charlton	337	1	White	Ebenzr 2d	1	1	1			1	1	2		1			9		
Charlton	337	22	White	Ebenzr 2d		1	1	1			2			1			6		
Hardwick	305	20	White	Elias	2		1			1	1		1				6		
Ashburnham	456	8	White	Elisha	2	1	1			2	1		1				8		
Royalston	231	11	White	Elisha															No Enumeration Listed
Uxbridge	474	9	White	Ezra	2			1	1	1			3	1			9		
Barre	406	3	White	James	1	1	1			1			2	1			7		
Westminster	454	14	White	James	2		1			1			1				5		
Northbridge	474	13	White	Jesse	2	2	3	1		1				1			10		
Charlton	338	27	White	John	3	1		1			1	1	1				8		
Grafton	199	11	White	John	3	1		1		2	2		1				10		
Milford	389	17	White	John	2			1		1			1				5		
Northborough	363	1	White	John		1	1					1					3		
Spencer	488	12	White	John	1		1						1				4		
Uxbridge	474	16	White	John	1	1	2		1		1	2		1			9		
Westminster	453	17	White	John		2	1		1	2	1	1		1			9		
Lancaster	358	27	White	John Jun	1		1			2		1					5		
New Braintree	312	21	White	Jonah	1		1	1				1					4		
Westminster	453	3	White	Jonas	2			1		2	1		1				7		
Spencer	488	14	White	Jonathan	3			1		1	2		1				8		
Uxbridge	474	11	White	Jonathan	2				1	2	1		1				7		
Hardwick	306	6	White	Joseph	1		1					2					4		
Lancaster	358	10	White	Joseph	3	1		1			2		1	1			9		
Sutton	167	40	White	Joshua		3	1			2		2	1				10		
Barre	408	11	White	Josiah			1	1		1			2	1			6		
Spencer	488	11	White	Josiah			1							1			2		
Sterling	348	4	White	Josiah	1		1			1			1				4		
Garry	274	13	White	Lucy			1							1			2		
Rutland	514	23	White	Moses	5	1		3	1	1	1	2	2				16		
Spencer	488	13	White	Nathan	1		1						1				3		
Uxbridge	473	13	White	Nathan			1	1					1				3		
Worcester	183	17	White	Nathan	3	2		1		1	2	2	1				12		
Lancaster	357	4	White	Nathaniel	2			1		1			1	1			6		
Barre	408	10	White	Noah								1		1			2		
Douglas	480	5	White	Paul	1		1						1	1			4		
Barre	406	4	White	Peter		1		1		3	1		1				7		
Boylston	369	3	White	Peter	1		1						1				3		
Douglas	479	28	White	Peter				1					1				2		
Uxbridge	473	4	White	Peter	1			1					2	1			5		
Spencer	487	15	White	Rand			2	1		1		1		1			6		
Western	251	8	White	Robert	1	1	1			1			1				5		
Sturbridge	327	6	White	Sarah Wd										2			2		
Douglas	480	3	White	Seth	1	2	1										11		
Garry	274	10	White	Simion			1			1		1					3		
Mendon	394	16	White	Smith	2		1	1		1	3		1				9	2d Parish	
Leicester	495	14	White	Stephen		2		1						1			4		
Petersham	286	14	White	Stephen	3			1		2			1	1			8		
Garry	274	9	White	Thomas	1		1	1	1					1			5		

TOWN	PG#	LN#	LAST NAME	FIRST NAME	M under 10	M 10 to 16	M 16 to 26	M 26 to 45	M 45 & over	F under 10	F 10 to 16	F 16 to 26	F 26 to 45	F 45 & over	TOTAL ALL OTHER	TOTAL SLAVES	TOTALS	DISTRICT/ TOWNSHIP	NOTES
Royalston	240	10	White	Thomas	2			1			2		1				6		
Spencer	488	1	White	Thomas			1										1		Most of enumeration covered by tap
Uxbridge	473	14	White	Thomas		3	1		1	1		2	1	1			10		
Spencer	488	10	White	William		1			1		1	2		1	1		7		
Sutton	167	39	White	William				1						1			2		
Uxbridge	474	15	White	William			1			1		1					3		
Western	251	6	White	William Jr	4	1		1	1		1	1	1				10		
Upton	383	15	White	Zuba Wd								1		1			2		
Northbridge	474	12	White	Joel		1		1		2	1		1				6		
Lancaster	355	17	White	John				1					1				2		
Garry	274	7	Whitehead	Gad	1			1		1	1		1				5		
Garry	274	12	Whitehead	George	4	1		1					1				7		
Princeton	518	12	Whiteker	William	3	1	3		1		1	1	1				12		
Hubbardston	416	10	Whitemore	Isaac	1			1		1		1					4		
Garry	274	4	Whitemore	Joseph	2			1				2	1	1			7		
Lancaster	355	15	Whitemore	Nathaniel		2		1	1			2		1			7		
Northbridge	474	7	Whiten	Paul	1		2	1				1					5		
Douglas	479	24	Whiting	Caleb		1		1						1			3		
Douglas	480	2	Whiting	David	2		1	1		2		1	1				8		
Hardwick	306	1	Whiting	Ebenz	1		1					1					3		
Barre	408	14	Whiting	Elijah	2			1		1	1						5		
Lunenberg	432	12	Whiting	Esek	2		2	1				1		1			7		
Barre	408	12	Whiting	Jason				1	1	1							3		
Douglas	480	7	Whiting	John	1	1		1			1		1				5		
Lancaster	355	13	Whiting	John	2	2		1		2	2	1	1	1			12		
Boylston	369	9	Whiting	John L.	1		1	1	1			1		1			6		
Barre	408	13	Whiting	Josiah				1						1			2		
Harvard	219	7	Whiting	Lucy									1	1			2		
Lunenberg	432	16	Whiting	Luther		1		1						1			3		
Lunenberg	432	13	Whiting	Nathaniel	1			1		3			1				6		
Douglas	479	30	Whiting	Timothy	2		1	1		1	2		1				8		
Lancaster	355	10	Whiting	Timothy	1	2	1	1		1	1	2		1			10		
Westminster	454	13	Whiting	William	2			1		1	2		1				7		
Douglas	479	32	Whiting	Abner		1		1		1		1					4		
Ashburnham	456	4	Whitman	Edward	1	1		1		3	1		1				8		
Ashburnham	455	5	Whitman	John	2		1	1		1	1	1	1				8		
Ashburnham	455	7	Whitman	Nicholas	2		1	1		1	1		1				7		
Westminster	453	9	Whitman	Zachn		1	2		1	2	3	2		1			12		
Fitchburg	424	3	Whitmore	Daniel	1			1		1	1	1					5		
Fitchburg	424	2	Whitmore	David	2			1		2			1				6		
Oakham	322	1	Whitmore	Ebenzr	1			1		2	1		1				6		
Rutland	514	24	Whitmore	Eber	1	1		1	1				1				5		
Royalston	240	14	Whitmore	Enoch	1			1		3			1				6		
Ashburnham	456	10	Whitmore	Isaac	1	1	1		1	2			1	1			8		
Royalston	237	4	Whitmore	Isaac	1			1		2			1	1			6		
Royalston	237	8	Whitmore	John	2		1	1		1			1				6		
Ashburnham	456	12	Whitmore	Joseph				1						1			2		
Oxford	154	5	Whitmore	Nathl	1		2	1		1	1	1					8		
Sutton	166	7	Whitmore	Nathll		1		2		1	1		1				6		
Sturbridge	329	23	Whitmore	Wm	1	2		1		1	1	1					7		
Harvard	217	1	Whitney	Aaron		1	1		1			1		1			5		
Lunenberg	432	20	Whitney	Abigail									1				1		
Ashburnham	455	17	Whitney	Abner				1						1			2		
Westminster	456	16	Whitney	Abner	1		2		1	1				1			8		
Harvard	218	17	Whitney	Abraham		1	3	1		3			1				9		
Westminster	456	19	Whitney	Alpohus			1						1				2		
Upton	384	9	Whitney	Amos	2		1	1		1	1	1	1				8		
Worcester	184	5	Whitney	Amos	1	1		1	1					1			5		
Princeton	518	13	Whitney	Andrew	2	2	1		1				1				8		
Petersham	286	10	Whitney	Benja	1		2	1		1	2	1		1			9		
Worcester	184	4	Whitney	Benja Jr		1	1	1						1			4		
Sterling	348	2	Whitney	Caleb		1	1			2		1	1				6		
Harvard	222	23	Whitney	Cyrus		1		1			1						3		
Harvard	222	14	Whitney	David			1						1				2		
Westminster	456	17	Whitney	David	2	1		1		1	1	1					8		
Harvard	218	28	Whitney	Ebenezar	3	1		1			2		1				8		
Hardwick	306	8	Whitney	Ebenz			1			1		2					4		
Worcester	184	17	Whitney	Ebenz			1			2		1	1				5		
Westborough	191	34	Whitney	Eli	1		1	1				1		1			6		
Milford	389	9	Whitney	Elias				1						1			2		
Milford	389	8	Whitney	Elias Jr			1	1	1	1	3		1	1			9		
Bolton	213	8	Whitney	Elijah		1	2		1	2	1	2		1			10		
Westminster	456	13	Whitney	Elisha	1	1			1	2	1		1				7		
Harvard	222	13	Whitney	Enoch		1		1		1	1	1					5		
Royalston	235	11	Whitney	Ephm	1			1		3			1				6		Name crossed off on census
Royalston	241	23	Whitney	Ephm	1			1		1	1		1				5		
Upton	384	10	Whitney	Ephm		1	1	1		2	1	1	1				8		
Upton	384	1	Whitney	Ezra			1			3			1				5		
Milford	389	12	Whitney	Hachaliah	1	1		1					1				4		
Winchendon	230	16	Whitney	Hanariah	3	1		1		1			1				7		
Templeton	242	13	Whitney	Hezekiah	3	1	1	1		1			1				8		
Harvard	222	20	Whitney	Hezikiah		1		1			1		1				4		
Harvard	221	14	Whitney	Isaac	1	1		1		1	1		1				6		
Harvard	218	16	Whitney	Isaiah	3	2			1	2	1	1	1				11		
Harvard	221	19	Whitney	Isaiah		1		1		1			1				4		
Harvard	218	15	Whitney	Israel		2		1	1		2	1					7		
Upton	384	7	Whitney	Jacob			1	1		2			1				5		
Winchendon	230	17	Whitney	Jacob	2			1		1			1				5		
Harvard	222	12	Whitney	James	1	1	1	1			1		1				6		
Milford	389	13	Whitney	Jesse					1					1			2		
Westminster	456	12	Whitney	Joel	2	1			1	3							8		

262

			HEADS OF HOUSEHOLD		FREE WHITE MALES					FREE WHITE FEMALES									
TOWN	PG#	LN#	LAST NAME	FIRST NAME	under 10	10 to 16	16 to 26	26 to 45	45 and over	under 10	10 to 16	16 to 26	26 to 45	45 and over	TOTAL ALL OTHER	TOTAL SLAVES	TOTALS	DISTRICT/ TOWNSHIP	NOTES
Bolton	209	3	Whitney	John		2	1		1	1	1	1		1			8		
Lunenberg	432	19	Whitney	John	1		2		1	1				1			6		
Westminster	456	18	Whitney	John	1	1		1		1			1				5		
Westborough	192	39	Whitney	Jonah		1				2			1				4		
Harvard	222	30	Whitney	Jonas	1		1	1		2	3	1	1		1		11		
Westminster	456	14	Whitney	Jonas	2		1	1		2	1		1	1			9		
Lancaster	355	9	Whitney	Jonathan		1	1	1	1		1	3		1			9		
Winchendon	229	7	Whitney	Joseph			1				1						2		
Gardner	448	5	Whitney	Joshua	4		1		1	1	1		1				9		
Worcester	183	18	Whitney	Joshua		1	1		1	1		2		1			7		
Lunenberg	432	23	Whitney	Lemuel		1	1		1			1	1	1			6		
Royalston	232	6	Whitney	Levi	1		1		1	2	1		1				7		
Sterling	348	14	Whitney	Mellon		1				3		1					5		
Harvard	217	2	Whitney	Moses		1	1			1		1					4		
Templeton	239	15	Whitney	Moses	1		1		1	1	1	1	3				9		
Uxbridge	473	2	Whitney	Moses		2		1		3		2	1				9		
Templeton	239	12	Whitney	Moses 2d	2			1				1					4		
Westminster	456	15	Whitney	Nathan				1					1				2		
Westminster	454	16	Whitney	Nathan Jr	2			1		1	2		1				7		
Harvard	220	25	Whitney	Oliver			1		1		1			1			4		
Upton	384	8	Whitney	Oliver			1	1				1	1				4		
Lancaster	355	16	Whitney	Paul	1	1		1		3			1				7		
Northborough	363	5	Whitney	Peter Revd		1			1			3		1			6		
Westminster	455	1	Whitney	Phenias	3			1		2	1		1				8		
Winchendon	229	6	Whitney	Phins	1			1		2		2					6		
Harvard	222	17	Whitney	Reuben	1		1	1				2	1				6		
Harvard	221	4	Whitney	Richard	1	1			1		1			1			5		
Templeton	239	11	Whitney	Samuel				1					1				2		
Westminster	455	2	Whitney	Samuel		3		1		2				1			7		
Ashburnham	455	14	Whitney	Sarah		2	2			2		1		1			8		
Petersham	285	1	Whitney	Simon	3	1	1	1		2	1		1				10		
Harvard	217	4	Whitney	Solmon	2	1		1		1			1	1			7		
Lunenberg	432	21	Whitney	Stephen		1	1	1	1		1	2	1	2			10		
Westminster	456	1	Whitney	Susanna	2								1				3		
Northborough	363	8	Whitney	Tho. L.			1	1		1	1		1				5		
Westborough	189	16	Whitney	Thomas				1			1		1				3		
Boylston	369	2	Whitney	Timothy		2	1	2	1	1	1	2		1			11		
Gardner	448	11	Whitney	William	3		1			2			1				7		
Winchendon	229	5	Whitney	Wm	1		2	1			1		1				6		
Lunenberg	432	8	Whitney	Zachariah		1	1		1	1	2	1					7		
Winchendon	229	11	Whiton	Israel	2	1		1		1		1					6		
Spencer	488	3	Whittemore	Aaron	3			1	2	1			1				8		
Leicester	498	13	Whittemore	Asa	2	2		1		2	1	2		1			11		
Leicester	498	6	Whittemore	Asa Jun			1					1					2		
Worcester	186	18	Whittemore	Clark	2	1		1		1		1	1		1		8		
Leicester	495	8	Whittemore	James		1	1		1			2	1	1			7		
Spencer	487	19	Whittemore	Jere Jun	1			1		2			1				5		
Spencer	488	2	Whittemore	Jeremiah			1	1			1	1	1				5		
Fitchburg	423	13	Whittemore	Jona	2			1		1			1				5		
Spencer	485	4	Whittemore	Reuben	2	1	1		1	2	1	1	1				10		
Worcester	184	6	Whitten	Abel	2			1				1		1			6		
Paxton	504	7	Wicker	David		1	1		1			1	2	1			7		
Paxton	504	6	Wicker	Samuel				1									1		
Hardwick	305	12	Wicker	Wm		3	2	1	1	2				1			10		
Leicester	495	4	Wickery	Benja				1			1			1			3		
Milford	391	30	Wight	Abner	4			1		1			1				7		
Sturbridge	329	22	Wight	Alpheus	2	1		1		3		1	1				9		
Sturbridge	327	8	Wight	David Jr	1	2	4			3	2	1	1	1			15		
Sturbridge	329	21	Wight	Oliver	1	1	2	1		4	3		1				13		
Worcester	186	15	Wight	Oliver			1		1	1			1				4		
Oakham	321	13	Wilcot	Oliver		2		1	1	1		1	1				7		
New Braintree	313	12	Wilcox	David	1		1	1	1			1	1	1			7		
New Braintree	313	18	Wilcox	Stephan			1			1			1				3		
Petersham	285	4	Wilder	Abel	2	2	2	1		3	2		1	1			14		
Winchendon	229	9	Wilder	Abel	5	1		1					1				8		
Winchendon	227	32	Wilder	Anna								1		1			2		
Winchendon	230	15	Wilder	Benja	4			1		2	2		1				10		
Ashburnham	455	15	Wilder	Bulah							1						1		
Ashburnham	456	7	Wilder	Caleb		2	1		1			2		1			7		
Ashburnham	455	12	Wilder	Caleb 2d				1						1			2		
Lancaster	358	16	Wilder	Calvin				1					1				2		
Petersham	285	5	Wilder	Cornelius		1	1		1		1			1			5		
Leominster	436	20	Wilder	David	1		1		1	1	2		1				7		
Leominster	436	16	Wilder	David Jun	1		2					1					4		
Leominster	436	12	Wilder	Edward	3	2		1		1			2				9		
Sterling	348	1	Wilder	Elihu	2		3	1		4		1	1				12		
Leominster	436	17	Wilder	Elisha	1	1	1			1				2			6		
New Braintree	313	2	Wilder	Ephraim	1				1		1		1				4		
Sterling	348	11	Wilder	Ephraim		1		1	1		1	1	1	1			7		
Lancaster	358	13	Wilder	Gardner				1		1				1			3		
Winchendon	229	1	Wilder	Gardner	1	1		1		1			1				5		
Leominster	433	29	Wilder	James	4	1	1	1		1	2		1	1			12		
Leominster	433	26	Wilder	Jemima		1						1	1	1			4		
Westminster	453	5	Wilder	Joel	1			1		1			1				4		
Lancaster	358	18	Wilder	John	2			1	1	1	1		1				7		
Petersham	285	8	Wilder	John	1	1	1		1		1	1					6		
Winchendon	229	2	Wilder	John				1		1		1					3		
Lancaster	358	26	Wilder	John 3d	2			1				1					4		
Lancaster	355	14	Wilder	Jonathan	5	2			1		1	1	1				11		

TOWN	PG#	LN#	HEADS OF HOUSEHOLD LAST NAME	FIRST NAME	FREE WHITE MALES under 10	10 to 16	16 to 26	26 to 45	45 and over	FREE WHITE FEMALES under 10	10 to 16	16 to 26	26 to 45	45 and over	TOTAL ALL OTHER	TOTAL SLAVES	TOTALS	DISTRICT/ TOWNSHIP	NOTES
Leicester	498	1	Wilder	Joseph			2					1					3		
Leominster	436	18	Wilder	Joseph		1	2	1	1	1	1		1				9		
Winchendon	229	8	Wilder	Joseph	1	2	2		1					1			7		
Gardner	448	13	Wilder	Josiah	1	2			1	1	1	2		1			9		
Templeton	233	17	Wilder	Josiah			2		1		1	1	1				6		
Templeton	233	18	Wilder	Josiah Junr				1				1					2		
Petersham	285	3	Wilder	Manasah			1	1						1			3		
Lancaster	358	20	Wilder	Menasseh		1		1		1	1			1			5		
Lancaster	358	19	Wilder	Moses	1	1			1	1		2					6		
Ashburnham	455	13	Wilder	Nahum			1										1		
Sterling	348	10	Wilder	Phinehas			1		1			1		1			4		
Sterling	348	15	Wilder	Phinehas Junr	2			1		1			1				5		
Lancaster	358	15	Wilder	Samuel	1				1			1					3		
Lancaster	355	18	Wilder	Samuel 2d	2	1	1		1	2		1	1				9		
Leominster	436	10	Wilder	Sarah										3			3		
Sterling	348	3	Wilder	Silas	1	1			1			1		2			7		
Lancaster	355	11	Wilder	Stephen			2		1					1			4		
Leominster	436	19	Wilder	Thomas	1	1	1	1	1	2		1	1	1			10		
Sterling	348	12	Wilder	Timothy	1	1			1	2		1	1				7		
Lancaster	358	21	Wilder	Titus	1	1			1	1		2		1			8		
Barre	406	11	Wilder	Wid			1			1		2		1			5		
Lancaster	358	17	Wilder	William			1		1	1		1					4		
Lancaster	355	12	Wiles	Joseph				1		1	2	2		1			7		
Templeton	238	2	Wilkinson	Ebenz			1	1	1		1	2	1				7		
Harvard	219	4	Willard	Abel			2						1				3		
Sutton	167	42	Willard	Abigail Wd							1		1				2		
Fitchburg	423	12	Willard	Abraham		1	2		1					1			5		
Holden	510	22	Willard	Ashbel	1			1				1		1			4		
Harvard	219	16	Willard	Barzilla	1		1		1	1	2	1		2			9		
Grafton	195	15	Willard	Benj		1			2	2	1	1	1				8		
Lancaster	355	21	Willard	Benjamin W.	1	1		1		1				2			6		
Harvard	218	1	Willard	Caleb		1	1					1					3		
Fitchburg	423	17	Willard	Charles			2		1		2	1		2			8		
Worcester	183	22	Willard	Clark	1		1			2		1					5		
Fitchburg	423	18	Willard	Daniel		1			1	3	2	1					8		
Harvard	218	2	Willard	Daniel	4		2	1	1	1	1		1				11		
Sterling	348	7	Willard	David			1		1	1	1	1		1			6		
Sterling	348	8	Willard	David Junr		2	1				1	1		1			6		
Dudley	342	1	Willard	Elijah			1				1		1				3		
Charlton	340	11	Willard	Ephraim	2		2	1		3	3	1	1				13		
Sterling	348	6	Willard	Ephraim	3			1	1			1		1			7		
Sterling	348	13	Willard	Ephraim Junr	1	2		2		1	2	1	1		1		11		
Lancaster	358	28	Willard	Ezra		1		1		1	1		1				5		
Grafton	196	3	Willard	Hannah								1		1			2		
Ashburnham	456	1	Willard	Henery			1										1		
Dudley	341	40	Willard	Henry	1			1		2	1	1					6		
Dudley	341	36	Willard	Hezekiah	1			1		2		1	1				6		
Winchendon	229	4	Willard	Isaac	1	1	1			1			1				5		
Worcester	183	19	Willard	Isaac				1			1		1				3		
Worcester	183	20	Willard	Isaac Junr	1		1	1		4			1				8		
Holden	510	20	Willard	Jacob			1			1		1					3		
Ashburnham	455	9	Willard	Jacob			1	1			2			1			5		
Lancaster	355	20	Willard	James	1		2	1		1		1	1	1			8		
Lunenberg	432	14	willard	Jepzibah								1		1			2		
Harvard	221	32	Willard	Jeremiah		1		1	12		3	6	20				43		
Harvard	218	4	Willard	Joel	2		1	1		3			1				8		
Ashburnham	456	5	Willard	John	2	1		1		1			1				6		
Lancaster	357	2	Willard	John	1	2		1	1	1	1	1		1			9		
Dudley	341	39	Willard	Jonath Junr		1		1	1	1	2		1	1			8		
Dudley	341	38	Willard	Jonathan				1						1			2		
Harvard	221	11	Willard	Joseph				1						1			2		
Holden	510	21	Willard	Joseph	1			1		1		1					4		
Harvard	221	12	Willard	Joseph Junr	4	1	1						1	1			8		
Grafton	196	1	Willard	Josephus	1			1		2			1				5		
Hubbardston	416	12	Willard	Joshua		3			1					1			5		
Sterling	348	5	Willard	Joshua	2		1		1	2		1	1				8		
Harvard	219	15	Willard	Josiah		1	3		2	1	1	2	1				11		
Petersham	285	19	Willard	Josiah			1					1					2		
Lancaster	357	3	Willard	Kenneth (or Sila	2							1					3		
Harvard	220	33	Willard	Lemuel		3	1	1	1	1		1					8		
Mendon	388	7	Willard	Levi Dr.	1		3	1			1	1	1				8	1st Parish	
Dudley	341	46	Willard	Nathan		1					1						2		
Lancaster	355	19	Willard	Paul	3			1		1		1					6		
Harvard	218	5	Willard	Phineas		1	1						1				2		
Uxbridge	473	7	Willard	Samuel	2	1	5	6	1		2	1	3	1	2		24		
Ashburnham	455	16	Willard	Silas		2	1	1		4		2		1			11		
Ashburnham	456	3	Willard	Simon	3			1		1			1				6		
Lancaster	358	9	Willard	Simon		1		1	1			1		1			5		
Lancaster	358	25	Willard	Solomon	3			1					1				5		
Holden	510	19	Willard	Thomas				1						1			2		
Worcester	184	15	Willard	Thomson	4	1		1		1	1	1					9		
Harvard	217	26	Willard	William	3	2		1			1		1				8		
Lancaster	357	1	Willard	William	3			1			1	1					6		
Petersham	285	20	Willard	Willm Jr	1			1		3		1	1				7		
Petersham	285	12	Willard	Wilm		1	2	1	1			1	1	1			8		
Spencer	485	3	William	Nathl		2	1	1		2	3		1				10		
Brookfield	251	7	William	Samuel	2					1		1	1				6	First Parish	
Charlton	337	25	William	Alpheus	1		1	1		3			1	1			8		
Northbridge	474	6	Williams	Chester		2		2		1			1				6		

264

TOWN	PG#	LN#	LAST NAME	FIRST NAME	FREE WHITE MALES					FREE WHITE FEMALES					TOTAL ALL OTHER	TOTAL SLAVES	TOTALS	DISTRICT/ TOWNSHIP	NOTES
					under 10	10 to 16	16 to 26	26 to 45	45 and over	under 10	10 to 16	16 to 26	26 to 45	45 and over					
Westborough	199	152	Williams	Cutting			2			1		1					4		
Charlton	337	24	Williams	Daniel		1			1		1	2		1			6		
Charlton	340	8	Williams	Daniel Junr	1			1		1	2		1				6		
Charlton	340	7	Williams	Daniel Maj	1			1				1	1				4		
Worcester	184	18	Williams	Ebenz	1			1		3			1	1			7		
Dudley	342	5	Williams	Henry	2			1					1	1			5		
Westminster	456	6	Williams	Isaac		1	1		2		1		1	1			7		
Oxford	154	6	Williams	James		1	1		1			1		1			5		
Worcester	184	8	Williams	James		1	1		1		2		1				6		
Petersham	286	9	Williams	Jarus	1			1		3			1				6		
Hubbardston	416	4	Williams	John	3	1	1	1			1		1				8		
Hubbardston	416	5	Williams	Jona	1	1		1		2		1	1				7		
Royalston	231	1	Williams	Joseph H			1	1		4	1		2				9		
Grafton	206	2	Williams	Moses	1			1					1				3		
Douglas	479	25	Williams	Samuel	2		1	1	2				1	1			8		
Rutland	514	21	Williams	Samuel	2	1		1		1			1				6		
Petersham	287	6	Williams	Seth	2	1	1		1	1	2		1				9		
Northborough	363	4	Williams	Stephen		2	2	2		1	1	1	2				11		
Uxbridge	473	3	Williams	Stephen		1	1		1		1		1				5		
Southborough	206	7	Williams	William			1			1		1					3		
Western	251	11	Williams		2			1		1			1				5		First name left blank
Milford	389	19	Williamson	John				1						1			2		
Worcester	183	34	Willington	Daniel		2	2		2	2	2		1				9		
Rutland	507	2	Willington	Ebenezer	2			1		2			1				6		
Worcester	183	33	Willington	Ebenz 3d	1		2	1					1				5		
Worcester	183	32	Willington	Ebenz Jun	2	1	1		1	1	1	1		1			9		
Rutland	507	1	Willington	John			2	1		2			1				6		
Leicester	498	15	Willington	Josiah				1					1				2		
Brookfield	251	2	Willis	Azariah		1	1		1			1	1				5	First Parish	
Oakham	321	17	Willis	Azariah	2			1		1	1	1	1				7		
Petersham	287	2	Willis	Caleb		1			1	2	1	1		2			8		
Hardwick	305	10	Willis	Ebenz	2		1	1	1	1		1		1			8		
Barre	405	19	Willis	John	2	1		1		4		1					9		
Hardwick	305	17	Willis	Lemll		1		1	1		1	1		1			6		
Barre	406	2	Willis	Seth		1			1			1		1			4		
Brookfield	266	14	Willister	Gad			1	1	1		1	1		1			6	Third Parish	
Ashburnham	455	8	Willmer	Jacob SG	2			1	1	3	1		1	1			10		
Athol	281	5	Willmouth	David				1					1	1			3		
Charlton	337	27	Wills	Jabez	1			1		2			1				5		
Paxton	504	8	Willson	Benjamin	2	1		1		2	1		1				8		
Sterling	348	16	Willson	Edward	2	1		1		1			1				6		
Spencer	488	4	Willson	Isaac			1					1					2		
Leicester	497	2	Willson	John				1					1				2		
Petersham	285	13	Willson	John	1			1		3		1	1				7		
Spencer	485	2	Willson	Lydia		1	1			2		1	1				6		
Spencer	488	15	Willson	Nathan			1			1		1					3		
Spencer	485	1	Willson	Nathl	1		1		1	2	1		1				7		
Barre	406	8	Willson	Saml				1						1			2		
Spencer	488	5	Willson	Samuel		1	1		2		1	1		2			8		
Sutton	167	23	Wilmarth	Benoni				1						1			2		
Mendon	394	17	Wilson	Alexander	3	1	1	1		2	1		1				10	2d Parish	
Fitchburg	423	16	Wilson	Benja				1	3				1	1			6		
Mendon	394	18	Wilson	Caleb	1			1		2		1	1				6	2d Parish	
Princeton	518	7	Wilson	Ephraim	3	1	2	1		1	1	2	1				12		
Holden	510	14	Wilson	Francis			1		1			1		1			4		
New Braintree	312	17	Wilson	James	1			1	1	1	1		1	1			6		
Worcester	184	2	Wilson	James	2			1		1	2		1				7		
Mendon	394	20	Wilson	Jeddediah		1	1		1		1	1					5	2d Parish	
Mendon	394	21	Wilson	John				1									1	2d Parish	
Gardner	448	8	Wilson	Joseph	2			1		2			1				6		
Winchendon	229	16	Wilson	Nathaniel	2	1			1	1		2	1				8		
New Braintree	312	18	Wilson	Robert			1		1					1			3		
Oakham	321	12	Wilson	Robert	4		1	1		2	1	2	1				12		
Upton	383	14	Wilson	Saml				1		2			1				4		
Oakham	321	16	Wilson	Samll		1		1				2	1				5		
Uxbridge	474	14	Wilson	Samuel		1		1			1		2				5		
Princeton	518	8	Wilson	Solomon			1				2						3		
Athol	281	9	Wilson	Willm			1	1						1			3		
Oakham	322	4	Wilton	Simon		1		1			1	1					4		
Barre	405	26	Winch	Aaron					1		1	1		1			4		
Winchendon	230	13	Winch	David				1									1		
Holden	510	13	Winch	Francis	2	1		1		1			1	1			7		
Holden	510	12	Winch	John	1	1		1					1				4		
Barre	405	27	Winch	Jonathan		1		1			1		1				4		
Ashburnham	455	18	Winchester	Ann											1		1		
Hardwick	306	17	Winchester	Benn				1									1		
Ashburnham	456	2	Winchester	Jonathan	2	2		1		2	1		1				9		
Hardwick	305	11	Winchester	Moses		1		1					2				4		
Hardwick	306	5	Winchester	Thos	3		1			1	1					6		
Southborough	202	14	Winchester	Willim				1			1		1				3		
Westminster	456	2	Winchip	Cyrus			1		2		1					4		
Westminster	453	11	Winchip	Jonas				1					2				3		
Westminster	456	4	Winchip	Jonas Jr	2		1		2		1	1				7		
Dudley	342	10	Windsor	William		1					1					2		
Charlton	337	7	Wing	Benj	3	1		1			1	1	1			8		
Northbridge	474	11	Wing	Jabez	1		1		2	1					5		
Hardwick	306	13	Wing	James	1		1		1						3		
Hardwick	305	18	Wing	Rebeckah							1			1		
Boylston	369	5	Winn	John	2		1		1	1		2			7		
Sterling	348	17	Winn	Rheuben	2	1								4		

TOWN	PG#	LN#	LAST NAME	FIRST NAME	FREE WHITE MALES					FREE WHITE FEMALES					TOTAL ALL OTHER	TOTAL SLAVES	TOTALS	DISTRICT/ TOWNSHIP	NOTES
					under 10	10 to 16	16 to 26	26 to 45	45 and over	under 10	10 to 16	16 to 26	26 to 45	45 and over					
Boylston	369	4	Winn	William		1			1	1		1					4		
Brookfield	264	16	Winslow	Ebenezer			1		1	2		2		1			7	Second Parish	
Uxbridge	473	9	Winslow	Ebenezer	1			1		1			1				4		
Western	251	9	Winslow	Jona	1			1		1			1				4		
Charlton	340	5	Winslow	Jonathan		1	2		1	1	1	2	1				9		
Barre	405	28	Winslow	Rhoda Wid		1						1		1			3		
Hardwick	306	15	Winslow	Rozamond		1	1				1			1			4		
Barre	405	29	Winslow	Seth	3		1	1		3		1	1				10		
Worcester	186	16	Winslow	Worcester											3		3		
Barre	405	30	Winslow	Zens Col.			2	1	1		2			1	1		8		
Sturbridge	327	3	Winter	Asa	2	1		1		2	3	1	1				11		
Northbridge	474	9	Winter	David		1		1		2	2	1	1				8		
Ashburnham	455	11	Winter	John	1			1	1		1		1	1			6		
Northbridge	474	8	Winter	John	3	1			1	1			1				7		
Northbridge	474	10	Winter	William			2			1		1	1				5		
Barre	405	24	Wintworth	Daniel				1	1			1	1				4		
Worcester	186	17	Wiswall	Ebenz Jun		1	1	1	2				1				6		
Worcester	184	12	Wiswall	Henry	1		2			2		1		1			7		
Milford	389	11	Wiswall	Noah		1		1		1			1				4		
Milford	389	10	Wiswall	Timothy	1	1	1		1		2	1		2			9		
Westminster	453	16	Wiswell	John	2		1						1				4		
Westminster	456	11	Wiswell	Noah	1	1	1		1	2	1	1	1				10		
Ashburnham	455	10	Wit	John	1	1		1		2			1				6		
Templeton	234	9	Withington	Benja	3			1		1			1				6		
Berlin	214	16	Witt	Asa	1			1			1	1					4		
Oakham	322	8	Witt	Benm	2			1	2		1						6		
Hubbardston	416	11	Witt	Eunas Wid	1	1	2					1	1				6		
Brookfield	264	18	Witt	Jonah		1	1			1		1					5	Second Parish	
Hubbardston	416	3	Witt	Oliver Capt.	4	2	1	1	1	1	3	1					15		
Oakham	322	2	Witt	Stephan	3			1	1		1		1				6		
Brookfield	251	5	Witt	Thomas			1	1						2			4	First Parish	
Oxford	154	8	Wolcott	Joshua			1	1				1					3		
Oxford	154	3	Wolcott	Naomi Wd				1						2			3		
Gardner	448	9	Wood	Aaron	1		1	1		2			1				6		
Westminster	456	9	Wood	Abel	2	2	2	1		2			2				11		
Royalston	233	14	Wood	Abiel	1		1			1		1					4		
Westminster	456	8	Wood	Abijah	1	1	1		1	3	1	1	1				10		
Northborough	362	13	Wood	Abraham	2	1		1	1	3	1	2		1			12		
Uxbridge	473	11	Wood	Amery	1			1		4			1				7		
Upton	384	15	Wood	Asa	2	1	2		1	3			1	1			11		
Upton	384	3	Wood	Benjamin			1							1			2		
Upton	384	2	Wood	Benjm Revd	1		2	1		1		1	1	1			8		
Brookfield	263	22	Wood	Buckmeister			3						1				4	Third Parish	
Leominster	433	22	Wood	Caleb		1		1					1				3		
Royalston	242	2	Wood	Daniel	2	1		1		1		1	1				7		
Lunenberg	432	9	Wood	David	3	1						2	1	1			9		
Uxbridge	474	7	Wood	David			1		1	2	2	2		2			10		
Uxbridge	473	6	Wood	Dexter			1	1	1			3		1			7		
Milford	389	18	Wood	Ebenezer			1	1				1	1				5		
Brookfield	266	13	Wood	Eli	3	1			1	1	1	2	1				10	Third Parish	
Athol	281	2	Wood	Elijah		1						1					2		
Uxbridge	474	8	Wood	Ezekiel	2	1	1		1	1		3		1			10		
Upton	383	13	Wood	Ezra Col.				1						1			2		
Upton	384	18	Wood	Ezra Esq	1	1	1	1		3	1	2	1				11		
Fitchburg	424	4	Wood	George	4	2		1		3	1		1				12		
Mendon	388	1	Wood	Grindal			1	1	1			1	2	1			7	1st Parish	
Uxbridge	474	17	Wood	Henry	1			1				1	1	1			6		
Upton	384	17	Wood	Hezekiah		1	1	2	1		2	1		1			9		
Gardner	448	16	Wood	Isabel			1						1	1			3		
Dudley	341	45	Wood	Jesse			1			1	1						3		
Leominster	436	15	Wood	John	1	2	2		1			1		1			8		
Westborough	198	127	Wood	John	1	1		1		3			1				7		
Fitchburg	423	14	Wood	Jonathan		1	1	1	1		1		1	1			7		
Gardner	448	6	Wood	Jonathan	1		2	1				1	1				7		
Grafton	201	16	Wood	Joseph	1	1	1		1	1		2	1				8		
Lunenberg	432	15	Wood	Joseph				1							1		2		
Grafton	206	1	Wood	Joseph Jun	2		3			2	1		1				10		
Leominster	433	21	Wood	Joshua				1			1		1				3		
Athol	281	4	Wood	Kimball				1				1		1			3		
Southborough	202	5	Wood	Lucrecia		1	2				1	1	1				6		
Uxbridge	473	1	Wood	Mark	2			2					1				5		
Brookfield	251	6	Wood	Mathew	2	1	1	1		2		1	1	1			11	First Parish	
Upton	383	20	Wood	Maynard			1					1					2		
Leominster	433	25	Wood	Michal			1					1		1			3		
Gardner	448	7	Wood	Nahum			1					1					2		
Dudley	341	32	Wood	Nathan	1		1			1		1					4		
Milford	389	3	Wood	Nathan			1						1				2		
Rutland	507	4	Wood	Nathaniel	3							1					5		
Mendon	388	3	Wood	Obadiah			1		1			1					3	1st Parish	
Milford	389	2	Wood	Obadiah		2		1		1		1		1			5		
Mendon	394	22	Wood	Peleg	3			1		2	1		1				8	2d Parish	
Rutland	514	13	Wood	Rebekah		1						1		2			4		
Upton	384	4	Wood	Reuben	1	1		1		3	1		1				8		
Milford	389	16	Wood	Robert				1						1			2		
Brookfield	252	16	Wood	Saml Jur				1				1	1				3	First Parish	
Brookfield	251	1	Wood	Samuel		1	2		1	1		2		1			8	First Parish	
Grafton	201	13	Wood	Samuel	1		1	1				1	1				5		
Northborough	362	14	Wood	Samuel				1						1			2		
Upton	384	11	Wood	Samuel		1						2	1	2			7		
Uxbridge	474	6	Wood	Samuel	1	1		1		2			1				6		

			HEADS OF HOUSEHOLD		FREE WHITE MALES					FREE WHITE FEMALES					TOTAL ALL OTHER	TOTAL SLAVES	TOTALS	DISTRICT/ TOWNSHIP	NOTES
TOWN	PG#	LN#	LAST NAME	FIRST NAME	under 10	10 to 16	16 to 26	26 to 45	45 and over	under 10	10 to 16	16 to 26	26 to 45	45 and over					
Upton	383	12	Wood	Seth			1		1	1	1	1		1			6		
Westborough	195	84	Wood	Seth		1			1		1	1		1			5		
Dudley	341	31	Wood	Simeon			2		1			1	1				5		
Mendon	388	4	Wood	Solomon Lt.			2		1	2	1	1	1				8		1st Parish
Mendon	388	2	Wood	Stephen		2	1		1	4	2	2	1				13		1st Parish
Westminster	456	5	Wood	Susanna									1				1		
Brookfield	263	16	Wood	Thomas			1		1		1	1		1			5		Third Parish
Uxbridge	473	8	Wood	Timothy	2	1		1	1				2	1			8		
Lunenberg	432	11	Wood	Zephaniah		1		1					1				3		
Lunenberg	432	17	Wood	David Jun	2			1		2		1	1				7		
Harvard	221	28	Wood	John			1						1				2		
Spencer	488	6	Wood	Sarah	2		1					3		1			7		
Harvard	221	27	Wood	Timothy				1				1	1				3		
Charlton	340	6	Wood	Wm	1			1		3			1				6		
Petersham	287	3	Wood	Carver	1			1		1			1				4		
Westminster	453	12	Wood	Nathan		1		1		2			1				5		
Charlton	337	3	Woodard	Joshua			1										1		
Sterling	348	18	Woodard	Pomp											2		2		
Charlton	337	4	Woodard	Sarah	2		1			1		1		1			6		
Worcester	183	27	Woodburn	Saml Junr			2	1	1	1		1	1	1	1		8		
Leicester	498	14	Woodbury	Aaron	3	1		1					1				6		
Sutton	166	12	Woodbury	Barthl				1			1		1	1			3		
Sutton	166	14	Woodbury	Benja	3			1		2	2		1				9		
Sutton	166	22	Woodbury	Benja Junr	1	1		1		2			1				6		
Charlton	340	13	Woodbury	Caleb	1		1	1				1					4		
Barre	405	20	Woodbury	Ezekiel		1		1				1		1			4		
Barre	405	21	Woodbury	Hubbard		2				1		1					4		
Bolton	209	10	Woodbury	Israel	3	1		1		1	1	1	1	1			10		
Winchendon	229	15	Woodbury	Jacob B.	2	2	1	1		2	1		1				10		
Sutton	166	20	Woodbury	John	1	1	1		1			1	1				6		
Sutton	166	9	Woodbury	John Junr		2		1		1		1	1				6		
Sutton	166	8	Woodbury	Jona				1			1	1	1				4		
Sutton	167	25	Woodbury	Jonah		1		1					1				3		
Sutton	166	21	Woodbury	Joseph		1		1		2	1		1				6		
Sutton	166	13	Woodbury	Lot	2	2		1		1			1				7		
Sutton	166	10	Woodbury	Nathan	3			1					1				5		
Royalston	242	1	Woodbury	Peter			1	1	1					1			4		
Bolton	209	9	Woodbury	Samuel			1							2			3		
Harvard	217	31	Woodbury	Samuel	1	1			1	2	1		1	1			8		
Sutton	166	11	Woodbury	Simeon			3			1		1		1			5		
Bolton	209	5	Woodbury	William	1	1		1		4		1	1	1			10		
Rutland	514	18	Woodcock	Bela	2		1	1		2	1		1				8		
Rutland	513	3	Woodcock	Daniel	1			1		1	1		1				4		
Royalston	237	11	Woodcock	Jeremiah				1				1		1			3		
Rutland	513	1	Woodcock	John	1		1			1	1						4		
Oakham	322	3	Woodis	Dorothy		1	1						1				3		
Oakham	322	6	Woodis	Ebenzr	2			1		1			1				5		
Oakham	322	5	Woodis	Edward	1	1		1	1		1		1	1			7		
Oakham	322	10	Woodis	Reuben	1		1			1	1						4		
Leominster	436	11	Woods	Asa	2	2		1		3			1				9		
New Braintree	313	11	Woods	Asa	1	1		1	1	2	1	1	1	2			11		
Princeton	518	6	Woods	Asa	1		2						1				4		
New Braintree	313	6	Woods	Daniel	1	1		1	1	2	1	1	1	2			11		
Harvard	217	8	Woods	Eliphalet				1			1			1			3		
New Braintree	313	3	Woods	George	2		1	1	1			1		1			7		
Harvard	217	7	Woods	Jabez	1		1						1				3		
Leominster	433	27	Woods	James			1				1						2		
New Braintree	312	19	Woods	James	3	1	1	1		1		2	1	1			11		
New Braintree	312	20	Woods	Jno	3			1	1	1	2	1	1	1			11		
Fitchburg	424	1	Woods	John			1			1			1				3		
Leominster	436	13	Woods	John				1	1			2		1			5		
Royalston	241	6	Woods	John	1	1		1		1			1				5		
Hubbardston	419	8	Woods	John Capt.			1		1			2		1			5		
Leominster	433	32	Woods	John Jun	2			1					1				4		
Hardwick	306	10	Woods	Nathl	1	1		1					1				4		
Leominster	436	14	Woods	Samuel	3			1		2	2		1				9		
Princeton	518	5	Woods	Samuel					1			2		1			4		
Hardwick	306	9	Woods	Wm	1			1					1				3		
Westminster	453	1	Woodward	Abel	2			1		1			1				5		
Oxford	154	9	Woodward	Amos	1			1		1			1				4		
Leicester	497	1	Woodward	Benja				1						1			2		
Leicester	498	8	Woodward	Caleb			1	1						1			3		
Oxford	154	10	Woodward	Caleb			1	1						1			3		
Hubbardston	416	2	Woodward	Daniel	3	1		1		2	2		1				10		
Hubbardston	416	7	Woodward	Ebenz				1						1			2		
Hubbardston	416	8	Woodward	Edward	3			2					1				6		
Petersham	286	15	Woodward	Elisha	1	2			1			1	1				6		
Hubbardston	419	14	Woodward	Elisha Esq		1		1	1	1		1		1			5		
Leicester	498	9	Woodward	John				1						1			2		
Sutton	167	38	Woodward	Jonah		1	1	1		2		1	1				7		
Sutton	167	37	Woodward	Jonas				1						1			2		
Petersham	286	11	Woodward	Joseph		2		1		3	1		1				8		
Petersham	286	12	Woodward	Nathl			1			1			1				3		
Westminster	454	17	Woodward	Nathll			1	1				1	1				4		
Spencer	487	14	Woodward	Noah	1	2		1		5	1		1				11		
Hubbardston	416	1	Woodward	Philemon		1	1	1	1	1		1		1			7		
Westminster	453	13	Woodward	Rebeckah							1	1	1				3		
Sutton	168	6	Woodward	Solomon				1					1				2		
Petersham	286	13	Woodward	Willm	1			1			1	1	1				5		
Spencer	488	17	Woodward	Wright				1			1			1			3		
Western	251	10	Woodworth	Arad	2		2	2		1			1				8		
Brookfield	263	6	Woolcot	John					1				2	1			4		Second Parish

267

TOWN	PG#	LN#	LAST NAME	FIRST NAME	FREE WHITE MALES					FREE WHITE FEMALES					TOTAL ALL OTHER	TOTAL SLAVES	TOTALS	DISTRICT/ TOWNSHIP	NOTES
					under 10	10 to 16	16 to 26	26 to 45	45 and over	under 10	10 to 16	16 to 26	26 to 45	45 and over					
Brookfield	266	8	Woolcot	John				1	1					1			3	Third Parish	
Brookfield	263	7	Woolcot	John Junr	2			1			2			1			6	Second Parish	
Leicester	498	7	Worcester	John			1	1		1			1				4		
Fitchburg	423	15	Worcester	Samuel			1	1		3	1	1					7		
Lancaster	358	22	Worcester	Samuel	1			1		2			1				5		
Oxford	154	7	Work	Jacob	1	1			1	1				1			5		
Princeton	518	15	Worster	Samson	2			1					1				4		
Brookfield	264	19	Wright	Abijah				1						3			4	Second Parish	
Templeton	235	7	Wright	Ebenz		1		1	2				1	1			6		
Brookfield	263	17	Wright	Ithamar				1	1					2			4	Third Parish	
Northborough	363	9	Wright	James			1	1	1	1			1				5		
Gardner	448	10	Wright	Joseph	3					2			1				7		
Hubbardston	419	9	Wright	Joseph		2	3		1	3		2		1			12		
Templeton	231	12	Wright	Joshua	1		1		1	1			1	2			7		
Templeton	231	14	Wright	Rufus	1	1	1						2				5		
Worcester	184	13	Wright	Samuel				1						1			2		
Rutland	507	5	Wright	Tabitha			1					1		1			3		
Sterling	348	9	Wright	Thomas	1	2	1	1		4	1		2				12		
Garry	274	5	Write	Nehemiah	1	2			1	1		2		1			8		
Templeton	235	10	Wyley	Moses	4		1		1			2	2	1			11		
Lancaster	355	8	Wyman	Benjamin	1			1		3	2		1	1			9		
Charlton	337	6	Wyman	Daniel	3			1		2	1	1					8		
Westminster	456	10	Wyman	David 2d	2			1		2			1				6		
Charlton	340	15	Wyman	John				1						1			2		
Northborough	363	3	Wyman	John		1	1	1		1	1	1		1			7		
Charlton	337	5	Wyman	Levi	1	1		1		1			1	1			6		
Princeton	518	14	Wyman	Thomas	4		1	1	1	1		1		1			10		
Winchendon	229	13	Wyman	Thomas Jr			1						1				2		
Winchendon	229	12	Wyman	Thos	2	2	1	1		1	1			1			9		
Westminster	454	15	Wynon	David	2	1		1		1	2		1				8		
Douglas	480	8	Yates	Abner		2		1						1			4		
Douglas	480	9	Yates	John	2			1					1				4		
Athol	281	11	Young	David	2	3		1	1	3			1	1			12		
Worcester	181	20	Young	James	2	1		1		1			1				6		
Athol	281	10	Young	Joel	1			1					1				3		
Northbridge	474	15	Young	Levi	1	1	2		1	4	1	1		1			12		
Worcester	181	19	Young	Mary									1				1		
Athol	281	12	Young	Saml	1	1	2		1	1	1	1		1			9		
Ward	176	28	Young	William		2	1		1		1	1		1			7		
Athol	281	13	Young	Willm	1		1		1	1		2	1				7		
Lancaster	357	7	Zware	Jacob				1			1		1				3		
Lancaster	357	8	Zware	Reuben	1		1				1						3		

NOTES